Glencoe

Writer's Choice

GRAMMAR and COMPOSITION

GRADE 7

on my mind...

Writing letters in a diary...

An old silent pond...
A frog jumps into the pond,
splash! Silence again.
— Bashō

My Journal

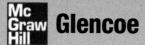

McGraw Hill Glencoe

ACKNOWLEDGMENTS

Grateful acknowledgment is given authors, publishers, photographers, museums, and agents for permission to reprint the following copyrighted material. Every effort has been made to determine copyright owners. In case of any omissions, the Publisher will be pleased to make suitable acknowledgments in future editions.

Cover (bkgd) © Gerry Charm/SuperStock **vi vii** Ralph J. Brunke; **viii** © Time, Inc.; **ix** Laura Derichs; **x** NASA; **xi** (t)Bettman/CORBIS, (b)Focus on Sports; **xii** *Circus Parade,* 1979. Kathy Jakobsen. Oil on canvas, 24" x 36". Museum of American Folk Art, New York, NY, gift of Robert Bishop 1979.11.1; **xv** Allan Landau; **xvi** Courtesy of R.H. Love Gallery; **xvii** Pete Saloutos/Photographic Resources; **xix** Courtesy Phyllis Kind Gallery, Chicago/New York; **xxi** Courtesy Brooke Alexander Gallery; **xxii** Hirshhorn Museum and Sculpture Garden, Smithsonian Institution, gift of the Joseph H. Hirshhorn Foundation, 1974. Photography by Lee Stalsworth; **xxiii** Allan Landau, *Atlas of the Living World* by David Attenborough. ©1989 by Marshall Editions Ltd. Reprinted by permission of Houghton Mifflin Co. All rights reserved; **xxiv** Giraudon/Art Resource, NY, with special authorization of the City of Bayeux; **xxv** Ralph J. Brunke; xxvii SEF/Art Resource, NY; **xxviii** Gilson Ribeiro; **xxix** Giraudon/Art Resource, NY

Acknowledgments continued on page 845.

 The **Facing the Blank Page** feature in this book was prepared in collaboration with the writers and editors of *TIME*.

6+1 Trait® is a registered trademark of Northwest Regional Educational Laboratory, which does not endorse this product.

The McGraw·Hill Companies

 Glencoe

Send all inquiries to:
Macmillan/McGraw-Hill • Glencoe/McGraw-Hill
8787 Orion Place
Columbus, OH 43240-4027

ISBN: 978-0-07-888768-0
MHID: 0-07-888768-2

Printed in the United States of America.

4 5 6 7 8 9 10 RJE/LEH 12 11 10

PROGRAM CONSULTANTS

Mark Lester is Professor of English Emeritus at Eastern Washington University. He served as Chair of the Department of English at Eastern Washington University and Chair of the Department of English as a Second Language at the University of Hawaii. He is the author of *Grammar and Usage in the Classroom* (Allyn & Bacon, 2000), co-author of *A Commonsense guide to Grammar and Usage* (Bedford/St. Martin's 2006), *Essential ESL Grammar* (McGraw-Hill 2008), and numerous other professional books and articles.

Sharon O'Neal is Associate Professor at the College of Education, Texas State University–San Marcos, where she teaches courses in reading instruction. She formerly served as Director of Reading and Language Arts of the Texas Education Agency and has authored, and contributed to, numerous articles and books on reading instruction and teacher education.

Jacqueline Jones Royster is Professor of English and Executive Dean of the Colleges of the Arts and Sciences at The Ohio State University. Her professional interests include the rhetorical history of women of African descent, the development of literacy, and contexts and processes related to the teaching of writing. In addition to her many years of teaching writing, directing writing programs and writing centers, and serving as a leader in several English professional organizations, she is also the author of numerous articles in literary studies and women's studies, and several books, among them: *Traces of a Stream: Literacy and Social Change Among African American Women; Critical Inquiries: Readings on Culture and Community;* and *Calling Cards: Theory and Practice in the Study of Race, Gender, and Culture.*

Jeffrey Wilhelm, a middle and high school English teacher for thirteen years, is currently Associate Professor of English Education at Boise State University, where he specializes in adolescent literacy, with research interests including gender and literacy, technology and literacy, and assisting struggling readers and writers. He is the founding director of the Maine Writing Project and Boise State Writing Project. He has authored fifteen books on literacy and education, and has won the top two research awards in English Education: the NCTE Promising Research Award for *You Gotta BE the Book* and the Russell Award for Distinguished Research for *Reading Don't Fix No Chevys.*

Denny Wolfe, a former high school English teacher and department chair, is Professor of English Education Emeritus, Director of the Tidewater Virginia Writing Project, and Director of the Center for Urban Education at Old Dominion University in Norfolk, Virginia. Author of more than seventy-five articles and books on teaching English, Dr. Wolfe is a frequent consultant to schools and colleges on the teaching of English language arts.

BOOK OVERVIEW

Part 1   Composition

Part 2   Grammar, Usage, and Mechanics

Part 3   Resources and Skills

Reference Section

v

CONTENTS

Part 1 Composition

UNIT 2   The Writing Process

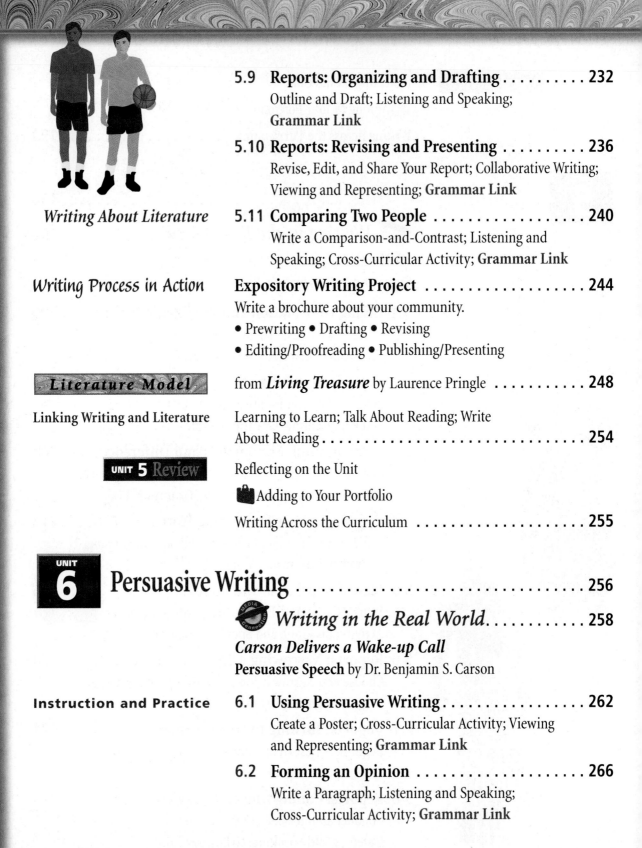

UNIT 6 Persuasive Writing **256**

Kathy Jakobsen, *Circus Parade*, 1979

Part 2 Grammar, Usage, and Mechanics

Part 3 Resources and Skills

Quick Help

Reference Section *Fast answers to questions about writing, research, and language*

LITERATURE MODELS

Composition Models

Each literature selection is an extended example of the mode of writing taught in the unit.

Skill Models

Excerpts from outstanding works of fiction and nonfiction exemplify specific writing skills.

LITERATURE MODELS

Skill Models *continued*

Language Models

*Each Grammar Review uses excerpts to link
grammar, usage, or mechanics to literature.*

FINE ART

*Fine art—paintings, drawings, photos, and
sculpture—is used to teach as well as to
stimulate writing ideas.*

FINE ART

GLENCOE

Writer's Choice

Grammar and Composition

Welcome to Writer's Choice!

Your writing and your choices are what this book is all about. Take a few minutes to get to know each of the book's four main parts: Composition; Grammar, Usage, and Mechanics; Resources and Skills; and the Writing and Research Handbook.

Part 1

Composition

How do you become a better writer? By writing! Four-page lessons give you the strategies you need to improve your writing skills. Each lesson focuses on a specific writing problem or task. The lessons offer clear instruction, show models of effective writing, and—most importantly—provide a variety of writing activities for you to practice what you've learned.

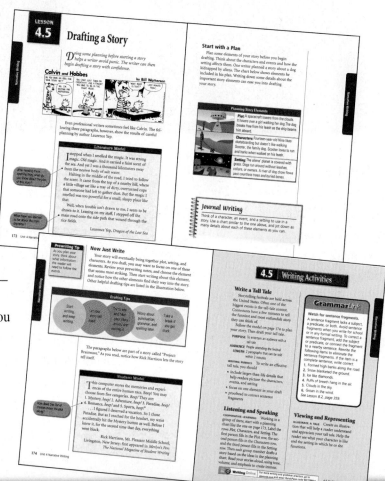

Part 2

Grammar, Usage, and Mechanics

Short focused lessons make learning grammar easy.
Rules and definitions teach you the basics, while
examples and literature models show you how the
concepts are used in real-life writing.

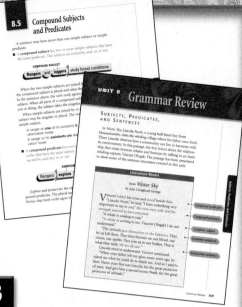

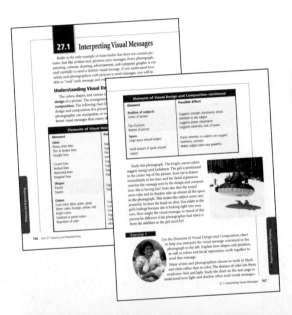

Part 3

Resources and Skills

Would you like to improve your study skills, learn
how to give a speech, or get better at taking tests?
The lessons in this part give you the skills you need
to do all these things and more. Each lesson is
complete, concise, and easy to use.

WRITING AND RESEARCH HANDBOOK

This user-friendly handbook
gives explanations, examples,
and tips to help you write
strong sentences, paragraphs,
compositions, and research
papers. Use it whenever you
get stuck!

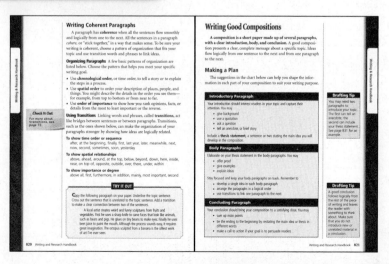

René Magritte, Le Printemps, 1965

"*The heat of the sun had melted the wax from his wings; the feathers were falling one by one, like snowflakes; and there was none to help.*"

—Josephine Preston Peabody,
"Icarus and Daedalus"

PART 1

Composition

**"Hold fast to dreams
For when dreams go
Life is a barren field
Frozen with snow."**

—Langston Hughes
"Dreams"

2

UNIT
1

Personal Writing

Writing in the Real World

On a visit to the Bahamas, singer and songwriter Ella Jenkins found a magical scene of dancers, calypso singers, and children playing. "Amidst all the things that were happening, the ocean had the loudest roar." She wrote about those ocean sounds in *Come Dance by the Ocean*, a record album with a message about planet Earth. Like other albums Jenkins has produced over the past fifty years, this one celebrates the lands, cultures, and oceans of our world.

Come Dance by the Ocean

by Ella Jenkins

Early this morning when I looked out,
I saw some dolphins playing about.
One chased two, then two chased one.
I'd say that all three had an ocean of fun.

Come on, come dance by the ocean.
Come on, come dance by the sea.
Come on, come dance by the ocean,
Come on, come dance with me.

Songwriter
Ella Jenkins

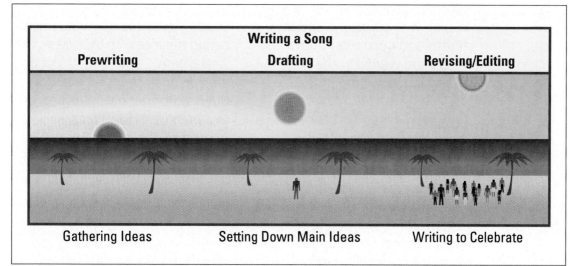

Writing a Song

Prewriting	Drafting	Revising/Editing
Gathering Ideas	Setting Down Main Ideas	Writing to Celebrate

A Writer's Process

Prewriting
Gathering Ideas

For Ella Jenkins, songwriting is a form of personal writing because, in her music, she talks about the things that matter the most to her. In writing the songs for the album *Come Dance by the Ocean,* Jenkins expressed her feelings about many things she loves. She wrote about the excitement of air travel, the wonder of nature, and the joy of encountering the world's amazing variety of cultures and lands.

Jenkins has had a lifetime interest in both music and other cultures. While she was in college, Cuban musicians taught her to play conga drums and maracas. At the same time, she read about other cultures and listened to songs from Africa, India, Egypt, and other lands. By her mid-thirties, Jenkins was carrying her message to young people through songs. "You have to respect that other people come from other places," she said. "They're trying to learn about you, and you want to learn about them."

As she travels, Jenkins does a lot of personal writing. She said, "I keep notebooks when I travel called 'Random Thoughts.' I use them to jot down notes about things that strike me." When Jenkins began creating the album *Come Dance by the Ocean,* she looked to this collection of personal notebooks for ideas.

Jenkins encourages every writer to keep a journal or a notebook of ideas. "Personal writing should be something you do on a regular basis because that

improves your skill and puts you in tune with yourself," she says. "Pretty soon you won't have just letters and words on the page but something very warm and alive."

Drafting
Setting Down Main Ideas

When Jenkins started writing poems for her album, the notes from "Random Thoughts" helped. For example, they provided material for the poem "A Winter Plane Ride." Jenkins had written the notes that inspired this poem on a flight from Portland, Oregon, to Chicago, Illinois. "It was so exciting to see the differences between one part of the country and another," she said. "I could have written a lot of little things that I was seeing, but all of a sudden I heard this voice, the pleasant voice of the pilot telling us about the sights. You'd have thought I was in class because I wrote down everything he said," she recalled.

Later these notes helped Jenkins recall and capture the moment. "Things grab you in life," she said. "No one experienced that plane ride as I did. Each person on that plane had a different experience, so no one could write about it as I did."

Once Jenkins knew what ideas and feelings she was going to put in her record album, she then had to figure out the words and melodies for each song. The title

song, "Come Dance by the Ocean," was easy. "I was remembering the music by the ocean, the steel drums," she said. "I loved the way they sounded and how the head of the group invited us to come on and enjoy ourselves. And I thought, 'come on' is a good way of beckoning people."

Revising/Editing
Writing to Celebrate

After writing each song and composing the music, Jenkins revised her drafts. She also settled on an opening verse for the album. With this playful song, she invited listeners to celebrate all the things we have in common—nature, music, new places, and people.

For her poem "A Winter Plane Ride," Jenkins used a free and informal style. In the poem, she describes her flight over snowy mountains and colorful canyons. She worked on the poem until each word was exactly right and conveyed her personal message: look around you, listen, and enjoy.

> I see light blankets of
>   snow
> Lying gently upon the
>   mountaintops
> Now the canyons are
>   coming—
> Rippled ridges wrapped
>   around colors, cleverly
>   shouting
> Yet not making a sound.

Examining Writing in the Real World

Analyzing the Media Connection

Discuss these questions about the song on page 4 and the poem on page 6.

1. How would you describe the mood of Jenkins's song "Come Dance by the Ocean"?

2. What effect does repetition have in the song's second verse?

3. How does Jenkins establish the setting for the poem "A Winter Plane Ride"?

4. What two sights does Jenkins celebrate in "A Winter Plane Ride"?

5. What effects does the repetition of consonant sounds have in the poem?

Analyzing a Writer's Process

Discuss these questions about Ella Jenkins's writing process.

1. What interests does Jenkins focus on in her personal writing?

2. How do Jenkins's personal notebooks help her in her writing?

3. While drafting "Come Dance by the Ocean," Jenkins decided to use and repeat the words "come on." Why did she think these words were so important to the song's message?

4. For what two reasons does Jenkins encourage others to do personal writing?

5. How is Ella Jenkins's personal writing process similar to or different from your own?

Grammar*Link*

Vary sentence length to make your writing more interesting.

To achieve variety in her writing, Ella Jenkins sometimes combines two related short sentences into one smooth longer sentence.

Early this morning when I looked out, I / I saw some dolphins playing about.

Combine the choppy sentences in each item into one sentence.

1. The game was almost over. We were losing.

2. Then Louise snagged the ball. She tied the score.

3. An opponent was passing the ball. She tripped.

4. Inez rushed toward the ball. She kicked it to me.

5. I received her pass. I scored the goal.

See Lesson 2.8, pages 74–77.

LESSON 1.1

Writing About What's Important to You

*P*ersonal writing, writing that you do for yourself, can be
like a conversation with your best friend. It allows you
to explore the things that matter most to you.

My family!

Music!

Doing my best!

Feeling good!

Time with friends!

Personal writing can include entries made in a private
journal, notes kept in a school journal, and letters or postcards
written to relatives or friends. Some personal writing is meant
for the writer alone. Often, private personal writing later
becomes a story, poem, or other form of writing that may
be shared.

To begin, ask yourself, "What is important to me?" Maybe
your answer is like that of a student in the picture; maybe it's
different. Whatever you write, it's about what matters to you.

Explore Thoughts and Feelings

When something incredibly good or bad occurs, put your reactions on paper. Writing about your thoughts and feelings makes them clearer and more accessible to you.

A letter to a friend is personal writing in which you share your thoughts and feelings.

Dear Lynn,

I wish we had never moved! It was so awful today. I got on the bus and didn't know anyone! All day long kids were staring at me. I felt like hiding in my locker or wearing a paper bag over my head.

I miss talking to you. I miss eating lunch with you. I even miss your jokes! Please write soon and tell me what's happening.

Your best friend,
Kara

July 12
Something happened tonight that I'll never forget. Everyone else was asleep. I walked a few yards from our camp and turned on my flashlight. Wherever I pointed the light, pairs of yellow eyes looked back. I never knew so many small animals lived in the woods right by our cabin.

Some kinds of personal writing are just for you.

TIME

For more about the writing process, see **TIME** *Facing the Blank Page*, pp. 97–107.

Journal Writing

You have probably had many ideas and experiences today. In your journal list as many of these as you can recall. You can use some of these ideas for personal writing.

Use Your Own Words

Personal writing is talking on paper. You can write as informally as you talk. Experiment by using words in unexpected ways or by expressing unusual ideas. Make up words, if you like.

Any subject might be worth writing about, perhaps in a poem, story, or letter you never send. Follow your thoughts wherever they may lead. One thought will lead to another. When you write for yourself, you don't have to worry about punctuation, spelling, or grammar—just focus on ideas. Use your own words and style to write about what is important to you. The model below shows how.

Student Model

The writer uses everyday language to write about a personal subject: herself.

Do you think most people Nancy's age share her concerns?

I am Nancy Young,
I remained at the age of twelve for too long,
• I cannot wait until I reach the mere age of thirteen,
Drive a car,
Go to college,
Go to the prom,
And finally,
Own my own life. . . .
• I just want feelings that I can express on paper. . . .
All I want is paper,
Pen and ink,
To bear down on,
Make an impression,
Of me.

Nancy McLaurin Young
Savannah Country Day School
Savannah, Georgia

Write a Letter

Imagine, ten years from now, opening a letter and finding a message you wrote to yourself when you were younger. Write a message to be opened in ten years. Include three things that are important to you now. The list you made for Journal Writing may help you.

PURPOSE To tell about yourself
AUDIENCE Yourself
LENGTH 1–2 paragraphs

WRITING RUBRICS To write an effective letter, you should

- include information about things that are important to you now
- share your thoughts openly

GrammarLink

Use the correct forms of _bad_.

The comparative and superlative forms of _bad_ are _worse_ and _worst_. In the letter on page 9, Kara describes her _bad_ day. Let's hope it doesn't get _worse_.

Complete each blank with _bad_, _worse_, or _worst_.

I thought I had a **1**_____ idea, but yours was **2**_____. His idea was the **3**_____ of all. This new idea is **4**_____ than the others; it's the **5**_____ I've ever heard.

See Lesson 12.3, pages 455–456.

Cross-Curricular Activity

MATHEMATICS Imagine that you have $50.00 to spend in a store of your choice. Write two questions that will help you decide how to spend the money. Then visit one of your favorite stores and take notes on merchandise that interests you. Include prices of the items you like. Use your questions and notes to help you make responsible choices of items you would buy while keeping within your budget.

Listening and Speaking

With a group, share your lists of the items you chose at your favorite store. Talk about ways in which the questions you wrote did or did not help you to make wise selections. Discuss how the group members' decisions are similar and different. Express and explain your ideas clearly and fluently.

LOG ON ▶ **Writing** Online For more writing and grammar practice, go to glencoe.com and enter QuickPass code WC77680p1.

11

Collecting Information

People use different forms of writing when they write just for themselves. They often create journal entries, lists, and graphic organizers that are never seen by anyone else.

Different forms fulfill different purposes in writing. Journal entries can give you ideas for creative writing, whereas lists and graphic organizers can help you organize—and remember—information. Look at the form the writer decided to use in each case above. How would you get these ideas down in writing?

Keep Track of Information

Your journal is your space for exploring ideas and keeping track of information. You may record the events of your day and your reactions to them in your journal. You may also list writing ideas that come to you. Reread your journal often. Think about what you have written. Try out some of your writing ideas.

Journal Writing

Write in your journal for at least five minutes a day for one week. At the end of the week, reread your entries. In your journal write one observation about any entry that seems interesting.

Journal Writing Tip

1. Try to write in your journal every day.
2. Date journal entries for future reference.
3. Write whatever comes to mind.
4. Use any form that feels comfortable.

Record Information

When you want to discover more about something you've covered in a class, use a learning log. A learning log is a place to write comments on what you are studying and to jot down questions that you have. You may use your journal or a separate notebook as a log. Study the log below in which one student listed information about an early civilization. Notice that the notes are informal and personal.

Did the runners wear shoes? What kind?

How far did each of these runners have to travel?

Can you visit Machu Picchu?

Ask Ms. Phillips where the Inca people are today.

Would I like to be an archaeologist?

Social Studies   chapter 3 notes

· The Inca built roads.
· I found a picture of a bridge built of rope cables.
· Runners took messages across the empire.
· They used these rope bridges.
· The Inca irrigated their fields.
· Archaeologists uncovered Machu Picchu, an Inca city in Peru.

SOUTH AMERICA

Cuzco
Potosi
Inca Empire

ATLANTIC OCEAN

BRAZIL

BOLIVIA

ATLANTIC OCEAN

Personal Writing

Write a Learning Log

Choose a chapter from another textbook, maybe a social studies or science book. Read the chapter, and make notes as you read. You may follow the form shown on page 14. Somewhere in the log, provide space to jot down questions or thoughts you might have as you are reading. Feel free to include drawings or graphics that might help you understand or recall the material. Remember, this is a personal study tool. Its purpose is to help you record and organize information. You will be the only one reading it, so make it meaningful to you.

PURPOSE To learn a study strategy
AUDIENCE Yourself
LENGTH 1 page

WRITING RUBRICS To write an effective learning log, you should

- organize the information
- use your own words
- include questions and ideas

Using Computers

If you decide to keep a computer journal, you can create separate files for different types of writing. For example, one file can be a record of daily activities. Writing ideas can be stored in a second file. In another file you can explore private thoughts and feelings. If you are concerned about privacy, you can create your files on a removable disk and keep it in a safe place.

GrammarLink

Use complete sentences in formal writing.

Don't worry about *sentence fragments* when you're writing notes or journal items. When you write for others, however, use complete sentences.

Archaeologists uncovered Machu Picchu, an Inca city in Peru.

Rewrite each fragment below as a complete sentence.

1. The best day of my life.
2. Every day after school.
3. Hate some kinds of vegetables.
4. Good at expressing ideas.
5. Prefer creative to expository writing.
6. A long soccer practice after a hard day at school.
7. The writing assignment that is supposed to be due on Friday.
8. Going to a movie or maybe skating this weekend.

See Lesson 8.2, pages 359–360.

Viewing and Representing

Examine an illustration, chart, or diagram from the chapter you chose for your learning log activity or from another book or Web site that is related to the topic you chose. Write a brief explanation of how the graphic adds to your understanding of the text. Share your explanation with the class.

LOG ON ▶ **Writing** Online For more writing and grammar practice, go to glencoe.com and enter QuickPass code WC77680p1.

15

Writing to Celebrate

A handwritten invitation to a celebration is one familiar type of personal writing you can share. A personal letter is another.

Dear Alan,
Get out your baseball cap. We're going to a game to celebrate my birthday. Meet at my house at 11:30 Saturday, May 12th. A barbecue will follow.
Hope to see you there!
Jih-Sheng
R.S.V.P.

Greeting card companies sell convenient fill-in-the-blank invitations. If you want that personal touch, however, you can write your own invitation. The handwritten invitation above includes all the information Alan needs to know about Jih-Sheng's birthday celebration.

All invitations should contain certain information. They should tell what the celebration is, the date and time and place of the celebration, and who the invitation is from. Additional information, such as special instructions or dress requirements, may also be included.

Spread Good News

Printed or written announcements tell of certain events, such as weddings and graduations. Greeting cards help celebrate holidays and important occasions, such as birthdays, recitals, and vacations. Other kinds of personal writing can be reminders of events and experiences. Some of the notes and cards on the bulletin board below will remind the person who saved them of special times she spent with friends and family members. What other events will they remind her of?

Journal Writing

Think of something that you would like to celebrate with others. Then, in your journal, design and write an invitation to your celebration. Supply all of the important information: who is giving the celebration, the purpose and form of the celebration, and the date, time, and location.

Write Personal Letters

When you write a personal letter, you choose your audience. Your relationship with that person helps you decide what to say and how to say it. Your choice of stationery and the photographs, drawings, or news clippings you might include are important to the person who receives your letter.

Read the letter from Eddie to his older brother. What does the letter tell about the relationship between them? What might be different about a letter from Eddie to a friend?

Dear Reggie,

What's happening? Is college life as cool as you thought it would be? Are the classes hard? Who's your roommate? Do you get to go to all the games for free?

It is weird around here without you. Mom really misses you. She's always saying, "I wonder how Reggie is doing." If you don't write or call soon, she may just show up at your dorm!

Thanks for letting me have your old room. It was awful sharing a room with Ray. He was always getting into my stuff and bothering me. Don't worry, though. I'll let you have your room back at Thanksgiving.

Your bro,

Eddie

Write an Invitation

Think about an upcoming party or celebration to which you might like to invite someone. Before you can write the invitation, you must plan the event. After you have made all of the important decisions about the celebration, decide whom you will be inviting and write the invitation. Be as creative as you can. You may use art or special paper to make your invitation.

PURPOSE To create an invitation
AUDIENCE A friend or relative
LENGTH 1 or 2 paragraphs

WRITING RUBRICS To write an effective invitation, you should

- make the invitation personal
- include the necessary information

Listening and Speaking

With a small group, discuss an upcoming celebration for which you would like to organize a party or an assembly in your school. Plan a public-address announcement and an invitation to share with those you wish to invite. Read each aloud and invite feedback from group members.

Spelling Hints

As you revise your invitation, remember that if a word ends with a consonant and a *y*, you must usually change the *y* to an *i* before you add a suffix.

try/tried   roomy/roominess
friendly/friendliness

Grammar*Link*

Capitalize proper names and titles correctly.

Eddie correctly capitalized the word *Mom* in his letter. He also did not capitalize a family relationship when it followed a possessive pronoun: *Your* bro,

Write each sentence below, correcting errors in capitalization.

1. My Uncle is only sixteen years old.
2. We have been invited to senator Louise Brigham's victory party.
3. Tell me more about your childhood, grandpa.
4. My sister had to report to her Sergeant for her assignment.
5. For the next few days mother will be away on a business trip.
6. On Saturday mornings I shoot hoops with my dad.
7. Have you met the new science teacher, ms. a. j. Lewellyn?
8. The commanding officer is captain Stephen Fong.
9. I'm going to help aunt Claudia with her garden today.
10. I predict dad will be late again.

See Lesson 19.2, pages 575–576.

Personal Writing

Writing About Yourself

Another kind of personal writing is about personal experiences. The words writers choose and the details they provide depend on how they feel about what happened.

Suppose you are trying out skating for the first time. The fast pace of the skaters speeding around the rink surprises you and makes you nervous about falling. Your account of the experience will probably reflect your nervousness.

In the model below, Farley Mowat, a writer and naturalist, describes a personal experience. Notice how Mowat uses precise details to describe his feelings as he comes face to face with one of the wolves he traveled to the Arctic to study.

Literature Model

Notice the writer's use of the word "quarry." The reader knows Mowat was looking for the wolf.

Which details express the writer's feelings about this experience?

My head came slowly over the crest—and there was my quarry. He was lying down, evidently resting after his mournful singsong, and his nose was about six feet from mine. We stared at one another in silence. I do not know what went on in his massive skull, but my head was full of the most disturbing thoughts. I was peering straight into the amber gaze of a fully grown arctic wolf, who probably weighed more than I did, and who was certainly a lot better versed in close-combat techniques than I would ever be.

Farley Mowat, *Never Cry Wolf*

Recall Your Experiences

When you want to write about a personal experience, begin by thinking about important or interesting events in your life. Concentrate on experiences that made you feel a strong emotion or that made you think about something or someone in a different way.

Trying out for the play scared me.

I can't believe I was elected class president.

Being a big brother for the first time is OK.

This student is recalling some experiences that may lead to personal writing.

Journal Writing

Recall three or four interesting experiences you have had in the last year. List them in your journal, mark one to share, and name an audience for whom you would write.

Select a Writing Idea

Consider an experience you would like to share with readers. Focus on how you felt about that experience. Think about the details that will help you explain your thoughts and feelings. One writer listed "I stepped on a snake" as one of her experiences. Then she listed thoughts about that experience to use in her writing. Look at the cluster diagram, and then read the student model below to see how Simone Tucker shared her encounter with a snake.

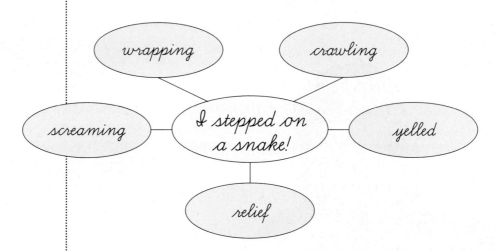

Notice the words Simone uses in the first paragraph to focus on her fear.

How does Simone let the reader know that her reaction to the snake changes?

Student Model

One day last summer my cousin and I went downstairs to iron our clothes. We entered the washroom and I stepped on something. It felt long, slimy, and as if it was crawling up and down my leg while wrapping around my foot. I screamed. My cousin immediately reached for the lights and turned them on, only to discover I was standing on a snake! We both yelled, "Snake!" Jumping and screaming, we ran upstairs.

Several hours later, we found the snake, captured it in a bottle, and let it go. What a relief!

Simone Tucker, Kirby Junior High, St. Louis, Missouri

Write About an Experience

Choose one experience from the list you made in the Journal Writing activity on page 21. Focus on your feelings about the experience. Make a cluster like the one on the previous page. Then write about your experience in a short piece of personal writing to share with your class.

PURPOSE To express your feelings about a personal experience

AUDIENCE Your teacher and classmates

LENGTH 1–2 paragraphs

WRITING RUBRICS To write effectively about an experience, you should

- include emotions and feelings
- use adequate detail

Torquato S. Pessoa, *Carousel*, 1960

Viewing and Representing

Look at the painting on this page. What emotions does the artist express in the painting? What elements of the painting communicate those emotions? Write your thoughts as a journal entry.

Cross-Curricular Activity

ART Recall an amusement park ride you have taken or any experience you think would make an interesting painting. List the details you would use in creating the painting. Would you use bold colors as the artist did for this painting? In one paragraph of personal writing, describe the picture you would create.

GrammarLink

Use the correct personal pronoun.

One day last summer my cousin and I went downstairs to iron our clothes.

Trying out for the play scared me.

Complete each sentence by inserting the correct pronoun, I or me.

1. Could Carlos's dad have cooked beef for Carlos and _____?
2. My mom says that Carlos and _____ have active imaginations.
3. Only Mom can talk that way about Carlos and _____.

See Lesson 11.3, pages 433–434.

LOG ON ▶ **Writing** Online For more writing and grammar practice, go to glencoe.com and enter QuickPass code WC77680p1.

23

Responding to a Character

In the excerpt below, Louise Bradshaw tells how she feels about her twin sister Caroline. Notice how author Katherine Paterson's characters bring her story to life.

Literature Model

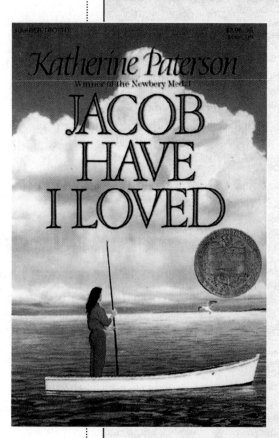

I would come in from a day of progging [poking, searching] for crab, sweating and filthy. Caroline would remark mildly that my fingernails were dirty. How could they be anything else but dirty? But instead of simply acknowledging the fact, I would fly into a wounded rage. How dare she call me dirty? How dare she try to make me feel inferior to her own pure, clear beauty? It wasn't my fingernails she was concerned with, that I was sure of. She was using my fingernails to indict my soul. Wasn't she content to be golden perfection without cutting away at me? Was she to allow me no virtue—no shard of pride or decency?

By now I was screaming. Wasn't it I who brought in the extra money that paid for her trips to Salisbury [a town where Caroline studied music]? She ought to be on her knees thanking me for all I did for her. How dare she criticize? How dare she?

Katherine Paterson, *Jacob Have I Loved*

Write Your Response

Using personal writing to respond to a character can help you better understand the character and the story. Perhaps you have read a story with a character you would like to talk to. Maybe you thought it would be interesting to stop reading and say, "Wait! That's not such a good idea!" or "I know just how you feel." Look at the examples below. One reader wrote a lesson in progging for Caroline. The other reader sympathized with Louise.

Progging Directions for Caroline

1. Get a bucket, a boat, and a pole.

2. In your boat go to the place your sister finds crabs.

3. Poke in the mud until you find a crab.

4. Pick up the crab, and put it into the bucket.

5. Are your fingernails clean?

Dear Louise,
I have an older sister like Caroline. Sometimes I think I don't really like her much. Then I feel like I must be horrible to think about my own sister that way. It made me feel better to know someone else felt the same way I do.
Sincerely,
Julie

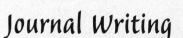

Journal Writing

In your journal list ideas you would like to share with either Caroline or Louise. What does your list show about your feelings toward the sisters' relationship?

Meet People in Books

Sometimes a fictional character proves to be an important influence in a reader's life. Jean Little wrote a book telling about things that influenced the way she felt and thought as a child. When Little was very young, she met a character named Mary Lennox in a book her mother read aloud. If you have read *The Secret Garden* or if you have seen the film, compare your own response to Mary. If you haven't read the book or seen the film, try to imagine what kind of person Mary is as you read Little's reaction.

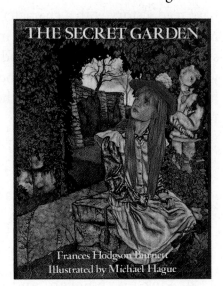

Literature Model

Mother opened the book and began.
When Mary Lennox was sent to Misselthwaite Manor to live with her uncle, everybody said she was the most disagreeable looking child ever seen. It was true, too.

I laid down my spoon. From the first sentence, *The Secret Garden* seemed especially mine. I did not wonder what Mary Lennox looked like. I knew. She looked exactly like me.

Mary had clearly not been born on a Sunday, either. She, too, was selfish and bad-tempered and lazy. She even tried to get Martha to put her shoes on for her. I wasn't the only one who had done such a reprehensible thing.

Yet little by little, she grew into somebody quite different. And the way it happened made perfect sense. I knew that I, too, would be different if I could find a hidden garden and friends like Dickon and Colin and the robin.

Jean Little, *Little by Little*

What is the effect of the sentence "I laid down my spoon"?

An old poem says that a child born on Sunday will have a happy personality. What does this reference tell a reader?

Why do you suppose Little included the last paragraph?

Write a Letter

Look through this book for a painting that has one or more people in it. Write a letter to a character in the painting. Ask the character questions or tell the character what you think of the painting. You might consider asking questions about the character's clothes or expression or about what he or she is doing in that scene.

PURPOSE To express thoughts and feelings about a character

AUDIENCE A character in a painting

LENGTH 2 paragraphs

WRITING RUBRICS To write your letter effectively you should

- think of the character as if he or she were real
- ask questions based on the painting

Listening and Speaking

In a small group, choose a person you have studied in history. Quickly brainstorm a list of the person's accomplishments. Within the group discuss what might have been the person's greatest accomplishments. Then discuss the extent of agreement within the group. Express and explain your ideas clearly and fluently. Finally, write a brief summary of your group's discussion.

Using Computers

With a partner, write a response to a writer whose work you both enjoy reading. Some contemporary writers publish e-mail addresses on their Web pages. If the writer you choose does not have a Web page, write a letter to that author. Use a word processing program to make sure that your letter or e-mail is clear and accurate.

Grammar**Link**

Use strong, vivid adjectives.

*She, too, was **selfish** and **bad-tempered** and **lazy**.*

Replace each numbered adjective with a strong, vivid adjective.

Jean Little is a **1**good writer. She gives an **2**interesting description of Mary Lennox and **3**fine examples to demonstrate Mary's **4**bad qualities. Little admits that she herself did **5**wrong things; that's why she identifies with the **6**bad Mary Lennox. She also admires the **7**good way the author shows the **8**slow change in Mary. I'd rather have **9**somewhat bad friends, like Mary Lennox and Jean Little, than **10**nicey-nice kids as my friends.

See Lesson 12.1, pages 451–452.

Writing Online For more writing and grammar practice, go to glencoe.com and enter QuickPass code WC77680p1.

27

Writing Process in Action

Personal Writing

In preceding lessons you've learned how to gather and organize your ideas to create a piece of personal writing that expresses your own thoughts, feelings, and memories of important personal experiences. Now it's time to make use of what you learned by writing about the events and feelings you experienced on a special day in your life.

Assignment

Context	You and other students will share articles that tell things you did and felt during a special day. It may have been an important day, a happy day, or a day of change.
Purpose	To communicate the importance of one special day through personal writing
Audience	Other students
Length	1 page

Planning to Write

The following pages can help you plan and write your article. Read and refer to them as needed. But don't be tied to them. You're in charge of your own writing process. Be sure

to set a time frame for your assignment, and keep in mind the controlling idea: to write about a special day in your life.

Writing
Online

LOG
ON

For prewriting, drafting, revising, editing and publishing tools, go to **glencoe.com** and enter QuickPass code WC77680p1.

Prewriting

First, you'll want to choose a special day to write about. To gather ideas, you might review your journal, look through old photos, or list some experiences important to you.

After selecting a special day, you'll be ready to develop your idea. Try making a cluster diagram to help you focus on your thoughts and feelings about the day you're considering.

Next, think about how you will order your ideas. Usually, the best way to tell a story is in the order in which events occurred.

Option A
Review your journal.

Option B
Look at photos and souvenirs.

Option C
List memorable events.

- First dance performance
- First week of jr. high
- Youth group camp
- Grandpa's visit
- Backpacking in Yosemite
- Work at child-care center
- Week Smoky was lost

Drafting

Now it's time to expand your ideas and notes into sentences and paragraphs. If you have difficulty getting started with your first draft, it may help to pretend that you are writing or talking to a close friend. Your friend would want to know what happened and how you thought and felt about it. Notice how Latoya Hunter focuses on her feelings in the following excerpt from her diary:

Literature Model

After church today I felt the urge to do something independent. I started walking and found myself heading home. . . . I got in trouble with both parents. . . . That's really embarrassing that they got upset for that! I thought I was more grown than that. I know I am, but they don't.

Latoya Hunter, from *The Diary of Latoya Hunter*

Writing Process in Action

Drafting Tip

For more information about using strong adjectives to make your details vivid, see Lesson 12.1, pages 451–452.

Hunter uses an event—getting in trouble for walking home from church—to express her frustration about being treated like a child.

As you write, refer to your prewriting notes to keep your writing on track. Remember to focus on what it is that makes this day special. Use vivid details, but don't worry now about including too many or too few. Just get your ideas down on paper. You can add, delete, or reorder details during revision.

Revising

To begin revising, read over your draft to make sure that what you have written fits your purpose and your audience. Then have a **writing conference.** Read your draft to a partner or a small group, or receive feedback from your teacher. Use your audience's reactions to help you evaluate your work so far. The questions below can help you and your listeners.

Question A

Have I explained why this event was special?

Question B

Is the order of events clear?

Question C

Have I used important details carefully?

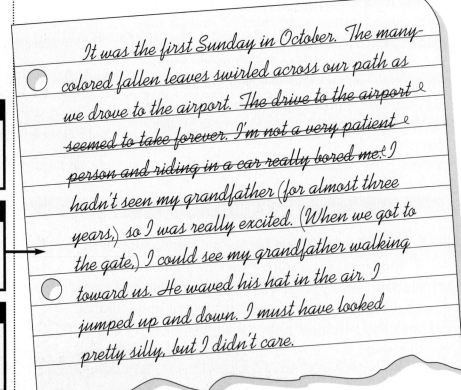

It was the first Sunday in October. The many-colored fallen leaves swirled across our path as we drove to the airport. ~~The drive to the airport seemed to take forever. I'm not a very patient person and riding in a car really bored me.~~ I hadn't seen my grandfather (for almost three years,) so I was really excited. (When we got to the gate,) I could see my grandfather walking toward us. He waved his hat in the air. I jumped up and down. I must have looked pretty silly, but I didn't care.

After considering those questions, you might discover that you need clearer or stronger details. Try doing some additional prewriting, such as listing details about the event. Remember, you can always return to the prewriting and drafting stages while revising.

Editing/Proofreading

The editing stage is your opportunity to clean up any errors in grammar, spelling, and punctuation. The checklist at the right will help you **proofread** your draft. Read through your revised draft several times, looking for one or two kinds of errors at a time. Careful editing can make your writing as special as the event that inspired it.

Publishing/Presenting

Although your writing is very personal, you may wish to share it with others. Be sure to write legibly, using print or cursive handwriting. You might want to exchange your writing with another student and ask for feedback. Finally, consider enhancing your presentation by including a memento, such as a photo or souvenir, of that special time.

Editing/Proofreading Checklist

1. Have I correctly capitalized names and titles?
2. Have I used the correct forms of adjectives?
3. Have I used the correct forms of pronouns?
4. Have I corrected any sentence fragments?
5. Have I spelled every word correctly?

Personal Writing

Proofreading

For proofreading symbols, see pages 80 and 847.

Journal Writing: Write to Learn

Reflect on your writing process experience. Answer these questions in your journal: What did you like best about your personal writing? What was the hardest part of writing it? What did you learn in your writing conference? What new things have you learned as a writer?

Literature Model

FROM

The Diary of Latoya Hunter

by Latoya Hunter

A diary is usually a very personal written record, but a book editor asked Latoya Hunter to keep a diary for everybody to see. Latoya's diary reflects the thoughts and feelings of a typical teenager. Notice how Latoya's personal writing illustrates changes within herself. Notice also how she considers the ways that she is connected to other people. Then try the activities in Linking Writing and Literature on page 38.

September 11, 1990

Dear Diary,

I never thought I'd get desperate enough to say this but I envy you. You don't have to live in this troubled world; all you do is hear about it. You don't have to go to J.H. and watch the clock, praying for dismissal time to come. You also don't have to go through a situation like sitting in a cafeteria watching others laughing and talking and you don't know anyone. To sit there and eat the food that is just terrible because there's nothing else to do.

You don't do any of those things. All you do is listen to pathetic[1] twelve-year-olds like me tell you about it.

I guess you can tell how my day went. Diary, what am I going to do? My best friend left to go to another school. I wish she could be with me. We had so much fun together. She moved right before summer started. She doesn't live anywhere close so it would be much easier if she stayed at the school closest to her. That's the only part of it that's easy. The hardest part is not being together.

September 30, 1990

Dear Diary,

I think I need a name for you. You've become like a best friend to me, you're someone I can talk to without being argued with. I think I know just the name for you. I'll call you Janice after my best friend from Jamaica. We were like sisters before I left. Over the years we've grown apart though, the letters have stopped but that friendship is still going on within me!

So today I christen[2] you diary, Janice Page.

---

[1] **pathetic** (pə thet′ik) causing pity or sorrow
[2] **christen** (kris′ən) to give a name to a person or thing

October 2, 1990

Dear Janice,

It's hard to believe but people change as rapidly as the world does. If I had kept you as a diary two years ago, you would have heard about Jimmy. He was the first guy who I was close to and who was a real friend to me. I liked him because other boys always seemed to be in a popularity contest, and he didn't care about that stuff. He was handsome and everything but he never let it get to his head. Well lately he's been going to the other side. He has a new walk, new talk, new look—the works! He ignores me, I guess I'm not popular enough for him! He just isn't the same.

. . . I felt the urge to do something independent.

My brothers just moved out recently. They don't live very far though, about 15 minutes away from the house. Their new house is nice. I like it there. They're both so funny. One is Dave and the other is Courtney. They're like twins except they look nothing alike and are a couple years apart. Dave is 23 and Courtney is 25. We don't communicate much anymore—they've got girlfriends and they're making new lives for themselves. It's impossible now to have a close relationship with either of them.

After church today I felt the urge to do something independent. I started walking and found myself heading home. Church and home aren't too close together so when I did get home I got in trouble with both parents— it's usually only my mom, but my father didn't approve either. That's really embarrassing that they got upset for that! I thought I was more grown than that. I know I am, but

October 7, 1990

Dear Janice,

This weekend was spent at home, at my brother's house and at church.

they don't. This whole entry is embarrassing. I'm not a baby, I can't believe they think that way of me. I only wanted to prove I could do something by myself. Even that is a crime these days in the parents law book. I can't do anything right these days.

October 8, 1990

Dear Janice,

Today I saw my old teacher, I was talking about the other day. I thought this should be the day I tell you about him. His name is Robert Pelka. He's a heavy man but that only means

Pierre Bonnard, *The Window*, 1925

Personal Writing

Bernice Cross, *In the Room*, c. 1950

there's more of him to love. There's just something about him that makes him impossible not to like. He's warm, caring, loving and everything else that comes with a great human being. He didn't only teach me academic things like math, English and so on. He taught me how to be open-minded to all kinds of people. He did that by making us empathize with other people, in other words, put ourselves in their place and write about it. I went from being a sister of a retarded boy named Victor to being a Jewish girl whose family was taken away from me back in the Hitler days.

Mr. Pelka made things we'd normally learn about from history books sort of come alive, it's like you're there. Those are just some of the things he introduced me to. The things he changed about me are innumerable. The world should know this man. He probably won't go down in any major history books but if this diary counts as a book of history, he just did.

November 18, 1990

Dear Janice,

I didn't go to church today. I got dressed up and everything but my cousins who I usual-ly go with weren't going so I came back home. I didn't do much back here. I just circulated around this house. The old me would have went straight outside to my friend's house. I find I've lost interest in going outside. I was usually like a magnet drawn to steel when it came to going outside. Now, I could spend

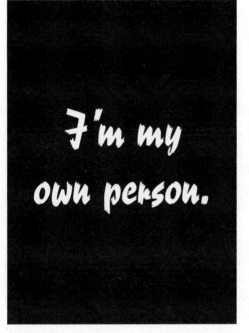

I'm my own person.

a whole week without stepping past the doorstep. Except for going to school of course. I think I've matured somewhat. I always was concerned about what I was missing outside. I never wanted to be left out of anything happening with my friends who are always doing something or going somewhere. In the way I've matured I've come to the sudden realization that there are many more things to life like being close to my family, before it's too late. Pretty soon I'll be off to college, then mar-ried with kids. I might be rushing things a bit, but these years go by very fast.

I'm my own person. I like to think that I'm not just my cousin's cousin or my friend's friend. I like to think I'm the individual Latoya Hunter.

Linking Writing and Literature

 Learning to Learn

Consider what you learned about Latoya after reading her diary. Take a few minutes to jot down a list of her likes and dislikes. Then consider whether you like or dislike any of the same things she does. Do you think the similarities or differences between you and Latoya affect the way you responded to this selection? If so, how?

 Talk About Reading

Talk with other students about the excerpt from *The Diary of Latoya Hunter.* Assign someone to keep everyone focused and someone to take notes. Then use the questions below to guide your conversation.

1. **Connect to Your Life:** How do Latoya's values about what is important in her life compare to your own? What did she say in her diary that helped you realize something new about your own values?

2. **Critical Thinking: Evaluate** What do you admire or respect about Latoya? What makes you feel impatient or annoyed with her? Give examples from the diary to support your opinions.

3. **6+1 Trait®: Voice** How does Latoya's writing help you understand how she feels? Name some specific passages, lines, or phrases from the diary that made you care about her as a person.

4. **Connect to Your Writing:** After reading this selection, what qualities do you think personal writing should have? Make a list of criteria for good personal writing.

 Write About Reading

Friendly Letter Write a friendly letter to Latoya, telling her what you two share in common or how you are different. Describe how your experiences, feelings, or values compare to hers. See the letter on page 329 for help with formatting your letter.

Focus on Voice Your letter will be more interesting for Latoya to read if you write about feelings and experiences in an open, direct voice. After you have written a draft of the letter, evaluate it. Ask yourself whether your ideas are clear, your sentences are varied, and your voice is true. Revise as you think necessary.

For more information on voice and the 6+1 Trait® model, see **Writing and Research Handbook,** pages 822–824.

6+1 Trait® is a registered trademark of Northwest Regional Educational Laboratory, which does not endorse this product.

Reflecting on the Unit: Summarize What You Learned

Focus on the following questions to help summarize what you learned in this unit.

1 What are the major purposes of personal writing?

2 Who is the audience for your personal writing?

3 What kinds of things can you put in your journal? What can they be used for?

4 Is personal writing formal or informal?

5 How can a journal serve as a learning log?

Adding to Your Portfolio

CHOOSE A SELECTION FOR YOUR PORTFOLIO Look over the personal writing you did for this unit. Choose a completed piece for your portfolio. Look for writing that shows one or more of the following:

- an idea or experience important to you
- a source of ideas for future writing
- thoughts and ideas you would like to share

REFLECT ON YOUR CHOICE Attach a note to the piece you chose, explaining briefly why you chose it and what you learned from writing it.

SET GOALS How can you improve your writing? What skill will you focus on the next time you write?

Writing Across the Curriculum

MAKE A HISTORY CONNECTION Select a man or woman from history. Jot down notes about the person's accomplishments or the important events in his or her life. Then use your notes to write a personal letter to the person, sharing your thoughts and feelings about his or her accomplishments or life.

" *Each mountain I face
is another pinnacle
in an internal adventure.* **"**

—Stacy Allison,
Beyond the Limits

The Writing Process

Writing in the Real World

MEDIA Connection
Newspaper Feature

"The Freep"? It's not a monster or a new soft drink. It's a weekly feature page in the *Detroit Free Press* that addresses topics of interest to today's young people. Readers enjoy "The Freep" for its eye-catching graphics and its lively content. Behind the scenes, though, there's a lot of work that goes into achieving that fun, contemporary style. The excerpt below is from a personality profile that highlights two talented local teens.

Smart, Cool and on the Air

by Maisha Maurant

Some use the word "nerd" to label smart folks, but you can be smart and cool. Standish-Sterling High School seniors Brooke Gillette and Anna Galvas certainly are.

They run their own radio talk show, spin records as disc jockeys, and work part-time at fast-food restaurants.

And they're honor students besides. Anna's got a 3.6 grade-point average; Brooke's average is 3.28.

Classmate Aaron Koin sure is impressed. "It's neat that they are on the radio and still in high school," he says.

Brooke and Anna are two of the people we heard about when "The Freep" asked

readers to name people they thought were smart and cool.

"It seems like these are the kinds of girls who, when I was in school, were looked up to as the trendsetters but weren't stuck up," says Tim LaVere, the 27-year-old news director at WSTD-FM (96.9).

from "Smart, Cool and on the Air," an article in "The Freep" section of *The Detroit Free Press*

Maisha Maurant, writer

Nunzio Lupo, editor

Keith Webb, designer

Creating a Feature Page		
Prewriting	**Drafting**	**Revising/Editing**

Planning the Page	Getting the Words Down	Meeting the Deadline

A Writer's Process

Prewriting
Planning the Page

Like most sections of a newspaper, "The Freep" reflects the collaboration of several people. Leading the effort is assistant features editor, Nunzio Lupo. He's assisted by designer Keith Webb and a staff of writers. One regular contributor is Maisha Maurant, who wrote the article "Smart, Cool, and on the Air."

Lupo usually begins planning each issue three to four weeks before publication. He mines many sources for ideas, including other sections of the *Detroit Free Press* and such youth magazines as *Spin* and *Sassy.* He also gets ideas from letters to the editor, such as the idea about two high school disc jockeys who were both smart and cool. Lupo gave the letter to Maurant and asked

her to explore the topic of smart and cool friends for a "Freep" article.

Another part of the prewriting stage is brainstorming ideas for graphics. Webb, a partner in this process, believes that graphics are just as important as words. "Graphics should help tell the story," he maintains, "not just decorate it."

Drafting
Getting the Words Down

The drafting stage belongs essentially to the writer— Maurant, in this case. Maurant usually has a week to write a feature. When she sits down to draft a manuscript, she looks over her notes on the subject. For "Smart, Cool, and on the Air," she took notes while conducting a telephone interview with the two student disc jockeys. During the interview, Maurant gathered facts for the story, including the subjects' grade-point averages and their activities in and out of school.

Maurant usually begins her drafting process by writing the lead, the opening that establishes the direction the feature will take. "I'm impatient," she explains. "I like to get a lead down to give me a feel for where I want to go."

Working at home, Maurant drafts the article in longhand. Once in the office, she transfers her draft into the computer. Maurant's drafting style is to write quickly without stopping. She never makes changes until she's got the whole piece down. After writing the first draft, Maurant will return to her notes so that she can "fill in things that make the story tighter."

Maurant keeps her young "Freep" audience in mind as she writes. "I try to use the most vivid words and images. My audience wants to be able to 'see' it."

Before she submits her article to Lupo, Maurant likes to set the manuscript aside for a day. She feels that a fresh mind helps her revise and perfect the story. After a day has passed, she reads the article once more, looking for unanswered questions and unclear information.

Revising/Editing
Meeting the Deadline

Maurant's story is due to Lupo the Friday before publication, which is press time—the day that copy goes to the printer. On deadline day, Maurant e-mails her copy to Lupo. Lupo reads the article, and then Maurant and Lupo work together to revise the article.

If Lupo and Maurant think the article seems flat or that something might be missing, they try to identify what's needed. Perhaps a stronger lead will help, or maybe they need to add more facts or new quotations. Lupo and Maurant toss solutions back and forth. "Sometimes," says Lupo, "reporters will think an idea is obvious, when, in fact, only they can see it. I can point out that their view isn't getting through."

After the copy is revised, Lupo meets again with designer Keith Webb. For "Smart, Cool, and on the Air," Webb created a graphic of a human brain. Lupo then wrote captions that described the smart and cool thoughts of this brain.

In the final step before publication, Lupo reviews the proofs. Copy editors have been working on the page, correcting spelling and grammar. With Lupo's sign-off, the page makes its way to press.

Examining Writing in the Real World

Analyzing the Media Connection

Discuss these questions about the excerpt on page 42.

1. What is the main idea that Maurant gets across in her lead? Do you agree that this idea is an interesting topic to young people? Explain your answer.

2. Why do you think Maurant gives information about the students' grades and activities?

3. Quotations help make writing come alive. Identify two quotations that Maurant uses. Explain why, in each case, she may have used a quotation instead of paraphrasing the speaker's words.

4. What is Maurant's purpose in this article? In your opinion, how well does this excerpt fulfill that purpose? Explain your answer.

Analyzing a Writer's Process

Discuss these questions about Maurant's writing process.

1. Where did Maurant gather material for "Smart, Cool and on the Air"? What other sources might she have used?

2. Why does Maurant begin drafting by establishing the lead? If you were writing a feature article, would you begin in the same way? Why or why not?

3. Maurant drafts straight through the first time with no changes. What is the advantage of drafting in that way?

4. What role does editor Nunzio Lupo play in the revision process? Why do you think this is helpful? How might you get the same kind of help for your own writing?

GrammarLink

Feature writers like Maurant follow set capitalization rules for direct quotations. They capitalize the first word of a quote but not the second part of an interrupted sentence.

"I try," says Maurant, "to use the most vivid words and images."

Correct the capitalization in the sentences below.

1. Webb says, "graphics should help tell the story."

2. "You know Maurant's approach," says Lupo, "Is to get a lead down right away."

3. "After I cover the facts," says Maurant, "Reviewing my notes helps me find anything I missed."

4. The reporter said, "press time is both exciting and challenging."

See Lesson 19.1, pages 573–574.

Using the Writing Process

Transforming a vacant lot covered with weeds and trash into a bright spot in the community isn't impossible. However, it takes planning and follow-through. It's the same with writing. Achieving a finished piece of writing requires planning carefully and following through.

The paragraph below is the result of Tai-Tang-Tran's thinking and planning. He began with an idea and worked through various stages of the writing process to describe Chinese New Year traditions.

Student Model

Many Chinese New Year traditions are about luck. One tradition that my family celebrates is the giving of lucky money. Parents give children money in a red envelope. The envelope symbolizes luck. Putting the money in the envelope means that the parent is sharing luck with a child. Both giving and receiving the red envelope bring luck.

Tai-Tang-Tran, Emerson Junior High School
Oak Park, Illinois

Having read this passage, what do you suppose Tai's complete piece is about?

Work in Your Own Way

Every writer works in his or her own way, but most writers take their writing through several stages before they finish. Before Tai finished his essay, he went through a process. First he listed his ideas about traditions. Then he organized them into paragraphs. Later he rearranged and polished his writing until he was satisfied.

Write from Start to Finish

Many writers use the following stages of the writing process. Not every writer follows them in strict order, however. Many writers go back to certain stages before they finish a piece of writing.

PREWRITING In this stage you find and explore ideas and then decide on a topic to write about. At this time you also decide on your audience, the people who will read or hear your writing, and you decide on the overall purpose of your writing.

DRAFTING Transforming thoughts, words, and phrases into sentences and paragraphs is called drafting. You can rearrange and revise your writing more easily once your ideas are in draft form.

Chinese New Year traditions:
lucky red money
spiri...
dra...
luc...

Around Chinese New Year adults and children feel lucky. Parents always give children lucky money. Both the parents and the children get luck when giving or receiving the lucky money. The red envelope symbolizes luck, and the money inside means the adult giving the money is taking some of the adult's luck and sharing it with the children.

Journal Writing

Think about the last time you wrote something. What challenges or rewards did that writing project present? Write your thoughts in your journal.

REVISING   In the revising stage you look at your writing to be sure it's clear and organized. You read your writing to a partner. Guide your revisions with questions like these: Does what I've written make sense? Have I presented my ideas in a sensible order? Have I kept my audience in mind?

Some pieces of writing need little revision. Others need revising two, four, even a dozen times before they satisfy their authors.

EDITING/PROOFREADING   The editing/proofreading stage, unlike the revising stage, focuses on the mechanics of your writing. When you edit and proofread, you make sure that you've spelled and punctuated your writing properly. You also try to correct any grammatical errors.

PUBLISHING/PRESENTING   In the last stage of writing, you present your work to your audience. You present some pieces of writing by handing them in to your teacher. You present other pieces more publicly. For example, you might read a research paper aloud in class, mail a letter to a local newspaper, or deliver a speech to members of a club or a community group.

The diagram below shows the stages of the writing process. Remember, it's up to you to decide how you move through the different stages.

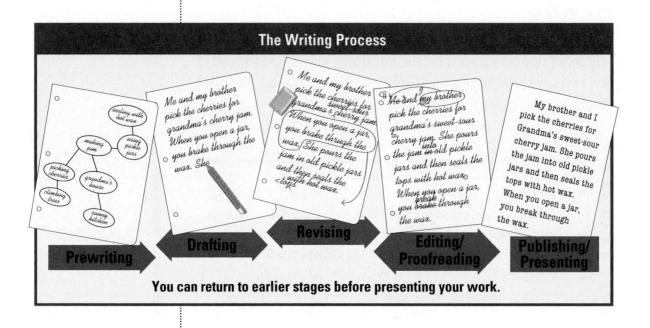

The Writing Process

You can return to earlier stages before presenting your work.

Write a Paragraph

Think about how you write. Do you go through a different process for different kinds of writing? For example, do you spend more time writing a report than writing a letter to a school newspaper? Write a description of your writing process.

PURPOSE To understand your writing process

AUDIENCE Yourself

LENGTH 1–2 paragraphs

WRITING RUBRICS To describe your writing process, you should

- decide what parts of the process are most challenging and most rewarding
- tell whether you move straight through the stages of the writing process or go back and forth between stages

Collaborative Writing

In a small group discuss the challenges that writing projects have presented. Each member of the group should take a few minutes to describe his or her writing experiences. Then take turns suggesting ways to approach the challenges described. Take notes.

Write a few paragraphs that describe any writing problems you may have and include solutions suggested by others.

GrammarLink

With a compound subject joined by *and*, use the plural form of the verb.

*Around Chinese New Year **adults and children feel** lucky.*

Rewrite each sentence, adding a noun or pronoun to make the subject compound. Use the correct form of the verb.

1. Bill jogs the ten blocks to school each day.
2. Mari watches for end-of-season sales.
3. Marcos belongs to the Carlton Junior High Science Club.
4. Jusef has played on the soccer team for two years.
5. In my opinion, the president was wrong about that.

See Lesson 16.5, page 543.

Cross-Curricular Activity

SOCIAL STUDIES Student Tai-Tang-Tran has described a Chinese New Year tradition on page 46. See if you can find out more about traditions that welcome in the new year in different countries around the world. Write a paragraph to share with classmates.

LOG ON ▶ **Writing** Online | For more writing and grammar practice, go to glencoe.com and enter **Quickpass** code WC77680p1.

49

Prewriting: Finding and Exploring a Topic

*O*ften *you write because you need to or want to. You might write a thank-you letter, a note asking for permission to do something, or a school assignment. At other times, however, you need to think of how to fill an empty sheet of paper.*

Some writers get their ideas easily. Other writers have their own special methods for getting ideas. Some take a walk; others take a shower. Some listen to music; others listen to friends. To come up with ideas, try a few basic techniques.

Identify Your Main Ideas

As a first step in ordering your thoughts, fig[ure] your main ideas. You may have only one main idea, [or] may have several. Remember your purpose for writing. W[hich id]eas will you need to include to help you meet your goal[s?]

Henry is reading a list of the main ideas he an[d] [o]thers will include in their proposal. They want to persuade [a com]munity improvement group to develop a neighborhood l[ot. Eac]h main idea is a point meant to help persuade the co[m]munity group to put the plan into action.

Journal Writing

Select a piece of writing you created earlier [f]or this unit. Read the piece to identify one or more mai[n] ideas. Underline each main idea you find.

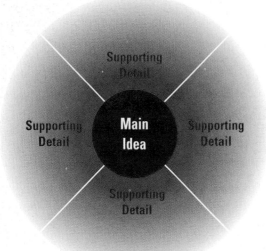

Find an Order That Works

Each main idea needs details, such as examples, facts, or reasons, to support it. The illustration on this page shows how a main idea and supporting details work together.

Brainstorm or use prewriting notes to make a list of details. Once you have the details, you can put them in order. The order will depend on your purpose.

- To persuade your reader, you might list details in the order of their importance. List the most important detail either first or last, depending on which order you think will be more convincing.

- To describe something, you might list the details in the order in which an observer would notice them, or you can begin with the more significant details.

- To explain something, you might work from the simplest details to the most difficult ones or from the first step to the last.

Supporting Detail

Supporting Detail

Main Idea

Supporting Detail

Supporting Detail

The empty lot is bad for the neighborhood

②businesses near the lot suffer

①it's unsafe *most important, mention first*

~~people think the lot makes our neighborhood the~~

~~ugliest in the city~~ *just an opinion, doesn't really fit here*

Notice that this group listed details first and ordered them later.

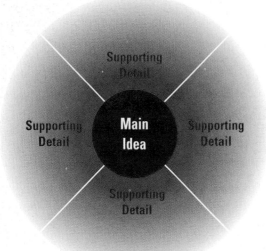

Make a Plan for Writing

Look at your topic and begin to plan your writing.

PURPOSE To plan your writing

AUDIENCE Yourself

LENGTH 1–2 paragraphs

WRITING RUBRICS To plan your writing, you should

• list your main ideas and supporting details

• arrange the main ideas and details in an order that suits your purpose

Henri Matisse, *The Bowl with Goldfish*, 1914

Grammar Link

Use *it's* and *its* correctly.

It's is a contraction. *Its* is a possessive pronoun used with a noun.

It's unsafe. **Its** bowl is clean.

Fill in each blank with *it's* or *its*.

The goldfish is floating in **1**_____ bowl. **2**_____ not very lively. Is that **3**_____ reflection at the bottom of the bowl? The fish tried to jump out of **4**_____ bowl. I hope **5**_____ going to be all right.

See Lesson 17.2, pages 555.

Viewing and Representing

SUMMARIZING IDEAS In a small group, discuss Henri Matisse's painting. What shapes do you notice? Where do you tend to focus as you look at the painting? How does the artist draw your eye to that spot? Finally, write a brief summary of your group's discussion.

Cross-Curricular Activity

SCIENCE Where do goldfish (*Carassius auratus*) live in nature? How do they survive? Research to learn more about them. Then plan your main ideas and supporting details. Write two paragraphs and share your findings with the class.

LOG ON ▶ **Writing** Online | For more writing and grammar practice, go to glencoe.com and enter QuickPass code WC77680p1.

61

LESSON 2.5

Drafting: Getting It in Writing

You're ready to write a first draft of your essay, story, or report. How should you begin?

By drafting, you turn your lists, clusters, and other prewriting work into sentences and paragraphs. The draft shown below didn't just write itself. The writer, Keshia, used her group's prewriting notes to guide her drafting.

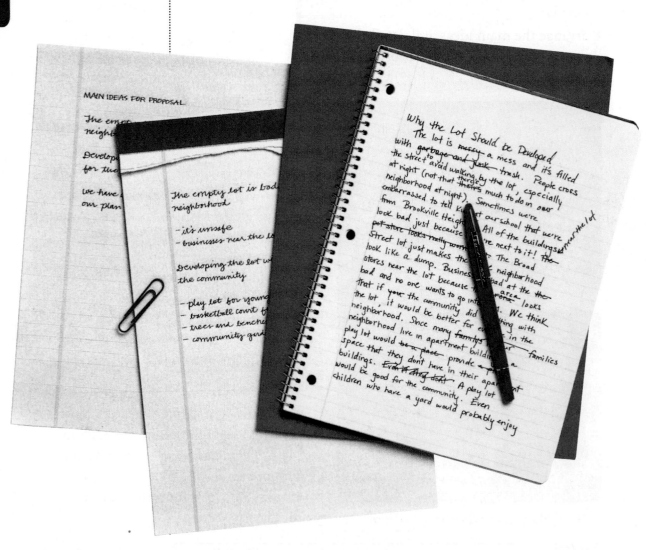

Try Different Ways

Sometimes stories and reports seem easy to write. At other times, your first page stays blank no matter how long you look at it. You might already have a way to begin drafting. If you don't or if you'd like to try another way, you might experiment with one of the following suggestions:

1. **Pretend you're writing to a friend.** Write as if you're talking about your idea with a friend who always listens and understands.
2. **Start on the easiest part.** You don't have to start at the beginning. Start by writing the easiest sections. Then the other parts will probably seem easier to write.
3. **Speak your ideas into a tape recorder.** Say what you're thinking on tape, and you'll have an instant first draft.
4. **Set reasonable goals.** The thought of writing an entire essay, report, or story can be scary. Decide that you are going to write just one paragraph or even one sentence at a time.

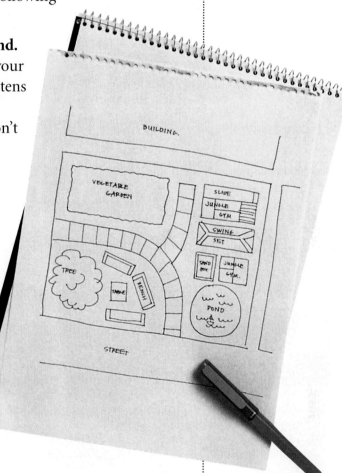

Journal Writing

Think about the techniques listed above or about one you have developed yourself. Then explain in your journal how these suggestions might help you with your drafting.

Write On

Once you've begun writing, the challenge is to continue writing. Keep your prewriting notes handy. Look back at them whenever you reach a stopping point in your writing.

Completing your first draft is more important than perfecting every sentence. Later you can rearrange your sentences or improve the way they're stated. You can also check grammar, spelling, and punctuation at a later stage.

Some writers like to draft on a computer. Others prefer to draft by hand. Do whatever works best for you. If you find yourself stuck, however, consider trying the suggestions below to get your writing back on track.

Write a Draft

Now it's time to face that blank sheet of paper. Just write. Skip every other line to leave room for changes. Don't worry about correctness. At this stage, you are still exploring what you want to say.

PURPOSE To create a draft

AUDIENCE Yourself

LENGTH 1–2 paragraphs

WRITING RUBRICS To begin drafting, you should

- use your prewriting notes
- get your ideas down on paper
- try to put your ideas down in an order that makes sense

Charles Goeller, *Third Avenue*, 1933–1934

Grammar*Link*

Use correct forms of *good*.

*If the community did something with the lot, it would be **better** for everyone.*

Fill in each blank with *good*, *better*, or *best*.

Third Avenue looks quite **1**_____ in this painting, but certain changes would make it even **2**_____. The market would look cleaner and **3**_____ with a paint job. For the street to look its **4**_____, someone should dispose of the litter. Is that man wearing the **5**_____ hat of all?

See Lesson 12.3, page 455.

Viewing and Representing

EVALUATING What old-fashioned and super-modern images do you see in Charles Goeller's painting? What message or story might the artist be presenting? In a small group, compare your ideas with those of others.

Cross-Curricular Activity

HEALTH What links do you think exist between health and school performance? What connections do you find between your physical and mental health? List your ideas and decide how to order them. Then draft a paper stating your opinions about this idea.

LOG ON ▶ **Writing** Online | For more writing and grammar practice, go to glencoe.com and enter QuickPass code WC77680p1.

65

Revising: Evaluating a Draft

L *ooking at the whole piece of writing rather than just its parts is important when you begin to evaluate and revise.*

Once your draft is finished, step back and look at it. Does it all go together, or do some parts not belong? Are any parts missing? Are all the parts in order?

When Henry, Mike, and Keshia looked at their sketch, they realized that some parts did not belong and would have to go.

Evaluate for Clarity

When your draft is done, set it aside for a while before you read it again. When you return to the draft, evaluate it for clarity and decide whether it makes sense. Answering the questions on this checklist will help you decide how to revise your draft for clarity.

Get a Second Opinion

One of the best ways to evaluate a draft is to have a peer reviewer examine it. Getting another opinion helps you gain distance from your writing. The remainder of this lesson explains how to be a peer reviewer and what to do once you get a peer reviewer's advice.

A WRITING CONFERENCE In a writing conference you read your draft to a partner or a small group. These are your peer reviewers. Peer reviewers try to answer these questions: What's the main idea of this paper? Do the details in the paper support that idea? Your goal as a peer reviewer isn't to label the writing good or bad. Instead, tell the writer what you understand to be the paper's main idea and purpose. Then tell how well you think the draft is working. Ask about anything that is unclear.

☑ Do I stick to my topic?

☑ Do I accomplish my purpose?

☑ Do I keep my audience in mind?

☑ Does my main idea come across clearly?

☑ Do I give enough details? too many?

Journal Writing

Think about the role of a peer reviewer. As you do, consider what kinds of advice you would like from a peer reviewer. What should your reviewer look for? How would you like your reviewer to evaluate your writing? Write your thoughts in your journal.

GIVING AND RECEIVING FEEDBACK Sometimes you may want to make or receive detailed comments on a draft. To make comments, you might find it helpful to fill out a peer-review form—either one from your teacher or a form of your own.

When you receive a review of your work, discuss the comments with your peer reviewer. If your reviewer has criticisms, remember that your writing is being evaluated, not you. Finally, remember that you're the writer. You decide which changes you'll make to your writing.

> The peer reviewer understood the purpose of the paper and for whom it was written. The draft forms a good foundation for the paper.

PEER REVIEW

1. What is the main idea of this paper?
   The Broad Street lot should be developed into a park, a play lot, and a community garden.

2. What is the writer's purpose? *To convince people to fix up the lot*

3. Who would be the intended audience for this paper? *Brookville Heights Community Improvement Group*

4. Which parts of the paper stand out for you? Name or describe them, and explain why they seem important. *The plans for developing the lot were great. I felt excited as I read about them. They convinced me that the proposal was a good idea.*

5. Identify any parts of the paper that seem puzzling or out of place. *Some comments, like ones about nothing to do in the neighborhood and being embarrassed to say where they're from, should have been left out.*

Why the Lot Sh...
The lot is a...
trash. People c...
avoid walking...
that there's n...
night). Some...
at our school...
Heights!
All of the...
because th...
just make...

Evaluate a Draft

Look again at your draft. Make sure some time has gone by before you begin to revise it. When you make your changes, remember that you can circle, delete, tape on—neatness is not a part of revising!

PURPOSE To prepare to revise
AUDIENCE Your peer reviewers
LENGTH 1 page of comments

WRITING RUBRICS To begin to revise your draft, you should

- use the checklist on page 67 to evaluate your draft for clarity
- read your paper to a peer reviewer or reviewers. Discuss your paper with them, using the Peer Review form on page 68

Using Computers

Use e-mail to share your writing with a peer reviewer. In your message, include the peer review checklist from page 68. Then attach a copy of your paper to your e-mail message. Ask your reviewer to respond to your paper by typing responses on the checklist and sending it back to you.

Cross-Curricular Activity

SCIENCE You are an archaeologist who has just unearthed a painting in an Egyptian tomb. Write a description of it. Then ask a fellow archaeologist (another student) to review your writing for clarity.

GrammarLink

Capitalize proper nouns.

Capitalize the specific names of places and groups, as well as the names of months and days of the week.

Rewrite the following paragraph, adding capital letters where necessary.

¹ Nella and Pietro belong to a neighborhood book club, the reading bugs. ² The club meets every thursday at the library on main street. ³ Once a month they go to memorial library on center street in mannville, where they visit with the fact and fiction club. ⁴ After the meeting everyone gathers at maury's pizzeria. ⁵ Since september, members of both clubs have been helping the children at rose park elementary school learn to read.

See Lesson 19.3, page 577, and Lesson 19.4, page 579.

LOG ON ▶ **Writing** Online | For more writing and grammar practice, go to glencoe.com and enter QuickPass code WC77680p1.

69

The Writing Process

Revising: Making Paragraphs Effective

An effective paragraph must have unity—that is, all sentences must work together to support a main idea.

Just as a garden is an arrangement of plants, a paragraph is an arrangement of sentences. All the sentences in the following paragraph present the main idea, a childhood memory.

Literature Model

Some of my earliest memories are of the storms, the hot rain lashing down and lightning running on the sky—and the storm cellar into which my mother and I descended so many times when I was very young. For me that little room in the earth is an unforgettable place. Across the years I see my mother reading there on the low, narrow bench, the lamplight flickering on her face and on the earthen walls; I smell the dank odor of that room; and I hear the great weather raging at the door. I have never been in a place that was like it exactly; only now and then I have been reminded of it suddenly when I have gone into a cave, or when I have just caught the scent of fresh, open earth steaming in the rain.

N. Scott Momaday, *The Names*

Notice that all the sentences in the paragraph support the idea in the first sentence.

Look for Main Ideas

As you review your draft, look for the main ideas. A main idea is like a magnet, pulling sentences toward it to form a paragraph.

Many paragraphs have a topic sentence that states the main idea. Sometimes a topic sentence is the first sentence in a paragraph. Other times it is the last sentence of a paragraph. Not all paragraphs need topic sentences, however. Many well-written paragraphs consist of sentences that suggest the main idea without directly stating it.

Although topic sentences are used in all types of writing, they're most common in paragraphs written to explain or persuade. When attempting to persuade, you don't want to make readers guess what you're thinking.

Notice the way this draft has been broken into paragraphs. Does each paragraph have a topic sentence? If so, what is it?

Since many families in our neighborhood live in apartments, a play lot would provide space that they don't have in their apartment buildings.

Topic sentence
A play lot would be good for the community. Even children who have a yard would enjoy a playground where there would be other children to play with.

New paragraph
For younger children the play lot would include a sturdy swing-and-slide set, a climbing frame, a sandbox, and a merry-go-round. Older kids could use two basketball hoops and backboards and a tetherball pole.

This idea doesn't fit in.
~~Regular exercise might improve school performance, as well.~~ These features would give children and teenagers something to do besides going to the mall or watching television.

Journal Writing

Select paragraphs from three different types of writing. You might choose paragraphs from a novel, a textbook, and an instruction manual. Is the main idea of each paragraph stated in a topic sentence? If so, copy the sentence into your journal. If not, write the main idea in your own words.

For more
information on
transitions, see
**Writing and
Research
Handbook,**
page 820.

The Writing Process

Link Thoughts Sensibly

Transitions are words and phrases that help connect sentences in some sensible manner. Transitions provide the links between ideas in a paragraph. *Also* and *as a result* are examples of these types of transitions.

Transitions such as *in front of* and *until then* help express a relationship in space or time. Other common transitions appear in the chart on this page. Notice how the revisions to the draft below use transitions to link thoughts within the paragraph and to show relationships.

Common Transitions			
after	before	because	although
now	therefore	however	for example
here	then	like	next to

This sentence was moved to the beginning because it provides a concrete example out of which the other sentences grow.

We don't think any store can be successful ~~next~~
in that location
~~to the lot.~~ Businesses nearby suffer because of
also
the lot's condition. *In the last two years*
Several businesses have come
and gone in the building next to the lot. We know
that developing the lot would make our neighbor-
Then
hood feel safer and look better. People might be
able to shop closer to home.

Why did the writer add the transition "Then"?

The Writing Process

Revise for Effective Paragraphs

Take another look at your draft. Evaluate each of your paragraphs.

PURPOSE To revise for paragraph unity
AUDIENCE Yourself
LENGTH Changes on the draft

WRITING RUBRICS To revise a paragraph for unity, you should

- make sure that all sentences are about one main idea
- decide if your paragraph needs a topic sentence, and if it does, add one
- add transition words to link thoughts and show relationships

Using Computers

To revise on the computer, make a copy of your paper. (Highlight your writing, copy it, and paste it on a new page or file.) Then revise—insert and delete words, move sentences, add new sentences. After revising, read both versions. Have you kept your important ideas? Have you organized them effectively?

GrammarLink

Use a comma after two or more introductory prepositional phrases.

You do not need to use a comma after a single short prepositional phrase at the beginning of a sentence. Do use a comma after two or more introductory prepositional phrases.

> **On the gate across the road,** a sign proclaimed "Town Forest."

Rewrite the paragraph below, adding commas where necessary.

[1]In the town forest I can observe a variety of plant life. [2]Along the path through the woods oaks and hemlocks compete for the light. [3]Among the roots of the trees partridgeberry and lady's slippers catch my eye. [4]In the sunny glade at the top of the hill wood lilies and wild geraniums flourish.

See Lesson 13.1, page 479, and Lesson 20.2, page 591.

Listening and Speaking

COOPERATIVE LEARNING In a small group, discuss your work so far. Each group member should share two things about his or her paper that are going well, as well as two problems. Brainstorm for solutions.

 **Writing** Online | For more writing and grammar practice, go to glencoe.com and enter QuickPass code WC77680p1.

73

The Writing Process

Revising: Creating Sentence Variety

*U*sing *a variety of sentences in your writing can make it more appealing.*

Think about the sentences in your paragraphs and the way you use those sentences. Varying the plantings and the size and shape of garden beds makes a garden more interesting to look at. Likewise, varying your sentences makes your writing more interesting to read.

Breaking run-on sentences makes them easier to understand.

*We know that it will take money to develop the lot**. and** we are willing to do our part to help raise the money. We could plan several fund-raising events**,** Such as a car wash, a raffle, and a rummage sale. **Also,** Many teenagers and grown-ups from the neighborhood have offered to help us, **also.***

Vary Sentence Length

Look at the length of your sentences. Too many short sentences make writing sound choppy. Too many long sentences make your thoughts difficult to follow.

Varying the order of words or phrases can add clarity to your writing. For example, you can write "The bat hit the ball with a loud crack," or "With a loud crack, the bat hit the ball."

Notice how revisions affect the rhythm of the paragraph.

Journal Writing

Select a passage of several sentences from your journal. Experiment with ways to vary the length and word order of the sentences. Write the variations in your journal.

SUNFLOWERS
LARGE
GRAY STRIPE

TOMATOES

CARROTS

SCARLET
NANTES

Revising Tip

For more information on varying sentences, see **Writing and Research Handbook,** pages 817–818.

Combine Sentences

You can also create variety by combining sentences that express similar ideas. Two or more sentences can be combined into one. Look at these sentences, and notice how they can be combined.

Wait until after the last frost to plant tomatoes. Wait until after the last frost to plant cucumbers, too.

Wait until after the last frost to plant tomatoes and cucumbers.

In both sentences, "Wait until after the last frost" expresses the same idea. "Tomatoes" and "cucumbers" are different nouns in those sentences. Consider combining sentences that express similar ideas but have different nouns, adjectives, or verbs.

When you combine sentences, certain words and phrases can clarify the relationships between ideas. For example, the sentence "Return that overdue book when you go to the library" uses the word *when* to express a relationship between two activities—*return* and *go*.

Notice how this writer combined similar thoughts and expressed the relationships between activities.

Another way that neighborhood people can help is by volunteering their time to work in the lot. Volunteers can pick up trash. They and can clear out weeds. They can also plant grass, trees, and flowers. This can happen once the work gets started.

The Writing Process

Vary Sentence Lengths

Adjust the sentences in your draft as you revise. Vary the lengths of your sentences.

PURPOSE To revise for sentence variety
AUDIENCE Yourself
LENGTH Changes on the draft

WRITING RUBRICS To revise for sentence variety, you should

- mix long and short sentences
- vary the beginnings of sentences
- combine sentences when it makes sense to do so
- use end punctuation correctly

Viewing and Representing

Notice the use of vertical and horizontal lines, as well as the use of space, in *Latticework*. Discuss with a partner

Josef Albers, *Latticework*, c. 1926

Grammar*Link*

To avoid repetition, use pronouns to replace nouns.

People can help by volunteering *their* time to work in the lot.

Write the paragraph below, replacing nouns with pronouns where appropriate.

[1]Juan plays the tuba in the school band. [2]Juan likes the low deep sounds of the tuba. [3]Juan's grandfather takes an afternoon nap. [4]Juan's grandfather always wakes up when Juan begins to play the tuba.

See Lessons 11.1–11.2, pages 429–432.

any patterns you see. Then create your own latticeworks and compare designs.

Cross-Curricular Activity

ART Rewrite the following passage about artist Josef Albers. Change the word order or combine sentences to vary the length of the sentences and to create effective sound and rhythm.

Josef Albers was born in Germany. He left Germany for the United States. Albers arrived in the United States in 1933. Albers made pictures out of pieces of colored glass. He used primary colors.

LOG ON ▶ **Writing** Online | For more writing and grammar practice, go to **glencoe.com** and enter QuickPass code WC77680p1.

77

Editing/Proofreading: Making Final Adjustments

O nce you've made all your revisions, you need to edit and proofread your work. Now you will check your spelling, punctuation, grammar, and usage.

Just as Keshia, Mike, and Henry are checking every part of their proposal, you need to look at every word in your writing to make sure that there are no errors or omissions. Before you present your work, make sure it looks good and reads as smoothly as possible.

Check Your Sentences

Editing/Proofreading is usually the last stage before you make your final copy and present your writing to an audience. At this point you have already reorganized paragraphs or inserted new ideas into your work.

When you edit and proofread, go over your writing line by line, word by word.

The checklist at the right will help you find many of your errors. If you're uncertain of a spelling, consult a dictionary. Make sure you know the meanings of the words you use and that you've chosen the right words. See that you've used a singular verb with a singular subject and a plural verb with plural subject. Check that you have used verb tenses appropriately. Examine your use of periods, commas, quotation marks, semicolons, and other punctuation marks.

Peer reviewers can help you edit. They can often spot errors in grammar, usage, and mechanics that you might overlook in your own work.

Editing/Proofreading Checklist

☑ Have I used all verbs properly?

☑ Do my subjects and verbs

☑ Have I used all pronouns properly?

☑ Have I used capital letters properly?

☑ Are my words spelled correctly?

☑ Have I used end punctuation marks correctly?

Journal Writing

Look in your journal for some writing that you have done recently. Choose a passage. Use the checklist above, a dictionary, and the Grammar, Usage, and Mechanics section of this book to edit the passage.

Drafting Tip

For more information on parallelism, see **Writing and Research Handbook,** page 818.

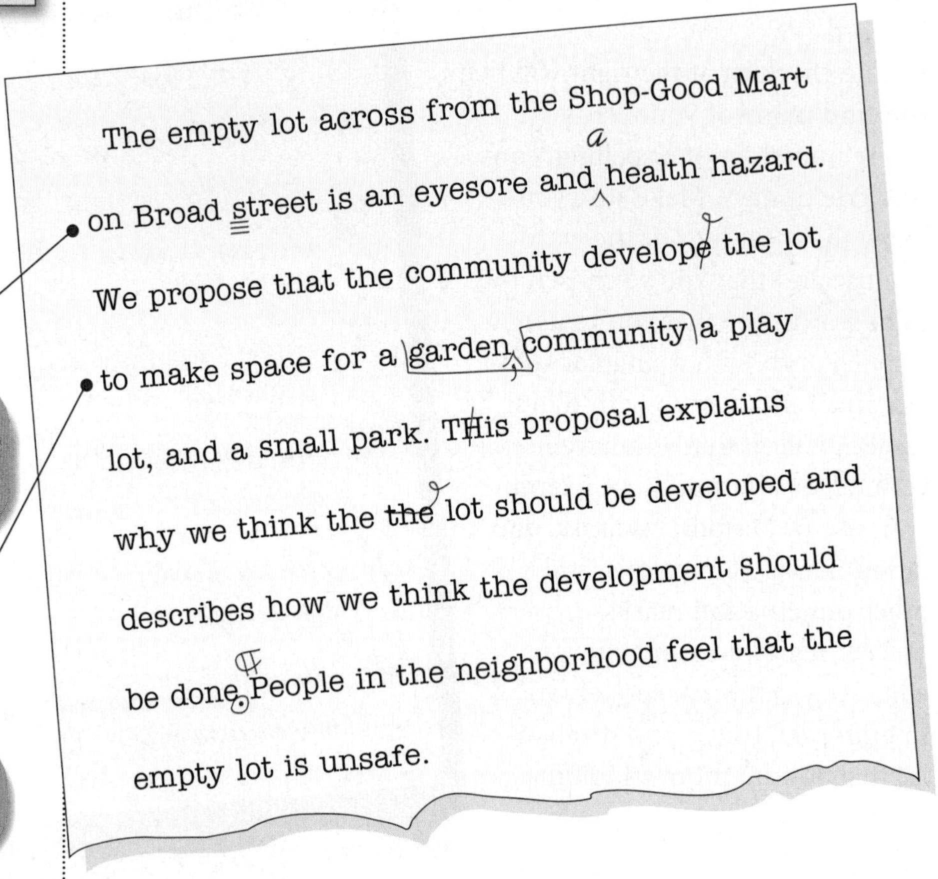

Proofread Your Copy

Proofreading symbols, like those shown below, make editing easier. Even if you do your own typing or word processing, use proofreading symbols as you edit. By clearly marking your copy, you can catch and correct errors before you prepare the final version of your writing.

The empty lot across from the Shop-Good Mart on Broad street is an eyesore and *a* health hazard. We propose that the community develope the lot to make space for a garden community a play lot, and a small park. This proposal explains why we think the the lot should be developed and describes how we think the development should be done. People in the neighborhood feel that the empty lot is unsafe.

Notice that the writer added the word *a* to create a more balanced, or parallel, construction.

Also notice the three parallel phrases in the second sentence.

Proofreading Symbols			
∧ Insert	⸜ Delete	⌐⌐ Reverse	⌗ New paragraph
⊙ Period	∧ Comma	＝ Capital letter	/ Lower-case letter

Writing Activities

Edit Your Writing

When you are satisfied that your writing says what you want it to say in the best possible way, the time has come to edit.

PURPOSE To edit for correctness
AUDIENCE Yourself
LENGTH Changes on the revised draft

WRITING RUBRICS To edit and proofread effectively, you should

- use the list on page 79 to edit your work
- check for one kind of error or problem at a time
- use proofreading symbols
- use end punctuation correctly

Listening and Speaking

SUMMARIZING IDEAS Write a half-page summary of what you have learned about the writing process in this unit. Then join two classmates to form a group, and pass your summaries around. Edit for spelling errors in the first paper you receive, for punctuation errors in the second, and for grammar or usage errors in the third. Look over your summary to see what changes your classmates suggested. Then discuss whether it was helpful to divide the editing into three separate steps.

GrammarLink

Use correct verb forms.

*By next week the development should be **done**.*

Write the past or past participle of the verb in parentheses to complete each sentence.

1. Tonya has (write) an essay.
2. My peer reviewer (teach) me to be more conscious of my audience.
3. Most of us have already (begin) to edit our drafts.
4. Laval (seek) out his peer reviewer to clarify her comments.
5. The editing process has (take) less time than I anticipated.
6. Working with my peer reviewer has (give) me greater confidence.

See Lesson 10.9, page 415, and Lesson 10.10, page 417.

Cross-Curricular Activity

ART Keshia, Mike, and Henry are making a proposal for the city. They are including a map of the playground they picture. Create a layout for an ideal park and recreation area. What features will you include? What symbols will you use for each type of playground equipment and recreation use? Include a paragraph that explains your design.

LOG ON ▶ **Writing** Online | For more writing and grammar practice, go to **glencoe.com** and enter QuickPass code WC77680p1.

81

Publishing/Presenting: Sharing Your Writing

You've said everything you wanted to say in the best way possible. You've fixed all the errors in your writing. Now it's time to make a clean, neat, legible version and to present your writing to its intended audience.

The completed sketch and the final, typed version of their proposal will help Mike, Henry, and Keshia make an impressive presentation to the community group.

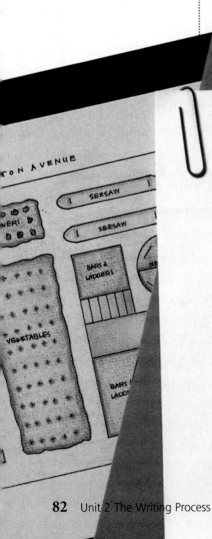

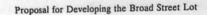

Proposal for Developing the Broad Street Lot

The empty lot on the corner of Broad Street and Washington Avenue is an eyesore and a health hazard. We propose that the community develop the lot to make space for a community garden, a play lot, and a small park. This proposal explains why we think the lot should be developed and describes how we think it could be done.

Why the Lot Should Be Developed
People in the neighborhood feel that the empty lot is unsafe. People cross the street to avoid walking by it, especially at night. It is overgrown with weeds and littered with trash. Glass from broken bottles is scattered over the ground. As a result, several children have been hurt while playing in the lot.
In the last two years several businesses have come and gone in the building next to the lot. We don't think any store can be successful in that location. Other businesses nearby also suffer because of the lot's condition. We know that developing the lot would make our neighborhood safer, and the neighborhood would look better. It might also mean that people would shop closer to home.

The Benefits of Improving the Lot
If our community developed the lot, people in the neighborhood would have a place to meet and spend time together. A park with benches and shade trees could be used by

Make a Good Impression

How you present your writing depends on your purpose and your audience. As you think about who will read your writing, you will decide if a formal presentation would be most impressive or if a casual or even artistic presentation would be better. Sometimes you may write it out by hand and give it a personal touch, such as when you write a letter to a friend. Remember to use your best cursive writing for handwritten letters. When you need something more formal, like a paper for a class, a letter to an editor, or a proposal to a community group, you'll want to use a typewriter or word processor. You might enclose your writing in a clear folder or binder to give it a more professional look.

Journal Writing

Think about a piece of writing you have completed recently. What two ways might you prepare it for presentation? In your journal, write a comparison of the two forms of presentation. Why did you choose them? What difference would a change in presentation make to your audience?

Presenting Tip

For more information on presentation and the 6+1 Trait® model, see **Writing and Research Handbook,** pages 822–823.

Reach Your Audience

Naturally, when you've finished your writing, you want to share it with the audience you've had in mind all along. How you reach an audience depends partly on who the audience is.

The illustration below shows several ways of presenting your work to different audiences. Forms of presentation include a printed report, a speech, a letter, a submission to a school literary magazine, a written invitation, a press release, a dramatic reading, or a banner. Keeping your audience in mind, ask yourself, How can I present my writing to reach this audience? Will visuals help?

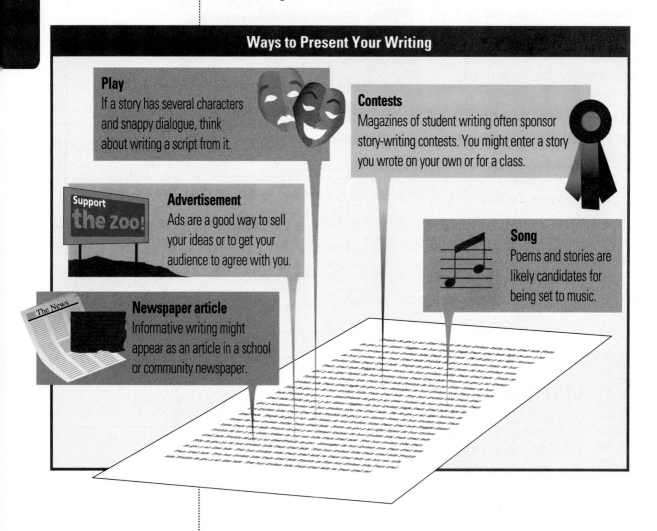

Ways to Present Your Writing

Play
If a story has several characters and snappy dialogue, think about writing a script from it.

Contests
Magazines of student writing often sponsor story-writing contests. You might enter a story you wrote on your own or for a class.

Advertisement
Ads are a good way to sell your ideas or to get your audience to agree with you.

Support the zoo!

Song
Poems and stories are likely candidates for being set to music.

Newspaper article
Informative writing might appear as an article in a school or community newspaper.

The News

Notice that some of these presentations are oral rather than written. Others might include illustrations or other types of images.

Present Your Writing

You have taken your writing through prewriting, drafting, revising, and editing/proofreading. Now it's time for the payoff—sharing your writing!

PURPOSE To share your finished work

AUDIENCE The audience you chose when you began to write

LENGTH Whatever is appropriate for your purpose

WRITING RUBRICS To share your finished work, you should

- choose a format that suits your purpose and your audience
- make your paper as neat, legible, and attractive as you can

Using Computers

If one of your presentations for the writing activity includes a poster, flyer, or other public notice, you might experiment with highlighting text by using different typefaces.

Try printing several versions of the same notice, using different combinations of type sizes and styles. Then compare the effects of the different versions.

Grammar*Link*

Use specific nouns to make your writing more interesting.

*The empty lot is an **eyesore** and a health **hazard**.*

Write a more specific noun to replace each noun in parentheses.

1. The woman's (clothing) was dirty, shabby, and ill-smelling.
2. I hope to study (science) in college someday.
3. My family has been reading (a book) aloud, a chapter a day.
4. I stayed up too late last night playing (a game).
5. Tom is crazy about his brand-new (bicycle).

See Lesson 9.1, page 379.

Viewing and Representing

Create a poster that shows the dos and don'ts of using the writing process. (For example, Do cluster or freewrite; Don't forget to proofread.) You may want to include photographs of classmates (with their permission) at work during various stages of the writing process. Present your poster to the class.

LOG ON **Writing** Online | For more writing and grammar practice, go to glencoe.com and enter QuickPass code WC77680p1.

85

Writing Process in Action

The Writing Process

In preceding lessons you've learned about the stages of the writing process. You've had a chance to explore a topic, write a draft and revise it, and finally present your feature writing. Now it's time to make use of what you learned by writing about courage—in yourself or in someone you admire.

Assignment

Context	A publication that prints stories, articles, and interviews by students about the bravery and endurance of young people
Purpose	To share your admiration of someone who overcame difficulty through bravery
Audience	Student readers
Length	3–4 paragraphs

Planning to Write

The following pages offer step-by-step advice on how to approach this assignment. Read through the pages before you begin. Then return to each step as needed while you work on your assignment. Set a time frame for completing this assignment so that you can pace yourself as you write. Be sure to keep in mind the controlling idea: to write about someone you admire because of their courage.

LOG ON ▶ **Writing** Online

For prewriting, drafting, revising, editing and publishing tools, go to **glencoe.com** and enter QuickPass code WC77680p1.

Prewriting

What's your definition of courage? Is it facing danger to save a life? Is it making a difficult decision? Or is it simply surviving in a situation that would make many people give up?

Begin looking for examples of courageous people. Decide on one person to write about. Choose one of the options at the right or an idea of your own. Then explore your subject by brainstorming, clustering, or listing. See pages 50–57 for more information about prewriting techniques.

Drafting

Look over your list, cluster diagram, or other prewriting notes. What problems did your subject face? Why do you think this person's act of bravery or courage is significant? Use your answers to these questions as foundations for sentences and paragraphs.

Remember that courage doesn't always come in a big, dramatic package. As in the model below, sometimes day-to-day life requires courage.

> **Option A**
>
> Talk to friends, teachers, or relatives.

> **Option B**
>
> Look through magazines or newspapers.

> **Option C**
>
> Read a biography.

courageous people–
  Helen Keller
from small town in Alabama
became deaf and blind in infancy
learned to speak at age ten
entered Radcliffe College at age
  nineteen

Literature Model

I know what you mean," she said slowly. "You try to hang on to older people—parents, uncles, grandmothers—and they disappear. You make friends, and they go off in different directions, never to be seen again. Everything crumbles so easily."

Minfong Ho, *The Clay Marble*

Drafting Tip

For more information about writing your first draft, see Lesson 2.5, page 62.

As you write your draft, think about specific actions that you admire in the person you're writing about. Remember, in the drafting stage you should let your ideas flow freely. Just get them down on paper. Try to express your ideas in sentences and paragraphs. You can always make changes later.

Revising

To begin revising, read over your draft to make sure that what you have written fits your purpose and your audience. Then have a **writing conference.** Read your draft to a partner or small group, or receive feedback from your teacher. Use your audience's reactions to help you evaluate your work so far. The questions below can help you and your listeners.

Option A

Have I explained why this person is courageous?

Option B

Does each paragraph add details to the picture?

Option C

Have I varied my sentences?

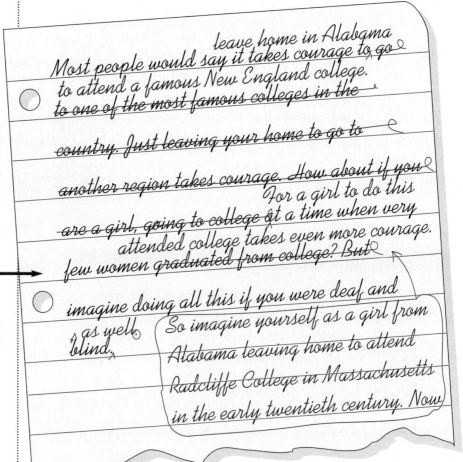

Most people would say it takes courage to ~~go~~ leave home in Alabama to attend a famous New England college. ~~to one of the most famous colleges in the country. Just leaving your home to go to another region takes courage. How about if you are a girl, going to college~~ For a girl to do this at a time when very few women ~~graduated from college? But~~ attended college takes even more courage. ~~imagine doing all this if you were deaf and~~ blind. So imagine yourself as a girl from Alabama leaving home to attend Radcliffe College in Massachusetts in the early twentieth century. Now

Editing/Proofreading

You've worked hard to determine what you want to say and how to say it well. As you prepare your article use the checklist at the right to help you get rid of any distracting errors.

In addition to proofreading, make sure your description does all the things you want to do. When you're satisfied, make a clean copy of your article and proofread it one more time.

Publishing/Presenting

Make sure your account of courage is neatly and legibly written or typed on clean white paper before you submit it. If possible, include a picture—a photograph or a drawing—of your subject so that readers will connect the actual person with what you've written.

As an alternative way of presenting your writing, you and others in your class might present your account as a play or a dramatic reading.

Try using spelling checker and grammar checker features on the computer to help you proofread your work.

Editing/Proofreading Checklist

1. Have I correctly capitalized proper nouns and direct quotations?
2. Have I used the correct forms of adjectives?
3. Have I used the correct forms of verbs?
4. Do my subjects and verbs agree?
5. Is every word spelled correctly?
6. Have I used possessive pronouns correctly?

Proofreading

For proofreading symbols, see pages 80 and 847.

Journal Writing: Write to Learn

Reflect on your writing process experience. Answer these questions in your journal. What do you like best about your article? What was the hardest part of writing it? What did you learn in your writing conference? What new things have you learned as a writer?

Literature Model

FROM

THE CLAY MARBLE

by Minfong Ho

In 1980, after North Vietnamese troops invaded Cambodia, writer Minfong Ho helped set up food programs for Cambodian children. Ho learned that these children, despite starvation and sickness, could enjoy making toys from clay. As you read, notice the details Ho uses to show how creative spirit can help people overcome the horrors of war. Then discuss the questions in Linking Writing and Literature on page 95.

After that marble, Jantu was interested only in playing with clay. She would spend the long afternoons crouched by the mud puddle by the stone beam, scooping up handfuls of moist clay to shape little figures.

For some reason, the massive stone beam attracted Jantu. She loved playing there. "It's so old, so solid," she said. "I like being near it. It makes me feel like a cicada[1] molting under some big rain tree."

At one end of the stone beam she had propped some fantail palm fronds,[2] to make a thatched shelter so that we could play in the shade. When we crouched under it, it was like being in a leafy cave.

We spent most of our spare time in there. I would sit on the stone beam, bouncing her baby brother in my lap, as Jantu sculpted her dainty clay figures.

"I wish we could always be together like this," I said one afternoon. "Don't you wish things would stay just the same?"

Jantu glanced up from the clay buffalo she was shaping and smiled at me. "But how can we always stay the same, Dara?" she asked. "We're not made of stone. You wouldn't want to lie half-buried in the fields for hundreds of years, anyway, would you?"

"No, I meant . . . I just meant that nothing nice ever lasts." I struggled to find words for what I wanted to say. "What we're doing now, just playing here together—I wish we could hang on to it, that's all."

Jantu put down the half-formed clay buffalo. "I know what you mean," she said slowly. "You try to hang on to older people—parents, uncles, grandmothers—and they disappear. You make friends, and they go off in different directions, never to be seen again. Everything crumbles so easily." Absentmindedly she picked up a dirt clod and crushed it in her fist, letting the crumbs of dirt dribble out. "We don't even have real families anymore," she said. "Just bits and pieces of one."

I stole a glance at my friend. I knew Jantu had lost both her parents and an older brother during the long war years, but she never talked about it.

"What do you mean?" I asked carefully.

"What I have, and what you have," she said, "are leftovers of families. Like fragments[3] from a broken bowl that nobody wants. We're not a real family."

"What's a real family, then?"

"A real family," Jantu said, "grows. It gets bigger. People get added to it. Husbands, mothers-in-law, babies."

---

[1] **cicada** (si kā′ də) a large, winged, flylike insect
[2] **fronds** (frondz) leaves
[3] **fragments** (frag′ mənts) parts broken off

I thought about this. It was true. My own family had been getting smaller, shrinking rather than growing. Was it just the fragment of a family now? "I'd like to be part of a real family again," I said wistfully.

"You could be," Jantu said. "And so could I."

"How?"

"You'll see. Watch," Jantu said. She started molding her clay buffalo again. With small twisting movements, her hands teased[4] out four legs, then shaped a pair of horns. Deftly[5] she smoothed and rounded the shape until it had become a miniature water buffalo.

Then, with a flourish, she lifted up a layer of straw in a corner of our shelter. Nestled in the straw was a group of other clay figures. Carefully she set the miniature buffalo next to them. "There," she said. "They're finished—the whole set of them."

"What are they?" I asked. "Can I see?"

Jantu smiled at me mysteriously. "I didn't want to show you until they were all ready."

Pierre Bonnard, *The Lesson*, 1926

"And are they ready?"

"They are!" Ceremoniously, Jantu took a clay doll and set it on the stone beam. Just then a few drops of rain started to fall.

_____

[4]**teased** (tēzd) pulled apart
[5]**deftly** (deft′ lē) skillfully

Jantu parted a section of the palm frond and scanned the sky anxiously. Thick gray clouds had drifted across to block out the sun. In the distance, a clap of thunder sounded.

The wind picked up and was sweeping up eddies[6] of dust into the air. Then the rain started in earnest, one of those sudden thunderstorms hinting of the monsoons[7] due to come soon. Jantu stretched her sarong[8] protectively over the pile of straw where her clay figures were. Hunched over them like that, she looked like a scruffy hen trying to hatch her precious eggs.

I huddled close to Jantu and listened to the rain drumming on the leaves. Raindrops pierced through the cracks of the palm fronds and felt light and cool on my bare arms. I thought of the long rainy afternoons I had spent on the porch at home when I was very young. As light and cool as the rain, my grandmother's fingers would massage my scalp while

I rested my head in her lap. Nearby, the murmur of my family surrounded me, like a soft blanket.

I closed my eyes now and tried to imagine them all sitting around me:

> I closed my eyes now and tried to imagine them all sitting around me...

Grandmother stroking me, Father and Sarun whittling on the steps, Mother stoking the embers of the cooking fire. It wasn't just the thick thatched roof that had sheltered me, I realized now. It was the feeling I had had then, of being part of a family as a gently pulsing whole, so natural it was like the breathing of a sleeping baby.

---

[6]**eddies** (ed′ ēz) currents of air moving in a circular motion against the main current

[7]**monsoons** (mon sōōnz′) southwesterly winds of southern Asia that bring heavy rains

[8]**sarong** (sə rông′) a long strip of cloth, often brightly colored and printed, worn around the lower part of the body like a skirt

Hung Liu, *Tale of Two Women*, 1991

When I opened my eyes, I saw that Jantu had a lost, faraway look in her eyes, and I knew that she was remembering, too, what it was like when her own family was whole and complete.

As the rain died down, Jantu turned to me and smiled. "You still want to play with my family of dolls?" she asked.

I'd rather have my own family back, I thought, but dolls were better than nothing. "Sure," I said.

Linking Writing and Literature

 ## Learning to Learn

Reflect on the importance of family to the girls in the story. What qualities do they seek in a family? Brainstorm to create a list of words and images that tell what the girls want in family life.Then brainstorm to create a new list of words that describe your ideas or values of family life.

 ## Talk About Reading

Talk with other students about the excerpt from *The Clay Marble.* Assign a group leader to keep everyone focused and a group secretary to take notes. Then use the questions below to guide your conversation.

1. **Connect to Your Life** How do Jantu's ideas about a "real family" compare with your own? What qualities do you think are important for a real family to have? Did this story help you look at your own family life in a new way?

2. **Critical Thinking: Draw Conclusions** Do you think Jantu has inner strength to face her life challenges? Use evidence from the story to support your conclusion.

3. **6+1 Trait®: Word Choice** Name some specific images that you remember from the selection. What words did the writer use to create these images? Discuss why you think these words are memorable.

4. **Connect to Your Writing** In this selection, the characters use analogies to talk about families and family love. How could you use analogies in writing that you do for school? How could you use them in writing that you do for yourself?

 ## Write About Reading

Description In the story, Dara vividly recalls an afternoon spent with her family. Write your own detailed description of a family scene, using either a real or an imaginary family. Describe the setting and what different family members are doing and feeling.

Focus on Word Choice Your description will take on a life of its own if you choose words and images that appeal to the senses. Before you begin writing, create a graphic organizer that lists the senses of sight, hearing, touch, taste, and smell. Fill the organizer with sensory details that describe your family scene. Read over your finished description to find places you might improve. Could you explain any complicated feelings or ideas by using analogies? Could you add transition words to smoothly connect your ideas?

For more information on word choice and the 6+1 Trait® model, see **Writing and Research Handbook,** pages 822–824.

6+1 Trait® is a registered trademark of Northwest Regional Educational Laboratory, which does not endorse this product.

Reflecting on the Unit: Summarize What You Learned

Focus on the following questions to help summarize what you learned in this unit.

1 What stages make up the writing process? How do writers use these stages in ways that work best for them?

2 How does prewriting help a writer find and explore topics for writing?

3 What does drafting mean?

4 What is the main purpose of revising? How can peer reviewers help?

5 What does the writer check when editing a piece of writing?

6 What is the publishing/presenting stage?

Adding to Your Portfolio

CHOOSE A SELECTION FOR YOUR PORTFOLIO Look over the writing you did for this unit. Choose a piece of writing for your portfolio. The writing you choose should show one or more of the following:

- a sharp focus on one interesting person or issue
- vivid details that give a strong impression
- a beginning that grabs the reader's interest
- paragraphs that show a clear development
- a sense of purpose and of the audience for which it is written

REFLECT ON YOUR CHOICE Attach a note to the piece you chose, explaining briefly why you chose it and what you learned from writing it.

SET GOALS How can you improve your writing? What skill will you focus on the next time you write?

Writing Across the Curriculum

MAKE A HISTORY CONNECTION What is happening in Cambodia now? The children of that time are grown. What has become of them? From your research notes write a paragraph about life in Cambodia today. Use vivid details. Write legibly and be sure to proofread for spelling and grammar errors.

TIME

Facing the Blank Page

Inside the writing process with TIME writers and editors

SPECIAL REPORT

TIME

MARS

JULY 4, 1997

Writing for TIME

The stories published each week in TIME are the work of experienced professionals—people who research, write, and edit for a living. The writing is clear; the facts are accurate; and the grammar, spelling, and punctuation are as error-free as possible.

Behind the scenes, however, another story emerges. TIME staffers face many of the same challenges that students do in the messy, trial-and-error process that is writing. Just like you, they must find a topic, conduct research, get organized, write a draft, and then revise, revise, and revise again. In these pages, they tell you how they do it.

Is there a secret to the quality of writing in TIME? Beyond experience and hard work, the key lies in collaboration. As the chart below illustrates, TIME stories are created through a form of "group journalism" that has become the magazine's hallmark. The writers and editors teach and learn from each other every week. You can do the same. Try out the writing and collaboration strategies presented in "Facing the Blank Page" to discover what's right for you.

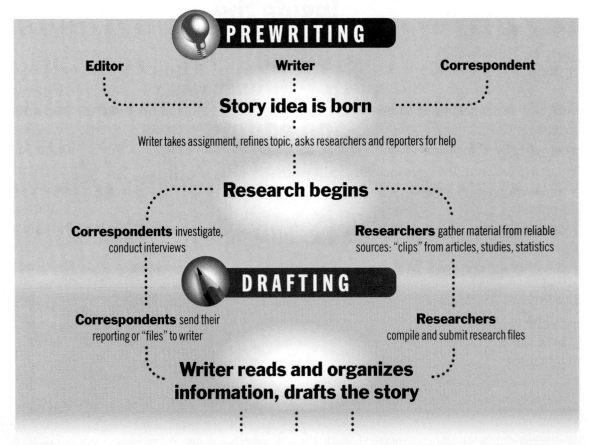

PREWRITING

Editor   Writer   Correspondent

Story idea is born

Writer takes assignment, refines topic, asks researchers and reporters for help

Research begins

Correspondents investigate, conduct interviews

Researchers gather material from reliable sources: "clips" from articles, studies, statistics

DRAFTING

Correspondents send their reporting or "files" to writer

Researchers compile and submit research files

Writer reads and organizes information, drafts the story

REVISING

Editor reads draft, suggests revisions

Correspondents
check interpretation,
make suggestions
◄·········►
**Writer revises,
sends draft to
members of the
team for comments**
◄·········►
Researchers
check accuracy,
details

Writer and editor revise again, "green" (edit for length)

 EDITING AND PROOFREADING

Checks for conformity to TIME
style and conventions
◄·······►
Copy Desk
◄·······►
Checks and corrects grammar,
mechanics, spelling

 PUBLISHING AND PRESENTING

**Managing Editor chooses to
print, hold, or "kill" (omit) story**

Circulation of TIME
rises or falls
◄········►
**Readers respond
to published story**
◄········►
E-mail and letters
to the editor

Prewriting

Getting Started: Finding Story Ideas

Generating good ideas for stories is as important—and can take as much time—as writing and editing the articles themselves. You may be assigned topics to write about; sometimes TIME writers get assignments, too. But just as often, writers are expected to come up with their own subjects and develop an interesting angle for a story.

Staff Writer and TV critic James Poniewozik tells how he gets started:
❝ Ideas for stories come from anything that surprises you. If you're watching a lot of television—for example, all the new pilots for the fall season—you might start noticing trends.

JAY COLTON FOR TIME

James Poniewozik: Write about what surprises you.

You might say, 'Gee, it seems that every other show has a voice-over on it, with characters talking directly to the camera.' You ask yourself, 'What does that mean? Is it a good thing or is it a bad thing? Is it a storytelling crutch, a way for writers to communicate characters' feelings without doing it through action and dialogue?' And so there's a story idea there—something that strikes you as a topic worth exploring.

The ideas part is pretty tough. I think one of the best ways to generate ideas is to talk to other people about things you're interested in. I've had a lot of story ideas that I didn't know were story ideas until I talked about them. I'll mention something in a conversation to others and they'll say, 'Oh, that sounds like it would make a topic for a story,' and I'll suddenly realize, 'Yes, it would!' Of course, I may have thought about the subject a half-dozen times before, but it never occurred to me to write about it. ❞

Janice Simpson, Senior Editor:
❝ If something is interesting to you as a writer or reporter—if something piques your curiosity and you want to know more about it—then probably there are other people who do, too. So I think we start there. What interests you? What catches your attention? ❞

A nother way to find story ideas is to work with your fellow writers. At TIME, the writers in each section hold "story meetings" to share news and ideas. Michael Lemonick, Senior Writer at TIME, discusses the collaborative process.

TED THAI FOR TIME

Michael Lemonick: Brainstorm with others.

Michael Lemonick writes for TIME's science section:

" Our group holds brainstorming sessions once a week, where we share ideas with each other. I keep my eyes and ears open all the time—with radio, TV news, friends, scientific journals, more specialized magazines, and local newspapers. Mostly I want to know what regular people are interested in or worried about.

Once the idea is there, we consult with each other about sources. Then the editor sends out a query to correspondents, and we start to shape the story we want. For example, with our cover story on microbes, we had heard a report about a new strain of drug-resistant tuberculosis, but someone then brought up another point. Working together, we came up with a concept for a big story: war against diseases. We all communicate with each other verbally, within staff meetings, by phone, and we get further ideas from correspondents in the bureaus.

After I'm assigned a story, I read everything I can find that's been printed to get a sense of the subject. I also conduct some of the interviews, along with the correspondents. **"**

LEARNING FROM THE WRITERS

TALK ABOUT IT

1. What benefits of working collaboratively do both James Poniewozik and Michael Lemonick point out?

2. Do you prefer working by yourself, with a partner, or with a group? List the pros and cons of each method.

TRY IT OUT

1. Have a class brainstorming session. Generate ideas for your next writing project as you work with a partner or a small group. See Lesson 2.2, "Prewriting: Finding and Exploring a Topic."

2. Find story ideas close to home. Work with James Poniewozik's notion that story ideas come from things that surprise you or thoughts that occur to you again and again. On an ordinary day at home or at school, is there a character, an observation, or an event that begs to be used in a piece of writing? Is there something that you hear or say routinely that you can use creatively? Select one of these as the basis for a piece of creative writing or for a school newspaper story.

LOOK IT OVER

1. Look at the writing you have done recently. Where did you get the idea for each piece? Is there a pattern in the way you find ideas, or do you find them in different ways?

2. Using Janice Simpson's advice, list things that pique your curiosity. Place stars in front of three that you want to develop in writing.

Drafting

Getting Words on Paper

Have you ever found it hard to start an assignment? You sit down at your desk, stare at the blank page, get up, wander around, come back, write a few words. This happens to professional writers, too!

Senior Writer Bruce Nelan:

" The biggest problem for me is organization. That's the hardest part. Sometimes, it's very tough. You sit and you stare. You flip through your material. And you say, 'Where do I start? What is it I want to say? How do I convey it?' But the clock is ticking. And so you sit down, you put the heading on, and you stare at the screen. You try this, you try that, and it starts to take shape. **"**

Nelan starts by making an outline:

" The first thing I do is make an outline. It doesn't necessarily have to be an elaborate, academic-style outline, but it at least has to tick off the main points, the most important elements. There's a period of discovery there that prepares you for writing. If I know that I'm at the second item on the outline and I want to get to the third item on the outline, something has to come in between, a transition of some sort. It'll sometimes become obvious to you, at the time that you're actually doing it. **"**

Lead with
— spy scandals
— link to China
— politics/Clinton

Background
— chronology/events
— 1980s
— 1998
— last month

Arrest and response

How Not to Catch a Spy

The government doesn't like to catch spies. Nabbing one tends to be embarrassing, seen as proof that the people in charge have been sloppy and lax on security. And it raises painful questions: How much damage has the spy done? Why wasn't he rooted out earlier? Who's making sure such pillaging of the country's vital secrets doesn't happen again? It's an unwinnable debate that no Administration wants to join.

But it is this kind of scandal that hit the White House last week—and the fact that it involved China made the mess even harder to clean up. Bill Clinton has already been bruised by accusations that illegal Chinese contributions found their way into his 1996 campaign and that he was overeager to allow U.S. firms to sell high-end computers and satellite technology to Beijing. Now the "soft on China" shouts are louder than ever, boosted by claims from critics in both parties that top Administration officials delayed and soft-pedaled the investigation into alleged Chinese spying at Los Alamos National Laboratory in New Mexico, birthplace of the atom bomb.

—Bruce Nelan

While Bruce Nelan favors outlining as a method of organizing his material, different writers work in different ways. Each has his or her own strategy for conquering the blank page, from starting to organize material to beginning the drafting process.

James Poniewozik, a Staff Writer who serves as TIME's TV critic, works this way:
❝ In theory, I think outlines are a good idea; in practice, I've never really used them, which is not necessarily good. What I might do is just free-associate on a page. I come up with a dozen topics or points that should be mentioned at some point in the piece, and then maybe I'll write numbers by them—either to show their relative importance or to put them in what seems to make for a smooth flow of the article. And an order emerges: I say, 'I should start with this, and then I'll jump to this, and this segues to that, and so on.' And then you go back and read through, see if it all makes sense, or if you need to change the beginning. ❞

Even with an outline in place, a writer can still get stuck. Poniewozik explains:
❝ I'm a really slow writer, and I'll spend minutes and minutes unnecessarily fussing over words or phrasing in a sentence. But you have to fight against that. It's important to force yourself to write, however bad the writing might be, and know that you can go back and improve it. If you're not writing anything, you'll never finish! Sometimes you just have to force the words out, kind of like warming yourself up when you are exercising. Then, once you're warmed up, you can move ahead and refine it, make it what you want it to be. ❞

Poniewozik's notes: An order emerges.

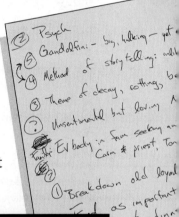

LEARNING FROM THE WRITERS

TALK ABOUT IT
1. Compare and contrast Nelan and Poniewozik's methods of organizing and outlining their work.
2. Look at Lesson 2.4, "Prewriting: Ordering Ideas," and Lesson 5.9, "Reports: Organizing and Drafting." How do the strategies suggested there compare with those Nelan and Poniewozik use in their work at TIME?

TRY IT OUT
Work from an outline. Choose your favorite of the topics that you decided to develop in writing. After gathering information on the topic, organize what you want to say by using one of the strategies mentioned here or by making an outline, as presented in Lesson 24.6. Use it as you write your first draft.

LOOK IT OVER
Which writer's method is most like your own? What tips for organizing material and ideas and for drafting can you offer your fellow writers?

Revising Too Many Adjectives?

In revising your work, it helps to focus on one language issue at a time instead of trying to attend to everything simultaneously. One way to do a quick, early edit is to cast a critical eye on your use of adjectives. As one editor advises: Weed out a few adjectives and you'll tighten up your writing.

Assistant Managing Editor Howard Chua-Eoan:

❝Adjectives should be used sparingly. I'm not at all against the use of adjectives; I think adjectives are very important. But if there are too many in one paragraph, then there are too many flowers and you don't see what the point of all the decoration is.**❞**

LEARNING FROM THE EDITOR

Read this excerpt from one of Howard Chua-Eoan's stories in TIME:

The Shaping of Jewel

With her blue cotton top worn inside out and with black riding sweats overlaid by suede chaps, Jewel lounges bareback on the Thoroughbred quarter horse she calls Jazz. She'd like to take him on the road. "Horseback riding is the most natural thing in my blood—that and singing," she says. She first rode a horse when she was two or three while growing up in Alaska, before the hard years—her parents divorcing, life with father in and out of bars, life with mother living out of cars, life alone. But now, at 23, she has sold more than 5 million copies of her album, *Pieces of You.* And she's got Jazz. Lovingly, she picks sawdust out of his hoof with a brush claw.

Jewel's is a fey, insidious charm, equal parts worldly and naive. Her flaws—the crooked nose and crooked teeth she is so proud of—only betray an uncommon beauty. Then there is the improbable match of slender youth and that voice—an astonishingly versatile instrument ranging from soul-shattering yodels to the most eloquent of whispers to arch Cole Porter tunes.

TALK ABOUT IT
What does Chua-Eoan mean by "too many flowers"? List the adjectives that Chua-Eoan uses in "The Shaping of Jewel." Does each one add something unique? Are there some he should omit?

TRY IT OUT
1. Compose an adjective-heavy sentence. Describe a summer morning or a scene of your choice. Now cut the adjectives out entirely. What is lost by doing this?
2. Improve the sentence. Use strong nouns and verbs and a few vivid adjectives to do the work of the edited adjectives.

LOOK IT OVER
Evaluate the use of adjectives in your first draft. If there are "too many flowers," revise.

Self-Editing: Reading Aloud

Several TIME writers share the same secret for editing their own work: reading aloud.

Howard Chua-Eoan: Beware of too many flowers.

Howard Chua-Eoan:

❝You should think of every sort of writing as a piece of theater. One thing I always suggest to young writers with trouble finding their voices is to read your story out loud, and find out if this is the way you want it to sound. Don't read just your stories out loud, but read other people's stories, too, to see why they sound the way they do, and why you like the way they sound.

I sometimes stop and read a paragraph—especially a lead paragraph—over and over and over again out loud just to see if that's the way I really want it to sound. If you're injecting some sort of artificial pace into it that isn't there as you read it, then you realize that the cadences and the syllables aren't giving that to you. So you do have to hear yourself. **❞**

Senior Editor Nancy Gibbs:

❝Sometimes when you read a story out loud, you find yourself editing it as you read it. You realize that the words that tripped you up, or the sentences that were too convoluted, need to be changed, and you correct them as you read it aloud. That's always the signal to go back and correct it on paper. **❞**

LEARNING FROM THE EDITORS

TALK ABOUT IT
1. What does Chua-Eoan mean when he says "think of every sort of writing as a piece of theater"?
2. Relate an experience you have had that is similar to Gibbs's finding herself correcting problem words and sentences as she reads aloud.

TRY IT OUT
1. Hear the writer's voice. Choose a piece of writing by one of your favorite authors and read it aloud. What does this help you notice about the writer's voice and the piece's rhythm, sentence length, and structure? How does this help you understand what it is you like about the way the writer uses language?
2. Swap first drafts with a partner. Read the papers aloud to each other. If you find that you change anything as you read, your partner should probably revise it in his or her draft too. Read aloud a literature selection from this textbook. What do you notice about it?

LOOK IT OVER
Read *your* first draft aloud. What changes do you find yourself making? Revise your work for clarity and style.

Editing and Proofreading

An Ever-Changing Language

The Copy Desk is the last stop for every TIME story. At this final stage in the editing process, Deputy Copy Chief Judy Paul and her colleagues check articles for errors in spelling, punctuation, style, and usage. There is only one problem: the rules they are supposed to apply keep changing! From the Copy Desk, these editors witness language and style evolving.

Judy Paul: Keeping up with the language.

Judy Paul:

❝We've changed a great deal. We used to follow some very strict style rules that no longer apply. For example, we were never allowed to say *Mid East* for *Middle East.* We were never allowed to use the abbreviation *L.A.;* we always had to spell out *Los Angeles.* And as times change, usage changes. We move with it and allow a lot more. Now you'll see *L.A.* in a Nation story, because that's something an American reader understands.**❞**

The new vocabulary of cyberspace is a challenge for copy editors. TIME's Copy Desk has had to decide how to "style" (that is, come up with a consistent way to use, spell, punctuate, and capitalize) words like *e-mail* and *dot.com.* Says Paul, "The most exciting part of working with the language right now is simply trying to keep up with it!"

LEARNING FROM THE EDITOR

TALK ABOUT IT
How does technological change force language to evolve? Look up *cyberspace* and *Internet* in a classroom dictionary. Are either of these terms defined? What other commonly used words may be missing from the dictionary? Why?

TRY IT OUT
1. List some words whose meanings and usages have evolved in recent years. How are these words, such as *web, net,* or *awesome,* defined in the dictionary? Write revised definitions for the words on your list.
2. List some informal terms

that you and your friends use in conversation. Define each of the terms and make a "style sheet" that indicates how to use and spell them correctly.
3. Edit and proofread your revised draft line by line. Fix errors in grammar, usage, spelling, and punctuation.

Publishing and Presenting

'Aha!' The Joy of Writing

Senior Editor Janice Simpson began writing when she was eight. She started out rewriting fairy tales, and though she now works in the realm of non-fiction, she sees a common thread in all writing: the ancient tradition of storytelling.

Janice Simpson reflects:

"I think the reason we use the term *story* so much in journalism is because there is a link to our pre-writing time, when griots in Africa and other storytellers in ancient civilizations would sit in a circle and tell people stories.

We journalists see what we do in that tradition. We're still telling stories. You can have wonderful information, but if you can't impart that information in a way that engages the reader, then people are just going to turn the page or put the magazine aside. You must have the power of a storyteller, because we are still sitting in the circle—today, it's a sort of global circle. Journalists are connected through the magazine or television to the other people in the circle, and we want to tell stories that explain what life is like, how we think about things, how things affect us. Like the griot, we need to do it in a narrative, engaging, explanatory way."

When writers and readers connect, the hard work of writing pays off:

"A writer's job is hard—very, very hard work. But there's also an element of fun about what we do, and the best writing reflects that joy. That joy is transmitted in writing. I think we've all had the experience of reading something and saying 'Aha! Let me write that down. That's just the way I felt about it.' When that happens, the writer has transmitted some of the joy he or she is feeling—some of the emotion—to you, the reader. And that's very much what writing and storytelling and journalism are all about."

LEARNING FROM THE EDITOR

TALK ABOUT IT
1. Tell a childhood story. Why has it stayed with you?
2. Do you agree that a writer's job is difficult but rewarding? Why? In what other difficult but rewarding activities do you participate?
3. Have you had the "Aha!" reading experience Simpson mentions? Describe it.

TRY IT OUT
1. Collect quotes. Keep a journal of "Aha!" quotations, their sources, and your reasons for including them.
2. Prepare a presentation copy of your draft. Read it in a storytelling circle and then display it in a class journal.

LOOK IT OVER
Look at three pieces of your writing, including your revised draft. How is each a form of storytelling?

" *The birds were hopping and twittering among the bushes, and the eagle was wheeling aloft . . .* **"**

—Washington Irving,
"Rip Van Winkle"

Descriptive Writing

Writing in the Real World

MEDIA Connection
Fantasy

Zilpha Keatley Snyder is a writer of imaginative fiction, so her descriptions must be first-rate. Otherwise, her readers could never see the fantasy characters and settings that exist in her imagination. The following excerpt is from Snyder's *Song of the Gargoyle,* a fantasy set in the Middle Ages. The book's main character, Tymmon, comes face to face with a gargoyle. Only, this gargoyle isn't made of stone. This one is alive!

Song of the Gargoyle

By Zilpha Keatley Snyder

The face was grinning, its loose lips stretched wide to reveal sharp white teeth, its long red tongue lolling to one side.

Frozen with fear, Tymmon gasped, "God help me," and sat motionless, waiting for death. Waiting for the cruel grip of sharp fangs.

But then suddenly he knew—and almost laughed out loud. It was only a gargoyle. Once again he had let himself be fooled by a gargoyle. He smiled sheepishly, excusing his foolish reaction by blaming it on the strange trancelike state he had been experiencing. A condition caused no doubt by hunger and exhaustion. But it was still more than a little embarrassing to give oneself up to die because of a harmless stone image.

The bulging eyes blinked, the grin disappeared, and the tongue flapped up to lick the sagging jowls. Not stone. Not of stone and, he belatedly realized, certainly not where gargoyles were usually to be found—on the eaves of church or castle. But what then? A monster certainly. A monster so ugly that the mere sight of it might well, like the evil Medusa, turn the viewer to stone.

Tymmon's hand crept up to test his cheek for evidence of hardening. Still soft and warm. He swallowed hard.

Swallowed again and tried to speak.

"What—what are you? What do you want of me?"

The monster cocked its head, its jagged batwing ears flopping. It certainly looked very like a gargoyle. A new thought occurred. Perhaps it was. Perhaps a magical gargoyle conjured into life by some powerful enchantment. . . .

. . . With its enormous head only inches from his face, its rank breath hot on his cheeks, it stared down at Tymmon and licked its chops.

Hungry. It was hungry, and its next meal might well be . . .

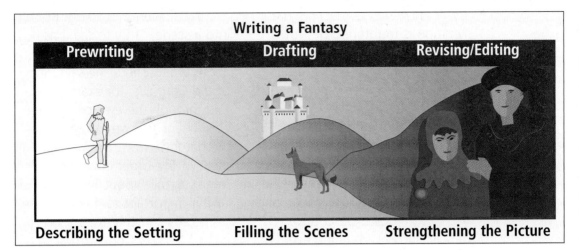

Writing a Fantasy

Prewriting	Drafting	Revising/Editing
Describing the Setting	Filling the Scenes	Strengthening the Picture

❝ *For me the whole joy of writing is the chance to let my imagination freewheel. I like to balance a story between reality and fantasy. Then I can use descriptive language to give exciting and delicious hints in both directions.* **❞**

—Zilpha Keatley Snyder

A Writer's Process

Prewriting
Describing Setting, Characters, and Plot

After Snyder has an idea for a fantasy, she begins by trying to fully imagine the setting. To do this, she draws sketches of the settings for various scenes. For *Song of the Gargoyle* she drew floor plans of castles. Photographs of real castles also helped Snyder visualize details about her imaginary castle.

From the setting, Snyder turns her attention to writing descrip-

tions of the story's main characters. She "writes down everything" she knows about the characters. How does she learn about them? "By trying to live in their shoes and react as they would," she says.

In *Song of the Gargoyle,* the main character, Tymmon, is searching for his kidnapped father. As he travels, Tymmon faces daunting challenges, such as meeting a living gargoyle named Troff. In the early stages of imagining these characters, Snyder played what she called the "what-if" game. What if Tymmon meets

Troff? How will he react? What if Tymmon is frightened by Troff's appearance? What if Tymmon isn't sure whether Troff is a gargoyle or a dog with batlike ears?

Snyder decided that Tymmon's first reaction would be fear, caused by Troff's ugliness. She asked herself what words and descriptions would communicate such a reaction to the reader. She then wrote down descriptive details, such as "bulging eyes" and "jagged bat-wing ears," that heightened Troff's scary features.

Snyder thinks even her characters' names can work as descriptive details. The name Troff, for example, "sounded a bit like a dog's bark," Snyder says.

Snyder's final step is to write what she calls the plot page. Here Snyder tries "to know the main thrust of the story and what the climax will be."

Snyder draws floor plans and details during the prewriting stage. These visual ideas help her describe a setting.

Drafting
Filling in the Scenes

Every morning Snyder sits down at her computer to write. When she's drafting a scene, she first writes two lists of goals. Snyder explains, "On the left-hand side is action—the events I want to happen. On the right-hand side is exposition. There I highlight the information I need to get across to the reader."

Snyder then tries to put herself into a scene. "I try to see it as vividly as possible. Then I tell about what I see," she says. *Song of the Gargoyle,* for example, is told through the eyes of Tymmon. This means that Snyder describes the gargoyle from Tymmon's point of view. The order in which she reveals details about Tymmon and Troff is important to the suspense of the story. In the excerpt on page 110, short descriptive phrases reveal Tymmon's mounting fear as he tries to figure out the creature standing before him.

Revising/Editing
Strengthening the Picture

Snyder revises each day's work the next morning. "I try to see if what I've written really calls forth my vision," she explains. This means making sure that her descriptive details suggest the two possible interpretations of Troff. Is he a gargoyle? Or is he a dog?

Snyder also uses her computer's thesaurus function to look for what she calls "more flamboyant adjectives and adverbs" to spice her descriptions. She seeks nouns and verbs that are precise.

When she's satisfied with the revised draft, Snyder shares it with a group of fellow writers. She says, "When you read aloud to other people, you hear things that you miss when reading

Examining Writing in the Real World

alone." Snyder wants to be certain that her readers see the picture she's described. In descriptive writing that means creating an overall impression with carefully chosen details.

Analyzing the Media Connection

Discuss these questions about the fantasy excerpt on page 110.

1. What descriptive details does Snyder use to show that the gargoyle is a frightening sight?
2. What descriptive details show the reader that Tymmon is afraid?
3. Snyder uses sensory language in her descriptions. What phrase in the excerpt evokes the reader's sense of smell? What phrase appeals to the sense of touch?
4. What verbal does Snyder use to describe the movement of the gargoyle's tongue (paragraph 1)? Find at least two other examples where Snyder uses precise verbals or verbs.
5. How does Snyder build suspense at the end of the excerpt?

Analyzing a Writer's Process

Discuss these questions about Zilpha Keatley Snyder's writing process.

1. What methods did Snyder use to help her clearly imagine the settings for *Song of the Gargoyle?*

2. What is Snyder's "what-if" game? How and why does she use it?
3. What two lists does Snyder make for herself when writing a draft? Why do you think it helps her to keep these parts separate?
4. How does Snyder use a thesaurus as she revises?
5. Why does Snyder read her work aloud to others?

Grammar*Link*

Snyder uses modifiers—adjectives or adverbs—to bring flair and precision to her writing.

> The **bulging** eyes blinked . . . Not of stone, and he **belatedly** realized . . .

Revise the paragraph below, adding vivid modifiers to describe each numbered word.

The ¹*trail* ended at a ²*cliff.* The ³*travelers* stopped. Below them lay the ⁴*city.* The travelers ⁵*looked* at each other and at the ⁶*sky* above them. The ⁷*sounds* and ⁸*smells* of the city rose up to meet them. They ⁹*turned* and ¹⁰*looked* for a new path.

See Lessons 12.1–12.2, pages 451–454.

Writing to Show, Not Tell

Descriptive Writing

People often use familiar words to label new things. That is how the sea anemone got its name. It resembles a flower—the anemone.

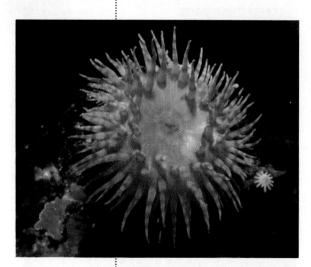

In *Journey Outside* a boy named Dilar has grown up on an underground river. When he discovers life on Earth's surface, he encounters new sights and sounds.

In the model below, Mary Q. Steele describes how Dilar reacts to an unfamiliar creature. Her use of familiar words shows the creature vividly.

Literature Model

He cried out abruptly. Something was coming toward him in the air, a little fish gliding through the air, helping itself along with great fins that stuck out from its sides and then folded tight against them. A wonder, a wonder! The fish stopped suddenly in the top of one of the little trees, put out little legs to hold itself up, threw back its head, and opening its mouth made such sounds as Dilar had never heard before. No water murmured so joyously or so sweetly or so triumphantly; nothing, nothing had ever rung upon his ears like that or made his heart feel it must burst open with that song's wild delight. Even when it had ceased it echoed in his head.

Mary Q. Steele, *Journey Outside*

> To what does Dilar compare the strange sights and sounds he encounters?

Use Effective Details

Using effective descriptive details can make a person, place, or thing come to life. When you write, select details so carefully that your reader can see, hear, smell, taste, and feel what you describe. In the passage below, Bethany Bentley does not merely tell the reader that a storm passed through her town. She uses descriptive details that show the storm.

Descriptive Writing

Student Model

I looked outside from the beaten-up restaurant and saw the vivid purple sky flashing with lightning, while the willow across the street swayed in the wind.

The lights from the neighboring store reflected on the window and blurred my view of the storm. The rain crashed down on the roof and pelted the windows, also contributing to my blurry view.

I could see pieces of bark flying off of the willow tree. Litter flew high into the evening sky.

The lightning struck again. I shuddered as a cold draft drifted through the cracked window nearby.

Bethany Bentley, Oak Creek School, Cornville, Arizona

Notice how the writer describes the movement of objects to show the violence of the storm.

How does the writer make this scene seem real?

Journal Writing

In your journal write several statements without any descriptive details, such as *The picnic was fun.* Then choose one of your sentences, and list five or six details that will help readers see, hear, smell, taste, or feel what you are describing.

Find Descriptions Everywhere

Descriptive words and phrases appear in all kinds of writing. A menu makes a sandwich sound so good that you can almost taste it. A travel brochure takes you to a place where you feel warm breezes, hear crashing waves, and smell the volcanic ash. A clear description of a lost pet leads to its safe return. A story fascinates you with its descriptions of a place or a person.

Descriptions catch a reader's interest and stay in the reader's memory.

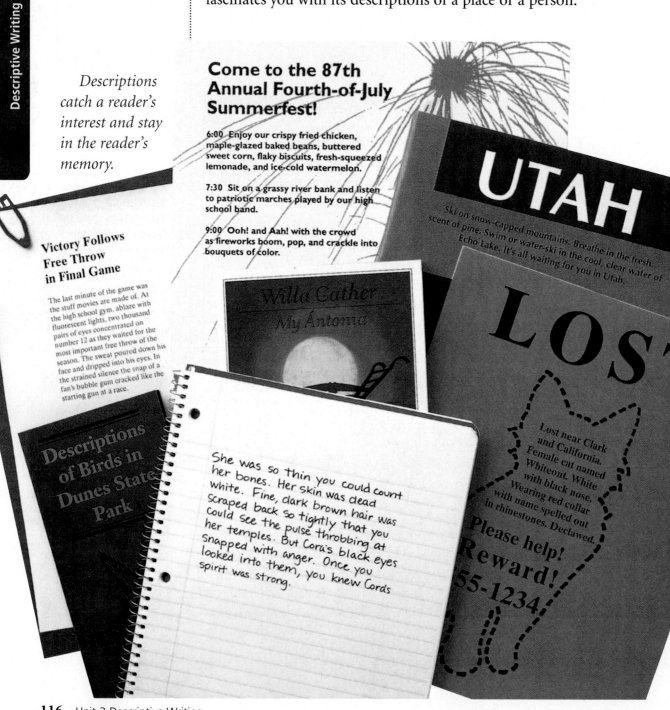

Come to the 87th Annual Fourth-of-July Summerfest!

6:00 Enjoy our crispy fried chicken, maple-glazed baked beans, buttered sweet corn, flaky biscuits, fresh-squeezed lemonade, and ice-cold watermelon.

7:30 Sit on a grassy river bank and listen to patriotic marches played by our high school band.

9:00 Ooh! and Aah! with the crowd as fireworks boom, pop, and crackle into bouquets of color.

UTAH

Ski on snow-capped mountains. Breathe in the fresh scent of pine. Swim or water-ski in the cool, clear water of Echo Lake. It's all waiting for you in Utah.

Victory Follows Free Throw in Final Game

The last minute of the game was the stuff movies are made of. At the high school gym, ablaze with fluorescent lights, two thousand pairs of eyes concentrated on number 12 as they waited for the most important free throw of the season. The sweat poured down his face and dripped into his eyes. In the strained silence the snap of a fan's bubble gum cracked like the starting gun at a race.

Willa Cather
My Ántonia

Descriptions of Birds in Dunes State Park

She was so thin you could count her bones. Her skin was dead white. Fine, dark brown hair was scraped back so tightly that you could see the pulse throbbing at her temples. But Cora's black eyes snapped with anger. Once you looked into them, you knew Cora's spirit was strong.

LOST

Lost near Clark and California. Female cat named Whiteout. White with black nose. Wearing red collar with name spelled out in rhinestones. Declawed. **Please help! Reward!** 55-1234.

Write a Description of an Object

Write a description of a familiar object or animal for someone who is seeing it for the first time. Describe what you see and hear. Choose details that make the description come alive for your reader.

PURPOSE To describe something clearly

AUDIENCE Your classmates

LENGTH 1 paragraph

WRITING RUBRICS To write a descriptive paragraph, you should

- use effective details
- use clear descriptions

Listening and Speaking

DESCRIBING Think of a busy scene at your school, such as a soccer game or lunch in the cafeteria. Orally describe the scene while listeners take note. Express your ideas clearly and fluently. Discuss which of the details you presented made the scene most vivid for your listeners and why.

Cross-Curricular Activity

ART Select a painting in this book. Choose one figure and list details about what the figure looks like. Then write a one-paragraph description of the figure for someone who has not seen the painting.

GrammarLink

Use adverbs to describe verbs.

Adverbs may describe *how, where, when,* or *in what manner* action is done.

*No water murmered so **joyously** or so **sweetly** or so **triumphantly**. . . .*

Write each sentence, adding an adverb to describe the action.

1. She swallowed _____ .
2. They walked _____ .
3. The bicyclist pedaled _____ .
4. The hiker climbed _____ .
5. The door opened _____ .
6. Mr. Jansen glowered _____ .
7. The child staggered _____ .
8. The wind blew _____ .
9. My sister stood _____ .
10. The man in the red convertible drove _____ .

See Lesson 12.6, pages 461–462.

Descriptive Writing

Combining Observation and Imagination

*W*hen artists paint and when authors write, they draw on observation and imagination. In Martin Charlot's painting and in Willa Cather's description on the next page, you can feel the power of observation and imagination.*

Imagine that you are flying in Charlot's fantasy world. Use your five senses. Look around. Notice the color, movement, and life. Close your eyes, and concentrate on sounds and scents. Touch the plants, the water, the fish, and the fruit. Now you, too, are combining the real and the imaginary.

TIME

For more about the writing process, see **TIME** *Facing the Blank Page*, pp. 97–107.

Martin Charlot, *Fruit of the Spirit,* 1983

Use Sensory Detail

Artists use color, shape, and pattern to pull you into a painting. Writers do the same thing with sensory language—language that appeals to the senses. Sensory language describes how something looks, sounds, feels, smells, or tastes. In the passage below, Willa Cather uses sensory details to pull the reader into a world that smells of strong weeds and where oak groves wilt in the sun. Her strong images pull the reader into another world.

Proofreading Tip

When proofreading, check for periods and other end marks after each sentence. For more information see pages 589–590.

Descriptive Writing

Literature Model

While the train flashed through never-ending miles of ripe wheat, by country towns and bright-flowered pastures and oak groves wilting in the sun, we sat in the observation car, where the woodwork was hot to the touch and red dust lay deep over everything. The dust and heat, the burning wind, reminded us of many things. We were talking about what it is like to spend one's childhood in little towns like these, buried in wheat and corn, under stimulating extremes of climate: burning when one is fairly stifled in vegetation, in the colour and smell of strong weeds and heavy harvests; blustery winters with little snow, when the country is stripped bare and grey as sheet-iron.

Willa Cather, Introduction to *My Ántonia*

To which senses does Willa Cather's language appeal? Give examples.

Journal Writing

Think of a sound you like to hear—maybe a song or the crack of a bat or someone's voice. In your journal list eight or ten words that describe the sound.

Use Your Experience and Imagination

You are able to describe people, places, things, and situations because you first perceive the details through your senses. You see that your friend has curly hair. You smell new tar on the street. You can take those details from your own experience and use them in descriptive writing. Nikki Housholder uses this technique in the poem below. She combines ordinary details to create images her readers can share.

Student Model

Waving trees,
Dark, lonely days
Sagging clouds over cold, crawling water,
Whispering leaves of short, furry bushes,
Surrounded by falling moonlight above,
With twinkling eyes spying from the dense darkness,
Opening the door to freedom.

Nikki Housholder, Oak Creek School
Cornville, Arizona

How is the sensory language in the fourth line different from that in the other lines?

You can also use your senses to help you describe imaginary things. The illustrator of the animal to the left created a new image by combining real details in unusual ways.

Write About an Imaginary Place

Write a description of an imaginary place. Use details that appeal to smell, feeling, or sight to describe the place.

PURPOSE To use sensory words in a description
AUDIENCE Your classmates
LENGTH 1 paragraph

WRITING RUBRICS To write a descriptive paragraph about an imaginary place, you should

- use details that describe what you might see, hear, touch, smell, or taste
- draw on your imagination to add detail to your description

Viewing and Representing

COOPERATIVE LEARNING In a group of five people, view the imaginary world pictured on page 118. Look carefully at the picture for two minutes, examining every detail. Then every person in the group should contribute three details that describe the scene. Base the details on one of the five senses: sight, hearing, smell, touch, and taste. Working as a group, combine these details to create a description that includes all the sensory details listed by group members. When your description is complete, share your group's work with the class.

Using Computers

Use the spelling checker option on your computer to check spelling on a final draft. You still have to read the draft for spelling errors, because the computer won't catch all mistakes. To make your description more vivid, compose your descriptive paragraph on the computer. Highlight nouns and decide whether to add adjectives. Then also highlight verbs and decide whether to add adverbs.

Grammar*Link*

Avoid run-on sentences.

Use main clauses correctly to avoid run-on sentences. Write them as two sentences, use a semicolon between them, or use a comma plus a coordinating conjunction between them.

Rewrite these items to avoid run-ons.

1. The sun beat down on the ripe grain the birds swooped over the fields.
2. Giant waves crashed over the boat, the mast shuddered.
3. Candles sputtered, soft shadows moved across the ceiling.
4. Students clustered in excited knots news buzzed in the air.
5. Outside the snow fell softly, inside the fire crackled cheerfully.

See Lesson 7.2, page 308.

Writing Online For more writing and grammar practice, go to glencoe.com and enter QuickPass code WC77680p1.

121

Descriptive Writing

Choosing Details to Create a Mood

Writers choose details that create a mood. A cave shimmering with sparkling columns sounds inviting. A dark cave where bats flitter seems eerie.

Imagine entering the cave in the picture, and think about how it feels to be there. List a few details you would use to describe the picture so others could share your feelings.

In the model below, Susan Cooper chooses details that make a cave seem threatening. These details help the reader to share Barney's feelings about the cave in the cliff called Kenmare Head.

Literature Model

"Hallo," Barney said tentatively into the darkness. His voice whispered back at him in a sinister, eerie way: not booming and reverberating round as it had in the narrow tunnel-like cave they had come through, but muttering far away, high in the air. Barney swung round in a circle, vainly peering into the dark. The space round him must be as big as a house—and yet he was in the depths of Kenmare Head.

Susan Cooper, *Over Sea, Under Stone*

> Why is the sound of Barney's whispered greeting an effective detail?

Use Details That Create a Mood

The details included in the literature model do more than help describe a scene. They also create a mood, or feeling. The cave, which you experience through Barney's senses, seems eerie and sinister. The writer wants you to understand that Barney feels frightened and a little desperate.

If Barney were exploring this cave for fun, he would probably have different feelings about it. The writer would select different details to show a different mood. Look at the notes below. What would the mood of the passage on page 122 be if the writer had used details such as these?

Grammar Tip

Adjectives help make a description more effective. Adjectives modify nouns. For more information see pages 451–452.

Descriptive Writing

Mood Details
- *spectacular colors and formations*
- *air-conditioned by nature*
- *a mysterious bottomless pit*
- *fascinating shadows dancing in the dim light*
- *friendly echoes talking back*

Journal Writing

Think of a place you have been that inspires a mood. In your journal make a list of mood details like the list above. Then write a brief description that creates the mood suggested by the details you wrote.

crisp, powdery snow
frostbitten ears
slushy, slippery sidewalks
biting wind
healthful exercise
sparkling sunlight
heavy, wet clothes
brilliant blue sky

Choose Words to Bring a Scene to Life

When you describe a scene, the words you choose set the mood and bring the scene to life for your reader. Try it out. Suppose you are describing a cold winter day. Select one of the photos shown below. Find details in the list that help create a cheerful or unpleasant mood. Then read Bryce Stoker's description of a personal experience. Notice his use of striking, specific words that bring details to life and create a mood.

Unpleasant

Cheerful

Student Model

Which phrases tell the reader how Bryce reacts to the attic visit?

One of the worst places I've been in is the attic. Whenever I'm told to go get something from the attic, I try to squirm my way out of it. When I can't get out of it, my skin begins to crawl, I get nervous and start to sweat while ascending the stairs, and my breathing and pulse go wild when I reach the trapdoor to the attic.

Bryce Stoker, Frontier School
Moses Lake, Washington

Write a Descriptive Paragraph

Write a description of a place where people are usually happy. The place might be a beach, an amusement park, or a street fair. Imagine that you are walking through this place. As you imagine your walk, take notes on the details that set the mood. Write a draft of your description. Then revise your description, adding other words and details that strengthen the mood. Read your paragraph to a classmate and have him or her identify the mood.

PURPOSE To create a mood in a description
AUDIENCE Your classmates
LENGTH 1 paragraph

WRITING RUBRICS To create a mood in a descriptive paragraph, you should

- select details that help create the mood
- choose striking, specific words to set the mood

Using Computers

Check to see if your word processing program has an electronic thesaurus. As you revise your description, use the thesaurus to find words that strengthen the mood you want to create.

GrammarLink

Use adjectives to create a mood.

Write each sentence twice, once with an adjective that creates a positive mood, and once with an adjective that creates a negative mood.

1. He decided to investigate the _____ sounds coming from next door.
2. She touched the _____ fabric with a/an _____ hand.
3. I watched the fish moving in the _____ water.
4. She woke up from the _____ dream.
5. The path stretched into the _____ woods.

See Lesson 12.1, page 451.

Listening and Speaking

COOPERATIVE LEARNING Divide into groups of four. In a container, place slips of paper labeled *sad*, *angry*, *happy*, and *scared*. Make sure each student picks one slip. Take turns orally describing a place, choosing sensory details to create the mood. Have listeners add more details to help strengthen the mood.

Descriptive Writing

Organizing Details in a Description

*W*hen you view a scene, your brain organizes what you see. In written descriptions, writers must organize information for the reader.

Imagine you are a radio reporter covering a hot-air-balloon festival. Your listeners cannot see the brightly colored balloons. How could you describe the scene, including the position of each balloon?

In the model below, Scott O'Dell creates a clear picture in your mind. He does so by ordering details so that you know just where Rontu is in relation to the wild dogs.

Literature Model

On this mound, among the grasses and the plants, stood Rontu. He stood facing me, with his back to the sea cliff. In front of him in a half-circle were the wild dogs. At first I thought that the pack had driven him there against the cliff and were getting ready to attack him. But I soon saw that two dogs stood out from the rest of the pack, between it and Rontu. . . .

Scott O'Dell, *Island of the Blue Dolphins*

Why might the position of the dogs in relation to Rontu be important in this scene?

Arrange Details to Suit Your Purpose

You can present details in various ways to give your reader a mental picture of a scene. Think about the location of each object and where it is in relation to other objects. How you describe them depends on your purpose. Describing a skyscraper from bottom to top emphasizes the building's height. A description of the Grand Canyon might show details in the order a descending hiker sees them.

The pictures below show three ways that details might be ordered to describe the photograph on page 126. Which order do you think would be most effective?

Prewriting Tip

During the prewriting phase for a description, think about the best order to present details.

Descriptive Writing

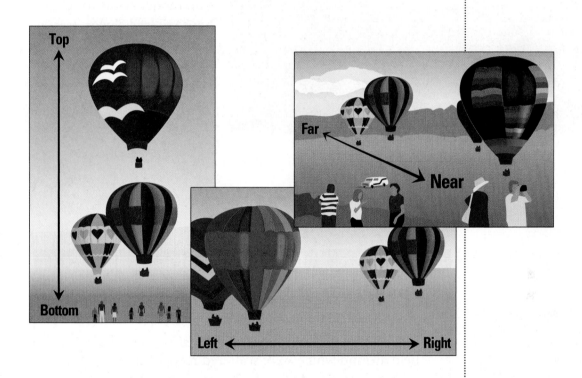

Journal Writing

In your journal describe a room at home or at school. Where is each important object? Where is it in relation to other objects? What kind of order works best to present your description?

Use Transitions to Show Relationships

Transition words and phrases help show how each detail in a description relates to the others. Look at the photograph and

In front of
Behind
To the right of
Next to

the phrases at the left. How can you use these transitions to answer such questions as *Where is the diving platform in relation to the trees?* and *Where is the falling boy in relation to the other boys?* Read the literature model below to see how Mildred Taylor uses transition words and phrases to describe a scene clearly.

> The school building is presented first. Then the writer describes objects in relation to it.

> How do the transition words connect the details?

Literature Model

They were headed for the Jefferson Davis County School, a long white wooden building looming in the distance. **Behind** the building was a wide sports field around which were scattered rows of tiered gray-looking benches. **In front of** it were two yellow buses, our own tormentor and one that brought students from the other direction, and loitering students awaiting the knell of the morning bell. **In the very center** of the expansive front lawn, waving red, white, and blue . . . was the Mississippi flag. **Directly below** it was the American flag.

Mildred D. Taylor, *Roll of Thunder, Hear My Cry*

Write a Painting Description

Select a painting from this book. Imagine that this painting has been stolen from the museum and you need to describe the painting to the police. Your description needs to be so clear that the detectives will recognize the painting immediately.

PURPOSE To describe a missing painting
AUDIENCE Police detectives
LENGTH 1 paragraph

WRITING RUBRICS To create a vivid description, you should

- present details in a logical order
- use transition words to show how details relate to one another

Viewing and Representing

COLLABORATIVE WRITING Draw a picture of a group of related objects, such as different kinds of tropical fish or items that make up a lunch. Trade drawings with a partner. Write a caption, using words such as *on the far right*, *next to*, and *in front of* to describe the order of the details. Work together to improve your captions.

Cross-Curricular Activity

MATHEMATICS Draw a design using geometric shapes such as triangles, rectangles, and circles. Write a description of your design, using transition words to show where shapes are on the page and in relation to one another. Test your description's accuracy by asking a classmate to re-create your design after reading the description.

Grammar*Link*

Use prepositional phrases to show position.

Phrases like *in front of* and *next to* can help readers picture a location. He stood facing me, **with his back to the sea cliff.**

Add a prepositional phrase to each sentence below.

1. The architect decided to put the stairway _____ .
2. The old barn was located _____ .
3. At the accident scene the police officer directed traffic _____ .
4. Ready to spring, the panther crouched _____ .
5. _____ we paused to check the map.

See Lesson 13.3, page 483.

Descriptive Writing

Describing a Person

*L*ike a jigsaw puzzle, a character is made up of pieces. Each piece is a detail: hair color, body shape, or the way a character smiles. Put together, these pieces make a complete picture.

In most puzzles the pieces fit together in only one way. However, you can mix and match details in endless ways when you set out to create a character in writing.

Show How the Character Looks

Begin your description of a character by picturing that person in your mind. Which details will help readers see the character? Choose the words and the order that fit your purpose.

In the following passage, Amy Tan looks at a picture of her mother, taken long ago. She describes the way her mother appears in that picture.

The speaker says that her mother looks "displaced." What is she wearing that supports this adjective?

Literature Model

In this picture you can see why my mother looks displaced. She is clutching a large clam-shaped bag, as though someone might steal this from her as well if she is less watchful. She has on an ankle-length Chinese dress with modest vents at the side. And on top she is wearing a Westernized suit jacket, awkwardly stylish on my mother's small body, with its padded shoulders, wide lapels, and oversize cloth buttons. This was my mother's wedding dress, a gift from my father. In this outfit she looks as if she were neither coming from nor going to someplace. Her chin is bent down and you can see the precise part in her hair, a neat white line drawn from above her left brow then over the black horizon of her head.

Amy Tan, *The Joy Luck Club*

Journal Writing

Visualize several of the most memorable people you've known. In your journal list five or six details someone else would notice first about them.

Grammar Tip

A pronoun must agree in number, gender, and person with its antecedent, the person, place, or thing to which it refers. See pages 431–432.

Show How the Character Acts

We decide what a person is like by judging what he or she does. One way we learn about people is to observe them in action, especially when their actions involve other people.

A writer can reveal a character's personality by showing how the character interacts with others. In the draft below, a writer begins to fill out the character visualized on page 131. Instead of simply telling readers what Andy looks like, the writer shows how Andy behaves at a skateboarding park. What does Andy's treatment of other people say about him?

When Cameron lost his board on a jump, Andy laughed. "Hey Cameron! Why don't you give up? My little sister can do that move better. Maybe you should come back during the little kids' hours, and she can help you." Ignoring Andy, Cameron retrieved his skateboard and limped to the end of the waiting line.

When Andy got onto the skateboarding course, he showed off his best stunts. Satisfied that he was again the center of attention, he called over his shoulder, "Look! Here's how Cameron skates the course!"

Andy made quite a show of waving his arms for balance, taking curves slowly, and failing to make it to the top of hills. The other kids couldn't help laughing at his imitation.

Write a Character Description

Write a description of a shoemaker. Use details from your imagination that will show the reader who this shoemaker is.

PURPOSE To describe a person's appearance and actions

AUDIENCE Your teacher and classmates

LENGTH 2 paragraphs

WRITING RUBRICS To write a character description, you should

- describe how the character looks
- describe how the character acts

Viewing and Representing

COOPERATIVE LEARNING With a partner, find several versions of Mark Twain's

The Adventures of Tom Sawyer. How does each illustrator picture Tom Sawyer? Considering each illustrator's work, discuss what the character is like and how he looks. How does your impression of the character change as you view different illustrator's pictures?

Using Computers

If you have access to a computer at home or at school, use it to complete the character description writing activity. The cut-and-paste option can help you revise the order of your details for clarity and impact. The editing functions will help you make corrections when editing your writing.

Grammar*Link*

Pronouns must have clear antecedents.

An *antecedent* is the noun referred to by a pronoun.

> When **Cameron** lost **his** board . . .

Revise each sentence below to make the antecedent clear.

1. Ms. Lee told Amy that she liked her description.
2. The boys threw stones at the birds, but they did not hit them.
3. The girls put the worms in a box so that they would stay healthy.
4. When the car hit the truck, it exploded.
5. After Mr. North gave Jim an apple, he smiled.

See Lesson 11.2, page 431.

LOG ON ▶ **Writing** Online | For more writing and grammar practice, go to glencoe.com and enter QuickPass code WC77680p1.

133

Relating a Poem to Your Experience

Poets are artists who share their thoughts and experiences by using words to draw mental pictures. Putting yourself into the picture makes a poem meaningful to you.

Descriptive Writing

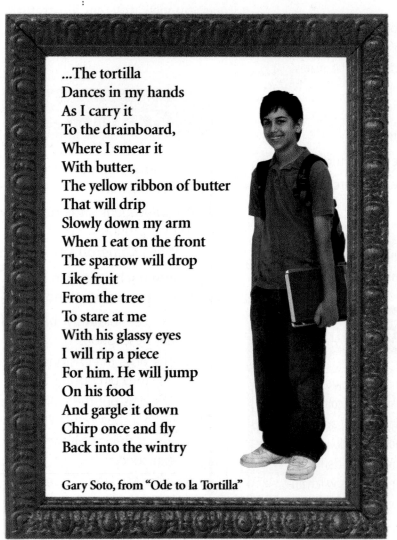

...The tortilla
Dances in my hands
As I carry it
To the drainboard,
Where I smear it
With butter,
The yellow ribbon of butter
That will drip
Slowly down my arm
When I eat on the front
The sparrow will drop
Like fruit
From the tree
To stare at me
With his glassy eyes
I will rip a piece
For him. He will jump
On his food
And gargle it down
Chirp once and fly
Back into the wintry

Gary Soto, from "Ode to la Tortilla"

In the poem at the left, Gary Soto uses sensory details to capture an ordinary experience and share it with the reader. As you read the poem, try to see, hear, feel, taste, and smell the things that Gary Soto describes. Notice the patterns of the words and the rhythm they create. How do they help you experience the tortilla?

Experience the Poem

Poets often use sensory language to share an impression. Gary Soto lets you feel what he probably feels as he prepares and eats a tortilla. You can experience "The yellow ribbon of butter / That will drip / Slowly down my arm . . ."

To understand a poem, relate it to what you already know. Recalling your own experience may help you understand how the poet feels as he prepares and eats the tortilla.

Descriptive Writing

Journal Writing

Think of an experience you have had that "Ode to la Tortilla" reminds you of. In your journal, use a graphic organizer to list sensory details describing the experience.

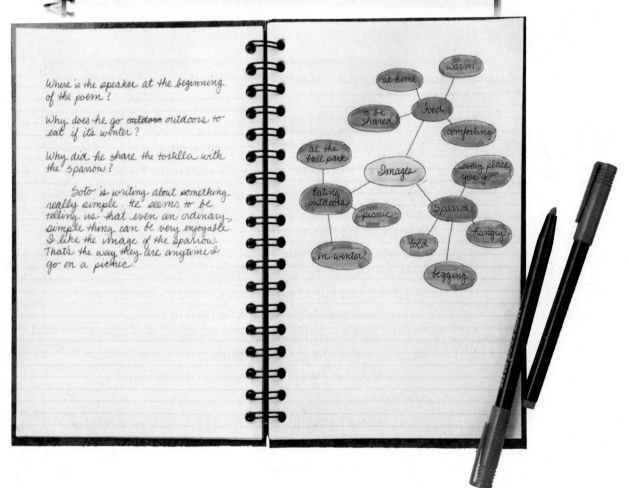

Where is the speaker at the beginning of the poem?

Why does he go ~~outdone~~ outdoors to eat if it's winter?

Why did he share the tortilla with the sparrow?

Soto is writing about something really simple. He seems to be telling us that even an ordinary, simple thing can be very enjoyable. I like the image of the sparrow. That's the way they are anytime I go on a picnic.

Prewriting Tip

You could respond to a poem in the form of a poster. Decorate your poster with pictures, colors, or shapes that help communicate your thoughts and feelings to your audience.

Respond to the Poem

You can respond to a poem in many different ways. One way is by telling the writer how the poem matches your own experiences. You can write your ideas in your journal or in a letter. Even better, you can create a poem of your own. Think about ordinary things in your life, things you enjoy or want to do. Are they like the ordinary things Soto writes about? Are they like the ordinary things in the poem below by Willow Star Wright?

Notice that Willow names ordinary things in each line of her poem.

In which lines of the poem did the writer surprise you by combining unlike things?

Student Model

Daydreams

I am a ballerina who strives to be a doctor in the delivery room of a widely known hospital.

I like boys, and the fish in my aquarium are gold and swim around plastic, purple and green seaweed.

I hear people cheering, wasps buzzing and summer is just around the corner.

I want to go swimming or horseback riding on a large Arabian horse from the oasis.

I don't like fall or this poem I wrote moments ago that will eventually be put into a final draft.

I dream of the day when all nations declare world peace or when the guy I like finds out I am alive.

But for now I will just have to settle for being a ballerina.

Willow Star Wright, Oak Creek School
Cornville, Arizona

Write a Poem

Reread "Ode to la Tortilla" and "Daydreams." Then write a poem describing an experience of your own. Choose an ordinary experience, possibly one from your writing journal. List sensory words or phrases that describe this experience. Write your poem, using details from your list.

PURPOSE To write a poem describing a personal experience

AUDIENCE Your teacher and classmates

LENGTH A poem of 8 to 12 lines

WRITING RUBRICS To write an effective poem, you should

- use a real experience
- recall the details of the experience
- use sensory details

Listening and Speaking

COOPERATIVE LEARNING In a small group, read aloud a poem selected by a member of your group or by your teacher. Be sure to speak clearly and fluently as you read. Within your group, talk about what the poem means and list the sensory images the poet uses.

Next, group members can relate the poem to their own experience. Discuss which images you like best. Which are surprising? Familiar? How does this poem relate to things that happen in your life?

Grammar*Link*

Use an appositive to identify or add information to another noun.

A comma or a pair of commas usually separates the appositive from the rest of the sentence.

Where I smear it with butter, **the yellow ribbon of butter . . .**

Complete each sentence with an appositive. Use commas correctly.

1. Lauren _____ fouled out of the game.
2. The prize _____ attracted many contestants.
3. The mountain _____ was hidden in the clouds.
4. Our school _____ publishes a newspaper.
5. Bo _____ wins most of his races.

See Lesson 9.6, page 389.

Cross-Curricular Activity

HEALTH Read again "Ode to la Tortilla." Investigate the food pyramid. Where would tortillas and butter be listed? Write a cluster diagram around the name of a favorite healthy food. List sensory details to describe how the food looks.

Writing Process in Action

Descriptive Writing

Descriptive Writing

In the preceding lessons you've learned about describing imaginary places and people and about using vivid words to make your descriptions come alive or to create a mood. You have written several descriptive paragraphs. Now it's time to make use of what you learned. This assignment invites you to apply your descriptive writing skills, using your powers of observation and imagination to create a special place of your own.

Assignment

Context	You've just visited a special place—real or imagined—that you want others to know about. You want to write an article for other students while the details are still fresh in your memory.
Purpose	To write an article describing a special place
Audience	Teenagers
Length	1 page

Planning to Write

The following pages can help you plan and write your article. Read through them and then refer to them as needed. But don't be tied down by them. You're in charge of your own writing process. First, set a time frame for your assignment. Keep in mind the controlling idea: to write an article describing a special place.

Writing
Online

For prewriting, drafting, revising, editing and publishing tools, go to **glencoe.com** and enter QuickPass code WC77680p1.

Prewriting

When you prewrite, draw from your experiences, knowledge, and emotions. The graphic on the right shows how freewriting helped one writer find a topic.

Once you've chosen a topic, continue prewriting to generate descriptive details. You might take notes or make a compare-contrast list. And, of course, you'll want to use all five senses to supply sensory impressions.

Drafting

Before you begin drafting, ask yourself how you can best organize your prewriting notes for a travel article. Should you describe a typical day in your special place? Should you hit the attractions from the most well known to the least? Choose an appropriate method to help you get started. You can change it later.

As you draft, make your descriptions vibrate with details. Appeal to your readers' senses. Notice how Virginia Hamilton describes a character's pleasure in discovering a special place.

Option A

Review your journal.

Option B

Build clusters.

Option C

Try freewriting.

> The places I like are different from home—different food, language, etc. I love the ocean. I can swim, body surf, fish. Telluride was cool, but no ocean. Baja California! Cabo San Lucas has it all.

Literature Model

But now, surrounding the pool on its banks were *things* growing in the dust. Nothing like them had ever grown. The pretty red, yellow. In an instant he knew the colors, knew to call them flowers, with greenery. Such bright growing extended three feet around the pool. He scented the plantings as he moved; the scent made him laugh.

Virginia Hamilton, *The Gathering*

Drafting Tip

For information about creating mood, see Lesson 3.3, pages 122–125.

Revising

To begin revising, read over your draft to make sure that what you have written fits your purpose and your audience. Then have a **writing conference.** Read your draft to a partner or a small group, or ask your teacher to give you feedback. Use your audience's reactions to help you evaluate your work so far. The questions below can help you and your listeners.

Look at the suggested revisions in the draft below. What revisions would you make?

Option A

Is the organization logical?

Option B

Are the details specific?

Option C

Is it clear why this place is special?

Even though it's small, there's lots to do in Cabo San Lucas. After siesta you can Meet new friends at the Cabo Wabo Cantina, owned by the rock group Van Halen. In the cool of the morning, you can go down to the dock to watch the fishing boats set out in hope of catching something. which marlin or sailfish. Take a stroll to The center of town features numerous craft shops. Here you can buy, or just admire, the black coral jewelry. And don't pass up the weird but delicious food: spicy fish unusual tacos with freshly grated cabbage or chicken in mole, a thick dark sauce flavored with cinnamon and chocolate.

Editing/Proofreading

During editing, your purpose is to locate and eliminate any errors in grammar, spelling, punctuation, and usage. Even one error, such as a misspelled word, can distract your audience from your message. A correct paper communicates your professional attitude as a writer.

Use the checklist at the right to **proofread** your work. Discovering an error you've overlooked before can bring a writer a great deal of satisfaction.

Publishing/Presenting

The goal of writing is to communicate with an audience. From the very first, you had a particular audience in mind—other students. Check to make sure that your writing is neat and legible. Then share your work with one or more of your classmates. You may want to have someone read your work, or you may read it to them. If you get a positive reaction, talk with your teacher about submitting your article for publication. Your teacher may be able to suggest publications to which you could send your writing. If others have written descriptive articles, perhaps you can publish them together in a class edition.

Editing/Proofreading Checklist

1. Have I corrected any run-on sentences?
2. Do my pronouns have clear antecedents?
3. Have I used the correct forms of pronouns?
4. Have I used commas correctly?
5. Have I used a dictionary to check my spelling?
6. Have I used regular and irregular verbs correctly?

Proofreading Tip

For proofreading symbols, see pages 80 and 847. If you have composed on the computer, try using the spelling checker feature to check your work.

Journal Writing: Write to Learn

Reflect on your writing process experience. Answer these questions in your journal: What do you like best about your description? What was the hardest part of writing it? What did you learn in your writing conference? What new things have you learned as a writer?

FROM

The Gathering

by Virginia Hamilton

In The Gathering *Virginia Hamilton presents four young mind-travelers, Justice and her brothers. They live in a universe where computers program themselves and everyone reads everyone else's thoughts. As you read, notice how Hamilton makes this strange world real through detailed descriptions and the everyday conversations all brothers and sisters have. In the following selection, join the mind-travelers on Sona. Led by someone (something?) called Celester, they see Colossus for the first time. Discuss the questions in Linking Writing and Literature on page 148.*

- -

They traveled the triway system down to the Oneway level and beyond the hydrafields to the rim of the enormous geodesic[1] dome that covered Sona. Celester pointed out the dome's tubular structure that had all of its parts under tension but never stress. Then he led them inside a silitrex sphere which sat above an opening in the ground, like a stopper in a bottle. Once the sphere closed around them, it began descending with a pneumatic swishing sound of air under pressure. Soft light from Celester's eyes illuminated the sphere, for the vivid sundown of Sona was left above as they plunged.

The gaseous light streaming from his eyes spread about them. Fascinated, Thomas thrust his hand into the stream. Light piled up on his palm like soft ice-cream on a cone. Thomas gasped, jumping back, jerking his hand out of the stream. The piled light scattered and regrouped in the stream coming from Celester's eyes.

"Wow! Magic!" said Dorian.

Celester hummed a comic toning, entertaining them with the light.

"Whatever it was, it got hot," Thomas said. He eyed Celester suspiciously.

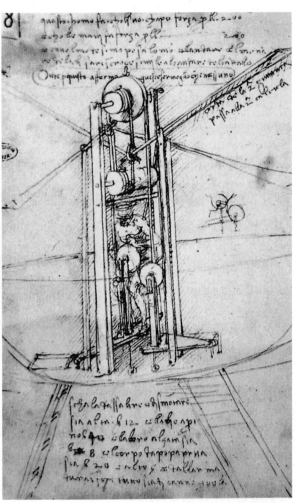

Leonardo da Vinci, sketch of an ornithopter, c. 1495–1510

"A property of light is heat," toned Celester. "He who puts hand in fire will singe his fingertips."

---

[1]**geodesic** (jē´ ə des´ ik) a structure having a strong surface made of bars that form a pattern of shapes having four or more sides

"I get the message," Thomas muttered.

"Celester, you have powerful gifts," Justice said.

The sphere seemed to float momentarily; then it stopped with a soft jolt. A door slid open. Celester moved smoothly out ahead of them.

"Colossus is like no other machine," he toned as they followed him. "There are tooling mills above and below this level built by Colossus. And there are functioning machines nearby that helped to build Colossus itself."

They were in a place of vague light, vastly mysterious because of the dimness. They could make out steep, over-hanging slopes and a wide, deep trench stretching away from them. In the entire emptiness of the trench there was but one object. It had to be Colossus.

What was there they saw, yet did not see.

The Colossus that Celester saw never varied. It was shaded mauve,[2] deepening in pulsations to black. It greeted him, he thought, with the light emitting from its smooth sur-

Peter Blume, *Light of the World,* 1932

face. Celester lifted off the ground, moving to the trench. Higher and higher he went until he was halfway to the summit of Colossus. There he stood on space in conjunction with Colossus, as Colossus tuned Celester until Celester felt no desynchronization[3] of any of his half-million

---

[2]**mauve** (mōv) a pastel shade of purple
[3]**desynchronization**
(dē sing′ krə nə zā′shən) adjustment of parts so that their movement does not occur at the same time or rate of speed

separate components. His brain was not yet middle-aged. His mind was peaceful.

Justice saw an enormous coiling, a Colossus whose awesome spring-release of time-force could whirl them home again. It changed form before her eyes. It was solid; it was ethereal. It was there, a brilliant silver coil, and it was not there.

Each of them saw Colossus differently. There before Thomas was what he loved, which was a science fiction. A silver spaceship was ready for lift-off. Upright in the trench, it was twenty stories high. Steam rose from it. He asked: Can I go, too?

He understood that the ship knew his wish to be master of himself, to speak for himself without stuttering. Only the ship knew the violent feelings he had because of his stutter and because he wanted to be free of Justice. But here and now was not for him. His here and now would come.

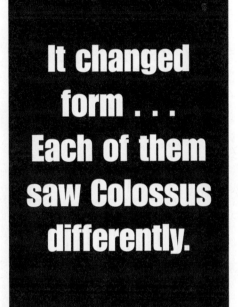

It changed form . . . Each of them saw Colossus differently.

No, he could not go a-flying with the ship.

Duster could not have comprehended a Colossus. But he had no need to name what he saw. It looked like his land of dust. He walked in it and the ground was moist under his feet. The area of the water pool was hardly recognizable. He knew it was water, glinting, refreshing to his senses, even though he was still a quarter-mile from it. But now, surrounding the pool on its banks were *things* growing in the dust. Nothing like them had ever grown. The pretty red, yellow. In an instant he knew the colors, knew to call them flowers, with greenery. Such bright growing extended three feet around the pool. He scented the plantings as he moved; the scent made him laugh. The odor was the best he'd smelled in all of the endless dust. He ran. He was there, putting his face down in the flowers.

A thought came, rising in his mind. Duster crawled to the water and thrust his hands under it, pulling his hands back toward himself on the bank. Drops of water did wet the shore. Duster stared at them. Suddenly he had his shove tool in his hand. It was a digger tool, sharp, broad and flat. He dipped the digger in the pool, then pulled it toward him in a straight line. He dug through the bank, half a hand under the dust. Water began flowing into the little ditch he made. Water filled the ditch and overflowed. That which was Colossus around Duster was aware of his learning. Now Duster knew how to keep moisture near the plantings. Tiny ferns grew quickly beside his first small irrigation ditch.

Then Duster was back in the underdome of Colossus. "Be wanting go to dust," he toned. "Where be my smooth-keep? Be wishing to be gone. Be doing to begin."

"It'll be okay, Duster," Levi said, patting his shoulder. He, too, had had a vision of Colossus. It had calmed him. He no longer feared being in the presence of such a wonder.

"Be touching leader, wrong," toned Duster to him. There was something of the old strength in his voice, which had made him leader of packens.

"It isn't like any machine I've even seen," Justice said about Colossus.

"That's the understatement of the year!" Thomas said in a hushed voice.

Dorian smiled to himself. He thought, Colossus must be the biggest computer ever built. It had to be a hundred, two hundred feet high, if not higher. The lights flashing at the top of it and the tape reels going a

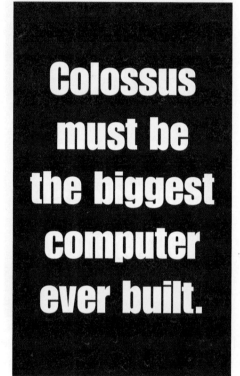

Colossus must be the biggest computer ever built.

mile a minute made him think of comets and stars. No sooner had he thought that Colossus could probably tape even their thoughts, than he heard the thought being transcribed[4] in a jumble of languages.

Smaller machines were connected to Colossus by what Dorian knew suddenly were coded physical quantities. They surrounded Colossus like flies, at a uniform height of about fifteen feet. They displayed differential equations and gave solutions to obscure problems through visuals, in electrical waves on fluorescent screens. Somehow the waves were transmitted to Colossus for it to read.

They do the small work of hydrafields, thought Dorian, of environments and life cycles. Colossus gives them direction, power.

They were all seeing Colossus differently but simultaneously. For Justice, it remained a brilliant silver coil. The space contained in the coiling caught her attention, causing her to go so near the trench she could have easily toppled in. Colossus was spectacular. It grew aware of her as distinct from the others. It saw her.

---

[4]**transcribed** (tran skrībd′) written

Linking Writing and Literature

 Learning to Learn

Think back on the characters in this science fiction story, including Colossus. Choose the character you find most compelling and write a couple of descriptive sentences about him, her, or it.

 Talk About Reading

Talk with other students about this excerpt from *The Gathering*. Assign a group leader to keep everyone focused and a group secretary to take notes. Then use the questions below to guide your conversation.

1. **Connect to Your Life:** How does the power of Colossus in the selection compare to the impact of machines in real life? Do you notice any connections between the real world and the imaginary world of *The Gathering?*

2. **Critical Thinking: Infer** What clues does Hamilton give to show that Colossus is powerful? What else do these clues suggest about Colossus?

3. **6+1 Trait®: Ideas** Name an idea in the story that you found of particular interest. Describe how Hamilton develops the idea to make it compelling.

4. **Connect to Your Writing:** What can you learn from Hamilton's writing about making imaginary elements appear lifelike?

 Write About Reading

Narrative Choose the character in the selection whom you find most interesting. (You may choose Colossus as a character.) Then write a new science fiction scene featuring that character.

Focus on Ideas Let your sci-fi imagination run free. Begin by skimming—reading quickly over—the story to review Hamilton's descriptions of the character. You may want to add to or change some of the character's traits in your narrative. Then write a new scene for the character, possibly having him or her face an unusual problem.

For more information on ideas and the 6+1 Trait® model, see **Writing and Research Handbook,** pages 822–824.

6+1 Trait® is a registered trademark of Northwest Regional Educational Laboratory, which does not endorse this product.

Reflecting on the Unit: Summarize What You Learned

Focus on the following questions to help summarize what you learned in this unit.

1 What is the purpose of descriptive writing?

2 What are the characteristics of strong descriptive writing?

3 Why should you use sensory details in descriptive writing?

4 What are the important elements of a character description?

5 Why is the order of details and the use of transition words important in descriptive writing?

 ## Adding to Your Portfolio

CHOOSE A SELECTION FOR YOUR PORTFOLIO Look over the writing you did for this unit. Choose a piece of writing for your portfolio. The writing you choose should show one or more of the following:

- descriptive details in an order that creates a strong image

- a mood so strong that a reader can share it

- exact and vivid words that clearly convey your meaning

REFLECT ON YOUR CHOICE Attach a note to the piece you chose, explaining briefly why you chose it and what you learned from writing it.

SET GOALS How can you improve your writing? What skill will you focus on the next time you write?

Writing Across the Curriculum

MAKE A GEOGRAPHY CONNECTION Write a two-paragraph description of the region in which you live for a person who has never been there. Describe common sights and sounds, especially ones that may be unique. Write about the climate and the ways people earn their livings. Try to imagine what would most interest a visitor, and try to make your description come alive with vivid sensory details. Be sure to write legibly and check your spelling before sharing your writing.

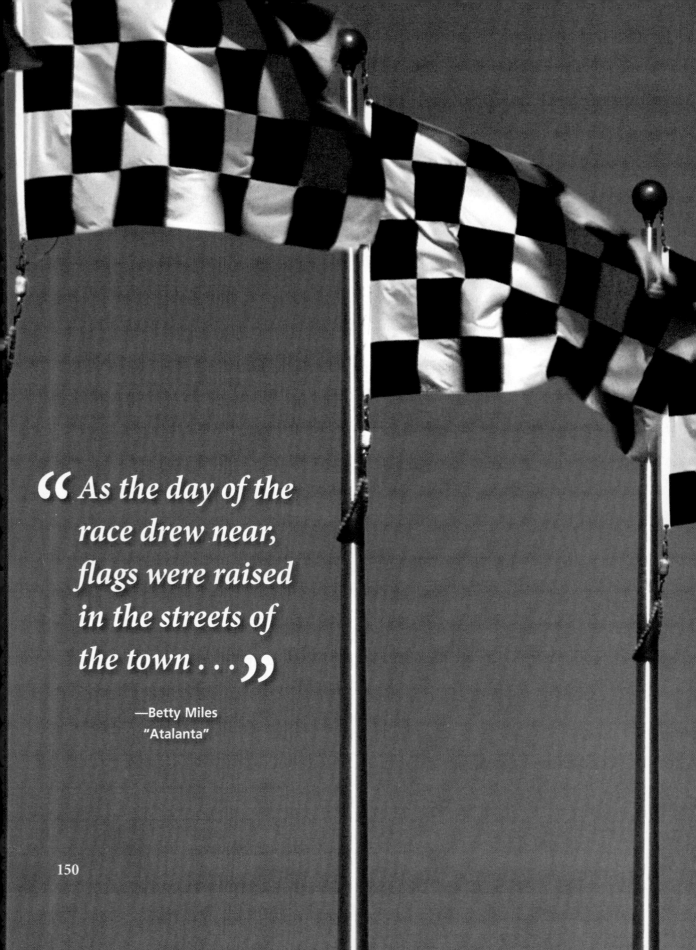

"As the day of the race drew near, flags were raised in the streets of the town . . . "

—Betty Miles
"Atalanta"

Narrative Writing

MEDIA
Short Story
Connection

Creating a good character is an important part of writing a short story. T. Ernesto Bethancourt invented a couple of great characters for his fantasy story "User Friendly." One is a junior high school student named Kevin. The other is Kevin's best friend, Louis—a super-computer that frighteningly develops a mind of its own.

from "User Friendly"

by T. Ernesto Bethancourt

My bowl of Frosted Flakes was neatly in place, flanked by a small pitcher of milk, an empty juice glass, and an unpeeled banana. I picked up the glass, went to the refrigerator, poured myself a glass of Tang, and sat down to my usual lonely breakfast. Mom was already at work, and Dad wouldn't be home from his Chicago trip for another three days. I absently read the ingredients in Frosted Flakes for what seemed like the millionth time. I sighed deeply.

When I returned to my room to shower and dress for the day, my history project was already printed out. I had almost walked by Louis, when I noticed there was a message on the screen. It wasn't the usual:

Printout completed. Do you wish to continue: Y/N?

Underneath the printout were two lines:

When are you going to get my voice module, Kevin?

I blinked. It couldn't be. There was nothing in Louis's basic programming that would allow for a question like this. Wondering what was going on, I sat at the keyboard, and entered:" *Repeat last message.* Amazingly, the computer replied:

It's right there on the screen, Kevin. Can we talk? I mean, are you going to get me a voice box?

I was stunned. What was going on here?

Writing a Fantasy

Prewriting	Drafting	Revising/Editing
Planning the Story	Introducing the Characters	Start from the Top

A Writer's Process

Prewriting
Planning the Story

Novelist T. Ernesto Bethancourt was inspired to write a fantasy about a computer when his first portable computer fizzled out. "I started going to all the computer shows," Bethancourt said, "and I was amazed at all the things that were being done with computers. Before long, I got heavily into the idea of artificial intelligence, and I thought, 'what a great companion a computer could be.' I said, 'Gee, what if the thing really had a personality and could be user friendly?'"

Once Bethancourt knew he had a good idea, he began mulling it over. For six weeks, he thought about characters and scenes.

All the while, Bethancourt followed his own map for short story writing. "You create a hero or heroine and place the figure in a problem situation," he said. "Then you have your hero use his or her inner resources—courage, intelligence, wit—to resolve the conflict. After the conflict is resolved, the main character is in some way changed."

Following this plan, Bethancourt created a hero named Kevin. Where did he get the inspiration for his character? Bethancourt modeled Kevin after a young friend of his—a quiet, smart boy with a sly sense of humor.

Bethancourt then broke his story line into individual scenes. He summarized each scene on an index card.

Once Bethancourt finished summarizing the scenes, he laid the index cards out on his desk. He looked for scenes that best showed the growing conflict. Those scenes would get the most space in his narrative.

Drafting
Creating the Plot

"Writing stories is fun," says Bethancourt. "You get to have adventures, except you're in control. And you get to use those swell remarks you don't think of until two days later and then say, 'Gee, I wish I'd said that.'"

Bethancourt started drafting "User Friendly" when he had the story events clearly in mind. Near the beginning of the story, Kevin notices the startling message on the computer screen: "When are you going to get me my voice module, Kevin?"

Bethancourt accomplished several tasks at the beginning of the story. First of all, he introduced two main characters, Kevin and the computer, using dialogue to bring them to life. Then he based events on everyday life to make the story believable. "The important thing in fantasy is that you've got to have a foot on the ground before you take off," Bethancourt said.

As Bethancourt moved into the middle of his story, he used action and dialogue to tell the story. These techniques also help him build suspense and hold the reader's attention. "This is largely a 'think' story," he said. To balance that effect with adventure, Bethancourt said, "action was important. I had to show that Kevin wasn't a total dweeb. I did this by having him outsmart a

Writing scene ideas on index cards helps Bethancourt organize the short story.

Scene 1
In Kevin's room.
Introduce Kevin and Louis.
Louis "talks"!

Scene 3
Kevin's confrontation with Chuck.
Kevin outsmarts the bully.

Last scene
At Kevin's house.
Dad pulls the plug on Louis.

jock who's trying to intimidate him."

Revising/Editing
Starting From the Top

After writing a draft, many writers—including Bethancourt—leave the draft alone for a period of time. For Bethancourt, the "shelf time" is about a week.

Typically, Bethancourt writes for two days, then goes back to page one. "I start at the top, and I rewrite it," he explains. Bethancourt lets this draft sit for at least a week before making any final changes.

Some key parts of "User Friendly" came into being because of Bethancourt's careful revising. One example is a scene between Kevin and a bullying character named Chuck. "In the first draft, I had Kevin running away from Chuck," Bethancourt said. "I wanted more physical action. But when I looked at it, it wasn't as good as when Kevin simply outsmarted Chuck. So I cut the running-away scene."

Bethancourt believes that the revision stage is a critical part of the writing process. He explains, "The best writing is rewriting. The idea is to get something down on paper. It doesn't matter how long you write— you can always cut stuff out."

Examining Writing in the Real World

Analyzing the Media Connection

Discuss these questions about the story excerpt on page 152.

1. What kind of details make the excerpt seem believable and ordinary?

2. How does Kevin feel as he eats breakfast? How does Bethancourt convey these feelings without actually stating them outright?

3. How does the mood of the excerpt's first scene differ from the mood of the scene that follows? How effective is this contrast?

4. What details does Bethancourt use to show that Kevin is surprised by his computer?

5. What immediate impression do you get of Louis, the computer? How does the author get this impression across?

Analyzing a Writer's Process

Discuss these questions about T. Ernesto Bethancourt's writing process.

1. After placing the main character in a problem situation, what inner resources does Bethancourt give to the character to resolve the conflict?

2. How did Bethancourt decide which scenes would receive the most attention in this story? Would you use Bethancourt's method? Explain.

3. What method of organization does Bethancourt use? What advantages does this method have?

4. Why does Bethancourt give his drafts "shelf time" before doing the final revision?

5. Do you agree with Bethancourt that "the best writing is rewriting"? Why or why not?

Grammar*Link*

While proofreading, check subject-verb agreement. In sentences that begin with *there*, look for the subject after the verb.

In the following sentence, the subject is *message*. It agrees with the singular verb *was*.

> *There was a message on the screen.*

Use each noun below as the subject of a sentence that begins with *there*. Be careful to make the verb agree with the subject.

1. cars
2. family
3. father
4. computer
5. music

See Lesson 16.2, pages 535–536.

Telling a Good Story

*W*hen you write a story, or narrative, you answer the question, "What happened?" To give your readers a complete picture of what occurred, your story will need a beginning, a middle, and an end. The story will also need a setting, a conflict and solution, characters, and dialogue.

Harold Lloyd in *Safety Last,* 1923

What happened in this photograph? How did this man get himself into this predicament? What will happen next? How will he get himself out of this dangerous situation? A good storyteller will answer all of these questions.

Describe What Happened

Suppose you've seen the movie in which this scene takes place, and a friend asks you what the movie is about. You would probably tell what happened through a series of events. This is called the **plot**.

As you talk about the events of the plot, you will find yourself talking about the characters. **Characters** are the people or animals that take part in the events. Notice how novelist Madeleine L'Engle introduces characters and plot in the following selection.

Narrative Writing

> What event begins the plot of this story?

"There are dragons in the twins' vegetable garden."

Meg Murry took her head out of the refrigerator where she had been foraging for an after-school snack, and looked at her six-year-old brother. "What?"

"There are dragons in the twins' vegetable garden. Or there were. They've moved to the north pasture now."

. . . She took her sandwich materials and a bottle of milk and set them out on the kitchen table. Charles Wallace waited patiently. She looked at him, scowling with an anxiety she did not like to admit to herself, at the fresh rips in the knees of his blue jeans, the streaks of dirt grained deep in his shirt, a darkening bruise on the cheekbone under his left eye. "Okay, did the big boys jump you in the schoolyard this time, or when you got off the bus?"

"Meg, you aren't listening to me."

"I happen to care that you've been in school for two months now and not a single week has gone by that you haven't been roughed up. If you've been talking about dragons in the garden or wherever they are, I suppose that explains it."

> What do you know about Meg and Charles Wallace by the end of the passage?

"I haven't. Don't underestimate me. I didn't see them till I got home."

Madeleine L'Engle, *A Wind in the Door*

Journal Writing

Think of a story you have read or heard recently that you really liked. In your journal, tell what it was about the story that interested you. Was it the plot or a character? Explain what a story must do to capture your attention.

Drafting Tip

When you write about a setting, use sensory details to make the scene as real as possible.

Set the Scene

A story has characters and a plot. It also has a **setting.** The setting puts the characters in a certain place at a certain time. Stories can be set in the present, the past, or the future. What happens in the story and how characters look and act often depend on the time when the events take place.

Where a story takes place may also affect what happens. A writer may set a story in a real place or in an imaginary one. A stormy lake, a summer camp, or another planet can be a setting for a story. Changing the setting will affect the kind of story you tell, as shown by the illustrations below.

Contrasting Three Settings

A story about a cowhand who rides a horse on the range could be a traditional Western adventure story.

A story about a cowhand who rides a horse in the city might be a modern-day comedy.

A story about a cowhand who rides a horse on the moon would probably be a science-fiction story.

Setting affects not only story events but also the way characters act. For example, the cowhand would probably act differently in each of the three settings illustrated above.

Write a Children's Story

Your class is writing a book of stories for children at a day-care center. Write an imaginative, entertaining story that will keep them interested. Think about some of the stories that were your favorites when you were younger and then write a story that a four- or five-year-old would enjoy.

PURPOSE To create an entertaining children's story

AUDIENCE Children at a day-care center

LENGTH 1–2 pages

WRITING RUBRICS To write a good children's story, you should

- structure your story so it has a clear beginning, middle, and end
- clearly define each character
- make sure the setting fits the characters and plot

Listening and Speaking

STORYTELLING In a group of three or four classmates, read your story aloud, using a voice and style appropriate for younger children. Critique each other's stories to make them more effective for that audience. Then arrange to read the stories to a group of preschoolers.

Viewing and Representing

ILLUSTRATING A STORY Create two or three visual images that illustrate your story. Display the images as you read your story in your group and, if possible, later when you read for a younger audience.

GrammarLink

Use a possessive noun to show ownership or possession of a thing or quality.

A possessive noun is formed in one of two ways. For all singular nouns and for plural nouns not ending in -s, add an apostrophe and -s ('s):

   cat's whiskers

   men's team

For plural nouns already ending in -s, add only an apostrophe ('):

   twins' vegetable garden

Write the correct possessive form for each underlined word.

1. This story captures the <u>reader</u> attention.
2. The <u>writer</u> opening line draws you into the story.
3. What were the <u>boys</u> reactions?
4. <u>Charles</u> attitude is clear.
5. The <u>children</u> relationship is implied.

See Lesson 9.3, page 383, and Lesson 9.4, page 385.

LESSON
4.2

Exploring Story Ideas

*T*he plot of most good stories centers on a problem faced by a character. Focusing on a problem that needs solving is one good way to come up with story ideas.

This cow's problem can spark ideas that would make a great story. Jot down some ideas about how the cow got the barrel on its head. Then list a few ideas about what will happen to it next and how it can get rid of the barrel.

TIME

For more about the writing process, see **TIME** *Facing the Blank Page*, pp. 97–107.

Identify the Problem

Look at the pictures at the top of the next page. Think about the problem involved in each situation. Take a few minutes to list some similar situations of your own. You can either use one of the pictures as a starting point or think of entirely new situations.

Car Breaking Down

Invisible Person

Monster in Town

Find a Solution

Once you have an idea you like, you can start developing it into a full-length story. Asking yourself questions like those listed in the chart below will help you plan a series of events. Some events will help solve the problem in your story. Others may make the solution more difficult.

As you answer these questions, let your imagination run wild. It is your story, and anything can happen! The journal entry to the right shows how one student answered questions about her story idea—a monster terrorizing Middleville.

Questions About Story Ideas

1. What is the problem?
2. What characters does it involve?
3. What happened before?
4. What will happen next?
5. What is the solution to the problem?

Problem—monster terrorizes Middleville

Characters—monster, Patrice (14-year-old girl), Matt (her 10-year-old brother)

Before—monster was lonely and came to town

Next—everyone scared of monster, except Patrice and Matt

Solution—Patrice and Matt put monster on a basketball team

Journal Writing

Think of a problem you have encountered that you can use as a base for a story. List one or two events leading up to the problem. Then list one or two events that might happen next and the solution.

Editing Tip

As you edit, check your story for appropriate use of personal pronouns. For more information, see Lesson 11.1, page 429.

Decide Who Is Involved

Once you have some ideas, try them out to see if they will work for a story. Many writers try out their story ideas by focusing on a particular character. What kind of a problem is that character likely to have? How would he or she try to solve that problem?

The paragraphs below involve Mellissa, who tells the story in the first person, and Eddie, who lives in an abandoned bus. The excerpt begins with Mellissa's father telling her some news.

Literature Model

After the reporter left Eddie's place today, Hendrikson showed up with a bunch of people. They barged right into the bus." He stopped, embarrassed. "Like I did tonight, I guess. Anyway, they told Eddie that the city was going to help him by moving him into the newest senior citizen housing complex."

I didn't like the sound of it. "They can't do that! Eddie will never go for it. He hates apartments. He told me. He likes to be free."

"I know. And I don't blame him. . . . But anyway, the thing that really upset him is they told him he can't take Shadow with him."

"Why not?"

"No dogs allowed."

Incredible! "Shadow isn't just a dog. He's like a relative to Eddie. They need each other."

"They don't care. He's a dog and they don't allow any animals."

Gloria Gonzalez, *The Glad Man*

When does Mellissa sense that Eddie faces a problem?

At what point does Mellissa recognize the seriousness of the problem?

Imagine that you are the author, Gloria Gonzalez, answering the questions in the chart on page 161. Think of some different solutions to Eddie's problem.

4.2 Writing Activities

Write a Narrative Message

Think of a story in your literature book in which a character gets into some kind of trouble or faces some kind of problem. Write a message from that character to a friend, asking the friend for help.

PURPOSE To narrate a brief story about a predicament

AUDIENCE A friend

LENGTH 2–3 paragraphs

WRITING RUBRICS To write an effective narrative message, you should

- explain the problem
- tell what led up to the problem
- tell what the character wants to happen—the solution
- include events that could happen, in order
- proofread for correct spelling and usage

Listening and Speaking

COOPERATIVE LEARNING In a group of three or four, read your messages aloud. See if the listeners in your group can tell what literary character "wrote" your message. Use feedback from your group members to help you refine your narrative message before you publish it in a collection assembled by the entire class.

Using Computers

Before you submit your work, you may want to make it look more appealing by experimenting with different type sizes and typefaces on your computer.

Grammar*Link*

Avoid using double negatives!

Two negative words together create confusing double negatives.

They **don't** allow **no** animals.

The correct version from the story is "They don't allow any animals."

Rewrite these sentences using only one negative word.

1. I didn't do nothing.
2. Hardly no one knew.
3. None never came to my house.
4. No one said nothing.
5. She doesn't never go to the movies.

See Lesson 12.10, page 469.

Using Time Order in a Story

*W*hich came first, the chicken or the egg?

Just as there is no right answer to this question, there is no one right way to tell a story. As a storyteller, you will want to narrate the events in an order that will make sense to your readers.

First, Think Time!

Time order—the order in which events occur from first to last—is a logical way to organize ideas in a story. Remembering the order in which events happen will help you plan your story and assist your readers in following the situation. Look at the illustrations at the top of the next page. They show a series of events arranged in time order.

Story Events in Time Order

| Fox sees the fire. | Fox runs away from the fire. | Fox reaches a ravine. |

This series of events is the basis for the paragraph below. Notice how the writer uses time order to tell the story and help her readers follow the action of a fox escaping a fire.

Student Model

Leaving my den in the morning, I felt an immense heat at my back. I turned around and there, before my eyes, was an enormous wall of fire and smoke! I bounded away from the fire and headed toward the safety of the ravine. The brush swept by my face. The fire kept gaining on me, threatening me. I tried to propel myself faster, but my tongue hung down and my energy began running out. Suddenly, the landscape sloped downwards, and the ravine came into view.

Jenny DeLong, Canyon Park Junior High School
Bothell, Washington

> How does time order help the writer tell the story?

Journal Writing

Think about the past week, and choose something that happened to you—something about which you might like to write a story. As you think of the events that you will include in your story, list them. Then number the events in the order in which they actually occurred.

Use Transitions

Certain words and phrases, called **transitions,** can help readers keep track of the order of events in your writing. Some examples of transitions include *before, after, until then, next, first,* and *finally.*

Read the story below. Then reread it, paying attention to the highlighted words. What do these transitions add to the story?

Literature Model

When John Cowles and his wife and baby moved to Wisconsin in 1843, they built a one-room cabin to live in. All the cabin needed was a front door. That was due to arrive before the weather turned cold. Until then they had hung a heavy quilt over the doorway.

John Cowles was a doctor. One night before supper, a messenger came for him. Someone was sick on a farm about twelve miles away. "I'll be home tonight or tomorrow morning," he told his wife. He quickly packed his things and rode off into the darkness.

His wife left a pot of beans simmering on the hearth in case he was hungry when he got home. Then she got into bed with her baby and went to sleep. Sometime during the night, Mrs. Cowles awakened. She sensed that someone was in the cabin with her, probably her husband. But when she opened her eyes, she saw a bear in front of the fireplace. He was eating the beans, mouthful after mouthful.

Suddenly he stopped. He looked up and stared across the room at her. In the darkness, his eyes looked like burning coals. She wondered if he could see her. If the baby cried out, what would he do? If he attacked, what could she do?

The bear turned back to the beans. When he finished with them, he pushed the quilt aside and left.

Alvin Schwartz, "A Pot of Beans"

What does the transition phrase "until then" tell the reader?

The transition word "suddenly" also adds drama and suspense to the story.

Write a Personal Narrative

Look in your journal at the entry for the activity on page 165. Using the events listed in your journal as a stimulus, write a one-page story.

PURPOSE To tell a personal story
AUDIENCE Your friends and family
LENGTH 1 page

WRITING RUBRICS To write an effective personal narrative, you should

- add details that develop plot, character, and setting
- use time order to develop the story
- use transitions to help your reader follow the action
- use consistent verb tenses
- write legibly

Viewing and Representing

SPEAKING WITH PICTURES Using your personal narrative as a guide, create a series of four or five drawings which tell the same story without words. Make sure the drawings follow the same order as the details in the narrative. Create a kind of exhibit guide by assembling the class's written narratives. Put the drawings on display and ask students to match the drawings with the written narratives.

GrammarLink

Make sure that your verbs do not shift unnecessarily from past to present tense.

Rewrite the following paragraph, avoiding tense shifts.

[1] The suspect sat squirming in his seat and does not meet my eyes. [2] "Tell me where you were," I say. [3] He hesitated, and in that instant I knew that he is trying to hide something. [4] I stare at him intently. [5] The color slowly drains from his face, and he finally looked up and met my eyes.

See Lesson 10.5, page 407.

Cross-Curricular Activity

SCIENCE Suppose that your science class has started a tutoring program for third-grade students. As part of the program, you have been asked to choose a science topic and write a story about it. For example, you might write a story to teach students how a plant grows.

Write a one-page story for younger students. Remember to use characters, plot, and setting to create your story. Be sure you use time order and transition words to relate events.

Narrative Writing

Narrative Writing

Writing Dialogue to Develop Characters

*W*hat characters say in a story will often reveal what they are like.

If you're familiar with *Alice in Wonderland,* you probably remember the line "Off with her head!" The Queen of Hearts said it quite often. What does that line tell you about the queen? How might the people she was angry with have felt?

Read the statements below. Describe what the lines tell you about each character who is speaking.

Dialogue

1. "Stand back, everyone! I'll take care of that dragon."
2. "Party? What party? It was your birthday? Ohhh. Sorry."
3. "If you won't help me, then I'll just do it myself."
4. "Hi, Mr. Elias! I'm here to take you for a wheelchair ride."

Let Them Speak for Themselves

Dialogue in stories consists of the characters' exact words. Dialogue can help reveal the moods, interests, and personalities of different characters. In the first passage on the next page, Mrs. Suárez is talking to her neighbor, Mr. Mendelsohn.

Literature Model

Another piece of bread?" she asked.
"No, thank you very much. . . . I'm full. But it was delicious."
"You too skinny — you don't eat right, I bet." Mrs. Suárez shook her head. "Come tomorrow and have Sunday supper with us."
"I really couldn't."
"Sure you could. I always make a big supper."

Nicholasa Mohr, "Mr. Mendelsohn"

What do you think Mrs. Suárez's words tell you about her personality?

In the next literature passage David, an American man who is spending a year in Wales, talks to Peter, his son. Peter is unhappy about celebrating Christmas away from home. David speaks first.

Editing Tip

When editing dialogue, make sure you've used quotation marks and commas appropriately. For more information, see Lesson 20.6, page 599.

Literature Model

Christmas is Christmas no matter where you are."
"I wish we were home," said Peter.
"You've made that plain over and over," retorted David. "There is no point in saying it again."
"You never seem to pay any attention."

Nancy Bond, *A String in the Harp*

What does the dialogue between Peter and David reveal about them?

Journal Writing

Look at three pieces of dialogue in a book or story you have read recently. In your journal jot down a few notes about how the dialogue made you feel toward the characters.

Use Descriptive Phrases Wisely

Tips for Writing Dialogue

 Use words that reflect the character's personality.

 Be sure the dialogue sounds like something that character would say.

 Put the character's exact words in quotation marks.

 Start a new paragraph when you move from one speaker to another.

 Use descriptive words to tell how the character said something.

Identifying the speaker helps your readers follow the dialogue. Describing how a character speaks helps the reader "hear" the lines. Think about how these characters say their lines.

"Anybody home?" she yelled cheerily.

"Anybody home?" Juan whispered.

"Anybody home?" the giant roared.

Use descriptive words or phrases such as *cheerily* sparingly. Attaching descriptions to every identifying phrase can make writing sound unnatural. In this excerpt Aztec ruler Montezuma and his advisers discuss the arrival of Cortez's army. Notice how the descriptive phrases convey Montezuma's reaction.

Literature Model

We must wait," Montezuma said in a dry voice.

"For what do we wait, my Lord?"

"We must see . . . we must discover if these strangers will leave us or if they will stay. We must find out what they want," Montezuma murmured so softly that I could hardly hear his words.

"My Lord," the councilmen asked, "will they come here? . . . Will they dare approach Tenochtitlán?"

"I do not know," the great Lord whispered, " . . . I do not know. . . ."

Jamake Highwater, *The Sun, He Dies*

How does Montezuma feel about the Spaniards' arrival? How do you know?

Write a Dialogue

Find a copy of a painting or a photograph in which two or three people seem to be engaging in a conversation. Imagine what the people might be saying to one another. Think of characteristics for each figure. Then draft a dialogue between the characters.

PURPOSE To use dialogue to make characters come to life

AUDIENCE Yourself

LENGTH 1–2 pages

WRITING RUBRICS To create effective dialogue, you should

- use language that reveals characters' moods and personalities
- use quotation marks to show characters' exact words
- use descriptive phrases when necessary to tell how the words should sound
- proofread to make sure you have made clear who is speaking

Listening and Speaking

COOPERATIVE LEARNING In a small group, review each other's pictures and dialogues. Use your group's comments to refine and revise your dialogue to make it clearer and more interesting. Then make a dramatic reading of the dialogue, having different students read aloud the parts you've written.

GrammarLink

Use quotation marks for dialogue.

Quotation marks go before and after the characters' exact words. Rewrite the sentences in the following dialogue, adding quotation marks.

1. Tim whispered, What's going on?
2. Hmm, responded Dave quietly, it looks like Joe's in trouble.
3. Let's get going! I'm not getting involved in his problems.
4. Hesitating, Dave replied, Wait! It looks as though he could use our help.
5. You stay, then. I'm out of here!

See Lesson 20.6, page 599.

Cross-Curricular Activity

DRAMA After all the small groups have reviewed and refined their dialogues and have made them into dramatic readings, hold a performance festival in class. Have each group choose one of its readings, display the picture on which it was based, and perform the dialogue for the entire class. Hold a follow-up discussion to find out how other students might have represented the characters differently.

LOG ON ▶ **Writing** Online | For more writing and grammar practice, go to **glencoe.com** and enter QuickPass code WC77680p1.

171

LESSON 4.5

Drafting a Story

Doing some planning before starting a story helps a writer avoid panic. The writer can then begin drafting a story with confidence.

Calvin and Hobbes   by Bill Watterson

Even professional writers sometimes feel like Calvin. The following three paragraphs, however, show the results of careful planning by author Laurence Yep.

Literature Model

I stopped when I smelled the magic. It was strong magic. Old magic. And it carried a faint scent of the sea. And yet I was a thousand kilometers away from the nearest body of salt water.

Halting in the middle of the road, I tried to follow the scent. It came from the top of a nearby hill, where a little village sat like a tray of dirty, overturned cups that someone had left to gather dust. But the magic I smelled was too powerful for a small, sleepy place like that.

Well, when trouble isn't drawn to me, I seem to be drawn to it. Leaning on my staff, I stepped off the main road onto the side path that wound through the rice fields.

Laurence Yep, *Dragon of the Lost Sea*

> After reading these opening lines, what do you know about the plot of this story?

> What have you learned so far about the main character?

Start with a Plan

Plan some elements of your story before you begin drafting. Think about the characters and events and how the setting affects them. One writer planned a story about a dog kidnapped by aliens. The chart below shows elements he included in his plan. Writing down some details about the important story elements can ease you into drafting your story.

Plotting Tip

A good story has the following elements:

- rising action
- a conflict or problem
- a climax or high point of interest
- falling action
- resolution

Planning Story Elements	
	**Plot:** A spacecraft lowers from the clouds. It hovers over a girl walking her dog. The dog breaks free from his leash as the ship beams him aboard.
	**Characters:** Fourteen-year-old Nina likes skateboarding but doesn't like walking Scooter, the family dog. Scooter loves to run and barks when walked on his leash.
	**Setting:** The aliens' planet is covered with grass. Dogs run around without leashes, collars, or owners. A river of dog chow flows past countless trees and buried bones.

Journal Writing

Think of a character, an event, and a setting to use in a story. Use a chart similar to the one above, and jot down as many details about each of these elements as you can.

Prewriting Tip

As you plan your story, think about what information the reader will need to follow the events.

Now Just Write

Your story will eventually bring together plot, setting, and characters. As you draft, you may want to focus on one of these elements. Review your prewriting notes, and choose the element that seems most striking. Then start writing about this element, and notice how the other elements find their way into the story. Other helpful drafting tips are listed in the illustration below.

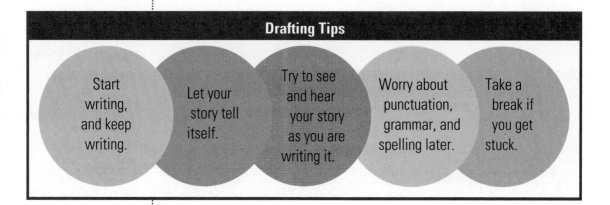

Drafting Tips

Start writing, and keep writing.

Let your story tell itself.

Try to see and hear your story as you are writing it.

Worry about punctuation, grammar, and spelling later.

Take a break if you get stuck.

The paragraphs below are part of a story called "Project: Brainwave." As you read, notice how Rick Harrison lets the story tell itself.

Student Model

This computer stores the memories and experiences of the entire human race. Beep! You may choose from five categories. *Beep!* They are: 1. Mystery, *beep!* 2. Adventure, *beep!* 3. Paradise, *beep!* 4. Romance, *beep!* and 5. Sports, *beep!*"

. . . I figured I deserved a vacation. So I chose Paradise. But as I reached for the headset, my wrist accidentally hit the Mystery button as well. Before I knew it, for the second time that day, everything went black.

Rick Harrison, Mt. Pleasant Middle School, Livingston, New Jersey; first appeared in *Merlyn's Pen: The National Magazine of Student Writing*

How does this list of choices move the plot along?

Write a Tall Tale

Storytelling festivals are held across the United States. Often one of the biggest events is the tall-tale contest. Contestants have a few minutes to tell the funniest and most outlandish story they can think of.

Follow the model on page 174 to plan your story. Then draft your tall tale.

PURPOSE To entertain an audience with a tall tale

AUDIENCE People attending the festival

LENGTH 2 paragraphs that can be told within 2 minutes

WRITING RUBRICS To write an effective tall tale, you should

- include larger-than-life details that help readers picture the characters, events, and setting
- focus on one element in your draft
- proofread to correct sentence fragments

GrammarLink

Watch for sentence fragments.

A sentence fragment lacks a subject, a predicate, or both. Avoid sentence fragments when you write for school or in any formal writing. To correct a sentence fragment, add the subject or predicate, or connect the fragment to a nearby sentence. Rewrite the following items to eliminate the sentence fragments. If the item is a complete sentence, write *correct*.

1. Formed high banks along the road.
2. Snow blanketed the ground.
3. Ice like diamonds.
4. Puffs of breath hang in the air.
5. Clouds in the sky.
6. Groan in the wind.

See Lesson 8.2, page 359.

Listening and Speaking

COOPERATIVE LEARNING Working in a group of three, start with a planning chart like the one on page 173. Label the rows *Plot, Characters,* and *Setting.* The first person fills in the Plot row, the second person fills in the Characters row, and the third person fills in the Setting row. Then each group member drafts a story based on the ideas in the planning chart. Read your stories aloud, using tone, volume, and emphasis to create interest.

Viewing and Representing

ILLUSTRATE A TALE Create an illustration that will help a reader understand and appreciate your tall tale. Help the reader see what your character is like and the setting in which he or she functions.

LESSON 4.6

Evaluating a Story Opening

A good story begins by grabbing the reader's attention. If the beginning is dull, the reader might decide not to continue. Notice how writer Isaac Asimov begins his story in the following model.

Isaac Asimov plunges into a tense scene to open this story, the first he ever published. He tells very little about the situation—directly. Yet, because Asimov's writing lets you hear and see the characters, you learn a great deal.

Asimov was only a teenager when he wrote this story. Yet the opening kept the editor of a science-fiction magazine reading long enough to decide to publish the story.

> ### Literature Model
>
> "Will you please stop walking up and down like that?" said Warren Moore from the couch. "It won't do any of us any good. Think of our blessings; we're airtight, aren't we?"
>
> Mark Brandon whirled and ground his teeth at him. "I'm glad you feel happy about that," he spat out viciously. "Of course, you don't know that our air supply will last only three days." He resumed his interrupted stride with a defiant air.
>
> Isaac Asimov, "Marooned off Vesta"

What makes this a good story beginning?

Grab Attention

Starting to read a story doesn't always mean finishing it. Think about what makes you keep reading a story. Is it an exciting plot? intriguing characters? an unusual writing style? Consider these questions as you read the following paragraphs written by a student.

Student Model

I only remember two things from when I was seven: The time I got a bingo chip stuck up my nose and had to go to the hospital to have it removed, and the fights I had with my sister, Jane. We used to argue endlessly.

When Mom and Dad weren't around, I'd always give her the "now I'M the boss" speech, she'd do something like pour shampoo in my sock drawer, and we'd both end up tearing each other's hair out. Then when Mom and Dad got back, I'd run to them and say, "YOU take care of her—I'm running away!" Jane would then waltz in and say, sweet as pie, "What's going on?"

Renee Albe, Maplewood, New Jersey
First appeared in *Cricket* magazine

> Renee uses dialogue to develop her characters and advance the story.

> Do you think this is an effective story beginning? Why?

Some writers work and rework the beginning of a story until they get it just the way they want it. They feel that once they have a beginning the rest of the story will fall into place. Other writers draft the entire story first. Then they look for the catchiest line or the first dramatic moment and move that to the beginning.

Revising Tip

To improve your story beginning, think about the most interesting detail of your story.

Journal Writing

Look at the opening paragraphs of a story you enjoyed reading recently. What elements in the opening did you find interesting? Record your answers in your journal.

Make an Impact

Sometimes revising a story opening means looking at the rest of what you've written to find the best place to start. You might look for the most engaging sentences and start your story at that point, as in the paper on the left below.

Other times you keep the beginning you have but make a few changes, as in the paper on the right. Cutting unimportant words or adding descriptive details can give more impact to your story beginning.

Either approach works well. You may try both methods several times before you write a beginning that satisfies you.

> What did the writer achieve by beginning where she did?

> Which of the revised openings do you find more effective? Why?

It was a lovely spring morning
when Kathy and I set out on the
bike trip we'd planned for so long.
I'd been so excited over breakfast
I'd hardly been able to eat.
It had never occurred to either
of us that anything would go
Start Here
wrong. So when my rear tire went
flat, I stood by the side of the road
and watched helplessly as Kathy
and her yellow bike receded into
the distance.

The
It was a lovely spring morning
overnight
when Kathy and I set out on the
bike trip we'd planned for so long.
was too   to eat
I'd been so excited over breakfast.
I'd hardly been able to eat.
It had never occurred to either
of us that anything would go
I was already starving
wrong. So when my rear tire went
only two hours into the trip
flat, I stood by the side of the road
and watched helplessly as Kathy,
and my lunch disappeared
and her yellow bike, receded into
over a hill
the distance.

4.6 | Writing Activities

Write a Story Opening

Look in your journal for story ideas. Select one idea to develop. Think of at least three beginnings to your story. Choose one version. Then draft and revise a possible beginning for the story you've selected.

PURPOSE To grab readers' attention
AUDIENCE Your teacher
LENGTH 1–2 paragraphs

WRITING RUBRICS To write a good story opening, you should

- capture your readers' attention
- include engaging details
- delete unnecessary words
- vary sentences by using adverb clauses

Allan Rohan Crite, *Last Game at Dusk*, 1939

Grammar*Link*

Use adverb clauses to modify verbs.

An *adverb clause* describes the verb in the main clause, telling how, when, where, why, or under what circumstances the action occurs. Adverb clauses begin with words such as *after, when, where, before, while,* and *as: Before cars were available, some people rode bikes.* Add an adverb clause to each of the following sentences:

1. Many people commute by bus.
2. Children must ride cautiously.
3. He watches television.
4. They returned from their trip.
5. I always brush my teeth.
See Lesson 14.4, page 507.

Cross-Curricular Activity

ART Brainstorm for ideas about characters, plot, and setting based on the painting on this page. Select one idea; then plan and draft a story opening. Refer to page 177 for different ways to revise your opening to give it more impact.

Listening and Speaking

COOPERATIVE LEARNING In groups of three or four, read your openings aloud. Use your group's comments to edit and refine your opening.

Narrative Writing

WRITING ABOUT LITERATURE
Responding to a Story

The response to a story is a reflection of the reader's experiences.

In the literature excerpt below, a young man has brought an injured owl to a doctor. Read to find out what the young man discovers during his visit.

Literature Model

Cage after cage of birds, Theseus saw, all down one wall of the room, finches and thrushes, starlings and blackbirds, with a sleepy stirring and twittering coming from them.

In the surgery [doctor's office] there was only one cage, but that one big enough to house a man. And inside it was such a bird as Theseus had never seen before—every feather on it pure gold, and eyes like candle-flames.

"My phoenix," the doctor said, "but don't go too near him, for he's vicious." . . .

"You are only just in time," Dr. Kilvaney said. "My hour has come. I hereby appoint you my heir and successor. To you I bequeath my birds. Feed them well, treat them kindly, and they will sing to you. But never, never let the phoenix out of his cage, for his nature is evil."

"No, no! Dr. Kilvaney!" Theseus cried. "You are in the wrong of it! You are putting a terrible thing on me! I don't want your birds, not a feather of them. I can't abide creatures in cages!"

Joan Aiken, "A Leg Full of Rubies"

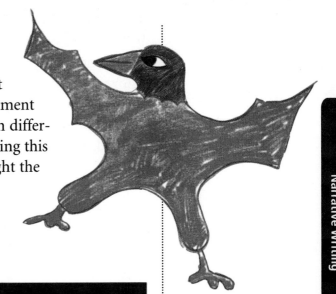

Connect with the Story

After reading this excerpt, were you curious about the phoenix? worried about Theseus? You can respond to any story element that intrigues you. You can also respond in different forms. One reader responded by drawing this picture of the phoenix. April Andry thought the story should end differently. Originally, Theseus safely rid himself of the phoenix. April responded by reworking the plot to provide a new ending.

Narrative Writing

Student Model

After several weeks, Theseus's curiosity about the phoenix became too much. Ignoring the doctor's warning, he decided to let the bird out of its cage.

He immediately regretted his decision. The bird quickly flew around the room, destroying the other cages and freeing the birds. Soon, there was a frenzy of birds all around Theseus. He couldn't see anything, but he could feel birds pecking him all over. Miraculously, he managed to escape.

Theseus's wounds healed eventually, but he still had the ugly scars to remind him of the phoenix. From then on, his sleep was haunted by visions of the golden phoenix and its glowing eyes.

April Andry, Emerson Junior High School
Oak Park, Illinois

> What other endings can you think of for the story?

Presenting Tip

When reading aloud from a narrative with more than one character, try using a different voice for each character.

Journal Writing

Which element of the literature excerpt on page 180 do you find the most intriguing? Explain why in your journal.

Use a Different Approach

Writing a story of your own is just one way to respond to a story. Use your imagination to explore other possibilities. Suppose that you have a chance to interview a character from the story. You may begin by writing down the questions you'd ask, and you might go so far as to imagine the character's answers.

Perhaps you are intrigued by a certain topic that the story suggests. One writer was fascinated by the phoenix in "A Leg Full of Rubies" and wanted to find out more about it. The journal entry below shows the writer's response.

> The story inspired this writer to do some additional reading to find out more about the phoenix.

I just finished reading a story about a phoenix. This was the first time I've heard about a phoenix. My teacher said it's a mythical bird and that it's in other stories, too. I checked out a book from the library that tells about different myths. It says that the phoenix lives for five hundred years! At the end of that time it builds a nest and goes up in flames. Out of the ashes comes a new phoenix.

In the story I read the phoenix is evil. But I don't think it would always be an evil bird. I'd like to write a story about a phoenix, but the bird wouldn't be evil. Because it lives for so long, it would probably be very wise. The phoenix could be an adviser to different rulers for hundreds of years.

Write a Response

Select a short story you would like to respond to. You can choose a new story or a story you have already read. Think of ideas for responding to it. Review the suggestions in this lesson or think of your own ideas. Then write a one-page response.

PURPOSE To respond to a story
AUDIENCE Yourself
LENGTH 2 paragraphs

WRITING RUBRICS To write an effective response to a story, you should

- be clear about your emotional reactions
- be creative in selecting a way to respond

Cross-Curricular Activity

MYTHOLOGY Use your school or public library to find out about the phoenix myth in Asian or Native American culture or in another culture. Make copies of the various images you find and display them in a class exhibit. Write a brief response to the images, discussing the similarities and differences you see in the images across cultures. Compare and contrast the images with the idea you had of the phoenix after you read the excerpt from "A Leg Full of Rubies."

GrammarLink

Use apostrophes correctly.

doctor's (possessive noun) *office*
don't (contraction of *do* + *not*)
its (possessive pronoun) *cage*
it's (contraction of *it* + *is*)

Add apostrophes where needed.

1. Its raining today.
2. Can I try on your sisters hat?
3. Is this book yours or ours?
4. The cat wants its food.
5. Give them the key—its theirs.

See Lesson 11.4, page 435, and Lesson 20.7, page 601.

 Using Computers

Extend your research on the phoenix by using the Internet to find additional information and images. In a small group, discuss the relative advantages and disadvantages of using electronic and print resources for research.

Writing Process in Action

Narrative Writing

In the preceding lessons, you learned about the elements that make up a short story—plot, character, and setting—and about the kinds of details, action, and dialogue that can make characters vivid and memorable. You have written stories of your own. Now, in this lesson, you're invited to write about someone you have known well. Tell the story of an event or a series of events that shows why this person is special to you.

Assignment

Context	You have been asked to share a story about a special person you have known well. Write about one event that makes this person special to you.
Purpose	To show in a story how you feel about a special person
Audience	Students
Length	1 page

Planning to Write

The following pages can help you plan and write your story. Read through them and then refer to them as needed. But don't be tied down by them. You're in charge of your own writing process. Begin by giving yourself a time frame to complete this assignment. Keep the controlling idea in mind: to show how you feel about a special person.

Writing Online

For prewriting, drafting, revising, editing and publishing tools, go to **glencoe.com** and enter QuickPass code WC77680p1.

Prewriting

Whom will you write about? You could choose a close friend, a relative, a teacher, or a camp counselor. Look through photo albums, letters, journals, or collections of objects to help you decide whom you want to write about. Brainstorming may help you explore what you want to say about the person. Find specific details about the person and your experiences with her or him to use in your story.

Drafting

After noting details about your subject, you need to look through your prewriting to get an idea of how to start your story. A strong opening paragraph will make the person you're writing about sound interesting from the very beginning. Choose a few details that set your character apart. Notice the details in the following paragraph that would let you recognize Delfina right away if you happened to meet her.

Option A

Look at important objects or mementos.

Option B

Browse through a photo album.

Option C

Review your journal.

My swimming trophies bear my name, but they should bear this name, too: Glenn Williams. I was afraid of the water until the summer he taught me to swim. His soft voice and steady gaze calmed me.

Literature Model

When she arrived at our house she was covered by a huge black umbrella. A white gardenia hung from her left ear. My sister Cynthia and I were bewitched by the sight of her. We were a little afraid, too. She seemed like an enormous fish or a shipwrecked lady far from home.

Marjorie Agosín, "A Huge Black Umbrella"

Drafting Tip

For information about creating mood, see Lesson 4.4, pages 168–171.

As you draft your story, keep your focus on the person you're writing about. If you get stuck, look again at your prewriting notes for fresh ideas. The most important thing to remember at the drafting stage is to get your ideas on paper. You can make changes later.

Revising

To begin revising, read over your draft to make sure that what you have written fits your purpose and your audience. Then have a **writing conference.** Read your draft to a partner or a small group, or receive feedback from your teacher. Use your audience's reactions to help you evaluate your work so far. The questions below can help you and your listeners.

Option A

Does every sentence contribute to the story?

Option B

Do the details let readers picture my subject?

Option C

Does the action of my story move along clearly?

I didn't even want to go to camp that summer. I hated the counselor who registered me, but as soon as I found out that Mr. the tall man with big ears who greeted us Williams was going to be my swimming teacher, I knew the summer would be all right. He yet sure talked in a soft voice that forced you to lean toward him. He wore a whistle like every other swimming teacher I'd ever had, but I never heard him use it.

Editing/Proofreading

Many writers will let their work sit for a day before they begin to edit. During the editing stage, you can **proofread** for any errors that might muddy the ideas and feelings you want to express. For instance, if your story contains dialogue, you'll want to make sure that your readers can follow who is speaking.

This Editing Checklist will help you catch errors you might otherwise overlook. You'll want your story to reflect your hard work. If some part of it still doesn't sound right, fix it.

Editing/Proofreading Checklist

✓ 1. Have I used quotation marks before and after direct quotations?
✓ 2. Are all my sentences complete?
✓ 3. Have I used possessive nouns and pronouns correctly?
✓ 4. Have I checked to be sure that all words are spelled correctly?
✓ 5. Have I used conjunctions and prepositions correctly?

Publishing/Presenting

It might help you to ask someone else who knows your subject to read your story. Your reader may have some last-minute suggestions to contribute. Copy your final draft neatly, using print or cursive handwriting. Consider putting your story in a folder or a clear plastic sleeve to make it more attractive. If you have a photograph of the person you've written about, include it with your story.

Proofreading Tip

Check for proper capitalization in sentences, quotations, and proper nouns and adjectives. For more information, see pages 573–574.

Journal Writing: Write to Learn

Reflect on your writing process experience. Answer these questions in your journal: What do you like best about your narrative? What was the hardest part of writing it? What did you learn in your writing conference? What new things have you learned as a writer?

Literature Model

Narrative Writing

A Huge
Black Umbrella

by Marjorie Agosín

In "A Huge Black Umbrella," Marjorie Agosín tells the story of Delfina,[1] a special woman who lived an extraordinary life. As you read, pay special attention to Agosín's effective use of detail to create the character of Delfina. Then try the activities in Linking Writing and Literature on page 192.

• • • • • • • • • • • • • • • • •

---

[1] **Delphina** (Del fēn′ə)

When she arrived at our house she was covered by a huge black umbrella. A white gardenia hung from her left ear. My sister Cynthia and I were bewitched by the sight of her. We were a little afraid, too. She seemed like an enormous fish or a shipwrecked lady far from home. Certainly, her umbrella was useless in the rain since it was ripped in many places, which let the rainwater fall on her—water from one of the few downpours of that surprisingly dry summer. It was the summer in which my sister and I understood why magical things happen, such as the arrival of Delfina Nahuenhual.[2]

My mother welcomed her, and Delfina, with a certain boldness, explained that she always traveled accompanied by that enormous umbrella, which protected her from the sun, elves, and little girls like us. My mother's delicate lips smiled. From that moment my mother and Delfina developed a much friendlier relationship than is usual between "the lady of the house" and "her servant."

Delfina Nahuenhual—we had to call her by her full name—was one of the few survivors of the Chilán earthquake in the south of Chile. She had lost her children, house, her wedding gown, chickens, and two of her favorite lemon trees. All she could rescue was that huge black umbrella covered with dust and forgotten things.

In the evenings she usually lit a small stove for cooking; the fire gave off a very lovely, sweet light. Then she wrapped herself up in an enormous shawl of blue wool that wasn't scratchy and she put a few slices of potato on her temples to protect herself from sickness and cold drafts.

As we sat by the stove, Delfina Nahuenhual told stories about tormented souls and frogs that became princes. Her generous lap rocked us back and forth, and her voice made us sleepy. We were peaceful children who felt the healing power of her love. After she thought we were asleep, Delfina Nahuenhual would write long letters that she would later number and wrap up in newspaper. She kept the letters in an old pot that was filled with garlic, cumin,[3] and slivers of lemon rind.

My sister and I always wanted to read the letters and learn the name and address of the person who would receive them. So whenever Delfina

---

[2]**Nahuenhual** (Nə' wen əl)
[3]**cumin** (kum' in) the fruits from a small plant in the parsley family, used for flavoring, pickles, soups, etc.

Nahuenhual was busy in the kitchen, we tried peeking into the pot to discover what she was hiding.

But we never managed to read the letters. Delfina Nahuenhual would smile at us and shoo us along with the end of her broom.

For many years, Delfina continued to tell us stories next to the stove. Not long after my brother Mario, the spoiled one of the family, was born, Delfina Nahuenhual told us she was tired and that she wanted to return to the south of Chile. She said she now had some savings and a chicken, which was enough to live on. I thought that she wanted to die and go to heaven because she had decided to return to the mosses and clays of her land.

I remember that I cried a lot when we said good-bye. My brother Mario clung to her full skirt, not wanting to be separated from the wise woman who, for us, was never a servant. When she bent over to give me a kiss, she said that I must give her letters to the person to whom she had addressed them but that I could keep the pot.

For many years, I kept her little pot like a precious secret, a kind of magical lamp in which my childhood was captured. When I wanted to remember her, I rubbed the pot, I smelled it,

and all my fears, including my fear of darkness, vanished. After she had left I began to understand that my childhood had gone with her. Now more than ever I miss the dish of lentils[4] that she prepared for good luck and prosperity on New Year's Eve. I miss the smell of her skin and her magical stories.

Many years later, my sister Cynthia had her first daughter. Mario went traveling abroad and I decided to spend my honeymoon on Easter Island, that remote island in the middle of the Pacific Ocean, six hours by plane from Chile. It is a place full of mysterious, gigantic statues called Moais.[5] Ever since I was a child, I had been fascinated by those eerie statues, their enormous figures seeming to spring from the earth, just as Delfina Nahuenhual and her huge black umbrella did when she first came to my house. I carried her letters, which I had long ago taken from the small earthen pot and placed in a large moss-green chest along with the few cloves of garlic that still remained. As a grown-up I never had the urge to

---

[4]**lentils** (lent′ lz) plants in the family to which peas and beans belong
[5]**Moais** (Mō′ īz)

read the letters. I only knew that they should be delivered to someone.

One morning when the sun shone even in the darkest corner of my hotel room, I went to the address written on Delfina's letters. It was a leper[6] colony, one of the few that still exist. A very somber employee opened the door and quickly took the packet of five hundred letters from me. I asked if the addressee was still alive and he said of course, but that I couldn't meet the person. When I gave him the letters, it seemed as though I had lost one of my most valuable possessions, perhaps even the last memories of my dear Delfina Nahuenhual's life.

So I never did meet the person to whom Delfina Nahuenhual wrote her letters nor learned why she spent her sleepless nights writing them. I only learned that he was a leper on Easter Island, that he was still alive and, perhaps, still reads the letters, the dreams of love Delfina Nahuenhual had each night. When I returned home, I knew at last that Delfina Nahuenhual was content, because when I looked up, as she had taught me to do, I saw a

Pierre-Auguste Renoir, *The Umbrellas*, 1881–1886

huge black umbrella hovering in the cloudy sky.

_____

[6]**leper** (lepʹ ər) a person having a severe skin disease that attacks and deforms skin, flesh, and nerves

Linking Writing and Literature

 Learning to Learn

Think back on the striking character of Delfina Nahuenhual. Brainstorm for a list of words, images, and phrases that describe her appearance, personality, and character.

 Talk About Reading

Talk with other students about "A Huge Black Umbrella." Assign a group leader to keep everyone focused and a group secretary to take notes. Then use the questions below to guide your conversation.

1. **Connect to Your Life** The images of the huge black umbrella and the small earthen pot always remind the narrator of Delfina. Is there some object that reminds you of another person?

2. **Critical Thinking: Interpret** How do the narrator and her family feel about Delfina? Why do you think they feel that way?

3. **6+1 Trait®: Sentence Fluency** How does Agosín achieve a smooth rhythm and flow to her writing? Cite one example in the story that you find especially fluent.

4. **Connect to Your Writing** What do you especially like about Agosín's style of writing? Select a paragraph in which this style trait is particularly evident.

 Write About Reading

Portrait Write a portrait of a person, either real or imaginary. Describe things that make that person unique, such as the person's appearance, habits, and favorite treasures.

Focus on Sentence Fluency Your portrait will have more rhythm and flow if you vary the structure and length of your sentences. Edit your portrait for fluency. Would it help to shorten or lengthen sentences? To begin some sentences with a dependent clause?

For more information on sentence fluency and the 6+1 Trait® model, see **Writing and Research Handbook,** pages 822–824.

6+1 Trait® is a registered trademark of Northwest Regional Educational Laboratory, which does not endorse this product.

Reflecting on the Unit: Summarize What You Learned

Focus on the following questions to help summarize what you learned in this unit.

1 What are the three basic elements of a story?

2 What is the purpose of a story plot?

3 Why is it important to arrange story events in time order?

4 What does dialogue contribute to a story?

5 What should be included in a strong story beginning?

 ## Adding to Your Portfolio

CHOOSE A SELECTION FOR YOUR PORTFOLIO Look over the narrative writing you did for this unit. Choose a piece of writing for your portfolio that shows one or more of the following:

- believable characters, an intriguing setting, and a clear plot
- a series of events in time order
- lively, realistic dialogue that reveals what characters are like
- a beginning that makes the reader want to read the whole story

REFLECT ON YOUR CHOICE Attach a note to the piece you chose, explaining briefly why you chose it and what you learned from writing it.

SET GOALS How can you improve your writing? What skill will you focus on the next time you write?

Writing Across the Curriculum

MAKE A GEOGRAPHY CONNECTION Picture your character in a setting in another part of the world. How would the sights, sounds, tastes, and smells differ in another place? Choose a country on another continent to research. Describe how your character would reach this destination and how the character would respond to the local situations.

MAKE A SCIENCE CONNECTION Science has shaped the world we live in today. Scientific discoveries have helped us live longer and healthier lives, explained the universe, and provided the technology that makes our lives easier and more productive. Imagine that you are a scientist. You have just made a discovery that does one of the things listed above. Write a personal narrative telling about your discovery, how you made it, and what you will do with the knowledge you have gained.

"It was a furious and compact storm, with an eye only eight miles wide and winds that reached out for 60 miles."

—Patricia Lauber
"Hurricanes: Big Winds
and Big Damage"

194

Expository Writing

Writing in the Real World

MEDIA
Signs and Labels
Connection

Visitors to the Monterey Bay Aquarium in California discover a fascinating world of underwater creatures. Most of the visitors, however, would understand little of what they were seeing without certain important information. That's where Judy Rand's job comes in. Rand writes information labels for the aquarium's exhibits. Her expository writing educates visitors eager to learn the mysteries of marine life.

Wolf-eel

Anarrhichthys ocellatus

This night prowler leaves its den for dinner.

Hardly a wolf, not really an eel, this fierce-looking fish spends the day quietly in a cave, wriggling out at night to feed.

Though some divers say the wolf-eel can bite a broomstick in half, this predator deserves a better reputation. Wolf-eels chomp on crabs, mussels, and urchins; they don't eat divers or their brooms.

by Judy Rand

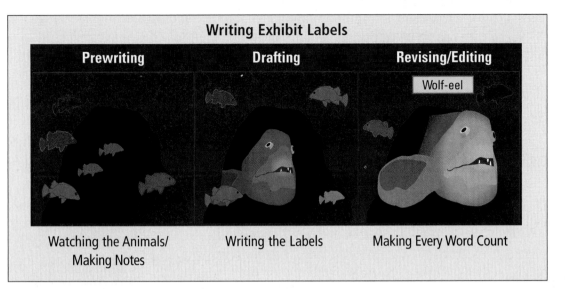

Writing Exhibit Labels

Prewriting	Drafting	Revising/Editing
		Wolf-eel
Watching the Animals/ Making Notes	Writing the Labels	Making Every Word Count

A Writer's Process

Prewriting
Observing, Learning, and Making Notes

Helping people see what's right in front of them is where Judy Rand's work begins. As master developer and senior editor at the Monterey Bay Aquarium, Rand writes the information labels that visitors read as they view an exhibit.

Before she can write the labels, Rand herself must become thoroughly acquainted with the marine creatures. She spends time watching each animal, and then she writes notes in a binder about that animal's appearance and behavior.

Rand gathers information from other sources as well. She interviews the scientists and curators who care for the aquarium's animals. She also talks to scientists from outside the aquarium, especially those who have worked directly with a particular animal. In addition, she reads field guides and scientific articles.

As she collects information, Rand fills in fact sheets about each animal's traits and habits. Afterwards, she writes each idea and fact on a separate index card. To organize the information, Rand scatters the cards on the floor. She explains, "I can shuffle my ideas around. I can set aside the ones that don't seem to fit and begin to find the ones that seem important."

During this process, Rand has to choose what information she will include on a card. She keeps the interests of her audience—the aquarium's visitors—firmly in mind. Rand explains, "The most important information on labels has to be about immediate and observable behavior. Visitors want to know about what they're seeing in the tank. 'Is this wolf-eel really an eel? What are those teeth for?'"

> ❝ *When aquarium visitors are face to face with a wolf-eel, they want to know, 'Does this animal want to eat me?' You need to begin with your reader's immediate experience. Then you can interpret the scientific facts in a friendly and relevant way.* ❞
>
> —Judy Rand

Drafting
Writing the Labels

With index cards spread around the room and with reference books lying open nearby, Rand plunges in to write.

The final label will be one to two paragraphs long. But, Rand says, "I can write ten or eleven different paragraphs for a single label. I can try out an idea that has the wolf-eel's teeth right up front. Then I can try out an idea that has popular misconceptions about the animal up front."

She finally decides to focus on the wolf-eel's undeserved bad reputation. She explains, "Visitors' immediate impression of the wolf-eel is that it's fierce looking and a predator. I wanted them to understand the idea that being a predator isn't bad."

Rand uses simple language, even for complex ideas. She describes the wolf-eel as a night prowler, rather than as a nocturnal fish. As Rand notes, "We want our labels to sound as if someone is talking to you. *Nocturnal* is a lovely word, but people don't usually use words like *nocturnal* in conversation."

She also uses strong examples. After reading that "some divers say the wolf-eel can bite a broomstick in half," visitors can imagine how strong those jaws must be.

Revising/Editing
Making Every Word Count

After setting her draft aside for a day, Rand puts on her editor's hat. She reads each label aloud, listening for a friendly and conversational sound. Then she asks several people to read each label and repeat the information in their own words. "If they can't tell me what it's about, then I know I have problems."

Finally Rand sits down at her computer to check for style. She asks herself, "Is there any unfamiliar language? Have I made every word count?"

When she feels satisfied with the labels she has written, Rand gets approval from two department supervisors, as well as the aquarium's executive director. The exhibit labels are then readied for display in the aquarium.

The Deep Reefs

Where is this habitat?
How are inhabitants (wolf-eel, lingcod, rockfishes, etc.) adapted to live in this habitat?

Deep Reefs

Lingcod

wolf-eel
. has a bad reputation it doesn't deserve-usually . attack unless / provoked

Analyzing the Media Connection

Discuss these questions about the model on page 196.

1. What effect do you think the opening sentence has on visitors to the aquarium? How does Rand achieve this effect?

2. How does Rand get across the point that the wolf-eel is a nocturnal creature, without actually using the word *nocturnal?*

3. What information does Rand convey about the wolf-eel's eating habits?

4. What if Rand had used the verb *consume* in place of the word *chomp?* How would that word choice change the tone of the writing? In your opinion, which word is more effective?

5. Where does Rand use humor to call attention to the wolf-eel's bad reputation?

Analyzing a Writer's Process

Discuss these questions about Judy Rand's writing process.

1. What methods does Rand use to gather information for her exhibit labels?

2. How does Rand organize the facts and ideas she has gathered? How does your own method compare to hers?

3. Rand can't use all the information that she gathers. What helps her decide what information she will include?

4. Does Rand use formal or informal language as she drafts her information labels? Why?

5. When editing, how does Rand make sure that the labels will be clear to her audience?

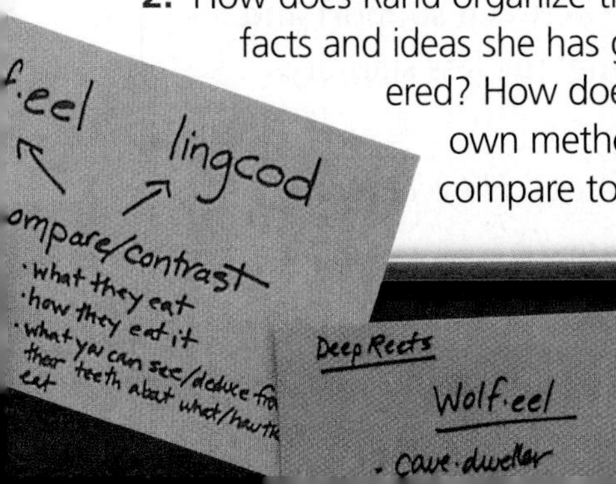

Grammar*Link*

Use commas to separate three or more items in a series.

Wolf-eels chomp on crabs, mussels, and urchins.

Use each set of words below as a series of items in a sentence. Use commas correctly.

1. bold, fierce, clever
2. furry, stout, clumsy
3. squirrels, mice, rats
4. lobsters, clams, shrimp
5. cats, dogs, goldfish

See Lesson 20.2, pages 591–592.

[handwritten notes]

f-eel

lingcod

ompare/contrast

· what they eat
· how they eat it
· what you can see/deduce fr
their teeth about what/how th
eat

Deep Reefs

Wolf-eel

· cave-dweller

Expository Writing

Giving Information and Explanations

The writing you do to explain and give information is expository writing. Most of the writing you do for school assignments is expository.

Heel counter

Sole

Midsole

If you wanted to explain to someone why running shoes are so comfortable, what information would you include? How would you order it? Read the paragraphs below to see how one writer solved this problem.

Literature Model

How does the writer use detail in the first paragraph?

The running shoe's few basic functions are extremely important to the runner. It provides cushioning to help absorb the impact of your foot striking an unyielding road surface.

The second paragraph names two parts of a shoe and tells how each part helps the runner.

Next, a shoe provides support, or stability. A stiff plastic **heel counter** cups the heel and keeps it from shifting laterally while you run. The **midsole** is shaped so that it helps keep your foot lined up in the shoe. Midsole design is a compromise between support and cushioning—the more cushioning, the less stability, and vice versa.

David Macaulay, "Running Shoe," *How Things Work*

Write to Explain and Inform

Expository writing gives readers information and explanations. One kind of expository writing tells readers how to do something: how to build a doghouse or make a salad. Another kind explains how something works. The model on page 200 explains how the parts of running shoes work together to help the runner.

Other kinds of expository writing explain what something is, how things are alike or different, or why something has happened. In the model below, Ben Rallo informs his readers about why something—water pollution—has happened.

Student Model

One cause of water pollution is careless campers and hikers throwing their garbage into virtually unpolluted water. They think that since there isn't anything dumped into it already, a bottle or two won't hurt. But before they know it, that same body of water, once so clean and beautiful, is sickeningly polluted by others like themselves who thought the same way.

Because of the campers' and hikers' carelessness, the natural beauty of the water is destroyed, and it no longer is a pretty sight for people to enjoy.

Ben Rallo, Springman Junior High School,
Glenview, Illinois

Notice that Ben uses the words "cause" and "because" to explain why something happened.

Journal Writing

Try explaining something to yourself, such as **why you made** a certain choice. In your journal list your **reasons,** and tell something about each one.

Grammar Tip

You often can combine two sentences that have the same subject by stating the subject once and using *and* between the verbs. For more information, see Lesson 8.6, page 367 and Lesson 18.7, p. 569.

Make Things Clear

The details you include in expository writing should help your readers understand your topic. The following chart lists other qualities that help produce strong expository writing.

Qualities of Good Expository Writing	
Clear	Easy to read
Concise	Exact, specific, and to the point
Inviting	Connects with the audience in direct, creative ways
Informative	Includes insights and ideas

In the selection below, the writer presents information about two rock formations. The last two paragraphs explain how the formations are alike and how they are different.

Notice how the writer uses elaboration to support the main ideas.

Which word supplies the clue that stalactites and stalagmites are alike in one way?

Literature Model

Stalactites are formed in caves by groundwater containing dissolved lime. The water drips from the roof and leaves a thin deposit as it evaporates. Growing down from the roof, stalactites increase by a fraction of an inch each year and may eventually be many yards long. Where the water supply is seasonal, stalactites may show annual growth rings like those of tree trunks.

Stalagmites are formed on the floor of caves where water has dripped from the roof or a stalactite above. Like stalactites, they develop as water containing dissolved lime evaporates.

Stalactites and stalagmites can grow together and meet to form pillars. These have been described as "organ pipes," "hanging curtains," and "portcullises."

R. F. Symes, *Rocks and Minerals*

Write Procedures

Think of a time you worked with others to make or do something, such as prepare a meal or plan an event. Explain the steps of the project you worked on.

PURPOSE To experiment with ways to present details clearly

AUDIENCE Your classmates

LENGTH 2 paragraphs

WRITING RUBRICS To explain a procedure effectively, you should

- include enough details to help readers follow your explanation
- make your steps clear, concise, and logical
- make your explanation lively and interesting
- print or write legibly

Listening and Speaking

GIVING INSTRUCTIONS Turn your explanation of a procedure into an oral presentation that you will deliver to a group of younger students. Use appropriate vocabulary, volume, and gestures to make your explanation clear. If possible, use visual aids or other tools to make your presentation more interesting. Present your explanation to a small group of classmates and ask for feedback on how to make it more effective for a younger audience.

Grammar Link

Make subjects and verbs agree.

When a subject and verb are separated by a prepositional phrase, always look back to the subject, and make the verb agree with it:

> One **cause** of water pollution **is** careless campers . . . .

Rewrite the following sentences, making sure that subjects and verbs agree. If they need no change, write *correct.*

1. The boy with the books look lost.
2. The cause of the false alarms were never discovered.
3. The search of the grounds was done quickly.
4. Damage from the recent rains total several million.
5. Only one of the triplets are going.

See Lesson 16.1, page 535, and Lesson 16.2, page 537.

Cross-Curricular Activity

SCIENCE Write a paragraph in which you explain to a third grader something you have recently learned in science class. Explain your topic clearly. Share your paragraph with a younger student or with someone to whom this information is new. Then consider what you learned from your "teaching experience."

LOG ON **Writing** Online | For more writing and grammar practice, go to **glencoe.com** and enter QuickPass code WC77680p1.

203

Organizing Informative Writing

*I*n expository writing the order in which you present information is extremely important. The directions below, to the Space Center, show why.

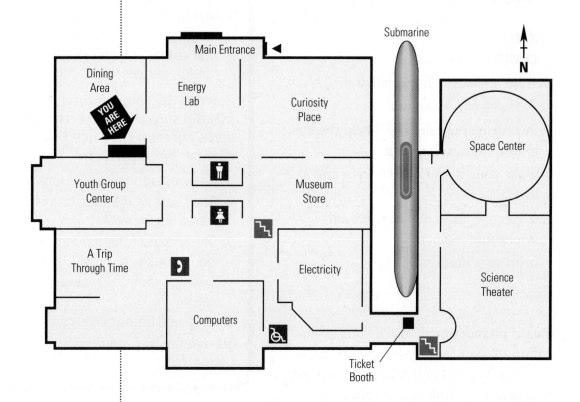

- At the pay phones, turn left.
- Leave by the door on the opposite side.
- Pass the ticket booth, and turn left immediately.
- Go into the Energy Lab, and turn right immediately.
- Pass the Science Theater. Turn right into the Space Center.
- Enter the Electricity exhibit.

The information is out of order, making the directions impossible to follow. On a sheet of paper, reorder these steps so that a visitor can go from the Dining Area to the Space Center.

Get Organized

How you organize information in expository writing depends on what you want to say. You may arrange steps in the order in which they would be performed. You may list facts in order of importance. You may tell about places and things according to their position. You may even list items according to how much you like or dislike them.

Examine the diagram below. How many different ways could you organize the information if you were going to write about the planets?

Drafting Tip

See **Writing and Research Handbook,** pages 820–821, for more information about how to organize information in paragraphs and in longer pieces of expository writing.

Expository Writing

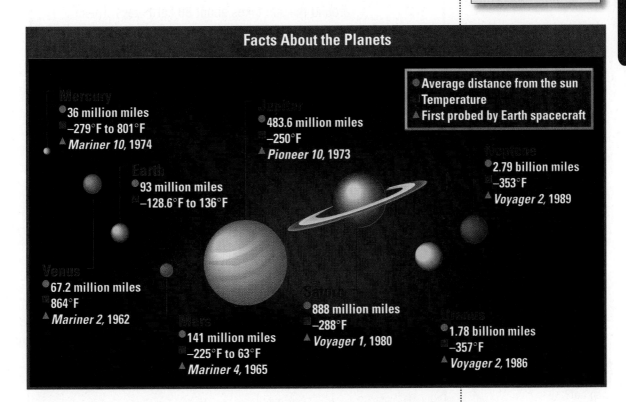

Facts About the Planets

Mercury
- 36 million miles
- −279°F to 801°F
- *Mariner 10,* 1974

Earth
- 93 million miles
- −128.6°F to 136°F

Venus
- 67.2 million miles
- 864°F
- *Mariner 2,* 1962

Mars
- 141 million miles
- −225°F to 63°F
- *Mariner 4,* 1965

Jupiter
- 483.6 million miles
- −250°F
- *Pioneer 10,* 1973

Saturn
- 888 million miles
- −288°F
- *Voyager 1,* 1980

Uranus
- 1.78 billion miles
- −357°F
- *Voyager 2,* 1986

Neptune
- 2.79 billion miles
- −353°F
- *Voyager 2,* 1989

- Average distance from the sun
- Temperature
- First probed by Earth spacecraft

Journal Writing

In your journal list five or six significant events that happened in the past year. Number the events in order of their importance to you.

Remember Details

Details are crucial in expository writing. Details can include facts, examples, reasons, and statistics (various kinds of numerical information). The chart below highlights different kinds of details.

Kinds of Details	
Facts	Mercury is nearer the sun than any other planet in our solar system.
Statistics	Mercury rotates once in about 59 Earth days. Its orbit around the sun takes about 88 Earth days. These numbers mean that a day on Mercury lasts about two-thirds of its year.
Examples	The temperature on Mercury could melt lead.
Reasons	Because it is so close to the sun, the daylight side of Mercury is extremely hot.

The writer of the following passage uses details to explain temperatures on Mercury. As you read, look for facts, statistics, examples, and reasons.

In what way do the details help you understand why Mercury is so hot?

Literature Model

Mercury is dry, hot, and almost airless. The sun's rays are about seven times as strong on Mercury as they are on the earth. The sun also appears about 2½ times as large in Mercury's sky as in the earth's. Mercury does not have enough gases in its atmosphere to reduce the amount of heat and light it receives from the sun.

"Mercury," *The World Book Encyclopedia*

Write Directions

Think of a time when you had to tell someone how to get from one place to an unfamiliar one. Describe the situation by writing detailed directions including landmarks, streets, and distances. Draw a map to accompany your directions. Be sure to use ordinal and cardinal directions when writing.

PURPOSE To present details clearly
AUDIENCE Your classmates
LENGTH 1–2 paragraphs

WRITING RUBRICS To give effective directions you should

- include enough details to help readers follow your directions
- make your directions clear, concise and logical
- print and draw legibly

Viewing and Representing

GIVING DIRECTIONS Make an oral presentation using your directions. Use appropriate vocabulary, volume and gestures to get your ideas across.

Using Computers

Tables and charts can help you organize information and make it clear for your reader. Try using a chart or table in your word processing program to help you organize the data in your final copy.

GrammarLink

Correct run-on sentences.

Run-on sentences are two or more sentences run together with no end punctuation or coordinating conjunction to separate them. Imagine if the sentences on page 206 were run together:

Mercury rotates once in about 59 Earth days its orbit around the sun takes about 88 Earth days.

To correct a run-on sentence you can make separate sentences, using a period or other end mark. If you prefer, combine the sentences, using a semicolon or using a comma followed by a coordinating conjunction.

Revise the following sentences to correct run-ons.

1.–3. The moon has no atmosphere it's unbearably hot when the sun shines on the lunar surface the daytime temperature there is high enough to boil water.

4.–5. Neil Armstrong and Buzz Aldrin were the first astronauts to walk on the moon and they went there in 1969 on the *Apollo* space mission.

See Lesson 7.2, Troubleshooter.

LOG ON ▶ **Writing** Online | For more writing and grammar practice, go to glencoe.com and enter QuickPass code WC77680p1.

207

Expository Writing

Writing About Similarities and Differences

As you read the model below, notice how the writer delves beneath the surface to show the differences between two things that are alike in many ways.

Model

Aquarium fish are cold-blooded, so they cannot adjust to abrupt changes in water temperature. As a result, you must keep the water temperature steady in any aquarium. The water's composition may be different, though, depending on the kind of fish you have. Marine (saltwater) fish need exactly the right amount of salt and other compounds dissolved in their water. Freshwater fish, on the other hand, cannot tolerate much salt. In general, marine fish are more delicate and more expensive. Many people think they are worth the extra trouble, however, because of their glorious colors and exotic shapes.

Notice the writer's use of "on the other hand." Does this phrase signal a similarity or difference?

After reading this comparison and contrast, which type of fish do you think would be more interesting?

Look Closely

On the surface two things may seem alike. If you examine them closely, however, you find differences. For example, two aquariums might both be made of glass and be filled with water, but the water in one might be fresh and the water in the other might be salt.

When you look at ways in which two things are alike, you are comparing them. When you examine their differences, you are contrasting them. Making a clear comparison-contrast list or diagram, such as the one below, can help you identify likenesses and differences.

Two Kinds of Aquariums

Freshwater	Freshwater and Saltwater	Saltwater

• less expensive	• can be made of glass or plastic	• more expensive
• variety of plants available	• need lids to keep dust out and fish in	• can use coral
• more fish can live in given space	• need light, thermostat, heater, filter, and aerator	• fewer fish can live in given space
• need fresh water	• need to be cleaned regularly	• need hydrometer to measure saltiness
	• need under-gravel filter	

Journal Writing

Think about talking with a friend or relative face to face and talking with that same person on the telephone. In your journal list how the experiences are alike and how they are different. Write a few sentences telling which method of communication you prefer and why.

Draw Comparisons

When you know how two things are alike and different, you can begin to organize your ideas for a written explanation. The chart below shows one way to organize details. It compares and contrasts two insects feature by feature. The passage following the chart also uses a feature-by-feature comparison.

Grammar Tip

A comparison-contrast explanation may include the adjectives *more*, *most*, *less*, and *least* to show degrees of similarity or difference. For more information, see Lesson 12.3, page 455.

Comparing Two Insects		
Feature	**Centipede**	**Millipede**
Legs	1 pair per segment	2 pairs per segment
Food	snails, slugs, worms	plants
Danger	poisonous	harmless
Movement	quick	moderate

Literature Model

Compare the centipede and millipede below. The centipede has one pair of jointed legs per segment, whereas the millipede has two pairs of legs per segment. Centipedes hunt for their food and have a pair of poison claws used to inject venom into their prey. Centipedes feed on snails, slugs, and worms. Their bites are very painful to humans. Millipedes don't move as quickly as centipedes and feed on plants.

Lucy Daniel, Edward Paul Ortleb, Alton Biggs, *Merrill Life Science*

Notice the writers' use of the word "whereas." Does the word signal a likeness or a difference?

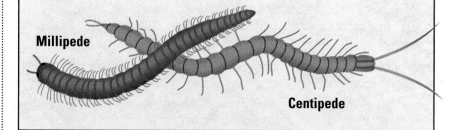

Millipede

Centipede

Write a Comparison-Contrast Letter

Think about how you spent the most recent summer vacation and how you spent any previous summer. What was similar about the two summers, and what was different about them? Make a Venn diagram comparing and contrasting the two summers, listing the things you did during both vacations in the intersecting portion of the two circles. Then, write a letter to a pen pal that compares and contrasts your two summers. Tell which vacation you preferred, and why. Include your diagram in your letter.

PURPOSE To compare and contrast two summer vacations
AUDIENCE A pen pal
LENGTH 2–4 paragraphs

WRITING RUBRICS To write a good comparison-contrast letter, you should

- include both similarities and differences in your Venn diagram
- use phrases that make clear comparisons and contrasts
- use comparative and superlative forms correctly
- write legibly in cursive or print

Cross-Curricular Activity

ART Find copies of two paintings or photographs that depict a similar subject—for example, a city sidewalk scene or a rural landscape. Make notes to identify similarities and differences between the two pictures. Then write a brief description comparing and contrasting the ways in which the two images depict their subjects.

Listening and Speaking

COMPARING AND CONTRASTING CUSTOMS
Work in a small group that includes at least one student who is familar with the customs of another country. Pick an event or ceremony—a wedding, a funeral, or some other formal occasion—and discuss the similarities and differences between customs in the United States and in another country. Present your findings to the class in an oral report.

Grammar*Link*

Use comparative and superlative forms correctly.

Most adjectives of one syllable add -*er* for the comparative and -*est* for the superlative. Longer adjectives are usually preceded by *more* or *most*.

*Centipedes tend to be fast**er** and **more** dangerous than millipedes*

Correct the following phrases.

1. the least shortest runner
2. the more taller building
3. the most chubbiest puppy
4. the less smaller sandwich
5. the most lowest grade

See Lesson 12.3, page 455, and Lesson 12.4, page 457.

LOG ON ▶ **Writing** Online | For more writing and grammar practice, go to **glencoe.com** and enter QuickPass code WC77680p1.

211

LESSON 5.4

Explaining How Something Works

*W*riters must explain steps in the proper order
when they want to show how something works.

You've probably never seen an apparatus as complicated as
this one. For all its moving pieces and dizzying action, the end
result is pretty simple. Can you figure out what it is? Follow the
steps in order from A to Q.

Write Step by Step

By putting items in the proper order, you can make a
complicated process clear. Consider a real process, such as
the operation of canal locks. Notice the way the following
passage explains how the locks work.

Model

First, a lock is filled with water by opening the filling valve. From the higher water level, the boat enters the first set of gates. The upper gates open easily because the water pressure is the same on both sides. After the upper gates are closed, water is pumped out of the lock through the drain valve. The water level begins to lower. Because of the angle of the gates, the higher water pressure at each level keeps them shut. When the water level in the lock is the same as it is on the lower part of the river, the lower gates open, and the boat continues its journey.

Which words does the writer use to signal the order in which the locks work?

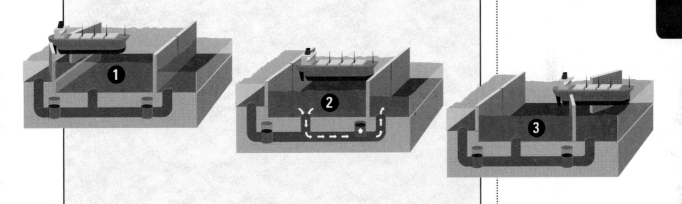

Ships can't travel through locks if the gates open out of order. In the same way, your writing about a process won't work for your readers if you put the steps in the wrong order.

Journal Writing

In your journal write down one of your dreams—for a career, a trip, or something else. Then list, in time order, the steps you would take to make that dream come true.

Guide Your Reader

Once you've placed the steps of a process in the correct order, use transition words and phrases that will help readers follow your explanation. Transitions show how the steps in a process are related to one another. Common transition words include *first, next, after, later, while, second, initially,* and *finally.*

Another way to make your writing clear is to organize it into paragraphs. Each paragraph should have one main idea and a clear topic sentence that states that idea. What is the main idea of the paragraph below? Notice how the writer rearranged a phrase and a sentence and added transition words to make the idea clearer.

What are the transition words in this paragraph? How do they help the reader?

The hydroelectric dam is the latest method of harnessing the power of rivers. It ~~is designed to~~ uses generate electricity ~~with~~ running water. First, Water from the dam's reservoir passes through large pipes called penstocks. The powerhouse is where electricity is generated. then The water flows to a powerhouse built on the other side of the dam. Next, The force of the water spins a large water wheel called a turbine. Finally, The turbine's action produces electricity, which goes out on power lines to homes, schools, factories, and businesses.

Write an Explanation

Explain to your class how something works. It could be something you use, such as a refrigerator or a bicycle, and it should be something you know well. Explain the steps in a logical order and, if you wish, use sketches or diagrams to illustrate your explanation.

PURPOSE To explain a process
AUDIENCE Classmates
LENGTH 4–6 paragraphs

WRITING RUBRICS To write an effective explanation, you should

- write a clear, interesting topic sentence for each paragraph
- explain each step in the process in the order in which it happens
- use appropriate transition words
- use precise verbs to make your writing vivid

Using Computers

Try turning your explanation into a magazine article. Some graphics or page-making software lets you lay out your page to look like a magazine or newspaper page. Design a magazine column for your piece. Include a headline, a byline, and room for your diagrams or sketches.

GrammarLink

Use precise verbs to help readers picture a process.

The right verb in a sentence can convey a clear, strong picture to the reader. Consider, for example, how much more meaning is communicated to the reader when *whispered* or *yelled* is substituted for **said** in dialogue.

Vague verb: goes
Precise verbs: passes, spins, flows

Revise the sentences below, replacing vague verbs with precise ones and adding verbs that make the action clear.

[1] To make a tossed salad, first get a large bowl. [2] Then deal with the lettuce. [3] Next, prepare tomatoes, carrots, and cheese. [4] Put sunflower seeds on top. [5] Finally, use salad dressing.

See Lesson 10.1, pages 399–400.

Listening and Speaking

COOPERATIVE LEARNING In small groups, take turns presenting your explanation orally, first, as you would do it for a group of fourth graders, and then as you would do it for adults. Discuss how you would alter your presentation for each audience.

Expository Writing

LOG ON ▶ **Writing** Online | For more writing and grammar practice, go to glencoe.com and enter QuickPass code WC77680p1.

215

Identifying Cause and Effect

One thing leads to another in the chain of events known as cause and effect.

Natural events cause changes in the weather. For example, ash from volcanic eruptions can partially block sunlight, which in turn can cause colder temperatures in parts of the world. The result can be ruined crops and more, as explained in the model below.

Literature Model

The coldest December temperatures in a century could wreak havoc with consumers' budgets this winter. Freezing weather has decimated [ruined] up to a third of Florida's citrus and 90 percent of the state's winter vegetable crop, estimates Doyle Conner, Florida's agriculture commissioner. Experts say that will translate into sharply higher prices for orange juice, grapefruits, and tomatoes.

Newsweek, January 8, 1990

What cause-and-effect relationship does the first sentence suggest?

Note the writer's use of statistics to show the effect of the cold weather.

Check Cause-and-Effect Relationships

A cause is an identifiable condition or event. An effect is something that happens as a direct result of that condition or event. Sometimes it seems that one event or condition causes another, when it really doesn't. Remember that causes must happen before effects, but not every event that precedes another is a cause.

Study the chart below. Notice which statements are not examples of cause and effect.

Editing Tip

When you edit, try combining a cause and its effect in a complex sentence. For more information, see Lesson 14.2, page 503.

 Expository Writing

Understanding Cause and Effect

| Cause | Lightning tends to strike the tallest object in the area. | | Effect | Single trees in open fields are often hit by lightning. |

This is true cause and effect. The cause is a condition that comes before and brings about the effect.

| Cause | Scientists hope someday to probe the planet Pluto. | | Effect | Scientists have collected information about the planets. |

A probe of Pluto did not precede the collection of information.

| Cause | In the spring melting snow filled the reservoir. | | Effect | This summer the city has a water shortage. |

Melting snow preceded the water shortage but did not cause it.

Journal Writing

Watch a television news program, and look for cause-and-effect relationships in the news reports. List three or four that the reporters identify. In your journal explain why one of them is a true example of a cause-and-effect relationship.

Examine How One Effect Leads to Another

Sometimes a cause and its effect form part of a chain of events. One cause may lead to an effect, and that effect may in turn change circumstances and lead to another effect. The diagram and the passage below show how this cause-and-effect chain works.

Below-freezing weather occurs.

Frost damages the oranges, and much of the crop is lost.

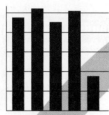

Fewer oranges are available than in previous years.

A rise in the price of oranges makes orange juice more expensive.

Consumers want as many oranges as before, but fewer are available, so prices rise.

Model

Is the "indoor air" mentioned in the first sentence a cause, an effect, or both?

Indoor air in winter has several effects on the human body. As the outdoor temperature drops, heat must be added indoors for comfort. However, added heat causes the indoor air to hold less moisture. This drier air often causes health problems, such as asthma or nosebleeds. People moving about in rooms where the air is too dry may also be irritated by static electricity, which is common when air moisture is low.

Write a Cause-and-Effect Letter

You are a responsible citizen. You are concerned about the number of accidents that occur when children play in the streets. Write a letter to your local representative explaining why children are playing in the streets and what will happen if no action is taken to correct this, including additional effects if it keeps up. Present some ideas the representative could use to effect change.

PURPOSE To present cause-and-effect analysis and present a plan

AUDIENCE Your local representative

LENGTH 1–2 paragraphs

WRITING RUBRICS To write an effective cause-and-effect letter, you should

- establish that there are cause-and-effect relationships
- show any chain effects
- include facts and statistics
- proofread and write legibly in print or cursive

Cross-Curricular Activity

HISTORY Use your history book to learn about a historic fire, or use other sources to find out about a more recent one. Write a few paragraphs in which you develop some cause-and-effect ideas. First, explain what caused or may have caused the fire. Then, write about what effects the fire may have had on the local community.

Listening and Speaking

MAKING A SPEECH Your student council has asked for ideas to help your school improve academically. Prepare a five-minute speech in which you propose one or two ideas (causes) and describe how they will improve students' academic performance (effects). In a small group, deliver your speech and ask for feedback about whether the causes you have suggested may produce the desired effects. Report the ideas your group suggests to the entire class. Express your ideas fluently, using Standard American English.

Grammar*Link*

Combine simple sentences to make complex sentences.

Complex sentences have a main clause and one or more subordinate clauses. Revise the paragraph below, combining causes and their effects in complex sentences where possible.

[1] Logging affects the ecosystem of a rainforest in several ways. [2] Trees are cut down. [3] The habitats of some organisms are destroyed. [4] More light and rain reach the forest floor. [5] The food supply of many organisms is wiped out.

See Lesson 14.2, page 503.

 **Writing** Online | For more writing and grammar practice, go to glencoe.com and enter QuickPass code WC77680p1.

219

Reports: Narrowing a Topic

A research report is a kind of expository writing. When you write a report, you gather information about your topic from a variety of sources. Then you take what you have learned, organize the information, and write about it in a way that your audience will understand.

Choose a Topic

Just as you can't play on every sports team in the same season, you can't say everything there is to say about a general topic in the same report. If a topic is too general or broad, you'll find too much information. If your topic is too narrow, you won't find enough. As you gain experience in writing reports, you'll learn to judge whether a topic is too broad, too narrow, or just right.

Keep three important things in mind when you're planning a research report:

1. Select a topic that you care about.
2. Narrow the topic so that you can cover it thoroughly.
3. Make sure that you can find several sources on your topic.

The diagram below shows how you can focus a topic. A focus on outdoor sports is too broad. There are too many outdoor sports to cover thoroughly. You can narrow the topic by focusing on a single sport—bicycling. But even this narrowed topic includes too much information. You can thoroughly cover one aspect of bicycling—bicycle safety, for example—in one report.

Editing Tip

When planning a report, remember that visual aids, such as photos, maps, and charts, can help your reader grasp your points.

Expository Writing

Journal Writing

What are your favorite sports or games? In your journal make a triangle diagram like the one above to identify which aspect of the one sport or game you enjoy most.

Know Your Audience

A report on bicycle safety could have a wide audience. It could be your class or the readers of your local paper or an adult community group. It's important to tailor a report to your audience.

The next time you are driving your car, think for a moment about others who are sharing the road. More and more people are riding bicycles these days, and too many of them are in accidents with moving cars. In a recent year, 460,000 people were injured in such accidents, and as many as 1,100 cyclists have been killed each year. Make the roads safe for all who use them.

▲ This paragraph is intended for drivers. Its purpose is to make drivers aware of the frequency of serious car-bicycle accidents.

Bike riding can be fun, but it also carries some responsibility. The next time you jump on your bike and get ready to take off, remember to (1) ride with the traffic and keep to the right; (2) never ride double on a bicycle; (3) wear a helmet, and (4) wear light-colored clothes, put reflective strips on your clothes and your bike, and use a bike light when light is poor.

▲ This paragraph is directed toward cyclists. The writer reminds bicycle riders of some basic safety rules. The purpose is to get readers to think about and follow precautions.

Choose and Narrow a Topic

Write down three or four topics that interest you—topics that you would like to research. Take some time to think about which one you would most enjoy researching and writing about. Use a conference or small-group discussion to help you choose.

PURPOSE To focus on a topic
AUDIENCE Audience of your choice
LENGTH A list

WRITING RUBRICS To choose and narrow a topic effectively, you should

- select a topic that you know and care about
- narrow the topic so you can cover it thoroughly
- make sure that several reliable sources of information on your topic are available

 Using Computers

Working on your own or with one or two others, look for information about your topic on the Internet. To find the most beneficial Web sites, you'll need to narrow your topic as much as possible before you begin. Look for Web sites devoted to your topic or use a search engine to find articles and other sources that can help you find a suitably narrow focus for your report.

Listening and Speaking

COOPERATIVE LEARNING Work in small groups to practice narrowing topics. Start with broad, general subjects, like sports, television, or fashion. Then brainstorm ways to narrow those broad subjects to topics appropriate for short papers that require some research. Report on your efforts to the class, describing what subjects you started with and what topics you ended with.

GrammarLink

Use correct subject-verb agreement with indefinite pronouns.

Indefinite pronouns do not refer to specific persons or things. Some, such as *anything* and *nobody,* are singular. Others, such as *both* and *many,* are plural. Still others, such as *all, any,* and *some,* can be either singular or plural, depending on the noun that follows.

All of the bacteria are alive. *All* of the money *is* gone.

Write the paragraph, inserting the correct verbs.

¹ Each of us (has, have) a job. ² Few (rests, rest) at all. ³ Some of us (finishes, finish) at 5:00 P.M. ⁴ All the effort (goes, go) into painting. ⁵ Everyone (admires, admire) our work.

See Lesson 16.1, page 535, and Lesson 16.4, page 541.

LOG ON ▶ **Writing** Online | For more writing and grammar practice, go to **glencoe.com** and enter QuickPass code WC77680p1.

223

Reports: Turning to Helpful Sources

In the preceding lesson you learned about narrowing a topic. The next task is research. What do you want to know, and where can you find the information that you need?

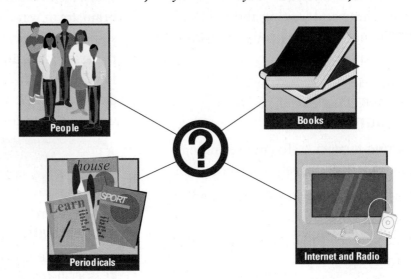

Ask Questions

Conducting research is like going on a treasure hunt. You won't know whether you've found the prize unless you know what you're looking for in the first place. Before you head off to the library or start searching the Internet, think about your topic. What do you think you know? Focus your thoughts by jotting down some ideas about your topic. What do you want to find out? Make a list of questions that you'd like your research to answer.

Find Answers

Your list of questions can guide your research the way a map can guide an explorer to a buried treasure. Let your research questions guide your research as you look for answers in a variety of sources. New questions will come to you as you learn more about your topic. Just add them to your list!

When you're researching a topic, the library can be your best resource. There, you're likely to find computers with access to the Internet, and you're sure to find a catalog that lists all the materials in the library according to subject, title, or author. You will find a variety of informative materials in the library:

- books and reference works, such as almanacs, atlases, and encyclopedias
- magazines, newspapers, and scholarly journals
- videotapes, audiotapes, and compact discs

An encyclopedia is a good place to begin reading about your topic. An encyclopedia article can give you a broad overview of a topic and can direct you to additional sources.

The best research reports include information from both primary and secondary sources. A **primary source** is a firsthand account of an event, written by someone who actually experienced or observed the event. Primary sources include diaries, letters, or historical documents from the period you're studying. An interview with a knowledgeable person is another kind of primary source. For example, an interview with someone who lives on a farm would be a primary source for a report on farm life. A **secondary source** is written by a person who has conducted original research, gathered information, and shaped that information in a certain way. Books and magazines are generally considered secondary sources.

Prewriting Tip

Learn to make the most of your library visit by reviewing Unit 22, Library and Reference Resources, pages 630–652.

Prewriting Tip

See **Writing and Research Handbook,** pages 825–826, for information about evaluating sources.

Prewriting Tip

It's important to examine more than one viewpoint on a topic, so be sure to read multiple sources. Compare and contrast their differing perspectives.

Expository Writing

Journal Writing

Review what you wrote for the Choose and Narrow a Topic activity on page 223. What kinds of primary and secondary sources might you look for on your topic? In your journal, jot down a preliminary plan for finding these sources and conducting research for your report.

Make Note Cards

The process of making note cards helps you learn about your topic and keep track of the information you find. As you scan your sources, look for information about your topic. When you find it, take notes on four-by-six-inch index cards. Use one card for each distinct piece of information. At the top of each card, write the main idea of the note. When you're ready to begin writing, you'll easily be able to sort and organize your information. At the bottom of each card, write the author's name, a page reference, and the source's title and publication information.

Each card for a report on bicycle safety contains notes on a different part of the topic.

Quotation marks indicate words copied from a source.

This primary source is an informal but helpful interview.

Prewriting Tip

You need to give credit to the source of the ideas and information you include in your report. That's why you should record source information on each note card. For more on giving credit and citing sources, see **Writing and Research Handbook,** pages 826–830.

Tips for Taking Notes

- Keep your notes in one place. Don't lose them!

- With every note, include the information source (title, author, publication information, and page numbers).

- List main ideas and details to support them. Record dates and names exactly.

- **Paraphrase** or **summarize** information, using your own words to record what you learn from a source.

- If you copy information word for word, use quotation marks to show that you're quoting from a source directly.

Begin Your Research

Write your narrowed topic at the top of a piece of paper. Write the headings *Books, Magazines and Newspapers, People, Technology,* and *Other Sources.* Under each one, list specific sources you can use and prepare note cards.

PURPOSE To gather information for a report
AUDIENCE Yourself
LENGTH 1 page of source ideas; at least 15 note cards

WRITING RUBRICS To begin your research effectively, you should

- find sources in the library
- find answers in your sources to the questions you have about your topic
- make note cards, following the tips on page 226

Using Computers

Try entering your notes into a computer file. Just as you would write a note's main idea on the top line of an index card, use boldface type to signify a note's main idea. At any point during your note-taking process, you can do a search for keywords in these main idea headings. Then sort your notes using the Cut-and-Paste feature, so that all your notes on the same aspect of your topic are in the same place in your computer file. Also be sure to record publication information for each note you enter into the computer.

Listening and Speaking

SHARE IDEAS With a small group of classmates, share ideas about how to find and evaluate sources of information for the topic you've selected. By talking about your topic with others, you can discover ways to limit—or expand—the scope of your topic. Be ready to listen to and act on the advice of your classmates.

GrammarLink

Use correct punctuation and capitalization.

Always capitalize proper nouns and titles, such as *M.D.* or *Jr.,* after a name. Underline or use italic type for titles of books and magazines. Use quotation marks for book chapters and song titles.

Revise the note card excerpts below to correct errors.

1. Comments made by Peter Hetzler jr., m.d.
2. Amy said that her favorite book is bicycling through North america.
3. Joe read A tale of two cities.
4. A chapter called Car Repair.
5. The Beatles wrote A Hard Day's Night in 24 hours.

See Lesson 19.2, page 575, and Lesson 20.6, page 599.

LOG ON ▶ **Writing** Online — For more writing and grammar practice, go to glencoe.com and enter QuickPass code WC77680p1.

227

Reports: Conducting an Interview

An interview with an expert can provide the kinds of details, dates, and stories that strengthen research reports.

An Illinois writer became curious about a program to promote safety among bicycle riders in Schaumburg, Illinois. Who ran the program? What did it do? An interview with an expert answered many of the writer's questions.

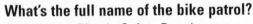

Interview with Schaumburg Police Intern Becky Stiefvater

What's the full name of the bike patrol?
Schaumburg Bicycle Safety Patrol

How does it operate?
We have six people, and we divide up into three teams of two. We ride around, and we look for kids who go through stop signs, ride on the wrong side of the road, or ride two people on a bike made for one—anything that's against the village ordinance.

What happens to people who get caught?
Sometimes we issue a warning ticket or a notice to appear in "bike court." We set up actual court proceedings for them, and they get assignments like community service.

How do you get around town when you're off-duty?
Since I'm riding a bike eight hours a day, I usually drive my car.

Prepare for an Interview

Your teachers or librarian might be able to suggest someone you could interview for a research report. Once you have identified an expert, contact him or her to see if and when an interview is possible. Be courteous: The interviewee is doing you a favor by setting aside the time to talk.

Prepare interview questions ahead of time. Ask yourself what you expect to learn through the interview. Do you want to discover new developments? Do you want personal observations or stories? The most effective interview questions are open-ended; that is, they ask for more than a yes or no answer. Note how one interviewer used open-ended questions when talking with Mrs. Rodriguez.

Interview : Mrs. Bianca Rodriguez
Founder of the Ready Riders Bike Safety Club
East side of town; weekly club meetings at the fieldhouse
1. Why did you organize this club?
2. What do you mean by bike safety?
3. How can kids contact you to join the club?
4. What are the benefits of joining this club?

How do the questions show that the interviewer prepared for this conversation?

Journal Writing

Decide on a topic someone could interview you about. In your journal write five open-ended questions an interviewer might ask you. Then answer the questions as honestly as you can.

Conduct an Interview

When you conduct an interview, use a notebook, tape recorder, or both. If you use a notebook, you may have time to write down only the most important points. A tape recorder captures everything that is said. A tape provides a record of the speaker's exact words; a notebook preserves a record of your strongest impressions. Using both may strengthen your report.

You can conduct your interview in person or, if necessary, by telephone. When you meet or first speak with an interviewee, thank him or her for taking the time to talk. If you can, conduct the interview in a quiet place. Before ending the interview, make sure that you have all the information you need.

Other hints for a good interview are listed below.

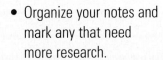

Tips for Conducting an Interview

- Prepare a list of open-ended questions ahead of time.

- Arrive on time, dressed properly.

- Ask permission before using a tape recorder.

- Listen carefully to the answers.

- If you don't understand an answer, politely ask for an explanation.

- Ask follow-up questions.

- Immediately after the interview, write a summary of what you heard.

- Organize your notes and mark any that need more research.

- Make sure that all numbers and names are correct.

- Review the interview and see if you can identify which comments are opinions and which are statements of fact.

Conduct an Interview

Identify a local or national expert on your subject. Plan an interview with her or him.

PURPOSE To gain first-hand information for a report

AUDIENCE Your interviewee; yourself

LENGTH 1 page of questions; several pages of notes

WRITING RUBRICS To plan and conduct an effective interview, you should

- make an appointment for the interview
- write some open-ended questions
- conduct the interview and review your notes, using the tips chart on page 230

Using Computers

ORGANIZE Use a computer to write and organize interview questions. First, list questions as they come to mind. Then block or highlight the questions and organize them in a logical order. Finally, add other questions that you might use.

Listening and Speaking

COOPERATIVE LEARNING Work with a partner to refine your questions. Read your questions to each other and give and take suggestions for improvement.

Grammar Link

Capitalize proper nouns and adjectives formed from proper nouns.

Proper nouns, such as *America*, and proper adjectives, such as *American*, must be capitalized. In addition to the names of people and places, other proper nouns include the names of clubs and organizations and the names of historical events.

> *Ready Riders Bike Safety Club, Boys and Girls Club, Civil War.*

Days of the week, months of the year, and holidays are also capitalized, as are the first and last words and all important words in titles of books, articles, films, and songs.

Correct capitalization errors in the following notes:

1. Interview: ms. Jan Tsai, student representative, national honor society
2. Meeting: Tuesday homeroom periods in the auditorium of john s. bradfield middle school
3. Visit planned: smithsonian institution in washington, d.c.
4. Write letter: principal j. w. smithers about the student election

See Lesson 19.2–19.4, pages 575–580.

Writing Online   For more writing and grammar practice, go to glencoe.com and enter QuickPass code WC77680p1.

231

Reports: Organizing and Drafting

*Y*ou've narrowed your topic and gathered ideas and details for a report. Now it's time to set a focus, organize your information, and write a draft of your report.

Prewriting Tip

Refer to **Writing and Research Handbook,** pages 817–824, for more information on how to put your ideas in the best order.

State the Main Idea

Before you can begin to organize all the information you've gathered, think about the big picture. What have you learned so far? What will be the main point of your report? Draft a **thesis statement**— a sentence or two that tells the main idea or that states what you want your writing to show, prove, or explain.

Get Organized

Let your thesis help you focus on what's important as you organize your thoughts—and your notes. You may need to set aside ideas and information that don't relate to your thesis. Get organized by following these steps.

- Make a list of the main points that you want to make in your report. All of these points should support your thesis statement.

- Begin creating an outline by listing your main points.

- Gather together your note cards and put them in groups according to their main-idea headings or subject matter.

- Complete your outline by adding details from your note cards and from your interview notes.

To see how a thesis statement and the parts of an outline fit together, review the sample outline shown on the next page.

Thesis Statement: Bike safety includes careful riding, regular maintenance, and proper equipment.

I. Introduction
II. Traffic regulations
    A. Ride on the right side of the road.
    B. Don't weave in and out.
    C. Ride single file.
    D. Obey traffic signs
       and use hand signals.
III. Maintenance of your bike
IV. Wearing a helmet

When you write an outline, use roman numerals to indicate main ideas and letters to indicate supporting details.

Drafting Tip

A thesis statement tells the main idea of a composition or report in the same way that a topic sentence tells the main idea of a paragraph.

Drafting Your Report

Now that you've developed a plan for your report, you're ready to start writing. Begin wherever you feel most comfortable—with your introduction or with a favorite section in the middle. Just make sure that you have one or more paragraphs for each heading in your outline and that you put the sections of your report in order before you review and revise your draft.

Remember that when you write a report, you make inferences, synthesize material, and draw conclusions from your research. Your goal is to present your own thinking—to say something new—using data from your research to support your ideas. Be careful not to **plagiarize,** or present someone else's ideas as your own. Therefore, when you write sentences from your note cards, put the source of the ideas in parentheses at the end.

Drafting Tip

See **Writing and Research Handbook,** pages 826–830, for more information about how to give credit to your sources as you write.

Journal Writing

List the steps that you have learned so far about writing a research paper. Put a check beside the step that you think will be most challenging for you. Write a plan about one paragraph long for meeting the challenge.

Know the Parts of a Report

Like other compositions, every report has three parts: an introduction, a body, and a conclusion. Each part has a specific purpose. An example of each part and its purpose appears below. (The picture shows only a section of the report on safety.) The **Writing and Research Handbook,** pages 817–832, provides more information about how to structure your report and the paragraphs within it.

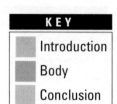

KEY
- Introduction
- Body
- Conclusion

The introduction sparks readers' interest and shows the writer's position on the issue.

> Millions of Americans today enjoy bike riding. At the same time, the number of cars on our streets keeps rising. With all these pe___ on the road, bike safe___ ___ everyo___

The body of the report develops the topic. The body includes at least one paragraph for each main idea in the outline.

> The safety rules that apply to biking can help young people when they begin to drive. Many bike programs and bike courts, like the one in Schaumburg, Illinois, have been developed to help cyclists. "The closer they are to driving a car," Becky Stiefvater says, "the more likely they'll end up in bike court. If they haven't learned safety rules for a bike yet, it's not too safe to send them out in a car."

The conclusion summarizes the topic or states the writer's final thoughts about it.

> Bike riding can be fun, but it also carries important responsibilities. By following the proper precautions and making safety a habit, cyclists can be sure that biking remains fun for everyone.

5.9 Writing Activities

Outline and Draft

Now you have the raw materials for your report. Look over your notes to see whether ideas changed as you researched. Are there new questions you would like to answer?

PURPOSE To outline and draft a report
AUDIENCE Yourself; peer reviewers
LENGTH 4–5 pages

WRITING RUBRICS To develop an effective outline and draft, you should

- write a clear, accurate thesis statement
- create an outline, using your note cards to arrange topics logically
- draft your report, creating an introduction, a body, and a conclusion

Listening and Speaking

COOPERATIVE LEARNING Read your draft to a partner or a small group. Ask your audience these questions:

—Is anything not clear?
—Where could I add more information?
—What do you find most interesting about my topic?
—What would you like to know more about?

Take notes on the responses of your peers, and use the notes to help you when you revise. Remember, the most important part of writing is to make your ideas clear to your audience.

GrammarLink

Use a comma to separate a phrase from the quotation itself.

Look back at the model on page 234. Notice how the writer uses commas with direct quotations.

"The closer they are to driving a car," Becky Stiefvater says, "the more likely they'll end up in bike court."

Write each quotation using correct punctuation.

1. Power said Lord Acton corrupts. Absolute power corrupts absolutely.
2. Don't look back Satchel Page said. Something could be gaining on you.
3. I never met a man I didn't like Will Rogers said.
4. My name is Luca the song goes. And I live on the second floor.

See Lesson 20.6, page 599.

Listening and Speaking

GETTING EXPERT ADVICE Arrange to have a teacher in an appropriate subject area or one of the experts you interviewed review your report for accuracy, clarity, and interest. Ask for advice about how to improve your report. Take notes on the feedback you receive and use those notes as you revise.

LOG ON ▶ **Writing** Online   For more writing and grammar practice, go to **glencoe.com** and enter QuickPass code WC77680p1.

235

Expository Writing

Reports: Revising and Presenting

By revising a report, you can test and strengthen the presentation of your ideas. Let your peers tell you whether your writing is clear.

Early bike-racing helmets consisted of padding and leather. The introduction of plastics allowed manufacturers to produce stronger and lighter helmets. Testing led to improvements that made helmets not only fit riders well but also keep them cool. It seems that the early version of just about anything can stand improvement. Consider how you can use a system of revising and testing with your research report.

Get It Right

When you revise, make sure that each section—the introduction, the body, and the conclusion—fulfills its purpose and engages your readers. Check that you've covered the main points in your outline and that your ideas flow in a logical order. You'll also want to confirm that your facts and statistics are correct, that you've quoted your sources accurately, and that you've given proper credit to any ideas that are not your own.

Create a Works-Cited List

The final step in the process of revising a research report is to create a works-cited list, which will become the last page of your report. A works-cited list gives complete publication information for all the sources you used and referred to in your paper. Entries should appear in alphabetical order. Refer to **Writing and Research Handbook,** pages 827–830, for more information about preparing your final draft and about the different bibliographic styles you can use for your works-cited list. Ask your teacher which style he or she prefers.

You may also want to review the model of a research paper on pages 831–832 of the **Handbook.** For your own paper, make sure that you put your list of works cited on its own page.

Revising Tip

When revising, check transitions between paragraphs. Good transitions create fluency by showing how one paragraph relates to the next.

Revising Tip

For a discussion of revision strategies, see Unit 2, Lessons 2.6–2.9.

Expository Writing

TIME

For more about the writing process, see TIME *Facing the Blank Page,* pp. 97–107.

Journal Writing

Evaluate your draft using the checklist on page 67. In your journal, jot down how well you accomplished each of the points on the checklist. Think critically about your draft and make notes about how you will revise your report.

Tell the World

When you start a report assignment, all you have is a topic that interests you. After completing a report, you have more knowledge. You're ready to share what you've learned.

You can share your work in a variety of ways. Bind your report in book form, present it on a computer disk, put it into a notebook binder, post it on an electronic bulletin board, or print it as part of a class newsletter or magazine. Think of things to include—covers, graphics, clippings, photographs— that will make your report attractive. Then share it with others!

Read the report page below to see how one writer used a diagram to illustrate information.

How does the diagram strengthen the report?

helmet

elbow pads

head light

rear reflector

proper shoes

Another safeguard that people often ignore is proper bike maintenance. Cyclists should inspect their bikes regularly to make sure the tires, brakes, handlebars, seats, and spokes are in proper shape. Some repairs can be done easily by the cyclist, but regular inspections at a bike repair shop are also recommended.

Proper clothing and equipment can also make a difference in bicycle safety. According to one study, only 12 percent of accidents involve a car and a bike. The rest occur when cyclists fall or are thrown from their bikes. Because of this, experts such as those from the National Safe Kids Campaign recommend that, when riding, cyclists wear bike helmets. The helmets protect against brain injuries.

Revise, Edit, and Share Your Report

Now is the time to make sure your report says what you want it to say. Does it support your thesis statement? Will it interest your readers?

PURPOSE To finish and share a research report

AUDIENCE Classmates, teacher, family

LENGTH 5–10 pages

WRITING RUBRICS To revise and edit your report before you share it, you should

- check the report for clarity, accuracy, organization, and interest
- proofread to correct errors in grammar, usage, spelling, and mechanics
- make a final copy for others to read and study

Collaborative Writing

Work in a small group to improve the following paragraph for readers. Brainstorm to make a good topic sentence. Work together to revise the paragraph for clarity, organization, and interest.

When people hear "old-fashioned bicycle," they think of a big front wheel and a small back one. Bicycles with a big front wheel were called ordinary. They were better. They were called "high wheelers." The first bicycle factory in the United States began making it in 1877. They were costly and unsafe with the rider so high. They gave a smooth ride and went fast.

Viewing and Representing

CREATING COVER ART Create a cover for your report. Reproduce or draw a visual image that will give a reader an idea of what to expect from your report. It can be funny or serious, depending on your subject.

Grammar*Link*

Use the correct form of the verb.

The principal parts of a verb include its base form, present participle, past form, and past participle.

ride, riding, rode, ridden

Write the correct form of the verb in parentheses.

1 Advertisers have (rely) on ads for decades. **2** Catchy jingles are (know) to be memorable. **3** Eye-catching images, often (create) on computers, draw people's attention. **4–5** Because so many ads have (appear) in the media, people often (ignore) them.

See Lesson 10.5, page 407, and Lesson 10.9, page 415.

LOG ON ▶ **Writing** Online For more writing and grammar practice, go to glencoe.com and enter QuickPass code WC77680p1.

239

WRITING ABOUT LITERATURE
Comparing Two People

Read what the writer of the passages below has to say about two women cyclists who gained fame. How are the women different? How are they alike?

Literature Model

[Margaret Le Long's] bicycle was a modern safety bicycle with the diamond frame, its top tube dropped to enable her—and other women—to pedal while wearing a dress. All she packed was a bag that strapped to her handlebars and contained a pistol, curl-papers, makeup box, and underwear. Her trip [from Chicago to San Francisco in 1896] took two months.

Predictably, Connie Young rose to become a world-class athlete. Her specialty was the explosive sprint events. She won two bronze medals in world speed-skating championships and made the Olympic speed-skating teams in 1980 and 1984. She also reigned as national and world cycling champion.

Peter Nye, *The Cyclist's Sourcebook*

Chart a Comparison

Organizing and answering questions such as those below can help you compare and contrast details. It's clear that Young and Le Long are different in important ways.

Revising Tip

When you edit, use verbals for variety in your writing style. For more information see Lessons 15.1, 15.2, and 15.3, pages 521–526.

Comparing and Contrasting
Margaret Le Long and Connie Young

1. In what decade did Le Long ride cross-country?

   In what decade did Young first participate in the Olympics?

2. What did Le Long wear when she rode? What did she carry with her? What does each item tell you about her?

   What do you think Young, a contemporary cyclist, wears when she rides?

3. Why is Margaret Le Long's ride considered an accomplishment?

   Why is Connie Young considered a "world-class" athlete?

| 1890s cyclist | modern cyclist |

Early cyclist
Margaret Le Long

Olympian
Connie Young

Journal Writing

Write brief answers to any pair of questions in the chart on this page. Then write one sentence telling which woman interests you more and why.

Expository Writing

Compare Real and Fictional Characters

When you read about a fictional character who reminds you of a real person, you might report on the fictional work by comparing and contrasting the character and the person. To help you organize your ideas, use a Venn diagram like the one on this page.

Read the passage below about The Goober, a character in Robert Cormier's novel *The Chocolate War*. Think about the qualities he shares with other athletes you know or have read about, especially Connie Young.

Literature Model

The Goober was beautiful when he ran. His long arms and legs moved flowingly and flawlessly, his body floating as if his feet weren't touching the ground. When he ran, he forgot about his awkwardness and the shyness that paralyzed him when a girl looked his way. Even his thoughts became sharper, and things were simple and uncomplicated—he could solve math problems when he ran or memorize football play patterns. Often he rose early in the morning, before anyone else, and poured himself liquid through the sunrise streets. Then everything seemed beautiful, everything in its proper orbit, nothing impossible, the entire world attainable.

Robert Cormier, *The Chocolate War*

What qualities do The Goober and Connie Young share with other athletes you know about but not with each other?

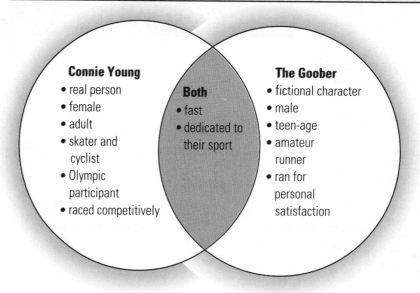

Connie Young
- real person
- female
- adult
- skater and cyclist
- Olympic participant
- raced competitively

Both
- fast
- dedicated to their sport

The Goober
- fictional character
- male
- teen-age
- amateur runner
- ran for personal satisfaction

5.11 Writing Activities

Write a Comparison-and-Contrast

Choose two characters you have read about recently. They can be fictional or real. Make a Venn diagram like the one on page 242 to show how they are alike and different. Then write two paragraphs comparing and contrasting them.

PURPOSE To compare and contrast two people

AUDIENCE Your classmates

LENGTH 2 paragraphs

WRITING RUBRICS To compare and contrast two characters effectively, you should

- identify both similarities and differences
- organize your paragraphs to make your points clearly
- proofread to correct mechanical errors

Listening and Speaking

COOPERATIVE LEARNING In a small group, hold a discussion about people's attitudes toward taking part in sports. Create a Venn diagram showing the similarities between those who play for fun and those who believe that "winning is the only thing." Think of people, real or fictional, who represent each type. Share your diagram and lists of people with the class.

Grammar*Link*

Make compound subjects and verbs agree.

When two or more subjects are joined by *either . . . or* or *neither . . . nor,* the verb agrees with the subject that is closest to it.

Neither the players nor the **coach** *is here yet.*

Write the correct form of the verb for each sentence below.

1. Either Janis or I (am, is) the fastest runner in seventh grade.
2. Neither my brothers nor my dad (runs, run) particularly fast.
3. Neither the choir director nor the orchestra conductor (encourages, encourage) students to choose track as an elective.
4. Either Sam or his sisters (is, are) going to wash the car.

See Lesson 16.5, page 543.

Cross-Curricular Activity

HISTORY From your history book, pick two historical figures who held similar positions or titles: for example, presidents, generals, or activists on certain issues. Compare and contrast the two in a brief essay that concludes with a statement about whether they were more similar to or different from each other.

LOG ON ▶ **Writing** Online For more writing and grammar practice, go to glencoe.com and enter QuickPass code WC77680p1.

243

Writing Process in Action

Expository Writing

In the preceding lessons you've learned about gathering, organizing, and writing the kind of details that are necessary for expository writing. You have written letters, an article, and a research report. Now, in this lesson, you're invited to write a brochure that will inform visitors about your community.

Assignment

Context	You are contributing to a brochure about your town. You need to gather details about the types of people in your town, including ages, races, customs, careers, and whatever other characteristics make them distinctive.
Purpose	To inform visitors and newcomers about the variety of people in your town
Audience	Visitors and newcomers to your town
Length	1–2 pages

Planning to Write

The following pages can help you plan and write your brochure. Read through them, and then refer to them as you need to. But don't be tied down by them. You're in charge of your own writing process. Set a time frame for completion, and keep in mind the controlling idea: to inform visitors and newcomers about the variety of people in your town.

Writing
Online

LOG
ON

For prewriting, drafting, revising, editing and publishing tools, go to **glencoe.com** and enter QuickPass code WC77680p1.

Prewriting

Sometimes just a few adjectives can start your ideas flowing. Ask yourself: What makes my community *distinctive* (or *popular* or *colorful*)?

Other ideas appear in the options at the right. Remember, too, that a writing partner can help you focus your thoughts and point out other ideas. As you review your notes, mark the ones you want to include in your draft, particularly those that will help show how your community is distinctive. Think about how to organize your information. You might show causes and effects. You might compare and contrast. You might use order of importance.

Option A

Brainstorm groups of people in your town.

Option B

Explore neighborhoods, taking notes on what you see.

Option C

Freewrite on news items about the community.

Town slogan: "You always can see a smile in Fairfield." Great Chinese shops and restaurants. Thriving African American neighborhoods. Street fairs and block parties. Walkathon for diabetes research.

Drafting

As you begin to draft, keep your main ideas in mind, and refer to your notes as necessary. It is important to get your ideas on paper. You'll have time to change things later, if you wish. Begin in a way that will catch your reader's interest. Notice how the writer Laurence Pringle begins in the passage below by speaking directly to you—the reader.

Drafting Tip

Jot down, in order of importance, the main ideas you want to get across. This helps you to plan your writing. For more information about organizing details, see Lesson 5.2, pages 204–206.

Literature Model

Pick up a handful of soil anywhere on earth. In it you will find more organisms—visible and microscopic—than exist on the entire surfaces of other planets.

Laurence Pringle, *Living Treasure*

Revising Tip

For more information about different ways of organizing and presenting information, see Lessons 5.9 and 5.10, pages 232–239.

Revising

To begin revising, read over your draft to make sure that what you've written fits your purpose and audience. Then have a **writing conference.** Read your draft to a partner or a small group or share it with your teacher. Use your audience's reactions to help you evaluate your work so far. The questions below can help you and your listeners.

Question A

Have I clearly explained unfamiliar terms?

Question B

Do I have enough details to support my main ideas?

Question C

Have I organized my information effectively?

The people of Fairfield enjoy diversity among their neighbors. The Mexican festival, Cinco de Mayo, is a yearly highlight for neighbors of many different ethnic origins. At the August art fair at
(Add Cinco de Mayo details)
Library Plaza, you'll find the works of local painters
hospital patients
who may be senior citizens, or college students. In
annual
"Life Steps," the walkathon for diabetes research,
Scandinavian Americans, African Americans, and
Hmong
~~Laotian Americans~~ to name just a few ~~join forces~~
as friends.

Editing/Proofreading

Small mistakes can cause confusion, especially in expository writing. Take the time to check the accuracy of your draft. You can do the editing yourself, and you might also ask a friend to be a peer reviewer.

One way to edit is to use a checklist such as the one shown here. Consider the questions, one by one, as you read your draft several times. Use **proofreading** marks to make changes.

You might find it helpful to first show your brochure to two long-time residents of your town. Have them read your work separately and comment about its thoroughness. Do they agree with what you've said about your subject?

Editing/Proofreading Checklist

1. Are quotations and other facts correct?
2. Have I used comparative and superlative forms correctly?
3. Do subjects and verbs agree in number?
4. Have I used standard spelling, capitalization, and punctuation?

Proofreading Tip

Check for proper use of quotation marks when editing dialogue. For more information see pp. 599-600.

Publishing/Presenting

Once you're happy with your brochure, you may want to prepare a set of photographs to accompany it. Perhaps you might combine your work with that of other students, and have compiled copies of *The People of (your town or city)* bound for your school or town library.

Journal Writing: Write to Learn

Answer these questions in your journal: What do you like best about your expository writing? What was the hardest part of writing it? What did you learn in your writing conference? What new things have you learned as a writer?

Literature Model

FROM

LIVING Treasure

by Laurence Pringle

In the following selection from his book Living Treasure, *Laurence Pringle brings to light a hidden, secret world filled with millions of plants and animals no one has ever seen. As you read, pay special attention to the way the author keeps his writing informative, lively, and engaging. Then try the activities in Linking Writing and Literature on page 254.*

Pick up a handful of soil anywhere on earth. In it you will find more organisms— visible and microscopic—than exist on the entire surfaces of other planets.

The planet Mars is icy cold—and lifeless. The planet Venus is fiery hot—and lifeless. Between these planets lies our home, Earth. Its atmosphere makes it an oasis in space, with a favorable climate, abundant water, and a rich variety of living things.

Scientists are dazzled and puzzled by the diversity of life on earth. No one knows how many different kinds

Patricia Gonzalez, *Heart Forest*, 1985

of plants, animals, and other organisms there are. But we do know that the organisms identified so far are only a small fraction of all living things. There are millions—perhaps many millions—that await discovery.

The study of living things is called biology (*bio* is a Greek term for "life"). Scientists who study living things are called biologists. And biologists have a name for the earth's incredible variety of life: biodiversity.

The first step toward understanding this biodiversity is naming and describing the different living organisms. Throughout human history and all over the world, people have given names to animals and plants they recognize. For example, in New Guinea, hunters can name sixteen different frogs, seventeen lizards and snakes, more than a hundred birds, and many more insects and worms. The New Guinea hunters are walking encyclopedias of information about the life around them.

Besides naming things, people have tried to make sense of the earth's biodiversity by considering similar organisms to be members of groups. The modern system of naming and classifying living things was devised by Swedish botanist Carl von Linné (Carolus Linnaeus) in the eighteenth century. At that time, Linné and other scientists believed that perhaps 50,000 kinds of organisms lived on earth.

Since then, more than 1.5 million kinds, or species, have been discovered and named. They include 250,000 species of flowering plants and 41,000 kinds of vertebrate animals. These animals with backbones include about 4,000 mammals, 19,000 fishes, about 9,000 birds, and more than 10,000 reptiles and amphibians. The largest group by far is the insects, with more than 751,000 named so far. The remainder includes worms, spiders, fungi, algae, and microorganisms.

Biologists believe that most of the earth's flowering plants and vertebrate animals have been discovered. They estimate that only a few thousand more fishes, birds, reptiles, and other vertebrates are likely to be found. The greatest riches of biodiversity remain to be discovered in the world of insects and other small creatures without backbones (invertebrates).

Biologists expect to find some of the earth's undescribed organisms living in coral reefs. There also may be other undiscovered habitats,[1] and species, on the floor of the deep ocean. In the 1980s, using small research submarines, scientists began to discover new forms of life—crabs, fishes, shrimps, tube worms—near geysers of hot, mineral-laden water that spew from the ocean floor.

The earth's greatest riches, however, lie in tropical rain forests. In the 1980s, as funds for tropical research

> # The earth's greatest riches . . . lie in tropical rain forests.

---

¹habitats (hab′ ə tats′) the places where plants or animals naturally grow or live

Kathryn Stewart, *Hummingbird Vision*, 1990

increased, biologists found astonishing numbers of animals there.

In Panama, entomologist[2] Terry Erwin of the Smithsonian Institution collected insects from nineteen trees of the same species. On those trees alone, he found more than 12,000 different kinds of beetles. He estimated that one out of seven species lived on that kind of tree and no other.

---

[2]**entomologist** (en´ tə mol′ ə jist) an expert in the branch of biology that deals with insects

Erwin also collected insects from one tree in the Amazon rain forest of Peru. He sent the ant specimens to be identified by biologist Edward O. Wilson of Harvard University. Wilson found forty-three kinds of ants, including several new species. This diversity of ants—from a single tropical tree— equaled the number of ant species that are known to live in all of Canada or Great Britain.

Tropical forests are also rich with plant life. In Borneo, a botanist discovered 700 species of trees growing on ten separate plots of land that totaled about twenty-five acres. This matches the number of tree species growing in all of North America. Also, the trunks and branches of rain forest trees are habitats for mosses, ferns, lichens, orchids, and other plants that grow far above the soil. In Costa Rica alone, more than 1,100 species of orchids have been identified.

In the 1980s, Terry Erwin and other biologists began for the first time to study insects, plants, and other organisms that live near the tops of tropical trees. The organisms living in the treetops, or canopy, of a rain forest are different from those living on or close to the ground. More than half of all rain forest species may live aloft. Most of them never touch the ground. Terry Erwin has called the tropical forest canopy "the heart" of the earth's biodiversity.

Until the 1980s, biologists estimated that 3 to 5 million species live on earth. However, since large numbers of tropical insects and other organisms may live on just one kind of tree, or in one small area of tropical forest, the biodiversity of earth may be much greater. Terry Erwin

> **More than half of all rain forest species may live aloft. Most of them never touch the ground.**

has estimated that the earth may be home to 30 million species of insects alone.

The total of all kinds of life could be much higher. Rain forest canopies harbor not only insects but also unknown numbers of mites,[3] roundworms, fungi, and other small organisms. Little is known about life in tropical soils. And most animals have other living things, called parasites, living on or inside them.

Whether the total number of species is 5 million, 30 million, or more, we know very little about the biodiversity of our planet. Our ignorance is great.

Suppose the number of species is "only" 10 million. This means that we have perhaps discovered just 15 percent of the total number of species. Then consider that we have not yet learned much about the plants and animals that *have* been identified. Many of these organisms are "known" only in the sense that a few individuals are kept as preserved specimens in scientific collections and that they have been given a formal name.

Their lives are a mystery. Their links with other living things, their importance in nature, and their possible value to humans are also mysteries.

> . . . we know very little about the biodiversity of our planet. Our ignorance is great.

---

[3]**mites** (mīts) tiny animals that look like spiders

Linking Writing and Literature

Learning to Learn

Jot down a few facts you remember from the article about the diversity of life forms on Earth. The author calls the vast amount of life species on our planet a *Living Treasure*. Think of another good title for the selection that reflects your opinion.

Talk About Reading

Talk with other students about *Living Treasure*. Assign a group leader to keep everyone focused and a group secretary to take notes. Then use the questions below to guide your conversation.

1. **Connect to Your Life** How does Pringle's information about the hidden world of life forms relate to your own physical environment? What kinds of life forms did Pringle mention that you were unaware of before?

2. **Active Reading Strategies: Summarize** In your own words, what is the main point the author tries to get across to readers in *Living Treasure*?

3. **6+1 Trait®: Conventions** How do you think your experience of reading the article would change if the author had been careless about his spelling and punctuation?

4. **Connect to Your Writing** After reading this selection, what kinds of evidence do you find compelling in an informational article? Make a list of criteria for good evidence that you can call upon when you write papers of your own.

Write About Reading

Review Write a review of *Living Treasure*. Tell whether you found the writing interesting and compelling and why or why not. Be sure to back up your opinions with evidence.

Focus on Conventions Your review will be more credible if you quote the text. Be sure you use quotation marks correctly. Proofread your writing carefully and correct any errors in grammar, usage, punctuation, and spelling.

For more information on conventions and the 6+1 Trait® model, see **Writing and Research Handbook,** pages 822–824.

6+1 Trait® is a registered trademark of Northwest Regional Educational Laboratory, which does not endorse this product.

Reflecting on the Unit: Summarize What You Learned

Focus on the following questions to help summarize what you learned in this unit.

1 What are the characteristics of strong expository writing?

2 What is the purpose of cause-and-effect writing?

3 How can you organize information for comparison and contrast?

4 What prewriting activities are usually necessary for a report?

5 What elements strengthen expository writing?

Adding to Your Portfolio

CHOOSE A SELECTION FOR YOUR PORTFOLIO Look over the writing you did for this unit. Choose a piece of writing for your portfolio. The writing you choose should show one or more of the following:

- clearly stated ideas supported by facts, statistics, or examples

- a sensible order in explanations or instructions

- charts, diagrams, or pictures that clearly show step-by-step activities, spatial relationships, or comparisons

- information based on close observation, careful research, or interesting interviews

- clear presentation of cause-and-effect relationships among events

REFLECT ON YOUR CHOICE Attach a note to the piece you chose, explaining briefly why you chose it, and what you learned from writing it.

SET GOALS How can you improve your writing? What skill will you focus on the next time you write?

Writing Across the Curriculum

MAKE A SOCIAL STUDIES CONNECTION Find out about your city or town history, landmarks, historic buildings, or parks. Choose one topic, and find out about it by doing research and interviews. You may want to work with a few classmates. Think of interesting ways to share your discoveries with your class or with an unfamiliar audience, such as city officials or town residents.

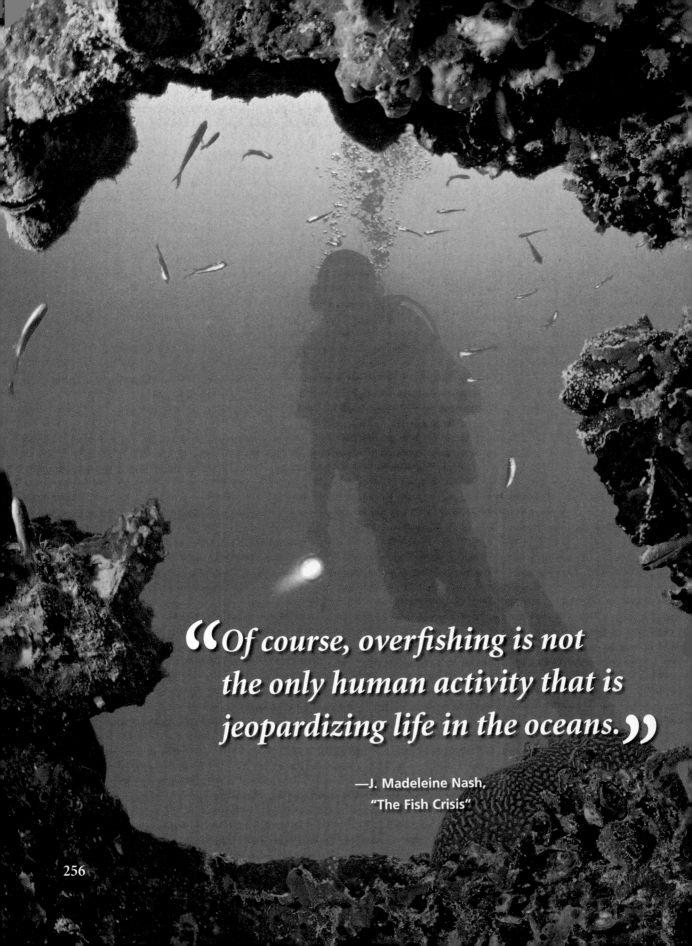

**Of course, overfishing is not the only human activity that is jeopardizing life in the oceans.**

—J. Madeleine Nash,
"The Fish Crisis"

Persuasive Writing

Writing in the Real World

MEDIA Connection · Persuasive Speech

Dr. Benjamin Carson is a world-famous children's brain surgeon. He's also a powerful, persuasive speaker. Carson takes time out from his medical work to talk to kids about success and the value of reading. He urges students to read books rather than to watch television. In the following excerpt, Carson underscores this point by relating an example from his own youth.

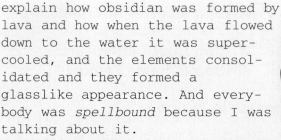

Carson Delivers a Wake-Up Call

by Dr. Benjamin S. Carson

"One day we were in science class, and the science teacher held up a dark, glassy rock. He said, 'Does anybody know what this is?'. . . I knew what it was because I'd been reading about this stuff, so I put my hand up. And I said, 'That's obsidian.' And the teacher said, 'That's right. That *is* obsidian.' And then I went on to explain how obsidian was formed by lava and how when the lava flowed down to the water it was super-cooled, and the elements consolidated and they formed a glasslike appearance. And everybody was *spellbound* because I was talking about it.

"For the first time, I could see in my classmates' eyes a look of admiration. This was a totally new experience for me; and I said, 'I like this; I can deal with this.' From that point on, I couldn't get enough to read."

A Writer's Process

Prewriting
Forming a Position

Like all persuasive speakers, Carson has taken a stand on an important issue. He believes that by turning off the television and by reading, reading, reading, any student can become a winner.

Carson bases his position on the facts and experiences of his life. When Carson was ten years old, he was in trouble. He didn't care about school. But Carson's mother came up with a plan to change all that. She told her children they could watch only two or three television shows a week. In their free time, they had to read two library books and give her a book report on each one.

Carson went along grumpily at first. But he quickly saw results. In a year and a half, he zoomed to the top of his class. He knew he was on his way.

From these and later experiences, Carson developed his position on reading. "The key thing about reading is what it does for the mind," he says. "I liken the mind to a muscle, which becomes flabby and weak if it's not used. Yet, if you use it frequently, it becomes firm and enlarged and very powerful.

"Reading," he says, "demands that you use your mind to make sense of words, sentences, and ideas. It makes you into a literate person who can express ideas."

Why is this important? "You have a great deal more confidence when you know you can express something," Carson says. "You probably know two people who have seen the same thing; one knows how to express himself and the other doesn't. That becomes a pattern through life. Clearly, the person who is able to state a position will be seen as the brighter individual. When it comes time for opportunities to be granted, the person who can express himself will almost always be chosen."

Drafting
Organizing the Case

To persuade people of another point of view, speakers like Carson often organize evidence into strong arguments. An example, such as Carson's personal story, is one form of persuasive evidence. Carson begins his story by describing his mother's reading plan and his journey into

Writing in the Real World

the world of the mind. He started reading about animals and plants. Soon he became fascinated by rocks.

Carson often continues his personal story by relating the school incident in the excerpt on page 258. His classmates' admiration for his knowledge is a convincing element in the anecdote.

Why does Carson tell a personal story in a persuasive speech? "People can remember stories and the points they make," he explains. In addition, Carson can form a bond with the audience by telling stories from his own life. I want to make it very clear that I had the very same experiences these students have had. Then they can say, 'This guy clearly knows what he's talking about. He's clearly been where I am or have been and is where I'd like to be in the future.'"

Carson adds, "I also need for them to understand that knowledge is power, not only in the eyes of teachers, but in the eyes of their friends. It's not a thing to be ashamed of."

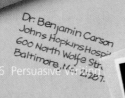

Mountains of letters from young students all around the world are evidence of Dr. Carson's ability to persuade.

Presenting
Telling the Story

Some persuasive writers and speakers are tempted to try too hard to make their points. They may speak too loudly or too expressively, thus failing to connect with the audience. Carson never falls into this trap. In making his presentation, Carson speaks softly and honestly, never preaching or raising his voice. Yet, his ideas and his tone help change students' minds.

"This way of speaking is effective because students believe the story is true," he says. "That's the bottom line. This is real. This is not made up in Hollywood. The fact that students can identify with me makes them believe success is possible for them, too."

Carson's story is powerful medicine. "I get tons of letters all the time, and almost everywhere I go people come up to me and say they've heard me or seen me," Carson says.

Schools in California, Texas, and other states have also started Ben Carson Reading Clubs—and the clubs work. An eighth-grade club member said to Carson one day, "Because I didn't read, I thought I was kind of dumb. Now I know better."

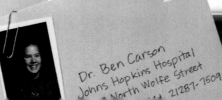

Analyzing the Media Connection

Discuss these questions about the speech excerpt on page 258.

1. Do you think the incident related in the excerpt effectively persuades listeners of the value of reading? Explain.

2. Carson could have cited statistics about poor reading scores instead of telling a story about his reading experience. Which evidence do you think would be more persuasive to his audience? Why?

3. How did Carson's classmates react when he started talking about obsidian? Why do you think Carson mentioned his classmates' reaction?

4. Dr. Carson's message is serious, but the tone of his speech is informal. Cite examples of Carson's informal style. Why do you think he adopts this tone?

Analyzing a Writer's Process

Discuss these questions about Carson's speeches and writing.

1. Every persuasive writer or speaker needs to state his or her opinion or stand on an issue. On what issue has Dr. Ben Carson taken a stand?

2. Where does Carson find the evidence to back up his position?

3. What is Carson's presentation style? Why is it effective?

4. How does Ben Carson know that his speeches are persuasive?

Grammar*Link*

Use a comma to separate main clauses joined by a coordinating conjunction.

"One day we were in science class, and the science teacher held up a dark, glassy rock."

Write each sentence, using commas correctly.

1. Alice is thirteen and her sister is ten.

2. Nelson will leave now but he will be back after lunch.

3. Chris will earn money babysitting or she will start a pet-walking service.

4. All of my friends are going to the concert and we plan to meet afterward.

See Unit 7, page 304.

Ben Carson Reading Club

THINK BIG

Unleashing Your Potential For Excellence

Ben Carson, M.D.

LESSON 6.1

Using Persuasive Writing

When you feel strongly about something, you may try to get others to think or act in a particular way. The model below, part of an advertisement by an animal-protection group, tries to persuade the reader to help save dolphins.

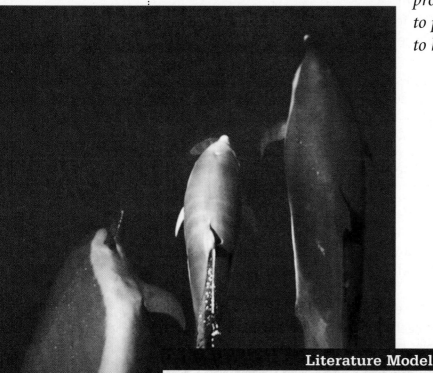

Literature Model

The ancient Greeks respected the dolphins for their kindness and intelligence. In fact, it was a crime punishable by death to harm or kill a dolphin. Today, though, over 100,000 dolphins are being needlessly killed every year, caught by tuna fishermen and driftnets.

Together we saved over 50,000 dolphins last year. But hundreds of thousands are still endangered. You can make the difference. Please join us.

Write us for further information and for a list of dolphin-safe tuna brands.

The Dolphin Project, Earth Island Institute

What exactly does the writer want you to do?

Do You Agree?

Persuasive writing can urge you to agree with the writer's opinions. Persuasive writing can also call you to action. For example, the Dolphin Project wants readers to agree that using driftnets harms dolphins. The organization wants people to help by buying only tuna that has been caught without the use of driftnets.

Read the two statements below. Think about the writer's purpose in making each.

What does the writer want you to do?

Join the Ten-Mile Walkathon, and walk to preserve our city's parks.

A vegetarian diet is the most healthful and most humane way to eat.

What two words do you think carry the writer's message most clearly?

Persuasive writers choose words carefully for their effects on readers. When you read persuasive writing, think about the special words and phrases the writer uses to persuade you.

Journal Writing

Find a newspaper or a magazine advertisement that makes you think about buying the item advertised. In your journal jot down the words that help persuade you that you might want to buy the item. Explain why these words appeal to you.

Presenting Tip

Consider the different forms in which you can present your persuasive statement, such as an ad, an editorial, a video, or a speech.

Look Around You

Magazines, newspapers, books, posters, letters, television programs—almost anything you read, see, or hear can include persuasion. All of these forms of persuasion try to get the reader, viewer, or listener to agree or to take action. What might an ad for a new cereal try to persuade you to do? What action would an editorial on sun exposure encourage you to take?

The illustration below shows everyday sources of persuasion. Those sources, which are labeled, range from written to oral to visual. As you look at the illustration, picture a room in your house, your school, or another place where you spend time. What sources of persuasion can you find there?

Sources of Persuasion

Poster

Television

Newspaper

Book

Advertisement

Radio   Magazine

Create a Poster

Create a poster advertising a fund-raising event to help homeless people. Try to convince people in your neighborhood to attend your fund-raiser, which may be a car wash, bake sale, or charity auction. Choose words that will motivate your readers.

PURPOSE To persuade readers to attend a fund-raising event

AUDIENCE Local adults and teenagers

LENGTH 3–5 lines

WRITING RUBRICS To write an effective advertisement, you should

- address people's strong beliefs
- choose words that will persuade
- appeal to the readers' emotions

Cross-Curricular Activity

RUNNING FOR STUDENT OFFICE Meet with a small group of classmates to plan an imaginary campaign for president of your class. Decide who in your group will be the candidate, and then brainstorm ideas for a brief statement to use in the campaign. Use words that will catch readers' attention. Discuss how persuasive each statement is. Finally, choose which statement you will use for the campaign.

GrammarLink

Use strong adjectives to create impact.

A **vegetarian** diet is the most **healthful** and most **humane** way to eat.

Complete the sentences below with strong adjectives.

1. The _____ man sat beside his _____ car.
2. If you are a _____ person, you must speak out against this _____ practice.
3. National parks offer _____ and _____ places to visit.
4. The special effects in her new film were _____.
5. Lashed by the _____ winds of the storm, the _____ waves crashed against the shore.

See Lesson 12.1, page 451.

Viewing and Representing

With your group, create a bulletin board display to present your candidate and his or her persuasive statement. Include original drawings, magazine illustrations, or other visuals of your choice that will help persuade your audience to vote for your candidate.

LOG ON ▶ **Writing** Online | For more writing and grammar practice, go to glencoe.com and enter QuickPass code WC77680p1.

265

LESSON 6.2

Forming an Opinion

People offer opinions on everything. We're always trying to persuade one another about something. Not all efforts to persuade are serious. In the model below, notice how Andy Rooney expresses his opinion of cats.

I ♥ MY BEAGLE

Pets' Rights

Literature Model

Cats Are for the Birds

I have never met a cat I liked. As an animal lover, I'm constantly disappointed with myself when there's a cat around.

Don't think I haven't tried to love cats, because I have. I always try to win their affection or, at the very least, try to establish some sort of relationship. Nothing. A cat will walk on my lap, jump on a table next to me where my host has put a dish of corn chips, or rub against my pants, but there is never any warmth in the cat's gesture.

"He likes you," the host will say.

Well, if those cats I've met like me, they have a plenty strange way of showing it. If I got the kind of affection from the people I like that I get from cats whose owners think they like me, I'd leave home.

Andy Rooney, *Not That You Asked . . .*

What does the writer think of cats?

Do you agree or disagree with the writer's opinion? Why?

What's Your Topic?

When searching for a topic, explore experiences from your daily life that inspire strong opinions. You can brainstorm and make a mental list. You can also freewrite. Write names of people, places, or things, and jot down your thoughts about each. Freewrite for about ten minutes to see where your writing leads you. Whether you brainstorm or freewrite, look at what you have noted, and ask yourself what you feel strongly enough about to use as a topic.

Journal entries also can help you find a topic. Sometimes just reading your entries will remind you of something about which you have a strong opinion. The example shows how the writer has circled possible topics.

Before making a final decision about your topic, look at each possibility. Then ask yourself the questions below.

> The only things I wanted for my birthday were my own phone and a job at the mall. I know I'm too young for a job, and Mom doesn't want to get me a phone. Still, the day wasn't a total loss. I heard about a program that trains teen-age babysitters, and now I'm old enough to sign up.

	Questions for Choosing a Topic
1	Is this a topic that makes me feel strongly?
2	Is this a topic that has more than one side, a topic on which people might disagree?
3	Do I have enough to say about this topic to persuade others to accept my position?

Journal Writing

Look through your journal for two or three possible persuasive-writing topics. Then use the questions in the chart to decide which one will work best for you.

Prewriting Tip

In the prewriting stage, brainstorm a list of strong words that apply to your topic. You can then refer to your list when you draft and when you revise.

Decide Where You Stand

Once you have a topic, think about your position on it. Sometimes when you learn more about a topic, your position on it changes. Other times you may discover that your opinion is similar to everyone else's. Exploring a topic helps you discover whether it's suitable for a writing project.

You can use a chart like the one below to explore your persuasive-writing topic. List the pros—reasons why people might agree with your opinion. Then list the cons—reasons why they might disagree with you. A pro-and-con chart can help you organize your thoughts, make your opinion clearer, and help you determine why or how others might argue against your opinion.

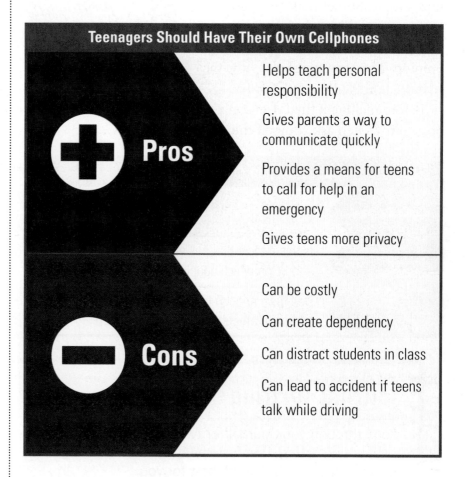

Teenagers Should Have Their Own Cellphones

Pros
- Helps teach personal responsibility
- Gives parents a way to communicate quickly
- Provides a means for teens to call for help in an emergency
- Gives teens more privacy

Cons
- Can be costly
- Can create dependency
- Can distract students in class
- Can lead to accident if teens talk while driving

Write a Paragraph

Suppose that people want to build a road through an unspoiled forest. The road will connect two cities, making travel and business between the cities easier. But it will also alter the area's natural beauty. What opinion do you have about this proposed construction? Brainstorm or freewrite to explore ideas. Write a paragraph to explain why you support one position or the other.

PURPOSE To clarify and explore an opinion
AUDIENCE Yourself
LENGTH 1 paragraph

WRITING RUBRICS To write a persuasive paragraph, you should

- make a chart showing pros and cons
- state your opinion clearly
- show that you have considered both sides of the issue

GrammarLink

Use correct pronoun forms in compound constructions.

You often need to choose between *I* and *me* in a compound construction.
  Ann and I differ.
To choose correctly, say the sentence with just the pronoun:
  I differ.

Write each sentence with the correct form: *I* or *me.*

[1] The cat was examining Josh and _____.[2] Josh and _____ agree on most things.[3] On cats, however, there is a big difference between Josh and _____ .[4] A room with a cat and _____ in it is too full. [5] Either the cat or _____ must go.
See Lesson 11.3, page 433.

Listening and Speaking

PRESENT A POINT OF VIEW Read to the class or to a small group your paragraph about the proposed road. Listen and respond to the opinions of those who agree and disagree with you.

Cross-Curricular Activity

HISTORY Choose a time in the United States' past when you might like to have lived. After making a chart detailing the pros and cons of living at that time, determine whether your opinion is still the same. Write a few paragraphs persuading the reader of your viewpoint.

LOG ON ▶ **Writing** Online | For more writing and grammar practice, go to **glencoe.com** and enter QuickPass code WC77680p1.

269

Gathering Evidence

How do you get permission to do something new and different? One way may be to write a proposal. Proposals need evidence to support them.

Suppose that you and your classmates want to use your school's public-address system to broadcast music. The music would be heard only in nonclassroom areas and only before school and during breaks between classes.

You already know your audience—teachers and administrators. Your goal is to convince them that a student-run music service is a good idea, one that they should seriously consider. One way to do this is to write a proposal in which you state what you want your audience to think and do, and then give reasons, or evidence, to back up your argument.

Find Support for Your Argument

In your proposal you should clearly state your position, or your opinion. One way to build an argument is to list reasons to support your opinion. Your list of pros and cons is a good source of reasons. The next step then is to gather evidence to support your reasons. The evidence consists of the facts, statistics, and examples that prove your argument. See the chart below for an explanation of three types of evidence. You may use any or all types in your argument. Your evidence should be presented in a logical way. It must offer a reasonable or sensible explanation in order to be convincing.

Persuasive Writing

Types of Evidence		
Type	**Definition**	**Example**
Fact	something that can be proven	The school already has the equipment needed for a music broadcast.
Statistic	fact expressed in numbers	A school poll shows that 84 percent of students are in favor of a music broadcast.
Example	particular instance or event	Two other schools in our area have similar broadcasts.

Test your argument to discover possible arguments against it. List the pros and cons to discover any weak links or places where your evidence is unconvincing. Decide how to strengthen any weaknesses you discover.

Journal Writing

Write about the last time you tried to convince someone to agree with you. Describe the position you took. List any evidence that you used, or could have used, to support your argument. Which piece of evidence do you think is the strongest? Explain why.

Consider Your Audience

To be effective in persuasion, you must choose a format that suits your audience. In the case of the proposal for music in school, for example, a newspaper editorial would be less successful than a written proposal.

You also need to think about your audience when you select your evidence. Consider the following questions.

- How much does my audience know and care about my topic?
- What evidence will be most interesting to my readers?
- What evidence will my readers find most convincing?

Notice how David Rauen considered his audience in this model.

Forms of Persuasive Writing
editorials
posters
letters to the editor
book reviews
advertisements
speeches

Student Model

I think wearing uniforms is a bad idea because it brings down the morale of the students. First of all, we feel uncomfortable in the uniforms. The pants are itchy. By the end of the day, our feet hurt from the school shoes. Secondly, wearing uniforms makes us feel like robots. After a few weeks we get tired of seeing the same colors and outfits every day. I believe the students at our school are responsible enough to choose what they wear. I think the principal should let students have a say about the school's uniform policy.

David Rauen, Hope Lutheran School
Chicago, Illinois

What evidence does he use to persuade his audience?

Write a Proposal

Suppose that you want to start a business, such as designing jewelry. First, though, you must persuade a relative or friend to lend you money. Gather some persuasive evidence, and write a short proposal to present.

PURPOSE To obtain a loan for your business
AUDIENCE An adult who might lend you money
LENGTH 1–2 paragraphs

WRITING RUBRICS To write an effective proposal, you should

- state your position clearly
- use a variety of evidence to support your position
- make sure your evidence suits your audience

Nancy Holt, *Sun Tunnels*, 1973–1976

GrammarLink

Use *good, better,* and *best* and *bad, worse,* and *worst* correctly.

*I think wearing uniforms is a **bad** idea...*

Rewrite each sentence, correcting errors in the use of adjectives.

1 Juan's was a more good song than Pat's. **2** It was the most good song in the concert. **3** Bob's outburst was the baddest moment. **4** It was more bad behavior than LaVerne's. **5** Too bad—he's the most good singer in school.
See Lesson 12.3, page 455.

Cross-Curricular Activity

ART The concrete tunnel shown here is one of four placed in the Utah desert by the artist. Each tunnel measures eighteen feet in length and more than nine feet in diameter. In the upper half of each tunnel, the artist cut holes in the pattern of various constellations. As the sun shines through these holes, light in the tunnel changes constantly.

Listening and Speaking

With a small group, discuss why an artist would place tunnels in the desert. Assess one another's arguments and presentations.

 **Writing** Online | For more writing and grammar practice, go to **glencoe.com** and enter QuickPass code WC77680p1.

273

Developing an Argument

In order to persuade, you must catch and hold the attention of your audience. Read how violinist Itzhak Perlman does that.

Persuasive Writing

Literature Model

I've been in public buildings throughout the world, and it's clear that the people who design them have no idea what it feels like to use crutches or sit in a wheelchair. One of the great architectural catastrophes of all time, from the point of view of any concertgoer, much less one who is disabled, is the Sydney Opera House in Sydney, Australia. A design contest was held and the winner was an architect who had conceived a truly fantastic-looking place with about a hundred steps leading to the entrance. There is no elevator—not for the general public, not for the poor musicians who have to lug instruments up all those stairs, and certainly not for the disabled. Why couldn't the prize have been given to the best design that was also barrier-free? Why, when it's possible to make *everyone* comfortable, is so little attention paid to accessibility?

Itzhak Perlman, "To Help the
Handicapped, Talk to Them"
Glamour, March 1987

> What change does the writer want? What evidence does he use to support his position?

State Your Position

A key statement in persuasive writing is the sentence that tells what you want your audience to do or think. Typically, a topic sentence, which may appear either at the beginning or at the end of your opening paragraph will contain that statement. Note that Perlman begins with a clearly focused topic sentence and gives strong evidence to support the opinion it expresses.

Where is the topic sentence in each paragraph?

The Whitebridge movie complex should have an entrance ramp. It has twelve theaters, four concession stands, and video games. You can see any movie, eat any snack, or play any game you want — if you can walk up a flight of stairs.

The other day my friend Tiffany and I went to Lily's Snacks. Tiffany uses a wheelchair to get around. I was shocked to realize that she couldn't come in with me. There are three steps to the door but no ramp. Why isn't Lily's accessible to everyone?

Revising Tip

In the revising stage, make sure you have organized your persuasive writing in a sensible way.

Journal Writing

Imagine a place you could not visit because of a disability. How would you feel about that place? What would you do to change it? Write a brief statement of your opinion, including a clear topic sentence and evidence that supports your proposal for change.

Organize Your Argument

The structure of a persuasive piece can resemble the three-part structure of a report. The introduction states the topic and your opinion on it. The body provides evidence to support your opinion. The conclusion summarizes your argument and suggests action.

To make your persuasive writing effective, place your most convincing evidence where it best supports your point. Your argument may work best when you present the strongest evidence first. At other times, putting the strongest evidence last will be more effective. Notice how Justin Pinegar introduces his topic and gets his opinion across.

Grammar Tip

Make sure that all your sentences express complete thoughts. To review the rules for sentences and fragments, see Lesson 8.2, page 359.

Tips for Structuring a Persuasive Piece

1	Decide how to arrange your evidence.
2	Write a strong opening that states your position.
3	Present all your supporting evidence in the best order.
4	Sum up your argument, and give your conclusions.

Student Model

How does Justin draw his audience into his argument?

Imagine that it is the year 2080. You are walking through a forest, when you see a five-legged frog jump out of a pool of orange and green water. Suddenly you realize that this is the first animal life you've seen on your walk. You are seeing one of the effects of toxic waste, caused by a world that relied too much on technology. Although many machines serve good purposes, we are relying too much on technology to solve our problems. We need to moderate technology now, before it is too late.

Justin Pinegar, Frontier Junior High School
Moses Lake, Washington

Write an Editorial

Consider what could be done with a large donation to your school. New sports equipment? Software? A new student lounge? Draft an editorial for the school newspaper to convince readers of your opinion.

PURPOSE To persuade others
AUDIENCE Students and teachers
LENGTH 1–2 paragraphs

WRITING RUBRICS To write an effective editorial, you should

- write a clear topic sentence
- organize your argument with an introduction, body, and conclusion
- present your evidence in a convincing order

Listening and Speaking

EVALUATE EDITORIALS With a small group, read aloud the editorials you wrote. Assess whether one another's arguments are convincing.

Cross-Curricular Activity

MUSIC Imagine that you are a musician in the 1800s, just before women were allowed to play in some orchestras. Write a letter trying to persuade a conductor to let female musicians perform in his orchestra.

GrammarLink

Use variety in your sentence structures.

One way to achieve variety is to use interrogative, imperative, and exclamatory sentences, as well as declarative ones.

Why isn't Lily's accessible to everyone?

Another technique is to use varied beginnings for your sentences.

Although many machines serve good purposes, *we are relying too much on technology to solve our problems.*

Revise the passage below, using varied kinds of sentences and varied sentence beginnings.

[1] You should now pretend that it is the year 1775. [2] You live on a small farm in the colony of Pennsylvania. [3] You are in favor of independence from England, but your father is against it. [4] A recruiter comes by, asking you to join a colonial army that will eventually fight the British. [5] You should now think about what you will do.

See Lesson 2.8, page 74, and Lesson 8.1, page 357.

LOG ON ▶ **Writing** Online For more writing and grammar practice, go to glencoe.com and enter QuickPass code WC77680p1.

277

Persuasive Writing

Polishing an Argument

All good writing deserves a second look. In persuasive writing, always double check your ideas.

The draft of your persuasive writing probably contains many solid ideas. But just as with any other writing, you should review your draft to be sure it makes sense. You want your argument not only to grab your readers' attention but also to hold it. If the argument lacks convincing evidence and sensible connections between ideas, your audience will feel confused and may lose interest in your topic. Review and revise your persuasive composition to keep it interesting and focused.

Look at the Big Picture

When you begin to revise your writing, look first at the big picture, the whole argument. Ask yourself, Have I stated my argument clearly and supported it with evidence? One way to answer this question is to have a classmate evaluate your writing. The draft below shows how one writer revised her work after a peer reviewer evaluated it.

Here are some questions that will help you evaluate your own and others' persuasive writing:

- Is the position stated clearly?
- Does the introduction grab attention?
- Is the evidence persuasive, and is it in the best order?
- Is enough evidence included?

Sally Lu should win the Student Community Service Award. Her efforts have helped bring the people in our community closer together. She started the Chinese-to-English Program to help Chinese children new to our area learn English. ~~She is a winning baseball and tennis player.~~ She also arranged a Get-Acquainted Night to bring the Chinese community into contact with other area groups. Vote for Sally Lu.

> Why did the peer reviewer suggest removing this sentence?

> What does this sentence add to the paragraph?

Journal Writing

Look at some editorials from your school newspaper or another local paper. Use the questions above to evaluate one of them. Note your evaluation in your journal.

Choose Strong Words

When you write to persuade, the words you choose are very important. Think about which bike ad makes you more likely to buy:

It's a great bike—and cheap, too!

It's the bike used by professional cyclists—and it doesn't cost a fortune!

Aim for strong words and phrases that grab your readers' attention. Look at the word changes made in this draft.

> **How do these changes affect the writing?**

David Lopez is ~~a good~~ *the most qualified* candidate for class president. He gets ~~good~~ *high* grades, and *both students and* teachers ~~like him. Students too.~~ *trust* He ~~belongs to~~ *takes part in* several school clubs: Theater Club, Chess Club, and Woodworking Club. He *also* plays on the basketball team. *Above all* He wants to make our school a better place for students and teachers.

What other words might the writer have used for *good* candidate? Why is *trust* a more effective word than *like* in this situation? Why is *takes part* more effective than *belongs to*?

The most effective test for the words you choose is your audience. If you wanted to persuade your parents to allow you to wait all night in line for tickets to a concert, you might use very different words than if you wanted to persuade one of your friends to wait with you.

Create a Leaflet

Think of an environmental concern. It could be the thinning of the ozone layer, the pollution of the ocean, or another problem. Consider the evidence you will need to persuade your classmates to take action. To present your argument, use persuasive writing in a leaflet that informs, as well as persuades. Then draft and revise your text.

PURPOSE To persuade people to take action on an environmental issue

AUDIENCE Your classmates

LENGTH 1–2 paragraphs

WRITING RUBRICS To write persuasively in a leaflet, you should

- state and support your position clearly
- arrange ideas in an order that suits your audience
- include enough evidence
- use attention-grabbing words

Using Computers

As you revise your leaflet for effective word choice, you might use your computer's thesaurus. The thesaurus suggests synonyms, words of similar meaning. Identify any words in your draft that you want to replace. Then look in the thesaurus for synonyms that may be more precise.

GrammarLink

Capitalize proper nouns and adjectives.

Capitalize the names of ethnic groups and nationalities. Also capitalize the name of languages and the adjectives formed from these words.

She started the Chinese-to-English Program to help Chinese children new to our area learn English.

Write each item, correcting errors in capitalization.

1. You must learn to speak Spanish.
2. Hillary traveled to rome when she was studying italian art.
3. Is polish a slavic language?
4. She is irish, so her ancestors may have spoken celtic.
5. I'll have the greek salad.

See Lesson 19.4, page 579.

Viewing and Representing

MAKE A FOOD POSTER Find pictures of a variety of foods from one country. Clip the pictures from magazines or download them from the Internet. Use them to make a poster advertising that country's cuisine. Accompany each picture with a brief description of the dish portrayed.

LOG ON ▶ **Writing** Online | For more writing and grammar practice, go to glencoe.com and enter QuickPass code WC77680p1.

281

Writing Publicity

*P*ublicity includes posters, radio ads, flyers, and other printed or spoken forms of persuasion. If you want to get the word out about an event or cause, publicize it.

Suppose that a band you're in is planning a concert. You could put announcements and advertisements on local radio shows and public-access television channels. You might make posters and display them all over town. You might also submit an article about your group to a local paper.

By the time the concert takes place, everyone in town will know about it. That's the result of good publicity.

Get Noticed

The first goal of publicity writing is to capture the attention of your audience. A striking image on a poster can make someone stop and stare. A short, snappy slogan on a flyer can invite someone to read. Think about any posters, flyers, leaflets, or other forms of publicity you've seen recently. What images or language made you notice them?

Publicity should ❶ get attention ❷ include all important information ❸ get results

When you plan to write publicity, you must think about your purpose. Decide what message you want to convey. Then think about your audience—the people whom you hope to convince. Once you have your purpose and audience in mind, consider what kind of language will most likely appeal to your audience. You should present all the necessary information in as few words as possible. Remember, too, that images can also be used to gain attention and convey meaning. Think about how your words can work with the images you use. You want your audience to understand your idea very quickly and react positively to it.

Grammar Tip

Check spelling and capitalization carefully when you edit. Because posters use few words, any mistakes stand out. To review capitalization guidelines, see Lessons 19.2–19.4, pages 575–580.

Journal Writing

Look through recent newspapers and magazines. Clip any especially eye-catching photographs or drawings. Tape or paste these images into your journal. Jot down ideas for persuasive statements to go with the images. One of the images may inspire a poster or another kind of publicity.

Post Your Message

Posters can be vivid, effective attention grabbers for some audiences. A poster could be the perfect way to persuade people to attend a school play or to recycle cans and bottles. This illustration shows four different uses for posters.

Uses for Posters

KAREN JONES
CLASS PRESIDENT
Get votes.

LOST
KAYO
123-4567
Find a lost pet.

CIRCUS
Advertise an event.

Support Our Band
Explain a cause.

Keeping your purpose in mind will help you decide what information to include on your poster. A poster announcing a lost pet, for example, needs certain information. You will want to have your pet's name, a picture or description, and any other important characteristics, such as whether it answers to its name and whether it likes strangers. In addition, be sure to provide your own name and phone number. Don't forget other special information, such as whether you are offering a reward.

Write an Advertisement

Think of how you might advertise a circus coming to town. Decide which form of publicity you will use—a poster, a leaflet, a flyer, or another form. Then write a persuasive advertisement.

PURPOSE To call attention to an event
AUDIENCE Adults and children
LENGTH 1–2 paragraphs

WRITING RUBRICS To create an effective advertisement, you should

- include a slogan or image that will get attention
- consider your purpose and audience
- include all necessary information

Cross-Curricular Activity

GEOGRAPHY Travel brochures try to lure people to visit certain places. With your group, design a brochure for a large, exciting city. Brainstorm the information you want to include. Divide up the tasks of researching information and visuals.

Then draft and lay out the visuals. Revise, edit, and place visuals so your brochure will be persuasive and appealing. Share your brochure with other groups.

GrammarLink

Use apostrophes in possessive nouns.

*Get a **viewer's** attention.*
*Get **people's** attention.*
*Get **customers'** attention.*

The text below is from a poster. Write each item, adding apostrophes where necessary.

1. Come hear great music at the citys benefit concert.
2. Listen to the beat of the musicians in the Top Bananas numbers.
3. Thrill to the sound of Tracy Westons songs.
4. Then comes the combined choruses performance.
5. These mens and womens voices will amaze you.

See Lesson 20.7, page 601.

Listening and Speaking

BE AN ANNOUNCER Pretend that you are the radio or television announcer who reads aloud the circus advertisement. Be as dramatic as you think appropriate.

Writing a Letter of Complaint

The most effective complaints often include positive suggestions.

NO SMOKING

SECTION

Sometimes it is not possible to do anything about an annoying situation at the time it takes place, but you may be able to do something later.

In the model below, Julia Mendoza writes a letter of complaint. Notice that she includes a constructive suggestion for a solution to the problem.

Student Model

Dear Sir or Madam:

My friends and I ate at El Jardín last Friday evening, and it upset us to find that your restaurant does not have a No Smoking section. The people at the tables on either side of us were smoking. Because the air around our table was full of smoke, we found it impossible to enjoy our dinner. We had to breathe the smoke, which is dangerous as well as unpleasant.

I suggest that you set aside one section of your restaurant as a smoking area. That way, customers who do not smoke will find it possible to enjoy your good food in a clean, smoke-free environment.

Sincerely,

Julia Mendoza

Julia Mendoza

What is the writer's complaint?

What solution does the writer suggest?

Draft Your Letter

A letter of complaint has the same purpose as other kinds of persuasive writing. A letter of complaint states the problem, explains the circumstances, and proposes a reasonable solution.

Letters of complaint follow the form of any business letter.

Heading: your address and the date

Inside address: the name and address of the person to whom you are writing

Greeting: begins with "Dear" and includes the name of the person to whom you are writing, followed by a colon

Closing: final words of the letter, such as "Sincerely," followed by a comma

Body: explains the problem and suggests a solution

Signature: your signed name, followed by your typed name.

71 Union Street
Tempe, AZ 85281
October 17, 200–

Sergeant Samuel Kincaid
Precinct 4
1106 Fortieth Street
Tempe, AZ 85281

Dear Sergeant Kincaid:

I want to call your attention to the dangerous intersection at Oak Street and First Avenue. Yesterday my younger sister was almost hit by a car speeding through the intersection. Because there are stop signs only on Oak Street, many drivers drive too fast through the intersection.

Would you please look into this problem? Perhaps stop signs can be placed on the First Avenue corners.

Sincerely,

Peter Raymond

Peter Raymond

Journal Writing

Think of something you would like to have changed. State the problem, explain it, and offer a reasonable solution. You may feel strongly enough to draft, revise, edit, and then send an actual letter. If your letter is handwritten, be sure to write legibly.

Grammar Tip

As you edit your letter, check that verb tenses agree with special subjects, such as business names. To review subject-verb agreement for special subjects, see Lesson 16.3, page 539.

Make a Good Impression

Think how you might react if you got a letter that was threatening, rude, or insulting. You probably wouldn't want to help the writer, even if some emotion was justified. When you write a letter of complaint, remember that your purpose is to use language that will persuade the reader to take action, not become angry. Notice the difference in language in the sentences below. How would you react to each approach?

Using Appropriate Language	
Inappropriate	**Appropriate**
I waited all day in the rain for concert tickets only to find that you stupid people advertised more tickets than you really had. I'll never use your ticket service again!	Your ad led me to believe that there would be plenty of tickets for next week's concert. I suggest that in the future you correctly advertise the number of tickets available.

In any letter of complaint, your explanation of the problem and your proposed solution should be clear, easy to follow, and reasonable. The overall impression of your letter should be businesslike and organized, as it is in the model that follows.

Student Model

What is the writer's complaint?

What solution does she offer for the problem?

For years I have been a content subscriber to *Outdoor Adventures,* but recently I have not been pleased. Neither the July nor the August issue has been delivered to my home.

I am writing to request that you deliver these issues when you deliver the September edition of the magazine. Thank you for your time.

Laurie Hedlund, Springman Junior High School
Glenview, Illinois

Write a Complaint Letter

Have you ever bought an item, used it once, and found it didn't work or that it broke entirely? Write a complaint letter to the manufacturer to express your disappointment.

PURPOSE To complain about a faulty product
AUDIENCE The manufacturer of the product
LENGTH 1–2 paragraphs

WRITING RUBRICS To write an effective complaint letter, you should

- state the problem, explain what happened, and propose a solution
- use language that will persuade, not anger
- make sure your argument is clear and easy to follow
- include the six parts of a business letter shown on page 287

Using Computers

When you write a letter of complaint to the government, you can increase its effect by sending it to more than one official. Use the merge function to insert the different names and addresses into the body of the letter.

Listening and Speaking

READING LETTERS ALOUD Exchange letters with a partner and take turns reading the letters aloud. Be dignified; don't overdramatize. Evaluate the effectiveness of the letters.

Grammar*Link*

Use correct capitalization and punctuation in letters.

Capitalize proper nouns and the first word of each sentence. Use commas in dates, between the names of cities and states, and in the closing of the letter.

*71 **U**nion **S**treet*
***T**empe, **AZ** 85281*
***O**ctober 17, 200-*

Write each item, correcting errors in capitalization and punctuation.

1. february 8, 1996
2. senator Della P. Storti
3. United states senate
4. Dirksen office building
5. washington, DC 20510
6. Dear senator storti:
7. Please give the enclosed paper your consideration.
8. I hope that your next vote on this issue is more in line with the views of your one-time supporters.
9.　　　　　　　Sincerely
10.　　　　　　　Calvina Booker

See Lesson 19.3, page 577; Lesson 19.4, page 579; and Lesson 20.4, page 595.

 **Writing** Online   For more writing and grammar practice, go to glencoe.com and enter QuickPass code WC77680p1.

289

WRITING ABOUT LITERATURE

Writing a Movie Review

An effective movie review gives readers enough information to help them decide whether they want to see the film.

"The best movie of the summer!" "I give it four stars!" "A real nail biter. Don't miss this movie!" Some movie reviews make you feel that you have to see the film. Others make you think that you shouldn't bother.

As you read the review that follows, think about how Kimberly Knapp tries to convince you to share her opinion.

Student Model

I enjoyed the movie *Honey, I Shrunk the Kids*. The special effects were very entertaining, especially the scene where the miniature kids rode on insects. I also thought the characters were realistic. In the beginning of the movie, the kids fought with each other. They behaved like real brothers and sisters. The movie had a lesson because at the end the kids had learned to get along with each other.

Kimberly Knapp, Hope Lutheran School
Chicago, Illinois

Does the reviewer convince you that the movie is worth seeing? Why or why not?

Weigh the Elements

A good movie review supports the writer's opinion with judgments about the various elements that make up the movie. (See the chart at right.) When you review a film, first note your overall reaction to it. Then jot down specific examples of characters, plot, acting, and effects that make you feel as you do. Such notes might look like this:

- The characters of the boy and girl were realistic, but the father's actions and words made him cartoonish.
- The plot was complicated, but good characters and smooth writing made it easy to follow.
- The acting was overdone at times. The actors seemed to be trying too hard to show the audience how good they are.
- The visual effects were stunning and realistic. During the stunt flying, I felt as though I were in the plane.
- The background music was pretty boring, but the concert segments were great.

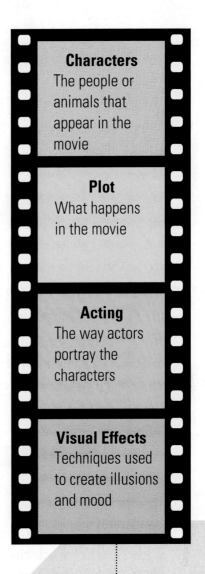

Characters
The people or animals that appear in the movie

Plot
What happens in the movie

Acting
The way actors portray the characters

Visual Effects
Techniques used to create illusions and mood

TIME

For more about the writing process, see **TIME** *Facing the Blank Page*, pp. 97–107.

Journal Writing

Think of a movie you have seen recently that has special effects. In your journal describe how these effects influenced your opinion of the movie.

Drafting Tip

As you draft your review, refer to the notes you took on the movie. They will help you keep the movie fresh in your mind.

Reveal Your Opinion

A reviewer may not always directly state an opinion about a film. Often that opinion is implied, or suggested, by the words and details the reviewer uses. Read the following passage from a review of director George Lucas's movie *Star Wars*.

What does the reviewer think of the film?

What words does the reviewer use to convince you of her opinion?

Literature Model

Lucas's talents lie more in the realm of film technique than film writing. The plot is a simplistic "shoot-em-up" war story of good *versus* evil, with stock characters such as the innocent hero, the beautiful damsel in distress, and the rogue with the heart of gold. The characters are shallow and always overshadowed by the technical aspects of the film and their dialogue is cartoonish and awkward. Although the sparse story line, weak characters, and lack of strong dialogue are obvious flaws, the visual effects are well done and so overwhelming that the impact of the film as a whole is not marred.

Ruth L. Hirayama,
"Star Wars," *Magill's Survey of Cinema*

Write a Review

Think of a movie you have seen recently. Write a review of it for your school newspaper. State your opinion clearly, and back it up with convincing evidence.

PURPOSE To express and support an opinion about a movie

AUDIENCE Readers of school newspaper

LENGTH 1–2 paragraphs

WRITING RUBRICS To write a convincing review, you should

- include enough background information for readers to understand what the movie is about
- use words that reveal your opinion rather than state it directly
- provide evidence that supports your opinion
- comments on the four elements shown on page 291

Listening and Speaking

COOPERATIVE LEARNING In a group of four students, choose a movie that you have all seen. Brainstorm to come up with comments on characters, plot, acting, and effects. Then discuss your group's overall opinion. Combine the group's thoughts into a well-organized oral review of the movie as a whole. Share your review with other groups.

GrammarLink

Use commas to separate items in a series.

If there are three or more items in a series, use a comma after each item except the last.

Although the sparse story line, weak characters, and lack of strong dialogue are obvious flaws . . .

Write each sentence, adding commas where necessary.

1. I thought this movie was a positive romantic charming and believable tale of friendship loyalty and resourcefulness.
2. I have to admit that the settings costumes and props were somewhat disappointing.
3. The director the actors and the producers are inexperienced, but perhaps they will improve.

See Lesson 20.2, page 591.

Viewing and Representing

MAKE A COLLAGE Check in newspapers or on the Internet to find photos from either of the movies you reviewed. Make a collage of the photos. Include comments about each one.

LOG ON **Writing** Online For more writing and grammar practice, go to glencoe.com and enter QuickPass code WC77680p1.

293

Writing Process in Action

Persuasive Writing

In the preceding lessons you've learned about forming an opinion and then gathering evidence to support it. You've also practiced developing and polishing an argument. Now it's time to make use of what you learned. In this lesson you will have the opportunity to argue for the preservation of something important—something that you believe is uniquely and irreplaceably American.

Assignment

Context	Your class is planning to publish one issue of This Is America, a magazine devoted to saving institutions, traditions, and culture that are unique and irreplaceable to the fabric that is America.
Purpose	To convince others through powerful persuasive writing to save something uniquely American
Audience	The readers of This Is America, your classmates, and teacher
Length	3–4 paragraphs

Planning to Write

The following pages can help you plan and write your persuasive piece. Read through them, and then refer to them as you need to. But don't be tied down by them. You're in charge of your own writing process. Be sure to set a time frame to complete this assignment. Always keep in mind the controlling idea: to convince others to save something uniquely American.

Writing
Online

LOG ON

For prewriting, drafting, revising, editing and publishing tools, go to **glencoe.com** and enter QuickPass code WC77680p1.

Prewriting

Try to find a topic that means something to you—one you can support with evidence. The chart on page 267 can help you test topic ideas. You can also use the options at the right.

Lay out your position and gather evidence. Review the chart on page 268 and review pages 270–272.

Option A
Freewrite for ideas.

Option B
Brainstorm with a peer reviewer.

Option C
Explore your journal.

Drafting

First, review pages 62–65. Then let your writing flow to get your argument down on paper. You can go back and fix any problems later.

Use examples to support your argument. In the model below, Kaufman uses a story about herself in her argument about preserving public libraries.

My dream of running for the Hawks next year. Not if the high school can't pay for sports. Photos of Hawk teams since the forties: the same jerseys. What's more American than high school sports?

Literature Model

I remember myself as a 12-year-old, newly arrived from Russia, groping toward the mastery of the English language in my neighborhood library. Guided by no reading lists, informed by no book reviews, I had no use for the card catalogue, since I worked each shelf alphabetically, burrowing my way from one end of the stacks to the other, relentless as a mole. I read by trial and error, through trash and treasure; like a true addict, I was interested not so much in quality as in getting the stuff.

Bel Kaufman, "The Liberry"

Drafting Tip

For more information about structuring a persuasive argument, see Lesson 6.4, pages 274–277.

Revising

To begin revising, read over your draft to make sure that what you have written fits your purpose and your audience. Then have a **writing conference.** Read your draft to a partner or a small group, or receive feedback from your teacher. Use your audience's reactions to help you evaluate your work so far. The questions below can help you and your listeners.

Question A

Is my position stated clearly?

Question B

Does the introduction grab attention?

Question C

Is my evidence in the best and most persuasive order?

polished glass
The pictures appear in the *polished glass* showcases in front of the auditorium. They show the *Ticu City* Hawks track team, *in the same staged pose, in the same crimson and* *black jerseys—* over more than sixty seasons. Now there might not be any more *to record* seasons.

can name the faces photographed in every season
~~I have known everyone on the team~~ since my sister ran, the year I entered grade school. That's when I decided to become a running Hawk. My dream was to come true next year, but then the school budget talks began.

Editing/Proofreading

Now you are ready to edit your persuasive piece. First, **proofread** your writing for errors in spelling, grammar, punctuation, and usage. Then use pages 78–81, especially the editing checklist on page 79, as a step-by-step guide to editing your writing. Refer also to the editing checklist on this page. This will save you both time and effort.

Finally, think about the language of your persuasive piece. Have you used the most persuasive language and chosen the most effective words? Will your words grab readers' attention and hold it? Look at page 280 for suggestions on this aspect of your editing.

Editing/Proofreading Checklist

1. Have I used correct pronoun forms in compound constructions?
2. Have I used the forms of <u>good</u> and <u>bad</u> correctly?
3. Have I used apostrophes correctly?
4. Have I used standard spelling and capitalization?
5. Have I used homophones correctly?

Publishing/Presenting

What would *This Is America* look like if your class were to put out an edition? Exchange papers with your classmates to see the range of topics and forms your classmates used to express their ideas of what should be preserved to keep America unique.

Finally, evaluate your work. Is there a means of presenting it that you haven't considered? Maybe you wrote a letter that you could publish in a local newspaper. Perhaps you wrote an essay that could find a home in a teen magazine. Whatever you do, be sure to consider including this piece in your portfolio.

Proofreading Tip

Check for the correct use of commas with words, phrases, or clauses in a series. For more information, see pages 591–592.

Journal Writing: Write to Learn

Reflect on your writing process experience. Answer these questions in your journal: What do you like best about your persuasive writing? What was the hardest part of writing it? What did you learn in your writing conference? What new things have you learned as a writer?

Literature Model

The Liberry

by Bel Kaufman

In this essay best-selling novelist Bel Kaufman argues persuasively for the importance of libraries. As you read, notice the tactics Kaufman uses to persuade her readers. Then try the activities in Linking Writing and Literature on page 302.

A small boy in one of William Saroyan's stories finds himself in the public library for the first time. He looks around in awe: "All them books," he says, "and something written in each one!"

I remember myself as a 12-year-old, newly arrived from Russia, groping toward the mastery of the English language in my neighborhood library. Guided by no reading lists, informed by no book reviews, I had no use for the card catalogue, since I worked each shelf alphabetically, burrowing my way from one end of the stacks to the other, relentless as a mole. I read by trial and error, through trash and treasure; like a true addict, I was interested not so much in quality as in getting the stuff.

Sometimes I would stumble upon a book that was special; a book unrequired, unrecommended, unspoiled by teacher-imposed chores—"Name 3 . . . Answer the following . . ."—a book to be read for sheer pleasure.

Where else was it allowed, even encouraged, to thumb through a book, to linger on a page without being shooed away from handling the merchandise? This was merchandise to be handled. I was not fooled by the stiff, impassive maroon and dark-green library bindings; I nosed out the good ones. If the pages were worn and dog-eared, if the card tucked into its paper pocket inside the cover was stamped with lots of dates, I knew I had a winner.

Those dates linked me to the anonymous fellowship of other readers whose hands had turned the pages I was turning, who sometimes left penciled clues in the margins: a philosophic "How True!"—a succinct[1] "Stinks."

Here, within walls built book by solid book, we sat in silent kinship, the only sounds shuffling of feet, scraping of chairs, an occasional loud whisper, and the librarian's stern "Shhh!"

The librarian was always there, unobtrusive[2] and omniscient, ready for any question: Where to find a book about Eskimos? A history of submarines? A best-selling novel?—unruffled even by a request I once overheard in the children's section: "Have you got a book for an eight-year-old with tonsils?"

---

[1]**succinct** (sək singkt′) clearly and briefly stated
[2]**unobtrusive** (un əb trōō′ siv) not calling attention to oneself

Jacob Lawrence, *The Library*, 1960

I am remembering this because today the public libraries are becoming less and less available to the people who need them most. Already shut part of the time, their hours reduced by 50 percent in the last five years, their budgets further curtailed as of July 1, and still threatened with continued cuts in staff and services, the public libraries have suffered more in the city's financial squeeze than any other major public-service agencies.

The first priority of our nation, according to former New York State Commissioner of Education, James E. Allen, is the right to read. Educators are inundating our schools with massive surveys, innovative techniques and expensive gimmicks to combat illiteracy and improve the reading skills of our children—at the same time that our public libraries are gradually closing their doors.

What are our priorities? Name 3.

It seems to me that especially now, when there are so many people in our city whose language is not English, whose homes are barren of books, who are daily seduced by clamorous offers of instant diversion, especially now we must hold on to something that will endure when the movie is over, the television set broken, the class dismissed for the last time.

For many, the public library is the only quiet place in an unquiet world; a refuge from the violence and ugliness outside; the only space available

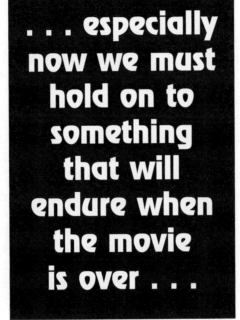

. . . especially now we must hold on to something that will endure when the movie is over . . .

for privacy of work or thought. For many it is the only exposure to books waiting on open shelves to be taken home, free of charge.

As a former student put it: "In a liberry it's hard to avoid reading."

When I taught English in high school, I used to ask my students to bring a library card to class, on the chance that if they had one they might use it. One boy brought in his aunt's. "Aw, I ain't gonna *use* it," he cheerfully assured me, "I just brought it to *show* you!"

Still—some did make use of their cards, if only because they were *there*. Some enter the library today because it is *there*. Inside are all them books, and something written in each one. How sad for our city if the sign on the door should say CLOSED.

Linking Writing and Literature

 ## Learning to Learn

In your own words, write what opinion Kaufman expresses about libraries in her persuasive essay. Then write down an opinion you have about your own local library.

 ## Talk About Reading

Talk with other students about "The Liberry." Assign a group leader to keep everyone focused and a group secretary to take notes. Then use the questions below to guide your conversation.

1. **Connect to Your Life** How do your experiences in the library relate to the experiences that Kaufman tells about in her introduction? Does her essay make you think any differently about your own library?

2. **Critical Thinking: Analyze** What is the main point that Kaufman makes in her persuasive essay? What would she like to see happen as a result of her essay?

3. **6+1 Trait®: Organization** How effective do you think it is for Kaufman to open her essay with a long anecdote?

4. **Connect to Your Writing** What did this essay teach you about making a solid argument?

 ## Write About Reading

Letter to the Editor Write a letter to the editor of your town or school newspaper. In your letter, give your opinion about your local library. Either suggest ways that the library could be improved or describe ways in which the library functions well.

Focus on Organization Your letter to the editor will be more effective if it is well organized. You might want to start with a personal anecdote, as Kaufman did in "The Liberry." Be sure to finish with a strong conclusion. When you edit your letter, see if you can add transitions that connect your ideas more smoothly.

For more information on organization and the 6+1 Trait® model, see **Writing and Research Handbook,** pages 822–824.

Reflecting on the Unit: Summarize What You Learned

Focus on the following questions to help summarize what you learned in this unit.

❶ What is the purpose of persuasive writing?
❷ How can you support an argument?
❸ In persuasive writing where is the opinion usually stated?
❹ What are some good techniques for exploring the pros and cons of a topic?
❺ What effect does your purpose and audience have on the way you develop your argument?

 ## Adding to Your Portfolio

CHOOSE A SELECTION FOR YOUR PORTFOLIO Look over the writing you did for this unit. Choose a piece of writing for your portfolio. The writing you choose should show one or more of the following:

- an opinion stated in a clear topic sentence
- different types of evidence to support an opinion
- evidence presented in an effective order
- precise word choice

REFLECT ON YOUR CHOICE Attach a note to the piece you chose, explaining briefly why you chose it and what you learned from writing it.

SET GOALS How can you improve your writing? What skill will you focus on the next time you write?

Writing Across the Curriculum

MAKE A SCIENCE CONNECTION Scientists often use facts to persuade. For example, a scientist might argue that, based on evidence of global warming, certain practices should be changed. Think of an environmental, health, or other science-related topic that interests you. Follow the writing process outlined in this unit to write an essay that persuades people to take some action on this issue.

" *I'll walk the tightrope that's been stretched for me. . .* **"**

—Margaret Danner,
"I'll Walk the
Tightrope"

Troubleshooter

Use Troubleshooter to help you correct common errors in your writing.

7.1 Sentence Fragment

Problem 1

Fragment that lacks a subject

frag Lucy bought a new tennis racket. Wanted to play today.

frag Oscar wrote a long essay. Read it in class.

frag My dog buried the bone. Dug it up later.

SOLUTION Add a subject to the fragment to make a complete sentence.

Lucy bought a new tennis racket. She wanted to play today.

Oscar wrote a long essay. He read it in class.

My dog buried the bone. He dug it up later.

Problem 2

Fragment that lacks a predicate

frag The beach is closed. The pool now too.

frag Spring is near. Flowers soon.

frag Marla wore a coat. That red woolen coat.

SOLUTION Add a predicate to make the sentence complete.

The beach is closed. The pool is closed now too.

Spring is near. Flowers soon will bloom.

Marla wore a coat. That red coat was woolen.

Problem 3

Fragment that lacks both a subject and a predicate

frag   Sophia ran very fast. During the relay race.
frag   My mother called me on the phone. At two o'clock.
frag   Ceara rode the sled. Down the hill.

SOLUTION Combine the fragment with another sentence.

Sophia ran very fast during the relay race.

My mother called me on the phone at two o'clock.

Ceara rode the sled down the hill.

If you need more help in avoiding sentence fragments, turn to Lesson 8.2, pages 359–360.

7.2 Run-on Sentence

Problem 1

Two main clauses separated by only a comma

run-on *Janet's book was published, it has twelve chapters.*

run-on *Jorge trained hard for the race, he expects to win.*

SOLUTION A   Replace the comma with a period or other end mark. Begin the second sentence with a capital letter.

Janet's book was published. It has twelve chapters.

SOLUTION B   Replace the comma between the main clauses with a semicolon.

Jorge trained hard for the race; he expects to win.

SOLUTION C   Insert a coodinating conjunction after the comma.

Jorge trained hard for the race, and he expects to win.

Problem 2

Two main clauses with no punctuation between them

run-on *Ravi went on vacation he will be home soon.*

run-on *Stanley left the party early he drove home.*

SOLUTION A   Separate the main clauses with a period or other end mark. Begin the second sentence with a capital letter.

Ravi went on vacation. He will be home soon.

SOLUTION B   Insert a comma and a coordinating conjunction between the clauses.

Stanley left the party early, and he drove home.

Problem 3

Two main clauses with no comma before the coordinating conjunction

run-on Vanna is going to Canada and her sister is going, too.

run-on Barry can leave today but he must return tomorrow.

SOLUTION   Insert a comma before the coordinating conjunction.

Vanna is going to Canada, and her sister is going, too.
Barry can leave today, but he must return tomorrow.

If you need more help in avoiding run-on sentences, turn to Lesson 8.6, pages 367–368.

7.3 Lack of Subject-Verb Agreement

Problem 1

A subject that is separated from the verb by an intervening prepositional phrase

agr   One of the books (were) sold.

agr   The actors in the play (is) good.

SOLUTION   Ignore a prepositional phrase that comes between a subject and a verb. Make sure that the verb agrees with the subject of the sentence. The subject is never the object of the preposition.

One of the books was sold.

The actors in the play are good.

Problem 2

A sentence that begins with *here* or *there*

agr   There (is) the books you want.

agr   Here (come) the school bus.

agr   There (is) trees in your backyard.

SOLUTION The subject is almost never *here* or *there*. In sentences that begin with *here* or *there*, look for the subject *after* the verb. The verb must agree with the subject.

There are the books you want.

Here comes the school bus.

There are trees in your backyard.

Problem 3

An indefinite pronoun as the subject

agr Several of the paintings (is) oils.

agr Each of the books (are) autographed.

agr All of my effort (were) worthwhile.

Some indefinite pronouns are singular; some are plural; and some can be either singular or plural, depending upon the noun they refer to.

SOLUTION Determine whether the indefinite pronoun is singular or plural and make the verb agree.

Several of the paintings are oils.

Each of the books is autographed.

All of my effort was worthwhile.

Problem 4

A compound subject that is joined by *and*

agr The car and the bus (was) hit by lightning.

agr Bacon and eggs (were) served for breakfast.

> **SOLUTION A** If the parts of the compound subject do not belong to one unit or if they refer to different people or things, use a plural verb.
>
> **The car and the bus were hit by lightning.**

> **SOLUTION B** If the parts of the compound subject belong to one unit or if both parts refer to the same person or thing, use a singular verb.
>
> **Bacon and eggs was served for breakfast.**

Problem 5

A compound subject that is joined by *or* or *nor*

agr Either a dog or a cat (make) a good pet.

agr Neither raisins nor an apple (make) a complete meal.

agr Either Jim or his friends (is) bringing the cake.

SOLUTION Make the verb agree with the subject that is closer to it.

Either a dog or a cat makes a good pet.

Neither raisins nor an apple makes a complete meal.

Either Jim or his friends are bringing the cake.

If you need more help with subject-verb agreement, turn to Lessons 16.1–16.5, pages 535–544.

7.4 Incorrect Verb Tense or Form

Problem 1

An incorrect or missing verb ending

tense   Have you ever (walk) all the way to school?

tense   Last Saturday we (pack) for our camping trip.

tense   Yesterday we (hope) for rain.

SOLUTION A   Add *-ed* to a regular verb to form the past tense and the past participle.

Have you ever walked all the way to school?

Last Saturday we packed for our camping trip.

Yesterday we hoped for rain.

Problem 2

An improperly formed irregular verb

tense   The water in the pond (freezed) overnight.

tense   Elena has (bringed) the girls to the dance.

tense   I (teared) my coat on the nail.

The past and past participle forms of irregular verbs vary. Memorize these forms, or look them up.

> **SOLUTION** Use the correct past or past participle form of an irregular verb.
>
> **The water in the pond froze overnight.**
>
> **Elena has brought the girls to the dance.**
>
> **I tore my coat on the nail.**

Problem 3

Confusion between the past form and the past participle

> *tense Diana had already (went) home when we arrived.*

> **SOLUTION** Use the past participle form of an irregular verb, not the past form, when you use the auxiliary verb *have*.
>
> **Diana had already gone home when we arrived.**

If you need more help with correct verb forms, turn to Lessons 10.1–10.10, pages 399–418.

7.5 Incorrect Use of Pronouns

Problem 1

A pronoun that could refer to more than one antecedent

pro   David always beats Hector to school, but (he) still gets there on time.

pro   When Tess leaves with Emma, (she) is home by noon.

> **SOLUTION A**   Rewrite the sentence, substituting a noun for the pronoun.
>
> **David always beats Hector to school, but Hector still gets there on time.**
>
> **When Tess leaves with Emma, Tess is home by noon.**

Problem 2

Object pronouns as subjects

pro   Velma and (me) went to the mountains today.

pro   (Her) and Glen rode to the farm on a bus.

pro   Terry and (them) read that book last year.

> **SOLUTION**   Use a subject pronoun in the subject of a sentence.
>
> **Velma and I went to the mountains today.**
>
> **She and Glen rode to the farm on a bus.**
>
> **Terry and they read that book last year.**

Problem 3

Subject pronouns as objects

> pro   *Jane will be at home with Akiko and ⓘ.*
>
> pro   *Please help ⓢⓗⓔ and ⓘ with the house painting.*
>
> pro   *Bart would like George and ⓘ to go to the movie.*

> **SOLUTION**   Use an object pronoun as the object of a verb or a preposition.
>
> **Jane will be at home with Akiko and me.**
>
> **Please help her and me with the house painting.**
>
> **Bart would like George and me to go to the movie.**

If you need more help with the correct use of pronouns, turn to Lessons 11.1–11.7, pages 429–442.

7.6 Incorrect Use of Adjectives

Problem 1

Incorrect use of *good, better, best*

> *adj*   The weather can't get (more) good than this.
>
> *adj*   This is the (most good) book in the library.
>
> *adj*   This is a (more) better exercise for you than that one.

> **SOLUTION**   The comparative and superlative forms of *good* are *better* and *best*. Do not use *more* or *most* before irregular forms of comparative and superlative adjectives.
>
> **The weather can't get better than this.**
>
> **This is the best book in the library.**
>
> **This is a better exercise for you than that one.**

Problem 2

Incorrect use of *bad, worse, worst*

> *adj*   This is the (baddest) movie I've ever seen.
>
> *adj*   These shoes are (more bad) than those shoes.
>
> *adj*   Yesterday I ate the (most) worst food I've ever tasted.

SOLUTION   The comparative and superlative forms of *bad* are *worse* and *worst*. Do not use *-er, -est, more,* or *most* with irregular forms of comparative and superlative adjectives.

This is the worst movie I've ever seen.

These shoes are worse than those shoes.

Yesterday I ate the worst food I've ever tasted.

Problem 3

Incorrect use of comparative and superlative adjectives

adj   Maple Drive is (more) wider than Elm Street.

adj   Daphne lives in the (most) smallest house in town.

SOLUTION   Do not use both *-er* and *more* or *-est* and *most* at the same time.

Maple Drive is wider than Elm Street.

Daphne lives in the smallest house in town.

If you need more help with the incorrect use of adjectives, turn to Lessons 12.3 and 12.4, pages 455–458.

7.7 Incorrect Use of Commas

Problem 1

Missing commas in a series of three or more items

com   *We visited the museum, the zoo, and the aquarium.*

com   *Sam drove down the block, around the corner, and into the parking lot.*

SOLUTION   Use commas to separate three or more items in a series.

We visited the museum, the zoo, and the aquarium.

Sam drove down the block, around the corner, and into the parking lot.

Problem 2

Missing commas with direct quotations

com   *"Biology class," said Ms. Blas, "meets tomorrow."*

com   *"Let's rake the leaves," said Ben, "before we leave."*

SOLUTION   The first part of an interrupted quotation ends with a comma, followed by quotation marks. The interrupting words are also followed by a comma.

"Biology class," said Ms. Blas, "meets tomorrow."

"Let's rake the leaves," said Ben, "before we leave."

Problem 3

Missing commas with nonessential appositives

com   *Our house$_\wedge$a split-level$_\wedge$was painted last year.*

com   *My bicycle$_\wedge$a black ten-speed$_\wedge$was shipped to Alaska.*

SOLUTION   Determine whether the appositive is truly essential to the meaning of the sentence. If it is not essential, set off the appositive with commas.

Our house, a split-level, was painted last year.

My bicycle, a black ten-speed, was shipped to Alaska.

If you need more help with commas, turn to Lessons 20.2–20.4, pages 591–596.

Problem 1

Singular possessive nouns

apos (Chriss) son borrowed the neighbor's rake.

The (womans) report is on the desk.

apos (Ettas) book is in (Ians) house.

SOLUTION Use an apostrophe and an -*s* to form the possessive of a singular noun, even one that ends in -*s*.

Chris's son borrowed the neighbor's rake.

The woman's report is on the desk.

Etta's book is in Ian's house.

Problem 2

Plural possessive nouns ending in -*s*

apos The (drivers) maps are in their cars.

apos The two (pilots) orders are to land in Springfield.

apos The (cats) owner fed them milk.

> **SOLUTION** Use an apostrophe alone to form the possessive of a plural noun that ends in -*s*.
>
> **The drivers' maps are in their cars.**
>
> **The two pilots' orders are to land in Springfield.**
>
> **The cats' owner fed them milk.**

Problem 3

Plural possessive nouns not ending in -*s*

apos   The (mens) department is at the rear of the store.

apos   Ida Stark is known as the (peoples) candidate.

> **SOLUTION** Use an apostrophe and an -*s* to form the possessive of a plural noun that does not end in -*s*.
>
> **The men's department is at the rear of the store.**
>
> **Ida Stark is known as the people's candidate.**

Problem 4

Possessive personal pronouns

apos   *The hat is (yours) but the jacket is (hers).*

SOLUTION   Do not use an apostrophe with any of the possessive personal pronouns.

The hat is yours, but the jacket is hers.

Problem 5

Confusion between *its* and *it's*

apos   *(Its) going to be a beautiful morning.*

apos   *Turn the rowboat over on (it's) side.*

SOLUTION   Use an apostrophe to form the contraction of *it is.* Do not use an apostrophe in the possessive of *it.*

It's going to be a beautiful morning.

Turn the rowboat over on its side.

If you need more help with apostrophes and possessives, turn to Lesson 20.7, pages 601–602.

7.9 Incorrect Capitalization

Problem 1

Words referring to ethnic groups, nationalities, and languages

cap   Mr. Dunn has studied several (asian) cultures.

cap   The (arabic) language is a difficult language to learn.

cap   Pierre is a (canadian) who speaks (russian).

SOLUTION   Capitalize proper nouns and adjectives that refer to ethnic groups, nationalities, and languages.

Mr. Dunn has studied several Asian cultures.

The Arabic language is a difficult language to learn.

Pierre is a Canadian who speaks Russian.

Problem 2

Words that show family relationships

cap   Denise told (uncle) Evan to go to the theater.

cap   Yesterday (mom) fixed the car.

SOLUTION   Capitalize words that show family relationships when such words are used as titles or as substitutes for people's names.

Denise told Uncle Evan to go to the theater.

Yesterday Mom fixed the car.

Problem 3

The first word of a direct quotation

cap "(we) didn't leave the house until evening," said Rosa.
cap Peter said, "(please) wash the dishes before you leave."

SOLUTION Capitalize the first word in a direct quotation. A direct quotation gives the speaker's exact words.

"We didn't leave the house until evening," said Rosa.

Peter said, "Please wash the dishes before you leave."

If you need more help in capitalizing, turn to Lessons 19.1–19.4, pages 573–580.

7.10 Lack of Parallelism

Problem 1

Failure to include articles before all the items in a series

*I met Karen, a teacher, Sam, **who is** a runner, and Jim, the butcher.*

SOLUTION Apply the pronoun, article, or phrase to all the items in the series, or only to the first item.

I met Karen, who is a teacher; Sam, who is a runner; and Jim, who is a butcher.

Problem 2

Failure to use similar verbs with all items in a series

> *I had purchased an MP3 player, downloaded some songs, and **had** enjoyed my music.*

SOLUTION Use verbs that have similar form.

I purchased an MP3 player, downloaded some songs, and enjoyed my music.

Problem 3

Failure to use similar phrases in sentences with correlative conjunctions

> *Not only the raging fire but also **running from** the hungry bear was a real danger.*

SOLUTION Rewrite the phrase that follows the second correlative conjunction to match the first.

Not only the raging fire but also the hungry bear was a real danger.

If you need more help with parallelism, see pages 80 and 818.

Business and Technical Writing

Contents

In every day life, we encounter a variety of nonfiction that we must read and respond to. Many of these materials are found in the home and in the workplace. Business and technical writing are broad categories that include nonfiction writing. Business writing includes business letters, summaries, application forms, contracts, interviews, proposals and multimedia presentations. Common examples of technical writing are product assembly instructions, product warranties, instructional manuals, insurance policies, and technical manuals.

Business Letters

Writing a Business Letter

A business letter is a formal communication tool that is used to give information or to request action.

The following business letter is written to express an opinion. Notice how the writer follows the tips suggested in the chart on the following page.

2317 Buckeye Ave.
Chadwick, OH 48276
November 10, 20--

Ms. Kate Callahan, Superintendent
Chadwick School Board
485 Cherry St.
Chadwick, OH 48276

> The letter is addressed to a specific person.

Dear Ms. Callahan:

The teachers at Chadwick High School have different opinions about what students can wear to their classes. I think Chadwick should have a dress code.

> The writer states his opinion in the first sentence.

A dress code would end arguments between teachers and students about what's appropriate to wear to school. Having a dress code would mean that kids wouldn't be so concerned over what they wear to school and could focus more on learning.

> He gives reasons for his opinion.

I think the dress code should allow jeans and plain tee shirts but not shirts or hats with slogans or pictures.

> He suggests a specific solution.

Respectfully,

Enrique Martinez, sophomore

Business Letters

Types of Business Letters

There are several types of business letters. You can use the formal business letter format to express your opinion; to request information or order a product; to make a complaint and describe a problem with a product or service; or to apply for a job, an award, or a scholarship.

When you write a business letter, keep your purpose in mind. Be brief. Don't include unnecessary information. Limit your letter to one page or less, if possible. A busy person is more likely to read your letter if it is brief.

A business letter is formal. Use polite language but a friendly tone. Avoid wordy language. For example, say "Thank you for your help" rather than "Thank you for your kind assistance in this matter."

TYPES OF BUSINESS LETTERS

Opinion Letter	Request Letter	Complaint Letter	Application Letter
State the issue briefly.	State your request briefly and clearly.	Be polite.	Write to a specific person.
State your opinion in the first sentence or two.	Make your request specific and reasonable.	Identify the product or service clearly.	Describe the job or program for which you're applying.
Support your opinion with reasons, facts, and examples.	Include all necessary information.	Describe the problem briefly and accurately.	List your qualifications.
Summarize your main points and offer a solution, if possible.	Include your phone number or a self-addressed, stamped envelope.	Request a specific solution.	Explain briefly why you're the best person for the position or the award.
		Keep a copy of your letter until your complaint has been resolved.	Request an application form or an interview.

Style

Business letters are usually written in one of two styles: block style or modified block style.

Block Style   In block style, all lines begin at the left margin. Paragraphs are not indented. They are separated by a line space. The letter on page 329 is typed in block style.

Modified Block Style   In modified block style, the heading, the closing, your signature, and your typed name begin at the center of the paper. Paragraphs may be indented—five spaces on a typewriter or half an inch on a computer—or not indented. If paragraphs are indented, there is no need to place a line space between them. The following letter is in modified block style with paragraphs indented.

---

708 Mount Vernon Rd.   **(Heading)**
Greenleaf, ME 10908
February 12, 20--

Mr. Bruce Chung, Manager   **(Inside Address)**
Greenleaf Department of Recreation
304 S. Main St.
Greenleaf, ME 10908

Dear Mr. Chung: **(Salutation)**
    I understand that next month (March) you will be arranging the schedule for the city softball fields for spring and summer. Please schedule some time for kids who are not part of any organized league.
    There are many kids in our community who do not belong to a league but who love to play softball. The   **(Body)**
parents of these kids pay taxes that are used for city recreation as do the parents of the kids in the leagues.
    I suggest reserving diamonds 4 and 6 on Wednesdays from 2:30 p.m. to 5 p.m. This would not interfere with evening or weekend games.

Yours truly,   **(Closing)**
Megan Payson   **(Name and Signature)**
Megan Payson

The Parts of a Business Letter

A business letter has six parts.

Heading
- your street address
- your city, state, and ZIP code
- the date

Inside Address
- the name of the person to whom you're writing
- the title of the person to whom you're writing (Place a comma after the name and write a short title on the same line. Use a separate line for a long title without a comma after the person's name.)
- the name of the business or organization
- the street address
- the city, state, and ZIP code

Business Letters

Salutation or Greeting When you know the name of the person to whom you're writing, the salutation should include a courtesy title: *Dear Mrs. Martin* or *Dear Mr. Marconi*. If you don't know the name of the person, the salutation should begin with *Dear* followed by the person's title: *Dear Manager* or *Dear President*. Place a colon after the salutation.

Body The body contains your message. It is the most important part of your letter.

Closing The closing is a final word or phrase, such as *Sincerely* or *Yours truly,* followed by a comma.

Name and Signature Type your name four lines below the closing. Then sign your name in the space between the closing and your typed name. If your first name could belong to either a male or a female, include *Miss, Ms.,* or *Mr.* in parentheses before both your typed name and your signature.

Neatness Counts

The person who reads your letter will pay more attention to your message if your letter is neat. Follow the formal rules for writing a business letter.

✔ Type or word process your letter.

✔ Use unlined white 81/2-by-11-inch paper.

✔ Leave a two-inch margin at the top of the page and margins of at least one inch at the left, right, and bottom.

✔ Single-space the heading. Allow one or more blank lines between the heading and the inside address, depending on the length of your letter.

✔ Single-space the remaining parts of the letter, leaving an extra line between the parts and between the paragraphs in the body if they are not indented.

Activity

Write a Business Letter Write a letter stating your opinion on an issue. Mail (or e-mail) your letter to someone who is in a position to take action.

PURPOSE to write a business letter
AUDIENCE person able to take action
LENGTH one page

WRITING RUBRICS To write an effective business letter, you should

- select an issue and state your opinion. Then use a library or the Internet to find the address of an appropriate person to write to
- trade letters with a classmate for feedback
- revise your letter so that all of your ideas relate to your subject, follow each other in a logical way, and are supported by the necessary details
- type, use word processing, or write neatly for your final draft
- send your letter

Summaries

Writing a Summary

A summary is a brief written statement of the main points of a larger work. Although some summaries include opinions, most only state facts in an objective way.

The following summary contains the minutes of a meeting. Notice how the writer follows the tips suggested in the chart on the following page.

Sea Oats School Yearbook Committee

Minutes for October 10, 20--

The meeting was called to order by Mrs. Akron at 3:25 P.M. in the journalism room.

Members present: Mrs. Akron, Jeremy Jefferson, Kim Lee, Tony Pascuzzi, Jennifer Bailey, and Maria Alverez.

> The names of those who are present are listed.

Minutes of Last Meeting
The minutes of the last meeting were read by Maria Alverez and approved.

Old Business
Kim Lee passed out copies of a letter to be sent to area businesses to solicit advertising for the yearbook. Tony Pascuzzi suggested that the letter would be more persuasive if it included statements by some of last year's advertisers telling how their ads brought in more business. The committee members decided this was a good idea, and Tony volunteered to call some of last year's advertisers to see if any of them would agree to be quoted.

> The business of the meeting is summed up briefly.

New Business
Mrs. Akron asked for a volunteer to take photographs of activities throughout the year. Jennifer Bailey volunteered. Mrs. Akron will lend Jennifer a camera, and film will be purchased with yearbook funds.

Next Meeting
The next meeting will be held on November 13, 20--, in the journalism room.

> The date, place, and time of the meeting are recorded.

The meeting was adjourned by Mrs. Akron at 4:03 P.M.

Types of Summaries

Summaries, which are shortened versions of larger works, take many forms: minutes, synopses, survey reports, and reviews.

Minutes are a record of when and where a meeting is held, who attends it, and what happens during the meeting. Minutes are usually kept in a file or a book so that they can be referred to as needed. A secretary or group member who is present at the meeting writes the minutes. A specific format is used for writing them, as shown in the model on page 333. When recording the minutes of a meeting, write what is said as accurately and briefly as you can.

A **synopsis** is a short statement that gives the general idea of a subject. A synopsis of a book is usually on its dust jacket or its back cover. Before writing a synopsis of a written piece, read all of it. Then sum it up in a few sentences or paragraphs.

A **survey report** is a summary of a detailed study that gathers facts and draws conclusions about a subject. An opinion poll is one form of survey. When writing a survey report, gather information from different sources and then create an overview of it. Sometimes a survey report includes charts or graphs.

A **review** is a brief summary and critical evaluation of an event or an artistic work, such as a movie, play, or concert. When writing a review, give your opinion of the quality of the event or of the work and its performance.

A summary can also be used to write a brief account of what happened in a business or a classroom during a certain period.

TYPES OF SUMMARIES

Minutes	Synopsis	Survey Report	Review
Record the date, time, and location of the meeting.	Include only the most important points of a report or other piece of writing.	Gather information from various sources.	Identify the event, work, or performance and its time and place.
List the names of those who attend it.	Write your statement in paragraph form.	Organize the data in some way, such as a table or a graph that makes it easy to understand at a glance.	Include a brief description of what was read, seen, or performed.
Sum up old and new business in brief sentences.	Be brief (one page or less).	State a conclusion drawn from the data.	Identify the most important people involved, such as the writer, the director, and the performers.
Record the date, time, and place of the next meeting.			State your opinion.
Note when and by whom the meeting is adjourned.			

Style

Some types of summaries, such as the minutes of a meeting, have a definite format (see model on page 333). Others—synopses, reviews, or summaries of a business or school day—can be written in paragraph form. Surveys and summaries of very large works are often divided into sections and include paragraphs, lists, tables, and graphs.

Seventh Grade Summary   (Title)
Week of February 10, 20––   (Date)

Subjects   (Heading)
English
Five students read their essays on Great American Poets this week, completing the essay presentations.
Science
This is the fourth week of the biology plant-growing experiment. Plants that get sun, water, and fertilizer are the tallest. Plants that get only sun and water are a bit smaller but are growing well. Plants that get only water or only sun have sprouted but are starting to look sick.

Class Fundraiser   (Heading)
The following table shows the results of gift-wrap sales so far.

Item	# Packages Sold	Price per Package	Total	(Table)
Cards	64	$7.00	$448.00	
Gift Bags	43	4.50	193.50	
Ribbon	64	5.50	352.00	
Wrapping Paper	89	4.50	400.50	

Subtotal $1,394.00
less 50% cost   697.00
Our profit $ 697.00

We are now more than half way to our goal of $1,200.00. Keep on selling and our new classroom computer will be here soon!   (Conclusion)

Summaries

The Parts of a Summary

A simple summary has just a title and one paragraph. Those that are more complex may also include a date, sections, graphic organizers, and a conclusion.

Title   The title lets readers know what subject or information is being summarized.

Date   The date shows the period of time covered by the summary.

Sections   Sometimes, sections may be needed to organize information.

Graphic Organizers   Some information is easier to understand if it is presented in a table, a graph, or a map.

Conclusion   The summary model on page 335 ends with a conclusion. Other summaries just state the facts and let readers come to their own conclusions.

Neatness Counts

Summaries that are neat and well organized can be read and understood easily.

✔ Create your summary on a computer, if possible.

Technology Tip

You can use the features of a word processing program to create an organized format for your summary. The table and column features can help you organize information into categories. Some word processing programs also make it easy to create simple tables, graphs, pie charts, and flow charts.

✔ Begin with a heading centered at the top of the page.

✔ Use bold type or underlining to identify each section.

✔ Leave a two-inch margin at the top of the page and margins of at least one inch at the left, right, and bottom.

✔ Leave a double space between sections and before and after organizers.

Activity

Write a Summary   Choose the kind of summary you would like to write. You may wish to write minutes for a meeting you attended; summarize what happened in your classroom during a day or a week; write a synopsis or a survey report; or review a play, a book, or a movie.

PURPOSE To write a summary
AUDIENCE Classmates
LENGTH One page or less

WRITING RUBRICS   To write a good summary, you should

- keep your summary as brief as possible
- include only the most important points
- make a graphic organizer if you have data to include
- trade summaries with a classmate and discuss ways they could be revised to make them briefer or easier to read
- revise your summary and then share it with your class

Forms

Creating a Form

A form is a document that has blanks for filling in required information. The model below is a form for scheduling family chores.

> The writer gives the form a title to show what it is for.

> The writer organizes the form into columns to make it easy to read.

O'Flarety Family Chore Schedule

	Sunday	Monday	Tuesday	Wednesday	Thursday	Friday	Saturday
Feed Buffy	Lisa	Lisa	Lisa	Kim	Matt	Kim	Matt
Take out trash	Lisa	Kim	Matt	Lisa	Lisa	Kim	Matt
Set table	Lisa	Kim	Kim	Kim	Matt	Kim	Lisa
Wash dishes	Matt	Kim	Matt	Lisa	Lisa	Kim	Matt
Clean bathroom	Kim	Kim	Matt	Kim	Matt	Lisa	Matt

> The writer provides spaces for filling in who does a chore and when the person does it.

Types of Forms

Forms are used to collect information in an organized way. There are forms for taking phone messages, writing memos, and filling out receipts (records of payment). Paying income tax requires filling out a form. Banks have forms for opening and closing accounts and for applying for loans. Accountants use forms to keep track of expenses and income. Forms fall into four basic types: schedules, tracking forms, application forms, and report forms.

A **schedule** is a form that lists the times at which certain events or things to do will take place. It usually lists events that have not happened yet. A vacation schedule shows when people working in the same office will be taking time off. An airline schedule shows flight arrival and departure times. The model on this page is a schedule.

Forms

A **tracking form** is used to record things as they occur. A teacher's grade book is a tracking form because the grades are recorded as they are earned. The model on page 339 is a tracking form.

An **application form** is used to gather information about a person who is requesting something, such as a job, membership in a group, or an award. When you fill out an application form, follow the instructions carefully and include information that will help persuade the person reading the application to choose you instead of other applicants.

A **report form** is used to record data or information on events that have already taken place so that it can be compared or combined. A form for recording the results of a class science experiment, a baseball score card, and a report card are different kinds of report forms.

You will fill out many forms during your life. You may also need to create forms. To create a form, first list all the kinds of information that you need to collect. Then decide on the best format for organizing the information.

TYPES OF FORMS

Schedule	Tracking Form	Application Form	Report Form
Give the schedule a title.	Give the form a title.	Give the form a title.	Give the form a title.
Use a column or grid format.	Use a column or grid format.	State the requirements for applicants.	Use a format that organizes the data so that it can be compared or combined easily.
List headings horizontally and vertically.	Include instructions for filling out the form.	Include instructions for filling out the form.	Use headings.
Include dates and times of events.	Use headings that show what information belongs in the blanks.	Include instructions on how and where to submit the form and the date by which it must be submitted.	Include dates and times.
	Arrange the headings in sequence.	Use a fill-in-the-blanks format for information about applicants.	Provide a space for the recorder's name.
	Provide a space for the recorder's signature.	Provide a space for an applicant's signature and the date.	

Style

Each type of form requires a particular style or format. Schedules and tracking forms are usually arranged in columns or grids. See the model on page 337 and the one below. Application forms use a fill-in-the-blank format and sometimes include large spaces in which essay questions can be answered. Report forms use any format that organizes their particular data or information best. The following application form uses a fill-in-the-blank format with a space in which to answer the open-ended question: "Why do you want to volunteer?"

Volunteer Application Form

Thank you for considering volunteer work at the Beckwith Library.

Name: _____Quinn Peterson_____ Date _____January 20, 20--_____

Address: _____3532 11th Avenue North_____

City: _____Grand Forks_____ State: __ND__ Zip: _____58203_____

Phone: _____701-555-1212_____ Fax: _____701-555-5510_____

DOB: __11/29/87__ SSN: _____123-45-6789_____

Best times to reach you: _____After 3:30 p.m. weekdays_____

Education (circle highest level completed):

     7   (8)   9   10   11   12

Is this experience for school credit?   Yes   (No)

School name and address: _____Lake Agassiz School_____

Why do you want to volunteer?

I have good organization skills and I know I would be an asset to the library staff. In addition, I am already very familiar with the layout of the library because I spend a lot of time there. I enjoy reading aloud to my little brother; I would especially like to be a volunteer reader during the story hour.

Describe previous volunteer experience.

     n/a

Signature: _____Quinn Peterson_____

The Parts of a Form

What parts a form has depends on what kind of information it will be used to record. Some or all of the following parts are used in various forms.

Title   The title, which is usually placed at the top of a form, shows what the form is used for.

Instructions   In some cases, a form includes instructions for filling it out and submitting it.

Headings   Headings indicate where information is to be placed on the form and what kind of information it should be.

Body   The body of a form is where information is recorded. It is usually columns, a grid, or text with blanks to be filled in. Sometimes the body is divided into sections.

Signature   A recorder's or an applicant's signature often appears on a form.

Neatness Counts

A form has to be organized so that it is easy for people to understand how to record information on it. A form should be created on a computer.

- ✔ Use unlined white 8 1/2-by-11 paper.
- ✔ Leave a two-inch margin at the top of the page and at least a one-inch margin at the left, right, and bottom.
- ✔ Single-space the heading. Use a double space between the sections of a form.

Technology Tip

You can use a computer word processing program to create columns and rows. Use the underline feature to create the blanks that are to be filled in. Experiment with using a word processing tables feature or a spreadsheet program to produce a grid.

Activity

Create a Form   Study the types of forms listed on this page. Then decide which type you want to create. Create your form and then have a partner fill it out. Discuss with your partner how easy or hard it was to understand and fill out the form. Discuss whether or not the form organized information in a logical way.

PURPOSE To create a form
AUDIENCE A classmate
LENGTH One page or less

WRITING RUBRICS   To create an organized, useful form, you should

- experiment with different formats to find the one that works best for your particular form
- include instructions on how to fill out the form if it isn't obvious
- create and revise your form on a computer
- use whatever sources are necessary to gather information for filling out your partner's form

Interviews

An interview is a meeting between one person (the interviewer) and a second person from whom the interviewer seeks information. It is also the name given to the written report of such a meeting. An interview has a question-and-answer format. The interviewer asks questions whose answers will provide specific information.

When you interview someone, your questions, manner, and tone determine how your subject answers. When someone interviews you, your appearance and ability to answer the questions make an impression on the interviewer. In the following interview, a reporter for the school paper interviews the school media specialist about new computer equipment available in the library.

Question: What new computer equipment was placed in the library over the summer?
Answer: There are four new computer stations, a black and white printer, and a color printer.
Q: When can students use the new equipment?
A: Students can use computer stations any time the stations are not already reserved or in use. They can reserve up to thirty minutes at a time by signing the sheet at the reference desk.
Q: How can students get help learning how to use the new equipment?
A: The computers are always turned on during library hours. There are instructions on the screen that tell users what to do. Also, all the librarians and assistants have been trained on the new computers and are available to assist students.
Q: What kinds of tasks can the computers be used for?
A: There are many ways to use the new computers. They can be used to look up books and reference materials available in the library. They will tell you whether a book is on the shelf or has been checked out. You can use the word processing software to write and print reports or essays. You can also use the new computers to access the Internet.
Q: Can students play computer games on the new stations?
A: There are math, spelling, and science games installed on the computers. There is also a word game that will help you improve your vocabulary. Students are not allowed to bring software from home.
Q: Is there anything else students should know about the new computer system?
A: We have a brand new Web site for our school. Space is available on it to publish student writing. I'm inviting students to submit essays, reports, and other forms of writing to be featured on the Web site.

The interviewer asks for the most important information first.

The interviewer asks for details that will be important to readers.

The interviewer asks for information that may be of interest but wasn't covered by other questions.

Types of Interviews

Interviews can be used to gather information in many different situations, but there are basically three types of interviews: a job interview, a news interview, and an investigation interview. An interviewer asks a subject questions and records the answers by taking notes or by tape recording the entire interview. The questions, which are planned carefully in advance, are designed to get the subject to provide specific information.

A **job interview** helps an employer determine whether an applicant is qualified for a specific job. When you are interviewed for a job, be prepared to answer questions about your experience and skills that are relevant to the job. A job interview also helps an interviewer get a sense of what kind of person an applicant is. The answers you give to questions about your accomplishments or what you would do in a given situation help the interviewer assess your values. The interviewer needs to determine whether you are a trustworthy person, a hard worker, and someone who would help the business.

A **news interview** is conducted to gather information that can be written into a news story. When you are planning to interview someone for a news story, first learn all you can about the person and the related topic. Then make up questions that will bring out information to fill the gaps in your knowledge. Tape the interview or take notes. Later, you can organize the information into story form. When you quote a person, be sure to copy his or her words exactly.

An **investigation interview** is used to gather information about something that has happened. For example, a police officer might interview a witness to an accident, or a school principal might interview a student witness to a school incident.

TYPES OF INTERVIEWS		
Job Interview	**News Interview**	**Investigation Interview**
Ask questions about the applicant's relevant experience.	Begin with a question that will introduce the subject to your readers.	Limit questions to those that will bring out relevant facts.
Ask questions about job skills.	Bring out the most important information by asking questions that contain a reporter's six favorite words: *who, what, where, when, why,* and *how.*	Ask specific questions about dates, times, and events.
Include questions that will bring out information about the applicant's ability to make decisions. You might ask, *What would you do if...?*		Ask for information that is based on the subject's personal knowledge rather than on hearsay.
	Always ask an open-ended question, such as *What other important point have I forgotten to ask about?* or *What else do readers need to know?*	

Style

An interview usually consists of questions and answers. An interview may be rewritten later in the same question and answer form. A news interview, however, is often rewritten in a news story format.

The following model is part of an interview in which a seventh grader is being considered for a job as a babysitter.

> **Mrs. Moore:** I am looking for someone to come in after school three times a week to watch and play with my two daughters, Megan, who is three, and Caitlin, who is eighteen months old. Sometimes I will be here working on the computer, but other times I will go out to do errands. Are you able to be here on Tuesdays, Thursdays, and Fridays from three to six in the afternoon?
>
> **Kristin:** Those times would work for me.
>
> **Mrs. Moore:** Have you ever babysat before?
>
> **Kristin:** I watch my little brother while my parents are out. He's three.
>
> **Mrs. Moore:** How old are you, Kristin, and how long have you been babysitting your brother?
>
> **Kristin:** I'm thirteen, and I have been helping to babysit Justin since he was born. I have been staying alone with him for the last year.
>
> **Mrs. Moore:** Do you know how to change a diaper?
>
> **Kristin:** Before Justin was potty-trained, I changed him a lot. I can change both disposable and cloth diapers.
>
> **Mrs. Moore:** Suppose while you were babysitting, Caitlin started crying and wouldn't stop. What would you do?
>
> **Kristin:** First I would ask her why she was crying. If she wouldn't answer, I'd look her over to be sure she wasn't hurt. Then I'd check to see if she needed a diaper change. If it seemed like nothing was wrong, I would hold her and tell her a story or carry her around the house and find some of her toys.
>
> **Mrs. Moore:** What would you do if one of the girls got hurt?
>
> **Kristin:** It would depend on how they were hurt. If it was something like a scraped or cut finger, I'd wash it with soap and water and put a bandage on it. If it was really serious, I'd call 911. If it was something in between, I'd call you and if I couldn't get you, I guess I'd call my mother for advice.
>
> **Mrs. Moore:** What would you do if you told Megan to do something and she refused?
>
> **Kristin:** I would probably tell her that I'm in charge and that she has to do what I say, even if she doesn't like it. I've found that if I pay attention to kids and have fun with them, they usually do what I tell them to do.
>
> **Mrs. Moore:** Would you like to meet Megan and Caitlin now?
>
> **Kristin:** I'd love to.

Question about whether the person is available when needed.

Question about the applicant's relevant experience.

Questions about the applicant's qualifications

Questions to determine how the applicant would handle a crisis.

The Parts of an Interview

An interview is made up of questions and answers. The questions should be crafted to bring out specific information and create a desired effect.

Introductory Question In a job interview, the first question should help to put the applicant at ease. In a news interview, the first question can be about the topic's most important point or be a general question about the topic. At the beginning of an investigation interview, the witness is usually asked to describe what happened during an incident.

Follow-up Questions Sometimes the answer to one question will suggest other questions that the interviewer hadn't thought of. The answers to such questions may provide important information.

Final Question The last question in an interview can be open-ended, inviting the person interviewed to add any information that he or she thinks is important.

Appearance Counts

How you look and how you act when you are being interviewed is as important as the answers you give, especially in a job interview. When you go to a job interview, dress neatly, smile, and shake hands with the interviewer. Be polite and answer each question but do not offer information that is not asked for. Try to appear relaxed and act naturally. Don't be afraid to ask questions.

If you are the interviewer, dress neatly, be businesslike but friendly, and help to put your subject at ease.

Activity

Conduct an Interview Work in pairs to interview each other for jobs or news stories. You may wish to produce a radio or television interview show.

PURPOSE to conduct an interview
AUDIENCE classmates
LENGTH ten minutes

WRITING RUBRICS To make sure that an interview is informative, you should do the following.

- Before you are interviewed, think of what questions you will probably be asked and decide on your answers.
- Before you interview a subject, use the models on pages 341 and 343 to help you write a list of questions.

Technology Tip

If your subject is far away, and if both of you have access to the Internet, you can conduct the interview by e-mail. Ask all of your questions in your first e-mail. After you have read your interviewee's responses, you can ask follow-up questions.

Proposals

Writing a Proposal

A proposal is a plan or suggestion that is presented to others for their approval. The following model is one student's proposal for a procedure to be followed in a school paper drive. Note how the writer follows the tips suggested in the chart on page 346.

Proposal
Procedure for Churchill School Paper Drive

Introduction: Last year's school paper drive caused confusion and was not very successful. Many students covered the same neighborhoods, and other neighborhoods were not covered at all. Residents were unsure of when to put their paper out for collection, and students were unsure of where and when to turn in the paper they did collect.

The writer describes a problem.

Proposed Solution: I propose that we use the following procedure for this year's school paper drive.
1. Students will pick up their neighborhood assignments and the flyers announcing the drive at the office. They will go door-to-door in their assigned neighborhoods to distribute the flyers on Monday or Tuesday, April 3 or 4.
2. Students will travel in pairs, never alone.
3. Students will go out only between 2:45 and 5:30 P.M.
4. Students will collect paper from front porches in their assigned neighborhoods on Saturday morning, April 8, between 8:30 and 10:30 A.M.
5. Students will bring all paper to the east parking lot immediately after collecting it.

The writer proposes a procedure to correct the problem.

The writer uses numbered steps to describe the procedure.

Respectfully submitted on February 28, 20--, by Hirokai Tanaka from Mrs. Benton's seventh-grade class.

The writer identifies himself.

Proposals

Types of Proposals

Proposals can be used to suggest many kinds of plans and solutions to problems. The four basic types of proposals are procedure, project, business, and grant proposals.

A **procedure proposal**, such as the model on page 345, outlines a new or better way of doing something. When you write a procedure proposal, introduce your idea by telling why the procedure is needed. Then describe the procedure.

A **project proposal** describes an intended project to a person or a committee to obtain permission to carry out the project. College students use proposals to describe projects they would like to do for credit.

A **business proposal** usually answers a request for goods or services that have to meet certain standards, such as how and when the goods or services must be provided. For example, in answer to a request from a city council member, a trucking company might submit a proposal to provide trash pick-up services.

A **grant proposal** requests money to pay for research or other projects. For example, a medical school might apply for a grant to study the effects of exercise on teenagers.

Proposals use persuasive writing and often require research. When you write a proposal, back up your request with reasons why it should be accepted. Support your argument with facts, statistics, and examples.

TYPES OF PROPOSALS

Procedure Proposal	Project Proposal	Business Proposal	Grant Proposal
Describe the problem that your procedure will solve.	Describe in detail the project you want to do.	State the request to which you are responding.	Describe your plan for using the grant money.
Explain your proposed procedure in step-by-step sequence.	Explain why the project is necessary.	Describe what goods or services you can provide and how they fit the requirements of the person or the group requesting proposals.	Explain how your plan meets the requirements for the grant.
Number the steps.	Explain what will be accomplished.		List your qualifications for carrying out your proposal.
Include your name, address, telephone number, and the date you submit the proposal.	Include the project's starting and ending dates.	Explain why your goods or services are better than those of others who may submit proposals.	Give reasons why the grant should be awarded to you.
	Tell what the project will cost and suggest ways to get the money to do it.	Include a quote (your price) and state exactly what the quote includes.	Include your name, address, telephone number, and the date you submit the proposal.
	Include your name, address, telephone number, and the date you submit the proposal.	Include your name, address, telephone number, and the date you submit the proposal.	

Style

Proposals usually have a title that tells what the proposal is for. The title is centered at the top of the page.

Some proposals are in paragraph form. Each line begins at the left margin in block style. Other proposals are divided into sections that have a line space between them. The model on this page is divided into sections in block style.

Field Trip Proposal **(Title)**
Submitted by: Ray Gomez **(Name of person submitting the proposal.)**
Date: September 2, 20— **(Date)**

I propose that our class take a field trip to the Stermann Apple Orchard and Cider Mill.

Activities: At the cider mill, we can go into the orchard **(Sections)** to pick apples. We can also watch a cider-making demonstration while Mr. Stermann explains the apple-pressing process. After the demonstration, we can taste free samples of cider.

Chaperones: Because our school requires one adult for every eight students on a field trip, we will need four chaperones. Our teacher, Mr. Welk, will count as one, so we need to find three more adults to accompany us. I suggest that we each ask an adult family member to volunteer.

Transportation: I have spoken to Mrs. Reed at the transportation office, and she says that we can reserve a school bus that will accommodate up to thirty passengers. Our class of twenty-four, plus four adult chaperones, would fit into one bus.

Costs: The cost per student would be $6.50. This amount covers $2.00 toward the cost of the bus and $4.50 for a bag of apples (the bag includes one caramel apple). If parents can be found to drive students in private cars, we can save the bus fee.

Dates: Mr. Stermann has November 5 and 6 and December 2 open for a group visit. I propose that we reserve November 6 since there are no school assemblies scheduled that day.

Proposals

The Parts of a Proposal

Title The title tells what the proposal is for.

Date The date is the day on which the proposal is submitted.

Body The body of a proposal can be a paragraph or it can contain many sections.

Name The name of the person submitting the proposal is always included. Some proposals are also signed by the writer. An address and phone number or some way of contacting the writer should also be included. Whoever is considering the proposal needs to have a way to get more information or to notify the writer of the proposal's acceptance or rejection.

Neatness Counts

- ✔ Your proposal will get more attention if it is neat, well organized, and easy to read. Type your proposal or create it on a computer.
- ✔ Use unlined white 8 1/2-by-11-inch paper.

Technology Tip

Create your proposal on a computer. Use the computer's formatting options, such as fonts, type sizes, and the bold feature, to organize your proposal so that it is easy to read and understand. If you have information that would be understood best in a table, create one with the table feature of a word processing program.

- ✔ Leave a two-inch margin at the top of the page and margins of at least one inch at the left, right, and bottom.
- ✔ Use a chart or a graph to organize information.

Activity

Write a Proposal Imagine that your class produced $1,000.00 in a fundraiser. Write a proposal for how the class should spend the money. Three class members can be appointed to a committee to consider the proposals and to decide which three of them the whole class should consider. Then the three proposals they have chosen can be presented to the class.

PURPOSE to write a proposal
AUDIENCE three classmates
LENGTH one page

WRITING RUBRICS To write a successful proposal, you should

- do research to find facts that support your plan
- develop your plan by categorizing ideas and organizing them into sections
- explain exactly how the money will be spent. If the money will be spent in different categories, provide a budget
- be persuasive but factual, appealing to the committee's logic
- include a table, a graph, or other organizer to make complex information easier to understand

Multimedia Presentations

Creating a Multimedia Presentation

A report that uses a combination of media (different types of communication) is called a multimedia presentation. Visuals (what you see, including written text) and sounds are combined to make a multimedia report.

Here are some parts of one student's multimedia presentation. Its purpose is to teach the audience about hummingbirds and to encourage people to plant flowers that attract them.

Business & Technical Writing

The writer uses a slide that shows the subject.

Hummingbird Facts

- more than 300 species of small birds
- rapid wing beat produces a humming sound
- feeds on nectar and tiny insects
- the only birds that can fly backwards

The writer uses a transparency to list facts.

The writer uses sound effects.

FLOWERS THAT ATTRACT HUMMINGBIRDS
- salvia
- lilies
- coral bells
- impatiens
- trumpet vine

The writer uses a handout so that the audience can keep the information.

Multimedia Presentations

Types of Media

Most media appeal either to sight (visuals) or hearing (sound). In a multimedia presentation, photos, slides, videos, illustrations, music, and other media are added to an oral presentation. The presenter becomes a narrator who guides an audience through the sights and sounds, and perhaps smells, tastes, and textures, of the presentation. The chart below lists examples of different types of media.

A multimedia presentation can be used for many purposes: to report in depth on a subject of interest, to present an opinion, to motivate an audience to do something, or to sell a product.

To prepare for a multimedia presentation, choose a thesis or a subject. Then do research at the library and on the Internet to find facts, statistics, and expert opinions on the subject. You can even interview experts by e-mail. Look for visuals and other media to enhance your subject.

If you are making a sales presentation, you aim is to make your product as appealing as possible. For example, if you are selling a new brand of dog food, you might want to demonstrate how much dogs love it by making a short video of a dog hungrily eating the food. You might also show a series of slides that tell why your brand is better than the other brands. You could even add a dog's bark as a sound effect every time you change slides. You could conclude your presentation by passing out samples of the food for dog owners to take home.

TYPES OF MEDIA		
Visuals	**Sound**	**Other Options**
Give a demonstration of how something works.	Play a cassette or CD to help your audience hear your subject (the sounds of a forest fire or an elk's bugle).	Appeal to your audience's sense of touch by having them handle an object (a blue jay's feather or part of an abandoned nest).
Use a photograph or a poster to show your subject clearly.	Use background music to help create a mood.	If you are selling a food product, pass out samples to taste and smell.
Show a video to add action.	Add sound effects to a slide show.	
Use a series of slides to show a process.		
Make charts and graphs into slides and transparencies.		
Make handouts of information you want your audience to take with them.		
Provide samples for the audience.		

Style

- Keep each visual simple.
- Use large type for words on visuals. Experiment with type sizes in the room where you will give your presentation.
- Avoid clutter. Two typefaces and three colors are plenty.
- Use the same border and background color on all of your visuals to tie them together.

An engaging picture is a good introduction to a subject.

A video can add interesting sights and sounds to the body of a presentation.

An easily read chart helps the audience make a judgment.

Dog's Delight Kibble		
Analysis	**Source**	**Health Benefit**
19% protein	turkey, lamb, eggs	strong bones and teeth
16% fat	canola oil	clear skin and shiny coat
5% fiber	rice, carrots	good digestion

Business & Technical Writing

The Parts of a Multimedia Presentation

Multimedia presentations have three parts.

Introduction In the introduction, sound, a visual, or both should be used to focus the audience's attention on the subject. For example, introduce yourself by saying, "I'm [your name] and I believe that Dog's Delight is the best dog food you can give your 'best friend.'" Here are some other ways to introduce a subject.

- ✔ Use a transparency or a slide to show a picture or the title of your subject in headline form while you introduce yourself.
- ✔ Use music to set the mood and then introduce yourself and your subject.
- ✔ Demonstrate a product while explaining who you are and what you are doing.

Technology Tip

If you have access to presentation software, do your multimedia presentation as a slideshow on a computer monitor. Such software allows you to combine written text, visuals (including movie clips and animation), and sound on a series of slides that can be shown automatically or slide by slide as a viewer pushes a button.

Body The body is the longest and most important part of a multimedia presentation. The topic should be explained and supported with facts gathered from reliable sources, such as encyclopedias, other reference books, and experts on the subject. A variety of media should be used to present facts and arguments in interesting ways. To make sure that the audience gets the message, a certain amount of time can be reserved for them to ask questions. Questions can be anticipated in advance so that extra facts and statistics will be available, if needed.

Conclusion In the brief conclusion of a presentation, the main idea is restated, the most important points are summed up, and the audience can be thanked for their attention.

Presentation Counts

To catch your audience's attention, should you begin with a video of a happy, playful dog; a transparency listing the healthy ingredients of the dog food; or a tape recording of a dog crunching kibble? Experiment with your presentation on your family and friends until you find the most successful combination of media. Use humor whenever possible. When it comes time to make your presentation, be enthusiastic and your audience will be too.

Business & Technical Writing

Activity

Create a Multimedia Sales Presentation Create a multimedia presentation to persuade an audience that a particular product or service is the best. Choose the form of your presentation and the kinds of media you will use. Make your presentation to the class.

PURPOSE To create and present a multimedia presentation

AUDIENCE classmates

LENGTH ten minutes

WRITING RUBRICS To create a persuasive multimedia presentation, you should

- make a list of products or services and then research them in a library or on the Internet
- choose a product or service. Then contact the customer service department of the company that sells it to gather facts and statistics about it. If you wish to invent a product or service, research the competition. Then make the statistics for your product more impressive than those for the competition
- summarize and organize ideas gathered from your research by making outlines, maps, organizers, or graphs
- document your sources in a bibliography
- include visuals and sound

Robert Delaunay, Rhythm no. 1

*"After all, a machine has feelings—
when it isn't a machine anymore."*

—Isaac Asimov
"Key Item"

PART 2

Grammar, Usage, and Mechanics

UNIT
8

Subjects, Predicates, and Sentences

- A **sentence** is a group of words that expresses a complete thought.

Different kinds of sentences have different purposes. A sentence can make a statement, ask a question, give a command, or express strong feeling. All sentences begin with a capital letter and end with a punctuation mark, which is determined by the purpose of that sentence.

- A **declarative** sentence makes a statement. It ends with a period.

    Ecologists study relationships in nature.

- An **interrogative sentence** asks a question. It ends with a question mark.

    Do animals and plants depend on each other?

- An **exclamatory sentence** expresses strong feeling. It ends with an exclamation point.

    What important work ecologists do!

- An **imperative sentence** gives a command or makes a request. It ends with a period or an exclamation point.

    Look at these animals.

Ecologists often do research in the field.

The work can be dangerous!

Do they also work in the lab?

Please preserve our wildlife.

Subjects, Predicates, and Sentences

Exercise 1   Identifying Kinds of Sentences

For each sentence, write whether it is *declarative, interrogative, exclamatory,* or *imperative.*

1. Environmentalists care about preserving the natural environment.
2. They also are concerned about conserving natural resources.
3. Does environmentalism involve recycling waste, too?
4. Ecologists tell us about the effects of air pollution.
5. Is "going green" a phrase that shows concern for the environment?
6. Examine the source of the water supply.
7. Aren't ecologists concerned about wildlife?
8. How awful that so many species are endangered!
9. Environmentalists can give us clues to saving endangered species.
10. What an important field this is!

Exercise 2   Punctuating Different Kinds of Sentences

Write each sentence, adding capital letters and punctuation marks where necessary.

1. ecologists and other environmentalists study the effects of air and water pollution
2. do you know how pollution affects your life
3. air pollution increases lung and breathing ailments
4. think about the effect of pollution on the water you drink
5. can fish live in poisoned water
6. look to the oceans for food in the future
7. what fascinating work marine biologists do
8. don't environmentalists use information from many sources
9. what other kinds of information do environmentalists use
10. they use knowledge from physics and mathematics
11. how important this field of study is
12. ecologists spread their message in many ways
13. ecologists often speak about the importance of a clean environment
14. they may appear before meetings of private organizations
15. do they also write magazine articles
16. read articles in the daily newspapers
17. what a need for publicity exists
18. colleges offer courses in ecology
19. students of ecology learn about the cycles of nature
20. think about becoming an ecologist

8.2 Sentences and Sentence Fragments

Every sentence has two parts: a subject and a predicate.

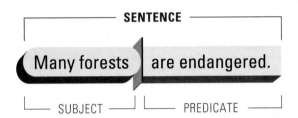

SENTENCE

Many forests | are endangered.

SUBJECT — PREDICATE

- The **subject part** of a sentence names whom or what the sentence is about.

- The **predicate part** of the sentence tells what the subject does or has. It can also describe what the subject is or is like.

A sentence must have both a subject and a predicate. It must also express a complete thought.

- A **sentence fragment** is a group of words that does not express a complete thought. It may also be missing a subject, a predicate, or both.

You often use sentence fragments when you speak. You should use complete sentences, however, in anything you write for school or business.

Correcting Sentence Fragments		
FRAGMENT	**PROBLEM**	**SENTENCE**
Lush forests.	The fragment lacks a predicate. *What do the lush forests do?*	Lush forests provide scenic land for recreation.
Inhabits the woodlands.	The fragment lacks a subject. *Who or what inhabits the woodlands?*	Wildlife inhabits the woodlands.
For animals.	The fragment lacks both a subject and a predicate.	Forests provide shelter for animals.

Exercise 3   Identifying Sentences and Fragments

Write *sentence* or *sentence fragment* for each group of words. If it is a sentence fragment, explain why.

1. Tall trees provide shade.
2. Groves of birches.
3. Under the shelter of trees.
4. Many plants grow in a forest.
5. Healthy forest land.
6. Forests provide benefits.
7. Among the trees.
8. Hardwood makes sturdy furniture.
9. Oak is a valuable hardwood.
10. Threatened by insect pests.

Exercise 4   Identifying Subjects and Predicates

Write each numbered item. Underline each subject part once and each predicate part twice. If the item is not a complete sentence, write *sentence fragment*.

1. Acres of forest land support many kinds of wildlife.
2. The great northern forest consists mostly of spruce.
3. Pine, fir, hemlock, and cedar, with birch and willow.
4. Giant redwood trees grow in the Pacific Northwest.
5. Pines are common in the South.
6. Forests of red and white pine.
7. Oak trees dominate the East.
8. Maple trees are also commonly found there.
9. Forests of evergreens cover parts of Asia.
10. Of birches and pines.
11. Tropical forests ring the middle of the globe.
12. Form a large patch in Africa, India, and Southeast Asia.
13. Remain green all year.
14. Teak is prized for its hard wood.
15. Chapparal and mesquite grow in dry areas.
16. Forests can provide food and shelter.
17. The tall trees of an ancient forest.
18. Each level of a forest has its own layer of life.
19. Even the forest soil teems with life.
20. Affected by air, water, and soil pollution.

8.3 Subjects and Predicates

A sentence consists of a subject and a predicate, which together express a complete thought. Both a subject and a predicate may consist of more than one word.

COMPLETE SUBJECT	COMPLETE PREDICATE
The capable foresters	study forests closely.
Foresters	are guardians of the environment.

- The **complete subject** includes all of the words in the subject of a sentence.

- The **complete predicate** includes all of the words in the predicate of a sentence.

Not all of the words in the subject or the predicate are of equal importance.

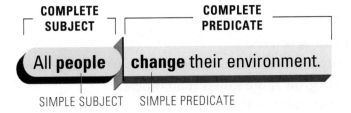

- The **simple subject** is the main word or group of words in the complete subject.

The simple subject is usually a noun or a pronoun. A **noun** is a word that names a person, a place, a thing, or an idea. A **pronoun** is a word that takes the place of one or more nouns.

- The **simple predicate** is the main word or group of words in the complete predicate.

The simple predicate is always a verb. A **verb** is a word that expresses an action or a state of being.

Sometimes the simple subject is also the complete subject. Similarly, the simple predicate may also be the complete predicate.

| Exercise 5 | **Identifying Complete Subjects and Complete Predicates** |

Write each sentence. Underline each complete subject once and each complete predicate twice.

1. Capable loggers cut only certain trees.
2. Some simple procedures preserve the conditions of the forest.
3. Several foresters study the trees in this region.
4. Their careful observations are useful to ecologists.
5. Their plans for lumber production seem reasonable.
6. Logging companies practice a variety of methods.
7. The most harmful method is clear-cutting.
8. This method totally destroys forest growth.
9. Only vast treeless areas remain.
10. New growth solves the problem in time.
11. A better way harvests only older trees.
12. Younger trees have a chance then.
13. Logging companies need plans for the distant future.
14. Concentration on short-term profits wastes natural resources.
15. Trees are a renewable resource.
16. Forest management requires a careful plan.
17. Forest workers plant new trees.
18. The bare land returns to forest eventually.
19. Some kinds of trees grow more slowly than others.
20. The slowest-growing trees are the most valuable.

| Exercise 6 | **Identifying Simple Subjects and Simple Predicates** |

Write each simple subject and each simple predicate.

1. Scientists control changes in the environment.
2. Ecologists counteract the effects of forest fires, erosion, and floods.
3. Everyone near a forest benefits from these efforts.
4. Careful people preserve natural resources.
5. Biologists observe the growth of plants.
6. Farmers improve the soil on their land.
7. The soil provides crops with valuable nutrients.
8. Some crops take few nutrients from the soil.
9. Lush green fields are a farmer's delight.
10. A temperate climate always helps.

8.4 Identifying the Subject

Most statements begin with the subject.

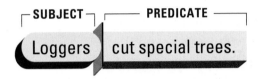

SUBJECT ┐ ┌───── PREDICATE ─────
Loggers cut special trees.

Not all sentences begin with the subject, however. Many questions begin with a word that is part of the predicate. The subject comes next, followed by the rest of the predicate.

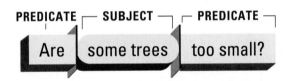

PREDICATE ┌── SUBJECT ──┐ ┌── PREDICATE ──┐
Are some trees too small?

To locate the subject in a question, it helps to rearrange the words to form a statement.

PREDICATE	SUBJECT	PREDICATE
Do	most people	understand the delicate balance of nature?
	Most people	do understand the delicate balance of nature.

The predicate also precedes the subject in statements beginning with *There is, There are, Here is,* or *Here are.*

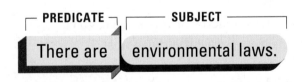

┌── PREDICATE ──┐ ┌────── SUBJECT ──────
There are environmental laws.

In commands the subject is usually not stated. The predicate is the entire sentence. The word *you* is understood to be the subject.

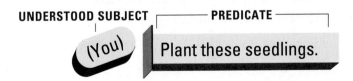

UNDERSTOOD SUBJECT ┐ ┌────── PREDICATE ──────
(You) Plant these seedlings.

Identifying the Subject in Different Sentences

Write the complete subject for each sentence. Write the word *(You)* for the subject if the sentence is a command.

1. The production of clean timber takes several years.
2. Lumber companies buy large amounts of timber.
3. Some simple procedures protect the conditions of the forest.
4. Growers of trees divide the forest into several sections.
5. Loggers work one section each year.
6. The workers cut individual trees.
7. Do the loggers leave some trees?
8. Think of the heavy chain saws.
9. Do plants sprout easily in the region?
10. Here is a book about ecology.
11. Other interesting books on the subject are in the library.
12. Many kinds of bacteria help the environment.
13. Do human beings change their environment?
14. Green plants need a certain amount of light.
15. Do ecologists study animal populations?
16. Scientists reduce the number of undesirable insects.
17. Look at the new plants in this region.
18. Some ecologists look for new methods of farming.
19. There are many helpful agricultural advances.
20. Learn about them when you have time.

Exercise 8 **Finding the Subject**

Write the complete subject from each of the following sentences.

1. Can the rain forest be saved?
2. Is the clearing of thousands of acres of forest necessary?
3. There are many reasons to preserve the rain forest.
4. List as many reasons as you can think of.
5. Is an important reason the effect on global weather patterns?
6. Think about the effect on wildlife.
7. Consider the valuable resources that are lost.
8. Does the rain forest release oxygen into the atmosphere?
9. Here is the world's greatest living resource.
10. Work to save it.

Subjects, Predicates, and Sentences

Compound Subjects and Predicates

A sentence may have more than one simple subject or simple predicate.

■ A **compound subject** has two or more simple subjects that have the same predicate. The subjects are joined by *and, or,* or *nor.*

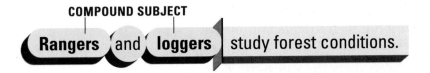

COMPOUND SUBJECT

Rangers and **loggers** study forest conditions.

When the two simple subjects are joined by *and* or by *both . . . and,* the compound subject is plural and takes the plural form of the verb. In the sentence above, the verb *study* agrees with the plural compound subject. When all parts of a compound subject refer to the same person or thing, the subject takes the singular form of the verb.

When simple subjects are joined by *or* or *nor,* the compound subject may be singular or plural. The verb must agree with the nearer simple subject.

A ranger or **one** of his assistants **is** always on watch in the observation tower.

A ranger or his **assistants are** always on watch in the observation tower.

■ A **compound predicate** has two or more simple predicates, or verbs, that have the same subject. The simple predicates are connected by *and, but, or,* or *nor.*

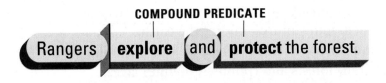

COMPOUND PREDICATE

Rangers explore and **protect** the forest.

Explore and *protect* are the simple predicates, or verbs, in the compound predicate. The plural noun *rangers* is the subject of both verbs. Notice that both verbs agree with the plural noun in the subject.

Exercise 9   Identifying Compound Subjects and Predicates

Write whether each sentence has a *compound subject* or a *compound predicate*.

1. Trees and grass hold soil in place.
2. Scientists observe and study the effects of erosion.
3. Both plants and minerals enrich the soil.
4. Erosion destroys and wastes valuable land.
5. Winds and rain sometimes harm the earth.
6. The wind lifts and blows away the topsoil.
7. Neither the soil nor its nutrients last forever.
8. Either rain or flood waters wash soil into streams.
9. Streams and rivers carry the soil away.
10. Crops wither and die in the poor soil.

Exercise 10   Making Subjects and Verbs Agree

Write each sentence, using the correct form of the verb in parentheses.

1. Rachel Carson and other biologists (warns, warn) people.
2. She and others (tells, tell) about the dangers of pollution.
3. *Silent Spring* (explains, explain) about pesticides.
4. Both plants and trees (releases, release) oxygen.
5. Some chemicals either (fights, fight) or (controls, control) pests.
6. Humans and animals often (eats, eat) the same foods.
7. The chemicals both (travels, travel) and (mixes, mix) in the food chain.
8. Insecticides and other chemicals (poisons, poison) insects.
9. Birds and mice (eats, eat) the poisoned insects.
10. Farmers (sprays, spray) and (harvests, harvest) grain crops.
11. Pesticides (turns, turn) up in milk and butter.
12. Other types of pollution (reaches, reach) and (harms, harm) us.
13. Power plants and cars (releases, release) gases into the air.
14. Some of these gases (mixes, mix) and (forms, form) acid rain.
15. Either smog or acid rain (injures, injure) the earth.
16. Air pollution and water pollution (affects, affect) the soil.
17. Acid rain (kills, kill) forests and (pollutes, pollute) lakes.
18. Both fertilizers and pesticides (leaks, leak) down through the dirt.
19. These (enters, enter) and (pollutes, pollute) underground water.
20. Either scientists or lab workers (studies, study) the effects of pollution.

Simple and Compound Sentences

■ A **simple sentence** has one subject and one predicate.

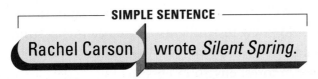

SIMPLE SENTENCE

Rachel Carson | wrote *Silent Spring*.

A simple sentence may have a compound subject, a compound predicate, or both, as in the following example.

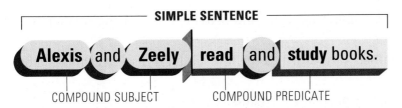

SIMPLE SENTENCE

Alexis (and) **Zeely** | **read** (and) **study** books.

COMPOUND SUBJECT · · · COMPOUND PREDICATE

■ A **compound sentence** is a sentence that contains two or more simple sentences joined by a comma and a coordinating conjunction or by a semicolon.

A compound sentence has two complete subjects and two complete predicates.

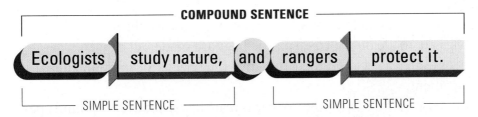

COMPOUND SENTENCE

Ecologists | study nature, (and) rangers | protect it.

SIMPLE SENTENCE · · · SIMPLE SENTENCE

A run-on sentence is two or more sentences incorrectly written as one sentence. To correct a run-on, write separate sentences or combine the sentences as shown below.

Correcting Run-on Sentences	
RUN-ON	**CORRECT**
Ecologists study nature they protect it.	Ecologists study nature. **They** protect it.
Ecologists study nature, they protect it.	Ecologists study nature**, and** they protect it.
	Ecologists study nature**;** they protect it.

Exercise 11 Identifying Simple and Compound Sentences

Write whether each sentence is *simple*, *compound*, or *run-on*. If it is a run-on sentence, rewrite it correctly.

1. Ecologists study forests, their research provides information for the rangers and for government agencies.
2. Ecologists study and work in modern, well-equipped laboratories.
3. The laboratories develop new instruments of science the instruments must work well in the field.
4. Some problems arise in forest environments; ecologists develop solutions to these problems.
5. Neither the animals' homes nor their food sources escape the effects of the unwise use of resources.
6. Small plants grow under tall trees and provide food for the smaller animals of the forest.
7. Sometimes animals can return to the forest after a disaster; this heartens ecologists.
8. Soil and leaves may be losing elements.
9. The burning of gas, oil, and coal pollutes the air and perhaps causes acid rain in certain regions.
10. A great many lakes in Canada and forests in the United States are harmed by acid rain.
11. Scientists develop antipollution devices farmers use natural fertilizers.
12. The Environmental Protection Agency establishes and enforces clean-air standards.
13. Ordinary people can help end pollution and save the earth.
14. Paper bags are made out of trees, plastic bags are made out of oil.
15. Many people are eager to do their part, but they need information and encouragement.
16. Americans use 50 million tons of paper a year that is about 580 pounds per person.
17. Americans should save newspapers and recycle them.
18. Newspaper is shredded and mashed into pulp, and the pulp is turned back into paper.
19. This could save millions of trees a year the effort is worth it.
20. There is only so much laws can do, people must cooperate.

SUBJECTS, PREDICATES, AND SENTENCES

In *Water Sky,* Lincoln Noah, a young half-Inuit boy from Massachusetts, visits the whaling village where his father once lived. There Lincoln observes how a community can live in harmony with its environment. In this passage, the boy learns about the relationship that exists between whales and humans by talking to an Inuit whaling captain, Vincent Ologak. The passage has been annotated to show some of the sentence structures covered in this unit.

Literature Model

from *Water Sky*
by Jean Craighead George

Vincent folded his arms and stood beside him. "Lincoln Noah," he said, "I have something very important to say to you." His eyes were soft, and his strength seemed to have returned.

"A whale is coming to you."

"A whale is coming to me, Vincent Ologak? I do not understand."

"The animals give themselves to the Eskimos. They let us kill them. They then become us: our blood, our voices, our spirits. They join us in our bodies. That is what they wish. We are all one."

Lincoln tried to understand. Vincent continued.

"When your father left my igloo many years ago, he asked me what he could do to thank me. And so I said to him: Name your first son Lincoln, for the great protector of men. And give him a second name, Noah, for the great protector of animals."

— Compound predicate

— Compound sentence

— Complete subject

— Complete predicate

— Declarative sentence

Subjects, Predicates, and Sentences

Grammar Review

> "He never told me that," Lincoln said. "I sure wish he had. I always hated my name. Kids made fun of it." He paused. "I guess I never asked about it."
>
> "Lincoln Noah is a fine name all right. I knew some-day there would be a whale who would come to one named Lincoln Noah. I have waited and waited for you to grow up and the whale to grow old."

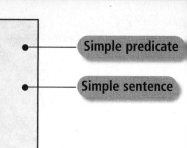

Simple predicate

Simple sentence

Review: Exercise 1   **Identifying Sentences and Sentence Fragments**

Write each sentence and underline each complete subject once and each complete predicate twice. If the item is not a complete sentence, write *sentence fragment*.

SAMPLE   Vincent said something important to Lincoln.
ANSWER   <u>Vincent</u> <u>said something important to Lincoln.</u>

1. Talked about the bond between men and animals.
2. Lincoln listened to Ologak.
3. The whaling captain knew Lincoln's father.
4. Had lived in Ologak's igloo long ago.
5. Lincoln's father was grateful to Ologak.
6. Ologak said to name the boy Lincoln Noah.
7. For Lincoln, the protector of men, and Noah, the protector of animals.
8. Lincoln Noah had hated his name.
9. Teased by the other kids because of his strange name.
10. Lincoln Noah was a fine name according to Ologak.
11. A whale who would come to one named Lincoln Noah.
12. Waited and waited for him to grow up.
13. And the whale to grow old.
14. The whaling captain told Lincoln about the whale.
15. Lincoln did not understand.
16. The animals give themselves to the Eskimos.
17. The whales and the Eskimos become one.
18. Their blood, their voices, their spirits.
19. The whales wished to do this.
20. Vincent continued with his story.

Review: Exercise 2 **Identifying Complete Subjects and Complete Predicates**

Write each sentence. Underline each complete subject once and each complete predicate twice.

SAMPLE The Inuits' way of life is rapidly disappearing.
ANSWER <u>The Inuits' way of life</u> <u>is rapidly disappearing.</u>

1. The land of the Inuit stretches from Siberia to Greenland.
2. This cold country is troubled by gales.
3. Inuits of the past were expert hunters.
4. They hunted whale, walrus, seal, and caribou.
5. Two kinds of boats carried them across the water.
6. The light, swift kayak was ideal for chasing seals.
7. The larger, heavier umiak transported entire families.
8. Inuits of former times lived in harmony with the seasons.
9. They hunted through the spring, summer, and fall.
10. Their winter homes were snowhouse villages on the sea ice.

Review: Exercise 3 **Identifying Simple Subjects and Simple Predicates**

Write each simple subject and each simple predicate.

SAMPLE Jean Craighead George studied science in college.
ANSWER Jean Craighead George / studied

1. George's family enjoyed nature and the outdoors.
2. Her father was an entomologist.
3. Her jobs involved writing or art.
4. George writes about nature and natural history.
5. Her first books were animal stories for children.
6. The author explores the places in her books.
7. This extensive research takes time and energy.
8. Natural history blends with good stories in her books.
9. Her most famous book is probably *My Side of the Mountain*.
10. However, her own favorite is *Spring Comes to the Ocean*.

Grammar Review

Review: Exercise 4   **Identifying Subjects and Predicates in Questions**

Rewrite each question as a statement. Then underline each simple subject once and each simple predicate twice.

SAMPLE   Do laws protect certain kinds of whales?
ANSWER   <u>Laws</u> <u>do protect</u> certain kinds of whales.

1. Are whales mammals?
2. Have people hunted whales since prehistoric times?
3. Can a whale produce sounds underwater?
4. Are some whales one hundred feet long?
5. Does size vary within species?
6. Have people confused whales with fish?
7. Does blubber insulate whales from the cold?
8. Are killer whales the fastest of all whales?
9. Do killer whales prey on seals, dolphins, and porpoises?
10. Are dolphins classified as whales?

Review: Exercise 5   **Identifying Compound Subjects and Compound Predicates**

Write whether the sentence has a *compound subject* or a *compound predicate*.

SAMPLE   Whales and dolphins have flippers instead of forelegs.
ANSWER   compound subject

1. The Greek philosopher Aristotle thought and wrote about whales.
2. Marine biologists observe and study marine mammals.
3. Whales and other marine mammals have traces of limbs.
4. They have lungs and breathe air.
5. Elephants and rhinos are tiny compared with blue whales.
6. Humpback whales and blue whales eat tiny sea creatures.
7. Sheets of baleen trap and strain their food.
8. Toothed whales navigate and find food by means of sound.
9. Humpback whales and gray whales migrate north in the summer.
10. Thirty-foot-long orcas attack and eat larger whales.

Review: Exercise 6   **Making Subjects and Verbs Agree**

Write the correct form of the verb in parentheses.

1. Both the Inuit hunter and his daughter (watches, watch) the old whale.
2. The whale and his pod (lives, live) in the Bering Sea in winter.
3. The lengthening day and warming waters (signals, signal) them.
4. The whales (leaves, leave) and (swims, swim) north.
5. Either adolescents or young adults (makes, make) up most of the first group.
6. Mothers, calves, and old whales (forms, form) the next wave.
7. Whales of assorted sizes and ages (migrates, migrate) last.
8. Neither scientists nor whalers (understands, understand) why they do this.
9. All the whales (rests, rest) and (feeds, feed) in their summer home.
10. Either the hunter or his daughter (waves, wave) goodbye to the whale.

Review: Exercise 7   **Identifying Simple and Compound Sentences**

Write whether each sentence is *simple* or *compound*.

1. One creature had a long, spiraling tusk.
2. It resembled the mythical unicorn, and they called it the unicorn of the sea.
3. That creature was the narwhal, but little could be learned of it.
4. Few people actually saw the narwhal, and it eventually became a fantasy itself.
5. Kings and queens desired and paid fortunes for narwhal ivory.
6. Narwhals live in the far North; they are creatures of the ice.
7. Male narwhals have two tusks, but only one tusk grows long.
8. Scientists and other people wonder about the tusk's purpose.
9. The narwhal's tasty, vitamin-rich meat provided food for Inuits and their sled dogs.
10. Narwhals were once widely hunted, but recent laws restrict hunting and protect these unique creatures.

Subjects, Predicates, and Sentences

Grammar Review

Review: Exercise 8 **Identifying Compound Sentences and Run-on Sentences**

Write *compound* if a sentence is a compound sentence. If it is a run-on sentence, rewrite it correctly.

1. Whales, dolphins, and porpoises are members of the order called cetaceans, and they are true air-breathing mammals.
2. Cetaceans are warm-blooded, they nurse their young on milk.
3. Cetaceans are divided into two subclasses; these are toothed whales and baleen whales.
4. Toothed whales are predators they pursue fish and squid.
5. Among the largest whales, only the sperm whale has teeth; the others are all baleen whales.
6. Baleen whales have fringed plates of baleen instead of teeth, and they strain small sea life out of the water.
7. These gentle giants were hunted almost to extinction, just a few hundred blue whales remain.
8. Whales need time to increase in number or they will die out.
9. The International Whaling Commission is working to end whaling, but some countries will not cooperate.
10. Norway hunts whales Japan, Iceland, and Korea do also.

Review: Exercise 9 **Writing Compound Sentences**

Use *and, but,* or *or* to combine each pair of simple sentences into a compound sentence.

1. Lincoln's father had lived in the village. He wanted his son to spend time there too.
2. The whale hunters had to locate and spear a whale. People in their village would starve.
3. The whale would provide them with meat and blubber. They would also use it for oil and leather.
4. Lincoln hunted for the whale. He killed it.
5. Lincoln loved the Inuit community. He felt he should return to his life in Massachusetts.

Review: Exercise 10

Proofreading

The following passage is about Siwidi, a mythological hero of the Kwakiutl. The whale mask below was used in ceremonial dances to reenact that hero's adventures. Rewrite the passage, correcting the errors in spelling, capitalization, grammar, and usage. Add any missing punctuation. There are ten errors.

The Legend of Siwidi

[1]Siwidi acquired many wonderful gifts during his adventures in an undersea kingdom [2]These gifts enabled Siwidi the great hero of the kwakiutl, to change his appearance. [3]When the hero rose from the sea, he appeared to his people as a whale with an eagle on it's back and a double tail. [4]People in canoes chased this great creature but they couldn't catch it. [5]As a result of Siwidis undersea adventures, him became known as "Born-to-Be-Head-of-the-World."

Artist unknown, Kwakiutl whale mask, nineteenth century

⁶The Kwakiutl developed a dance to celabrate Siwidi's appearance as a whale. ⁷The performer imitates the movements of a whale throughout this dance; also wears a large whale mask. ⁸By recognizing the bond between animals and people, Vincent Ologak of *Water Sky* showed his respect for whales the dance reflects the respect the Kwakiutl have for Siwidi and for all whales.

Review: Exercise 11

Mixed Review

Identify the underlined word or words in each of the following sentences as a *complete subject*, a *complete predicate*, a *simple subject*, a *simple predicate*, a *compound subject*, or a *compound predicate*.

¹The <u>greatest event in an Inupiaq village</u> is the whale hunt. ²One whale <u>can feed</u> many people. ³Each <u>village</u> may take only a limited number of whales, however. ⁴The Inupiaq people <u>respect and honor</u> the whales they hunt. ⁵They <u>think of the meat as a gift from the animal itself</u>. ⁶Inupiaq children learn an important lesson. ⁷<u>Humans</u> and <u>animals</u> must live in harmony with each other and with nature.

⁸Everyone <u>joins in the work of bringing in the whale</u>. ⁹Even the youngest <u>boys and girls</u> help pull the whale onto the ice. ¹⁰<u>Many children</u> hope to become whaling captains someday. ¹¹Whaling captains earn money from the whales they catch. ¹²More important, a successful captain <u>divides and shares</u> his catch. ¹³In the Arctic, <u>no one</u> goes hungry when a whale hunt is successful. ¹⁴<u>The elderly and the sick</u> receive their share of food. ¹⁵<u>Young people in the Arctic</u> have been taught sharing as a way of life for centuries.

¹⁶Inupiaq <u>schoolchildren</u> learn both English and their native language in school. ¹⁷They also <u>learn the traditional ways of their people</u>. ¹⁸Not all Inupiaq children <u>stay and live</u> in their home villages. ¹⁹High school <u>graduates</u> often go on to college, but some return to the Arctic. ²⁰Many college graduates <u>teach or work</u> in the native government system.

Writing Application

TIME

For more about the writing process, see **TIME Facing the Blank Page,** pp. 97–107.

Sentence Types in Writing

Madeleine L'Engle uses different kinds of sentences in *A Wind in the Door* to convey her speakers' tones and to make her writing clearer and more interesting. Examine the passage below, noting the italicized sentences.

"Okay, did the big boys jump you in the schoolyard this time, or when you got off the bus?"

"Meg, you aren't listening to me."

"I happen to care that you've been in school for two months now and not a single week has gone by that you haven't been roughed up. If you've been talking about dragons in the garden or wherever they are, I suppose that explains it."

"I haven't. *Don't underestimate me.* I didn't see them till I got home."

Techniques with Sentence Types

Try to apply some of Madeleine L'Engle's techniques when you write.

❶ Use interrogative sentences to capture a speaker's tone and show that he or she is asking a question. Compare these:

DECLARATIVE VERSION the big boys jumped you when you got off the bus

L'ENGLE'S VERSION did the big boys jump you in the schoolyard this time, or when you got off the bus?

❷ Make your writing more effective by using imperative sentences to convey a speaker's feelings as he or she makes a demand or request.

DECLARATIVE VERSION I wish you wouldn't underestimate me.

L'ENGLE'S VERSION Don't underestimate me.

Subjects, Predicates, and Sentences

Practice Practice these techniques by revising the following passage. Pay particular attention to the underlined words, changing the sentence types as necessary to make the passage more interesting, varied, and effective.

"By dinnertime we should be there," said Marshall. "The stream might still be frozen." He leaned eagerly over the front seat to nudge his father's shoulder. "Might it be, Marsh?" replied Ed. "We'll check it out as soon as we get there." "I want to know how long it will be until we get there."

"Oh, about an hour, I'd guess," said his father. "You could sit back and relax."

"Dad, I want to hear about how we're going to ice fish in the stream," said Marshall as the car turned off the highway for Naylor's Peak.

Nouns

Kinds of Nouns

Look at the incomplete sentence below. Decide which of the words in the box that follows can complete the sentence.

The inventor created many new  .

across	processes	dramatic	the
goes	products	things	machines

The words *processes, products, things,* and *machines* can complete the sentence. These words are called nouns.

■ A **noun** names a person, place, thing, or idea.

There are two basic kinds of nouns: proper nouns and common nouns.

■ A **proper noun** names a *specific* person, place, thing, or idea.

■ A **common noun** names *any* person, place, thing, or idea.

The first word and all other important words in proper nouns are capitalized.

Nouns can be either concrete or abstract.

■ **Concrete nouns** name things that you can see or touch.

■ **Abstract nouns** name ideas, qualities, or characteristics.

KINDS OF NOUNS		
PROPER NOUNS	**COMMON NOUNS**	
	Concrete	**Abstract**
Thomas Edison	inventor	idea
Naples, Florida	city	progress
Monday	calendar	time
African American	trumpet	culture

Nouns

Identifying Nouns, Capitalizing Proper Nouns

Write each noun that appears in the following sentences. Indicate whether each is a *common noun* or a *proper noun*. Remember to capitalize each proper noun.

1. Guglielmo marconi sent the first electronic signals through the air.
2. With his equipment, marconi sent the first signals across the atlantic ocean.
3. Reginald fessenden was the first person to transmit his voice on radio.
4. The radio was first used for communication between ships at sea.
5. Messages on the radio helped save many victims of disasters at sea.
6. Radios were used to help rescue survivors from the shipwrecked *titanic*.
7. The first musical broadcast occurred two years earlier.
8. The broadcast was from the metropolitan opera house in new york city.
9. The program starred enrico caruso, a famous singer from naples, italy.
10. A station in pittsburgh announced the results of the 1920 presidential elections.
11. The first commercial station was started in that same year.
12. Franklin roosevelt often spoke to the nation on the radio.
13. Radio was once the most popular entertainment in the united states.
14. Fred allen, jack benny, and bob hope had popular comedy shows on the radio.
15. A beam from a radio was able to guide a plane from cleveland to new york.
16. Later, radar helped locate planes or ships in dark or stormy weather.
17. Then police began to use radar to locate cars that were speeding.
18. Radios were first used by soldiers during world war II.
19. People can now call from a phone inside a car, a boat, or other places.
20. A personal pager, or "beeper," can tell a person to call the office or home.

Exercise 2 **Identifying Nouns**

Write the nouns you find below in two lists: *concrete nouns* and *abstract nouns*.

1. People with imagination have been inventing things from the earliest time.
2. The first inventions were based on the need for food and protection.
3. Early tools were created from natural things—wood, bone, stone, and hides.
4. The discovery by early people that heated metal could be shaped was important.
5. Our entire industrial civilization grew out of this important knowledge.
6. With the improvement in vehicles, people began to travel to other lands.
7. These travelers traded goods and brought back knowledge of new inventions.
8. The creation of new inventions has not always been greeted with enthusiasm.
9. New inventions have often caused anger among workers in factories.
10. The workers had the great fear that machines might replace them.

Nouns

9.2 Compound Nouns

Some nouns consist of more than one word. The noun *hometown*, for instance, is made up of the two words *home* and *town*. These nouns are called compound nouns.

■ **Compound nouns** are nouns that are made up of two or more words.

Compound nouns can be written as one word—*hometown*— or as more than one word—*ice cream*. Other compound nouns are written as two or more words joined by hyphens—*mother-in-law*. If you're unsure of how to write a compound noun, check a dictionary.

Compound Nouns	
One word	doorknob, homeroom, strongbox, bookmark, fireplace
Hyphenated	age-group, runner-up, great-grandmother, kilowatt-hour
More than one word	dining room, motion picture, maid of honor, music box

Most nouns can be singular or plural. A singular noun names one person, place, thing, or idea. A plural noun names more than one. Most plural nouns are formed by adding *-s* or *-es* to the singular form of the noun.

To write the plural forms of some compound nouns, however, you need to know special rules.

Forming Plural Compound Nouns		
	To Make Plural	**Examples**
One word	Add **-s** to most words. Add **-es** to most words that end in **ch, sh, s,** or **x**.	fireplace**s**, bookmark**s**, strongbox**es**
Hyphenated	Make the most important part of the word plural.	runner**s**-up, mother**s**-in-law, great-grandmother**s**
More than one word	Make the most important part of the word plural.	music box**es**, dining room**s**, maid**s** of honor

| **Exercise 3** | **Making Compound Nouns Plural** |

Write the plural form of each compound noun below.

1. steam engine	6. jack-of-all-trades	11. chainsaw	16. baby-sitter
2. wheelbarrow	7. governor-general	12. dishwasher	17. basketball
3. housekeeper	8. father-in-law	13. cotton gin	18. public school
4. ice skate	9. box seat	14. mailbox	19. great-aunt
5. headache	10. stepsister	15. home team	20. go-cart

| **Exercise 4** | **Making Compound Nouns Plural** |

Write each sentence. Use the plural form of the compound noun in parentheses to complete each sentence.

1. The newspaper gave all the reporters new _____.   (personal computer)
2. The reporters used _____ to interview their subjects.   (tape recorder)
3. Because of heavy use, the _____ kept breaking down.   (copy machine)
4. The paper's _____ never stopped running.   (printing press)
5. The city's major newspapers were invited to witness the launching of the two _____ .   (space probe)
6. The four _____ decided to attend with their staffs.   (editor in chief)
7. The _____ of several countries were present.   (vice president)
8. All reporters carried _____ to keep in touch with the office during the blizzard.   (cellular phone)
9. Several local _____ predicted a record snowfall.   (weather bureau)
10. Half the town's _____ broke down during the storm.   (snowplow)
11. All the _____ at a nearby ski resort were even shut down.   (ski lift)
12. Both _____ opposed the mayor's reelection.   (political action committee)
13. The _____ were sealed before the votes were recounted.   (ballot box)
14. The new mayor presented the city with five new _____ .   (fire engine)
15. Two _____ escaped injury when they interrupted a robbery. (attorney-at-law)
16. Detectives went to _____ all over the city looking for one injured suspect. (emergency room)
17. The other robbers were stopped at one of the _____ outside of town. (roadblock)
18. Photographers were asked to make _____ of the ceremony.   (videotape)
19. Four retired _____ stood while the monument was dedicated. (sea captain)
20. The general's two _____ also attended the ceremony. (great-granddaughter)

9.3 Possessive Nouns

A noun can be singular, naming only one person, place, thing, or idea; or it can be plural, naming two or more. A noun can also show ownership or possession of things or qualities. This kind of noun is called a possessive noun.

■ A **possessive noun** names who or what owns or has something.

Possessive nouns can be common or proper nouns. They can also be singular or plural. The following pairs of sentences show how possessive nouns are formed.

> **Miko** owns a book about inventions.
> **Miko's** book is about inventions.

> Several **books** have indexes.
> Check several **books'** indexes.

Possessive nouns are formed in one of two ways. To form the possessive of most nouns, you add an apostrophe and -*s* ('*s*). This is true for all singular nouns and for plural nouns not ending in -*s*. To form the possessive of plural nouns already ending in -*s*, you add only an apostrophe. These rules are summarized in the chart below.

Forming Possessive Nouns		
Nouns	**To Form Possessive**	**Examples**
Most singular nouns	Add an apostrophe and **-s** ('**s**).	a girl—a girl**'s** coat Wichita—Wichita**'s** population
Singular nouns ending in **-s**	Add an apostrophe and **-s** ('**s**).	Joseph Ives—Joseph Ives**'s** clock Alexis—Alexis**'s** book
Plural nouns ending in **-s**	Add an apostrophe (').	boys—boys**'** shoes the Wrights—the Wrights**'** plane
Plural nouns not ending in **-s**	Add an apostrophe and **-s** ('**s**).	children—children**'s** toys women—women**'s** organization

Forming the Possessive

Write the possessive form of each underlined word below.

1. Marie Curie discovery
2. scientist experiments
3. Gus house
4. Ellie jacket
5. machines designers
6. monkeys tails
7. coach speech
8. Queen Isabella policy
9. principals offices
10. men store
11. Hawaii climate
12. Alice Ross address
13. children plans
14. skiers clothing
15. library books
16. turkey feathers
17. Henry music
18. boss office
19. brothers room
20. cow milk

Identifying Singular and Plural Possessives

Write the possessive nouns. Add or insert apostrophes where needed, and label each possessive noun as *singular* or *plural*.

1. Benjamin Franklin was one of Americas greatest citizens.
2. Among Franklins many occupations were printer, publisher, author, scientist, and statesman.
3. Although this mans interests were many, he probably liked science best.
4. The weathers many changes interested Franklin.
5. Electricitys mysteries were of particular interest to this inventive scientist.
6. One of Franklins experiments led to the invention of the lightning rod.
7. The inventors idea came during a violent thunderstorm.
8. Franklin sailed a silk and metal-tipped kite into a stormy clouds interior.
9. Soon a spark of electricity traveled down the kites string.
10. A metal key hanging from the kite string attracted the electrical charges, and Franklins nearby hand drew sparks.
11. Lucks fortune was with Franklin that day.
12. Others who tried it did not escape the sparks danger and were killed.
13. Franklin was sure of his experiments meaning—that lightning is electricity!
14. Cities buildings are safer because of the lightning rod.
15. Placed on a buildings highest point, a metal rod connects to a heavy wire that leads to another rod deep in the ground.
16. Lightnings electricity is attracted to the rod.
17. It is then guided into the ground, ensuring the peoples safety.
18. Lightning rods have also protected many ships crews from storms at sea.
19. At one time, lightning storms destroyed many citizens homes.
20. Lightning rods even saved the Franklin familys home.

9.4 Distinguishing Plurals, Possessives, and Contractions

It can be easy to confuse plural nouns and possessive nouns. Most plural nouns and possessive nouns end with the letter -*s*. They sound alike, but their spellings and meanings differ.

Plural and Possessive Nouns		
	Example	**Meaning**
Plural Noun	The **scientists** met.	more than one scientist
Plural Possessive Noun	The **scientists'** discovery was important.	the discovery of the scientists
Singular Possessive Noun	This **scientist's** photograph is in the newspaper.	the photograph of one scientist

Notice that plural nouns do not have apostrophes. Plural possessive nouns end with an apostrophe. Singular possessive nouns end with an apostrophe and an -*s*.

An apostrophe is also used to indicate where letters have been left out in a contraction.

- A **contraction** is a word made by combining two words into one by leaving out one or more letters.

In the sentence *Elaine's going to the exhibit,* the word *Elaine's* is a contraction. It is made by combining the singular proper noun *Elaine* and the verb *is.* The apostrophe takes the place of the letter *i.* The contraction *Elaine's* sounds the same and is spelled the same as the singular possessive form of the proper noun *Elaine.*

Possessive Nouns and Contractions		
	Example	**Meaning**
Possessive	**Elaine's** invention is a new bell.	the invention by Elaine
Contraction	**Elaine's** going to the exhibit.	Elaine is going

Exercise 7   Using Contractions

Write the sentence in each pair that contains a contraction. Underline the contraction; above it, write the two words that have been combined.

1. This article's topic is space flight. This article's about space flight.
2. The satellite's an invention with many uses. The satellite's uses are many.
3. Russia's the first nation with a space satellite. Russia's satellite was *Sputnik*.
4. A rocket's used to launch satellites. A rocket's launch is exciting to watch.
5. Rockets break free of earth's atmosphere. Earth's beautiful from space.
6. Space flight's technology grows in the 1960s. Space flight's always in the news.
7. Our nation's first manned space flight is May 5, 1961. The nation's happy!
8. Shepard's the first American in space. Shepard's flight lasts fifteen minutes.
9. Russia's first astronaut traveled earlier. Russia's ahead in the space race!
10. The next decade's filled with flights. At decade's end, men walk on the moon!

Exercise 8   Using Plural and Possessive Nouns

Write each sentence, choosing the correct word in parentheses.

1. Modern (rockets, rockets') carry satellites into orbit around Earth.
2. Some of the (satellites, satellites') equipment is powered by sunlight.
3. Ground (stations, stations') antennae send signals to satellites.
4. These (stations, stations') also receive signals from satellites.
5. (Farmers, Farmers') crops need good weather.
6. Satellites in space send weather (reports, reports') back to earth.
7. Some satellites take photographs of distant (galaxies, galaxies') stars.
8. Other (satellites, satellites') relay telephone calls between countries.
9. My friend in Omaha can speak to her (friend's, friends) relatives in Australia.
10. The goal of the space (probes, probes') was to explore the solar system.
11. The Soviet (Unions, Union's) *Venera* probes were the first to land on Venus.
12. The *Viking* (rockets, rockets') purpose was to explore the planet Mars.
13. After two (year's, years') travel, *Pioneer 10* left the solar system.
14. *Voyager 1* took (pictures, pictures') of the rings of Saturn.
15. *Voyager 2* flew by the (planets, planets') Jupiter, Saturn, Uranus, and Neptune.
16. (Plans, Plans') called for *Voyager 2* to fly past Jupiter first.
17. It took ten (years, years') time for *Voyager 2* to reach Neptune.
18. Of all the space (probes, probes'), *Helios 1* came closest to the sun.
19. The (scientists, scientists') next project was to build space shuttles.
20. The (shuttles, shuttles') goals were to launch and repair satellites.

9.5 Collective Nouns

Certain nouns name a group made up of a number of people or things. These nouns are called *collective nouns.*

■ A **collective noun** names a group of individuals.

Collective Nouns			
committee	audience	swarm	club
family	team	crowd	orchestra
flock	class	jury	herd

Nouns and verbs in sentences must always show agreement. Collective nouns, however, present special agreement problems. Every collective noun can have either a singular meaning or a plural meaning. If you are speaking about the group as a unit, then the noun has a singular meaning. If you want to refer to the individual members of the group, then the noun has a plural meaning.

> The whole **flock** enters the meadow through a gate.
>   [a unit, singular]
> The **flock** enter by different gates. [individual members, plural]
>
> The entire **audience** applauds the performers. [a unit, singular]
> The **audience** take their seats. [individual members, plural]

When the collective noun is a single unit, use a singular verb. When the collective noun refers to the individual members of the group, use a plural verb. Other words in the sentence can help you tell whether a collective noun is singular or plural.

> The **family** begins <u>its</u> trip. [its, singular]
> The **family** eat <u>their</u> sandwiches. [their, plural]

The entire
audience applauds
the performers.

The **audience strain**
their necks to see.

Exercise 9   Identifying Collective Nouns

Write each sentence. Underline each collective noun and write whether its meaning is *singular* or *plural*.

1. The crowd shakes the stadium with its school cheer.
2. The crowd leave their seats.
3. The committee argue with one another over the rules.
4. The committee holds its first meeting tonight.
5. The class give their various opinions about the issue.

Exercise 10   Using Collective Nouns

Write each sentence. Underline each collective noun and write whether its meaning is *singular* or *plural*. Use the verb form in parentheses that agrees with the collective noun.

1. The chorus (agrees, agree) about which song it will sing.
2. The chorus (sings, sing) its five favorite songs.
3. The baseball team (plays, play) its first game of the season tonight.
4. The school of dolphins (attacks, attack) their enemies, the sharks.
5. The musical group (performs, perform) its latest hit.
6. The crew of volunteers (tosses, toss) their shovels onto the truck bed at sundown.
7. The family (cleans, clean) their rooms.
8. The jury (sits, sit) in its special section of the courtroom.
9. The enthusiastic audience (shows, show) its approval with a standing ovation.
10. After the intermission, the audience (straggles, straggle) toward their seats.
11. Each political party (works, work) untiringly for its candidate.
12. After a month's preparation, the class (presents, present) their projects.
13. When a dog disturbs them, the flock of blackbirds (scatters, scatter) in many directions.
14. In fall the flock (flies, fly) south to its winter home in Florida.
15. Every summer before school starts, the band (attends, attend) summer camp.
16. The water polo club (swims, swim) their laps on empty stomachs after school.
17. The pack of hyenas (forages, forage) near their den for food.
18. The President's cabinet (attends, attend) the State of the Union address.
19. The U.S. Congress (meets, meet) in the Capitol in Washington, D.C.
20. The herd of cows (chews, chew) their cuds under the gathering rain clouds.

9.6　Appositives

■ An **appositive** is a noun placed next to another noun to identify it or add information about it.

> Nicolas-François Appert, **a chef,** made an important discovery.

The noun *chef* identifies *Nicolas-François Appert,* the noun next to it. *Chef* tells what Appert was. In this sentence, *a chef* is an appositive.

An appositive is sometimes accompanied by other words.

The noun *chef* still identifies Appert, as it did in the original sentence. Here, however, the word *French* is used to describe the word *chef.* The words *a French chef* form an appositive phrase.

> Nicolas-François Appert, **a French chef,** made an important discovery.

Ken

■ An **appositive phrase** is a group of words that includes an appositive and other words that describe the appositive.

You always use an appositive or appositive phrase together with another noun. An appositive phrase can come at the beginning, middle, or end of a sentence, as long as it appears next to the noun it identifies.

> An **expert on food,** Appert worried about food spoilage.
> Appert, **an expert on food,** worried about food spoilage.
> The government gave Appert, **an expert on food,** a cash award.
> A simple solution had occurred to Appert, **an expert on food.**

Usually, appositives are set off from the nouns they identify by commas. Notice that a single comma follows an appositive that appears at the beginning of a sentence. A comma is used before an appositive that appears at the end of a sentence. Two commas set off an appositive in the middle of a sentence.

Ken, John's friend

Nouns

Ken, the artist

Exercise 11   Identifying Appositives

Write each sentence. Underline each appositive or appositive phrase and add commas where needed. Circle the noun the appositive identifies.

1. Nicolas-François Appert a French chef found a method for preserving food.
2. Food spoilage a serious social health problem was causing disease.
3. A prize a large sum of money was the government's reward for a solution.
4. A determined person Appert worked on the problem for years.
5. Finally, Appert discovered an answer a rather simple method.
6. His method included packing food into containers wide-mouthed glass bottles.
7. Each bottle had its own tight seal cork and wire.
8. A cloth sack one more protection was wrapped around each bottle.
9. Next the bottles were lowered into a boiler a large pot of boiling water.
10. The large boiling pot a giant water bath was covered with one more lid.
11. Appert's idea worked, but his theory protection from air proved incomplete.
12. The sealed jars an important contribution did help preserve the foods.
13. Another contribution the tin can was invented around the same time.
14. The inventor of this container Peter Durand was English.
15. No one knew why Appert's method use of sealed containers worked so well.
16. Then Louis Pasteur a French scientist found an explanation.
17. Pasteur discovered bacteria the real cause of food spoilage.
18. It was bacteria an invisible enemy in the air that caused foods to spoil.
19. Appert's high heating method had destroyed the bacteria the source of disease.
20. Bacteria the food spoilers could not enter when the containers were sealed.

Exercise 12   Using Appositives

Rewrite the sentences, using the appositives and inserting commas correctly.

1. Johann Gutenberg invented movable type. (the basis of the printing press)
2. Alexander Graham Bell invented the telephone. (a former speech teacher)
3. Kirkpatrick Macmillan is given credit for the bicycle. (a Scottish blacksmith)
4. The zipper was invented by W. L. Judson. (a slide fastener)
5. The inventor of the elevator was Elisha G. Otis. (a device for vertical lifting)
6. The stethoscope was developed by René Laënnec. (a French physician)
7. J. H. Loud is given credit for the ballpoint pen. (an American inventor)
8. The Wright brothers flew a biplane. (the first successful flying machine)
9. X rays were discovered by Wilhelm Roentgen. (the basis of the X-ray machine)
10. Van Leeuwenhoek made a successful microscope. (a lens for seeing tiny things)

Grammar Review

NOUNS

In this passage, Anne Morrow Lindbergh, a veteran of many historic airplane flights, describes the launching of *Apollo 8*, the first crewed spacecraft to orbit the moon. The craft took off from Cape Kennedy, Florida, early on the morning of December 21, 1968. The passage has been annotated to show some of the kinds of nouns covered in this unit.

Literature Model

from *Earth Shine*
by Anne Morrow Lindbergh

With the morning light, *Apollo 8* and its launching tower become clearer, harder, and more defined. One can see the details of installation. The dark sections on the smooth sides of the rocket, marking its stages, cut up the single fluid line. Vapor steams furiously off its side. No longer stark and simple, this morning the rocket is complicated, mechanical, earth-bound. Too weighty for flight, one feels.

People stop talking, stand in front of their cars, and raise binoculars to their eyes. We peer nervously at the launch site and then at our wrist watches. Radio voices blare unnaturally loud from car windows. "Now only thirty minutes to launch time . . . fifteen minutes . . . six minutes . . . thirty seconds to go . . . twenty . . . T minus fifteen . . . fourteen . . . thirteen . . . twelve . . . eleven . . . ten . . . nine. . . . Ignition!"

A jet of steam shoots from the pad below the rocket. "Ahhhh!" The crowd gasps, almost in unison.

- Proper noun
- Singular noun
- Common noun
- Concrete noun
- Compound noun
- Plural noun
- Collective noun

Nouns

Grammar Review

Review: Exercise 1 **Identifying Nouns**

The following sentences are about the life of Anne Morrow Lindbergh, the author of *Earth Shine*. Find all the nouns in the sentences and write them in lists. First, list all *proper nouns*, capitalizing them correctly. Then list the *common nouns*.

SAMPLE In *Earth Shine,* Anne Morrow Lindbergh talks about fear.
ANSWER *Earth Shine,* Anne Morrow Lindbergh; fear

1. Anne morrow married charles lindbergh.
2. Lindbergh had already gained fame for his solo flight from new york to paris.
3. Anne morrow lindbergh soon shared his love of aviation.
4. Anne accompanied her husband on many expeditions as copilot and navigator.
5. Anne came to share Charles's great enthusiasm for adventure.
6. After they were married, Anne joined charles on a flight to south america.
7. The lindberghs also spent some time in hollywood with amelia earhart.
8. Anne lindbergh became a successful author, writing many articles and books.
9. Anne won praise from critics and gained huge popularity among readers.
10. Biographer dorothy herrmann paints a vivid picture of this remarkable woman.

Review: Exercise 2 **Forming the Possessive**

Write the possessive form of each underlined noun.

1. <u>Anne Morrow Lindbergh</u> book
2. <u>husband</u> flight
3. <u>critics</u> praise
4. <u>airplane</u> pilot
5. <u>lawyers</u> case
6. <u>crowd</u> gasp
7. <u>Charles</u> airplane
8. <u>Anne</u> biographer
9. <u>couple</u> wedding
10. <u>friends</u> congratulations
11. <u>children</u> pictures
12. <u>parents</u> encouragement
13. <u>sisters</u> letters
14. <u>Franklin Roosevelt</u> presidency
15. <u>women</u> opinions
16. <u>brother</u> house
17. <u>Paris</u> liberation
18. <u>astronauts</u> explorations
19. <u>Ciardi</u> criticism
20. <u>Kennedys</u> compound

Review: Exercise 3   **Using Possessives and Contractions**

The following sentences are based on the *Apollo 8* mission. Rewrite each sentence, inserting apostrophes where needed in the possessive nouns and contractions.

SAMPLE   The announcers voice breaks the silence.
ANSWER   The announcer's voice breaks the silence.

1. "Wow, that rockets tall," said a boy in the crowd.
2. The rockets height is 465 feet.
3. The mens families anxiously await the launch.
4. The rockets engines ignite following the countdown.
5. The peoples eyes follow the spaceship as it lifts off the launch pad.
6. At last the spacecrafts on its way to the Moon.
7. The first stage of the rockets called the booster stage.
8. The boosters power, called its thrust, is 7,500,000 pounds.
9. Its been about two and one-half minutes since the booster began firing.
10. By then the rockets speed is 6,100 miles per hour.
11. Its height above Earths about thirty-eight miles.
12. The second stages burn is about six and one-half minutes.
13. Now the rockets speed is about 15,000 miles per hour.
14. The third stage fires, and the rockets in orbit around Earth.
15. While the spacecrafts in orbit, the crew checks the equipment.
16. The third stage fires again, and the rockets headed for the Moon.
17. "Earths so beautiful," exclaims one astronaut.
18. The lunar craters shadows lie across the moon.
19. The firing of the crafts retro-rockets slows it into an orbit around the Moon.
20. The spacecraft comes within sixty-nine miles of the Moons surface.
21. The main rocket fires, and now the crafts headed for home.
22. The crafts surface becomes very hot as it reenters the atmosphere.
23. Now a parachutes opened to slow the fall of the spacecraft.
24. "I can see the capsules parachute!" a sailor shouts.
25. The spacecrafts parachute lowers it gently to the water for the splashdown.

Nouns

Grammar Review

Rewrite each sentence, using the form of the verb in parentheses that agrees with the collective noun.

SAMPLE   A group of reporters (follow, follows) the president wherever he goes.

ANSWER   A group of reporters follows the president wherever he goes.

1. The crew aboard the spacecraft (prepares, prepare) their vehicle for flight.
2. The team (hopes, hope) its mission will be successful.
3. One astronaut's family (stands, stand) together to watch the liftoff.
4. The crowd (holds, hold) its breath as the rocket pushes into the sky.
5. After the launch, the crowd (heads, head) quietly back to their cars.

Review: Exercise 5   **Using Appositives**

Rewrite each sentence below, inserting the appositive or appositive phrase in parentheses. Remember to add commas where needed.

SAMPLE   *Apollo 8* orbited the Moon ten times. (a highly sophisticated spacecraft)

ANSWER   *Apollo 8,* a highly sophisticated spacecraft, orbited the Moon ten times.

1. Frank Borman, James Lovell, and William Anders took pictures of the Moon. (the crew of *Apollo 8*)
2. They were the first to see the Moon's far side. (a cold, forbidding place)
3. Borman was a veteran space explorer. (the commander of the crew)
4. During a Christmas Eve broadcast, half a billion people listened to an incredible dialogue. (a conversation between the crew and mission control)
5. The *Apollo 8* crew marveled over their view. (bright Earth in a black sky)
6. The astronauts said Earth was beautiful. (a bright royal blue disk)
7. Control Houston announced that *Apollo 8* was orbiting the Moon. (the backup crew on Earth)
8. They wished the astronauts a safe journey in *Apollo 8*. (the "best bird" they could find)
9. Houston's view of the Moon could not compare with the view from *Apollo 8*. (beautiful Earth)
10. For the first time, human beings had orbited another celestial body. (the Moon)

Review: Exercise 6

Proofreading

The following passage is about the space shuttle *Challenger*, the subject of the work below. Rewrite the passage, correcting the errors in spelling, grammar, and usage. Add any missing punctuation. There are ten errors.

Challenger's Last Flight

¹In the center of this painting, artist Robert McCall pays tribute to the final mission of *Challenger* the ill-fated space shuttle. ²Just seconds after liftoff on January 28, 1986, an explosion teared the space shuttle apart, killing it's seven crew members. ³The shuttles destruction was not the space programs first tragedy. ⁴During a test of the *Apollo 1* command module, three astronauts died in a fire on the luanching pad. ⁵Nonetheless, scientist's continued to improve the spacecraft. ⁶It was less than three year later that two men Neil Armstrong and Edwin Aldrin, walked on the moon. ⁷McCalls painting celebrates the human spirit.

Robert McCall, Challenger's *Last Flight*, 1987

Review: Exercise 7

Mixed Review

Identify the underlined nouns in each sentence as *common, proper, compound, collective, possessive,* or *appositive.* More than one label may apply to a single noun.

1. Anne Morrow Lindbergh saw the dramatic launching of <u>*Apollo 8*</u> from Cape Kennedy.
2. Twenty years before, she had visited Cape Canaveral, which was the former <u>name</u> of Cape Kennedy.
3. She and her <u>family</u> had camped behind the dunes next to an empty beach.
4. That was long before the great NASA <u>space center</u> was built there.
5. Now the once-empty shore is lined with the towers that launch <u>rockets</u>.
6. She and her husband, <u>Charles Lindbergh</u>, enjoyed lunch with the astronauts.
7. They spoke of Robert Goddard, who had the <u>idea</u> of multistage moon rockets.
8. Lindbergh was amazed at the amount of <u>fuel</u> used for an *Apollo* launching.
9. Just the first second used ten times as much fuel as his transatlantic <u>flight</u>.
10. The Lindberghs were impressed with the <u>astronauts'</u> courage and knowledge.
11. The astronauts knew the hazards but had <u>faith</u> in the technology.
12. The night before the launch, the <u>Lindberghs</u> decided to visit the site.
13. The roadside was already lined with a <u>crowd</u> of people.
14. From miles away, *Apollo 8* shone like a blazing <u>star</u> in the dark night.
15. In the morning, within sight of the <u>launching pad</u>, the suspense grew.
16. With the last number of the <u>countdown</u>, the crowd gasped as one person.
17. Flames and <u>smoke</u> burst forth, and the rocket rose slowly.
18. <u>Explosions</u> thundered on and on, and the earth shook for a long time.
19. In sudden panic, a great <u>flock</u> of marsh birds rose up and filled the air.
20. With its mighty <u>power</u>, the rocket blasted upward and out of sight.
21. Within eleven minutes, *Apollo 8* was already in <u>Earth's</u> orbit.
22. Anne Lindbergh was awed by the technology she observed that <u>day</u>.
23. However, the human beings, the <u>people</u> in control, mattered most to her.
24. After the launch, the Lindberghs explored NASA's nearby wildlife <u>refuge</u>.
25. Here, out of sight of the rocket <u>towers</u>, they found nature flourishing.

Writing Application

TIME

For more about the writing process, see **TIME Facing the Blank Page,** pp. 97–107.

Nouns in Writing

As he describes his encounter with a wolf in this passage from *Never Cry Wolf,* Farley Mowat uses nouns that enliven his writing and create a vivid picture. Note the italicized nouns.

> My *head* came slowly over the crest—and there was my *quarry.* He was lying down, evidently resting after his mournful *singsong,* and his *nose* was about six *feet* from mine. We stared at one another in *silence.* I do not know what went on in his massive *skull,* but my *head* was full of the most disturbing *thoughts.* I was peering straight into the amber *gaze* of a fully grown *arctic wolf,* who probably weighed more than I did, and who was certainly a lot better versed in close-combat *techniques* than I would ever be.

Techniques with Nouns

Experiment with some of Farley Mowat's writing techniques as you write and revise your own work.

❶ Create more engaging images for readers by replacing general words with specific and vivid nouns. Compare the following:

GENERAL WORDS My head came slowly over the hill—and there was the wolf.

MOWAT'S VERSION My head came slowly over the *crest*—and there was my *quarry.*

❷ Whenever possible, identify people, places, or things by the most specific name available. Notice the extra information Mowat gives in the following example.

GENERAL NOUN a fully grown wolf

MOWAT'S VERSION a fully grown *arctic wolf*

Nouns

Practice Read the following passage, focusing especially on the underlined words. Practice the techniques discussed above as you revise the passage on a separate sheet of paper.

The <u>girls</u> climbed steadily up the <u>trail</u>, following the <u>signs</u> posted along their <u>trail</u>. As they wound around a <u>curve</u>, Jinnie called out, "Look, there's a <u>deer</u>!" She quickly took off <u>one pair of glasses</u> and peered through her <u>other</u> glasses at the deer. "Wow, she's a <u>nice</u> <u>one</u>! Here, you look," she said, handing the glasses to her <u>friend</u>.

10.1 Action Verbs

Many sports are games of fast action. The actions in sports can be named by verbs. If a word expresses action and tells what a subject does, it is an action verb.

■ An **action verb** is a word that names an action. It may contain more than one word.

Notice the action verbs in the following paragraph.

> Sports experts **write** about the football player Jim Thorpe even today. Thorpe **blocked** like a tank. He **tackled** like a tornado. In every game, Thorpe **attacked** his opponents with all his might. He **caught** the ball skillfully and **charged** ahead fearlessly. Experts still **remember** and **honor** Thorpe's greatness.

Action verbs can express physical actions, such as writing and running, or mental activities, such as thinking and honoring.

ACTION VERB

Action Verbs	
Physical	write, block, tackle, attack, catch, charge
Mental	remember, honor

Have, *has*, and *had* are often used before other verbs. They can also be used as action verbs when they name what the subject owns or holds.

Tonio **remembered** Thorpe's famous play . . .

These players **have** red uniforms.
The pitcher **has** a sore arm.
The stadium **had** an electronic scoreboard.
Our cheerleader **had** a megaphone.

. . .as he **snared** the ball.

Verbs

Exercise 1   **Identifying Action Verbs**

Write each action verb from the following sentences.

1. The French probably invented tennis in about 1150.
2. At one time, people called the game lawn tennis.
3. In 1874 Mary E. Outerbridge observed tennis in Bermuda.
4. She brought a net, tennis balls, and racquets back to the United States.
5. She established the first court in New York City.
6. Maud Wilson won the first women's championship at Wimbledon in 1884.
7. Ellen Hanson earned the first singles crown at the U.S. Open in 1887.
8. Women excelled at tennis during the 1920s.
9. Suzanne Lenglen of France won at Wimbledon from 1920 to 1924.
10. She developed an athletic style of play.
11. In 1926 Lenglen starred in the first U.S. professional tennis tour.
12. Helen Moody set a record of eight Wimbledon singles titles.
13. Players in Wimbledon compete on grass courts.
14. Many players prefer clay courts.
15. Althea Gibson learned tennis on the streets of New York City.
16. She won her first championship in her home neighborhood of Harlem.
17. In 1949 Gibson entered college.
18. Fans regarded her as the foremost woman amateur in the 1950s.
19. She dominated the game in 1957 and 1958.
20. She established herself as one of the world's greatest tennis players.

Exercise 2   **Using Action Verbs**

For each sentence, write an appropriate action verb.

1. People have _____ against each other in bowling for thousands of years.
2. The sport probably _____ in ancient Egypt.
3. In Germany during the Middle Ages, people _____ bowling at village dances.
4. The Germans _____ stones at wooden clubs.
5. In the Netherlands, pin setters _____ tall pins far apart.
6. The Dutch _____ their game to America during the 1600s.
7. Americans first _____ the game at Bowling Green in New York City.
8. The game soon _____ in popularity throughout New England.
9. Eventually people all over the country _____ for recreation.
10. Thousands still _____ the game today.

Transitive and Intransitive Verbs

Every sentence has a subject and a predicate. In some sentences the predicate consists of only an action verb.

The punter **kicks.**

Usually sentences provide more information. The predicate often names who or what received the action of the verb.

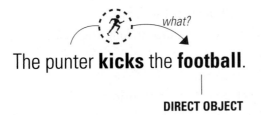

The punter **kicks** the **football**.

DIRECT OBJECT

In the sentence above, *football* receives the action of the verb *kicks.* It answers the question *what?* after the action verb. *Football* is called a direct object.

■ A **direct object** receives the action of a verb. It answers the question *whom?* or *what?* after an action verb.

A verb can also have a compound direct object. That is, it can have more than one direct object.

The team carried **gloves** and **bats** into the stadium.

Sometimes the action verb does not have a direct object.

The team played well.

In the sentence above, *well* does not answer the question *whom?* or *what?* after the verb *played.* Therefore, it is not a direct object. Action verbs that have direct objects are called transitive verbs. Action verbs that do not have direct objects are called intransitive verbs.

■ A **transitive verb** has a direct object.

■ An **intransitive verb** does not have a direct object.

Exercise 3   Distinguishing Transitive and Intransitive Verbs

Write each sentence. Underline each action verb. If the verb has a direct object, write *transitive*. If it does not, write *intransitive*. Draw a circle around each direct object.

1. Few athletes rival Jim Thorpe.
2. Thorpe gained fame as one of the greatest athletes in history.
3. Jim Thorpe ran fast as a boy in Oklahoma.
4. Thorpe came from a Native American family.
5. In 1909 Jim Thorpe entered Carlisle College.
6. Thorpe played football there under Coach Pop Warner.
7. He starred as the starting halfback on the team.
8. He excelled as a spectacular runner, placekicker, and tackler.
9. In 1912 Thorpe scored 129 points.
10. Thorpe entered the 1912 Olympics.
11. He participated in the decathlon and pentathlon.
12. He competed against many other athletes.
13. He jumped higher and farther than the others.
14. Thorpe ran with great strength and concentration.
15. Other track athletes copied Jim Thorpe's style.
16. Thorpe defeated his rivals in the ten events of the decathlon.
17. He even set world records.
18. He began his professional football career in 1915.
19. He served as the first president of the football association.
20. Thorpe retired from football in 1929 at the age of forty-one.

Exercise 4   Using Transitive and Intransitive Verbs

Write each sentence. If the verb is transitive, add a direct object in the blank space. If the verb is intransitive, leave the space blank. Direct objects will vary.

1. Track meets provide _____ of many kinds.
2. The first track competitions appeared _____ in ancient Greece during the Olympic Games.
3. Individual athletes, as well as teams of athletes, demonstrate _____ at track events.
4. Many athletes perform well _____ in a variety of events.
5. Hurdle races challenge _____.

10.3 Verbs with Indirect Objects

Nouns or pronouns that answer the question *whom?* or *what?* after an action verb are called direct objects.

> Michael Jordan led his **team** to the championship.
> Michael Jordan tossed the **ball.**

Sometimes two kinds of objects follow an action verb. The object that directly receives the action of the verb is the direct object. The object that tells *to whom* or *for whom* the action is done is called the indirect object.

■ An **indirect object** answers the question *to whom?* or *for whom?* an action is done.

Michael Jordan **shows** his **teammates** new shots.

INDIRECT OBJECT

The direct object in the sentence above is *shots.* The indirect object is *teammates. Teammates* answers the question *to whom?* after the action verb *shows.*

An indirect object appears only in a sentence that has a direct object. Two easy clues will help you recognize indirect objects. First, the indirect object always comes before a direct object. Second, you can add *to* or *for* before the indirect object and change its position. The sentence will still make sense, although it will no longer have an indirect object.

> The helper gives the **players** towels.
> The helper gives the towels **to the players.**

You can figure out that in the first sentence *players* is the indirect object. First, it comes before the direct object. Second, its position can be changed to follow the word *to.*

Exercise 5　Identifying Direct and Indirect Objects

Write each sentence. If the sentence contains a direct object, underline it once. If the sentence contains an indirect object, underline it twice.

1. The tournament sometimes attracts good athletes.
2. The university gave the tournament its support.
3. The level of play interested the onlookers.
4. One player earned his team a three-point edge.
5. For a few minutes, no player could stop him.
6. In the first game of the season, the teams showed their fans some skillful plays.
7. A number of fans cheered loudly at each game.
8. Many fans paid the players tribute with colorful banners.
9. The coach gave the players new instructions.
10. Students from many different schools cheered their favorite players.
11. Mr. Romero refereed the game.
12. Clayton's shooting skill gave his team's offense a potent advantage.
13. All of the players paid him many compliments.
14. All of the players admired his ability.
15. Several players gave him a pat on the back.
16. A top reporter wrote an article about the game for the *Times Gazette*.
17. She asked Clayton some questions about his game.
18. Clayton explained his strategy to her.
19. The coach gave his players all the credit.
20. The team, in turn, praised its coach.

Exercise 6　Using Indirect Objects

Without changing the meaning of the sentence, rewrite each so that it contains an indirect object. Underline the indirect object.

SAMPLE　A good show was given to us by the field events.
ANSWER　The field events gave us a good show.

1. The competitors are given height and speed by long fiberglass poles.
2. The vaulters are shown each move by the coaches.
3. Well-prepared competitors are brought victory by constant practice.
4. A vaulter earns another chance by a successful jump.
5. The competitors are given encouragement by the crowd's cheers.

10.4 Linking Verbs and Predicate Words

Action verbs tell what the subject of a sentence does. Other verbs tell what the subject is or is like. These verbs are called linking verbs.

■ A **linking verb** connects the subject of a sentence with a noun or an adjective in the predicate.

John McGraw **was** the manager.

LINKING VERB

LINKING VERB

In the sentence above, the word *was* is a linking verb. It connects, or links, the subject, *John McGraw*, to a word in the predicate, *manager*.

■ A **predicate noun** is a noun that follows a linking verb. It tells what the subject is.

■ A **predicate adjective** is an adjective that follows a linking verb. It describes the subject by telling what it is like.

Sam is a **pitcher.** [predicate noun]
The pitcher is **skillful.** [predicate adjective]

Common Linking Verbs			
be	appear	turn	smell
become	look	taste	sound
seem	grow	feel	

Many of these verbs can also be used as action verbs.

Chandra **turned** thirteen. [linking verb]
The car **turned** the corner. [action verb]

Verbs

Exercise 7 — Distinguishing Action and Linking Verbs and Predicate Nouns and Adjectives

Write each sentence. Underline each verb, and write whether it is an *action verb* or a *linking verb*. If it is a linking verb, circle the predicate noun or predicate adjective. Write whether it is a *predicate noun* or a *predicate adjective*.

1. Our pitcher appears very nervous today.
2. He shows a serious lack of concentration.
3. The catcher ran very quickly.
4. She seems quite agile.
5. She caught the ball.
6. The pitcher was a good hitter.
7. He was also a fine fielder.
8. The player at third base threw the baseball.
9. It sailed into the outfield.
10. Fans of the team grew ecstatic.
11. One player turned a pop fly into a home run.
12. The ball flew into the bleachers.
13. Fans of the home team seem confident today.
14. The team looked wonderful for the first three innings.
15. The home team was the winner yesterday.
16. The players on both teams seem eager at the start of the game.
17. The mayor walks onto the field.
18. She looks very proud of the team.
19. All of the team members flock around her.
20. She is an honorary member of the team.

Exercise 8 — Using Predicate Nouns and Adjectives with Linking Verbs

Write each sentence, adding a predicate noun or adjective to fill the blank.

1. Sports are _____ in many schools.
2. Athletes feel _____ after a workout.
3. Hot dogs taste _____ at the ball park.
4. Beth is a _____ on the basketball team.
5. Josh and Sam are _____ in the school band.

10.5 Present, Past, and Future Tenses

A verb changes its form to show tense and to agree with its subject. The **tense** of a verb tells when an action takes place.

■ The **present tense** of a verb names an action that is happening now or that happens regularly. It can also express a general truth.

In the present tense, the base form of a verb is used with all subjects except singular nouns and the words *he, she,* and *it*. When the subject is a singular noun or *he, she,* or *it, -s* is usually added to the verb.

Present Tense Forms	
Singular	**Plural**
I **race.**	We **race.**
You **race.**	You **race.**
He, she, *or* it **races.**	They **race.**

■ The **past tense** of a verb names an action that already happened.

The past tense of many verbs is formed by adding *-ed* to the base form of the verb.

The runner **trained** hard.   I **slapped** the buzzer.

■ The **future tense** of a verb names an action that will take place in the future.

In the future tense, the word *will* is used with the verb. Sometimes *shall* is used when the pronoun *I* or *we* is the subject.

Future Tense Forms	
Singular	**Plural**
I **will (shall) go.**	We **will (shall) go.**
You **will go.**	You **will go.**
He, she, *or* it **will go.**	They **will go.**

Exercise 9   Using the Past Tense of Verbs

Write the past tense of each verb.

1. Jesse Owens achieves a national reputation during the 1930s.
2. He lives his early years in Oakville, Alabama.
3. At the age of seven, he moves with his family to Cleveland.
4. In 1933 he enters Ohio State University.
5. Almost immediately he succeeds in track and field events.
6. At a college meet, he establishes three world records in forty-five minutes.
7. He gains great fame at the Summer Olympics of 1936.
8. The games occur in Berlin, Germany.
9. Owens walks away with seven world records.
10. His success earns him a position as one of history's most famous athletes.

Exercise 10   Using Present, Past, and Future Tenses

Write the appropriate tense of the verb in parentheses. Then write whether it is in the *present, past,* or *future* tense.

1. Wilma Rudolph (enter) many races in the 1950s.
2. She (gain) victory in a great many of those.
3. During her youth, Rudolph (suffer) many difficulties.
4. Her hard work (allow) her to overcome all of them.
5. She (practice) hour after hour and day after day.
6. Wilma Rudolph (encourage) other young runners.
7. Her record (offer) hope to any young runner.
8. She (work) every day for it.
9. In future years, people (remember) her success on the track.
10. At an early age, Wilma Rudolph (learn) the importance of good health.
11. The young Wilma (want) an active life.
12. As a girl, she (enjoy) several different sports.
13. She (triumph) over many illnesses.
14. For many years, she (train) long and hard.
15. All her work finally (count).
16. In 1960 Rudolph (receive) an Olympic medal in track.
17. Her medal (prove) the importance of hard work.
18. This great runner no longer (describe) sports on television.
19. Rudolph died in 1994, but her performance (inspire) many young athletes.
20. In the years ahead, young runners (follow) Rudolph's example.

Verbs

Main Verbs and Helping Verbs

Verbs have four principal parts that are used to form all tenses. The chart below shows how the principal parts of most verbs are formed.

Principal Parts			
Base Form	Present Participle	Past Form	Past Participle
jump	jumping	jumped	jumped

The principal parts of a verb are often combined with helping verbs to form verb phrases.

■ A **helping verb** is a verb that completes the meaning of the main verb.

■ A **verb phrase** consists of one or more helping verbs followed by a main verb.

The students **are jumping** rope now.

In the sentence above, the word *are* is the helping verb, and the present participle *jumping* is the main verb. Together they form a verb phrase.

The most common helping verbs are *be, have,* and *do.* Forms of the helping verb *be* include *am, is,* and *are* in the present and *was* and *were* in the past. They combine with the present participle of the main verb.

Forms of the helping verb *have* include *has* and *had.* They combine with the past participle form of a verb.

Have, Has, and *Had* with the Past Participle			
Singular	Plural	Singular	Plural
I **have** jumped.	We **have** jumped.	I **had** jumped.	We **had** jumped.
You **have** jumped.	You **have** jumped.	You **had** jumped.	You **had** jumped.
She **has** jumped.	They **have** jumped.	She **had** jumped.	They **had** jumped.

Exercise 11 — Using Helping Verbs with Present and Past Participles

Write each sentence, choosing the correct helping verb from the parentheses. Underline the verb phrase once, and draw a second line under the participle. Then write whether it is a *present* participle or a *past* participle.

1. We (are, have) learning about archery this year.
2. Slowly but surely, champions (are, had) making archery a more popular sport throughout the country.
3. During the last forty or fifty years, competitive archery equipment (are, has) changed very little.
4. Many people (are, have) playing in tournaments each year.
5. Archers (was, had) founded the National Archery Association in 1879 for annual tournaments.
6. Tournaments (have, are) increased people's interest in archery.
7. People (have, are) competing in tournaments in target archery, field archery, flight shooting, and shooting at ground targets.
8. Many more people (have, are) enjoyed target archery than any other type of archery.
9. In target archery, competitors (are, have) shooting down a long course at straw targets.
10. Concentric wire circles (are, have) dividing the target into sections.
11. Similar wire circles (have, are) dividing the bull's-eye into sections.
12. An archer (is, has) earning ten points by a direct hit in the bull's-eye.
13. The archers in the competition (are, have) practiced for at least three hours every day.
14. Archers (are, had) marking their targets.
15. Archers (are, have) working hard in today's competition.
16. That archer in the colorful red jacket (is, has) earned the most points so far in the tournament.
17. She (is, has) scored several bull's-eyes.
18. Sarafina's arrow (is, has) landed away from the target.
19. She (is, has) adjusting for her next shot at the target.
20. A good archer (is, has) planning each and every shot.
21. Her concentration (is, has) improved greatly.
22. Last year archery (had, was) taking up most of her free time.
23. The best archers (have, are) devoted countless hours to their sport.
24. Some archers (are, have) bringing new arrows.
25. Tomorrow's champion (is, has) profited from old mistakes.

10.7 Progressive Forms

You know that the present tense of a verb names an action that occurs repeatedly. To describe an action that is taking place right now, you use the present progressive form of the verb.

■ The **present progressive form** of a verb names an action or condition that is continuing in the present.

> I **am enjoying** this baseball game at Candlestick Park.
> The home team **is winning** at the moment.

The present progressive form of a verb consists of the present participle of the main verb and the helping verb *am, are,* or *is.*

Present Progressive Form	
Singular	**Plural**
I **am looking.**	We **are looking.**
You **are looking.**	You **are looking.**
He, she, *or* it **is looking.**	They **are looking.**

■ The **past progressive form** of a verb names an action or condition that continued for some time in the past.

> They **were winning** the game.

The past progressive form of a verb consists of the present participle and the helping verb *was* or *were.*

Past Progressive Form	
Singular	**Plural**
I **was trying.**	We **were trying.**
You **were trying.**	You **were trying.**
He, she, *or* it **was trying.**	They **were trying.**

Exercise 12 Using Present and Past Progressive Forms

Rewrite each sentence, using the present progressive or past progressive form of the verb.

1. Soccer (develop) into the most popular sport in the world.
2. I (watch) a great soccer game on television now.
3. The players (try) very hard.
4. Yesterday fans (cheer) this same team.
5. Every play (gain) my undivided attention.
6. The fans (follow) every play.
7. No one (miss) a moment of the action.
8. Today the crowd (applaud) wildly.
9. The players (think) very hard about every play.
10. After the game, the players (search) for the bus.
11. They (look) up and down each street.
12. They (search) behind houses and barns.
13. They (get) desperate.
14. The coach (laugh) at the players.
15. He (give) them some hints.
16. He (suggest) some possible locations.
17. Finally, they (look) at a bus.
18. They (go) up to it.
19. They (examine) the bus closely.
20. They (climb) onto the bus.

Exercise 13 Using the Progressive Forms

Rewrite each sentence. If the verb is in the present tense, change it to present progressive. If the verb is in the past tense, change it to past progressive.

1. The soccer coach plans a team for the next season.
2. She asked players from other teams to the tryouts.
3. Many new players tried out also.
4. Some players train for the next season.
5. My friend watched the players at the tryouts.
6. Some players stand by the goal post.
7. The players kick the ball back and forth.
8. Several players exercised.
9. A goalie inspected the field.
10. Some enthusiastic players practice daily.

10.8 Perfect Tenses

■ The **present perfect tense** of a verb names an action that happened at an indefinite time in the past. It also tells about an action that happened in the past and is still happening now.

My family **has attended** many sports events.
We **have watched** baseball games for years.

The present perfect tense consists of the helping verb *have* or *has* and the past participle of the main verb.

Present Perfect Tense	
Singular	**Plural**
I **have watched.**	We **have watched.**
You **have watched.**	You **have watched.**
He, she, *or* it **has watched.**	They **have watched.**

■ The **past perfect tense** of a verb names an action that happened before another action or event in the past.

The past perfect tense is often used in sentences that contain a past tense verb in another part of the sentence.

By the time we found our seats, the game **had** already **started.**
I **had** never **seen** a baseball game before.

The past perfect tense of a verb consists of the helping verb *had* and the past participle of the main verb.

Past Perfect Tense	
Singular	**Plural**
I **had studied.**	We **had studied.**
You **had studied.**	You **had studied.**
He, she, *or* it **had studied.**	They **had studied.**

Exercise 14   Using the Present Perfect Tense

Write each sentence, using the present perfect tense of the verb in parentheses.

1. Some players (recognize) the need for practice.
2. They (start) their warm-up routines.
3. They (walk) to the practice field very early.
4. They (arrive) in time to hear the coach's instructions.
5. They (follow) every bit of advice.
6. They (devote) the extra time.
7. The coach (watch) the games.
8. She (notice) some real weaknesses.
9. She (identify) items for practice.
10. She (plan) an intensive practice.
11. She (call) an early practice this evening.
12. Some players (complain) about the work.
13. Most players (agree) to the new rules.
14. They (realize) their weaknesses.
15. They (experience) the benefits of practice.
16. They (arrive) at school early for more practice.
17. Some (practice) for three hours.
18. Others (promise) weekend practice.
19. The students (hope) for a victory.
20. They (work) very hard for it.

Exercise 15   Using the Past Perfect Tense

Write each sentence, using the past perfect tense of the verb in parentheses.

1. The skater (earn) a medal by the age of six.
2. She (want) a place on her school's skating team.
3. The speed skater (try) twice before.
4. She (practice) daily.
5. The team (welcome) her into the group.
6. They (wish) her the best of luck.
7. The spectators (notice) the new skater.
8. Her skating (improve) dramatically.
9. They were pleased that she (earn) a place on the team.
10. They (celebrate) her first victory.

Verbs

10.9 Irregular Verbs

The irregular verbs below are grouped according to the way their past form and past participle are formed.

Present Perfect Tense			
Pattern	**Base Form**	**Past Form**	**Past Participle**
One vowel changes to form the past and the past participle.	begin	began	begun
	drink	drank	drunk
	ring	rang	rung
	shrink	shrank *or* shrunk	shrunk
	sing	sang	sung
	spring	sprang *or* sprung	sprung
	swim	swam	swum
The past form and past participle are the same.	bring	brought	brought
	buy	bought	bought
	catch	caught	caught
	creep	crept	crept
	feel	felt	felt
	get	got	got *or* gotten
	keep	kept	kept
	lay	laid	laid
	lead	led	led
	leave	left	left
	lend	lent	lent
	lose	lost	lost
	make	made	made
	pay	paid	paid
	say	said	said
	seek	sought	sought
	sell	sold	sold
	sit	sat	sat
	sleep	slept	slept
	swing	swung	swung
	teach	taught	taught
	think	thought	thought
	win	won	won

hit
hit
hit

swing
swung
swung

throw
threw
thrown

fling
flung
flung

win
won
won

Verbs

Exercise 16   Using the Past Forms of Irregular Verbs

Write the past form or past participle of the verb in parentheses.

1. The public first (sing) Sonja Henie's praises in the late 1920s as her fame began to spread internationally.
2. Experts have (say) that she made figure skating popular all by herself.
3. Sports historians have (think) highly of her.
4. She (get) gold medals at the 1928, 1932, and 1936 Olympic games.
5. After her victories, she (win) roles in several American movies in which she appeared with other major stars.
6. Peggy Fleming and Dorothy Hamill of the United States had also (begin) professional careers after Olympic victories.
7. They have (bring) high standards to the sport.
8. Ballet has (lend) many movements to figure skating.
9. It has (make) figure skating very graceful.
10. Last night the skater (spring) into the rink.
11. Her sudden appearance had (catch) the spectators by surprise.
12. The silver skate blades (ring) on the ice.
13. The skater has (lead) her partner onto the ice.
14. The skater's partner has (catch) the woman expertly.
15. Hours of practice had (bring) them to a perfect and flawless performance that could keep the audience spellbound.
16. We (feel) the excitement of the moment.
17. We (keep) our eyes on the expert pair.
18. The judges (begin) their voting immediately after each performance ended.
19. The coach had (teach) the skaters to perform as well and as perfectly as possible.
20. That skating team (win) last year's gold medal.
21. One judge has (seek) the opinion of another judge.
22. The judges have (keep) the performances very clearly in mind.
23. We (think) that each skater did his or her best to entertain the vast audience that filled the arena.
24. The judges (think) the performance spectacular, despite a few imperfections during the closing moments.
25. Even the skills of the losers (leave) us breathless.

10.10 More Irregular Verbs

Irregular Verbs			
Pattern	**Base Form**	**Past Form**	**Past Participle**
The base form and the past participle are the same.	become come run	became came ran	become come run
The past form ends in -ew, and the past participle ends in -wn.	blow draw fly grow know throw	blew drew flew grew knew threw	blown drawn flown grown known thrown
The past participle ends in -en.	bite break choose drive eat fall give ride rise see speak steal take write	bit broke chose drove ate fell gave rode rose saw spoke stole took wrote	bitten *or* bit broken chosen driven eaten fallen given ridden risen seen spoken stolen taken written
The past form and the past participle do not follow any pattern.	be, am, are, is do go tear wear	was, were did went tore wore	been done gone torn worn
The base form, past form, and past participle are all the same.	cut let put hit	cut let put hit	cut let put hit

Verbs

Exercise 17   Identifying Past Forms of Irregular Verbs

Write each verb, and identify it as *past tense* or *past participle* form.

1. Hockey has become one of the world's most popular sports.
2. It has grown into a financially successful sport as well.
3. The spectators have given hockey their support.
4. Last night's game was particularly impressive.
5. A half hour passed without a score.
6. The players had driven up and down the ice.
7. Never had we seen such fierce play.
8. We saw several shots on the goal.
9. The goalies had fallen on several.
10. The crowd went wild.

Exercise 18   Using the Past Forms of Irregular Verbs

Write the past tense or the past participle form of the verb in parentheses, whichever the sentence requires.

1. I once (know) almost nothing about handball.
2. I have (see) several games of handball in the city recently.
3. When I felt the excitement of the game, I (know) that handball was for me.
4. The speed of the game (take) my breath away.
5. Several of us have (choose) to join a handball club.
6. Gail has (speak) with the director.
7. He has (write) out her membership card.
8. He also (give) Gail a few visitors' passes.
9. Gail (become) interested in handball last year and now plays regularly.
10. She has (become) a very fine player.
11. She has (give) hours to her new sport.
12. The handball (fly) across the room.
13. Juan (drive) the shot against the front wall.
14. One of the players has (tear) her sweatshirt.
15. A player has (fall) during an exciting play.
16. The player (take) time out for a few moments.
17. The director (draw) the four lines across the handball court.
18. Two players have (choose) a date for their next game.
19. The winner (give) a victory speech.
20. She (rise) from her chair to say a few words to the audience.

Grammar Review

Verbs

Douglas, the hero of this novel, craves a new pair of sporty tennis shoes. In this passage, which has been annotated to show various concepts covered in the unit, he tries to persuade a shoe-store owner to sell him a pair.

Literature Model

from *Dandelion Wine*
by Ray Bradbury

"Please!" Douglas held out his hand. "Mr. Sanderson, now could you kind of rock back and forth a little, sponge around, bounce kind of, while I tell you the rest? It's this: I give you my money, you give me the shoes, I owe you a dollar. But, Mr. Sanderson, *but*—soon as I get those shoes on, you know what *happens*?"

"What?"

"Bang! I deliver your packages, pick up packages, bring you coffee, burn your trash, run to the post office, telegraph office, library! You'll see twelve of me in and out, in and out, every minute. Feel those shoes, Mr. Sanderson, *feel* how fast they'd take me? All those springs inside? Feel all the running inside? Feel how they kind of grab hold and can't let you alone and don't like you just *standing* there? Feel how quick I'd be doing the things you'd rather not bother with? You stay in the nice cool store while I'm jumping all around town! But it's not me really, it's the shoes. They're going like mad down alleys, cutting corners, and back! There they go!"

Annotations (right margin):
- Action verb
- Indirect object
- Direct object
- Future tense
- Present progressive form
- Predicate noun

Side tab: Verbs

Grammar Review

Review: Exercise 1 Identifying Action Verbs and Direct Objects

Write each sentence. Then underline each action verb (including any helping verbs) and circle the direct object.

SAMPLE Douglas spends his money for shoes.
ANSWER Douglas <u>spends</u> his (money) for shoes.

1. Douglas owes a dollar for the shoes.
2. Douglas suggests a solution to his problem.
3. Douglas asks a favor of Mr. Sanderson.
4. Douglas will do many things.
5. Douglas will deliver packages.
6. Douglas will bring coffee to Mr. Sanderson.
7. Douglas will also burn the trash.
8. He will attempt odd jobs for Mr. Sanderson.
9. He will take the mail to the post office.
10. Douglas will perform these chores.

Review: Exercise 2 Distinguishing Transitive and Intransitive Verbs

Write each sentence. Underline each verb and circle any direct objects. Then write *T* if the verb is transitive or *I* if the verb is intransitive.

SAMPLE Douglas and his father and brother pick dandelions for salad.
ANSWER Douglas and his father and brother <u>pick</u> (dandelions) for salad. *T*

1. Ray Bradbury wrote about a special summer in the twelfth year of Douglas's life.
2. Bradbury reveals a great deal about Douglas.
3. A boy's twelfth year provides durable memories.
4. Young boys make new discoveries all the time.
5. Douglas valued his experience.
6. He learned during that summer.
7. His daily experiences caused wonder.
8. Douglas felt exhaustion.
9. Douglas slowly learns many things about life.
10. Writers learn by writing.

Verbs

Review: Exercise 3   **Distinguishing Direct and Indirect Objects**

Write each direct object. If the sentence contains an indirect object, write it and underline it.

SAMPLE   Please hand me the shoes.
ANSWER   shoes, <u>me</u>

1. Those shoes always give him blisters.
2. People wear different shoes for different purposes.
3. Shoes give people support.
4. People need special shoes for play.
5. A number of styles meet the requirements of various sports.
6. Football and baseball players wear special designs.
7. Many people buy their children sturdy shoes for active wear.
8. He asked me a question about the history of shoes.
9. People in cold climates wore shoes of animal fur.
10. People in warmer climates designed themselves open shoes.

Review: Exercise 4   **Identifying Action and Linking Verbs and Predicate Words**

Write each sentence. Circle each verb, and write whether it is an *action* or a *linking verb.* Then write whether the underlined word or words is a *direct object*, an *indirect object*, a *predicate noun*, or a *predicate adjective.*

SAMPLE   A dandelion is a bright yellow <u>flower.</u>
ANSWER   A dandelion (is) a bright yellow <u>flower.</u> (linking verb, predicate noun)

1. Dandelions dot <u>lawns and meadows</u>.
2. The temperate regions of the world encourage the <u>growth</u> of dandelions.
3. The flowers have given <u>us</u> great beauty.
4. Gardeners of the world have declared <u>war</u> on the dandelion.
5. Garden and lawn lovers hunt <u>dandelions</u> mercilessly.
6. The dandelion is not a native American <u>weed</u>.
7. The early colonists brought <u>them</u> from Europe.
8. The root of the dandelion is <u>long</u>.
9. Roots, young leaves, and flower buds are <u>tasty and nutritious</u>.
10. Some gardeners give <u>friends</u> dandelion greens for salad.

Grammar Review

Review: Exercise 5   Distinguishing Present, Past, and Future Tenses

Write the correct form of the verb in parentheses. Then write whether it is in the *present*, *past*, or *future* tense.

SAMPLE   Every year Susan (grow) more weeds in her garden than vegetables.
ANSWER   grows — present

1. Beautiful plants (demand) great care.
2. Farmers in the United States (spend) more than $6 billion last year.
3. They (use) the money on weeds.
4. Weeds always (compete) with crops for sunlight and water.
5. In spite of the money, farmers last year (lose) a fortune because of weeds.
6. Weeds (appear) in gardens, parks, and playgrounds.
7. Unless they are controlled, they (grow) along highways and railroad tracks.
8. Some weeds (poison) people and animals last year.
9. Every year others (produce) severe skin reactions in people.
10. Next autumn ragweed pollen (cause) hay fever in many sufferers.

Review: Exercise 6   Identifying Verb Phrases and Participles

Write each verb phrase, and draw a line under the main verb. Then write whether the main verb is a *present participle* or a *past participle*.

SAMPLE   This year's races are capturing everyone's attention.
ANSWER   are <u>capturing</u> — present participle

1. In early March, a number of people are readying themselves for a big race.
2. The course is plotted between Anchorage and Nome in Alaska.
3. In the past, several dozen people and their dogs have competed.
4. The Iditarod International Sled Dog Race has occurred yearly since 1973.
5. Drivers are scheduling eleven days for the race.
6. Racers are always preparing for difficult conditions.
7. Cold, snow, and howling winds have turned the course into a nightmare.
8. The wind-chill factor has dropped the temperature to an effective –100°F.
9. The race has tested both dogs and racers.
10. Success in the race has made people and dogs celebrities.

Review: Exercise 7 **Using Progressive Forms**

Write each sentence, using the verb form indicated in italics.

SAMPLE   I (read) an exciting type of fiction. *present progressive.*
ANSWER   I am reading an exciting type of fiction.

1. Ray Bradbury (write) fantasy novels. *past progressive*
2. He (experiment) with science fiction topics. *past progressive*
3. A writer of fantasy (examine) a world of dreams. *past progressive*
4. He or she (make) the unusual understandable. *past progressive*
5. Some science-fiction authors (deal) with the future. *present progressive*
6. They (create) an unbelievable and fantastic world. *present progressive*
7. The most interesting writers, however, (describe) possible events. *present progressive*
8. We (enjoy) their realistic characters. *present progressive*
9. I (relate) to their hopes and dreams. *present progressive*
10. Ray Bradbury (worry) about the future of humanity. *past progressive*

Review: Exercise 8 **Using Perfect Tenses**

Write each sentence, using the tense indicated in italics.

SAMPLE   I (complete) an interesting summer project. *present perfect*
ANSWER   I have completed an interesting summer project.

1. I (collect) a number of fascinating books. *past perfect*
2. All of these (hold) my interest. *present perfect*
3. Each story (feature) fantasy. *past perfect*
4. The stories (include) strange settings and unusual characters. *past perfect*
5. A few stories also (contain) very imaginative situations. *present perfect*
6. Some of these (remain) fresh in my mind. *present perfect*
7. I (remember) a story set in the very distant future. *present perfect*
8. I (recall) the characters in the story. *present perfect*
9. They (abandon) their feet as a means of transportation. *past perfect*
10. They (wish) themselves somewhere else. *past perfect*

Verbs

Grammar Review

Review: Exercise 9   **Using the Past and Past Participles of Irregular Verbs**

Write the past tense or the past participle of the verb in parentheses, whichever the sentence requires.

SAMPLE   The sport of automobile racing had (begin) in the 1890s.
ANSWER   begun

1. The first racers (take) their cars to regular public roads.
2. Many of these were (make) of dirt.
3. Drivers on these roads often (lose) control of their cars.
4. They (swing) from the course into groups of spectators.
5. The spectators (pay) a high price for their curiosity.
6. The first racing organization in the world had (get) a start in 1895.
7. The course had (lead) from Paris to Bordeaux—732 miles.
8. Twenty-two drivers (begin) the race.
9. Only nine had (bring) their cars across the finish line.
10. The winner (creep) along at fifteen miles per hour.

Review: Exercise 10   **Using the Past and Past Participles of Irregular Verbs**

Write the past tense or the past participle of the verb in parentheses, whichever the sentence requires.

SAMPLE   For many years, racing has (be) a very popular form of competition.
ANSWER   been

1. Early race cars (be) the same as family autos.
2. Today's race cars are (drive) just at races.
3. They have (become) very special vehicles.
4. A race car has (come) to be a very expensive item.
5. Auto racing has (grow) into a very special sport.
6. In the last few years, it has (draw) only very wealthy competitors.
7. No race car is (give) away.
8. A dedicated racer has (go) to great trouble.
9. He or she has (choose) to race.
10. It has already (take) years of preparation.

Review: Exercise 11

Proofreading

The following passage is about the artist Gregg Spears, whose painting appears on the next page. Rewrite the passage, correcting the errors in spelling, grammar, and usage. Add any missing punctuation. There are ten errors.

¹Gregg Spears's *My Back Porch,* like Ray Bradbury's *Dandelion Wine,* has catched lifes everyday happenings. ²Spears has always seeked to create new understanding of such comon themes.

³Spears growed up in Chicago and it is there that most of his works have been exhibited. ⁴Gregg Spears has participate in exhibits at the DuSable Museum of African American History. ⁵And the Chicago Cultural Center. ⁶The location of Spear's studio are an abandoned building that has been rebuilt instead of having been teared down.

Mixed Review

Number your paper from one to ten. For each item in parentheses, write a verb form that makes sense for the passage.

The World of Science Fiction

Ray Bradbury ¹(*linking verb*) one of the leading American science-fiction writers. People ²(*action verb*) science fiction. Common themes include time travel, fantastic inventions, and space travel. A large number of science-fiction stories ³(*action verb*) in the future. Some, including Bradbury's, describe ⁴(*direct object*) engaged in ordinary activities.

Science fiction's beginnings ⁵(*linking verb*) in prehistoric myths. These stories commonly offered ⁶(*indirect object*) fantastic voyages and adventures. In the first century A.D., a Greek writer ⁷(*past progressive form*) stories that described trips to the moon.

In the current century, magazines ⁸(*present perfect tense verb*) the fame of science fiction. Movies ⁹(*action verb*) the popularity of science-fiction themes. In the 1970s and 1980s, a number of science-fiction authors increased in popularity with the general reader. Writers like Ray Bradbury are now ¹⁰(*predicate adjective*) to readers throughout the world.

Gregg Spears, *My Back Porch,* **1992**

Writing Application

TIME

For more about the writing process, see **TIME Facing the Blank Page,** pp. 97–107.

Verbs in Writing

Notice the way Minfong Ho uses verbs in this passage from *The Clay Marble*. They vividly capture the rainy setting and bring Jantu's and Dara's moods and actions to life for readers. Read the passage, focusing especially on the italicized verbs.

> The wind *picked* up and *was sweeping* up eddies of dust into the air. Then the rain *started* in earnest, one of those sudden thunderstorms hinting of the monsoons due to come soon. Jantu *stretched* her sarong protectively over the pile of straw where her clay figures *were*. Hunched over them like that, she *looked* like a scruffy hen trying to hatch her precious eggs.
>
> I *huddled* close to Jantu and *listened* to the rain drumming on the leaves. Raindrops *pierced* through the cracks of the palm fronds and *felt* light and cool on my bare arms.

Techniques with Verbs

Try to apply some of Minfong Ho's techniques when you write and revise your own work.

❶ Keep your writing lively by varying the kinds of linking verbs you use:

COMMON LINKING VERB . . . she *was* a scruffy hen

HO'S VERSION . . . she *looked* like a scruffy hen trying to hatch her precious eggs

❷ Whenever possible, replace bland and common verbs with vivid action verbs. Compare the following:

GENERAL VERB raindrops *fell* through the cracks of the palm fronds . . .

HO'S VERSION raindrops *pierced* through the cracks of the palm fronds . . .

Practice Try out these techniques by revising the passage below. Use a separate sheet of paper. As you work, focus especially on the underlined words.

There was Quentin standing on the diving board. He was a taut rubber band. A blast of sound filled the air as the referee blew his whistle. Quentin then moved his long arms, first back and then forward, adding energy with each movement. Jumping off the board, he rose high into the air above the shimmering pool. Falling toward the pool, Quentin made three complete turns. Then, arms pointed out in front of him, he dove cleanly through the water to complete his dive.

Verbs

Pronouns

11.1 Personal Pronouns

■ A **pronoun** is a word that takes the place of one or more nouns.

The most frequently used pronouns are called personal pronouns. The words *It* and *her* in the second sentence below are personal pronouns.

> The myth amuses Kim. **It** amuses **her.**

■ Pronouns that are used to refer to people or things are called **personal pronouns.**

Some personal pronouns are used as the subjects of sentences. Other personal pronouns are used as the objects of verbs or prepositions. In the example above, the pronoun *It* replaces the noun *myth* as the subject of the sentence. The pronoun *her* replaces *Kim* as the direct object of the verb *amuses.*

■ A **subject pronoun** is a personal pronoun in the nominative case. It is used as the subject of a sentence.

> **She** especially likes "Atalanta's Race."

■ An **object pronoun** is a personal pronoun in the objective case. It is used as the object of a verb or a preposition.

> The librarian recommended **it** to **us.**

Study the personal pronouns in the chart below.

Pronouns

Personal Pronouns		
	Singular	**Plural**
Used as Subjects	I	we
	you	you
	he, she, it	they
Used as Objects	me	us
	you	you
	him, her, it	them

| **Exercise 1** | **Identifying Personal Pronouns** |

List the pronouns and identify each pronoun as a *subject pronoun* in the nominative case or an *object pronoun* in the objective case.

1. I will tell you a story about three characters in mythology.
2. They are named Daphne, Apollo, and Cupid.
3. Apollo loved Daphne, but Daphne did not love him.
4. The malice of Cupid caused the dissention between them.
5. Apollo said, "Cupid's arrows are not worthy weapons for me."
6. Cupid replied, "This arrow is small but still can wound you."
7. Then he stood on a rock and pulled two arrows from a quiver.
8. Aiming at Daphne, Cupid pierced her with a tiny leaden arrow.
9. From then on, she refused all offers of marriage.
10. Cupid's golden darts bring love, and leaden darts repel it.

| **Exercise 2** | **Using Pronouns in the Nominative and Objective Cases** |

Write each sentence, replacing the underlined word or words with a pronoun. Identify each pronoun as a *subject pronoun* in the nominative case or an *object pronoun* in the objective case.

1. Greek poets developed myths from old stories.
2. Rita studied the myths for their factual information.
3. Myths about historical events interest Dan.
4. Rita traced the different versions of one myth.
5. "Atalanta's Race" is an interesting Greek myth, according to Rita and Dan.
6. The myth of Atalanta tells about a foot race.
7. Atalanta is a beautiful woman and a very fast runner.
8. Many men want Atalanta as their bride.
9. Atalanta refuses the men time after time.
10. Atalanta arranges a race to find the fastest runner.
11. Atalanta will marry a man faster than she is.
12. Atalanta passes the runners with graceful ease.
13. Hippomenes wants Atalanta as his wife.
14. Hippomenes asks Aphrodite for help in his race against Atalanta.
15. Aphrodite helps Hippomenes.
16. She gives three golden apples and instructions to Hippomenes.
17. Hippomenes drops the apples along the way.
18. Atalanta picks the golden apples up and so forsakes her victory.
19. Hippomenes takes Atalanta as his bride.
20. Aphrodite brings Hippomenes and Atalanta together.

11.2 Pronouns and Antecedents

Read the following sentences. Can you tell to whom the word *She* refers?

Arachne competes against Athena. **She** weaves skillfully.

The sentence is not clear because the word *She* could refer to either Arachne or Athena. Sometimes you must repeat a noun or rewrite the sentence. Read the sentences below. Repeating the noun makes it clear who weaves skillfully.

Arachne competes against Athena. Athena weaves skillfully.

■ The noun or group of words that a pronoun refers to is called its **antecedent.**

When you use a pronoun, you should be sure that it refers to its antecedent clearly. Be especially careful when you use the pronoun *they*. Read the following sentence.

They have several books about Greek myths at the library.

The meaning of *They* is unclear. The sentence can be improved by rewriting it in the following manner.

Several books on Greek myths are available at the library.

When using pronouns, you must also make sure that they agree with their antecedents in **number** (singular or plural) and gender. The **gender** of a noun may be masculine (male), feminine (female), or neuter (referring to things). Notice how the pronouns in the sentences below agree with their antecedents.

The myth of Arachne is amusing. I enjoyed **it.**
The bystanders see Athena. **They** watch **her** at the loom.

Write the second sentence in each pair. Use the correct pronoun in each blank. Then write the antecedent of the pronoun and its number.

1. The maiden Arachne lives in Lydia. _____ is a country in Asia.
2. Arachne is a skillful weaver. _____ boasts about her weaving.
3. Arachne first forms woolen threads. _____ feel as soft as clouds.
4. People watch Arachne and admire her work. They tell her, "Pallas Athena must have taught _____."
5. The angry Arachne replies, "So you think my art comes from a teacher? I tell _____ that I am a better weaver than Athena herself!"
6. Athena and Arachne enter into a contest. The people watch the two of _____.
7. The weaving hands work with great speed. _____ are a blur.
8. There has never been such a contest. _____ is amazing to see.
9. Both weavers do their best. Both of _____ try to win.
10. Athena weaves pictures of a story about the male god Poseidon. In her story, _____ loses a contest to her.
11. Poseidon is the ruler of the sea. _____ is his domain.
12. Poseidon carries a trident. This symbol identifies _____.
13. The people look at Athena's pictures. The curious audience observes _____ woven into cloth.
14. Athena is in the pictures. _____ is shown dressed in armor.
15. Arachne weaves a story about the male god Zeus. _____ looks alive and seems to speak.
16. Her weaving also shows a swan and a bull. _____ look real.
17. At the end of the contest, Athena is the winner. _____ has woven a fabric like a rainbow.
18. Arachne is the loser. _____ feels guilty about the challenge.
19. Arachne's pictures displease Athena. Athena destroys _____.
20. Arachne is punished. _____ is turned into a spider.
21. Arachne will weave webs forever. _____ will weave them in old houses.
22. All Arachne's descendants are spiders. _____ get their scientific name, *arachnid*, from her name.
23. Edmund Spenser was an English poet. _____ wrote a poem about Arachne.
24. You and I can find the poem on the Internet. _____ must look in the literature section.
25. The literature section is always crowded. _____ is very popular.

11.3 Using Pronouns Correctly

Subject pronouns in the nominative case are used in compound subjects, and object pronouns in the objective case are used in compound objects.

> **He** and Carmen wrote a report on the subject. [not *Him and Carmen*]
>
> Tell John and **me** about Hercules. [not *John and I*]

A preposition takes an object, just as many verbs do. The object of a preposition can be simple or compound. In either case, use an object pronoun as the object of the preposition. In the sentences below, the pronouns in dark type are the objects of the preposition *to.*

> Lee read a famous Roman myth to **me.**
>
> Lee read a famous Roman myth to Irma and **me.**

If you are not sure which form of the pronoun to use, say the sentence aloud with only the pronoun as the subject or the object. Your ear will tell you which form is correct.

Whenever the pronoun *I* is part of a compound subject, it should always be placed after the other parts of the subject. Similarly, when the pronoun *me* is part of a compound object, it should go after the other parts of the object.

> Lee and **I** read some ancient Roman myths. [not *I and Lee*]
>
> Mythology interests Lee and **me.** [not *me and Lee*]

In formal writing and speech use a subject pronoun after a linking verb.

> The writer of this report was **she.**
>
> It is **I.**

Pronouns

Exercise 4 | **Using Pronouns in the Nominative and Objective Cases Correctly**

Write each sentence. Use the correct word or words in parentheses. Then identify each pronoun you selected as a *subject pronoun* or an *object pronoun*.

1. (She, Her) and Chen told the class about Roman mythology.
2. They told Earl and (I, me) about Jupiter and Mars.
3. Mars and (he, him) were the most important gods.
4. Two planets were named after Mars and (he, him).
5. Dom and (me, I) asked questions about Jupiter.
6. Dom described a famous Roman myth to Chen and (I, me).
7. Earl and (he, him) know about Roman culture.
8. Sandra and (we, us) listened to the ancient Roman story of Romulus and Remus.
9. The founders of the city of Rome were (they, them).
10. Romulus and (he, him) were twin sons of a god and a human.
11. A basket with Romulus and (he, him) in it was set adrift.
12. A she-wolf cared for Remus and (he, him).
13. Romulus, Remus, and (she, her) became popular figures in Roman art.
14. Later (he, him) and Remus founded a city.
15. Remus and (he, him) quarreled; Romulus won.
16. The city is named after (he, him), not Remus.
17. (Us, We) can read about the beginning of Rome in a poem.
18. Virgil, an ancient Roman poet, wrote about (they, them).
19. (He, Him) was the author of the *Aeneid*, a great epic poem.
20. Mary says that the feats in the poem are exciting to (she, her).

Exercise 5 | **Using Pronouns in the Nominative and Objective Cases**

Write each sentence. Change the underlined noun or group of words to a pronoun, and identify it as a *subject pronoun* or an *object pronoun*.

1. Readers may be interested in learning a myth of the goddess Echo.
2. Echo, fond of woods and hills, lived in the woods and hills.
3. Echo loved to chat and always wanted to have the last word.
4. One day in the woods, the goddess Juno was looking for the nymphs.
5. Echo and the nymphs were friends.
6. Echo and Juno talked about where the nymphs could be.
7. Echo, by talking, delayed the goddess until the nymphs escaped.
8. Juno discovered Echo's trickery.
9. Echo's trick prompted Juno to punish Echo.
10. Juno said, "Juno will now pass sentence on Echo."

11.4 | Possessive Pronouns

You often use pronouns to replace nouns that are subjects and nouns that are objects in sentences. You can use pronouns in place of possessive nouns too.

- A **possessive pronoun** is a pronoun in the possessive case. It shows who or what has something. A possessive pronoun may take the place of a possessive noun.

Read the following sentences. Notice the possessive nouns and the possessive pronouns that replace them.

> Homer's story is famous. **His** story is famous.
> This story is Homer's. This story is **his.**

Possessive pronouns have two forms. One form is used before a noun. The other form is used alone. The chart below shows the two forms of possessive pronouns.

Possessive Pronouns		
	Singular	**Plural**
Used Before Nouns	my your his, her, its	our your their
Used Alone	mine yours his, hers, its	ours yours theirs

Possessive pronouns are not written with apostrophes. The pronoun *its*, for example, shows possession. The word *it's*, on the other hand, is a contraction of *it is*. Read the following sentences. Notice the meaning of the words in dark type.

> **Its** central character is Odysseus. [possessive pronoun]
> **It's** about the adventures of Odysseus. [contraction of *It is*]

Identifying Pronouns in the Possessive Case

Write each sentence. Underline each possessive pronoun. Then write *before a noun* or *stands alone* to tell how the pronoun is used.

1. His adventures interested all types of readers.
2. Its title comes from the name Odysseus.
3. Few characters possess a personality like his.
4. The Romans renamed him Ulysses in their list of heroes.
5. I like that translation better than ours.
6. A romantic poem about Ulysses will engage your attention and mine.
7. It narrates the wanderings of Ulysses in his return from Troy.
8. My literature book describes where the ships landed in Ithaca.
9. The inhabitants wanted to claim the ships as theirs.
10. Does your book describe what other adventures Ulysses has?

Exercise 7 **Using Pronouns in the Possessive Case**

Write each sentence. Replace each underlined word or group of words with the correct possessive pronoun.

1. Athena helped the Greeks, and soon the city of Troy was the Greeks'.
2. With Athena's help, the Greeks defeated the Trojans.
3. Athena said to Odysseus, "Return to Odysseus's home."
4. The sailors told Odysseus, "The sailors' ships stand ready."
5. Odysseus saved Odysseus's crew many times.
6. Many adventures were the sailors'.
7. Odysseus told his crew, "His crews' homes are waiting for you."
8. Tell me the reader's own version of how the Trojan War began.
9. Once, three goddesses did not use the goddesses' wisdom well.
10. All citizens except one goddess got the citizens' invitations.
11. That goddess did not get that goddess's invitation.
12. "Where is this goddess's invitation?" she asked angrily.
13. For revenge, she tossed a golden apple in the guests' midst.
14. The apple's inscription read, "For the fairest."
15. Athena, Hera, and Aphrodite each claimed the apple as each one's own.
16. A shepherd named Paris was ordered by Zeus to make Zeus's decision.
17. Hera said to Paris, "Great power is Paris's if you pick me."
18. Glory and renown would be Athena's gift to Paris.
19. Paris could have a beautiful wife if he called Aphrodite's name.
20. Paris chose Aphrodite and gave her the contest's prize.

11.5 Indefinite Pronouns

■ An **indefinite pronoun** is a pronoun that does not refer to a particular person, place, or thing.

Does **anyone** know the story of Midas?

Most indefinite pronouns are either singular or plural.

Some Indefinite Pronouns			
Singular			**Plural**
another	everybody	no one	both
anybody	everyone	nothing	few
anyone	everything	one	many
anything	much	somebody	others
each	neither	someone	several
either	nobody	something	

The indefinite pronouns *all, any, most, none,* and *some* can be singular or plural, depending on the phrase that follows them.

When an indefinite pronoun is used as the subject of a sentence, the verb must agree with it in number.

Everyone discusses the plot. [singular]
Both talk about King Minos. [plural]
All of mythology **is** about beliefs and ideals. [singular]
All of the myths **are** about beliefs and ideals. [plural]

Possessive pronouns often have indefinite pronouns as their antecedents. In such cases, the pronouns must agree in number. Note that in the first example the intervening prepositional phrase does not affect the agreement.

Each of the characters has **his** or **her** motive.
Several have conflict with **their** rivals.

Exercise 8   Using Indefinite Pronouns

Write each sentence. Use the word in parentheses that correctly completes the sentence. Underline the indefinite pronoun and write whether it is *singular* or *plural.*

1. Many (knows, know) the tale of Midas.
2. Few (has, have) more gold than King Midas.
3. Some of the gods, however, (possesses, possess) more gold than the king.
4. One of them (is, are) the object of Midas's jealousy; he is Apollo, the sun god.
5. Others (punishes, punish) mortals who are jealous of the gods, but not Apollo.
6. "Anything (is, are) yours," Apollo tells Midas.
7. In mythology someone may be granted (his or her, their) wish.
8. No one (thinks, think) harm will come of Midas's wish that all he touches turns to gold.
9. Several wish (his or her, their) fate were the same as Midas's.
10. Everybody (know, knows) that Midas meant no harm.
11. All of Midas's gold (bring, brings) him little happiness.
12. Several of life's joys (is, are) taken away from Midas.
13. One of his touches (is, are) fatal to any living thing.
14. Midas touches his daughter; each of his other children (is, are) safe.
15. All of his food (turn, turns) to gold, and so he cannot eat.
16. Soon Midas regrets his wish; nothing retains (its, their) life once he touches it.
17. "Nothing (is, are) more precious than life," Midas admits, "not even gold."
18. Apollo forgives Midas; all of the golden objects regain (its, their) original form.
19. All of life (is, are) now a pleasure for Midas.
20. Many now (think, thinks) the name Midas means "rich man."

Exercise 9   Using Indefinite Pronouns Correctly

Write each sentence. Use the correct indefinite pronoun.

1. (Each, All) of Zeus's brothers was asleep in his own bed.
2. Nearby were many giants; (several, one) raised their voices.
3. The brothers awoke; (everybody, all) jumped from their beds.
4. Typhon was (one, many) of the giants; his voice was loudest.
5. (Both, One) had one hundred arms and breathed fire from his nose.
6. The brothers and giants battled; (each, most) fought his best.
7. The giants lost; (all, either) of them took their punishment.
8. (All, Everybody) were imprisoned under the island of Sicily.
9. (Much, Others) of the island moves; its ground quakes.
10. (Another, Many) blow their breath up through the mountain.

Pronouns

11.6 Reflexive and Intensive Pronouns

Reflexive and intensive pronouns are formed by adding *-self* or *-selves* to certain personal and possessive pronouns.

Reflexive and Intensive Pronouns	
Singular	**Plural**
myself	ourselves
yourself	yourselves
himself, herself, itself	themselves

Sometimes *hisself* is mistakenly used for *himself* and *theirselves* for *themselves*. Avoid using *hisself* and *theirselves*.

■ A **reflexive pronoun** refers to a noun or another pronoun and indicates that the same person or thing is involved.

The woman found **herself** a book of folk tales.

REFLEXIVE PRONOUN

■ An **intensive pronoun** is a pronoun that adds emphasis to a noun or pronoun already named.

George **himself** bought a copy of *American Tall Tales.*
He **himself** paid for the book.

Never use reflexive and intensive pronouns as the subject of a sentence or as the object of a verb or preposition.

Roy and **I** read a tale. [not *Roy and myself*]
It intrigued Roy and **me.** [not *Roy and myself*]

Pronouns

Identifying Reflexive and Intensive Pronouns

Read each sentence. Write each reflexive and intensive pronoun. Then write whether each pronoun is a *reflexive* or *intensive* pronoun.

1. Today occupy yourselves by reading the legend of King Arthur.
2. The legend itself may be based on historical evidence.
3. Arthur's mother admired herself for giving birth to such a son.
4. Arthur's father himself was the elected sovereign of Britain.
5. Arthur himself is said to have had twelve victories in battle.
6. In the last battle, his armies outdid themselves.
7. They were very effective, and Arthur himself honored them.
8. His people considered themselves lucky to be living in peace.
9. The country itself was peaceful for twenty years.
10. Then Arthur's nephew Modred showed himself to be a traitor.

Exercise 11 **Using Reflexive and Intensive Pronouns Correctly**

Write each sentence. Use the correct pronoun in parentheses. Write whether the pronoun is a *reflexive, intensive, subject,* or *object* pronoun.

1. I recently bought (me, myself) a book about Paul Bunyan.
2. (He, Himself) is a legendary giant lumberjack of the north woods.
3. The book (it, itself) is a collector's item.
4. The imaginative legends provide (us, ourselves) with a sense of folk tradition.
5. Perhaps settlers on the frontier would tell (them, themselves) these stories.
6. My friends and (I, myself) find the legends amusing.
7. Paul Bunyan (he, himself) has a good sense of humor.
8. (We, Ourselves) call Paul Bunyan's adventures tall tales.
9. The students bought (theirselves, themselves) a copy of the tales.
10. In the tales, Bunyan forms much of America (it, itself).
11. (He, Himself) digs Washington's Puget Sound.
12. The lumberjacks thank (him, himself) for his help.
13. Now the logs (they, themselves) float easily to the mills.
14. The giant blue ox, Babe, makes (it, itself) Bunyan's friend.
15. Bunyan gives (it, itself) many gifts during their friendship.
16. The Great Lakes (they, themselves) are Babe's drinking water.
17. The north woods (them, themselves) are in the United States and Canada.
18. (I, Myself) know one story about Paul Bunyan.
19. (It, Itself) tells how the ten thousand lakes of Minnesota formed.
20. Tall tales have always been amusing to (us, ourselves).

Pronouns

11.7 Interrogative Pronouns

■ An **interrogative pronoun** is a pronoun used to introduce an interrogative sentence.

> **Who** is Pandora?
> For **whom** does Hephaestus make a staff?
> **What** is Pandora's curiosity about?
> **Whom** does Zeus call?
> **Whose** is the gift of hope?

The interrogative pronouns *who* and *whom* both refer to people. *Who* is used when the interrogative pronoun is the subject of the sentence. *Whom* is used when the interrogative pronoun is the object of a verb or a preposition.

> **Who** gives Pandora her name? [subject]
> **Whom** does Zeus dislike? [direct object]
> To **whom** does Zeus give a gift? [object of preposition]

Which and *what* are used to refer to things.

> Some gifts are for Pandora. **Which** are they?
> Athena makes Pandora a robe. **What** does Hephaestus make?

Whose shows that someone possesses something.

> The jar is in Pandora's house. **Whose** is it?

Do not confuse *whose* with *who's.*

> **Who's** reading the myth? [contraction of *Who is*]
> **Whose** is it? [interrogative pronoun]

Exercise 12   Using Interrogative Pronouns

Write each sentence. Use the correct word given in parentheses.

1. (Who, Which) is the myth about a quest for a great treasure?
2. To (whom, who) do you read those myths?
3. (What, Whom) is the object of the quest?
4. (Who, Which) is the hero in the first story?
5. (Who's, Whose) reading these myths?
6. (What, Which) does the word *myth* mean?
7. (Whom, Which) of the Roman myths are known by most people?
8. (Who, Whom) was the first person to make up a myth?
9. To (whom, whose) can the first tall tale be credited?
10. (Whose, Who's) are the most vivid imaginations, children's or adults'?

Exercise 13   Using Interrogative Pronouns and Contractions

Write each pair of sentences. Use the correct word given in parentheses. If the word you selected is a contraction, write *contraction.*

1. Jason is a famous hero of classical Greek mythology. (Whose, Who's) Jason?
2. His quest is for the Golden Fleece, the wool of a winged ram. (What, Whom) is the Golden Fleece?
3. Jason's father, Aeson, is the king until Pelias removes him. (Who,Whom) does Pelias remove?
4. When Jason grows up, he wants Pelias's throne. (Whose, Whom) is the throne currently?
5. Pelias promises him the throne if he retrieves the Golden Fleece. (Whose, What) is Pelias's demand?
6. Jason sails on the Argo with a group of brave friends, called the Argonauts. (Who's, Which) is the Argonauts' ship?
7. The ship is named after Argo, the shipbuilder. (Who, Whom) is the ship named after?
8. The famous Hercules was among the crew. (Who, Whom) is among the crew?
9. They rowed until they reached the eastern end of the sea. (Whose, Which) way did they row?
10. In Greece Jason tamed the king's two fire-breathing bulls. (Who's, Whose) were the fire-breathing bulls?

Grammar Review

PRONOUNS

In Greek mythology, Phaethon is the son of Apollo, the sun god, and Clymene, a mortal. Although Phaethon's mother has told him that Apollo is his father, Phaethon seeks proof from Apollo himself. Phaethon approaches the sun god, who solemnly promised to grant his son any wish the boy might have. Unfortunately, Phaethon asks to drive the sun god's chariot for a day, a job only Apollo himself can handle.

In the following excerpt from "Phaethon," retold by Edith Hamilton, Phaethon sets out on his disastrous ride. The passage has been annotated to show some of the kinds of pronouns covered in this unit.

Literature Model

from "Phaethon"
retold by Edith Hamilton

For a few ecstatic moments Phaethon felt himself the lord of the sky. But suddenly there was a change. The chariot was swinging wildly to and fro; the pace was faster; he had lost control. Not he, but the horses were directing the course. That light weight in the car, those feeble hands clutching the reins, had told them their own driver was not there. They were the masters then. No one else could command them. They left the road and rushed where they chose, up, down, to the right, to the left. They nearly wrecked the chariot against the Scorpion; they brought up short and almost ran into the Crab. By this time the poor charioteer was half fainting with terror, and he let the reins fall.

> Reflexive pronoun

> Possessive pronoun

> Indefinite pronoun

> Subject pronoun agrees with its antecedent, *the poor charioteer*

Grammar Review

| Review: Exercise 1 | **Using Pronouns in the Nominative, Objective, and Possessive Cases** |

Write each sentence. Replace the underlined word or words with a pronoun and write whether it is a *subject pronoun*, *object pronoun*, or *possessive pronoun*.

1. Phaethon was <u>Apollo's</u> and <u>Clymene's</u> son.
2. <u>Apollo</u> was the sun god, and <u>Clymene</u> was an ocean nymph.
3. <u>Apollo's and Clymene's</u> son wanted to drive <u>Apollo's</u> horses.
4. The sun god let <u>Phaethon</u> ride off with the <u>sun god's team</u>.
5. <u>The horses</u> carried <u>Phaethon</u> high into the sky

| Review: Exercise 2 | **Using Pronouns and Antecedents Correctly** |

Write the second sentence in each of the following pairs. Use the correct pronoun in each blank. Then write the antecedent of the pronoun.

SAMPLE After a long journey, Phaethon approaches the palace of his father. _____ is excited.

ANSWER He is excited. Phaethon

1. Phaethon walks up the steps. _____ are made of white marble.
2. The boy enters the great hall. His footsteps echo in _____.
3. There sits Apollo, dressed in a splendid robe. _____ is deep purple and trimmed in gold.
4. At the right and left hands of Apollo stand servants dressed in flowing garments. _____ make the servants look regal.
5. Spring stands with her crown of flowers. _____ looks radiant.
6. The lovely Summer carries a garland of ripened grain. The garland is _____ symbol.
7. Autumn's feet are stained from grapes. She stomps on _____ to press out the juice.
8. Frost stiffens Winter's hair. Icicles hang from _____.
9. Around the great hall stand Day, Month, Year, and—at regular intervals—Hours. _____ watch as Phaethon approaches.
10. Apollo looks at Phaethon with pride. "_____ welcome you to my palace," Apollo says.

Review: Exercise 3 **Using Pronouns in the Nominative and Objective Cases Correctly**

Read each sentence. Write the correct word or words in parentheses. Then write whether each pronoun you selected is a *subject pronoun* or an *object pronoun*.

1. (He, Him) and Apollo admired the chariot and the horses.
2. Apollo told Phaethon and (they, them) to be careful.
3. The horses and (he, him) would soar through sky and clouds.
4. "The team and (I, me) thank mother and father," said Phaethon.
5. "(We, Us) and Apollo bless you and the team," said the gods.
6. The wheels and axles were cleaned by servants and (he, him).
7. Phaethon and (they, them) had a breakfast of ambrosia and honey.
8. (They, Them) and Phaethon needed energy and courage.
9. The first two horses lifted the chariot and (he, him) at dawn.
10. Al and (I, me) think Phaethon and the chariot represent the sun.

Review: Exercise 4 **Using Indefinite Pronouns**

Write each sentence. Use the word or words in parentheses that correctly complete the sentence. Then underline the indefinite pronoun and write whether the pronoun is *singular* or *plural*.

SAMPLE Everyone (watches, watch) in horror as the chariot plunges to earth.
ANSWER <u>Everyone</u> watches in horror as the chariot plunges to earth. singular

1. Some (tries, try) to hide from the fiery car.
2. Others (appeals, appeal) to Zeus, the ruler of the gods, to stop the falling chariot.
3. Something (shine, shines) in Zeus's hand as he climbs his tower.
4. Zeus rules clouds and lightning; both (is, are) under his control.
5. Everyone (gasps, gasp) as he hurls a thunderbolt at the charioteer.
6. No one (is, are) sadder than the sun god to see Phaethon struck dead by the bolt.
7. Few (point, points) as Phaethon, hair on fire, falls from the sky.
8. Many (describe, describes) him as like a shooting star.
9. Each tells (his or her, their) own story.
10. Much (happen, happens) as the river receives and cools his body.

Grammar Review

Review: Exercise 5   **Using Subject, Object, Reflexive, and Intensive Pronouns**

Write each sentence. Use the correct pronoun in parentheses. Write whether the pronoun is a *reflexive, intensive, subject,* or *object* pronoun.

1. Phaethon told Father, "I want to drive the chariot (me, myself)."
2. Father objected strongly; (he, himself) knew his son's fate.
3. Phaethon positioned (him, himself) in the chariot.
4. (It, Itself) was a gift from Vulcan, who makes Zeus's lightning.
5. Father hugged the boy and gave (him, himself) the reins.
6. "(You, Yourselves) and I will drive the sun through the sky," declared Phaethon to the horses.
7. The horses (himself, themselves) were eager to start.
8. At dawn the horses carried (he, him) high into the sky.
9. But the horses seized control of the chariot, and (they, themselves) sped past the constellations.
10. Alas, only the sun god (him, himself) can drive the chariot.

Review: Exercise 6   **Using Interrogative Pronouns**

The following sentences are about figures in Egyptian mythology. Write each question, using the correct interrogative pronoun in parentheses.

1. Nut represented the heavens. (What, Which) did Nut represent?
2. Geb was the earth god. (Who, Whom) was Geb?
3. Nut and Geb married, but Ra, the sun god, opposed their marriage. (Which, What) did Ra oppose?
4. Ra had the head of a hawk. (Who, Whom) had the head of a hawk?
5. Ra wore a solar disk as a crown. (What, Who) did Ra wear as a crown?
6. Ra ordered Shu, the god of the air, to separate Nut from Geb. (Who, Whom) did Ra order to separate Nut from Geb?
7. Shu separated heaven from earth. (Who, What) moved heaven away?
8. Isis's head had the horns of a cow. Horns were worn by (who, whom)?
9. Isis was the wife of Osiris. (Who, Whom) was the wife of Osiris?
10. Osiris was god of the underworld. (Who, Whom) ruled the underworld?

Proofreading

The following passage is about chariot racing. This event inspired *Charioteers*, the painting shown on the Greek vase below. Rewrite the passage, correcting the errors in spelling, capitalization, grammar, and usage. Add any missing punctuation. There are ten errors in all.

Artist unknown, Greece, *Charioteers*, fifth century B.C.

(continued)

Grammar Review

Charioteers

[1]A four-horse chariot race became part of the ancient Olympics in greece. [2]The race proved to be so popular that they became the opening spectacle at the games. [3]As many as forty chariot drivers competing in the race. [4]Each chariot driver were hired by the owner of the chariot and horses. [5]Sometimes an owner enter as many as seven chariots in the same race.

[6]The competitors has to run laps down a straight track for a total distance of nearly nine miles. [7]When the four horses pulling a chariot turned around to double back down the track. [8]The chariot would swing wildly. [9]As Phaethon discovered when he tried to drive the sun god's chariot, the horses were very hard to control. [10]Spills and collisions occured frequently. [11]As a result, very few of the chariot drivers manages to finish the race.

Review: Exercise 8

Mixed Review

On your paper, list in order the twenty numbered pronouns that appear in the following paragraphs. Identify each pronoun as *personal*, *possessive*, *indefinite*, *reflexive*, *intensive*, or *interrogative*.

One day in summer, Phaethon went to visit[1] his father, Apollo the sun god. Apollo[2] himself lived in a faraway palace, and Phaethon had never seen[3] it. [4]Nothing would stop Phaethon from seeing the palace today. After a long journey, Phaethon found [5]himself at the palace. [6]What did [7]he see there?

[8]All of the palace's columns glittered with gold. Precious stones such as diamonds and rubies studded [9]them. [10]Nothing but polished ivory formed the ceilings. The front doors [11]themselves were made from silver, and they shone in the sun like mirrors. Colorful murals covered [12]some of the palace walls. [13]They represented the earth, the sea, the sky, and [14]their inhabitants. The largest mural depicted a group of nymphs frolicking by the sea. [15]Some were riding the sea waves. [16]Others were riding on the backs of fishes. [17]One was sitting on a rock and drying [18]her long, sea-green hair.

Phaethon was amazed. [19]Which was the most spectacular sight? He couldn't choose. How would [20]you decide?

Writing Application

Pronouns in Writing

Pronouns can replace nouns to make your writing more varied. Study how Latoya Hunter uses pronouns in this passage from *The Diary of Latoya Hunter*. Notice the italicized pronouns.

> Dear Diary,
> *I* never thought *I*'d get desperate enough to say this but I envy *you*. *You* don't have to live in this troubled world; all *you* do is hear about it. *You* don't have to go through a situation like sitting in a cafeteria watching others laughing and talking and *you* don't know *anyone*. To sit there and eat the food that is just terrible because there's *nothing* else to do . . .
> I guess *you* can tell how *my* day went. Diary, what am *I* going to do? *My* best friend left to go to another school. *I* wish *she* could be with *me*.

Techniques with Pronouns

Try to apply some of Latoya Hunter's techniques when you write and revise your work.

❶ Lend variety to your writing by alternating pronouns and nouns.

CONFUSING VERSION *She* left. I wish *she* could be with me.

HUNTER'S VERSION *My best friend* left. I wish *she* could be with me.

❷ Keep your writing clear by making pronouns agree with their antecedents.

CONFUSING VERSION You don't have to live in *this troubled world*; all you do is hear about *them*.

HUNTER'S VERSION You don't have to live in *this troubled world*; all you do is hear about *it*.

TIME
For more about the writing process, see **TIME Facing the Blank Page**, pp. 97–107.

Pronouns

Practice Practice some of these pronoun techniques by revising the following passage. Focus particularly on the underlined words.

Every day <u>it</u> was the same torture. Chants of "Charlie Brown! Charlie Brown!" filled the bus the minute Walker boarded. He was mortified. Alex, <u>his</u> buddy, kept saying "<u>They</u> are only teasing." He couldn't know how <u>he</u> felt. No one ever teased <u>him</u>. Walker had tried every solution. First, he'd ignored <u>it</u>. Then he'd plunged into reading. Finally, he'd camped out at the front of the bus under the driver's eagle eye. Nothing helped. But today <u>they</u> would be different. <u>He</u>, the school principal, had given <u>him</u> special permission to ride a bike to school. He really seemed to understand <u>his</u> problem.

LOG ON ▶ **Writing** Online | For more grammar practice, go to **glencoe.com** and enter QuickPass code WC77680p2.

Writing Application **449**

An adjective describes a person, place, thing, or idea. An adjective provides information about the size, shape, color, texture, feeling, sound, smell, number, or condition of a noun or a pronoun.

Many groups of visitors admire the **huge new** building.

In the sentence above, the adjective *many* describes the noun *groups,* and the adjectives *huge* and *new* describe the noun *building.*

■ An **adjective** is a word that modifies, or describes, a noun or a pronoun.

Most adjectives come before the nouns they modify. Sometimes adjectives follow linking verbs and modify the noun or pronoun that is the subject of the sentence, as in the example below.

Some architects are **skillful** and **creative.**

In the sentence above, the adjectives *skillful* and *creative* follow the linking verb *are* and modify the subject, *architects.* They are called predicate adjectives.

■ A **predicate adjective** is an adjective that follows a linking verb and modifies the subject of the sentence.

Forms of verbs are often used as adjectives and predicate adjectives.

The architect created a **surprising** design. [present participle]

The building is **decorated.** [past participle]

Adjectives and Adverbs

Exercise 1   Identifying Adjectives

Write each adjective and then write the noun or pronoun it modifies.

1. Good architects often have an artistic background.
2. They arrange many different materials into beautiful shapes.
3. Reliable architects have studied engineering.
4. They want to design attractive, sturdy, and useful buildings.
5. Often you will see rectangular buildings.
6. You can also find buildings with other shapes.
7. The big city of Chicago has a circular building.
8. Famous old cathedrals have tall, graceful towers.
9. Most designs aim for true beauty and creative form.
10. Look for graceful lines as attractive features of buildings.
11. Architectural styles change along with other fashions.
12. Good architects have simple but unique plans.
13. Commercial buildings must have good designs.
14. The efficient use of space is a challenging requirement for many designs.
15. Careful designs provide comfortable areas for workers.
16. A good design also provides easy access to equipment.
17. Successful architects know about potential problems.
18. Advanced designs produce practical buildings.
19. The original skyscraper was a triangular sail.
20. In a calm sea, it was set high above the ordinary sails.

Exercise 2   Predicate Adjectives

Write the sentence in each pair that has a predicate adjective. Underline the predicate adjectives. (In one pair, both sentences have predicate adjectives.)

1. John Muir's early life was difficult. He worked hard at home.
2. However, that didn't stop him. Muir was willing and strong.
3. Muir was studious. His father discouraged his reading, though.
4. Muir was also inventive. He created many labor-saving devices.
5. After college Muir got some bad news. He might be blind soon.
6. Muir became adventurous. He started a journey west.
7. Muir traveled by foot. His journey was slow but meaningful.
8. The Sierra Nevada captivated him. They were beautiful.
9. Finally he reached San Francisco. For a time he was content.
10. He became a farmer. But travel was too tempting for him.

12.2 Articles and Proper Adjectives

The words *a, an,* and *the* make up a special group of adjectives called **articles.** *A* and *an* are called **indefinite articles** because they refer to one of a general group of people, places, things, or ideas. *A* is used before words beginning with a consonant sound. *An* is used before words beginning with a vowel sound.

> **a** unit   **a** pilot   **an** hour   **an** astronaut

The is called a **definite article** because it identifies specific people, places, things, or ideas.

> Neil Armstrong was **the** first man to walk on **the** moon.

- ■ **Proper adjectives** are formed from proper nouns.
  A proper adjective always begins with a capital letter.

> On my vacation in Italy, I ate only **Italian** food.

Some proper adjectives are the same as the related proper nouns: *United States government, June wedding.* Although many proper adjectives use one of the endings listed below, some are formed differently. Check the spellings in a dictionary.

Common Endings for Proper Adjectives				
Ending	**Examples**			
-an	Mexico Mexic**an**	Morocco Morocc**an**	Alaska Alask**an**	Guatemala Guatemal**an**
-ese	China Chin**ese**	Bali Balin**ese**	Sudan Sudan**ese**	Japan Japan**ese**
-ian	Canada Canad**ian**	Italy Ital**ian**	Nigeria Niger**ian**	Asia As**ian**
-ish	Spain Span**ish**	Ireland Ir**ish**	Turkey Turk**ish**	England Engl**ish**

Adjectives and Adverbs

Exercise 3   Using *A* and *An*

Write each word or groups of words, adding the correct indefinite articles.

1. satellite
2. electrical storm
3. transmitter
4. vehicle
5. hurricane
6. expedition
7. universe
8. unexplored part
9. unknown rock
10. typical day
11. surface
12. awkward age
13. instrument
14. high altitude
15. honest effort
16. activity
17. irregular heartbeat
18. total loss
19. unknown cause
20. civil tongue

Exercise 4   Identifying Proper Adjectives

Write the proper adjective from each phrase.

1. Peruvian mountain
2. Alaskan railway
3. Lithuanian dictionary
4. Yugoslavian background
5. Balinese dancer
6. Hungarian map
7. Asian viewpoint
8. Belgian detective
9. African adventure
10. Norwegian pilot
11. Pakistani restaurant
12. Mexican vote
13. Italian film director
14. Israeli consul
15. Japanese costume
16. Indian elephant
17. Moroccan musician
18. Vietnamese landscape
19. Ukrainian dance
20. Jordanian speaker

Exercise 5   Forming Proper Adjectives

Rewrite each group of words, using a proper adjective to describe the noun. Change the indefinite article if necessary.

1. a car from Germany
2. a spice from India
3. a tour of Europe
4. an exhibition in June
5. a song from Brazil
6. a uniform from Canada
7. a shawl from Spain
8. a ring from Bolivia
9. a cowhand from America
10. a coat from England
11. a baseball from Taiwan
12. a carpet from Turkey
13. a dress from Java
14. a harp from Ireland
15. a scientist from Mexico
16. a holiday in November
17. a painting from ancient Persia
18. an athlete from Sweden
19. a recipe from Nepal
20. a delegate from Russia

12.3 Comparative and Superlative Adjectives

Adjectives can also compare two or more nouns or pronouns.

■ The **comparative form** of an adjective compares two things, groups, or people.

> The stone building is **larger** than the wooden building.

■ The **superlative form** of an adjective compares more than two things, groups, or people.

> The **largest** building of the three is made of stone.

For most adjectives of one syllable and some of two syllables, *-er* and *-est* are added to form the comparative and superlative.

Comparative and Superlative Forms	
Adjective	The architect designed a **tall** building.
Comparative	Her new building is **taller** than her last project.
Superlative	Her next building will be the **tallest** of all her buildings.

Some adjectives form irregular comparatives and superlatives.

Irregular Comparative and Superlative Forms		
Adjective	**Comparative**	**Superlative**
good	better	best
well	better	best
bad	worse	worst
many	more	most
much	more	most
little	less	least

For each sentence, write the correct form of the adjective given in parentheses.

1. Remains of huts from about 120,000 years ago are the (old) buildings yet found.
2. The (good) discoveries of all may come from future digs by archaeologists.
3. We now have (many) examples of prehistoric remains than we have ever had.
4. The (early) structure of all is a circle of blocks that may go back more than a million years.
5. The (tall) office building in the world is the Taipei 101 building in Taiwan.
6. The Petronas Towers in Kuala Lumpur are (tall) than the Sears Tower.
7. The Petronas Twin Towers have (little) space than the Sears Tower.
8. The Pentagon covers the (large) area of any office building.
9. If you are entertaining 240,000 people, the stadium in Prague in the former Czech Republic is the (roomy) stadium of all.
10. Of all the students, Iko has the (much) interest in architecture.
11. The auditorium has (good) acoustics than the gymnasium.
12. One day other buildings may become the (big) buildings in the world.
13. (Strange) of all are those structures built mostly underground for safety or security reasons.
14. The (safe) buildings of all have automatic sprinkler systems in case of fire.
15. The better the indoor air quality, the (healthy) the building.
16. In Boston the old State House may be the (little) changed of the old public buildings.
17. The new State House is in the (hilly) part of that area.
18. Boston streets have (many) twists than a monkey's tail.
19. The Back Bay section is (new) than the Beacon Hill area.
20. Charles Bulfinch may be the architect who had the (great) influence of all on what the city looks like.
21. The Charles River Basin is one of Boston's (nice) spots of all for walking, jogging, or biking.
22. The Boston Common may be the (green) spot downtown.
23. Harvard University, across the Charles River, is (old) than any of the other local colleges.
24. Boston's ocean breezes make it (windy) than inland cities.
25. Unlike many old buildings, (late) structures are very tall.

12.4 More Comparative and Superlative Adjectives

The comparative and superlative forms of most one-syllable and some two-syllable adjectives are formed by adding *-er* and *-est* to the adjective.

For most adjectives with two or more syllables, however, the comparative and superlative are formed by adding *more* and *most* before the adjective.

Comparing Adjectives of More than One Syllable	
Adjective	The archeologist made an **impressive** discovery while digging in the ruins.
Comparative	Her latest discovery is **more impressive** than her first finding.
Superlative	Her new discovery is the **most impressive** finding of the decade.

The words *less* and *least* are used before both short and long adjectives to form the negative comparative and superlative.

Negative Comparative and Superlative Forms	
Adjective	The public was unusually **curious** about the discovery.
Comparative	The public was **less curious** about ancient ruins than about prehistoric fossils.
Superlative	Of all the ancient buildings unearthed in this century, historians were **least curious** about that Greek temple.

Do not use *more*, *most*, *less*, or *least* before adjectives that already end with *-er* or *-est*. This is called a double comparison.

Adjectives and Adverbs

Exercise 7   Using Comparative and Superlative Adjectives

Write the correct comparative or superlative form of each adjective in parentheses.

1. Architecture is certainly one of the (interesting) careers of all.
2. Very few people have (challenging) jobs than architects do.
3. The public is usually (curious) about the architects themselves than about the work they do.
4. Art, mathematics, and engineering are among the (important) subjects of all for architects to study in school.
5. For architects in the Middle Ages, roofs presented the (difficult) problem of all.
6. Buildings became (massive) than they had ever been before.
7. As roofs grew heavier, the supporting walls became (solid).
8. These structures are among the (imposing) buildings ever constructed.
9. In the twelfth century, architects found better ways to support roofs, and buildings became (graceful) than they had been in the past.
10. Buildings could now support huge stained-glass windows, perhaps the (beautiful) windows people had ever seen.

Exercise 8   Using Comparative and Superlative Negatives

Write the correct negative comparative or negative superlative form of the adjective in parentheses.

1. Early humans may have found that caves were smaller and (convenient) than structures they could build.
2. Unlike huts, caves were (available) in areas with few hills or mountains.
3. Before humans learned to work with stone and brick, they were forced to construct (complex) buildings.
4. Perhaps the (famous) architect was the first to build a stone dwelling.
5. Cretan architecture was (ancient) than that of Egypt.
6. Although the Romans learned from the Greeks, many people think that Roman buildings are (attractive) than Greek buildings.
7. A few people argue that Roman architecture is the (appealing) of all ancient types.
8. Some of the (popular) buildings may be among the best examples of Romanesque architecture.
9. Some people believe that the (important) question one can ask is which type of architecture—Roman or Greek—is more beautiful.
10. In general, older buildings are (graceful) than newer buildings.

12.5 Demonstratives

The words *this, that, these,* and *those* are called demonstratives. They "demonstrate," or point out, people, places, or things. *This* and *these* point out people or things near to you, and *that* and *those* point out people or things at a distance from you. *This* and *that* describe singular nouns, and *these* and *those* describe plural nouns.

This, that, these, and *those* are called demonstrative adjectives when they describe nouns.

- Demonstrative adjectives point out something and describe nouns by answering the questions *which one?* or *which ones?*

The words *this, that, these,* and *those* are demonstrative pronouns when they take the place of nouns and point out something.

"I can almost reach **those** buildings from **this** one."

Demonstratives	
Demonstrative Adjectives	**Demonstrative Pronouns**
That bridge is unusual.	**That** is an unusual stadium.
Look at **this** cathedral.	**This** is a glass dome.
Those windows are enormous.	**Those** are enormous windows.
Who designed **these** homes?	How did workers construct **these?**

The words *here* and *there* should not be used with demonstrative adjectives. The words *this, these, that,* and *those* already point out the locations *here* and *there.*

This bridge is interesting. [not *this here bridge*]

The object pronoun *them* should not be used in place of the demonstrative adjective *those.*

I took a photo of **those** skyscrapers. [not *them skyscrapers*]

Exercise 9　Identifying Demonstrative Adjectives

Write the demonstrative adjective found in each sentence.

1. The castles in these pictures are all in England.
2. The ones you see in that first set were built by the Saxons.
3. You can see the Norman influence on that castle.
4. This tower is called the keep.
5. Don't those buildings look like fortresses?
6. Do you recognize that ditch filled with water?
7. The builders used these moats for added protection.
8. These later castles are more comfortable.
9. Can you tell which of these strongholds was built first?
10. This picture is of Windsor Castle, home of England's rulers.

Exercise 10　Using Demonstrative Adjectives

For each sentence write the correct demonstrative adjective.

1. (This, These) buildings date from the 1700s.
2. (That, Those) style is a typical colonial home.
3. People built (that, those) houses for the cold climate.
4. (That, Those) fact is the reason for the small rooms.
5. Snow could easily slide off (that, those) sloping roof.
6. (That, This) house we are now touring is a typical Cape Cod house.
7. I like (this, these) exhibit of colonial architecture.
8. What are (these, those) pamphlets on the table over there?
9. (That there, That) booklet describes the architecture.
10. (This, These) model shows a southwestern American scene.
11. Missionaries built (them, those) churches with sun-dried brick or adobe.
12. (That, Those) churches combined Native American and Spanish styles.
13. (This, This here) model shows colonial New York.
14. The Dutch settlers built (that, those) type of house.
15. (Them, Those) houses were of brick or stone with small windows.
16. We know (this, these) buildings are representative of colonial-style houses.
17. The brick for (this, these) buildings came from Holland.
18. (This, This here) exhibit is devoted to public buildings.
19. (That, Those) building is still standing in Philadelphia.
20. How many of (them, those) other buildings have been torn down?

12.6 Adverbs

■ An **adverb** is a word that modifies, or describes, a verb, an adjective, or another adverb.

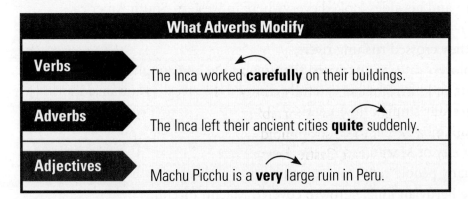

What Adverbs Modify	
Verbs	The Inca worked **carefully** on their buildings.
Adverbs	The Inca left their ancient cities **quite** suddenly.
Adjectives	Machu Picchu is a **very** large ruin in Peru.

When modifying a verb, an adverb may describe *how* or *in what manner* the action is done. It may describe *when* or *how often* an action is done. Also, it may describe *where* or *in what direction* an action was done.

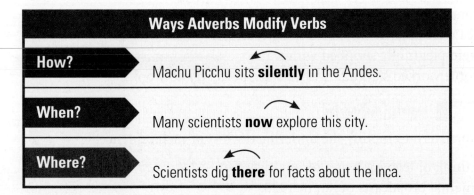

Ways Adverbs Modify Verbs	
How?	Machu Picchu sits **silently** in the Andes.
When?	Many scientists **now** explore this city.
Where?	Scientists dig **there** for facts about the Inca.

Many adverbs are formed by adding *-ly* to adjectives. However, not all words that end in *-ly* are adverbs. The words *friendly, lively, kindly,* and *lonely* are usually adjectives. Similarly, not all adverbs end in *-ly*.

Adverbs not Ending in *-ly*			
afterward	often	there	hard
sometimes	soon	everywhere	long
later	here	fast	straight

Exercise 11　Identifying Adverbs

For each of the following sentences, write the adverb and then write the word it modifies.

1. Hiram Bingham searched diligently for the lost Incan cities.
2. Bingham and his aides looked everywhere in western South America.
3. They traveled slowly through thick jungles.
4. Slowly they crossed rushing rivers.
5. The explorers cautiously carried their own food and supplies.
6. Bingham and his searchers carefully climbed the steep mountainsides.
7. They carefully studied the legends.
8. The Urubamba River snaked below.
9. The lost city of Machu Picchu lay above.
10. Once many people came to the Incan city.
11. Now the Peruvian jungle growth covered Machu Picchu.
12. The mist lifted briefly over the walled city.
13. The city's emptiness affected them greatly.
14. They felt strongly the passage of centuries.
15. Bingham's group worked hard at their task of discovery.
16. The Inca's irrigation system carried water efficiently.
17. They constructed their houses solidly.
18. The Inca were apparently skilled in agriculture.
19. They were plentifully supplied with water.
20. The people worked skillfully with metals, pottery, and wool.

Exercise 12　Using Adverbs

Write an adverb to modify the underlined word in each sentence.

1. People think of television as a recent invention.
2. Experimental broadcasts began in 1928.
3. The quality of the broadcasts was not good.
4. Two important inventions came after 1930.
5. Philo T. Farnsworth patented a scanning cathode ray tube in 1930.
6. Kate Smith sang on one of the first scheduled broadcasts.
7. By the early 1940s, twenty-three TV stations were operating.
8. TV grew after the lifting of wartime restrictions.
9. By 1949 more than a million families had bought TV sets.
10. Ten years later the number had multiplied to 50 million.

When modifying a verb, an adverb may give information about *when, where,* or *how* the action of a sentence takes place. When describing an adjective or another adverb, an adverb often emphasizes or intensifies the word it modifies.

■ An adverb that emphasizes or intensifies an adjective or adverb is called an **intensifier.**

Read the sentences below.

> The people of Rapa Nui (Easter Island) built large statues.
> The people of Rapa Nui (Easter Island) built **extremely** large statues.

In the first sentence you learn that the people built large statues. The adjective *large* describes the noun *statues.* In the second sentence you learn that the statues were extremely large. The intensifier *extremely* describes the adjective *large.*

Now read the following sentences.

> Scientists examined the old statues carefully.
> Scientists examined the old statues **very** carefully.

In the first sentence you learn that scientists carefully examined the statues. The adverb *carefully* describes the action verb *examined.* In the second sentence you learn how carefully the scientists examined the statues. The intensifier *very* describes the adverb carefully.

Here is a list of intensifiers often used to describe adjectives and other adverbs.

The people of Rapa Nui (Easter Island) built extremely large statues.

Intensifiers			
almost	nearly	rather	somewhat
extremely	practically	really	too
just	quite	so	very

Exercise 13　Identifying Intensifiers

For each sentence below, write the intensifier and the word it modifies.

1. The Rapa Nui statues are somewhat mysterious.
2. Most visitors are astounded by their quite enormous size.
3. Scientists have tried extremely hard to explain their origin.
4. The statues were made almost exclusively of volcanic rock.
5. We have learned just recently about their beginnings.
6. Some scientists very carefully built a copy of one of the ancient statues.
7. Scientists worked rather laboriously on the new statue.
8. They spent such long days at their task.
9. For most of the scientists, the project was simply thrilling.
10. The scientists' tools were nearly identical to the ancient ones.
11. The really difficult work took many months of steady labor.
12. Very slowly a sixty-foot copy of an old statue took shape.
13. The ancient builders must have been enormously happy with their work.
14. Rapa Nui is the most easterly island of Polynesia.
15. The island has some extremely interesting stone walls.
16. They are made up of blocks rather carefully fitted together.
17. They are remarkably like the walls of the Inca.
18. The builders of these walls kept their secrets too well.
19. Their identity is essentially hidden from us.
20. It is fairly certain that they lived at least nine hundred years ago.

Exercise 14　Using Intensifiers

Write each sentence, adding the intensifier that appears in parentheses.

1. Being a tourist can be difficult sometimes.　(extremely)
2. Often there are long lines to get through.　(quite)
3. Not speaking the language makes it harder.　(much)
4. You are also at the mercy of the weather.　(somewhat)
5. The food that's available may be unfamiliar.　(quite)
6. If you stay in a hotel, it may be expensive.　(very)
7. Yet traveling remains popular all over the world.　(extremely)
8. Traveling in the off-season can be helpful.　(most)
9. Special package tours can be cheaper than single tickets.　(much)
10. For many people, seeing new sights is its own reward.　(really)

12.8 Comparative and Superlative Adverbs

- The **comparative form** of an adverb compares two actions.
- The **superlative form** of an adverb compares more than two actions.

Long adverbs require the use of *more* or *most.*

Comparing Adverbs of More than One Syllable	
Comparative	The Cretans lived **more peacefully** than the Greeks.
Superlative	They lived the **most peacefully** of all Aegean peoples.

Shorter adverbs need *-er* or *-est* as an ending.

Comparing One- and Two-Syllable Adverbs	
Comparative	The Cretans built cities **earlier** than the Greeks.
Superlative	The Cretans built cities the **earliest** of all Europeans.

Here are some irregular adverbs.

Irregular Comparative Forms		
Adverb	Comparative	Superlative
well	better	best
badly	worse	worst
little (amount)	less	least
far (distance)	farther	farthest
far (degree)	further	furthest

The words *less* and *least* are used before both short and long adverbs to form the negative comparative and superlative.

I work **less often.** I work **least efficiently.**

Do not use *more, most, less,* or *least* before adverbs that already end in *-er* or *-est.*

Exercise 15   Using Comparative and Superlative Forms

Write the correct comparative or superlative form given in parentheses.

1. The Egyptians came to Crete (earlier, earliest) than all other peoples.
2. Did the Cretans arrive in Greece (later, more later) than the Egyptians?
3. Some people think the Cretans built the palace of Knossos (better, best) of all their buildings.
4. Its hundreds of rooms sheltered people (more, most) comfortably than other palaces.
5. Cretan ships sailed (more, most) swiftly of all early vessels.
6. Knossos was powerful and needed protection (less, least) frequently than other cities.
7. This civilization developed commercial trade (further, furthest) than the arts of war.
8. Cretans practiced their arts (more, most) enthusiastically than any other activity.
9. Noted for artistic achievements, perhaps they painted scenes of sports (better, best) of all.
10. Lively scenes appeared in their palace rooms (more, most) often than serious pictures.
11. Despite considerable research, we understand Cretan writings (less, least) well of all early languages.
12. Crete's culture began (earlier, earliest) than most.
13. We'll know more when we can (more, most) readily read the early Cretan inscriptions.
14. Sir Arthur Evans was the person who (more, most) successfully unearthed important discoveries.
15. Evans went even (further, furthest) by discovering the palace of King Minos, located in Knossos.
16. It is laid out (more, most) complexly than other buildings on Crete.
17. Evans decided it was (more, most) likely the labyrinth long-described in Greek legend.
18. (More, Most) recent discoveries may change our thinking.
19. In the legend, Theseus found his way out of the twisting passages (sooner, more soon) than was expected.
20. Theseus entered the labyrinth (more, less) readily, knowing he would be able to escape later.

12.9 Using Adverbs and Adjectives

Adverbs and adjectives are often confused, especially when they are used after verbs. Predicate adjectives follow linking verbs, such as *be, seem, appear,* and *become.*

> The labor at Stonehenge was **hard** without machinery.
> This accomplishment still seems **brilliant** to some visitors.

In the first sentence the predicate adjective *hard* modifies the subject, *labor.* In the second sentence the predicate adjective *brilliant* modifies the subject, *accomplishment.*

Now read the sentences below.

> Bronze Age people worked **hard** at building Stonehenge.
> The sun shines **brilliantly** between two stones each year.

In each sentence the word in dark type is an adverb that describes an action verb. *Hard* describes *worked,* and *brilliantly* describes *shines.*

■ Use a **predicate adjective** after a linking verb, such as *be, seem, appear,* or *become.*

■ Use an **adverb** to describe an action verb.

People often confuse *good, bad, well,* and *badly.*

> They were **good** at studying the sky. [predicate adjective]
> An earthquake was **bad** for the project. [predicate adjective]
> Stonehenge still works **well** as a kind of calendar. [adverb]
> Weather **badly** affected Stonehenge's usefulness. [adverb]

Good and *bad* are adjectives. Use them after linking verbs. *Well* and *badly* are adverbs. Use them to describe action verbs. *Well* may also be used as an adjective when describing someone's health.

Exercise 16   Identifying Adjectives and Adverbs

Write *adjective* or *adverb* to identify the underlined word in each sentence.

1. The first bridges humans used were <u>natural</u>.
2. A tree trunk might lie <u>conveniently</u> across a stream.
3. One could <u>nervously</u> cross a stone bridge over a canyon.
4. Someone swung <u>daringly</u> across a river on a twisted vine.
5. The stone bridges of the Romans are still <u>visible</u>.
6. Bridges were <u>necessary</u> for military operations and communication.
7. Too much rhythmic shaking was <u>bad</u> for a bridge.
8. That's why soldiers <u>usually</u> broke step as they crossed a bridge.
9. Some Roman bridges still operate <u>well</u> after hundreds of years.
10. Their engineering skills were <u>amazing</u>.

Exercise 17   Distinguishing Between Adjectives and Adverbs

Write the correct word given in parentheses.

1. The work on Stonehenge seemed (impossible, impossibly).
2. Each stone at Stonehenge is (enormous, enormously).
3. Several groups worked on Stonehenge (separate, separately).
4. The inhabitants of Salisbury Plain were (energetic, energetically).
5. Their project at Stonehenge was (incredible, incredibly).
6. They worked (diligent, diligently) on a large, circular ditch.
7. Then they searched (careful, carefully) for huge stones.
8. They worked (good, well) on the construction of a stone wall inside the ditch.
9. The opening in the circle of stones is (intentional, intentionally).
10. The position of the stone at the opening is (different, differently).
11. An earth wall is (visible, visibly) at Stonehenge.
12. The wall (complete, completely) surrounds the area.
13. The work on Stonehenge progressed (bad, badly).
14. Did Druids build the stone circle so (solid, solidly)?
15. They may have (cruel, cruelly) sacrificed victims there.
16. Many (definitely, definite) believe an older people built it.
17. Even today the first sight of it is (powerful, powerfully).
18. The spaces between the huge stones are (equal, equally).
19. How were such heavy stones raised (horizontal, horizontally)?
20. Tourists cannot get (close, closely) to the stones.

12.10 Avoiding Double Negatives

The adverb *not* is a negative word. **Negative words** express the idea of "no." *Not* often appears in a shortened form as part of a contraction. Study the words and their contracted forms below.

Contractions with *not*		
is not = isn't	cannot = can't	have not = haven't
was not = wasn't	could not = couldn't	had not = hadn't
were not = weren't	do not = don't	would not = wouldn't
will not = won't	did not = didn't	should not = shouldn't

In all of these words, the apostrophe replaces the *o* in *not.* In *can't* both an *n* and the *o* are omitted. *Will not* becomes *won't.*

Other words besides *not* may be used to express the negative. Each negative word has several opposites. These are **affirmative words,** or words that show the idea of "yes." Study the following list of negative and affirmative words.

Negative and Affirmative Words	
Negative	**Affirmative**
never	ever, always
nobody	anybody, somebody
none	one, all
no one	some, any
nothing	everyone, someone
nowhere	something, anything
scarcely, hardly	somewhere, anywhere

Two negative words used together in the same sentence create a **double negative.** You should avoid using double negatives in your writing. Only one negative word is necessary to convey a negative meaning.

You can correct a sentence that has a double negative in two ways: remove one of the negative words, or replace one of the negative words with an affirmative word.

Exercise 18   Using Negative Words Correctly

Write each sentence, using the correct word or words given in parentheses.

1. Houses with flat roofs (were, weren't) hardly useful in the North.
2. Thick snow (couldn't, could) never fall off the roof.
3. Snow wasn't (any, no) problem in the South.
4. No one in the West (could, couldn't) build better homes than the Pueblo Indians.
5. Before 1851 the world (had, hadn't) never seen a building like the Crystal Palace.
6. (No one, Anyone) ever missed visiting it.
7. The Crystal Palace was built of hardly (nothing, anything) except iron and glass.
8. Sir Joseph Paxton, the architect, didn't have (any, no) earlier models for the Crystal Palace.
9. No one (could, couldn't) believe the size of the Crystal Palace.
10. Sir Joseph (wasn't, was) not interested in a trial he was watching.
11. He (didn't, did) listen but instead planned the Crystal Palace.
12. Some people thought his dream (wouldn't, would) never be built.
13. Nothing (wasn't, was) spared for this giant structure.
14. Not even the trees on the site (weren't, were) left outside.
15. Visitors (couldn't, could) hardly believe their eyes.
16. Exhibitors (were, weren't) limited to one country.
17. Only a few countries didn't have (nothing, anything) there.
18. Visitors never (did, didn't) lose interest in seeing it.
19. The Crystal Palace didn't have (any, no) fireproofing.
20. In 1936 nothing (couldn't, could) stop it from burning down.

Exercise 19   Forming Contractions

Write the contraction or the words that form the contraction.

1. was not	6. did not	11. haven't	16. wouldn't
2. does not	7. must not	12. hasn't	17. mightn't
3. won't	8. will not	13. didn't	18. wasn't
4. are not	9. should not	14. isn't	19. can't
5. shouldn't	10. is not	15. aren't	20. couldn't

Grammar Review

ADJECTIVES AND ADVERBS

The treasures of ancient Egypt were sought by many archaeologists, explorers, and fortune hunters. The following passage is from a story about the British archaeologist Howard Carter, who describes a king's burial place that he discovered. It is the pharaoh Tutankhamen's tomb, which is today the most famous of Egypt's royal treasures. The passage has been annotated to show some of the kinds of adjectives and adverbs covered in this unit.

Literature Model

from *Mummies, Tombs, and Treasure*
by Lila Perl

Carter was looking into the first of four rooms of a surprisingly small royal tomb. The Antechamber, as the first and largest room was called, was only about twelve by twenty-six feet, the measurements of a fair-sized living room. It was heaped with chairs, footstools, and chests of alabaster, ebony, and ivory, and strange couches of gilded wood in the form of animals, including a cow and a lion. Piled beneath the cow-bed were egg-shaped food containers made of clay.

Sealed doorways, one guarded by two gold-encrusted statues of Tutankhamen, led to the other three rooms of the tomb—an Annex that was even more jumbled than the Antechamber, the Burial Chamber in which the mummy lay, and a small room beyond that called the Treasury.

Intensifier

Superlative form of the adjective *large*

Adjective

Past participle used as an adjective

Comparative form of the adjective *jumbled*

Definite article

Adjectives and Adverbs

Grammar Review

Review: Exercise 1   **Identifying Adjectives**

For the sentences below, write the adjectives and the nouns they modify. Underline the adjectives. (Do not include articles *a, an, the.*)

SAMPLE   The passage gives a brief description of what Carter discovered.
ANSWER   <u>brief</u> description.

1. Howard Carter was a British archaeologist.
2. Carter hired some Egyptian workers to help him on the dig.
3. The team began to dig under ancient huts.
4. They had avoided the old huts, which were in front of another tomb.
5. The empty tomb of Ramses VI was a popular attraction for tourists.
6. Carter's first view of the Antechamber was through a small hole.
7. Before he went in, he sent for his wealthy patron, Lord Carnarvon.
8. The Antechamber turned out to be a large, cluttered room.
9. Carter had to go through sealed doorways to reach the other rooms.
10. The mummy lay in a windowless room.

Review: Exercise 2   **Using Comparative and Superlative Adjectives**

Write the correct comparative or superlative form of the adjective given in parentheses.

SAMPLE   The discovery was (good) than he had hoped.
ANSWER   better

1. The (early) graves of all Egyptians were small, shallow pits in the sand, covered with rocks.
2. As time went on, rich Egyptians wanted (elaborate) tombs.
3. Thieves got (daring) about breaking into the tombs and robbing them.
4. Unfortunately, the pyramids proved to be even (secure) than the old tombs.
5. Grave robbers were even (curious) about the riches inside of them.
6. As a result, archaeologists were finding (few) treasures than ever.
7. Carter knew that his discovery was (important) than anything he'd ever done.
8. Lord Carnarvon was even (happy) about opening the tomb.
9. "Can you see anything?" he asked in his (anxious) voice.
10. Tutankhamen's tomb was (small) than Carter had expected it to be.

Review: Exercise 3   Identifying Adverbs

Write each adverb and the word or words it modifies. Underline the adverb.

SAMPLE   He slowly opened the door.
ANSWER   <u>slowly</u> opened

1. Carter gazed through the small hole he had carefully made in the door.
2. The contents of the Antechamber were piled carelessly about the room.
3. Carter and Lord Carnarvon stared into the surprisingly small royal tomb.
4. Two statues of Tutankhamen led directly to three other rooms in the tomb.
5. Carter was not very surprised at the disorder that met his eyes.
6. He felt strongly that grave robbers had discovered the tombs before.
7. But they may have left hastily.
8. Cemetery officials had apparently surprised the thieves.
9. It seemed that they had tidied up the tomb incompletely.
10. The workers' huts had completely covered the entrance.

Review: Exercise 4   Using Comparative and Superlative Adverbs

Write the correct comparative or superlative form of the word given in parentheses.

SAMPLE   Carter worked (diligently) on the Antechamber than on any other room.
ANSWER   more diligently

1. Lord Carnarvon died (early) than expected, never having seen King Tut's coffin.
2. His death was viewed (suspiciously) by some than others.
3. People now approached the tomb (warily) than before.
4. Things also went (unpleasantly) for Carter for a while.
5. Government officials behaved (cooperatively) than he would have wished.
6. Even (unbelievably), they sealed the tomb, stopping Carter's work.
7. He left the country much (soon) than he had hoped.
8. He did return to work even (tirelessly) to finish the job.
9. He understood the tomb's significance (clearly) than the others did.
10. Nothing Carter had found so far could be valued (highly) than the innermost coffin of solid gold.

Grammar Review

Review: Exercise 5   Using Comparative and Superlative Adjectives and Adverbs

Write each sentence, correctly inserting the comparative or superlative form of the adverb or adjective in parentheses.

1. The contents of the Annex were in even (bad) disarray than the nearby Antechamber.
2. The (early) mummies of all occurred naturally when people buried their dead in dry, sandy areas.
3. When the bodies dried out quickly, they lasted (long) than they would have lasted otherwise.
4. Drying out the body before burial meant that it would be (good) preserved than usual.
5. Wood, clay, and stone figures of servants were placed inside the tomb, but these figures were (small) than the dead person they were to serve.

Review: Exercise 6   Distinguishing Between Adjectives and Adverbs

Write the correct word given in parentheses and label it *adverb* or *adjective*.

SAMPLE   He wrote down each discovery (careful, carefully).
ANSWER   carefully, *adverb*

1. At first Carter could see nothing, as hot air escaping (sudden, suddenly) from the chamber caused his candle to flicker.
2. Then details of the room began to emerge (slow, slowly).
3. That's when Lord Carnarvon began to press him (anxious, anxiously).
4. Carter himself was (silent, silently) with wonder.
5. (Final, Finally), he managed to answer Lord Carnarvon.
6. Was there (actual, actually) such a thing as a mummy's curse?
7. Lord Carnarvon's death was somewhat (mysterious, mysteriously).
8. An insect bite on his cheek had become (bad, badly) infected.
9. Carter himself lived many more years, dying (natural, naturally) at the age of sixty-five.
10. One may wonder, though, why Tutankhamen reigned so (brief, briefly), dying at eighteen.

Review: Exercise 7

Proofreading

The following passage is about Charles Simonds, whose sculpture *Untitled* appears below. Rewrite the passage, correcting the errors in spelling, grammar, and usage. Add any missing punctuation. There are ten errors in all.

Charles Simonds

¹Charles Simonds created this here sculpture from clay. ²He use only water, glue, and the simplest tools to form the clay into both landscape and architecture. ³In many of his most simplest works, the color distinctions are very basic: red clay for landscape and gray clay for stone. ⁴The color of the clay helps define and separate different parts of them sculptures. ⁵Simonds's miniature dwellings demonstrate a interest in how people live and how their beliefs affect the structures they build. ⁶Clay is the material Simonds has been comfortablest with since childhood. ⁷While saveing money and increasing the variety of soil types and colors, Simonds enjoys the pleasure of recycling clays and sands from around the world.

⁸Simonds's sculptures convey a sense of history but they are his own archaeological interpretations. ⁹They arent miniature reconstructions. ¹⁰Of actual buildings or sites.

Adjectives and Adverbs

Charles Simonds, *Untitled*, 1982

Review: Exercise 8

Mixed Review

Write the word or words described in the parentheses after each sentence.

1. Because of the pyramids, we have a good picture of the way Egyptians lived. (adjective + the word it modifies)
2. These painted tomb walls tell us a lot.   (demonstrative adjective)
3. We can see that the Egyptians greatly enjoyed music and beautiful things. (adverb + the word it modifies)
4. We learn of Egyptian beliefs about death.   (proper adjective)
5. There is also most interesting information about the gods people believed in. (superlative adjective + the word it modifies)
6. Some pictures were carved directly into stone.   (adverb + the word it modifies)
7. This picture writing is called hieroglyphics (hī ₔr ₔ glif′iks).   (demonstrative adjective)
8. For many years, no one understood these sacred carvings.   (three adjectives)
9. Then in 1799 an officer of the famous French general Napoleon found a black stone covered with very strange lettering.   (intensifier)
10. The stone was immediately named after the nearby town of Rosetta.   (adjective + the word it modifies)
11. The same message was written in three different languages.   (three adjectives)
12. A French language specialist translated the Greek.   (two articles)
13. He used the Greek inscription to figure out the other two forms, which were Egyptian hieroglyphics.   (two proper adjectives)
14. Archaeologists could more readily decode the writings in the tombs. (comparative adverb)
15. These were spells and charms to help the dead pass safely through dangers. (adverb + the word it modifies)
16. Other writings also supplied helpful information.   (two adjectives)
17. Papyrus was one of the earliest forms of paper.   (superlative adjective + the word it modifies)
18. Tall stalks of papyrus grow along the banks of the Nile.   (number of articles in the sentence)
19. After strips of the stalk were soaked in water, they were compressed firmly to form sheets.   (adverb + the word it modifies)
20. Papyrus sheets were expensive.   (predicate adjective)

Writing Application

TIME

For more about the writing process, see **TIME Facing the Blank Page,** pp. 97–107.

Adjectives in Writing

The following passage is from *The Names* by N. Scott Momaday. Examine the passage, focusing on the italicized adjectives. Notice how Momaday brings his memories to life with adjectives that describe the people and places of his experience.

> Some of my earliest memories are of the storms, the *hot* rain lashing down and lightning running on the sky—and the storm cellar into which my mother and I descended so *many* times when I was very *young.* For me that *little* room in the earth is an *unforgettable* place. Across the years I see my mother reading there on the *low, narrow* bench, the lamplight flickering on her face and on the *earthen* walls; I smell the *dank* odor of that room; and I hear the *great* weather raging at the door.

Techniques with Adjectives

Try to apply some of N. Scott Momaday's writing techniques when you write and revise your own work.

❶ Use sensory adjectives when appropriate to help readers see, hear, feel, touch, and smell the objects of your description:

GENERAL WORDS I smell the odor of that room.

MOMADAY'S VERSION I smell the *dank* odor of that room.

❷ Use comparative and superlative adjectives to more specifically define time and place in your descriptions:

GENERAL WORDS Some of my memories are of the storms . . .

MOMADAY'S VERSION Some of my *earliest* memories are of the storms . . .

Practice Practice these techniques by revising the following passage. Rewrite the following passage, adding adjectives in the places indicated by carets ∧.

Shelly fanned her ∧ face with a ∧ piece of paper, struggling to keep cool in the ∧ heat. She crouched farther into the ∧ corner of the ∧ bus stop, but it was no use. Sweat was dripping down her neck in ∧ streams and her skirt was a ∧ mess. She had purposely waited for a ∧ bus, hoping to avoid the ∧ part of the day. Now she'd be ∧ to reach her grandmother's before dessert. Mmmm!

Adjectives and Adverbs

Prepositions, Conjunctions, and Interjections

Prepositions and Prepositional Phrases

■ A **preposition** is a word that relates a noun or a pronoun to some other word in a sentence.

The paint **on** the canvas will dry very slowly.

The word *on* in the sentence above is a preposition. It shows the relationship of the nouns *paint* and *canvas*.

Commonly Used Prepositions				
about	at	down	of	to
above	before	during	off	toward
across	behind	for	on	under
after	below	from	out	until
against	beneath	in	outside	up
along	beside	inside	over	upon
among	between	into	since	with
around	beyond	like	through	within
as	by	near	throughout	without

A preposition can consist of more than one word.

You can use acrylic paint **instead of** oils.

Compound Prepositions			
according to	aside from	in front of	instead of
across from	because of	in place of	on account of
along with	far from	in spite of	on top of

■ A **prepositional phrase** is a group of words that begins with a preposition and ends with a noun or pronoun, which is called the **object of the preposition.**

Michelangelo was born **in a small town.**

Prepositions, Conjunctions, & Interjections

Exercise 1   Identifying Prepositional Phrases and Objects of Prepositions

Write each prepositional phrase. Draw a line under the preposition and circle the object of the preposition.

1. Some artists study Michelangelo's work for inspiration.
2. His work had a great influence on many other artists.
3. Artists see perfection in his paintings.
4. They also see it in his sculpture.
5. Everyone admires the passion he conveyed in his statues.
6. Architects study building designs by Michelangelo.
7. Most think him the embodiment of genius.
8. He painted the ceiling of the Sistine Chapel.
9. He lay on his back on a scaffold.
10. The chapel work was completed in three years.
11. His fellow artists honored him after this project.
12. Michelangelo was a man with many artistic talents.
13. He carved sculpture from marble.
14. His *David* is one of his best-known statues.
15. According to art historians, the *Pietà* in Rome is Michelangelo's only signed sculpture.
16. This sculpture was the most important work of his youth and won him much admiration.
17. Among his other statues are *Victory* and *Cupid Kneeling*.
18. Michelangelo sometimes painted on wet plaster.
19. In his artwork, he depicted the human body very realistically.
20. The artist designed a dome for a church.
21. Michelangelo once worked with Leonardo da Vinci.
22. Michelangelo was also the author of many poems.
23. He is often considered the greatest sculptor of the Italian Renaissance.
24. Today Michelangelo's beautiful paintings and sculpture can be seen in many Italian museums.
25. The physical strength and emotional tension in Michelangelo's sculpture still inspire viewers.

13.2 Pronouns as Objects of Prepositions

When a pronoun is the object of a preposition, remember to use an object pronoun and not a subject pronoun.

> Nick handed the easel to Martha.
> Nick handed the easel to **her.**

In the example above, the object pronoun *her* replaces *Martha* as the object of the preposition *to.*

Sometimes a preposition will have a compound object consisting of a noun and pronoun. Remember to use an object pronoun in a compound object.

> I borrowed the palette from Nick and Martha.
> I borrowed the palette from Nick and **her.**
> Lloyd painted with Ayisha and **me.**

Object pronouns are used in the sentences above. In the second sentence, *Nick and her* is the compound object of the preposition *from.* In the third sentence, *Ayisha and me* is the compound object of the preposition *with.*

If you are unsure about whether to use a subject pronoun or an object pronoun, try saying the sentence aloud with only the pronoun following the preposition.

> I borrowed the palette from **her.**
> Lloyd painted with **me.**

The subject pronoun *who* is never the object of a preposition; only the object pronoun *whom* can be an object.

> The artist of **whom** I spoke has a show at the Whitney Museum.
> To **whom** did you lend the paint brushes?

Using Pronouns After Prepositions

Write the correct pronoun in parentheses. Be sure each pronoun you choose makes sense in the sentence.

1. Nina said that a paper on Rembrandt has been assigned to Bernard and (she, her).
2. Rembrandt is an artist about (who, whom) many historians have written.
3. According to H. W. Janson and (them, they), Rembrandt's early work is highly realistic.
4. Bernard showed some slides to Nina and (I, me).
5. Then I set a series of pictures in front of everyone, including Bernard and (she, her).
6. They all felt familiar with Rembrandt. I asked if they could tell the difference between the artist Caravaggio and (he, him).
7. Aside from Bernard, Laticia, and (I, me), no one recognized Rembrandt's work.
8. In the seventeenth century, Rembrandt was very popular. Many residents of Amsterdam wanted portraits painted by (him, he).
9. Rembrandt painted many life-size portraits of (they, them).
10. Rembrandt's self-portraits were described by Nina and (I, me).
11. Besides Janson, many experts have analyzed Rembrandt's work. The writings by Janson and (them, they) have called Rembrandt's lighting dramatic.
12. Many students learned about art from (he, him).
13. Through (he, him) we are able to see the man's inner strength.
14. No one knows for (who, whom) Rembrandt painted many of his pictures.
15. Because of (they, them), Rembrandt could finally afford to paint whatever pictures he wanted.
16. Rembrandt showed the innermost feelings within (they, them).
17. Rembrandt painted the people and places he saw around (he, him).
18. Rembrandt was unique. Few painters in history can compare with (he, him).
19. Frans Hals portrayed his subjects in a different way from (he, him).
20. There were other famous seventeenth-century Dutch painters besides Frans Hals and (he, him).

Prepositional Phrases as Adjectives and Adverbs

■ A prepositional phrase can function as an **adjective,** modifying or describing a noun or a pronoun.

The fabrics **from Asia** were quite beautiful.

These ancient hangings are tapestries **from other lands.**

In the first sentence above, the prepositional phrase *from the Orient* describes the subject of the sentence, *fabrics.* In the second sentence, the prepositional phrase *from other lands* describes the noun in the predicate, *tapestries.*

■ A prepositional phrase can also function as an **adverb,** modifying or describing a verb, an adjective, or another adverb.

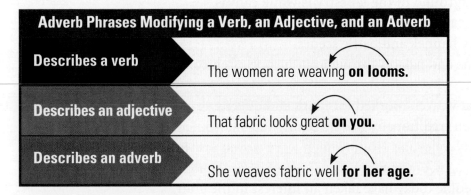

Adverb Phrases Modifying a Verb, an Adjective, and an Adverb	
Describes a verb	The women are weaving **on looms.**
Describes an adjective	That fabric looks great **on you.**
Describes an adverb	She weaves fabric well **for her age.**

An adverb phrase tells *when, where,* or *how* an action takes place. The prepositional phrases in the chart below all modify the verb *work.*

How Adverb Phrases Modify Verbs	
When?	Weavers work **during the day.**
Where?	They work **in shops.**
How?	They work **with care.**

Identifying Adjective and Adverb Phrases

Write each prepositional phrase and identify the phrase as an *adjective* phrase or an *adverb* phrase. Then write the word each phrase modifies.

1. Weavers around the world practice an ancient craft.
2. Early weavers worked with long grass strands.
3. Paintings from ancient Egypt show that weaving had developed by 5000 B.C.
4. Tapestries with complex patterns hang in museums.
5. These tapestries often illustrate stories about great people.
6. Many tapestries depict stories from the Bible.
7. Other tapestries show scenes of famous battles fought between great armies.
8. The famous *Bayeux Tapestry* illustrates William the Conqueror's invasion of England.
9. The tapestry hangs in a French museum.
10. You can walk the length of the tapestry—230 feet—and examine it closely, but you cannot touch it.
11. The background of the tapestry is white canvas.
12. You can easily see soldiers on horseback, the boats used crossing the English Channel, and battle scenes.
13. Museums and palaces throughout Europe often contain collections of tapestry.
14. Medieval weavers worked for kings and queens.
15. Hopi men traditionally wove clothing for the women.
16. Pueblo, Navajo, and Hopi women wore woven sashes during ceremonial dances.
17. Many people today have taken an interest in the craft.
18. They often may be found around the country diligently at work on big or small looms.
19. Contemporary weavers use a variety of materials—like wool, cotton, linen, angora, mohair, and synthetics—in their work.
20. Young weavers usually begin with simple patterns.
21. Patterns from many nations teach the necessary skills.
22. Weavers may become famous for their designs.
23. A tapestry made at home may become valuable after a while.
24. Articles made by weavers and quilters are often sold at craft shows.
25. Weavers can produce shawls, dresses, vests, and other articles of clothing on their looms.

13.4 Conjunctions

■ A **coordinating conjunction** is a single word used to connect parts of a sentence, such as words or phrases. *And, but, or, so, yet, for,* and *nor* are used as coordinating conjunctions.

Using Coordinating Conjunctions	
Compound Subject	Ann **and** Flo studied art.
Compound Predicate	Georgia O'Keeffe studied art **and** taught it.
Compound Object of a Preposition	Art appeals to you **and** me.
Compound Sentence	I could go to art school, **or** I could study on my own.

To make a relationship between words or groups of words especially strong, use a correlative conjunction.

■ **Correlative conjunctions** are pairs of words used to connect words or phrases in a sentence. Correlative conjunctions include *both . . . and, either . . . or, neither . . . nor,* and *not only . . . but also.*

> **Both** New York **and** Paris are major art centers.

When a compound subject is joined by *and,* it is a plural subject. The verb must agree with the plural subject.

When a compound subject is joined by *or* or *nor,* the verb must agree with the nearest part of the subject.

> Jaime **and** Sue are artists.
> **Neither** the twins **nor** Carla **is** a good painter.

Exercise 4   Identifying Conjunctions

Write each conjunction. Then write whether it joins a *compound subject,* a *compound predicate,* a *compound object of a preposition,* or a *compound sentence.*

1. Mari mixed the paint, for she wanted various colors.
2. Nora rented a studio and painted there on weekends.
3. Both painters and sculptors need good lighting.
4. The painter took many lessons, but students now learn from her.
5. Yvonne will attend the high school of art and design.
6. Either Maria or Cathy will accept the award for the class.
7. Jonathan enjoyed the art class but found it hard to paint with oils.
8. The school offers courses in architecture, computer graphics, and painting.
9. Not only is she a painter, but she is also a sculptor.
10. No admission is charged at the museum on Monday and Tuesday.

Exercise 5   Making Compound Subjects and Verbs Agree

Write each sentence, using the correct verb form. Underline each conjunction.

1. Painters or sculptors (enter, enters) the exhibition.
2. Both this sketch and that sculpture (is, are) beautiful.
3. Neither the students nor their teacher (attends, attend) the show.
4. The judge and the artist (have, has) different opinions.
5. Either a famous painter or some critics (is, are) judging the show.
6. Neither this canvas nor the frame (look, looks) sturdy.
7. Watercolors or oils (provides, provide) rich tones.
8. Patty, George, and Peter (enjoys, enjoy) walking to the gallery on weekends.
9. The books and their favorite picture (was, were) on sale.
10. Neither the students nor the teacher (minds, mind) working in the art studio.
11. Either the artist or her students (plans, plan) to carry the heavy artwork.
12. Tracy or Scott (is, are) expected to take first prize in the competition.
13. Claudia and her friend (tours, tour) the modern art museum.
14. Neither the sculptures nor the painting (appeals, appeal) to the tour group.
15. Boston, New York, and Washington (is, are) exhibiting the artist's works.
16. Neither Matisse nor Picasso (has, have) paintings in the city's museums.
17. Both the students and their teacher (laughs, laugh) at a colorful mobile.
18. Light and atmosphere (figures, figure) prominently in Impressionist art.
19. Degas's paintings and sculpture often (depicts, depict) dancers.
20. Both the glass collection and the jewelry (sparkles, sparkle) brilliantly.

Sometimes people express very strong feelings in a short exclamation that may not be a complete sentence. These exclamations are called interjections.

■ An **interjection** is a word or group of words that expresses strong feeling. It has no grammatical connection to any other words in the sentence.

Any part of speech can be used as an interjection. These are some of the more common interjections.

Awesome! Great! Wow!

Commonly Used Interjections			
aha	good grief	no	well
alas	ha	oh	what
awesome	hey	oh, no	whoops
come on	hooray	oops	wow
gee	look	ouch	yes

An interjection that expresses a very strong feeling may stand alone, either before or after a sentence. Such interjections are followed by an exclamation mark.

Oh, no! The art museum is closed today.

When an interjection expresses a milder feeling, it appears as part of the sentence. It is separated from the rest of the sentence with a comma.

Oh, well, I'll just have to go tomorrow.

Interjections should be used sparingly. Overusing them will spoil their effectiveness.

Exercise 6   Identifying Interjections

Write the interjections.

1. Oh, I am going to be late for my painting class.
2. My! I have never seen anyone who could sketch that fast.
3. It certainly is hard work to stretch this canvas tight. Phew!
4. We may be able to get an interview with a famous artist. Hooray!
5. Golly, I hope she will autograph one of her prints for me.
6. Wow! The colors in that painting hurt my eyes.
7. Hey! Where are you going?
8. Yes! That one's definitely my favorite.
9. Come on, I want to show you a painting by Salvador Dali.
10. Have you ever seen such images? Look!
11. That clock looks as though it melted. Awesome!
12. No way! I prefer this painting by Chagall.
13. Oops, those people seem to be floating.
14. Well, don't you think these young artists make Picasso look serious?
15. Gee, I don't know.
16. Really! He seems old-fashioned by comparison.
17. I would like to see a few more paintings, but it is time to leave, alas.
18. Sorry, I didn't notice you already had a brush.
19. Gosh! I never knew you could draw such a good likeness.
20. Oh, no! The paint spilled all over the floor.

Exercise 7   Using Interjections

Write each sentence, adding an interjection in the blank space. Be sure that the interjection you choose expresses the correct feeling for the sentence.

1. Up close you can hardly tell this is a bridge. _____!
2. _____! Did you know that the Impressionists were criticized at first?
3. _____! These paintings by Monet are all of the same cathedral.
4. _____, drawing in the style of the Impressionists is hard.
5. I knew I would finally get the color right. _____!
6. _____, this is certainly the prettiest one so far.
7. _____! The violin in this painting by Picasso is in pieces.
8. This canvas is solid black. _____!
9. _____, Picasso's *Guernica* is an enormous painting.
10. My feet are too tired to walk any farther, _____.

13.6 Finding All the Parts of Speech

Each word in a sentence performs a particular job. Each word can be put into a particular category called a **part of speech.** The part of speech of a word depends on the job that the word performs in the sentence. The same word may be classified as one part of speech in one sentence and as a different part of speech in another.

You have learned about all eight parts of speech. They include *nouns, pronouns, verbs, adjectives, adverbs, prepositions, conjunctions,* and *interjections.* The following sentence contains at least one example of each part of speech

Wow, she is artistic and paints well with watercolors.

**Artist unknown, China,
Woman Painting, 18th c.**

Parts of Speech		
Word	**Part of Speech**	**Function**
Wow	Interjection	Expresses strong feeling
she	Pronoun	Takes the place of a noun
is	Verb (linking)	Links *she* with *artistic*
artistic	Adjective	Describes the subject *she*
and	Conjunction	Joins two parts of compound predicate
paints	Verb (action)	Names an action
well	Adverb	Describes the verb *paints*
with	Preposition	Relates the words *paints* and *watercolors*
watercolors	Noun	Object of the preposition *with*

Exercise 8   **Identifying Parts of Speech**

Write each underlined word and its part of speech. If the word is a verb, identify it as an *action verb* or a *linking verb*.

1. <u>I</u> often sculpt with <u>colored</u> <u>clays</u>.
2. <u>Sometimes</u> the clay <u>dries</u> too <u>quickly</u>.
3. <u>Wow</u>! That <u>statue</u> <u>is</u> enormous.
4. Does <u>Aretha</u> sculpt <u>with</u> clay <u>or</u> stone?
5. <u>He</u> sculpts <u>realistic</u> heads.

Exercise 9   **Using Parts of Speech**

The parentheses in each of the following sentences describe a word that you must add to complete the sentence. Be sure your finished sentences make sense.

1. Hector, Marisol, and (proper noun) visited an art museum (preposition) New York City.
2. To get (preposition) the museum, they took a (common noun).
3. At Fifth Avenue, (pronoun) transferred to a (common noun).
4. (Pronoun) saw a great many (common noun).
5. Hector liked the Impressionist paintings (adverb).
6. (Pronoun) thought Claude Monet's paintings were (adjective).
7. Marisol (action verb) two Americans: Mary Cassatt (conjunction) Winslow Homer.
8. (Adverb) they (action verb) the Post-Impressionists.
9. Hector loved (correlative conjunction) van Gogh (correlative conjunction) Rousseau.
10. "(Interjection)!" said Marisol. "I think we've (action verb) too much art."
11. Walking (adverb), they headed (preposition) the cafeteria.
12. Hector wanted (correlative conjunction) a bowl of chili (correlative conjunction) a hamburger.
13. (Proper noun) selected a dish of chocolate ice cream for (common noun).
14. Marisol paid the bill (preposition) money she earned baby-sitting.
15. Hector and Marisol (action verb) the museum guide while they were eating.
16. "(Interjection)! I want to (action verb) the Egyptian mummies," Hector said.
17. "We're too (adjective)," (action verb) Marisol.
18. Instead, they strolled (adverb) through Central Park.
19. Bicyclists, walkers, and (common noun) crowded the streets and sidewalks (preposition) the park.
20. "(Interjection)!" Hector said. "It's so (adjective) outside."

Grammar Review

PREPOSITIONS, CONJUNCTIONS, AND INTERJECTIONS

This Chinese American folktale tells the story of a painted horse that comes to life. The passage has been annotated to show some of the parts of speech covered in this unit.

Literature Model

from *The Magical Horse*
by Laurence Yep

As the boy sat with his body aching from the hard work and eating his cold rice, he gazed up at the painting. His father had caught the horse as if it were suspended upon one hoof. And as he watched, the horse's sides seemed to heave in the moonlight—as if it were breathing in the incense. On a whim, Sunny set out feed for his painted horse just as he did for the other animals.

He slept among the beasts for warmth, so he was not surprised when he felt an animal's warm breath blow on him. When a nose nudged him, he sat up irritated, intending to shove the creature away, but his hand paused in the air.

By the light of the moon, he saw a silvery horse standing over him. He looked over at the wall where the painting had been and saw that the canvas was empty. The next thing he knew, he was on the back of the horse, his hands clinging to the flying mane, the horse's hooves booming rhythmically along a road that gleamed like a silver ribbon winding up into the sky.

> Preposition

> Prepositional phrase (adverb phrase)

> Pronoun as object of the preposition *on*

> Prepositional phrase (adjective phrase)

> Coordinating conjunction

Grammar Review

Write each prepositional phrase. Underline the preposition and circle the object. Note that there may be more than one prepositional phrase in each sentence.

SAMPLE   The horse on the canvas that his father painted seemed alive.
ANSWER   on the (canvas)

1. Sunny set out food for him.
2. The boy slept among the animals.
3. When he awoke, the empty canvas stood against the wall.
4. The horse and the boy galloped down the road.
5. Painting is only one form of art.
6. Other forms include sculpture, photography, printmaking, and designs for industrial products.
7. Among the different kinds of art, sculpture is very popular.
8. Throughout the museum are many examples of fine sculpture.
9. Large pieces are located in the sculpture garden beside the museum.
10. Because of weather, sculpture that is placed outdoors can change in color and texture.
11. When you look at sculpture, moving around it helps you see it all.
12. Sculpture can be made from many materials—lumps of clay, slabs of marble, even small pieces of stone.
13. Carving a statue from marble takes great technical skill.
14. Some artists use clay for models.
15. Rodin cast his sculptures in bronze.
16. Degas added ribbons and bits of cloth to his dancers.
17. Some artists make their sculptures from wood.
18. Old, recycled materials can be incorporated into a sculpture.
19. Sculptures that move in the wind are called mobiles.
20. The giant Calder mobile in front of the building revolves.
21. Some mobiles hang from the ceiling.
22. One piece of sculpture—the Statue of Liberty—is 151 feet in height.
23. The sculptor of the statue, Bartholdi, was from France.
24. On account of its great size, the statue was shipped from France to the United States in several pieces.
25. Visitors can go inside the Statue of Liberty.

Review: Exercise 2 **Using Pronouns After Prepositions**

Write the correct pronoun in parentheses. Be sure each pronoun you choose makes sense in the sentence. Remember to use an object pronoun and not a subject pronoun after a preposition. The subject pronoun *who* is never the object of a preposition; only the object pronoun *whom* can be used after a preposition.

1. Alicia and Mark stared at the height of the buildings around (they, them).
2. "Look at the buildings in front of (we, us)!" Mark exclaimed.
3. Alicia added, "Because of (they, them), no sun reaches us here on the street."
4. *Skyscrapers* is the word used for (they, them).
5. Before (they, them), most tall buildings were made of stone.
6. Mark pointed out to (she, her) a beautiful library made of granite.
7. "Stand between the library and (I, me)," Mark said.
8. The skyscraper above (she, her) dwarfed the library.
9. Tall buildings are supported by steel framing inside (they, them).
10. Two buildings near Mark and (she, her) were designed by the famous architect Louis Sullivan.
11. Because of (he, him) and other innovative architects, Chicago became famous for its architecture.
12. Skyscrapers in the Art Deco style, Alicia explained, often have towers on top of (they, them).
13. The columns near Mark and (she, her) help support the building.
14. The Gothic-style building across from (they, them) has arched entrances and small arched windows.
15. Mr. Smith went with (they, them) to the city.
16. He visited the Sears Tower without (they, them).
17. The tower, then the tallest building in the world, appealed to (he, him).
18. According to (he, him), the Sears Tower is a very safe building.
19. Mark and Alicia took the elevator to the skydeck, and six other students rode with (they, them).
20. From (they, them) the students learned that the tower has 110 stories.
21. Below Paul and (they, them) lay Lake Michigan.
22. The aluminum-clad exterior next to (she, her) felt smooth.
23. The columns between you and (I, me) resemble those of ancient Greece.
24. Paul examined the fierce-looking gargoyles above (he, him).
25. Behind Alicia and (he, him) stood the famous Wrigley Building.

Grammar Review

Review: Exercise 3　**Identifying Adjective Phrases**

Write each adjective prepositional phrase. Then write the word the phrase modifies.

SAMPLE　The computer drawing of the sports car was extremely realistic.
ANSWER　of the sports car, drawing

1. I am learning a drawing program on the computer.
2. It's the only computer with a newer monitor.
3. The program gives me a wide choice of colors.
4. The color of the new wallpaper is too bright.
5. I can easily copy this detailed and colorful design from Mexico.
6. The picture for my mother will surely please her.
7. This screen image of dancers can actually move.
8. The circle around the word was drawn by a computer.
9. Only a few of the students have computers they can use.
10. Michael, Christopher, and Jennifer greatly enjoyed taking the computer class for beginners.

Review: Exercise 4　**Identifying Adverb Phrases**

Write each adverb prepositional phrase. Then write the word the phrase modifies.

SAMPLE　The students and their chaperones traveled by train.
ANSWER　by train, traveled

1. The entire class went to Boston last week.
2. The students walked along the Freedom Trail.
3. They stopped for a moment at the Old Granary Burial Ground.
4. The students crossed with great care.
5. They walked into the Old South Meeting House.
6. The display showed in detail the city's growth and history.
7. Tall ships once sailed from those docks.
8. American patriots protested unfair taxes in that room.
9. They saw where tea splashed into the harbor.
10. Peter, Sylvia, and John rode on the famous swan boats.

Prepositions, Conjunctions, & Interjections

Review: Exercise 5   **Identifying Adjective and Adverb Phrases**

Write each prepositional phrase, and write whether it is an *adjective* phrase or an *adverb* phrase. There may be more than one prepositional phrase in each sentence.

SAMPLE   People express through folklore their beliefs and customs.
ANSWER   through folklore, adverb

1. Fairy tales, legends, myths, even dances—all are considered part of folklore.
2. Some folklore is handed down through games.
3. There must be two versions of a story.
4. The story must have been told in more than one place and in more than one time period.
5. Ancient songs tell stories from the past too.
6. Jakob and Wilhelm Grimm collected folk stories from common people in Germany.
7. They published the stories in a book called *Grimm's Fairy Tales.*
8. Myths help explain the origins of people and of the world.
9. Fictional stories about animals or human beings are called folk tales.
10. Many folk tales have been changed into very successful movies.

Review: Exercise 6   **Using Conjunctions**

Rewrite each sentence, inserting the most appropriate conjunction (word or word pair) in the blank or blanks provided.

SAMPLE   The father wanted to create a perfect horse,
_____ _____ he painted without resting.

ANSWER   The father wanted to create a perfect horse,
and so he painted without resting.

1. When the painting was finished, _____ Sunny _____ his father admired the magnificent horse.
2. _____ Sunny _____ his father knew that the horse would come to life.
3. The father was old _____ tired from hard work.
4. The painter died, _____ his spirit entered into the horse in the painting.
5. Sunny _____ _____ buried his father, _____ _____ earned the money for the funeral.

Grammar Review

Review: Exercise 7   **Making Compound Subjects and Verbs Agree**

Write each sentence, using correct verb form. Write each coordinating or correlative conjunction.

SAMPLE   Neither Alexandra nor her mother (wants, want) to carry the camera.
ANSWER   <u>Neither</u> Alexandra <u>nor</u> her mother wants to carry the camera.

1. Both Alexandra and her parents (likes, like) to take pictures.
2. Neither San Francisco nor Los Angeles (is, are) on their itinerary.
3. Eating in a Chinese restaurant and riding on a cable car (is, are) on their list of things to do.
4. Either the fog or the clouds often (blocks, block) the view from Twin Peaks.
5. Both the sea otters and the crashing surf (makes, make) the trip worthwhile.
6. Neither the redwoods nor the shoreline (captures, capture) their interest.
7. Carmel and the Hearst Castle (is, are) on the way to Los Angeles.
8. Neither Carmel nor Monterey (lacks, lack) art galleries.
9. The city and its suburbs (sprawls, sprawl) for miles in every direction.
10. Both the beaches and homes along the coast (suffers, suffer) every time there's a big storm.

Review: Exercise 8   **Using Interjections**

The following sentences are based on passages in "The Magical Horse" that do not appear in this textbook. Rewrite each sentence, inserting an appropriate interjection in the blank. More than one answer may be possible.

SAMPLE   "_____!" cried Sunny when he rode the horse for the first time.
ANSWER   "Hooray!" cried Sunny when he rode the horse for the first time.

1. Sunny woke up the next morning and found that the feed for the painted horse was gone. "_____!" exclaimed the boy. "It wasn't a dream."
2. Every night Sunny called out, "_____! Let's go for a ride."
3. One evening the boy said, "_____, I'd like to see the king's palace."
4. "_____!" shouted the prince to his servant as the horse sped past the palace.
5. _____, the prince decided then and there to take the horse away.

Proofreading

The following passage is about artist Helen Oji, whose work appears below. Rewrite the passage, correcting the errors in spelling, grammar, and usage. Add any missing punctuation. There are ten errors.

Helen Oji

[1]Helen Oji paints subjets from nature. [2]A row of volcanoes are shown in one painting by she. [3]Horses, a group of fish swimming in swiftly moving water and a brightly colored bird in flight is some of her subjects. [4]Both movement and intense energy characterizes Oji's explosive style.

[5]In the painting on this page, neither the cool white horse nor the fiery red swirls is the focus. [6]Instead, the viewer's attention is pulled to the interaction between they. [7]The works bold, thick brushstrokes help raise the picture from the canvas. [8]Neither the magical horse in Laurence Yep's folktale nor the horse in the painting seem quite real.

Helen Oji, *H.P.*, 1986

Grammar Review

Review: Exercise 10

Mixed Review

In this exercise, you can practice what you have learned about prepositions, conjunctions, and interjections. Write each sentence, filling in the blank or blanks as directed.

1. One _____ the primitive American artists was Edward Hicks. (preposition)
2. Revere was _____ a silversmith _____ a patriot. (correlative conjunction)
3. Revere's portrait was painted _____ John Singleton Copley. (preposition)
4. _____ an early engraving, we can get an idea of how colonial Boston looked. (preposition)
5. _____, this painting is the only way we know what happened. (interjection)
6. Sometimes people who were not present at an event are shown in a painting, _____ some who were there are not shown. (coordinating conjunction)
7. That is a well-known painting _____ the Revolutionary War. (preposition)
8. _____ the early years of our Republic, George Washington was a favorite subject for painters. (preposition)
9. Native Americans were sometimes shown as heros _____ sometimes as victims of American growth. (coordinating conjunction)
10. _____ George Catlin _____ Alfred Miller visited Native American encampments and painted them. (correlative conjunction)
11. Catlin recorded Native American life _____ great detail. (preposition)
12. _____ Catlin, we have an idea of what Native American life was like in the early days. (compound preposition)
13. The works of Catlin and Bierstadt amazed and inspired Americans living _____ the East. (preposition)
14. Early Americans saw America's beauty only _____ art. (preposition)
15. In the *Last of the Buffalo* by Bierstadt, a Native American is shown bravely plunging his spear into a charging buffalo. _____! (interjection)
16. George Caleb Bingham depicted scenes of the frontier, _____ his paintings are reflective and quiet. (coordinating conjunction)
17. Mathew Brady was a photographer _____ the Civil War. (preposition)
18. _____ industrialization came many abuses. (compound preposition)
19. In the late nineteenth century, some writers and artists depicted injustice and cruelty _____ their works. (preposition)
20. Those works helped improve conditions _____ factories. (preposition)

Writing Application

TIME

For more about the writing process, see **TIME Facing the Blank Page,** pp. 97–107.

Prepositions in Writing

Mary Q. Steele uses prepositions in this passage from *Journey Outside* to give readers a detailed understanding of the movements and actions in a boy's first encounter with a bird. Examine the passage, paying particular attention to the italicized prepositions and prepositional phrases.

> He cried out abruptly. Something was coming *toward him in the air*, a little fish gliding *through the air*, helping itself along *with great fins* that stuck out *from its sides* and then folded tight *against them*. A wonder, a wonder! The fish stopped suddenly *in the top of one of the little trees*, put out little legs, . . . threw back its head, and opening its mouth made such sounds as Dilar had never heard before.

Techniques with Prepositions

Try to apply some of Mary Q. Steele's writing techniques when you experiment with drafting and revising your own work.

❶ Use prepositions to settle readers within a situation and to make your writing clearer and more detailed.

WITHOUT PREPOSITIONS Something was coming.

STEELE'S VERSION Something was coming *toward him in the air*.

❷ Make your writing more specific and engaging by adding prepositional phrases that tell readers how, when, and where an action is taking place. Compare the following:

GENERAL WORDS great fins that stuck out and then folded tight

STEELE'S VERSION great fins that stuck out *from its sides* and then folded tight *against them*

Prepositions, Conjunctions, & Interjections

Practice Practice these techniques by revising the following passage, using a separate sheet of paper. As you work, expand or clarify the passage's meaning by adding prepositional phrases in the places marked with carets (∧).

It must be Tuesday. Sharon Urstand was pulling her little sister Gina ∧. They rolled quickly ∧ to Everett Street, stopping at the traffic light. Suddenly Gina climbed out ∧ and began to jump up and down in distress. Gina's yells reached all the way ∧. "But I can't go to school ∧ !" she shouted. Sharon, steered the wagon around and headed ∧ . Gina sat ∧ , wearing a look of relief ∧ , as they climbed steadily ∧ .

LOG ON ▶ **Writing** Online For more grammar practice, go to **glencoe.com** and enter QuickPass code WC77680p2.

Writing Application **499**

Clauses and Complex Sentences

14.1 Sentences and Clauses

A **sentence** is a group of words that has a subject and predicate and expresses a complete thought.

■ A **simple sentence** has one complete subject and one complete predicate.

The **complete subject** names whom or what the sentence is about. The **complete predicate** tells what the subject does or has. Sometimes it tells what the subject is or is like.

Complete Subject	Complete Predicate
Some people	travel.
Neither cars nor jets	are completely safe.
Trains and buses	carry passengers and transport luggage.
Freight trains	transport products to various cities.

■ A **compound sentence** is a sentence that contains two or more connected simple sentences. Each simple sentence in a compound sentence is called a main clause.

■ A **main clause** has a subject and a predicate and can stand alone as a sentence.

In the compound sentences below, each main clause is in black. The connecting elements are highlighted in red.

Millions of people live in cities, **but** many others reside in the suburbs.

Most people travel to work, **and** many of them use public transportation.

Commuters take trains, buses, and cars; some even fly.

Helicopters are often used to monitor traffic conditions, **but** computers can more accurately predict traveling time.

If the main clauses are connected by *and, but,* or *or,* a comma precedes the conjunction. If the main clauses are not joined by a conjunction, a semicolon can be used as the connector.

Exercise 1   Identifying Simple and Compound Sentences

Identify each sentence as *simple* or *compound.*

1. Long-distance travel was difficult for early Americans.
2. In those days, people traveled in stagecoaches and covered wagons.
3. Long-distance travel was possible, but it was not very fast or comfortable.
4. Eventually railroads were built; tracks were laid across the country.
5. Distant cities were connected, and people could travel between them.
6. The growth of railroads changed the lives of many Americans.
7. Americans found trains a pleasant alternative to stagecoaches and wagons.
8. Railroads were popular for long journeys, and they made short trips easier, too.
9. Workers moved out of crowded cities, and commuters used trains.
10. Family members moved across the country, but trains reunited them.

Exercise 2   Punctuating Simple and Compound Sentences

Write each sentence, and underline each main clause. Add a comma or a semicolon if needed.

1. Four million miles of roadways exist in the United States and problems with them do arise.
2. Accidents cause delays poor road conditions often result in traffic jams.
3. Traffic can be annoying for drivers but it can often be bypassed.
4. Radio listeners hear traffic reports and can avoid trouble spots.
5. Drivers could allow more driving time but many decide to take alternate routes.
6. The problem may not be a traffic jam it might be poor road conditions.
7. Roadways can become damaged by time and use.
8. This damage could be dangerous and it can cause accidents.
9. Crews are sent to make repairs the workers and equipment can block the roads.
10. Drivers take detours around these trouble spots.
11. Detours are usually long and they can take more time to travel.
12. Most drivers dislike detours but they prefer not to travel on damaged roads.
13. Travelers on public transportation usually avoid delays and detours.
14. Public transportation is often faster than driving and it can be much easier.
15. Subway commuters never need to find parking spaces.
16. Riding the train is not free but it is often less expensive than driving.
17. Drivers must pay for gas and they often pay tolls on the highway.
18. There are many other advantages to public transportation.
19. Passengers on trains or buses have additional freedoms.
20. A driver can't read in her car she could read the newspaper on the train.

14.2 Complex Sentences

A **main clause** has a subject and a predicate and can stand alone as a sentence.

Sometimes sentences have more than one clause, with only one of the clauses being a main clause. The other clause is called a subordinate clause.

■ A **subordinate clause** is a group of words that has a subject and a predicate but does not express a complete thought and cannot stand alone as a sentence. A subordinate clause is always combined with a main clause in a sentence.

■ A **complex sentence** is a sentence that has one main clause and one or more subordinate clauses.

In each complex sentence below, the main clause is in light type, and the subordinate clause is in dark type.

When the sun set, the caravans stopped for the night.
The dromedary has one hump, **which stores fat.**
Most people know **that camels are stubborn.**

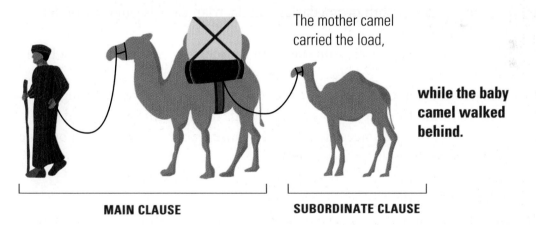

The mother camel carried the load,

while the baby camel walked behind.

MAIN CLAUSE   SUBORDINATE CLAUSE

Identifying Complex Sentences

Write each sentence. Underline each main clause once and each subordinate clause twice. Then identify each sentence as *complex* or *simple*.

1. The desert is a place where most animals are not able to live or work.
2. Camels are useful because they cross the desert easily.
3. Camels provide necessary transportation in the desert.
4. Long caravans of camels carry heavy loads across these dry, hot regions.
5. Camels have double eyelashes, which protect their eyes from the blowing sand.
6. Its eyelashes also help protect a camel's eyes from the strong glare of the sun.
7. Did you know that a camel's hump contains fat and muscle?
8. People usually ride dromedary camels, which have only one hump.
9. It is the Bactrian camel that has two humps.
10. People have found that camels can survive sandstorms.
11. Until the sun sets, camels maintain a 105-degree temperature.
12. We have learned that the camel's temperature drops to 93 degrees at night.
13. Camels survive desert life because they can live with little water.
14. Scientists have not always understood how a camel could endure a lack of water.
15. Although people once believed camels store excess water in their humps, this belief is a myth.
16. For short periods, both dromedaries and Bactrian camels can exist on fat from their humps.
17. If a camel nourishes itself with the fat in its hump for several days, the hump will sag and lean to one side.
18. Because they can tolerate desert conditions so well, camels were brought to America in the 1850s for use as pack animals in California and Nevada.
19. The camels annoyed stagecoach drivers, whose teams of horses often became frightened at the sight of the camels.
20. Camels were also brought to Australia as pack animals since they could endure arid conditions better than horses.
21. Many people do not know that a Bactrian camel can swim for short distances.
22. Although a camel is relatively tall, a rider can easily climb up onto the back of a kneeling camel.
23. Pads on its knees act as cushions when the camel kneels in the sand.
24. A baggage camel can carry a load of several hundred pounds.
25. Mehari camels are special camels that are bred for warfare and racing.

14.3 Adjective Clauses

Sometimes a subordinate clause acts as an adjective. Each subordinate clause in dark type in the sentences below is an adjective clause. An adjective clause adds information about a noun or pronoun in the main clause.

Ed's bicycle, **which he bought on sale,** is a ten-speed.

He paid a price **that was incredibly low.**

■ An **adjective clause** is a subordinate clause that modifies, or describes, a noun or pronoun in the main clause of a complex sentence.

An adjective clause is usually introduced by a relative pronoun. Relative pronouns signal that a clause is a subordinate clause and cannot stand alone.

Relative Pronouns			
that	who	whose	what
which	whom	whoever	

A relative pronoun that begins an adjective clause is usually the subject of the clause.

Allene bought the ten-speed **that is the most popular.**

She is a person **who truly loves bicycling.**

In the first sentence above, *that* is the subject of the adjective clause. In the second sentence *who* is the subject of the adjective clause.

An adjective clause can also begin with *where* or *when.*

Allene likes trails **where she can see flowers.**

Exercise 4   Identifying Adjective Clauses

Write each sentence. Underline each adjective clause. Circle the noun that each adjective clause modifies.

1. Bicycle riding is an activity that many people enjoy.
2. Reckless bicyclists ignore the rules that others obey.
3. Some athletes who ride bicycles enjoy competing in races.
4. Many amateurs who are extremely dedicated decide to race professionally.
5. The first recorded bicycle race, which took place in a park near Paris in 1868, was slightly more than a mile long.
6. Some cyclists who are devoted to the sport of bike racing travel great distances to compete in races.
7. The most famous bike race is the Tour de France, which draws teams of riders from around the world.
8. It is not only professional racers who take pleasure from bicycle riding.
9. People who follow the simple rules of bicycle riding can benefit from this healthful and pleasant activity.
10. Rules that exist are for the protection of the bike riders and the people around them.

Exercise 5   Identifying Adjective Clauses and Relative Pronouns

Write each sentence. Underline each adjective clause. Circle the subject of the adjective clause.

1. Disregarding safety rules can result in accidents that could harm bike riders or anyone in their path.
2. All bicyclists should have helmets that are worn for protection against serious head injuries in accidents.
3. Those bicyclists who ride in cities should be especially cautious.
4. Bicycle riders should always be aware of pedestrians who may be in their path.
5. Careful riders also use arm signals, which can alert drivers and pedestrians.
6. Arm signals show the direction that a cyclist will turn.
7. Some people who ride bicycles professionally are not racers.
8. These are the people who ride for business purposes.
9. Packages can often be delivered faster by a messenger who is on a bike.
10. A messenger who travels through a city by bicycle follows the same laws as automobile drivers.

Sometimes a subordinate clause is an adverb clause. It may add information about the verb in the main clause. An adverb clause tells *how, when, where, why,* or *under what conditions* the action occurs.

Before Julia bought a bicycle, she compared models.

She likes ten-speeds **because they are versatile.**

In the first sentence, the adverb clause *Before Julia bought a bicycle* modifies the verb *compared.* The adverb clause tells *when* Julia compared bicycles. In the second sentence, the adverb clause *because they are versatile* modifies the verb *likes.* The adverb clause tells *why* she likes ten-speeds.

■ An **adverb clause** is a subordinate clause that modifies, or describes, the verb in the main clause of a complex sentence.

An adverb clause is introduced by a subordinating conjunction. Subordinating conjunctions signal that a clause is a subordinate clause and cannot stand alone. Some common subordinating conjunctions are listed below

Julia crossed the finish line . . .

Subordinating Conjunctions			
after	before	though	whenever
although	if	unless	where
as	since	until	whereas
because	than	when	wherever

You usually do not use a comma before an adverb clause that comes at the end of a sentence. When an adverb clause introduces a sentence, however, you do use a comma after the adverb clause.

before the other bicyclists arrived.

Exercise 6   Identifying Adverb Clauses

Write each sentence. Underline each adverb clause. Circle the verb that each adverb clause modifies.

1. Before automobiles were available, some people rode bicycles.
2. Travelers covered miles easily when they used this simple vehicle.
3. When people wanted company and exercise, they rode tandem bicycles.
4. Two people could enjoy this type of bicycle, since they could ride it together.
5. No self-propelled bicycles existed until the first one was built in 1839 by the Scottish inventor Kirkpatrick Macmillan.
6. Many Americans probably purchased bicycles after 1878 because bicycles were first manufactured in the United States that year.
7. Eventually many people chose automobiles over bicycles, since automobile travel was easier and faster.
8. When gasoline prices rose, many people used bicycles.
9. Bicyclists behave dangerously when they speed.
10. At crosswalks cautious cyclists reduce speed before they proceed.

Exercise 7   Identifying Adverb Clauses and Subordinating Conjunctions

Write each adverb clause. Circle the subordinating conjunction.

1. Although it may have been less convenient than driving, bicycle riding was more economical.
2. Some bicyclists are inconsiderate and unsafe because they disregard rules.
3. Unless cyclists are careful, they can cause injury to themselves and to others.
4. If a cyclist rides in the street, the bicycle is considered a motor vehicle.
5. Whenever they ride their bicycles on the road, cyclists must follow most motor vehicle rules.
6. Although some riders ignore these rules, cyclists should stop at red lights and use hand signals for turns.
7. After they finish work, many people commute by bicycle to their homes.
8. Many messengers use bicycles when they make local deliveries.
9. These messengers face heavy traffic when they are working.
10. Today you will see cycling messengers whenever you visit a large city.

14.5 Noun Clauses

A subordinate clause can be an adjective clause or an adverb clause.

Other subordinate clauses act as nouns. Notice how the noun in dark type in the sentence below can be replaced by a noun clause.

> **Bicyclists** should wear a helmet.
> Should **whoever rides a bike** wear a helmet?

In the second example above, the clause in dark type, like the noun it replaces, is the subject of the sentence. Since this kind of clause acts as a noun, it is called a noun clause.

■ A **noun clause** is a subordinate clause used as a noun.

You can use a noun clause in the same ways that you can use a noun—as a subject, a direct object, an object of a preposition, or a predicate noun.

How Noun Clauses Are Used	
Subject	**Whoever uses a bike** rides for fun or exercise.
Direct Object	Suki says **that she wants a ten-speed bike.**
Object of a Preposition	She is interested in looking at **whatever is on sale.**
Predicate Noun	The flea market is **where she can find a good deal.**

Some of the words that can introduce noun clauses are given in the chart below.

Words That Introduce Noun Clauses		
how, however	where	whose
that	which, whichever	why
what, whatever	who, whom	
when	whoever, whomever	

Exercise 8   Identifying Noun Clauses

Write each noun clause.

1. That bicycles outnumber cars in most countries may surprise you.
2. Bicycling is how the majority of people in Danish cities travel.
3. The flat terrain is what makes the Netherlands an ideal place for biking.
4. Where you will find many cyclists is along the many bridges of Amsterdam.
5. The fact is that many people ride bicycles to and from school and work.
6. Chongqing, China, is where most people travel locally by bike.
7. The people of Beijing own what equals one bike for every two people.
8. A drawback to commuting by bicycle is that the weather isn't always pleasant.
9. Many cities provide special lanes for whoever rides a bicycle in traffic.
10. That bike lanes exist does not guarantee a cyclist's safety on the streets.

Exercise 9   Identifying Noun Clauses

Write each noun clause. Then write *subject, direct object, object of a preposition,* or *predicate noun* to tell how it is used.

1. Where you ride is your choice.
2. The late 1800s was when bicycle racing became a popular spectator sport.
3. Did you know that bicycle racing has been an Olympic event since 1896?
4. Do you know when the forty-nine-mile women's bicycle race was added?
5. I know that this race became an Olympic event in 1984.
6. What many consider the most important race each year is the Tour de France.
7. A special indoor track is where some bicycle races are held.
8. This article says that outdoor races are held on roads, trails, and tracks.
9. Time trials are held for whichever racers wish to compete.
10. You know that many cyclists prefer team competitions.
11. Strength and endurance are what a race demands.
12. One consideration in the triathlon is how the participants should be judged in running, swimming, and cycling.
13. Whoever is eligible may compete at the Winterlude triathlon in Ottawa.
14. Whoever races bicycles must prepare for steep roads.
15. The bicycle gears are what a cyclist shifts for easier pedaling uphill.
16. Whoever keeps the best pace will win the race.
17. Bob knows where the next race will be held.
18. Most amateur races are open to whoever fills out an application.
19. Competitive riders must be ready for what a race requires.
20. Which kind of equipment a racer uses depends on the race.

Grammar Review

CLAUSES AND COMPLEX SENTENCES

John Steinbeck, a celebrated American author, won the Pulitzer Prize in 1940 for *The Grapes of Wrath*. In 1962 he won the Nobel Prize for Literature. The following passage is taken from *The Pearl*. Set on the coast of the Gulf of California, the novel is constructed around a young fisherman, Kino, who discovers an extraordinary pearl. In this passage, Kino and his wife, Juana, are preparing to paddle Kino's canoe out to the oyster beds. The passage has been annotated to show some of the kinds of clauses and sentences covered in this unit.

Literature Model

from *The Pearl*
by John Steinbeck

Kino and Juana came slowly down to the beach and to Kino's canoe, which was the one thing of value he owned in the world. It was very old. Kino's grandfather had brought it from Nayarit, and he had given it to Kino's father, and so it had come to Kino. It was at once property and source of food, for a man with a boat can guarantee a woman that she will eat something. It is the bulwark against starvation. And every year Kino refinished his canoe with the hard shell-like plaster by the secret method that had also come to him from his father. Now he came to the canoe and touched the bow tenderly as he always did. He laid his diving rock and his basket and the two ropes in the sand by the canoe. And he folded his blanket and laid it in the bow.

- Adjective clause
- Compound sentence
- Complex sentence
- Adverb clause
- Simple sentence

Grammar Review

Review: Exercise 1   **Identifying Simple and Compound Sentences**

Write *simple* or *compound* to identify each sentence.

SAMPLE   Kino's grandfather came from Nayarit.
ANSWER   simple

1. The state of Nayarit lies on the western coast of Mexico.
2. The Santiago River flows through Nayarit; it empties into the Pacific Ocean.
3. Kino's grandfather moved north from Nayarit to a village near La Paz.
4. La Paz is in Baja, or Lower California, but this peninsula is part of Mexico.
5. Baja is divided into two states, and La Paz is the capital of the southern state.
6. The Gulf of California and the Pacific Ocean surround the Baja Peninsula.
7. La Paz is on the southeastern tip of Baja; this coast is on the Gulf of California.
8. Spanish explorers settled Baja in 1697, but Native Americans already inhabited the land.
9. In 1811 the city of La Paz was settled by the Spanish.
10. Pearls were found in oyster beds in area waters, and La Paz grew rapidly.

Review: Exercise 2   **Punctuating Simple and Compound Sentences**

Write each sentence and underline each main clause. Add a comma or a semicolon as needed.

SAMPLE   Pearls are found in oysters some oyster beds lie in the gulf.
ANSWER   <u>Pearls are found in oysters;</u> <u>some oyster beds lie in the gulf</u>.

1. Pearl fisheries are on the gulf's western shore the beds are on the eastern shore.
2. The formation of a pearl inside an oyster is actually an act of self-protection.
3. Oysters are a type of mollusk and they have a shell like other mollusks.
4. A foreign substance may enter the oyster's shell and irritate the oyster.
5. The foreign substance can be a grain of sand or it can be a harmful parasite.
6. An oyster will secrete nacre and this secretion protects the oyster.
7. Oysters line the insides of their shells with thin layers of nacre.
8. Nacre is a substance oysters make but they are not the only mollusks to make it.
9. The thin, smooth layers of nacre enclose a foreign body this forms the pearl.
10. Nacre has the physical characteristics of the inside shell of the oyster.

Clauses and Complex Sentences

Review: Exercise 3 **Distinguishing Between Simple and Complex Sentences**

Write whether each sentence is *simple* or *complex*. If it is complex, write the subordinate clause.

SAMPLE The Gulf of California, which was explored by the Spanish explorer Hernando Cortez, was once called the Sea of Cortez.

ANSWER complex, which was explored by the Spanish explorer Hernando Cortez

1. John Steinbeck wrote a book that was titled *The Sea of Cortez*.
2. In this book, Steinbeck told about a story that he heard in Mexico.
3. The story, which was about a great pearl, gave Steinbeck the idea for *The Pearl*.
4. According to Steinbeck, the story may or may not be true.
5. An Indian boy found a pearl in the waters near La Paz.
6. The boy, who had never imagined a pearl of such size and worth, was excited.
7. This valuable pearl would surely bring him and many others happiness.
8. After he found the pearl, the boy had a series of terrible experiences.
9. He was almost killed by people who wished to steal the pearl.
10. Finally, he threw the pearl back into the sea.

Review: Exercise 4 **Distinguishing Between Compound and Complex Sentences**

Write *compound* or *complex* to identify each sentence. If it is complex, write the subordinate clause.

SAMPLE Steinbeck's story *The Pearl* is about a man and woman who are very poor.

ANSWER complex; who are very poor

1. The man's name is Kino, and his wife's name is Juana.
2. Kino, who earns a living as a pearl diver, is barely able to support his wife and their baby son Coyotito.
3. A crisis occurs when a scorpion bites the baby and injects him with its deadly poison.
4. The local doctor refuses to treat the baby because the couple is too poor to pay.
5. Juana prays that she and Kino will go out in the canoe and find a pearl.

Grammar Review

Review: Exercise 5   **Identifying Adjective Clauses**

Write each adjective clause. Underline each relative pronoun. Write the noun or pronoun that each adjective clause modifies.

SAMPLE   People who fish for a living face many difficulties.
ANSWER   <u>who</u> fish for a living, People

1. The fishing industry is important to those who live near the sea.
2. Fishing, which people have done for thousands of years, is the livelihood of millions of people.
3. Most commercial fishing occurs in the sea, which is the main source of fish.
4. The weather, which is often unpredictable, can be an enemy of fishers.
5. Rough, stormy seas can end a fishing trip that is vital to a person's income.
6. Today, there are other problems that threaten the security of fishing families.
7. Some areas, where fish were once bountiful, have been overfished.
8. Fishers whose nets are empty do not earn much money.
9. Families cannot pay bills or maintain the boats that are vital to their livelihood.
10. People who have always made a living from the sea must find other work.

Review: Exercise 6   **Identifying Adverb Clauses**

Write each adverb clause. Underline each subordinating conjunction. Write the verb or verb phrase that each adverb clause modifies.

1. People eat seafood because it is a good source of protein.
2. Since oysters provide nourishment, they have become a popular seafood.
3. Oysters are often found where the water is quiet, calm, and shallow.
4. When they are twenty-four hours old, oysters develop shells.
5. After being allowed to grow for three to five years, oysters are harvested.
6. An oyster is called a *bivalve* because it consists of two parts, or valves.
7. Unless an enemy approaches, the oyster will keep its two valves open.
8. The oyster snaps its valves shut tight whenever it senses danger.
9. Because they harvest millions of oysters each year, humans are the oyster's greatest enemy.
10. A crab will crush the tender shell of a young oyster before it eats the oyster.

Review: Exercise 7 **Distinguishing Between Adjective and Adverb Clauses**

Write each sentence. Underline each subordinate clause once and the word that the clause modifies twice. Then write whether the clause acts as an *adjective* or *adverb.*

SAMPLE A canoe is very important to a simple man who fishes for a living.
ANSWER A canoe is very important to a simple <u>man</u> <u>who fishes for a living</u>. (adjective)

1. Early canoes were made from tree trunks, which dwellers in the Caribbean islands hollowed out.
2. The North American peoples also used canoes, which they made from birchbark and wooden frames.
3. Birchbark canoes provided excellent transportation because they were light and relatively fast.
4. When they explored parts of North America, Marquette and Joliet traveled in birchbark canoes.
5. Today's canoes, which are used for recreation, are made from aluminum, canvas, fiberglass, or wood.

Review: Exercise 8 **Identifying Noun Clauses**

Write each noun clause, and label it *subject, direct object, object of a preposition,* or *predicate noun.*

SAMPLE That canoeing is a popular outdoor sport is no surprise.
ANSWER That canoeing is a popular outdoor sport—subject

1. Can you guess what makes canoeing so popular today?
2. That canoes are easy to use and affordable may help their popularity.
3. Another reason may be that they are easily transported from place to place.
4. Where you go canoeing adds to the pleasure.
5. Whoever has paddled a canoe down a quiet stream understands.
6. Instead of a noisy motor, a paddle is what propels a canoe.
7. People are delighted at how peaceful the world seems from a canoe.
8. Did you know that kayaks are popular with outdoor enthusiasts?
9. Whoever rides in a kayak must be prepared for an occasional dunking.
10. Kayakers know that kayaks can turn over and go under water.

Grammar Review

Review: Exercise 9 **Writing Complex Sentences**

Combine each pair of sentences below, using the correct relative pronoun or subordinating conjunction in parentheses. You may have to delete some words.

1. John Steinbeck wrote *The Pearl*. He has written many novels. (who, which)
2. Steinbeck was born and raised in northern California. Many of his stories take place in northern California. (whatever, where)
3. This area had fish canneries and farms. Steinbeck's stories are often about fish canneries and farming. (because, until)
4. Steinbeck worked at a series of temporary jobs. He attended Stanford University. (while, as if)
5. The characters in Steinbeck's novels were based on people. He knew and respected these people. (whom, which)
6. *Of Mice and Men* and *The Red Pony* were published in 1937. Steinbeck became a popular writer. (wherever, after)
7. *The Grapes of Wrath* may be Steinbeck's best book. It won the Pulitzer Prize in 1940. (which, who)
8. The story is about a poor farm family. They are the Joads. (who, which)
9. The family leaves Oklahoma and moves to California. They lose their farm during the Depression. (when, than)
10. *The Grapes of Wrath* seems to be about the Great Depression of the 1930s. Many people feel that this story is about human dignity. (where, although)
11. You enjoyed the book. You will enjoy *The Grapes of Wrath* movie. (if, as)
12. During World War II, Steinbeck traveled to Italy and North Africa. He was a war correspondent in those places. (whom, where)
13. Steinbeck traveled to the Gulf of California. He wrote *The Pearl*. (until, after)
14. He went with Ed Ricketts. Ricketts was a marine biologist. (which, who)
15. *The Pearl* first appeared in a magazine. It also became a film. (which, who)
16. The movie *Viva Zapata* is about a leader of the Indians during the Mexican Revolution. Steinbeck wrote the screenplay for this film. (whereas, which)
17. John Steinbeck had a poodle. The dog's name was Charley. (which, whose)
18. *Travels with Charley* is a nonfiction book by Steinbeck. It is an account of his travels with his pet poodle. (whom, that)
19. John Steinbeck died in 1968. He received many awards, including the 1962 Nobel Prize for Literature. (because, before)
20. Steinbeck had a belief. He believed writers should celebrate the greatness of the human spirit. (which, that.)

Proofreading

The following passage is about the artist Paul Sierra, whose painting *A Place in Time* appears below. Rewrite the passage, correcting the errors in spelling, capitalization, grammar, and usage. Add any missing punctuation. There are 10 errors.

Paul Sierra, *A Place in Time*, 1989

(continued)

Clauses and Complex Sentences

Paul Sierra

¹Born in a cuban community in 1944, Paul Sierra was expected to enter a profession. ²Although he receive little encouragement he spent hours drawing in notebooks and reading books on painting. ³When he was sixteen Sierra moved to the united States, and he lived first in Miami and then in Chicago. ⁴The only formal art training Sierra recieved was three years at the Art Institute of Chicago, where he enrolled in 1963. ⁵Today Sierra work as the creative director of a small advertising agency. ⁶His job allow him the freedom to paint for himself and he can ignore the expectations of others. ⁷"I only hope," he says "to live long enough to make a good painting."

Review: Exercise 11

Mixed Review

Write whether the sentence is *simple, compound,* or *complex.* If a sentence is complex, write the subordinate clause. Then write whether the subordinate clause is an adverb clause, an adjective clause, or a noun clause.

¹That someone might find a precious pearl inside an oyster is intriguing and exciting. ²Although it is possible to find a natural pearl in an edible oyster, it isn't likely. ³Most natural pearls come from the Persian Gulf and Sri Lanka; the Red Sea and the Philippines are also a source of natural pearls. ⁴Pearls are valued for their color, shape, clarity, and weight. ⁵In areas where natural pearls are scarce, pearls are cultured. ⁶A cultured pearl, which looks deceptively like a natural pearl, has fewer and thicker layers of nacre inside. ⁷Unless you are a gem expert, you cannot see the difference between a natural and a cultured pearl. ⁸Only an X-ray of the pearl would reveal the truth. ⁹For centuries people had tried to culture pearls, but no one found commercial success until 1893. ¹⁰Then Kokichi Mikimoto, who is sometimes called the Pearl King, produced the first good cultured pearls in Japan. ¹¹Most pearls that are made into jewelry and sold today are cultured. ¹²Whoever is interested in science and the habits of certain sea creatures would be fascinated by the process of culturing pearls. ¹³The fact is that oysters are still a very necessary and essential element in the production of a pearl. ¹⁴The oysters just get a little assistance from humans. ¹⁵The process takes several years; it is part technology and part nature.

Writing Application

TIME

For more about the writing process, see **TIME Facing the Blank Page**, pp. 97–107.

Sentence Variety in Writing

In this passage from *The Diary of Latoya Hunter*, the writer varies her sentence structure to capture the natural flow of her thoughts. Notice the underlined words.

> It's hard to believe <u>but</u> people change as rapidly as the world does. <u>If I had kept you as a diary two years ago</u>, you would have heard about Jimmy. He was the first guy who I was close to and who was a real friend to me. I liked him <u>because</u> other boys always seemed to be in a popularity contest, and he didn't care about that stuff.

Techniques in Sentence Variety

Try to apply some of Latoya Hunter's writing techniques when you write and revise your own work.

❶ When appropriate in dialogue or personal writing, mix *simple*, *compound*, and *complex* sentences to help your writing sound lively and realistic.

FLAT SENTENCE PATTERN It's hard to believe. People change as rapidly as the world does.

HUNTER'S VERSION It's hard to believe *but people change as rapidly as the world does.*

❷ Make your writing more specific by using subordinate clauses to tell readers which ideas and information are the most important:

LESS SPECIFIC VERSION I liked him. Other boys always seemed to be in a popularity contest.

HUNTER'S VERSION I liked him *because other boys always seemed to be in a popularity contest.*

Clauses and Complex Sentences

Practice Practice these techniques as you revise the following passage. Identify the ideas that might be subordinated, and experiment with different sentence structures to create variety.

A strong wind tore across the fields. It rippled the wheat. Pieces scattered to the skies. Splinters of wheat struck the boy's face. Ernest struggled on toward the house. He could see Pa on the tractor in the far field. He hollered. His voice was lost on the wind. Slowly but steadily, Ernest inched his way against the gusts. He reached the house. His mother quickly opened the door. He plunged into the stillness.

UNIT
15

Verbals

Participles and Participial Phrases

A present participle is formed by adding *-ing* to a verb. A past participle is usually formed by adding *-ed* to a verb.

A participle can function as the main verb in a verb phrase or as an adjective to modify nouns or pronouns.

> The biplane was **soaring.** [verb]
> The flight had **astounded** skeptics. [verb]
> The **soaring** biplane flew 120 feet. [adjective]

In the first sentence above, the present participle *soaring* is the main verb, and *was* is the helping verb. In the second sentence, the past participle *astounded* is the main verb, and *had* is the helping verb. In the third sentence, the present participle *soaring* is used as an adjective to describe the noun *biplane.*

Sometimes a participle that is used as an adjective is part of a phrase called a participial phrase.

> **Sailing across the dunes,** the *Flyer* made history.

■ A **participial phrase** is a group of words that includes a participle and other words that complete its meaning.

A participial phrase that begins a sentence is always set off with a comma. Participial phrases in other places may or may not need commas. If the phrase is necessary to identify the modified word, it should not be set off with commas. If the phrase simply gives additional information about the modified word, it should be set off with commas.

> The biplane **displayed here** is a model of the *Flyer.*
> The model, **shaped with care,** attracts many visitors.

A participial phrase can appear before or after the word it describes. Place the phrase as close as possible to the modified word; otherwise, the meaning of the sentence may be unclear.

Verbals

Exercise 1   Identifying Participles

Write each participle, and write whether it is *part of a verb phrase* or is used as an *adjective*.

1. People throughout the world have considered the flying Wright brothers the first pilots.
2. Even as young children, the Wright brothers were fascinated by machines of all types.
3. Otto Lilienthal did pioneering work.
4. In the 1890s, he had experimented with gliders.
5. The Wrights had learned of his work.
6. Soon they were experimenting in North Carolina.
7. They had selected Kill Devil Hill near Kitty Hawk for their experiments.
8. Their first two models lacked enough lifting power.
9. In 1903 they built an advanced model.
10. This model became the world's first working airplane.

Exercise 2   Identifying Participial Phrases

Write each sentence and underline the participial phrase. Then draw two lines under the word that the phrase describes. Add commas as needed.

1. Witnessed by only a few the first successful flight gained little recognition for the Wright brothers.
2. A statement issued to the press about the Wright brothers' achievements received almost no attention.
3. The brothers, however, were inventors committed to their work.
4. Believing that airplanes eventually would transport passengers the Wright brothers perfected their invention.
5. Later flights lasting up to five minutes each attracted attention.
6. Working hard the Wrights built a wooden biplane.
7. By 1908 the Wright brothers had signed a government contract financing their invention.
8. Wilbur made many flights in the eastern United States demonstrating the brothers' new machine.
9. The Wright brothers' basic principles used in airplanes even today have stood the test of time.
10. Piloted by bold aviators airplanes still thrill the public.

15.2 Gerunds and Gerund Phrases

The previous lesson explains that the present participle may be used as an adjective. A verb form ending in -*ing* may also serve as a noun, in which case it is called a *gerund*.

■ A **gerund** is a verb form that ends in -*ing* and is used as a noun.

Sometimes a gerund functions as the subject of the sentence.

Moving involves a lot of work.

At other times, a gerund functions as the direct object of a verb. Remember, a direct object of a verb receives the action of the verb. It answers the question *whom?* or *what?* after an action verb.

People enjoy **traveling.**

Do not confuse gerunds with other verb forms that end in -*ing*. You can tell them apart by distinguishing their functions in a sentence. A verb form ending in -*ing* may be the main verb in a verb phrase. It may be used as an adjective to describe a noun or pronoun. It also may function as a noun. Then it is called a gerund.

Megan has been **packing.** [main verb in a verb phrase]
She will take an **exciting** trip. [participle used as adjective]
Traveling will be fast. [gerund]

In some sentences a gerund is part of a gerund phrase.

■ A **gerund phrase** is a group of words that includes a gerund and other words that complete its meaning.

Many jobs require **long-distance traveling around the country.**
Choosing the best mode of travel takes some consideration.

Exercise 3   Identifying Verbs, Gerunds, and Participles

Write whether the underlined word is the *main verb in a verb phrase*, a *participle used as an adjective*, or a *gerund*.

1. Commerce requires <u>moving</u> goods between places.
2. For centuries people had <u>exchanged</u> one kind of goods for another.
3. People had been <u>transporting</u> objects long before the invention of the wheel.
4. Trade produced increased contact among <u>differing</u> groups of people.
5. In this way, new ideas were <u>carried</u> to many distant places.
6. <u>Trading</u> also presented problems.
7. For example, <u>traveling</u> could prove dangerous and expensive.
8. Ancient merchants depended on animals for their <u>growing</u> businesses.
9. Some merchants preferred <u>riding</u> in long caravans of people and animals.
10. People began <u>using</u> litters for heavy packages.

Exercise 4   Identifying Gerund Phrases

Write each gerund phrase. Write whether it is used as a *subject* or a *direct object*.

1. Hauling packages on these litters simplified work.
2. Workers started using logs as rollers for litters.
3. Eventually people began floating crude rafts of logs.
4. Transporting various goods on these vehicles created new problems.
5. Steering these rafts was difficult.
6. Raft builders liked experimenting with the design.
7. Adding a wall of logs along each edge of the raft formed a boat.
8. Shipping goods became easier with the rafts.
9. The Phoenicians later began voyaging throughout the Mediterranean.
10. Trading raw materials and finished goods was the basis of their civilization.
11. They even started traveling as far away as Britain.
12. Sailing the Mediterranean was also important to the Greeks.
13. The Romans began building roads throughout the known world.
14. Finishing these roads took many years.
15. Exchanging goods also depended on rivers.
16. Large cities began growing along important trade routes.
17. Searching for new trade routes to Asia led to an age of exploration.
18. Europeans enjoyed acquiring Asian silks and spices.
19. They also liked learning about the East from explorers.
20. They began searching for a sea route to Asia.

15.3 Infinitives and Infinitive Phrases

Verb forms that are used as adjectives and nouns are called *verbals.* Participles and gerunds are two kinds of verbals. Participles can act as adjectives. Gerunds act as nouns. A third kind of verbal is called an infinitive.

■ An **infinitive** is formed from the word *to* together with the base form of a verb. Infinitives are often used as nouns in sentences.

When the word *to* helps to form an infinitive, it is not a preposition. Remember, a preposition is a word that relates a noun or a pronoun to another word in the sentence. A prepositional phrase is a group of words that begins with a preposition and ends with a noun or pronoun as its object.

> Many children like **to skate.** [infinitive]
> Some adults skate **to their jobs.** [prepositional phrase]

In the first sentence, the words in dark type form an infinitive. In the second sentence, the words in dark type form a prepositional phrase.

Sometimes an infinitive functions as the subject of a sentence. It names *whom* or *what* the sentence is about. At other times, the infinitive may function as the direct object of a verb. The direct object receives the action of the verb. It answers the question *whom?* or *what?* after an action verb.

> **To stop** is sometimes difficult. [subject]
> Beginning skaters need **to practice.** [direct object]

Sometimes an infinitive is part of an infinitive phrase.

■ An **infinitive phrase** is a group of words that includes an infinitive and other words that complete its meaning.

> **To skate on cracked sidewalks** demands practice.

Exercise 5   **Distinguishing Infinitives from Prepositional Phrases**

Write whether each underlined group of words is an *infinitive* or a *prepositional phrase*.

1. <u>To wait in city traffic</u> is difficult for people in a hurry.
2. Some people can walk <u>to their jobs</u>.
3. Others like <u>to bicycle</u>.
4. <u>To skate</u> is often the best choice of city transportation.
5. Skaters speed across town <u>to their destinations</u>.
6. They do not need <u>to stop for slow traffic</u>.
7. Some people want <u>to learn this new skill</u>.
8. Skaters must learn <u>to keep their balance</u>.
9. They often enjoy skating <u>to music</u> at indoor rinks.
10. The invention of the roller skate is attributed <u>to Joseph Merlin</u>.

Exercise 6   **Identifying Infinitive Phrases**

Write each infinitive phrase and whether it is used as a *subject* or a *direct object*.

1. To improve on Merlin's design became the goal of James Plimpton.
2. To sit in a car amid traffic is a waste of time.
3. Experienced skaters have learned to move through crowds easily.
4. Some skaters like to speed.
5. To race professionally is the desire of others.
6. To compete in skating races seems quite a challenge.
7. Some skaters prefer to work in teams.
8. Free skaters learn to perform difficult jumps and spins.
9. The practice each day helps to perfect their moves.
10. Most people no longer want to own old-fashioned skates.
11. In the past, to make wheels of wood or metal was essential.
12. Many skaters prefer to use in-line skates.
13. Some skaters want to move as fast as possible.
14. To glide silently through the park is a skater's idea of a perfect afternoon.
15. Some people like to spend all of their free time skating.
16. The best skaters learn to move very fast.
17. To play roller hockey is the goal of some skaters.
18. Players like to score points against an opposing team.
19. Beginning skaters may want to rent their equipment at first.
20. To purchase skates and safety pads can be expensive.

Grammar Review

VERBALS

Amelia Earhart: First Lady of Flight, by Peggy Mann, is a biography of one of the world's most famous aviators. One of Earhart's greatest achievements occurred in 1932, when she became the first woman to successfully complete a solo flight across the Atlantic Ocean. The following excerpt from the book describes the early part of that historic flight. The passage has been annotated to show some of the types of verbals covered in this unit.

Literature Model

from *Amelia Earhart: First Lady of Flight*
by Peggy Mann

At first the flight seemed a dream coming true. The view was vast and lovely. As she looked about, she felt she was gulping beauty. The clouds were marvelous shapes in white, some trailing shimmering veils. In the distance the highest peaks of the fog mountains were tinted pink with the setting sun.

Gradually she flew into darkness, star-flecked, with moonlight shimmering through the endless skies.

Then, suddenly, the dream turned into nightmare. Something happened that had never occurred in all her twelve years of flying. The dials of the altimeter started to spin crazily. She could no longer tell how high she was above the sea. And she was flying through thick darkness—flying into a storm.

Present participle as main verb

Present participle as adjective

Participial phrase

Infinitive phrase

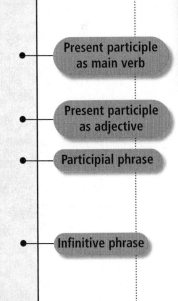

Verbals

Grammar Review

Review: Exercise 1 **Identifying Participial Phrases**

Write each sentence, and underline each participial phrase. Then draw two lines under the word that the phrase describes. Add commas as needed.

1. Setting a record Amelia Earhart was the first woman to fly across the Atlantic alone.
2. Working as a nurse's aide during World War I she became interested in flying.
3. Entered as a contestant in flying meets the young aviator gained experience.
4. Earhart flying as a passenger was the first woman to cross the Atlantic by air.
5. Fascinated by machines she also worked on airplane engines.
6. Soaring high above the clouds her planes were small and fast.
7. Interested in all types of flying Earhart also performed stunts.
8. Crowds welcoming her home often greeted her safe return.
9. Some of Earhart's flights lasting many hours were exhausting.
10. Earhart attempting to fly around the world was lost in 1937.

Review: Exercise 2 **Using Participles and Participial Phrases**

Rewrite each sentence, inserting the participle or participial phrase in parentheses. Add commas as needed.

SAMPLE Amelia Earhart watched the earth fade from view. (gazing down from the cockpit)

ANSWER Gazing down from the cockpit, Amelia Earhart watched the earth fade from view.

1. She was awestruck by the beauty. (breathtaking)
2. The stars danced in the night sky. (twinkling)
3. Clouds glowed warmly in the sunset. (pink-tinted)
4. Earhart encountered some rough weather. (traveling across the Atlantic)
5. The pilot peered into the darkness. (flying through the storm)
6. She stared at the controls with dread. (spine-tingling)
7. Earhart could see nothing but black sky. (looking outside)
8. She sat rigidly. (frozen with fear)
9. Clouds completely hid the earth from view. (black-tipped)
10. This was only the beginning of Amelia Earhart's journey. (history-making)

| **Review: Exercise 3** | **Identifying Gerund Phrases** |

Write each gerund phrase, and then write whether it is used as a *subject* or a *direct object*.

SAMPLE Achieving your goals can be very satisfying.
ANSWER Achieving your goals, subject

1. Receiving a pilot's license is an important achievement.
2. Being the first woman to cross the Atlantic made Amelia Earhart a hero.
3. Earhart disliked needing so many months for preparation.
4. Waiting eleven months made her restless.
5. She would try flying around the world at the equator.
6. Attempting such a feat would test her courage and endurance.
7. No man or woman had ever even tried piloting a plane that far.
8. After her announcement, she began making arrangements for her flight.
9. Flying across the Atlantic was the first real test of her ability.
10. Navigating by instinct was a necessary skill.

| **Review: Exercise 4** | **Using Gerunds and Gerund Phrases** |

Write a sentence that answers each question. Use the word or words in parentheses in your answer.

SAMPLE What was Amelia Earhart's biggest achievement? (pioneering aviation for women)
ANSWER Pioneering aviation for women was Amelia Earhart's biggest achievement.

1. What event filled Earhart with wonder in her youth? (seeing an airplane in the sky)
2. What was Earhart's first claim to fame? (flying across the Atlantic as a passenger in 1928)
3. What was Earhart's greatest passion? (flying faster, higher, and farther than anyone else had ever flown before)
4. What action gained Earhart renewed respect in 1935? (becoming the first person to successfully fly from Hawaii to California)
5. What was one of Earhart's major goals in her speeches? (promoting the rights of women)

Grammar Review

Review: Exercise 5   Identifying Infinitive Phrases

Write each infinitive phrase, and then write whether it is used as a *subject* or a *direct object*.

SAMPLE   Amelia Earhart loved to fly.
ANSWER   to fly, direct object

1. Amelia Earhart wanted to prove herself.
2. Throughout her life, to promote women's rights was important for her.
3. Earhart even wanted to draft women into the armed services.
4. To earn money for flight lessons was the reason she worked as a file clerk, truck driver, and nurse's aide.
5. To spend her life as a pilot was her greatest dream.
6. To make a nonstop, solo flight from Mexico City into Newark, New Jersey, was a notable achievement.
7. She tried to earn a living as a pilot in her twenties.
8. She promised to risk her life on a transatlantic flight.
9. Despite her shyness, Earhart needed to become a forceful speaker.
10. To pursue a dangerous goal fascinated Earhart.

Review: Exercise 6   Using Infinitives and Infinitive Phrases

Write a sentence that answers each question, using the word or words in parentheses.

SAMPLE   What did Amelia Earhart want? (to earn money for lessons)
ANSWER   Amelia Earhart wanted to earn money for lessons.

1. What did Amelia Earhart start to do in 1937? (to fly around the world)
2. What was Fred Noonan's mission on the flight? (to serve as Earhart's navigator)
3. What did Earhart and Noonan manage to do before they ran into trouble? (to complete two-thirds of their journey)
4. What have searchers failed to do ever since? (to find a trace of Earhart)
5. What do researchers continue to do? (to study Earhart's disappearance)

Verbals

Review: Exercise 7

Proofreading

The following passage is about Yvonne Jacquette, whose painting appears on the next page. Rewrite the passage, correcting the errors in spelling, capitalization, grammar, and usage. There are ten errors.

Yvonne Jacquette

¹Born in 1934 in Pittsburgh, Pennsylvania Yvonne Jacquette began her artistic career by painting landscapes. ²Later, she became facsinated with painting these scenes from a distance. ³Breaking with tradition she began painting landscapes from the vantage point of a single-engine plane.

⁴Flying high above the earth Jacquette selects particular views and makes sketches of they. ⁵Uses these drawings to help her make her paintings. ⁶In the painting on the next page, Jacquette has paint the view overlooking a stretch of rural landscape. ⁷Filled with cloud shapes the painting could illustrate what Amelia Earhart seen on her solo flight across the french countryside so long ago.

Review: Exercise 8

Mixed Review

Write each underlined word or phrase in the following paragraph. Tell whether each is a *participle*, a *gerund*, an *infinitive*, a *participial phrase*, a *gerund phrase*, an *infinitive phrase*, or a *main verb*.

Shortly before Amelia Earhart's <u>amazing</u> solo flight across the Atlantic, Charles A. Lindbergh had <u>accomplished</u> a similar feat. He managed <u>to become the first man</u> who flew across the Atlantic alone. <u>Flying such a mission</u> required <u>astonishing</u> endurance and bravery. Like Earhart, Lindbergh had <u>found</u> the <u>exciting</u> new field of aviation very attractive. He had left school <u>to perform</u> daredevil stunts in the air. <u>Gaining respect</u> as a careful pilot required time and practice. <u>Hoping for prize money</u>, Lindbergh took off from New York in May 1927. When he landed in Paris, he saw thousands of people. They <u>had gathered</u> to greet him. Soon the crowd started <u>calling his name</u>. They began <u>applauding</u> <u>wildly</u>. The spectators <u>organized</u> parades and celebrations in honor of the flight. As Amelia Earhart would five years later, Lindbergh had <u>become</u> a hero, <u>enjoying the admiration of people around the world</u>.

Yvonne Jacquette, *Clouds over Farmland, Forked Tree Masses,* **1988**

Writing Application

TIME

For more about the writing process, see **TIME Facing the Blank Page**, pp. 97–107.

Phrases in Writing

Minfong Ho uses gerund, infinitive, and participial phrases along with participles in this passage from *The Clay Marble* to add detailed imagery, as well as variety, to her sentences. Read the passage carefully, noting the italicized phrases.

> I closed my eyes now and tried *to imagine them all sitting around me:* Grandmother stroking me, Father and Sarun whittling on the steps, Mother stoking the embers of the cooking fire. It wasn't just the thick thatched roof that had sheltered me, I realized now. It was the feeling I had had then, of being part of a family as a gently *pulsing* whole, so natural it was *like the breathing of a sleeping baby.*

Techniques with Phrases

Try to apply some of Minfong Ho's writing techniques when you write and revise your own work.

❶ Use infinitive phrases when appropriate to expand meaning in your sentences. Compare the following:

GENERAL VERSION I closed my eyes now and thought.

HO'S VERSION I closed my eyes now and tried *to imagine them all sitting around me.*

❷ Create specific and vivid imagery by describing nouns with participles.

GENERAL VERSION part of a family as a whole

HO'S VERSION part of a family as a gently *pulsing* whole

Verbals

Practice Use a separate sheet of paper to practice these techniques as you revise the following passage. Choose places to insert infinitive and participial phrases, working to make the passage more specific and engaging. Let the underlined words be starting points for your changes.

"<u>This</u> will take at least a week," sighed Tabitha. Sandy's bike, <u>in a heap</u>, rested sadly against the wall of Tabitha's shop. "<u>If I work hard</u>, maybe I can do it in five days. Will that be fast enough?" she <u>said</u>. "Before I fix the frame, I need <u>help</u> with these. Hand me the wrench <u>over there</u>," Tabitha said, pointing to the opposite wall. "Don't worry. We'll get it done. I love <u>work</u>!"

Subject-Verb Agreement

Making Subjects and Verbs Agree

A subject and its verb are the basic parts of a sentence. A singular noun subject calls for a singular form of the verb. A plural noun subject calls for a plural form of the verb. The subject and its verb are said to agree in number. Read the sentences below. You can see that the subjects and verbs agree in number.

Notice that in the present tense the singular form of the verb usually ends in *-s* or *-es.*

Subject-Verb Agreement with Nouns as Subjects	
Singular	**Plural**
A **poet explores** beauty.	**Poets explore** beauty.
The **theme touches** readers.	The **themes touch** readers.
Robert Frost writes about farms.	**Frost and Robinson write** about farms.

Verbs and subject pronouns must also agree. Look at the chart below, and notice how the verb changes. In the present tense, the *-s* ending is used with the subject pronouns *it, he,* and *she.*

Subject-Verb Agreement with Pronouns as Subjects	
Singular	**Plural**
I **read.**	We **read.**
You **read.**	You **read.**
He, she, it **reads.**	They **read.**

The irregular verbs *be, do,* and *have* can be main verbs or helping verbs. They must agree with the subject, regardless of whether they are main verbs or helping verbs.

I **am** a poet. They **are** talking to a poet. He **is** a poet.
She **does** well. She **does** write poetry. They **do** write.
He **has** books. He **has** read poetry. They **have** written.

Exercise 1   Identifying Subject and Verb Forms

Write the subject and verb of each sentence. Underline the subject once and its verb twice. If they agree, write *correct*. If they do not agree, change the verb.

1. Anne Bradstreet's poems appears first in this book.
2. She was an early American poet.
3. Her poetry have charm and wit.
4. She was a teenager in 1630.
5. Many people enjoys her poems today.
6. Her strong spirit shines through her work.
7. Her shorter poems have the most appeal.
8. Directness mark her style.
9. In 1666 her house and library was destroyed by fire.
10. She discusses the fire in a famous poem.

Exercise 2   Making Subject and Verb Forms Agree

For each sentence, write the subject and the correct form of the verb in parentheses.

1. This book (contain, contains) poems by Frost.
2. Frost (has, have) a great reputation as a lyric poet.
3. Readers (find, finds) his use of symbols interesting.
4. He (was, were) a teacher in his youth.
5. Most libraries (has, have) collections of Frost's work.
6. Certainly our local library (do, does).
7. Students (talk, talks) about Frost's poem "Fire and Ice."
8. This poem (is, are) rather bleak.
9. Several works (share, shares) common themes.
10. Robert Frost's poems (do, does) much for the American spirit.
11. They (have, has) meaning for us today.
12. Some people (think, thinks) his poems are cold.
13. Most people (do, does) admire his work, however.
14. Frost's poetry (do, does) require close study.
15. Even his short poems (have, has) hidden meanings.
16. Certain poems (is, are) apparently simple.
17. His poetry (focus, focuses) on ordinary people.
18. Most students (have, has) read some of his work.
19. His book *In the Clearing* (have, has) some of his most beautiful poems.
20. Frost's poetry (continue, continues) to be popular.

16.2 Problems with Locating the Subject

Making a subject and its verb agree is easy when the verb directly follows the subject. Sometimes, however, a prepositional phrase comes between the subject and the verb.

The **city,** in all its moods, **inspires** poets.
The **cities** of the Midwest **inspire** poets.

In the first sentence above, *in all its moods* is a prepositional phrase. The singular verb *inspires* agrees with the subject of the sentence, *city,* and not with the plural noun *moods,* which is the object of the preposition. In the second sentence, *of the Midwest* is a prepositional phrase. The plural verb *inspire* agrees with the plural subject, *cities,* and not with the singular noun *Midwest,* which is the object of the preposition.

Some sentences begin with *here* or *there. Here* or *there* is never the subject of a sentence. Look for the subject after the verb.

There **is** a great **poem** about Chicago.

To more easily identify the subject, rearrange the sentence so that the subject and verb are in their usual order.

A great **poem** there **is** about Chicago.

In some interrogative sentences, a helping verb may come before the subject. The subject appears between the helping verb and the main verb.

Do these **poems interest** you?

You can check the subject-verb agreement by making the sentence declarative.

These **poems do interest** you.

Exercise 3 Identifying the Subjects and Verbs

Write the subject and verb for each sentence. Underline the subject once and its verb twice. If they agree, write *correct*. If they do not agree, correct the verb.

1. These lines of the poem describes the city of Chicago.
2. Here is the phrase "Hog butcher of the world."
3. Does it introduce a certain viewpoint?
4. A list of adjectives are in another line.
5. Sandburg, with a few words, show us the city.
6. There are longer phrases after the introduction.
7. A string of verbs appear among the long phrases.
8. Another nickname for Chicago is City of Big Shoulders.
9. Sandburg's reputation as the Chicago poet come from these lines.
10. The words of this poem echoes American popular speech.

Exercise 4 Making the Subject and Verb Forms Agree

For each sentence, write the subject and the correct form of the verb in parentheses.

1. The writer of these poems (is, are) Carl Sandburg.
2. This son of Swedish immigrants (is, are) famous.
3. Ideas for his work (arise, arises) from his travels.
4. His days in Puerto Rico (inspire, inspires) his earliest poems.
5. Does the young man (succeed, succeeds) in his career?
6. Critics around the world (praise, praises) his work.
7. Poems about modern industry (is, are) unusual.
8. (Do, Does) Sandburg's work appear in many collections?
9. The idioms of mid-American speech (marks, mark) his work.
10. The six volumes of his Lincoln biography (is, are) widely read.
11. The sights and sounds of the country also (interests, interest) Sandburg.
12. Bedtime stories for his family (appear, appears) in *Rootabaga Stories*.
13. (Do, Does) you know about Sandburg's school career?
14. Nature, especially in late summer and autumn, (is, are) a favorite subject.
15. The events of Lincoln's early life (forms, form) the basis of *The Prairie Years*.
16. (Has, Have) critics changed their view of Sandburg in recent years?
17. There (is, are) many jobs in Sandburg's past.
18. Poetry of other cultures (was, were) important to Sandburg's work.
19. Here (is, are) the sound of American speech as poetry.
20. A famous poem of his later years (is, are) titled "Timesweep."

16.3 Collective Nouns and Other Special Subjects

It is difficult to tell whether certain special subjects are singular or plural. For example, collective nouns follow special agreement rules. A collective noun names a group. The noun has a singular meaning when used to tell about a group that acts as a unit. The noun has a plural meaning when used to describe members of the group acting as individuals.

The **audience sits** in silence. [one group, singular]
The **audience sit** on chairs and pillows. [individuals, plural]

Certain nouns, such as *mumps* and *mathematics*, end in -*s* but take a singular verb. Other nouns that name one thing, such as *pliers* and *binoculars*, end in -*s* but take a plural verb.

News is important to us all. [singular]
Scissors are useful and often attractive. [plural]

When the subject refers to an amount as a single unit, it is singular. When the subject refers to a number of individual units, it is plural.

Fifty years seems a long time. [single unit]
Fifty years pass quickly. [individual units]
Five dollars is the admission price. [single unit]
Five dollars are on the table. [individual units]

A title of a book or work of art is always singular even if a noun within the title is plural.

"The Victors" is a poem by Denise Levertov. [one poem]
***Collected Earlier Poems* was** published in 1979. [one book]

The class . . .

. . . **studies** modern poetry.

The class . . .

. . . **study** for their exams.

Exercise 5   Identifying the Subject and Verb Forms

Write the subject and verb of each sentence. Underline the subject once and the verb twice. If they agree, write *correct*. If they do not agree, correct the verb.

1. Langston Hughes's work include more than fifty volumes.
2. The class is studying Hughes's poems for a performance.
3. *The Weary Blues* celebrates Harlem in the 1920s.
4. The class has practiced their poems for the performance.
5. The audience sits quietly, waiting for the curtain to rise.
6. The crowd looks at their programs to find the poem titles.
7. The band plans the blues pieces to be played.
8. The band take out their instruments.
9. Binoculars help those people in the back of the auditorium.
10. Two dollars are the admission price for the performance.

Exercise 6   Using the Correct Verb Form for Special Subjects

For each sentence, write the subject and the correct form of the verb in parentheses.

1. The crowd (gather, gathers) outside the room.
2. The crowd (look, looks) at their programs.
3. Ten minutes (seem, seems) like a long time.
4. The audience (find, finds) their seats.
5. The class (attend, attends) the poetry reading.
6. Our class (is, are) in the first row.
7. The class (discuss, discusses) the Pulitzer Prize among themselves.
8. A committee (award, awards) the prize each year.
9. The committee (accept, accepts) nominations of American poets.
10. A thousand dollars (is, are) the amount of the prize.
11. The audience (include, includes) the poet laureate of the United States.
12. His book *Promises* (win, wins) a prize for Robert Penn Warren.
13. Two dollars (is, are) the price of admission.
14. The poetry club (read, reads) their favorite poems.
15. *Winter Trees* (is, are) a book by Sylvia Plath.
16. *Winter Trees* (contain, contains) some of Plath's best poems.
17. News of other events (is, are) posted at the reading.
18. "Women" (is, are) a poem by Alice Walker.
19. Walker's *Revolutionary Petunias* (was, were) published in 1973.
20. Twenty-five dollars (is, are) the average price of a new book.

Indefinite Pronouns as Subjects

■ An **indefinite pronoun** is a pronoun that does not refer to a specific person, place, thing, or idea.

Some indefinite pronouns are singular. Others are plural. When they are used as subjects, the verb must agree in number with these indefinite pronouns. Study the indefinite pronouns in the chart below.

Indefinite Pronouns			
Singular			**Plural**
another	everybody	no one	both
anybody	everyone	nothing	few
anyone	everything	one	many
anything	much	somebody	others
each	neither	someone	several
either	nobody	something	

The indefinite pronouns *all, any, most, none,* and *some* may be singular or plural, depending on the phrase that follows. Notice how indefinite pronouns are used below.

> **Everyone admires** the poems of Emily Dickinson.[singular]
> **Many** of the poems **deal** with death and love. [plural]
> **Most** of her world **is** within four walls. [singular]
> **Most** of the poems **are** very short. [plural]

Often a prepositional phrase follows an indefinite pronoun that can be either singular or plural. To determine whether the pronoun is singular or plural, look at the object of the preposition.

For example, in the third sentence above, *most* refers to *world.* Because *world* is singular, *most* is singular. In the fourth sentence *most* refers to *poems.* Because *poems* is plural, *most* is plural.

Exercise 7 — Identifying Subject and Verb Forms

For each sentence, write the indefinite pronoun and the correct form of the verb.

1. Anyone (is, are) invited to read poems at this poetry reading.
2. Most of the audience (has, have) found seats.
3. Others (stands, stand) in the back of the room.
4. Someone (reads, read) six recently written poems.
5. Everyone (listens, listen) with quiet attention to the poems.
6. Few of the poets (has, have) published their work yet.
7. Several of the poems (is, are) funny.
8. Everybody (laughs, laugh) at a poem about slippery foods.
9. Most of the work (is, are) more serious in tone.
10. Several of the poets (seems, seem) quite young.

Exercise 8 — Using the Correct Verb Form for Indefinite Pronoun Subjects

For each sentence, write the subject and the correct form of the verb in parentheses.

1. Much of Emily Dickinson's life (was, were) solitary.
2. Few (understand, understands) her need for quiet.
3. Many (study, studies) her life and times.
4. Each (learn, learns) about her lonely adulthood.
5. Everything in nature (inspire, inspires) the poet.
6. One of the poems (use, uses) a spider as its focus.
7. Another in this tradition (is, are) Walt Whitman.
8. Everyone (know, knows) "O Captain! My Captain!"
9. Someone in class (prefer, prefers) "When Lilacs Last in the Dooryard Bloom'd."
10. Both of these poems (is, are) in memory of Abraham Lincoln.
11. Few (use, uses) rhythm in such a musical way.
12. No one (appreciate, appreciates) Whitman's poetry without effort.
13. Many of Dickinson's poems (is, are) not titled.
14. Few (write, writes) as sparely as Dickinson.
15. Most of Whitman's work (sound, sounds) powerful.
16. Each (have, has) an individual style.
17. All of us (reap, reaps) benefits from the study of these poets.
18. Both of the poets (rely, relies) heavily upon the use of symbolism.
19. Few of Dickinson's poems (was, were) published in her lifetime.
20. Nobody (use, uses) dashes in the same way as Dickinson.

16.5 Agreement with Compound Subjects

■ A **compound subject** contains two or more simple subjects that have the same verb. The way the subjects are joined determines whether the compound subject takes a singular or a plural verb. When two or more subjects are joined by *and* or by the correlative conjunction *both . . . and,* the plural form of the verb should be used.

> Chicago, Boston, **and** Paris **inspire** many poets.
> Maya Angelou **and** Nikki Giovanni **are** poets.
> **Both** Angelou **and** Giovanni **write** about their times.

All of these sentences refer to more than one person, place, thing, or idea.

Sometimes *and* is used to join two words that are part of one unit or refer to a single person or thing. In these cases, the subject is considered to be singular. In the example below, notice that *teacher* and *adviser* refer to the same person. Therefore, the singular form of the verb is used.

> Her teacher **and** adviser **is** a famous writer.

When two or more subjects are joined by *or, nor,* or the correlative conjunction *either . . . or* or *neither . . . nor,* the verb agrees with the subject that is closest to it.

> The listener **or** the reader **responds** to the rhythm.
> **Either** music **or** street sounds **inspire** urban poets.

In the first sentence, *responds* agrees in number with *reader,* which is the subject closer to it. The verb is singular because the subject is singular. In the second sentence, *inspire* agrees with *sounds,* which is the closer subject. The verb is plural because *sounds* is a plural subject.

Using the Correct Verb Form for Compound Subjects

For each sentence, write the subject and the correct form of the verb in parentheses.

1. Countee Cullen and Langston Hughes (write, writes) of Africa.
2. Africa and the South (is, are) settings in Hughes's poems.
3. Drums or pianos (appear, appears) often in Hughes's poetry.
4. Heritage and history (form, forms) Cullen's main themes.
5. W. S. Merwin and John Ashbery (is, are) poets.
6. Both Merwin and Ashbery (live, lives) in New York state.
7. The woods and gorges there (stir, stirs) these poets' emotions.
8. Neither cold nor snow (keep, keeps) them from their work.
9. Both Hughes and Cullen (influence, influences) young poets.
10. Blues, jazz, or gospel music often (provide, provides) a background for a poem.
11. Personal concerns and hope for a better world (drive, drives) poet Maya Angelou's work.
12. A poet and novelist (is, are) scheduled to read from her work in the next month.
13. Children and adults (enjoys, enjoy) Angelou's poetry.
14. Either a boy or a girl (appears, appear) in many of these poems.
15. Her inspiration and her subject (is, are) African American life.
16. Maya Angelou and Alice Walker (is, are) African American women and poets.
17. Neither Angelou nor Walker (has, have) ignored the problems of real people.
18. Either Africa or the rural South (is, are) the setting for much of Walker's work.
19. Both the novel and the film of Walker's *The Color Purple* (was, were) very popular.
20. A Welsh mother and a Russian Jewish father (was, were) Denise Levertov's parents.
21. Both her verse and her essays (is, are) lively and precise.
22. Either Levertov or Walker (was, were) a member of the award panel.
23. Neither yesterday's poets nor today's poets (has, have) found all the possibilities of poetry.
24. Both the sound and the meaning of a poem (is, are) important.
25. Poets and readers of poetry (contributes, contribute) to the future of poetry.

Grammar Review

SUBJECT-VERB AGREEMENT

In this passage from "Robert Frost: Visit to a Poet," Octavio Paz describes the wooded area near Robert Frost's cabin in Vermont. The passage has been annotated to show examples of subject-verb agreement.

Literature Model

from "Robert Frost: Visit to a Poet"
by Octavio Paz
translated from the Spanish by Michael Schmidt

In the air there was a scent of green, hot growth, thirsty. Not a tree, not a leaf stirred. A few clouds rested heavily, anchored in a blue, waveless gulf. A bird sang. I hesitated: "How much nicer it would be to stretch out under this elm! The sound of water is worth more than all the poets' words." I walked on for another ten minutes. . . . When I reached the top I could see the whole little valley; the blue mountains, the stream, the luminously green flatland, and, at the very bottom, the forest. The wind began to blow; everything swayed, almost cheerfully. All the leaves sang. I went toward the cabin. It was a little wooden shack, old, the paint flaked, grayed by the years. The windows were curtainless; I made a way through the underbrush and looked in. Inside, sitting in an easy chair, was an old man. Resting beside him was a woolly dog. When he saw me the man stood up and beckoned me to come around the other side. I did so and found him waiting for me at the door of his cabin.

> After the word *there*, a singular verb is followed by its singular noun subject.

> Agreement between a singular subject and verb that have a prepositional phrase between them

> Agreement between a singular pronoun subject and a singular verb

Grammar Review

Review: Exercise 1 **Making Verbs Agree with Noun and Pronoun Subjects**

For each sentence, write the subject and the correct form of the verb in parentheses. Underline the subject.

SAMPLE Octavio Paz (walk, walks) toward Robert Frost's cabin.
ANSWER <u>Octavio Paz</u> walks

1. He (listen, listens) to the still air.
2. Clouds (float, floats) lazily in the sky above.
3. One bird (begin, begins) to sing a song.
4. It (inspire, inspires) other birds to sing as well.
5. The flock (continue, continues) to sing their songs all afternoon.
6. Beside Robert Frost (lie, lies) his dog.
7. Both (notice, notices) Paz's arrival.
8. They (greet, greets) him with pleasure.
9. The summer day (please, pleases) each of them.
10. The distant mountains (appear, appears) blue.

Review: Exercise 2 **Making Forms of *Be, Do,* and *Have* Agree with Subjects**

For each sentence, write the subject and the correct form of the verb in parentheses.

SAMPLE The pine needles (is, are) soft under foot.
ANSWER needles are

1. The air (has, have) the scent of hot, green growth.
2. The clouds (is, are) anchored in the blue, waveless gulf.
3. A bird (has, have) started to sing.
4. The mountains (is, are) blue in the distance.
5. Frost's cabin (is, are) old, with flaking grayed paint.
6. It (do, does) look like a good place for a poet to work.
7. The windows (has, have) no curtains.
8. The dog (have, has) a woolly coat.
9. Paz and Frost (has, have) arranged this visit in advance.
10. The two men (do, does) feel glad for the chance to talk.

Review: Exercise 3   **Locating Subjects and Making Verbs Agree**

Write each sentence and complete it with the correct form of the verb in parentheses. Then underline the subject once and the verb twice. If the verb consists of two words, underline both words.

1. There (is, are) a few clouds hanging heavily overhead.
2. Paz (wants, want) to talk with Frost.
3. There (is, are) the sound of water running in a small brook.
4. (Do, does) Paz enjoy the sound of the water?
5. The fields at the bottom of the valley (is, are) luminously green.
6. Here (is, are) Frost's cabin at the top of the hill.
7. (Do, Does) Frost's cabin seem remote?
8. Where (is, are) the woolly dog and his master?
9. There (is, are) signs of movement inside the cabin.
10. The windows (is, are) curtainless.

Review: Exercise 4   **Making Verbs Agree with Collective Nouns and Other Special Subjects**

For each sentence, write the subject and the correct form of the verb in parentheses.

1. Binoculars (offer, offers) a view of the valley.
2. The woods (is, are) home to many small animals.
3. A cluster of trees (provides, provide) a moment of coolness.
4. Frost's "Fire and Ice" (discusses, discuss) heat and cold.
5. Twenty minutes of walking (makes, make) Paz feel hot.
6. A few minutes under the elms (seems, seem) appealing.
7. In the sun, the audience (waves, wave) small fans to stay cool.
8. A flock of crows (moves, move) like many shadows in the blue sky.
9. The fleet of clouds (clumps, clump) together, darkening the hills.
10. Mathematics (was, were) not of much interest to the young Frost.

Subject-Verb Agreement

Grammar Review

Review: Exercise 5   **Making Verbs Agree with Indefinite Pronoun Subjects**

For each sentence, write the subject and the correct form of the verb in parentheses.

1. Most of Robert Frost's poetry (deals, deal) with the landscape.
2. Most of his poems (uses, use) simple language.
3. Some of us (remembers, remember) his reading at Kennedy's inauguration.
4. Anyone present that day (treasures, treasure) the memory of Frost's reading.
5. Everybody (remembers, remember) Angelou's reading at Clinton's inauguration.
6. Nobody (puts, put) together a collection of American poetry without including Frost.
7. Something in his poems (makes, make) them touch our hearts.
8. Few (has, have) never read any of his works.
9. Most of us (knows, know) "Stopping by Woods on a Snowy Evening."
10. No one (is, are) likely to miss this poem's meaning.

Review: Exercise 6   **Making Verbs Agree with Compound Subjects**

For each sentence, write the subject and the correct form of the verb in parentheses.

1. Frost and Paz (discusses, discuss) their countries' landscapes.
2. Vermont and Mexico (does, do) not look much alike.
3. According to Frost, either fear or loneliness (drives, drive) people away from the countryside.
4. According to both men, failure or adventures (awaits, await) every poet.
5. Neither Frost nor Paz (trusts, trust) people who cannot laugh, especially at themselves.
6. According to Frost, neither solemn poets nor humorless professors (is, are) worthy of trust.
7. Neither fantasy nor science fiction (appeals, appeal) to Frost.
8. Both the work of young poets and the work of philosophers (interests, interest) him.
9. According to Paz, Frost and the Spaniard Antonio Machado (has, have) much in common.
10. Neither Frost nor Machado (has, have) any fondness for solemn topics.

Proofreading

The following passage is about French artist Pierre Bonnard, whose work appears below. Rewrite the passage, correcting the errors in spelling, capitalization, grammar, and usage. Add any missing punctuation. There are ten errors.

Pierre Bonnard

¹Pierre Bonnard (1867–1947) began his career as one of the french artists who rejected the more brighter colors and broken brush strokes of a popular style of art. ²Later Bonnard begun painting scenes of everyday life. ³Brighter colors and textured brush strokes marks his work.

⁴The painting below reflect Bonnard's change of style. ⁵Full of light and color, the painting capture the effect of sunlight streeming into a room. ⁶The view of the trees and woods are peaceful. ⁷The picture could show what Octavio Paz saw when he reached Robert Frosts cabin. ⁸The vivid blues and greens in the picture contrasts sharply with the deep red colors.

Pierre Bonnard, *Dining Room in the Country,* 1913

Review: Exercise 8

Mixed Review

For each sentence, write the correct form of the verb in parentheses.

Octavio Paz: Mexican Poet

1. Octavio Paz (is, are) a poet, an essayist, and a diplomat.
2. The Nobel Prize committee (has, have) awarded him its highest honor.
3. With his family, he (live, lives) in Mexico City.
4. His literary output (includes, include) poems, essays, and translations.
5. Most of his poems (is, are) written in Spanish.
6. His early poems (is, are) among his most powerful.
7. *On Poets and Others* (contains, contain) Paz's interview with Frost.
8. The poem "Renga" (shows, show) his grasp of languages.
9. Languages or literature (are, is) Paz's primary interest.
10. Mixcoac, one of Mexico City's suburbs, (was, were) his childhood home.
11. The colonial buildings of Mixcoac (reflects, reflect) a long heritage.
12. Paz's place in literary reference books (seems, seem) secure.
13. His six years as ambassador to India (influences, influence) his poetry.
14. The Eastern idea of *yin* and *yang* (appeals, appeal) to him.
15. The two sides of the Mexican coin (forms, form) an important image in Octavio Paz's work.
16. Anybody interested in literature (needs, need) to read Octavio Paz.
17. Many of his works (is, are) available in English.
18. *Selected Poems* (was, were) published in 1963.
19. Harvard and the University of Texas (is, are) important in Octavio Paz's educational career.
20. The United States, France, and Japan (was, were) early posts in his diplomatic career.
21. For younger writers, Paz (serves, serve) as a teacher and as a guide.
22. Both his father and his grandfather (was, were) involved in politics.
23. A lawyer and liberal reformer (was, were) Paz's grandfather Ireneo.
24. (Has, Have) Paz's writings become more available recently?
25. News of Octavio Paz's receiving the honor (was, were) no surprise to readers of his work.

Subject-Verb Agreement

Writing Application

TIME

For more about the writing process, see **TIME Facing the Blank Page**, pp. 97–107.

Subject-Verb Agreement in Writing

As he discusses the earth's complex biology in this passage from *Living Treasure*, Laurence Pringle is careful not to distract his readers with unmatched subjects and verbs. Read the passage, focusing especially on the italicized words.

> *Scientists are* dazzled and puzzled by the diversity of life on earth. *No one knows* how many different *kinds* of plants, animals, and other organisms there *are*. But we do know that the *organisms* identified so far *are* only a small fraction of all living things. There are *millions*—perhaps many millions—that *await* discovery.

Techniques with Subject-Verb Agreement

Try to apply some of Laurence Pringle's writing techniques when you revise your own work.

❶ Watch carefully for phrases and unusual sentence structures that make the subject difficult to identify. Notice below how removing a phrase from the sentence or rearranging the sentence to place the subject at the beginning allows you to check for subject-verb agreement:

HARD TO CHECK The *study* of living things *is* called biology

EASIER TO CHECK The *study is* called biology

❷ Pay special attention to subject-verb agreement when the subject is an indefinite pronoun. You must determine whether the indefinite pronoun is singular or plural.

INCORRECT VERSION *No one know* how many different kinds . . . there are.

CORRECT VERSION *No one knows* how many different kinds . . . there are.

Practice Practice these techniques by revising the following passage, using a separate sheet of paper. At each blank space, insert a verb that agrees with the sentence subject.

"The words of this song _____ me every time," complained Lucia. Look, both characters _____ throughout the song, yet she _____ never named. Still, the lovely melody _____ audiences to their feet every time. Very few songs _____ that. Here _____ some copies of the music. Let's give it a try." With that speech, Lucia signaled the beginning of our new school Chorus Club.

Glossary of Special Usage Problems

17.1 Using Troublesome Words I

Like all languages, English contains a number of confusing expressions. The following glossary will help you understand some of the more troublesome ones.

Word	Meaning	Example
accept	"to receive"	Most stores readily **accept** credit cards as well as cash.
except	"other than"	I have no money **except** a dollar.
all ready	"completely prepared"	I am **all ready** to go shopping.
already	"before" or "by this time"	I **already** spent all of my allowance for this week.
all together	"in a group"	We will shop **all together.**
altogether	"completely"	The shirts I liked were **altogether** too costly.
amount	"quantity of things thought of as a unit"	That **amount** of money will buy a large **number** of roses.
number	"quantity of things thought of as separate units"	
beside	"next to"	The shoe store is **beside** the bank.
besides	"in addition to"	**Besides** shoes it carries socks.
between	Use *between* for two people or things.	Choose **between** two styles.
among	Use *among* when talking about groups of three or more.	Distribute the suits **among** the seven stores.
bring	"to carry from a distant place to a closer one"	We **bring** goods into this country.
take	"to carry from a nearby place to a more distant one"	They **take** goods from this country to other lands.
choose	"to select" (present)	We **choose** items to import.
chose	"selected" (in the past)	Buyers **chose** silk last year.
in	"inside"	Factories are often **in** cities.
into	indicates movement from outside to a point within	Imports come **into** a country.

Glossary of Special Usage Problems

Exercise 1   Choosing the Correct Word

Write each sentence, choosing the correct word or words in parentheses.

1. Most countries (accept, except) foreign goods.
2. Trade (between, among) China and the United States has grown.
3. Food distribution has (all ready, already) improved in China.
4. Jan (choose, chose) silk from Hong Kong.
5. (Bring, Take) enough money, or yuan, with you when you go to Guangzhou.
6. The buyers flew (all together, altogether) to Shanghai.
7. Exports go out of a country, whereas imports come (in, into) it.
8. Most countries export all goods (accept, except) those needed by their people.
9. (Beside, Besides) machinery, China imports grain, cotton, and fertilizers.
10. China trades with (many, a lot of) countries, including Japan.

Exercise 2   Using the Correct Word

Write each sentence, using a word or words from the lesson. A definition of the word or a clue appears in parentheses.

1. Nigeria _____ to lower the price of oil. (selected)
2. Oil is loaded on tankers _____ the docks. (next to)
3. That tanker is _____ to sail to foreign lands. (completely prepared)
4. Nigeria produces most of its major foods _____ fish. (other than)
5. _____ oil, Nigeria exports rubber. (in addition to)
6. He will _____ our order to the mill. (carry to a distant place)
7. Many foreign companies operate oil wells _____ Nigeria. (inside)
8. Oil causes money to flow _____ Nigeria and the United States. (two places)
9. Farming, mining, and fishing are _____ their activities. (group of three)
10. Nigeria _____ foreign goods from trading partners. (receives)
11. Foreign ships _____ imports to Nigeria. (carry from a distant place)
12. The Nigerians stood on the dock _____, waiting for the ship. (in a group)
13. A person can _____ to be a farmer or a miner. (select)
14. When I arrived, the tanker was _____ at the dock. (by that time)
15. The oil was pumped _____ a tanker. (movement from outside to within)
16. That ship carried no goods _____ oil. (other than)
17. The captain and crew stood _____ their ship. (next to)
18. _____ this crop to the nearest market. (carry to a distant place)
19. Nigeria _____ to lease oil wells to foreign companies. (selected)
20. _____ Nigerian wells produce millions of barrels of oil daily. (in a group)

Word	Meaning	Example
its	the possessive form of *it*	A country may limit **its** imports.
it's	the contraction of *it is*	**It's** vital to protect jobs.
lay	"to put" or "to place"	Vendors **lay** shoes in rows.
lie	"to recline" or "to be positioned"	Fish **lie** packed in ice.
learn	"to receive knowledge"	We **learn** about trade.
teach	"to give knowledge"	Economists **teach** in colleges.
leave	"to go away"	I will **leave** on a sales trip.
let	"to allow"	**Let** them buy our product.
loose	"not firmly attached"	A **loose** bolt damages a product's quality.
lose	"to misplace" or "to fail to win"	Buyers often **lose** trust in a product.
raise	"to cause to move upward" or "to grow"	We **raise** the nets. They **raise** corn.
rise	"to move upward"	Porpoises **rise** from the water.
set	"to place" or "to put"	They **set** products on display.
sit	"to place oneself in a seated position"	**Sit** here and take orders.
than	*Than* introduces the second part of a comparison.	My price is lower **than** hers.
then	"at that time"	If prices are low, **then** buy.
their	*Their* is the possessive form of *they.*	**Their** products are well made.
they're	*They're* is the contraction of *they are.*	**They're** taught to work carefully.
who's	*Who's* is the contraction of *who is.*	**Who's** a great economist?
whose	*Whose* is the possessive form of *who.*	She is a person **whose** views are valued.

Exercise 3 — Choosing the Correct Word

Write each sentence, choosing the correct word in parentheses.

1. Italians are proud that (their, they're) country's products are in demand.
2. Italy produces more olives (than, then) any other country.
3. Tourists agree that (its, it's) a beautiful country.
4. Many Italian students (learn, teach) skills in industry.
5. We drove into Milan and (than, then) brought back fabrics.
6. We feared we would (loose, lose) our way.
7. The Alps (lay, lie) along Italy's northern border.
8. Italy looks like a boot (whose, who's) toe points toward Sicily.
9. Sardinia seems to (raise, rise) out of the Mediterranean Sea.
10. Many statues (sit, set) in the plazas of Italy's large cities.

Exercise 4 — Using the Correct Word

Write each sentence, using a word from the lesson. A definition of the word or a clue appears in parentheses.

1. Britain _____ its trade with Europe expand. (allows)
2. North Sea oil rigs _____ on steel pilings. (are positioned on)
3. These oil rigs can become _____. (not firmly attached)
4. Workers on these rigs _____ their families for months. (go away from)
5. Visits home _____ the spirits of these workers. (cause to move upward)
6. They can then _____ down and rest. (recline)
7. Great Britain is proud of _____ oil wells. (possessive form of *it*)
8. Today oil production is better _____ in the past. (used in comparisons)
9. Now oil rigs _____ from the North Sea. (move upward)
10. Once the people had to import _____ oil. (possessive form of *they*)
11. The British had much to _____ about mining oil. (receive knowledge)
12. By the 1970s, they could _____ others about oil rigs. (give knowledge)
13. First they pumped the oil, and _____ they exported the surplus. (at that time)
14. Britain is a country _____ mines are well known. (possessive form of *who*)
15. Much of the country _____ above rich deposits of coal. (is positioned)
16. _____ a fact that coal output has declined lately. (contraction of *it is*)
17. Most people use gas or oil to heat _____ homes. (possessive form of *they*)
18. The British will _____ little export revenue. (fail to win)
19. _____ still mining coal and natural gas. (contraction of *they are*)
20. They _____ above other minerals. (place themselves in a seated position)

Grammar Review

GLOSSARY OF SPECIAL USAGE PROBLEMS

The Clay Marble, by Minfong Ho, tells of a Cambodian family forced to flee when Vietnamese troops invaded Cambodia in 1980. In the following passage, the narrator, twelve-year-old Dara, and her friend Nea load rice seed onto a cart.

Literature Model

from *The Clay Marble*
by Minfong Ho

Half running and half stumbling with the sack of rice held between us, Nea and I headed for one of the oxcarts, probably looking very much like a crab scuttling across the sand. But we managed to reach the cart, and even to swing the sack neatly into it. Nea wiped the sweat off her forehead. "We did it," she said, sounding very surprised.

"I told you we could," I grinned, panting.

Again and again we did this, moving sack after sack from the shelter of the blue tarp and into the wagon. After a while there was a layer two-deep of the precious rice-seed bags on the bottom of the oxcart.

If we planted the rice seeds with care and if the weather was good, I knew that the seeds we brought home in the cart would be enough to supply half the village next year. I felt a deep satisfaction that these seeds, at least, would not be broken and crushed to feed the soldiers here.

> *Between* used with two people

> *Into* used to indicate movement from outside to within

> *Brought* used to mean "carried from a distant place to a closer one"

Grammar Review

Review: Exercise 1   **Making Usage Choices**

The following sentences were suggested by passages from *The Clay Marble*. Write the correct word in parentheses to complete each sentence.

SAMPLE   Carrying each sack of rice (between, among) them, the two girls loaded the cart.

ANSWER   between

1. Dara and Nea planned to (bring, take) the rice back to their home in Cambodia.
2. The countries of Asia (raise, rise) much rice.
3. They had (all ready, already) repaired the oxcart.
4. Oxcarts find much use (between, among) the people of Cambodia.
5. They placed the sacks (beside, besides) each other.
6. Dara hoped her family would be ready to plant the seeds (all together, altogether).
7. When the girls finished their work, the oxcart was (all ready, already) for the trip home.
8. Jantu (leave, let) Dara play with the clay toys.
9. Many poor people must make (their, they're) own toys.
10. Clay gets (its, it's) color from the materials in it.
11. Farmers (learn, teach) their children that too much clay is bad for crops.
12. One day Jantu gathered some (loose, lose) clay, rolled it into a perfect sphere, and gave it to Dara.
13. "(Its, It's) a magic marble," said Jantu.
14. Dara believed in (its, it's) magical powers.
15. The girl had to (learn, teach) that the magic was in her.
16. Thick layers of clay (lay, lie) under the rich, black soil.
17. Artists often use clay when (their, they're) sculpting a person or an animal.
18. Jantu, (who's, whose) brother was hurt, had to go to the hospital with him.
19. Dara was afraid to (leave, let) her friend.
20. (Than, Then) she remembered the magic marble.
21. Bravely the girl (choose, chose) to look for her family on her own.
22. Dara knew that it was (all together, altogether) possible for her to fail.
23. But she would not (accept, except) defeat.
24. Now her hopes of finding her family began to (raise, rise).
25. Dara's determination, rather (than, then) the marble, gave her courage.

Review: Exercise 2

Proofreading

The following passage is about the cultivation of tea in China, which is illustrated in the work below. Rewrite the passage, correcting the errors in spelling, grammar, and usage. Add any missing punctuation. There are ten errors.

Tea Cultivation in Ancient China

[1]By the ninth century into China, the cultivation of tea was subject to well-established procedures and traditions. [2]The seeds first had to be planted in sandy soil to leave them drain properly. [3]When the seeds sprouted, the farmers lightly watered the plants, using the same water in which the seeds had all ready been washed. [4]The figures in *Tea Cultivation* is watering the young tea plants and fertilizing them. [5]According to Lu Yü, who's essay on tea helped popularize tea cultivation, fertilizer made from the wastes of silkworms was prefered.

Artist unknown, China, *Tea Cultivation*, nineteenth century

(continued)

Glossary of Special Usage Problems

⁶Rice is another major crop rose in China and in many other Asian countries. ⁷To Dara and her family in *The Clay Marble,* rice meaned life. ⁸Planting the seeds enabled them to rebuild they're lives. ⁹Accept for the rice, they might have starved.

Review: Exercise 3

Mixed Review

In the following exercise, you will learn more about rice, which was so important to Dara and Nea. Write the correct word or words in parentheses to complete each sentence.

1. About half of the world's people eat rice as (their, they're) main food.
2. Although wheat is important here, (its, it's) rice that's important in Asia.
3. (Accept, Except) for rice, many Asians have little to eat.
4. In Asia (a lot of, many) people eat rice three times a day.
5. Rice plays a role in the religious life (between, among) people of India.
6. (Its, It's) thought that the throwing of rice at weddings came from India.
7. Many Asian farmers (raise, rise) rice on their land.
8. Cereal grains (beside, besides) rice include oats, rye, wheat, and barley.
9. Rice farmers must (choose, chose) to plant in areas that have much rain.
10. Mature rice plants (raise, rise) from two to six feet above the ground.
11. Rice farmers (leave, let) the grains in the head of each plant ripen.
12. A rice grain has a rough hull, or shell, (in, into) which the kernels are found.
13. Each kernel is surrounded by (its, it's) brown skins, called bran coats.
14. Kernel, bran coats, and hull are (all together, altogether) in the rice grain.
15. We usually (loose, lose) the bran coats when rice is milled.
16. Valuable vitamins and minerals (lay, lie) within the bran coats.
17. Rather than (accept, except) this loss, we add these ingredients back to milled rice.
18. When rice plants are (all ready, already) to harvest, their stalks are cut.
19. The stalks are (than, then) left in the sun to dry.
20. Some farmers (bring, take) their sun-dried stalks to a thresher.

Writing Application

TIME

For more about the writing process, see **TIME Facing the Blank Page,** pp. 97–107.

Usage in Writing

A persuasive argument can be seriously weakened by a usage error. In Bel Kaufman's article about the value of public libraries, she avoided confusing certain similar words. Note the italicized words as you read this passage from "The Liberry."

> It seems to me that especially now, when there are so many people in our city *whose* language is not English, *whose* homes are barren of books, who are daily seduced by clamorous offers of instant diversion, especially now we must hold on to something that will endure when the movie is over, the television set broken, the class dismissed for the last time.
>
> For many, the public library is the only *quiet* place in an *unquiet* world; a refuge from the violence and ugliness outside; the only space available for privacy or thought.

Techniques with Usage

Try to apply some of Bel Kaufman's writing techniques when you write and revise your own work.

❶ Make your meaning clear by using *whose* correctly to indicate possession and *who's* when a contraction of *who* and *is* is appropriate:

INCORRECT USAGE *who's* language

KAUFMAN'S VERSION *whose* language

❷ Be alert to frequently confused word pairs, such as *quiet* and *quite.* Choose the correct word to help keep your writing accurate and precise.

INCORRECT USAGE the public library is the only *quite* place in an un*quite* world . . .

KAUFMAN'S VERSION the public library is the only *quiet* place in an un*quiet* world . . .

Glossary of Special Usage Problems

Practice Gain practice distinguishing confusing pairs of words as you revise the passage below. Check each underlined word. If the word is correct, write *correct* on your paper. If the word is wrong, write the correct word.

"Be sure to <u>take</u> your costume when you come to dress rehearsal. <u>It's</u> our last chance to get everything <u>already</u> for the show." Mr. Oberg, <u>who's</u> voice filled the theater as he spoke to the cast, then <u>sat</u> each student's script on a pile <u>beside</u> the stairs to the stage. "Pick these up as you <u>leave</u>. <u>There</u> all marked with last-minute reminders and tips. And don't <u>loose</u> them," he implored, "or I won't <u>leave</u> you attend the cast party!"

Diagraming Simple Subjects and Simple Predicates

Every sentence contains a subject and a predicate. To diagram a sentence, first draw a horizontal line. Then draw a vertical line that crosses the horizontal line.

To the left of the vertical line, write the simple subject. To the right of the vertical line, write the simple predicate. Use capital letters as they appear in the sentence, but do not use punctuation.

Apples grow.

| Apples | grow |

Be sure to write only the simple subject and the simple predicate in this part of the diagram. Remember that the simple predicate can include a helping verb.

Some **apples are falling** already.

| apples | are falling |

Exercise 1   Diagraming Simple Subjects and Simple Predicates

Diagram each simple subject and simple predicate.

1. Apples fell.
2. They have ripened.
3. Joan tastes one.
4. Workers pick the fruit.
5. Some people are resting.
6. The orchard is busy.
7. Many people are working.
8. We trimmed the tree.
9. Mom removed the old branches.
10. Birds fill the orchard.

Diagraming the Four Kinds of Sentences

The simple subject and simple predicate of the four kinds of sentences are diagramed below. Note that the location of the simple subject and simple predicate in a sentence diagram is always the same, regardless of the word order in the sentence.

DECLARATIVE

Many **people eat** pears.

people	eat

INTERROGATIVE

Do many **people eat** pears?

people	Do eat

IMPERATIVE

Eat a pear.

(you)	Eat

EXCLAMATORY

How many pears **people eat!**

people	eat

Note that in an interrogative sentence, the subject often comes between the two parts of a verb phrase. In an imperative sentence, the word *you* is understood to be the simple subject.

Exercise 2   **Diagraming Simple Subjects and Predicates**

Diagram the simple subject and the simple predicate of each sentence.

1. I brought a pear for lunch.
2. Do you like pears?
3. Taste this one.
4. This pear is delicious.
5. How delicious this pear is!
6. Pears are good in salads.
7. Do you eat pears often?
8. Try some pear juice.
9. Have you ever eaten pear pie?
10. Slice these pears.
11. Pear trees grow everywhere.
12. Do the trees grow high?
13. Pears have few calories.
14. How tall these trees are!
15. American pears came from France.
16. Many pears grow in California.
17. Are these pears ripe?
18. Most pears ripen in the fall.
19. How juicy these pears are!
20. Wash these pears.

18.3 Diagraming Direct and Indirect Objects

In a sentence, a direct object usually comes after the verb. In a sentence diagram, place the direct object to the right of the action verb. Use a vertical line to separate the direct object from the verb. The vertical line does *not* extend below the horizontal line.

The Cruzes grow **apples.**

Cruzes	grow	apples

They have an **orchard.**

They	have	orchard

A sentence can also have an indirect object. In a sentence diagram, place an indirect object on a line below and to the right of the verb. Join it to the verb with a slanted line.

Rosa showed **us** the trees.

Rosa	showed	trees
	us	

Exercise 3 Diagraming Sentences

Diagram the simple subject, the simple predicate, and the direct object of each sentence. If there is an indirect object, diagram it also.

1. Our class was studying agriculture.
2. Mrs. Hong showed us some peaches.
3. She told the students many historical facts.
4. The ancient Chinese discovered peaches.
5. They gave the trees care.
6. Artists painted pictures of the lovely fruit.
7. People gave their friends this treat.
8. Travelers took Europeans some peaches.
9. Europe developed different varieties.
10. American colonists brought them to Virginia.

18.4 Diagraming Adjectives and Adverbs

An adjective modifies a noun or a pronoun. In a diagram, write the adjective on a slanted line beneath the noun or pronoun it modifies. Diagram the articles *a, an,* and *the* as you would diagram other adjectives.

Many workers had picked **the ripe** tomatoes.

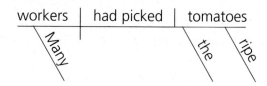

An adverb can modify a verb, an adjective, or another adverb. Note how adverbs are diagramed.

We eat **very ripe** tomatoes **quite often.**

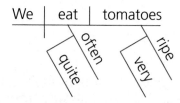

Exercise 4 **Diagraming Sentences**

Diagram each sentence.

1. Ancient people used wild plums.
2. Many medicines contained the fruit.
3. The Romans first ate the purple delicacy.
4. Early Americans ate plums quite often.
5. New settlers then encountered the plums.
6. This rather tart fruit did not please the new settlers.
7. The Europeans had already cultivated plums.
8. Japanese plums please many people.
9. Varieties include many popular types.
10. All plums have smooth skins.

Diagraming Predicate Nouns and Predicate Adjectives

In a sentence diagram, a direct object follows the action verb.

We bought grapefruit.

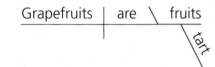

A predicate noun follows a linking verb in the complete predicate of a sentence. In a sentence diagram, place the predicate noun after the linking verb. Draw a slanted line to separate the linking verb from the predicate noun.

Grapefruits are tart **fruits.**

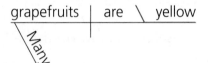

Diagram a predicate adjective as you would a predicate noun.

Many grapefruits are **yellow**

grapefruits | are \ yellow

Many

Exercise 5   Diagraming Sentences

Diagram each sentence.

1. Grapefruit is a healthful food.
2. Fruits are nutritious.
3. Some grapefruits are seedless.
4. They were popular.
5. Many grapefruits taste sour.
6. This can be an enjoyable taste.
7. Heavy grapefruits are juicy.
8. The grapefruit is a favorite breakfast food.
9. The fruit is a West Indian native.
10. It is popular lately.

Diagraming Sentences

In a sentence diagram, connect modifiers to the words that they modify. If the modifier is a prepositional phrase, connect the phrase to the word that it modifies. The model below shows a prepositional phrase used as an adjective.

The berries **on those bushes** are ripe.

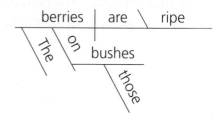

In this sentence, the prepositional phrase *on those bushes* modifies the noun *berries*.

The same phrase can be used as an adverb.

Raspberries grow **on those bushes.**

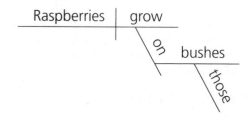

In this sentence, the adverb phrase modifies the verb *grow*.

Exercise 6   Diagraming Sentences

Diagram each sentence.

1. Pineapples come from the tropics.
2. Explorers discovered them in the Caribbean.
3. The people of the area ate pineapples frequently.
4. Crowns of pineapples hung over the huts.
5. Many pineapples grow in Hawaii.

18.7 Diagraming Compound Sentence Parts

Coordinating conjunctions such as *and, but,* and *or* are used to join words, phrases, and sentences. To diagram compound parts of a sentence, place the second part of the compound below the first. Then write the coordinating conjunction on a dotted line connecting the two parts.

COMPOUND SUBJECT

Lemons or limes add flavor.

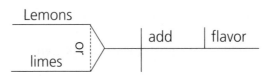

COMPOUND PREDICATE

Trees **grow and blossom.**

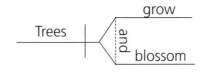

COMPOUND DIRECT OBJECT

Lemon trees produce **leaves and blossoms.**

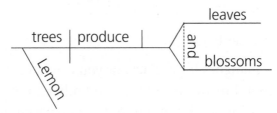

Exercise 7 — Diagraming Sentences

Diagram each sentence.

1. Oranges and peaches came from China.
2. Traders bargained or bartered.
3. Traders sought fruit and spices.
4. Oranges provide flavor and color.
5. Oranges and peaches are sweet and flavorful.

Diagraming Compound Sentences

To diagram compound sentences, diagram each main clause separately. If the main clauses are connected by a conjunction such as *and, but,* or *or,* place the conjunction on a solid horizontal line, and connect it to the verbs of each clause by vertical dotted lines. If the clauses are connected by a semicolon, use a vertical dotted line to connect the verbs of each clause.

Mangoes are grown in tropical climates, **and** people enjoy them.

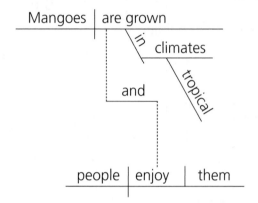

Exercise 8   Diagraming Sentences

Diagram each sentence.

1. You can eat mangoes for a snack, or you can have them for dessert.
2. Explorers found mangoes in India, and other countries soon grew them.
3. Mango leaves are slender, and pink flowers bloom on the trees.
4. Sometimes mangoes are snacks, but at other times, they are a staple food.
5. The mango is the fruit of an evergreen tree, and it grows in tropical regions.
6. The mango came to America, but it has not been very popular here.
7. The mango tree is very attractive, and it may grow quite tall.
8. The fruit resembles an apple, but it is heavier.
9. The fruit can be eaten with a spoon, or it can be enjoyed from the hand.
10. The mango is quite common in local markets, and we must try some.

Diagraming Complex Sentences with Adjective and Adverb Clauses

To diagram a complex sentence with an adjective clause, place the adjective clause below the main clause. Draw a dotted line between the relative pronoun of the adjective clause and the word it modifies in the main clause. Position the relative pronoun according to its function in the adjective clause.

ADJECTIVE CLAUSE

People **who grow fruit** work hard.

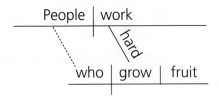

Similarly, diagram an adverb clause below the main clause. Draw a dotted line between the verb of the adverb clause and the verb in the main clause. Write the subordinating conjunction on the dotted line.

ADVERB CLAUSE

As a banana ripens, it turns yellow.

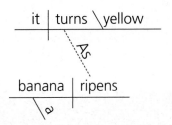

| Exercise 9 | **Diagraming Sentences** |

Diagram each sentence.

1. Bananas are green before they ripen.
2. A banana that is brownish is very ripe.
3. Bananas smell fragrant when they are ripe.
4. When a banana has turned yellow, its seeds have matured.
5. Bananas are shipped before they are ripe.

Capitalization

19.1 Capitalizing Sentences, Quotations, and Letter Parts

A capital letter appears at the beginning of a sentence. A capital letter also marks the beginning of a direct quotation and the salutation and closing of a letter.

RULE 1: Capitalize the first word of every sentence.

Pioneers pushed the American frontier westward.

RULE 2: Capitalize the first word of a direct quotation that is a complete sentence. A direct quotation gives a speaker's exact words.

Tyrone said, "**T**he pioneers acted very bravely."

RULE 3: When a quoted sentence is interrupted by explanatory words, such as *she said*, do not begin the second part of the sentence with a capital letter.

"They left their homes," said Lee, "**s**o they could improve their lives."

When the second part of a quotation is a new sentence, put a period after the interrupting expression and begin the second part of the quotation with a capital letter.

"Many pioneers went west for the rich farmland," said Maria. "**T**hey also wanted to build new homes."

RULE 4: Do not capitalize an indirect quotation. An indirect quotation does not repeat a person's exact words and does not appear in quotation marks. It is often introduced by the word *that*.

Tanya read **that m**any pioneers traveled in Conestoga wagons.

RULE 5: Capitalize the first word in the salutation and closing of a letter. Capitalize the title and name of the person addressed.

Dear **M**rs. **J**ohnson,   **Y**ours truly,
Dear friend,   **S**incerely,

Exercise 1   Capitalizing Sentences, Quotations, and Letter Parts

Write each sentence, using capital letters where needed. If an item contains no error, write *correct*.

1. we were preparing a report on westward expansion.
2. Joan said, "the pioneers needed many skills."
3. "they hunted," said Carlos, "and farmed."
4. Ann added, "some pioneers were trappers."
5. "they also had skill in building," she said. "many pioneers built their own homes."
6. Joan said, "most pioneers made their own clothing."
7. "can you imagine life without stores?" asked Ann. "pioneers had to take with them everything they couldn't make themselves."
8. we decided that pioneers had to be self-sufficient.
9. "most pioneers kept a cow for milk, butter, and cheese," said Carlos. "they also raised chickens for meat and eggs."
10. "before the railroads," said Joan, "pioneers traveled by wagon."
11. Carlos said that the wagons were pulled by oxen.
12. he added, "a loaded wagon might weigh a ton."
13. most families traveled in groups.
14. in one book, Ann read, "the normal speed for a wagon was two miles an hour."
15. "the trip from Missouri to California was long," said Joan. "it often took five months."
16. "one trail the pioneers followed was the Santa Fe trail," Joan added, "which went from Missouri to New Mexico."
17. "we followed part of that trail last summer," Lee told us. "in some places you can still see wagon ruts!"
18. pioneers wrote letters that began, "dear loved ones."
19. they signed them, "with much love."
20. pioneers and other travelers left their letters at the trading posts that dotted the trails.
21. Joan asked, "would you have gone west, Carlos?"
22. Carlos replied, "no, I would have stayed home."
23. "the railroad," said Ann, "opened the West."
24. "stagecoach company owners resented the railroads' competition," Joan said. "the railroads won in the end."
25. "they were faster than stagecoaches," Lee added, "and more comfortable too."

"Most of these people," said Mihn, "live in cities or towns."

Capitalizing People's Names and Titles

A common noun is the general name of a person, place, thing, or idea. A common noun is not capitalized. A proper noun names a particular person, place, or thing and is capitalized.

RULE 1: Capitalize the names of people and the initials that stand for their names.

> Meriwether Lewis   Susan B. Anthony   J. F. Cooper

RULE 2: Capitalize a title or an abbreviation of a title when it comes before a person's name or when it is used instead of a name.

> General Lee   Sen. John Glenn   Mrs. Adé
> Did Lieutenant Clark say, "Yes, Captain, I'll go with you"?

Do not capitalize a title that follows a person's name or is used as a common noun.

> Clark himself was later promoted to captain.
> Thomas Jefferson, then president, planned the expedition.

RULE 3: Capitalize the names and abbreviations of academic degrees that follow a person's name. Capitalize *Jr.* and *Sr.*

> M. Katayama, M.D.   Jan Rangel, Ph.D.   Robert Ayers Jr.

RULE 4: Capitalize words that show family relationships when used as titles or as substitutes for a person's name.

> In 1960 Father retraced the steps of Lewis and Clark.
> He was accompanied by Uncle Bill.

Do not capitalize words that show family relationships when they follow a possessive noun or pronoun.

> Sharon's aunt Janet wrote an article about the trip.

RULE 5: Always capitalize the pronoun *I.*

> Social studies is the subject I like most.

Exercise 2   Capitalizing People's Names and Titles

Write each item, using capital letters where needed.

1. john c. frémont
2. c. w. peale
3. king george
4. aunt lena
5. lynn bader, m.d.
6. his uncle ted
7. dr. chiang
8. max bond jr.
9. general ellen jones
10. ms. amanda swenson
11. president thomas jefferson
12. cartier, an explorer
13. grandma shepard
14. governor barbara roberts
15. mr. william p. scholz
16. representative kasich
17. uncle morris
18. susan curtis, m.s.w.
19. jedediah strong smith
20. queen elizabeth II

Exercise 3   Using Capital Letters

Write each sentence, using capital letters where needed for names, titles, and abbreviations.

1. Meriwether lewis and william clark explored the Northwest all the way to the Pacific Ocean.
2. President jefferson sponsored their expedition.
3. The president had known meriwether lewis as a young boy.
4. He chose his former neighbor—now captain lewis—to lead the expedition.
5. Jefferson wrote, "i could have no hesitation in confiding the enterprise to him."
6. Lewis himself invited clark, his former company commander, to serve as coleader.
7. A Shoshone woman named sacajawea was one member of the expedition.
8. Sacajawea and her husband, toussaint charbonneau, served as interpreters.
9. Sacajawea's brother, cameahwait, a Shoshone chief, provided the expedition with pack horses.
10. Captain clark adored sacajawea's son, i believe.
11. Clark helped the boy, jean baptiste, with his schooling.
12. Can you imagine his saying, "Thank you, captain"?
13. Later jean baptiste led jefferson clark to the West Coast.
14. Of course, jefferson's father had helped lead the lewis and clark expedition.
15. In 1807 captain lewis became governor of Louisiana.
16. Lewis's uncle, fielding lewis, had married general george washington's sister.
17. His uncle charles was a patriot who fought in the Revolutionary War.
18. The story of lewis and clark's great adventure was published in 1814.
19. A magazine editor, mr. nicholas biddle, edited the book.
20. Journals kept by patrick gass and john ordway, two sergeants, helped biddle.

19.3 Capitalizing Place Names

The names of specific places are proper nouns and are capitalized. Do not capitalize articles and prepositions that are part of geographical names, however.

RULE 1: Capitalize the names of cities, counties, states, countries, and continents.

    Houston   Orange County   Iowa   Japan

RULE 2: Capitalize the names of bodies of water and geographical features.

    Mediterranean Sea   Gulf of Mexico   Cape Ann
    Niagara Falls   Mojave Desert   Atlantic Ocean

RULE 3: Capitalize the names of sections of the country.

    New England   the Midwest   the Far West

RULE 4: Capitalize compass points when they refer to a specific section of the country.

    the West Coast   the Southeast   the North

Do not capitalize compass points when they indicate direction.

    Los Angeles is south of San Francisco.

Do not capitalize adjectives derived from words indicating direction.

    easterly wind   western Texas

RULE 5: Capitalize the names of streets and highways.

    Monroe Street   Route 66

RULE 6: Capitalize the names of buildings, bridges, and monuments.

    Chrysler Building   Brooklyn Bridge

RULE 7: Capitalize the names of celestial bodies.

    Pluto   North Star   the Milky Way

Capitalization

Exercise 4   Capitalizing Place Names

Write each word or group of words, using capital letters where needed.

1. europe
2. the pacific northwest
3. south dakota
4. the east coast
5. omaha
6. canada
7. mojave desert
8. lexington avenue
9. the great lakes
10. the big dipper
11. sioux city
12. northern california
13. montague expressway
14. mount rushmore
15. franklin county
16. rocky mountains
17. empire state building
18. west virginia
19. lincoln memorial
20. saturn

Exercise 5   Using Capital Letters

Write each sentence, using capital letters where needed for geographical names.

1. Adventurers from spain came to the New World in the early sixteenth century.
2. From island bases in the caribbean sea, they set sail to conquer mexico, central america, and south america.
3. Like Hernando Cortés, they came to the americas looking for gold.
4. These adventurers crossed the harsh, lonely deserts of mexico and reached monterey.
5. In mexico, Cortés conquered the Aztec capital city, tenochtitlán.
6. This great city was built on an island in lake texcoco.
7. Spanish explorers searched for the Fountain of Youth in florida.
8. They explored several islands in the caribbean sea.
9. These Spaniards encountered natural wonders, like the grand canyon, but they cared only for riches.
10. A mine on mount potosí in bolivia yielded tons of silver.
11. Spanish treasure ships sailed across the atlantic ocean to spain.
12. American gold and silver made spain the richest nation in europe.
13. By 1600 spain controlled mexico, peru, all of central america, and florida.
14. The Spaniards even explored what is now called the southwest.
15. One explorer reached the mississippi river in 1541.
16. Other explorers traveled up the pacific coast as far as northern california.
17. They established military posts and missions along a road called el camino réal.
18. Spanish heritage can be seen today in the san josé mission in san antonio, texas, and other missions.
19. Many United States cities have Spanish names, such as san diego.
20. Spain held its outposts in north america for more than two hundred years.

19.4 Capitalizing Other Proper Nouns and Adjectives

Many nouns besides the names of people and places are proper nouns. Adjectives that are formed from proper nouns are called proper adjectives. For example, the proper adjective *Egyptian* is formed from the proper noun *Egypt.*

RULE 1: Capitalize the names of clubs, organizations, businesses, institutions, and political parties.

    Data Corporation   Boy Scouts   Republican Party

RULE 2: Capitalize brand names but not the nouns following them.

    Cruncho peanut butter   Spiffy cleaning fluid

RULE 3: Capitalize the names of important historical events, periods of time, and documents.

    Battle of Yorktown   Bronze Age   Bill of Rights

RULE 4: Capitalize names of days of the week, months of the year, and holidays. Do not capitalize names of the seasons.

    Thursday   April   Memorial Day   summer

RULE 5: Capitalize the first word, the last word, and all important words in the title of a book, play, short story, poem, essay, article, film, television series, song, magazine, newspaper, and chapter of a book.

    A Wrinkle in Time   "The Raven"   *Washington Post*

RULE 6: Capitalize the names of ethnic groups, nationalities, and languages.

    Asian   German   Spanish

RULE 7: Capitalize proper adjectives that are formed from the names of ethnic groups and nationalities.

    Asian languages   Italian food

Exercise 6   Capitalizing Proper Nouns and Adjectives

Write the following items, using capital letters where needed.

1. sierra club
2. thanksgiving day
3. belgian waffles
4. *los angeles times*
5. war of 1812
6. halloween
7. the middle ages
8. sneezo tissues
9. october
10. french horn
11. world war II
12. *national geographic*
13. chase manhattan bank
14. *anne of green gables*
15. "casey at the bat"
16. saturday
17. presidents' day
18. girl scouts
19. associated press
20. best friend dog food

Exercise 7   Using Capital Letters

Write each sentence, using capital letters where needed for proper nouns and adjectives. Write *correct* if the sentence has no errors.

1. James Marshall found gold in California on january 24, 1848.
2. In the spring, thousands of prospectors arrived at Sutter's Mill.
3. Hawaiian, japanese, chinese, european, and american fortune seekers joined the rush.
4. The song "my darling clementine" immortalized these miners as '49ers.
5. One woman's letters appeared in the *california monthly magazine.*
6. Have you read *the california gold rush?*
7. The book *three weeks in the gold mines* was popular.
8. A similar rush to Colorado took place in 1858.
9. In 1859 a newspaper called the *rocky mountain news* reported on the search for gold in Colorado.
10. In 1875 the homestake mine was the West's most productive gold mine.
11. Long after the civil war, gold was found in Alaska.
12. During autumn 1898, three scandinavian men found gold near Nome.
13. The alaska gold mining company tried to steal miners' claims.
14. Its owner was sentenced to jail on february 11, 1901.
15. In 1906 a federal mint opened in Denver.
16. In 1942 the war production board shut down gold mines until the end of world war II.
17. People have prized gold down through the ages.
18. Alchemists in the middle ages tried to create gold from other metals.
19. Gold covers the massachusetts statehouse dome.
20. Gold was even used as medicine by chinese doctors.

Grammar Review

CAPITALIZATION

In "The Pomegranate Trees," a short story by William Saroyan, the narrator's uncle Melik attempts to grow pomegranates in the middle of a desert. In the following excerpt from the story, the narrator reflects on his uncle's dream of creating a garden on the land. The passage has been annotated to show some of the rules of capitalization covered in this unit.

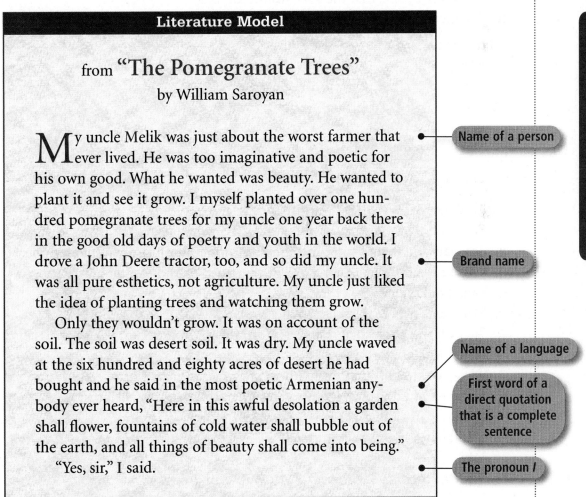

Literature Model

from "The Pomegranate Trees"
by William Saroyan

My uncle Melik was just about the worst farmer that ever lived. He was too imaginative and poetic for his own good. What he wanted was beauty. He wanted to plant it and see it grow. I myself planted over one hundred pomegranate trees for my uncle one year back there in the good old days of poetry and youth in the world. I drove a John Deere tractor, too, and so did my uncle. It was all pure esthetics, not agriculture. My uncle just liked the idea of planting trees and watching them grow.

Only they wouldn't grow. It was on account of the soil. The soil was desert soil. It was dry. My uncle waved at the six hundred and eighty acres of desert he had bought and he said in the most poetic Armenian anybody ever heard, "Here in this awful desolation a garden shall flower, fountains of cold water shall bubble out of the earth, and all things of beauty shall come into being."

"Yes, sir," I said.

Name of a person

Brand name

Name of a language

First word of a direct quotation that is a complete sentence

The pronoun I

Capitalization

Grammar Review

Review: Exercise 1 **Capitalizing Sentences and Quotations**

Find any errors in capitalization. Write the words correctly.

1. uncle Melik wanted to bring beauty to the desert.
2. "I think you understand," he said, "Why I bought this land."
3. "Yes," I said. "you want to plant a garden here."
4. The narrator thought that His Uncle was a poet.
5. "most farmers don't try to grow pomegranate trees on dry desert land," explained the narrator.
6. "I'll help you plant the trees," the narrator said, "But they won't grow in this soil."
7. he told his uncle that the soil was too dry.
8. his uncle was convinced that beauty would grow on his land.
9. He said that Fountains of fresh, cold water would bubble out of the ground.
10. Uncle Melik said, "here in this awful desolation a garden shall flower.

Review: Exercise 2 **Capitalizing Direct Quotations**

Find any errors in capitalization. Write the words correctly.

1. "William Saroyan," said Marge, "Wrote about people he met."
2. She added, "one story was about a Parisian shoemaker with a pet owl."
3. Saroyan said that Chance meetings are sometimes the most memorable.
4. "I read," said Jorge, "That Saroyan cherished most meeting his newborn son and daughter."
5. "He met a lot of characters!" said Nicki. "my favorite is Aram Joseph."
6. "Joseph was a wrestler," Marge put in, "Who drove a car backward at sixty miles per hour."
7. "Yes," Nicki said. "that was a funny story."
8. Jorge asked, "do you remember the story about Saroyan's job at the cemetery in San Francisco?"
9. "All the best jobs," he reminded us, "Were held by men named Johnson."
10. "One of them," added Nicki, "Made up funny slogans."

Review: Exercise 3 **Capitalizing People's Names and Titles**

Find any errors in capitalization. Write the words correctly.

1. William saroyan wrote about strange jobs he had had.
2. For a few days, he worked for mr. papulius, who published *The Macaroni Review.*
3. A man and a woman named mr. and mrs. Goostenhouse shared the office with Papulius.
4. Papulius called his dentist, dr. john r. skouras, d.d.s., while Saroyan was in the office.
5. Saroyan had a job helping his Uncle Melik plant pomegranate trees.
6. Saroyan wrote a short story about uncle melik.
7. Saroyan also worked at a cemetery owned by the johnson family.
8. The man Saroyan remembers best was vice president, mr. Johnson.
9. Among other things, the Vice President wrote slogans for the cemetery.
10. "When i quit after a month, he was terribly disappointed," Saroyan wrote.

Review: Exercise 4 **Capitalizing Place Names**

Find any errors in capitalization. Write the words correctly.

1. Armenia is an ancient kingdom of western asia.
2. Today its land is divided among iran, turkey, and the republic of Armenia.
3. Armenia is located Southeast of the black sea and southwest of the caspian sea.
4. A mountainous region, it reaches 13,418 feet at mount aragats.
5. The euphrates river and the araks river have their sources there.
6. A few Armenians were invited to the americas by the early Colonists.
7. Fleeing from Turkish oppression between the 1890s and the 1920s, many Armenians went to other countries, such as greece, russia, bulgaria, france, england, and the balkans.
8. Because of trouble in the middle east, another wave of immigration started in 1975.
9. New York, massachusetts, and rhode island attracted the most Armenians.
10. Many Armenian farmers settled in the san joaquin valley of california.

Grammar Review

Review: Exercise 5   **Capitalizing Other Proper Nouns**

Find any errors in capitalization. Write the words correctly.

1. William Saroyan was born in the summer, on august 31, 1908.
2. That was before the beginning of world war I.
3. His parents were armenians who came to the United States.
4. Armenia's fight for independence was opposed by the russians and the turks.
5. The russo-Turkish treaty of 1921 divided the country.
6. Saroyan's autobiography described his life as an armenian american.
7. Its title is *my name is aram.*
8. Saroyan was awarded the Pulitzer Prize for his play *the time of your life.*
9. In Joseph Pulitzer's will, he gave money to columbia university so that annual awards for journalism, the Pulitzer Prizes, could be awarded.
10. Saroyan also wrote short stories such as "the daring young man on the flying trapeze."

Review: Exercise 6   **Capitalizing Proper Adjectives**

Write each of the following phrases correctly.

SAMPLE   armenian language
ANSWER   Armenian language

1. chinese people
2. roman ruins
3. spanish olives
4. indian subcontinent
5. alaskan sled dogs
6. mexican food
7. french fashions
8. swiss cheese
9. greek dances
10. hawaiian volcanoes
11. african nations
12. russian winters
13. polish sausages
14. english countryside
15. brazilian coffee
16. egyptian pyramids
17. italian movies
18. vietnamese jungles
19. cuban government
20. japanese cars

Review: Exercise 7

Proofreading

The following passage is about artist Rudy Fernandez, whose work appears below. Rewrite the passage, correcting the errors in spelling, capitalization, grammar, and usage. Add any missing punctuation. There are ten errors.

Rudy Fernandez, *Hot and Cold: Cold,* 1987

(continued)

Rudy Fernandez

¹Rudy fernandez was born in 1948 and grew up in the southwest. ²The mexican American artist feels an intense affection for the area's landscape. ³He especially loves the high deserts of new mexico. ⁴Many of Fernandez paintings capture the beauty of the desert landscape.

⁵Fernandez celebrates the dessert by using abstract images of a flowering cactus in his picture. ⁶the simply-drawn cactus glows warmly against the blue background. ⁷Like uncle Melik in "The Pomegranate trees," Fernandez believes that beauty can survive in the desert. ⁸The plants and flowers of the desert has their own beauty.

Review: Exercise 8

Mixed Review

The following passage contains twenty errors in capitalization. Find them, and write the words correctly.

¹William Saroyan's Uncle Melik had come from armenia to the West with the dream of creating beauty out of desolation. ²He wanted to create a garden on the west Coast. ³Along with many others, Melik settled in california. ⁴The author wrote about his Uncle in a story titled "the Pomegranate Trees."

⁵Saroyan's uncle purchased 680 acres of land at the foot of the sierra Nevada. ⁶Melik hired workers to clear the land and bought a John Deere Tractor. ⁷The author asked his uncle Why he wanted to plant pomegranate trees. ⁸Saroyan said, "he knew i would understand the impulse that was driving him to ruin." ⁹"I like the idea of planting trees," Melik told his nephew, "And watching them grow." ¹⁰In the armenian language, Uncle Melik spoke like a poet. ¹¹"But this is desert soil," the author told his uncle. "it's too dry." ¹²However, saroyan helped his Uncle Melik plant hundreds of pomegranate trees. ¹³The hot Summer sun baked the young trees, and they failed to thrive in the desert soil. ¹⁴When Melik finally raised a crop, the pomegranates didn't sell because the american people didn't know what they were.

¹⁵Eventually Melik had to give the land back to mr. Griffith, the man who had sold it to him. ¹⁶At the end of the story, the pomegranate trees had died, and cactus had returned to the Western desert land.

Writing Application

TIME

For more about the writing process, see **TIME** **Facing the Blank Page,** pp. 97–107.

Capitalization in Writing

Correct capitalization makes your writing clearer. Mistakes in capitalization can distract readers from the substance of your writing. As you read the passage below from "A Huge Black Umbrella," notice how author Marjorie Agosín uses capitalization to identify proper nouns. Notice the italicized words.

> Mario went traveling abroad and I decided to spend my honeymoon on *Easter Island,* that remote *island* in the middle of *the Pacific Ocean,* six hours by plane from *Chile.* It is a place full of mysterious, gigantic statues called Moais. Ever since I was a child, I had been fascinated by those eerie statues, their enormous figures seeming to spring from *the earth,* just as *Delfina Nahuenhual* and her huge black umbrella did when she first came to my house.

Techniques with Capitalization

Try to apply Agosín's writing techniques when you write and revise your own work.

❶ Be alert to the difference between a word used within a proper noun to identify a specific place and the same word used as a common noun to identify a general place.

INCORRECT VERSION on *Easter Island,* that remote *Island* in the middle

AGOSÍN'S VERSION on *Easter Island,* that remote *island* in the middle

❷ Except when beginning a new sentence, remember to capitalize only the main words in a proper noun that names a geographical place:

INCORRECT VERSION The *Pacific Ocean,* six hours by plane

AGOSÍN'S VERSION the *Pacific Ocean,* six hours by plane

Capitalization

Practice Practice these capitalization techniques as you revise the following passage, using a separate piece of paper.

the bus came to a halt at the head of the road leading to treetop farm. as clarice headed down to the dusty road to the farm, she tossed a quick farewell to the driver, "see ya, frank. i've got to run and finish my chores. i want to ride into town to the library before dark." clarice hurried through her chores, wishing she lived at the hortense place, where hired staff did the farm chores. within an hour, she was entering the river view park town square, pedaling full speed towards the pearson memorial library.

Punctuation

Using the Period and Other End Marks

Three punctuation marks signal the end of sentences. The period is used for declarative and imperative sentences. The question mark is used for interrogative sentences. The exclamation point is used for exclamatory sentences and interjections.

RULE 1: Use a period at the end of a declarative sentence. A declarative sentence makes a statement.

> I enjoy traveling by train.
> Almost every country in the world has at least one major railroad line.

RULE 2: Use a period at the end of an imperative sentence. An imperative sentence gives a command or makes a request.

> Read about Russia's long rail system. [command]
> Please explain the meaning of the word *railroad*. [request]

RULE 3: Use a question mark at the end of an interrogative sentence. An interrogative sentence asks a question.

> Do we still use steam trains in this country?
> Why are diesel engines used now?

RULE 4: Use an exclamation point at the end of an exclamatory sentence. An exclamatory sentence expresses strong feeling.

> What a high-speed train this is!
> How fast it moves!

RULE 5: Use an exclamation point at the end of an interjection. An interjection is a word or group of words that expresses strong emotion.

My!	Alas!	Oops!
Well!	Whew!	Sh!
Wow!	Gee!	Ouch! Oh, no!

Exercise 1   **Using End Marks**

Write the correct end mark for each sentence. Then write whether the sentence is *declarative*, *imperative*, *interrogative*, or *exclamatory*.

1. Railroads provide an important means of transportation
2. Are we going to learn about the history of railroads
3. When was the first steam locomotive invented
4. Wood was shoveled into a firebox attached to the boiler that makes steam for the locomotive
5. What do you think were the dangers of this means of locomotion
6. Read about railroads in your book
7. An English inventor named Richard Trevithick built the world's first steam locomotive
8. Please tell me about the race between a horse and the tiny steam locomotive called the *Tom Thumb*
9. What an exciting race that was
10. In 1830 Peter Cooper built the *Tom Thumb*
11. This small locomotive raced against a horse but lost
12. The *Tom Thumb* led until an engine belt slipped
13. What a disappointment for Peter Cooper
14. Railroads grew rapidly in the mid-nineteenth century
15. The Union Pacific Railway company built track westward from eastern Nebraska toward the Rocky Mountains
16. The Central Pacific Railroad company laid track eastward from the coast of California across the Sierra Nevada
17. How were the railroads able to find enough workers to build the railroad across California's high mountains
18. More than five thousand Chinese workers were brought to California from China to work on the railroad
19. What excitement when the tracks met in Utah
20. Picture the scene when spikes made of gold and silver were hammered into the last section of track for the transcontinental railroad
21. Did these early railroads have high accident rates
22. As a safety measure, George Westinghouse developed an air brake for railroads
23. Explain the difference between an air brake and a hand brake
24. What a wonderful invention the air brake was
25. Isn't rail travel still a wonderful way to see the country

Using Commas I

Commas make sentences easier to understand by signaling a pause or separation between parts of a sentence.

RULE 1: Use commas to separate three or more words, phrases, or clauses in a series.

> Columbus commanded the *Niña*, the *Pinta*, and the *Santa Maria*.

RULE 2: Use a comma after two or more introductory prepositional phrases, after a long introductory phrase, or when a comma is needed to make the meaning clear.

> For thousands of years, shipbuilders constructed large ships. [two prepositional phrases—*For thousands* and *of years*]
>
> For many years people crossed the ocean in ships. [one prepositional phrase—*For many years*. A comma could be used, but it is not needed.]

RULE 3: Use a comma after introductory participles and introductory participial phrases.

> Daydreaming, I found myself on an ancient ship.
> Traveling the Mediterranean, the Minoans became seafarers.

RULE 4: Use commas to set off words that interrupt the flow of thought in a sentence.

> Ships, you might imagine, were invented thousands of years ago.

RULE 5: Use commas to set off an appositive if it is not essential to the meaning of the sentence.

> The Egyptians, the inventors of sails, built barges from planks of wood. [The appositive, *the inventors of sails,* is not essential.]

RULE 6: Use commas to show a pause after an introductory word and to set off names used in direct address.

> Ms. Mar, did the Romans have a large fleet?
> Yes, that was one of the reasons for their power.

Write the following sentences, adding any needed commas. Write *correct* if a sentence needs no changes.

1. Packet ships clipper ships and ocean liners are three kinds of ships.
2. By the early part of the nineteenth century trade between the United States and Europe had grown.
3. At that time according to newspaper reports American shipowners built packet ships for carrying cargo and passengers.
4. Packet ships you might imagine were not comfortable.
5. The first packet ship a ship that measured about one hundred feet did not travel very fast.
6. Clipper ships carried prospectors miners and traders to Gold Rush country.
7. In the 1850s clipper ships the most beautiful of all sailing ships provided speed and comfort.
8. Driving at top speed the captain of a clipper could cut through the water at twenty knots.
9. Merchants and sailors in America lost interest in the speedy clipper ships after a while.
10. The British sailed the fast clipper ships to China for tea, spices, and silk.
11. The age of the huge swift and luxurious ocean liner began in the early 1900s.
12. The *Titanic* a British liner began her maiden voyage in April 1912.
13. Luxuriously furnished the ship carried many wealthy and important people.
14. Racing across the Atlantic the *Titanic* hit an iceberg and sank.
15. The boat's builders had as it turned out claimed the ship was unsinkable.
16. More than fifteen hundred men women and children died in that tragic disaster.
17. For the first half of the twentieth century the only way to cross the Atlantic was by ship.
18. Among the famous luxury liners were the *Queen Mary* the *Queen Elizabeth* and the *United States.*
19. Beginning in the late 1940s airplanes attracted passengers.
20. Most ocean liners could not compete with airplanes.
21. Yes in the 1960s some European shipping companies tried to compete with jet planes.
22. Juanita do you enjoy sailing?
23. Yes Peter I love to go sailing.
24. It is more fun to sail in the sunshine you must admit.
25. After an hour of sailing we will need to head back to the boathouse.

20.3 Using Commas II

Commas clarify meaning in sentences with more than one clause. A clause is a group of words that has a subject and a predicate and is used as part of a sentence. A main clause can stand alone as a sentence.

Two or more main clauses can be joined by a comma plus the conjunction *and, or,* or *but.*

> **RULE 7:** Use a comma before *and, or,* or *but* when they join main clauses.
>
> Camels can travel great distances, and their strength enables them to carry heavy loads.
> Camels can live alone, but most travel in small herds.
> Camel's hair is used for making blankets, or it is woven into cloth for suits and coats.
>
> Subordinate clauses cannot stand alone as sentences. They are always joined with a main clause to make a complex sentence. One common kind of subordinate clause is an adverb clause which tells how, when, why, or where an action takes place. Some adverb clauses are separated from the main clause by commas.
>
> **RULE 8:** Use a comma after an adverb clause that introduces a sentence. Adverb clauses begin with subordinating conjunctions, such as *after, although, as, because, before, considering (that), if, in order that, since, so that, though, unless, until, when, whenever, where, wherever, whether,* or *while.*
>
> Since camels are the main means of transportation in many dry areas, they are called ships of the desert.
>
> Usually commas are not used with adverb clauses that come at the end of sentences.
>
> Nomads value their camels because these animals are vital to desert life.

Exercise 3　Using Commas with Clauses

Write each sentence. Add a comma or commas where needed. For a sentence that needs no commas, write *correct*.

1. Ever since ancient people began trading camels have been used as beasts of burden.
2. Some camels were bred for speed and they were then used in warfare.
3. Because camels were considered stupid malicious stories told about them were not very complimentary.
4. Camels were linked with evil and some people considered them unclean.
5. Since camels supply so many needs millions of people depend on them.
6. In the desert, camels pull plows or they turn water wheels.
7. Because they carry nomads to places without roads camels are highly valued in the desert.
8. These animals walk easily on soft sand and they go where trucks cannot pass.
9. When camels travel they go without water for days.
10. Because camels can go without water people thought they stored water in their humps.
11. The humps are actually fat and camels store food as fat in their humps.
12. A camel's hump gets smaller when the animal goes without food for a while.
13. Since camels do not sweat easily they retain their bodily fluids.
14. Camels are well adapted to their environment and they can live where other animals could not survive.
15. If camels pass through sandstorms their nostrils shut.
16. Because camels provide such a practical means of transportation nomads use them regularly.
17. Camels may seem strange to us because they are not native to our country.
18. When a person gets on a camel the beast usually whines.
19. Until a camel begins moving it grunts and groans.
20. After a camel starts walking it carries its load quietly.
21. Since camels do not work willingly they never learn obedience.
22. If camels become upset they may bite.
23. Because camels are easily annoyed they often kick with their hind legs or bite.
24. Camels may look larger than they are because they are covered with very thick, woolly fur.
25. Camels have very strong, sharp teeth and they will eat almost anything put in front of them.

20.4 Using Commas III

Several rules for using commas—including those for punctuating dates and addresses, titles, direct quotations, and salutations—are a matter of standard usage

RULE 9: Use commas before and after the year when it is used with both the month and the day. Do not use a comma if only the month and the year are given.

> The bus trip began on July 5, 2001, and lasted four weeks.
> The journey ended in August 2001.

RULE 10: Use commas before and after the name of a state or a country when it is used with the name of a city. Do not use a comma after the state if it is used with a ZIP code.

> People came from as far away as Buffalo, New York, to travel with the tour.
> The address on the envelope was as follows:
> 136 East Main St., Huntington, NY 11743.

RULE 11: Use a comma or pair of commas to set off an abbreviated title or degree following a person's name.

> Carol Warren, M.D., studied the effects of motion sickness.

RULE 12: Use a comma or commas to set off *too* when *too* means "also."

> Dr. Warren, too, rode on the bus with us.

RULE 13: Use a comma or pair of commas to set off a direct quotation.

> Kerry said, "Buses are more efficient than cars."
> "Train travel," Sarah said, "is pleasant and safe."

RULE 14: Use a comma after the salutation of a friendly letter and after the closing of both a friendly and a business letter.

> Dear Dad,   Your pal,   Yours truly,

RULE 15: Use a comma to prevent misreading.

> Instead of two, five teachers made the trip.

Exercise 4 — Using Commas

Write each sentence. Add a comma or commas where needed.

1. A letter from Troy, New York arrived in May 2001.
2. Alan said "I'm planning a tour of Canada."
3. "I hope" said Nora "that we can go in July."
4. The bus will go from New York to Quebec City Canada and then back.
5. Pamela Chin M.A. will lead the tour.
6. Nora said "I have always wanted to visit Quebec City."
7. Patty and Jennifer asked too if they could go.
8. "Tomorrow" Alan said "we will ask John Cage M.D. to accompany us."
9. "I hope we go through Burlington Vermont" Patty said.
10. The tour stops in Montreal Canada on July 15 2001.
11. Like Quebec City Montreal has many interesting sights.
12. "In Montreal" Alan explained "French and English are both used."
13. Montreal too is an important seaport.
14. Montreal Canada was the site of the World's Fair in August 1967.
15. Quebec City too is on the St. Lawrence River.
16. The group will be in the city from July 20 to July 24 2001.
17. "Jean LeGrand Ph.D. will be our guide in Quebec" Pamela announced.
18. Instead of Patty Maria will be my roommate.
19. The British took Quebec City from the French on September 14 1759.
20. The group will tour the State Capitol in Albany New York.

Exercise 5 — Using Commas

Add commas if needed to the following numbered items.

[1]98 Heritage Road
[2]Somers New York 10589
[3]August 8 2001

[4]Dear Keith

[5]I have just returned from a terrific bus trip. [6]We went from Troy New York to Quebec City Canada. [7]Mike went too. [8]On the bus, I read a great book about Quebec by Carlos Espinoza Ph.D. [9] Instead of three hours four hours were allotted for our meals.

[10]Your friend
Ahmad

20.5 Using Semicolons and Colons

The semicolon and the colon are punctuation marks that separate parts of a sentence that might otherwise be confused.

RULE 1:   Use a semicolon to join parts of a compound sentence when a conjunction, such as *and, but,* or *or,* is not used.

> In the 1890s the electric car became the most popular car in America; people liked electric cars because they ran quietly and cleanly.

RULE 2:   Use a semicolon to join parts of a compound sentence when the main clauses are long and are subdivided by commas. Use a semicolon even if the clauses are joined by a coordinating conjunction such as *and, but,* or *or.*

> Before the invention of the automobile, people rode horses, bicycles, or streetcars for short distances; and they took horse-drawn carriages, trains, or boats for longer trips.

RULE 3:   Use a colon to introduce a list of items that ends a sentence. Use a phrase such as *these, the following,* or *as follows* to signal that a list is coming.

> A few years ago you could order a car only **in the following** colors: black, white, blue, and brown.

Do not use a colon immediately after a verb or a preposition. Either leave out the colon or reword the sentence.

> Large automobile companies **sell** cars, trucks, and vans.
>
> Most of the world's cars are built **in** the United States, Japan, or Europe.

RULE 4:   Use a colon to separate the hour and the minute when you write the time of day.

> Ms. Cole starts her car at 7:15 A.M. each day.

RULE 5:   Use a colon after the salutation of a business letter.

> Dear Sir or Madam: Dear Ms. Delgado:

Tasha drove downtown at rush hour

she found a parking space in front of the library.

Exercise 6   Using Semicolons and Colons

Write each sentence, adding semicolons or colons as needed. Write *correct* if the sentence needs no changes.

1. Large automobile clubs aid travelers these travelers often write to the clubs for information.
2. I wrote to one of these organizations last month it promised to send me a packet of information.
3. Within a week, the organization sent me the following items a road map, a guidebook, and a car manual.
4. I plan to leave next Saturday at 530 A.M.
5. For possible emergencies, I am taking these items a flashlight, a first-aid kit, and a spare tire.
6. I also have a set of flares with instructions in case I have an accident.
7. It will take approximately nine hours for me to reach my destination I plan to stop every two hours to rest during the trip.
8. When you drive long distances, it's important to stay awake, stay alert, and drive safely but it's easy to get tired and bored on long trips.
9. I have taken everything I need in my suitcase, including the following a bathing suit, a pair of sunglasses, and a good book.
10. On the return trip, I will leave at 830 A.M. and expect to be home by 800 P.M.

Exercise 7   Using Semicolons and Colons in a Letter

Add semicolons or colons, if needed, to punctuate the following numbered items.

[1]Dear Sir or Madam

[2]I am planning a trip. I am, therefore, seeking information about Virginia, Tennessee, and North Carolina. [3]I would like to visit the following cities Richmond, Raleigh, and Atlanta. [4]Please send the following a road map and a guidebook and hotel information. [5] If I leave my home in Baltimore, Maryland, at 800 A.M., at what time will I arrive in Richmond?

Sincerely,

An-Mei Cho

20.6 Using Quotation Marks and Italics

Quotation marks signal a person's exact words, as well as the titles of some works. Italic type—a special slanted type that is used in printing—identifies titles of other works. You can show italics on a typewriter or in handwriting by underlining.

RULE 1: Use quotation marks before and after the exact words in a direct quotation.

> "For centuries people dreamed of flying," Iris said.

RULE 2: Use quotation marks with both parts of a divided quotation.

> "Leonardo da Vinci," said Ray, "drew plans of flying machines."

RULE 3: Use a comma or commas to separate a phrase such as *he said* from the quotation itself. Place the comma inside closing quotation marks.

> Chan said, "Orville and Wilbur Wright invented the airplane."
> "It was a great advance for civilization," Lou said.

RULE 4: Place a period inside closing quotation marks.

> Ed said, "An Air Force captain made the first supersonic flight."

RULE 5: Place a question mark or an exclamation point inside the quotation marks when it is part of the quotation.

> Amy asked, "When did jumbo jets begin carrying passengers?"

RULE 6: Place a question mark or an exclamation point outside the quotation marks when it is part of the entire sentence.

> Did I really hear Sam say, "Jumbo jets are just big airplanes"?

RULE 7: Use quotation marks around the title of a short story, essay, poem, song, magazine or newspaper article, or book chapter.

> "Araby" [short story]   "Trees" [poem]

RULE 8: Use italics (underlining) for the title of a book, play, film, television series, magazine, newspaper, or work of art.

> The Pearl [book]   Seventeen [magazine]

Exercise 8 — Using Quotation Marks and Underlining for Titles

Write each item, adding quotation marks or underlining for italics where needed.

1. Through the Tunnel (short story)
2. Denver Post (newspaper)
3. Dream Variations (poem)
4. Much Ado About Nothing (play)
5. Kilimanjaro (essay)
6. Nova (television series)
7. Hook (film)
8. Newsweek (magazine)
9. Stardust (song)
10. The Budget Amendment Riddle (article)

Exercise 9 — Using Punctuation Marks

Write each sentence, adding quotation marks, italics, and other punctuation marks where needed.

1. Dolores said Supersonic planes travel at great speeds
2. Only spacecraft added Randy travel faster than these airplanes
3. Is it true supersonic transports cross the Atlantic in three hours asked Ms. Chu.
4. Dolores shouted What an exciting ride that must be
5. Randy asked Is that plane a supersonic transport
6. Ms. Chu answered Yes a supersonic transport appeared in the film Airport
7. Isn't that plane called the Concorde asked Akira.
8. Yes said Ms. Chu it flies between New York and Paris
9. How fast does the Concorde travel asked Randy.
10. Dolores looked up the information in The World Book Encyclopedia
11. The article in Time explained why no American company built such a plane
12. Roberto did you say That surprises me
13. Some countries Ms. Chu continued have very fast trains
14. The article Japan's Bullet Trains talks about the fast trains in Japan
15. Randy exclaimed Riding on a train like that sounds terrific
16. The ride is very quiet and smooth on the bullet train Ms. Chu said.
17. Then Ms. Chu said I have been on such a train
18. Have you ever been on France's fast trains Dolores asked.
19. Peter asked Do you know why train travel in America is not popular
20. The article states Most Americans seem to prefer traveling by plane

20.7 Using Apostrophes

An apostrophe can show possession. It can indicate that letters are missing within a contraction. It can also signal the plurals of letters, numbers, or words when they refer to themselves

> **RULE 1:** Use an apostrophe and an *s* *('s)* to form the possessive of a singular noun.
>
>   James + **'s** = James**'s**   nation + **'s** = nation**'s**
>
> **RULE 2:** Use an apostrophe and an *s* *('s)* to form the possessive of a plural noun that does not end in *s*.
>
>   men + **'s** = men**'s**   geese + **'s** = geese**'s**
>
> **RULE 3:** Use an apostrophe alone to form the possessive of a plural noun that ends in *s*.
>
>   boys + **'** = boy**s'**   Thompsons + **'** = Thompson**s'**
>
> **RULE 4:** Use an apostrophe and an *s* *('s)* to form the possessive of an indefinite pronoun, such as *everyone, everybody, anyone, no one,* and *nobody*.
>
>   anybody + **'s** = anybody**'s**   someone + **'s** = someone**'s**
>
> Do not use an apostrophe in a possessive pronoun, such as *mine, its, yours, his, hers, ours,* and *theirs*.
>
>   That car is **ours**.   Is that cat **yours**?
>   The bird flapped **its** wings.   This cassette is **hers**.
>
> **RULE 5:** Use an apostrophe to replace letters that have been omitted in a contraction.
>
>   it + is = it**'s**   I + will = I**'ll**
>   we + are = we**'re**   is + not = isn**'t**
>
> **RULE 6:** Use an apostrophe to form the plurals of the names of letters, figures, and words. Underline the name to show its special use. Do not underline the *'s*.
>
>   three <u>b</u>**'s**   five <u>4</u>**'s**   <u>if</u>**'s**, <u>and</u>**'s**, or <u>but</u>**'s**

Exercise 10 Using Apostrophes in Possessive Forms

Write the possessive form of each word or group of words below. Use an apostrophe and an -s (*'s*) or an apostrophe alone (*'*).

1. teacher
2. teachers
3. Ms. Sandoval
4. adults
5. deer
6. man
7. country
8. countries
9. dog
10. Celia
11. women
12. heroes
13. Gladys
14. dessert
15. friends
16. dress
17. islands
18. mice
19. Thomas
20. wind
21. tents
22. people
23. youth
24. teeth
25. teams

Exercise 11 Using Apostrophe Items

For each sentence, write any words that require apostrophes. Insert apostrophes where needed. Write *correct* if the sentence needs no changes.

1. The friends bicycles are ready for the long trip.
2. Ada has made sure shes prepared.
3. "Im ready to start," Ada said.
4. "Were ready when you are," replied Jess and Kim.
5. "Is the bicycle with the basket yours?" asked Kim.
6. The friends stopped cycling to watch two soccer games.
7. "Why do all the shirts have *T*s on them?" asked Isamu.
8. "Its anyones guess," said Inez.
9. That shirt is hers.
10. A train went by with its horn blaring.
11. Theres more food for everyone in the kitchen.
12. The picture book on sale in the store next door is perfect for teaching your cousin her ABCs.
13. "We should take umbrellas with us," Jack said, "since it looks as if its raining outside."
14. The tickets date seems to be incorrect.
15. The jackets all had large *J*s on the back.
16. The coach gave rings to the girls.
17. According to Jon, its yours.
18. Its clear that the people in charge of the event planned carefully.
19. Claudias watch broke when she fell off her bicycle.
20. His parents told him to watch his *p*s and *q*s.

20.8 Using Hyphens, Dashes, and Parentheses

RULE 1: Use a hyphen to show the division of a word at the end of a line. Always divide the word between its syllables.

> Astronauts operate spacecraft and conduct engi-
> neering, medical, and scientific experiments in space.

RULE 2: Use a hyphen in compound numbers from twenty-one through ninety-nine.

> seventy-six   twenty-three

RULE 3: Use a hyphen to spell out a fraction.

> Some astronauts receive **one-half** pay upon retirement. [modifier]
>
> **One-half** of all astronauts have a master's degree. [noun]

RULE 4: Use a hyphen or hyphens in certain compound nouns. Check the dictionary to see which ones need hyphens.

> great-grandmother   sister-in-law   attorney-at-law

RULE 5: Use a hyphen in a compound modifier when it precedes the word it modifies.

> She is a **well-trained** astronaut.   She is **well trained**.

RULE 6: Use a dash to show a sudden break or change in thought or speech. If the sentence continues, use a second dash to mark the end of the interruption.

> Dr. Owens—he lives nearby—teaches astronomy.

RULE 7: Use parentheses to set off words that define, or helpfully explain, a word in the sentence.

> Flight training for the space program consists of training in simulators **(**devices that reproduce the conditions of space flight**)** and in other special equipment.

Using Hyphens

Write the items below, using a hyphen or hyphens where needed. Write *correct* if an item needs no changes.

1. one half interest
2. great uncle
3. thirty five
4. Anglo Saxon
5. well liked leader
6. merry go round
7. thirty two missions
8. three fourths majority
9. forty two
10. high powered speaker
11. first lady
12. forty minute class
13. English speaking actor
14. ninety five
15. red haired girl
16. twenty story building
17. soft boiled egg
18. sight seeing
19. two thirds vote
20. five mile walk

Exercise 13 **Using Hyphens, Dashes, and Parentheses**

Write each sentence, adding hyphens, dashes, and parentheses where needed. Write *correct* if a sentence needs no changes.

1. Astronauts undergo a six month training course.
2. Most astronauts are pilots they already know about flying.
3. At first no civilians could be astronauts only military men were selected.
4. Now men and women both scientists and other professionals can fly into space.
5. Astronauts must follow a low fat diet as part of their training.
6. The astronauts and cosmonauts in the Apollo Soyuz Test Project visited each other's countries.
7. The astronauts familiarized themselves with the equipment, with the flight plan, with but you know that.
8. The space travelers participated in joint rehearsals of the mission.
9. Dr. Ilych he is a fine teacher led the sessions.
10. As a scientist, Dr. Ilych is well regarded in Russia.
11. He trained two thirds of the participants.
12. Russian scientists sometimes schedule four week missions.
13. American space trips these are space shuttle flights are fairly short.
14. The crew is well trained to carry out scientific experiments.
15. Thanks to much improved technology, we can watch them on television.
16. It's possible to speak directly to the astronauts they can answer directly too.
17. Astronauts study distant stars some in other galaxies.
18. Space flights have resulted in income producing inventions.
19. Only one accident a very tragic one has occurred with the space shuttle.
20. The shuttle lifted off one half hour late.

20.9 Using Abbreviations

RULE 1: Use the abbreviations *Mr., Mrs., Ms.,* and *Dr.* before names. Abbreviate professional or academic titles that follow names.

Mr. Carl Baird **Jr.**   Vivian Huang, **M.D.**   Ana Elias, **Ph.D.**

Ms. Leona Wilson, **M.A.**   James Nichols, **R.N.**

RULE 2: Use all capitals and no periods for abbreviations that are pronounced letter by letter or as words. Two exceptions are *U.S.* and *Washington, D.C.,* which do use periods.

NHS National Honor Society   **PDT** Pacific daylight time

NATO North Atlantic Treaty Organization

PIN personal identification number

RULE 3: With exact times use A.M. (*ante meridiem,* "before noon") and P.M. (*post meridiem,* "after noon"). For years use B.C. (before Christ) and, sometimes, A.D. (*anno Domini,* "in the year of the Lord," after Christ).

8:45 A.M.   6:30 P.M.   30 B.C.   A.D. 476

RULE 4: Abbreviate days and months only in charts and lists.

Mon. Tues. Wed.   Apr. Aug. Sept. Oct. Nov. Dec.

RULE 5: In scientific writing, abbreviate units of measure. Use periods with abbreviations of English units but not of metric units.

inch(es) **in.**   pound(s) **lb.**   gallon(s) **gal.**

centimeter(s) **cm**   gram(s) **g**   liter(s) **l**

RULE 6: On envelopes, abbreviate words such as *Street, Avenue, Road, Boulevard, Court, Drive,* and *Circle.* Spell out these words everywhere else.

St.   Ave.   Rd.   Blvd.   Ct.   Dr.   Cir.

Let's meet at the corner of First **Avenue** and Elm **Street**.

RULE 7: On envelopes, use the U.S. Postal Service two-letter abbreviations for state names.

AL Alabama   **MO** Missouri   **WA** Washington

KY Kentucky   **ME** Maine   **MA** Massachusetts

Punctuation

Exercise 14 Using Abbreviations

Write the correct abbreviation for each underlined item.

1. after Christ 1000
2. Mister Roosevelt
3. 76 Melrose Avenue
4. Don Newell Junior
5. Wednesday
6. 1 inch
7. Atlanta, Georgia
8. Lexington, Kentucky
9. Tat Lam, Medical Doctor
10. Internal Revenue Service
11. 42 Bradford Drive
12. 32 feet
13. November 23
14. 1100 before Christ
15. 15 liters
16. April 23
17. 7 inches
18. United Nations
19. Fred Jackson, Doctor of Philosophy
20. Blake Road
21. October 24
22. January 15
23. Kansas City, Missouri
24. Seattle, Washington
25. Portland, Maine

Exercise 15 Using Abbreviations

Write the abbreviation for each underlined item. Write *correct* if no abbreviation should be used.

1. Our new house is at 14 Laurel Street.
2. The letter from Gail R. Momaday, Registered Nurse, contained information about the public-health seminar.
3. It stated that a meeting will be held from 11:30 in the morning until 4:45 in the afternoon.
4. The meeting will be held on Monday, August 17.
5. Scheduled speakers include Doctor Hilario Reyes.
6. Carol McQuaid, Master of Arts, plans to speak on art therapy.
7. Write to the Environmental Protection Agency.
8. The nearest office is in Boston, Massachusetts.
9. That office is twenty kilometers from my house.
10. That large building houses the Federal Bureau of Investigation.
11. The mall is full of shoppers on Saturday and Sunday.
12. Our tour begins on August 13 and ends on September 4.
13. The bus leaves from Newark, New Jersey, at 8:30 at night.
14. On Tuesday we will be in Baltimore, Maryland.
15. That cathedral is a copy of one built in after Christ 1000.
16. The students from Ohio State University toured with us.
17. The Central Intelligence Agency's headquarters are not open to the public.
18. [on an envelope]   Doctor Amy Salazar
19.   6758 Bradley Drive
20.   Jackson, Missouri 63755

20.10 Writing Numbers

In charts and tables, you always write numbers as figures. However, in an ordinary sentence you sometimes spell out numbers and sometimes write them as numerals

---

RULE 1: Spell out numbers that you can write in one or two words.

In the early nineteenth century, stagecoaches traveled at a speed of less than **twenty-five** miles per hour.

RULE 2: Use numerals for numbers of more than two words.

The first coaches traveled a distance of **392** miles.

RULE 3: Spell out any number that begins a sentence, or reword the sentence so that it does not begin with a number.

Three thousand one hundred coaches existed in England by 1836.

RULE 4: Write a very large number as a numeral followed by the word million or billion.

Did these coaches carry more than **25 million** passengers?

RULE 5: If related numbers appear in the same sentence, use all numerals.

For a trip of **390** miles, drivers changed horses every **20** miles.

RULE 6: Spell out ordinal numbers (such as *first* or *second*).

In America, Wells, Fargo & Company ranked **first** for its coach service.

RULE 7: Use words to express the time of day unless you are writing the exact time or using the abbreviation A.M. or P.M.

The journey began at **six o'clock** in the morning.
It ended at **9:15 P.M.**

RULE 8: Use numerals to express dates, house and street numbers, apartment and room numbers, telephone numbers, page numbers, amounts of money of more than two words, and percentages. Write out the word *percent*.

July **19, 1832**   **15** Summit Road   Apartment **6E**   **40 percent**

Exercise 16   Writing Numbers

Write the correct form for the underlined numbers in the following sentences. Write *correct* if a sentence needs no changes.

1. The first stage line came into existence in England in about <u>sixteen hundred seventy</u>.
2. This stage line covered a distance of <u>six hundred and fifty-one</u> kilometers.
3. Did coaches in England travel at least <u>fifty-five million</u> miles before the rail-ways replaced them?
4. <u>200</u> years ago the United States Congress began mail service by stagecoach.
5. For a trip of <u>360</u> miles, <u>eighteen</u> drivers each traveled about <u>twenty</u> miles.
6. Some trips from Philadelphia to Ohio began at <u>six-thirty</u> a.m.
7. The <u>1st</u> stagecoach lines were established in colonial America in <u>seventeen hundred fifty-six</u>.
8. Horse-drawn coaches rode along at <u>ten</u> miles per hour.
9. Now Americans can fly to London in the Concorde jet at nearly <u>fourteen hundred</u> miles per hour.
10. Before <u>eighteen hundred seventy-five</u> the streetcar (or tram) had replaced the horse-drawn coach.
11. The <u>1st</u> streetcars were called horsecars because teams of horses pulled the wooden cars.
12. <u>Four</u> horses were needed to haul the cars up the steep hills of San Francisco, California.
13. The <u>first</u> trolley line in San Francisco was opened in <u>eighteen hundred seventy-three</u>.
14. A trolley line in Portland, Oregon, was the <u>2nd</u> steepest ever built in the United States.
15. Most of the trolley lines in San Francisco had been abandoned by the beginning of the <u>20th</u> century.
16. American cities were growing quickly—<u>fifty</u> cities had more than <u>one hundred thousand</u> inhabitants.
17. By <u>nineteen hundred and ten</u> electric streetcars had replaced horsecars.
18. In the <u>1920s</u> and <u>nineteen thirties,</u> car travel made streetcars obsolete.
19. It costs <u>one dollar and twenty-five cents</u> to buy one token for the bus or subway.
20. The new subway system built recently in the city carries <u>forty</u> percent of all commuters.

Grammar Review

PUNCTUATION

Time travel is one of Jack Finney's favorite subjects. In the story "The Third Level," Finney's narrator believes there are three levels at Grand Central Station, the monumental railroad station located in the heart of Manhattan. Finney writes, however, that "the presidents of the New York Central and the New York, New Haven and Hartford railroads will swear on a stack of timetables that there are only two." The passage has been annotated to show some of the rules of punctuation covered in this unit.

Literature Model

from "The Third Level"
by Jack Finney

I turned into Grand Central from Vanderbilt Avenue, and went down the steps to the first level, where you take trains like the Twentieth Century. Then I walked down another flight to the second level, where the suburban trains leave from, ducked into an arched doorway heading for the subway—and got lost. That's easy to do. I've been in and out of Grand Central hundreds of times, but I'm always bumping into new doorways and stairs and corridors. Once I got into a tunnel about a mile long and came out in the lobby of the Roosevelt Hotel. Another time I came up in an office building on Forty-sixth Street, three blocks away.

Sometimes I think Grand Central is growing like a tree, pushing out new corridors and staircases like roots. There's probably a long tunnel that nobody knows about feeling its way under the city right now, on its way to Times Square, and maybe another to Central Park.

> **Period at the end of a declarative sentence**

> **Comma before *but* that is joining main clauses**

> **Hyphen in a compound number**

> **Apostrophe in a contraction**

(continued)

Grammar Review

> **Dashes to show an interruption in thought**
>
> And maybe — because for so many people through the years Grand Central has been an exit, a way of escape — maybe that's how the tunnel I got into . . . But I never told my psychiatrist friend about that idea.

Review: Exercise 1   Using End Marks

Write the correct end mark for each sentence. Then write whether the sentence is *declarative, imperative, interrogative,* or *exclamatory.*

1. The narrator, a young man named Charley, claimed that there were three levels at Grand Central Station
2. What a crazy idea
3. His friends didn't believe him
4. Would you believe him
5. Think of when your friends didn't believe you
6. If you think Grand Central Station is complicated, you should see the train stations in Tokyo, Japan
7. Some stations have as many as twenty-five exits to the street
8. Did you know that you can do all your shopping—from groceries to shoes—in the train station
9. Buy your ticket before you get on the train
10. Do you need a map of the transit system

Review: Exercise 2   Using Commas

Write each sentence, adding commas where needed.

1. The main waiting room at Grand Central Station unbelievably is large enough to hold a football field.
2. Many large cities have an underground transport system a bus system and streetcars.
3. Public transportation as you can tell is often ignored and not well funded.
4. Washington and Los Angeles two large cities have just built public transit systems to make commuting easier.
5. Did you know Dr. McFarlan that France and Japan have trains that operate much faster than ours?

Review: Exercise 3   **Using Commas with Introductory Words and Phrases**

Write each sentence, adding commas where needed. Write *correct* if a sentence needs no changes.

1. For centuries people have dreamed about space travel.
2. On October 4, 1957, the first artificial satellite was placed in orbit.
3. For the Russians in the 1950s the launch of *Sputnik* was a major achievement.
4. Staying in orbit for twenty-three days Sputnik relayed information to Earth.
5. At the age of twenty-seven Yuri Gagarin became the first person in space.
6. At first unfortunately many of America's rocket tests were unsuccessful.
7. Blasting off in May 1961 Alan Shepard became America's first astronaut.
8. America was finally able to claim it had entered the space age.
9. Orbiting the Earth three times John Glenn found the view magnificent.
10. Unfortunately accidents have marred the American space program.

Review: Exercise 4   **Using Commas in Compound Sentences**

Write each compound sentence, adding commas where needed. If a sentence needs no commas, write *correct.*

1. Some ferries just carry people and some transport people and vehicles.
2. Oil tankers load oil in one port and pump it out at its destination.
3. Oil tankers are very efficient for oil but they cannot transport other cargoes.
4. Tugs help push big ships into position and turn ships around.
5. A cruise can be very relaxing and many cruise lines offer a wide variety of trips for vacationers.
6. Most cruise ships offer several restaurants and provide a range of activities.
7. The ship can dock at a deep-water port or passengers can be ferried ashore in small boats.
8. You can cruise for a few days or sail for up to a month.
9. Iron ships played a role in the Civil War but they were soon replaced with ships built of steel.
10. Outdated warships are mothballed or they are sold for scrap.

Grammar Review

Review: Exercise 5 **Using Commas with Introductory Adverb Clauses**

Write each sentence, adding commas where needed. If a sentence needs no commas, write *correct*. Remember that an adverb clause is a subordinate clause that tells *how, when why,* or *where* an action takes place.

1. The Pony Express is very famous even though it lasted just eighteen months.
2. Before it was founded mail was transported to California by ship.
3. When a ship docked in California everyone rushed to hear the latest news and pick up mail.
4. Delivering mail overland was difficult because winter weather was harsh.
5. Even when a southern route was used the trip across the country by stage-coach took more than three weeks.
6. When it was proposed the Pony Express promised a ten-day crossing.
7. The Pony Express used stagecoach stations wherever it was possible.
8. Other stations were built so that riders could get fresh horses.
9. Although hundreds applied to be riders only eighty were chosen.
10. When the first run was completed the riders were hailed as heroes.

Review: Exercise 6 **Using Commas**

Write each sentence, adding commas where needed. If a sentence needs no commas, write *correct*.

1. The game will be played in Stanford California at Maples Pavilion.
2. The last time the team won was February 1991.
3. Will Roy Williams M.D. travel with the team?
4. The date of the championship game is March 4 2005 at eight o'clock.
5. Address the ticket request to 231 North Ridge Road Palo Alto CA 94301.
6. Parents will be traveling with the team too.
7. Along with shoes shirts and jackets were donated by the booster group.
8. The award ceremony on March 10 2005 will be held in San Francisco.
9. Bands from Sacramento California and Reno Nevada will be playing.
10. Instead of rings scholarships will be given to the winners.

Review: Exercise 7   **Using Commas with Direct Quotations**

Write each sentence, adding commas where needed.

1. "The first around-the-world nonstop flight took place in 1986" Mark said.
2. "The pilots" Jessica stated proudly "were Dick Rutan and Jeanna Yeager."
3. "In order to make the trip without refueling" Mark explained "the plane had to carry its own fuel supply."
4. "The plane's long, narrow wings" he said "were designed to carry fuel."
5. "The trip took nine days" Jessica added.
6. "This was so different from Charles Lindbergh's flight across the Atlantic" Mark said.
7. "Lindbergh's flight" Jessica stated "took thirty-three hours."
8. "His plane was called the *Spirit of St. Louis*" she said.
9. "Lindbergh was hailed as a hero when he landed in France" stated Mark.
10. "He was revered in America" Jessica added.

Review: Exercise 8   **Using Commas and End Marks in Direct Quotations**

Write each sentence, adding commas and end marks where needed.

SAMPLE "When did man first step on the moon" Jamie asked.
ANSWER "When did man first step on the moon?" Jamie asked.

1. "How long did the astronauts train for their mission" Sam asked.
2. "Three astronauts were on the *Apollo 11* flight to the moon" Jamie explained.
3. "Neil Armstrong, you know" Mark announced "was not a military man"
4. Jamie exclaimed, "I found Neil Armstrong's words so inspiring"
5. Sam asked "What exactly did he say when he stepped on the moon"
6. "I wonder" Sam said "what he expected to find on the moon's surface"
7. Peter asked "Does anyone remember the name of the second man to walk on the moon"
8. Who heard Armstrong say "*The Eagle* has landed"
9. Sam said "Millions of Americans watched the landing on television"
10. Jamie asked "What happened to the rock samples they brought back"

Grammar Review

Review: Exercise 9   **Punctuating Direct Quotations**

Write each sentence, adding quotation marks, commas, and end marks where needed.

1. Juan asked How many interstates are there in the United States
2. Theresa explained The major roads are all numbered
3. With interstates she said the highways that go east-west across the country are given even numbers
4. The interstates that go north-south she continued are given odd numbers
5. Todd asked Is Interstate 90 in the north or the south of the United States
6. Interstate 90 Juan answered runs from Massachusetts to Seattle
7. Where is Interstate 5 Theresa asked
8. Juan exclaimed That's one of the newest roads in the country
9. Did I hear you say that it's easy to find your way around Boston asked Juan.
10. I like to navigate when my parents drive Theresa said as long as I have a good map to follow

Review: Exercise 10   **Using Apostrophes**

For each sentence, write any words that require apostrophes. Insert apostrophes where needed. Write *correct* if a sentence needs no apostrophes.

SAMPLE   Its snowing hard right now.
ANSWER   It's

1. Whats it like to ride on a monorail?
2. Some monorails hang down from a single rail.
3. In Disney Worlds monorail system, the car straddles the track.
4. Is their system like yours in Seattle?
5. Its a transportation system that has not been very popular in America.
6. My seat is here, but theirs is on the other side of the car.
7. The womens packages were accidentally left on the train.
8. Only tickets marked with As and Bs are accepted for the ride.
9. The conductor said that it was someones seat.
10. Dr. Adamss invention will make train travel more comfortable.

Review: Exercise 11

Proofreading

The following passage is about Russian artist Simon Faibisovich, whose work appears on the next page. Rewrite the passage, correcting the errors in spelling, capitalization, grammar, and usage. Add any missing punctuation. There are ten errors.

Simon Faibisovich

[1]Simon Faibisovich a russian painter who lives in Moscow. [2]Trained as an architect he teached himself to paint. [3]His work was never shown publically before American gallery owner Phyllis Kind discovered him in 1987. [4]There have been several shows of his work in New York, New York since then.

[5]Mister Faibisovich paints large pictures of ordinary people doing ordinary things, such as standing at a bus stop or waiting in line for food. [6]His portraits are more better than snapshots. [7]The faces of the people he paints reflects a yearning for something else in their lifes. [8]Just as Charley views a train station as an opportunity to escape the boy in the painting on the next page is clearly longing for something besides a bus ride.

Review: Exercise 12

Mixed Review

Write correctly the sentences with spelling and punctuation errors. There are twenty errors in all. If the sentence contains no errors, write *correct*.

[1]When a person lives in a big city with a large population its easy to feel lonely sometimes. [2]Trucks and buses speed by on the roads and crowds jam the sidewalks. [3]Are you ever afraid of just crossing the street [4]Getting away may mean going to the country or it may mean taking a walk in a big park.

[5]In Central Park in New York City you can forget that youre in the middle of one of Americas biggest cities. [6]The parks trees shade people on summer days you can take long walks on a five mile path through the woods. [7]You can even go boating if you want. [8]On Sundays people arent allowed to drive their cars through the park.

[9]Imagine what an escape a space trip must be [10]Looking down on

(continued)

Earth from a spaceship you would have the most magnificent view. ¹¹Its so quiet out in space no one would bother you. ¹²When Buzz Aldrin landed on the moon he looked around and said Beautiful, beautiful, beautiful—a magnificent desolation.

Simon Faibisovich, *Boy*, 1984

Writing Application

TIME

For more about the writing process, see **TIME Facing the Blank Page**, pp. 97–107.

Quotation Marks in Writing

In this passage from *The Gathering*, Virginia Hamilton brings her characters to life by presenting their exact words. She uses quotation marks and commas to clearly identify where those words, known as dialogue, begin and end. Note the punctuation marks.

> "Wow! Magic!" said Dorian. Celester hummed a comic toning, entertaining them with the light.
>
> "Whatever it was, it got hot," Thomas said. He eyed Celester suspiciously.
>
> "A property of light is heat," toned Celester. "He who puts hand in fire will singe his fingertips."
>
> "I get the message," Thomas muttered.
>
> "Celester, you have powerful gifts," Justice said.

Techniques with Quotation Marks

Try to apply some of Virginia Hamilton's writing techniques as you write and revise your own work.

❶ Make your characters vivid by capturing their exact words. Use quotation marks before and after each direct quotation. Compare the following:

BLAND VERSION Dorian was surprised.

HAMILTON'S VERSION "Wow! Magic!" said Dorian.

❷ Keep your dialogue clear by using commas to signal the shift from a quoted sentence to surrounding text.

INCORRECT VERSION "A property of light is heat" toned Celester.

HAMILTON'S VERSION "A property of light is heat," toned Celester.

Punctuation

Practice Try out these techniques by revising the following passage, using a separate piece of paper. Decide which information might be better presented as dialogue in quotation marks. Use commas as necessary to separate that dialogue from other text.

Nan's toes felt frozen. She looked around in wonder at all the snow. Seeing her dismay, her father told her about the Blizzard of 1888. He explained that cities had been buried under several feet of snow. People were stranded on trains and at work. Nan suggested that it might have been interesting to see that much snow. It might help her feel happier about living in Tucson where it never snows. Her father laughed at her suggestion and headed back inside.

UNIT 21 Grammar Through Sentence Combining

Prepositional phrases are useful in sentence combining. Like adjectives and adverbs, prepositional phrases enable you to give more information about nouns and verbs. Because prepositional phrases show relationships, they often express complex ideas effectively.

> **EXAMPLE**   **a.** Latoya Hunter faithfully kept a diary.
>   **b.** Latoya's home was **New York City. [from]**
>   **c.** She wrote the diary **in seventh grade.**

Latoya Hunter **from New York City** faithfully kept a diary **in seventh grade.**

The new information (in dark type) in sentences *b* and *c* takes the form of prepositional phrases when added to sentence *a*. In the new sentence, the phrase *from New York City* modifies the noun *Latoya Hunter*. The phrase *in seventh grade* modifies the verb *kept*. Prepositional phrases that modify nouns follow the nouns they modify. Prepositional phrases that modify verbs come before or after the verbs they modify. (For a list of common prepositions see page 479.)

- A **prepositional phrase** is a group of words that begins with a preposition and ends with a noun or pronoun. Prepositional phrases modify nouns, pronouns, and verbs.

Exercise 1   **Combining Sentences with Prepositional Phrases**

The following sentences are based on passages from *The Diary of Latoya Hunter,* which you can find on pages 32–37. Combine each group of sentences, turning the new information into a prepositional phrase. In the first few items, the new information is in dark type.

1. **a.** Latoya missed her old social life.
   b. She was **attending her new school. [at]**
2. **a.** Latoya envied her diary.
   b. She envied the diary **for its detachment.**

3. **a.** Latoya's best friend had moved away.

  b. She moved **during the spring.**

4. **a.** Latoya's progress is revealed in her diary.

  b. Her progress was toward greater maturity.

5. **a.** Each new entry is like a snapshot.

  b. The entry is in her diary.

  c. The snapshot is of the writer's mind.

6. **a.** Latoya's diary traces her development.

  b. Her development was from an unhappy girl.

  c. Her development was into a self-confident young woman.

7. **a.** Latoya named her diary Janice.

  b. She named it after her best friend.

  c. Janice was her friend in Jamaica.

8. **a.** One Sunday Latoya got in trouble.

  b. There was trouble at home.

  c. She was in trouble with both parents.

9. **a.** Latoya was feeling desperate.

  b. She wrote about her situation.

  c. Her main concern was how she felt in school.

10. **a.** A book editor wanted the diary.

  b. She wanted the diary of a teenager.

  c. The teenager had been in distress.

Exercise 2   Combining Sentences

Rewrite the paragraphs below, using prepositional phrases to combine sentences. Make any other changes in wording that you feel are necessary.

Latoya devoted one entry to a former teacher. The entry is in her diary. Her words create a wonderful picture. The words are about Mr. Pelka. The picture is of a warm and caring man. The class learned to empathize with other people. They learned this from Mr. Pelka. One day Latoya learned the moving story of a Jewish girl. This girl lived in the time of the Holocaust. Mr. Pelka should go down in history. This is according to Latoya.

Mr. Pelka made history come alive. He did that for all his students. He made them understand that history is like a story. It's like a story from a movie. History is about major events. It's also about people. It's about people like us. Latoya learned to understand major events through her reading. She read about real people. Those stories helped her understand herself better. Now she knew more. Now she knew something about other people's feelings.

21.2 Appositives

You can use appositives to combine sentences in a compact and informative way. Single word appositives and appositive phrases identify or tell something new about a noun or a pronoun.

EXAMPLE **a.** Mars is too cold to support life.
b. Mars is **Earth's neighbor.**

Mars, **Earth's neighbor,** is too cold to support life.

The appositive phrase *Earth's neighbor* tells us more about the noun *Mars.* Note that the appositive phrase is set off with commas because it gives extra information about Mars. If an appositive supplies information that is essential for identifying a noun, it is not set off with commas. (For more information about appositives, see pages 389–390.)

■ An **appositive** is a noun placed next to another noun to identify it or give additional information about it. An **appositive phrase** includes an appositive and other words that describe it.

Exercise 3   Combining Sentences with Appositives

The sentences below are based on an excerpt from *Living Treasure* by Laurence Pringle, which you can find on pages 248–253. Combine each group of sentences so that the new information is turned into an appositive or an appositive phrase. In the first few items, the new information is in dark type. The information in brackets indicates that you should add a comma or commas to the new sentence.

1. **a.** Earth lies between icy Mars and hot Venus.
   b. Earth is **our home planet.** [, + ,]
2. **a.** Because of its climate, our own planet is an oasis.
   b. The planet is **Earth.** [, + ,]
3. **a.** According to the writer, scientists are astounded by the great diversity of life forms on Earth.
   b. The writer is **Laurence Pringle.**

4. a. The Swedish botanist developed the Linnaean system.
   b. The botanist was **Carl von Linné.**
   c. The Linnaean system is **the modern means of classifying plants and animals. [,]**

5. a. One threat to humanity is the loss of biodiversity.
   b. Biodiversity is the variety of life on Earth.

6. a. The tropical rain forest is valuable to all of us.
   b. The rain forest is the heart of Earth's biodiversity.
   c. All of us are the inhabitants of this planet.

7. a. New species may have the ocean floor as a habitat.
   b. New species are undescribed organisms.
   c. A habitat is a place where plants and animals naturally grow or live.

8. a. Terry Erwin collected insects in Panama for the Smithsonian.
   b. Terry Erwin is an entomologist.

9. a. Edward O. Wilson found forty-three kinds of ants from one habitat.
   b. Wilson is a Harvard University biologist.
   c. The habitat was a single tropical tree.

10. a. Some scientists specialize in biology.
    b. Biology is the study of living things.

Exercise 4 **Combining Sentences**

Rewrite the following paragraphs. Use appositives and appositive phrases to combine sentences. Make any changes in wording that you feel are necessary.

Funding for tropical research increased in the 1980s. These years were a period of discovery of the rain forest. From one tree in Peru, for example, an entomologist collected many ants. The entomologist was Terry Erwin. His ants were examined by Edward O. Wilson. Wilson was a biologist at Harvard University. In that one tree, Wilson discovered as many ant species as have been identified in all of Canada or Great Britain. These countries are areas far to the north of the rain forest. The biodiversity of the planet is probably unique in the solar system. The planet is Earth.

These entomologists made their discoveries in the rain forest. The entomologists are experts in the branch of biology that deals with insects. The rain forest has also led to new discoveries in botany. Botany is the branch of biology dealing with plant life. Terry Erwin and these other biologists are especially interested in studying the rain forest's canopy. Terry Erwin has called the canopy "the heart" of Earth's biodiversity.

21.3 Adjective Clauses

Adjective clauses are useful in sentence combining. When two sentences share information, one of them can often be made into an adjective clause modifying a word or phrase in the other.

EXAMPLE **a.** Dara and Jantu had both lost part of their families
b. Dara and Jantu **were good friends. [, who . . . ,]**

Dara and Jantu, **who were good friends,** had both lost part of their families.

The new information (in dark type) in sentence *b* becomes an adjective clause modifying *Dara and Jantu. Who* now connects the clauses. Notice the commas in the new sentence. Adjective clauses that add nonessential information require commas. Those that add essential information do not. (For more information see pages 505–506.)

■ An **adjective clause** is a subordinate clause that modifies a noun or pronoun in the main clause. The relative pronouns *who, whom, whose, which,* and *that* are used to tie the adjective clause to the main clause.

Exercise 5 **Combining Sentences with Adjective Clauses**

The following sentences are based on an excerpt from *The Clay Marble* by Minfong Ho, which you can find on pages 90–94. Combine each numbered group of sentences so that the new information is turned into an adjective clause. In the first few items, the new information is in dark type; the information in brackets indicates the relative pronoun to use and that a comma or commas are needed.

1. **a.** Jantu spent afternoons under the stone beam.
   b. Jantu **loved to play with clay. [, who . . . ,]**
2. **a.** Palm fronds shaded one end of the beam.
   b. The beam **became a cavelike shelter. [, which]**

3. **a.** Jantu made delicate figures from clay.

    b. **She had scooped** this clay **from a mud puddle. [that]**

4. **a.** Dara watched Jantu.

    b. Dara **would hold Jantu's baby brother. [, who . . . ,]**

5. **a.** The girls talked of family members.

    b. **They had lost** family members. **[whom]**

6. **a.** Continuity in her life was important to Dara.

    b. Dara hated change.

7. **a.** The war made many people suffer.

    b. The war had broken Jantu's family.

8. **a.** Jantu described a real family as a loving group.

    b. This group grows with new members all the time.

9. **a.** Dara's memories helped her feel her family around her.

    b. Those memories were a great comfort to her.

10. **a.** The rain on the roof was like the soft touch of Dara's grandmother.

    b. Her grandmother would massage the girl's head.

Exercise 6   Combining Sentences

Rewrite the paragraphs below, using adjective clauses to combine sentences. Make any changes in wording and punctuation you feel necessary. If any sentence doesn't make sense when trying to combine it, leave it as is.

Jantu created a thatched shelter. The shelter was like a leafy cave. Dara would sit in the shelter holding Jantu's baby brother and watch Jantu. Jantu was sculpting clay figures. Dara wished aloud. She wished that everything would stay the same. This of course couldn't happen. But Jantu understood her friend. Her friend had endured so much change already. Jantu and Dara had both once had whole families. The families were just bits and pieces of ones now. Jantu spoke of their families as leftovers. The leftovers were like fragments from a broken bowl. Both girls wanted to be part of a real family. A real family was one that was growing and not shrinking. Jantu hoped to make her friend feel better with a surprise. She had been working on the surprise.

Jantu showed Dara some clay figures. Jantu wanted to comfort her. The girls were interrupted by a rainfall. The rainfall reminded Dara of long-lost rainy afternoons with her family. Dara imagined her family as a soft blanket. The blanket sheltered her. Jantu invited Dara to play with the family of dolls. Jantu was remembering her own lost family. In the clay figures, Dara recognized her own family members, as well as members of Jantu's family. Jantu had made their broken families whole again. Jantu had the skill and the imagination of an artist.

21.4 Adverb Clauses

You can use adverb clauses to combine sentences. Adverb clauses are especially effective in establishing clear relationships between two or more actions. For example, adverb clauses can indicate that one action follows another or causes another.

EXAMPLE   **a.** Bel Kaufman read a great deal a a girl.
b. She was trying to master the English language. **[because]**

Bel Kaufman read a great deal as a girl **because she was trying to master the English language.**

In the new sentence, the adverb clause *because she was trying to master the English language* modifies the verb *read.* The adverb clause tells why Bel Kaufman was reading so much. Note that the subordinating conjunction *because* makes the relationship between the action and its reason very clear. An adverb clause may occupy different positions within a sentence. If it begins the sentence, it is followed by a comma. (For more information about adverb clauses, see pages 507–508.)

■ An **adverb clause** is a subordinate clause that modifies the verb in the main clause. Adverb clauses are introduced by subordinating conjunctions, such as *after, although, because, before, since, when, whenever, if,* and *while.*

Exercise 7   Combining Sentences with Adverb Clauses

The following sentences are based on "The Liberry" by Bel Kaufman, which can be found on pages 298–301. Use adverb clauses to combine each group of sentences. Vary the position of the adverb clause and vary the subordinating conjunction too. In the first few items, the information in brackets signals the subordinating conjunction and the punctuation you should use.

1. **a.** Bel Kaufman came to New York City at the age of twelve.
   [Before . . . ,]
   b. She had lived in Russia.

2. **a.** She never felt the need to use the library's card catalog.
   b. She went through the bookshelves alphabetically. [**because**]
3. **a.** She found a book with dog-eared pages and many dates on its card. [**Whenever . . . ,**]
   b. She recognized a book that she would probably want to read.
4. **a.** Kaufman enjoyed reading comments scribbled in the margins.
   b. Kaufman glanced through a book's pages. [**When . . . ,**]
   c. She knew it was wrong to mark up a library book. [**although**]
5. **a.** One reader might write "How true!" in a book's margins.
   b. Another reader would write "This book stinks." [**, whereas**]
6. **a.** Kaufman wrote an essay about the importance of libraries.
   b. She was very concerned about cuts in funds for libraries.
7. **a.** People are increasingly troubled about children's reading skills.
   b. Public libraries are closing their doors.
8. **a.** People have less leisure time.
   b. They are less inclined to read.
9. **a.** In a library, it is hard to avoid sitting down and reading a book.
   b. You are surrounded by large numbers of books and readers.
10. **a.** It has a vast selection of reference works.
    b. They need information on a special assignment or project.
    c. The public library is also invaluable for many people.

Exercise 8   **Combining Sentences**

Rewrite the following paragraphs, using adverb clauses to combine sentences. Make any other changes in punctuation or wording that you feel are necessary.

What needs do libraries fill? According to Bel Kaufman, libraries offer us a quiet refuge. We seek peace and privacy. Libraries also give people a chance to read. They have no other access to free books.

Bel Kaufman is very distressed about library closings. She remembers libraries so fondly. She taught high school English in New York City. She required her students to bring a library card to class. They actually had a card. They might go to the library. One student brought in his aunt's card. He did not have one of his own. Nevertheless, some of her students did use their cards. The cards were there. Some people still go to the library. The library is still there. According to Kaufman, the city will suffer. Everyone's neighborhood library is forced to close.

Review: Exercise 9

Mixed Review

The following sentences are based on "A Huge Black Umbrella" by Marjorie Agosín, which you can find on pages 188–191. Combine each group of sentences so that the new information is turned into the kind of phrase or clause indicated in dark type. Any necessary pronouns or punctuation are also indicated.

1. a. She was covered by a huge black umbrella.
   b. Delfina Nahuenhual arrived at their house. **[adverb clause; When . . . ,]**
   c. The umbrella was ripped in many places. **[adjective clause; that]**
2. a. The umbrella was useless in the rain.
   b. It had many holes. **[adjective clause; ,which . . . ,]**
   c. It let the rainwater fall on her. **[adverb clause; because]**
3. a. Delfina explained to Mother that she always traveled with the umbrella.
   b. Mother welcomed her. **[adjective clause; ,who . . . ,]**
   c. The umbrella protected her from the sun, elves, and little girls. **[adjective clause; ,which]**
4. a. Delfina Nahuenhual was a survivor.
   b. We called her by her full name. **[adjective clause; ,whom . . . ,]**
   c. She was a survivor of a Chilean earthquake. **[prepositional phrase]**
5. a. Mother was really a friend of Delfina.
   b. Mother was the lady of the house. **[appositive phrase; , . . . ,]**
   c. Delfina was my mother's servant. **[appositive phrase; ,]**
6. a. Delfina Nahuenhual told us many stories.
   b. The stories were about tormented souls and frogs. **[prepositional phrase]**
   c. The frogs became princes. **[adjective clause; that]**
7. a. Delfina Nahuenhual would write long letters.
   b. The letters she would number and wrap up. **[adjective clause; that]**
   c. She would wrap them up in newspaper. **[prepositional phrase]**
8. a. She kept the letters in an old pot filled with lemon rind, garlic, and cumin.
   b. Cumin is a kind of spice. **[appositive phrase; ,]**
9. a. Cynthia and her sister tried to read those letters.
   b. Delfina was busy in the kitchen. **[adverb clause; Whenever,]**
10. a. After Mario was born, Delfina Nahuenhual said she was tired and wanted to go back to Chile.
    b. Mario was the spoiled one of the family. **[appositive phrase; , . . . ,]**

Romare Bearden, Sunday After Sermon (detail), 1969

"*In the old days it was not unusual to find several generations living together in one home.*"

—Rudolfo Anaya,
"The Boy and His Grandfather"

PART 3

Resources and Skills

UNIT 22

Library and Reference Resources

LOG ON ▶ **Writing** Online   For research tools and additional skills practice, go to **glencoe.com** and enter QuickPass code WC77680p3.

The Arrangement of a Library

The library is a good place to satisfy your curiosity about anything from aardvarks to Zuñis. It also offers a wealth of information you can use for school assignments and projects.

A trip to the library can be eye opening even when you don't have a purpose in mind. Just browsing, you might find a new magazine that's all about your favorite hobby. You might spot a DVD of a movie you've been wanting to see. You might find a book you'd like to read or a Web site where you can take notes about a place you've always wanted to visit.

You can expect to make discoveries at a library. You can also expect most libraries to be arranged in roughly the same way. Turn the page to learn more about what you can find at a library.

No two libraries are alike, but most of them share the same characteristics and have similar resources.

Librarian A librarian can be the most important resource of all. He or she can help you use the library wisely by directing you to different resources, showing you how to use them, and giving you advice when needed. You might want to prepare your questions for the librarian ahead of time. Librarians are prepared to help their patrons and will be glad to answer your questions.

Young Adult and Children's Section Young readers can find books written for them in a separate area of the library. Sometimes reference materials for students are also shelved here, along with periodicals and audiovisual materials.

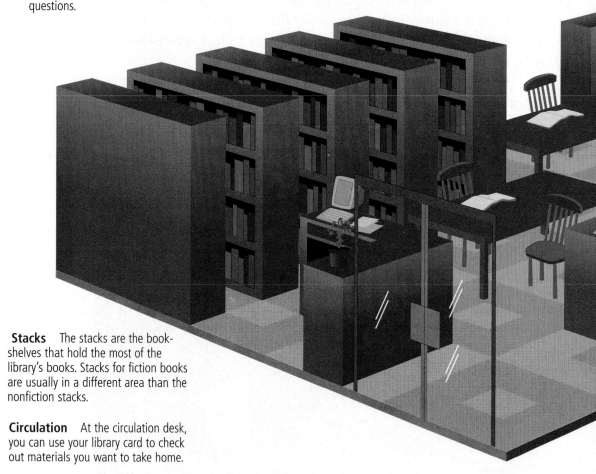

Stacks The stacks are the bookshelves that hold the most of the library's books. Stacks for fiction books are usually in a different area than the nonfiction stacks.

Circulation At the circulation desk, you can use your library card to check out materials you want to take home.

Periodicals You can find current issues of periodicals—newspapers, magazines, and journals—in a general reading area. Here you can read local newspapers as well as newspapers from around the world. Periodicals are arranged alphabetically and by date. Older issues may be available in the stacks or online. Use the computer catalog to locate them or ask a librarian to help you. Some libraries allow you to check out the older issues of periodicals.

Reference   The reference area holds dictionaries, encyclopedias, atlases, and other reference works. Usually you are not allowed to check out these materials. They are kept in the library so that everyone may have access to them. Computer databases are also part of the reference area. These systems allow you to search for facts or articles from periodicals. For example, InfoTrac provides complete articles and article summaries from more than one thousand newspapers and magazines. Some computer databases allow you to search for particular types of information, such as history or art.

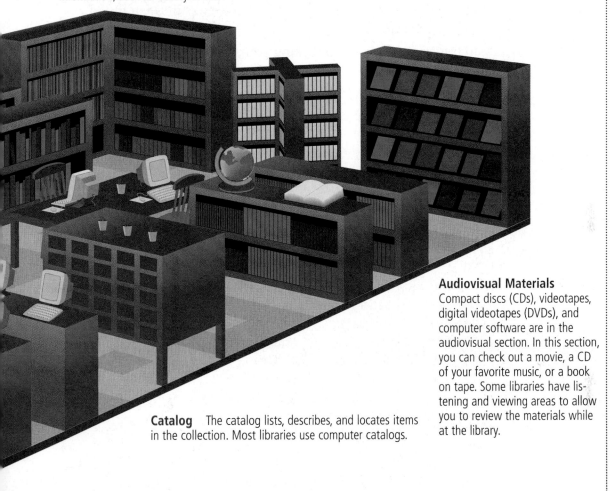

Catalog   The catalog lists, describes, and locates items in the collection. Most libraries use computer catalogs.

Audiovisual Materials
Compact discs (CDs), videotapes, digital videotapes (DVDs), and computer software are in the audiovisual section. In this section, you can check out a movie, a CD of your favorite music, or a book on tape. Some libraries have listening and viewing areas to allow you to review the materials while at the library.

Exercise 1

In which section of the library might you find each of the following items?

1. A DVD of the film *March of the Penguins*.
2. *The Times Atlas of World Exploration*
3. This week's issue of *Sports Illustrated*
4. *Dictionary of the Middle Ages*
5. *A Wrinkle in Time* (a fantasy novel for young readers)

22.2 The Dewey Decimal System

Suppose a library had no system for organizing its books. You'd have to search every shelf to find a book you wanted. Many public libraries use the Dewey decimal system of classification to organize their books. This system groups books into ten broad categories of knowledge, as shown on the chart below. As you search for a book, begin by asking yourself in what group it might be classified.

Dewey Decimal System			
Category Numbers	**Major Category**	**Example of a Subcategory**	**Sample Book Title**
000–099	Computers, information, and general reference	Encyclopedias	World Book Encyclopedia
100–199	Philosophy and psychology	The senses	The Amazing Five Senses
200–299	Religion	Mythology	Greek Mythology
300–399	Social sciences	Law	We, the People
400–499	Language	Chinese language	Speaking Chinese
500–599	Science	Astronomy	The Night Sky Book
600–699	Technology	Medicine	Sports Medicine
700–799	Arts and recreation	Dance	Ballet Basics
800–899	Literature	Plays	Our Town
900–999	History and geography	Mexican history	The Ancient Maya

Books in each major category are labeled with a similar number. For example, all books about science have a number in the 500s. Books about the arts—for example, painting, sculpture, photography, dance, theater—have numbers in the 700s.

Each major category is broken up into smaller categories. Each added digit, or single numeral, in the Dewey decimal number narrows the category further. A book about photography would have a number in the 770s. Look at the Dewey decimal number on the following page for *Mountains of Fire*. This book by Robert W. Decker is about volcanoes. Notice how each digit in the number further narrows down the topic.

500	**Science**	A book about science is listed in the 500s.
550	**Earth Sciences**	This book is about a subcategory of science.
551	**Geology**	Geology is a subcategory of earth sciences.
551.21	**Volcanoes**	The numbers after the decimal narrow down the topic even further.

Books are shelved in order according to the Dewey decimal number and then alphabetically by author's last name. For example, among all the books with number 551.21, a book by Robert W. Decker would come before a book by Margaret Poynter.

A fiction book is not usually given a Dewey decimal number. Instead, the first line of the call number is either an *F* or *FIC*, for *fiction*. The second line almost always shows the first three letters of the author's name. Fiction books are arranged on the shelves by the author's last name. Books by the same author are further alphabetized by title.

Exercise 2

Go to the nonfiction stacks in your school or neighborhood library. Find a book that looks interesting in each category listed below. Write down the book's Dewey decimal number, author, title, and topic.

1. 000–099
2. 100–199
3. 300–399
4. 600–699
5. 700–799

Using a Library Catalog

How do you find the book you want in a library filled with books? The library catalog is the best place to start. Your library may have a computer catalog, a card catalog, or both. Either catalog can tell you which books the library owns.

Using a Computer Catalog

The computer catalog lists all the books, periodicals, and audiovisual materials in the library. You can search for these materials by title, author, subject, or keyword. A **keyword** is a word or phrase that describes a topic. If you type an author's name, you can view a list of all the books written by that author. Typing a subject enables you to view all the books about that particular topic. The computer catalog tells you the title, author, and call number of each book, and whether it is available for checkout. Be sure to take notes or print out the information to help you find the book.

For example, suppose you are looking for books about career guidance for young actors. Your computer search might proceed as follows:

1. Type in the subject, *acting—vocational guidance.*
2. The computer will show a list of all the books in the library on this subject. Each item is numbered.
3. Now, for more detailed information on an item, click on the entry you want.
4. You will then see a screen, like the one shown here, with detailed information about the book.

> You searched subject: acting—
> vocational guidance—juvenile
> literature
>
> Title: Stars in your eyes—feet on
> the ground: a practical guide for
> teenage actors (and their parents!) /
> by Annie Jay with LuAnne Feik;
> illustrated by Ron Crawford.
>
> LOCATION   CALL #
> STATUS
> MAIN–2 Adult   792.028 Ja DUE
> Nonfiction   12-14-08

The way the computer catalog works may differ slightly from library to library. Follow the on-screen directions to use any computer catalog. If you have trouble with your search, ask a librarian for help.

Using a Card Catalog

The card catalog, a cabinet of long, narrow drawers, holds cards describing each book in the library. The cards are arranged in alphabetical order. The book's Dewey decimal number, or call number, is usually printed in the upper-left corner of the card. This number also appears on the spine of the book.

Most fiction books have two cards: an author card and a title card. Nonfiction books usually have several catalog cards: an author card, a title card, and subject cards. In some libraries, subject cards are grouped separately from author and title cards.

You may also see cross-reference cards in the catalog. These cards direct you to other ways a subject is listed in the catalog.

Finding a Book

When you have located a book you want in the catalog, write down its call number. In the stacks locate the shelf that holds books with numbers close to your call number. For example, if your number is 862.12, first find the 800s section. Then look for the 860s. If several books have the same call number, they will be shelved alphabetically by author.

Identify the book by the specific author, title, or subject.

Look up the book in the computer catalog or the card catalog.

Find the book in the stacks or in the reference section.

Check out the book at the circulation desk unless it must be used only in the library.

Exercise 3

Use the catalog to find a book for each of the following topics. List the author, title, and call number of each book you find.

1. Types of sailing ships
2. Rocks and minerals
3. Japan's economy
4. Castles
5. Egyptian mythology
6. Poems by Myra Cohn Livingston
7. Geometry
8. African masks
9. Guide dogs
10. Olmec civilization

22.4 | Basic Reference Sources

The next time you want to satisfy your curiosity about the world, try the library's reference section. The reference section contains many general information sources, both in print and online. These sources are useful when you are doing research or working on a class assignment. They're useful any time you need an answer to a question. The chart below gives some examples of the kinds of questions basic references can answer.

Using Basic Reference Books to Answer Questions		
Question	**Where to Look**	**Examples of Sources**
When did Elizabeth I rule England?	**Encyclopedias** include general information on a variety of topics.	• *World Book Encyclopedia* • *Grolier Online* • *Encyclopaedia Britannica*
What is the average temperature in Lagos, Nigeria?	**Atlases** are collections of maps. They often include special maps on climate, population, and other topics.	• *Hammond World Atlas* • *The Rand McNally World Atlas*
Who won the Nobel Prize for literature in 2007?	**Almanacs** provide lists, statistics, and detailed information on recent events.	• *Information Please Almanac* • *World Almanac and Book of Facts*

Encyclopedias

You have probably used encyclopedias for research papers and class projects. These basic reference books may be contained in a single volume or in many volumes. General encyclopedias have articles on a wide variety of topics. Some examples are countries, animals, noteworthy people, historical events, and scientific ideas. Whatever you're looking for, you'll probably find something about it in an encyclopedia.

An encyclopedia is a good place to start a research project. An encyclopedia article will give you an overview of the topic. It may provide a list of books for further research.

In addition to general encyclopedias, most libraries have some specialized encyclopedias. These provide more detailed information on a specific subject. Two examples are the *Encyclopedia of Muscle Tone and Strength* and *Encyclopedia of Ancient Greece.*

Articles in an encyclopedia are arranged alphabetically. To find out if an encyclopedia has information on your topic, look up the topic in the index. The index may be contained in a separate volume. The index will tell you the volume and page numbers on which the information appears. Below is a sample encyclopedia page. Do you think the photographs on the page below help communicate important information? Explain.

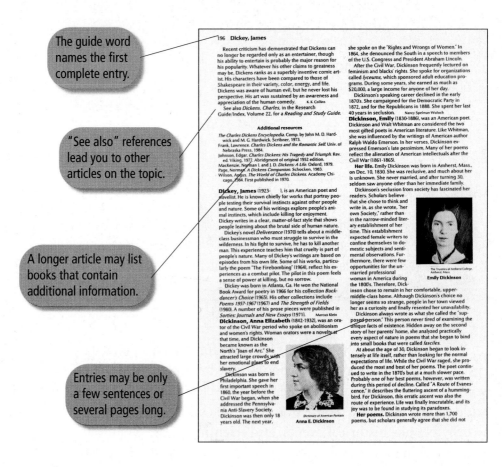

The guide word names the first complete entry.

"See also" references lead you to other articles on the topic.

A longer article may list books that contain additional information.

Entries may be only a few sentences or several pages long.

Atlases

An atlas is a collection of maps. Some atlases contain maps of all the countries in the world. The *Times Comprehensive Atlas of the World* is an example of a large general atlas. Other atlases may focus on one continent or one country. An atlas of the United States, for example, generally includes one or more maps of each state.

The maps in an atlas show various land and water areas—mountains, plateaus, oceans, lakes, and rivers. These are called natural, or physical, features. Maps also show cities, towns, roads, countries, and boundaries between places. These are called cultural features because they were made by people. Many atlases have special maps showing climate, population, natural resources, and other special information.

Almanacs

Who first ran a mile in less than four minutes? What's the population of Bolivia? When is the next eclipse of the sun? What is the world's highest mountain? largest ocean? longest river? deepest lake? coldest place? The answers to these and thousands of other questions are in an almanac.

An almanac is a book of up-to-date general information. Almanacs are usually published once a year. They contain the most recent information for the preceding year. An almanac includes lists of important people and events and facts about governments, history, geography, and weather. It gives figures on population, industry, farm production, and much more.

Because an almanac presents a huge amount of information in very concise form, you can locate a specific fact very quickly. To look up a specific fact, use the index. An almanac's index is often placed at the front of the book rather than at the back.

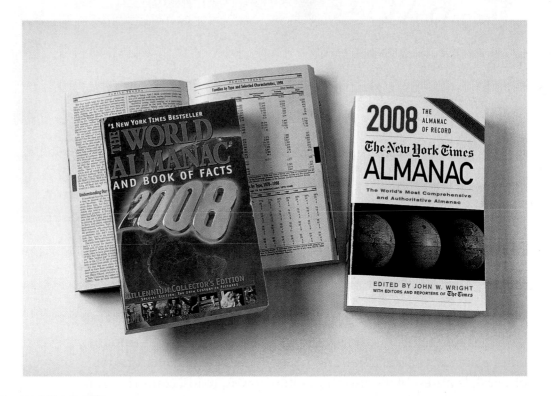

Exercise 4

Which would be the best resource to answer each of the following questions—an encyclopedia, an atlas, or an almanac? Find the answer to each question.

1. Of what country is Maputo the capital?
2. Who was Victoria Woodhull?
3. Who was the winner of the Newbery Medal in 1977?
4. Is Thailand primarily forest or crop land?
5. What is a kookaburra, and where does it live?
6. What is the major cause of acid rain?
7. Who won the World Cup in soccer in 2002?
8. In what ocean are the Cook Islands located?
9. What countries border Lake Chad in Africa?
10. What film won the Academy Award for best picture of 2004?

Other Library Resources

When you think about a library's resources, you probably think of books. However, most modern libraries offer much more than books. Some libraries are now called resource centers or media centers to show that they include resources other than books.

Internet Access

Computers at your public library also provide access to the Internet, a valuable source of information. The Internet—also known as *The Net*, *Cyberspace*, or *The Information Highway*—is the largest computer network in the world. The World Wide Web is the part of the Internet that provides information in various formats, including print, sound, graphics, and video.

Because there are so many Internet sites, the best way to find worthwhile information on the Net is by using a *search engine*. Search engines work by sending out software agents called *spiders*. Spiders search every Internet link they can find. If you do not get any useful results with one search engine, try several others. They each search the Internet differently.

All Internet sources are not equally reliable, however. Always check any site for accuracy and timeliness. Check to see when it was last updated. Check for errors and omissions. Check to see what agency sponsors the site. Many libraries now provide a collection of recommended Web sites.

Online Libraries Online libraries on the Internet are important reference sources. These sites are available 24 hours a day. You can connect from home if you have access to a computer and a modem. Examples of excellent online reference sites include *The Internet Public Library,* hosted by Drexel University's College of Information Science and Technology and the Virtual Reference Shelf, a site with selected Web resources compiled by the Library of Congress.

Other Nonprint Resources

Nonprint resources can take many different forms. Microforms, digital video discs, compact discs, and videotapes are some of the nonprint resources you can find in libraries.

Library and Reference Resources

Microforms   Libraries often store old issues of magazines and newspapers on microforms. Microforms are reduced images on either rolls of film (microfilm) or small film cards (microfiche). An entire issue of a magazine can be stored on a three-by-five-inch or four-by-six-inch microfiche. Microforms save space and are less likely to be damaged by use.

Special viewing machines enlarge the photographs for viewing. Some viewing machines can also produce copies of the enlarged image. Such machines are usually located in the newspaper and magazine section.

Sound Recordings   If you want to listen to music, a poetry reading, or a drama reading, try your library's collection of audiotapes and compact discs (CDs). The library may have players for each of these sound resources in the audiovisual section. You can check these recordings out to take home.

Video Recordings   Most libraries with audiovisual sections have a collection of DVDs and videotapes. There you may find films, documentaries, how-to videos, and travelogues. Videos, like sound recordings, are usually listed in a special catalog in the audiovisual section and may be checked out.

Exercise 5

In what library resource would you expect to find each of the following? (Resources include the Internet, microform of periodicals, audiotape, CD, and videotape.) More than one answer may be possible in some cases.

1. The results of a political poll taken just before the presidential election of 2000
2. The musical *Into the Woods* by Stephen Sondheim
3. An issue of *Sports Illustrated* describing an auto race held last month
4. An article about a new bridge now being built in your community
5. Information on a hurricane currently approaching the east coast

22.6   Searching for Periodicals

Suppose you wanted to find information on the latest developments in computer technology. How would you find magazine articles on your topic?

Until the early 1990s, most searching for periodicals articles was done with printed indexes and then by searching either bound periodicals or microforms (copies of magazines and newspapers stored on film). Today you can do periodicals searches electronically on the Internet and on various databases. A database is a collection of electronic files that are easily retrieved by a computer.

If you are searching for older publications, however, such as a magazine from about 1980 or before, you still need to search the older way. Scan for your topic in a bound copy of *Readers' Guide to Periodical Literature* and then follow your citation to the correct issue of the magazine in the periodical section.

But often you will search online. Most libraries provide two types of electronic databases: general periodical ones, and ones specific to a subject. *eLibrary,* which searches newspapers, general magazines, maps, and TV and radio transcripts, is an example of a multimedia database. *Social Issues Resource Series (SIRS)* is an example of a database that is focused on one main subject area, sociology and current social problems.

All databases share common features. Most offer the option to do a basic search or a more advanced search. Each has a query screen. On it you key in the search term(s)—either one word or a search phrase. Many databases allow you to use natural language. In other words, you ask the question the way you would ask it of a friend.

Sample Periodical Search

This search was done on a database called *MasterFILE Premier,* which searches current magazines and newspapers.

Screen One   The researcher here is looking for information on connections between the Internet and radio. The search has been limited by date.

Screen Two   Examine the first five references that came up for this search.

Find: <u>Internet and radio</u>   Search
     For a natural language search, enter a phrase or sentence that describes what you are looking for. Quoted phrases or keywords will always be included in your results. For search examples, see Search Tips.
Limit Your Search:
___ Full Text
___ Magazine
_X_ Date Published Mo. Jan Yr. 99 to Mo.
   Oct. Yr.99
___ Publication Type
New Search/Subject Search/Magazine Search/Choose Databases/Online Help

Keyword Search/Advanced Search/Natural Language Search/Options/Search Tips

Examine the first five references that came up for this search. An X indicates Full text; that is, the entire text of the article is available.
Records (1 to 5) of 349
Mark Full Text Select Result for More Detail
X How CBS Is Bartering Its Way Into the Dot.com World; By: Kover, Amy. Fortune, 09/27/99, Vol. 140 Issue 6, p. 312, 2 p, Ic Full Page Image
X Web key in CBS, Viacom merger.; By Garrity, Brian., Billboard, 09/18/99, Vol. 111 Issue 38, p5, 2p
Old Media Get a Web Windfall.; By: Hwang, Suein L., Wall Street Journal—Eastern Edition, 09/17/99, Vol. 234 issue 55, pB1, 0p, 1bw
MTV Networks Unit Sues Imagine Radio Founders., Wall Street Journal—Eastern Edition, 09/15/99, Vol. 234 Issue 53, pB9, 0p
X Fun. (cover story); by: Pappas, Ben. and Schifrin, Matthew. And Berentson, Ben. and Solan, Joshua. And Manzo, Emily and Nathan, Adit. and Leitzes, Adam., Forbes, 09/13/99, Vol. 164 Issue 6, p105, 1p, 2c
(1 to 5) of 349 Refine Search Print/Email/Save

Look over your display results carefully. The display screen gives you important information about each article. It includes the titles, the author, the source, the date of the article, its length, and availability of photographs or other graphics.

Exercise 6

Look at the sample screens and answer these questions.

1. Which of these articles has a full page image?
2. Which of these periodicals did a cover story on this topic? Why might a cover story be more valuable than just any story?
3. How many of these articles have full text available?

Library and Reference Resources

The Dictionary and the Thesaurus

A dictionary and a thesaurus can help put more words on the tip of your tongue and at the tip of your pencil. Both references are essential tools for writers. Both can be found in print, on CD, and online.

The Dictionary

A dictionary contains entries in alphabetical order. An entry is a single term, or word, along with its pronunciation, definition, and other information. Some characteristics of three types of dictionaries are summarized below.

Types of Dictionaries

	Characteristics	Examples
Unabridged Dictionaries	• Detailed word histories • Detailed definitions • Found mostly in libraries	• *Random House Webster's Unabridged Dictionary* • *Webster's Third New International Dictionary*
College Dictionaries	• Detailed enough to answer most questions on spelling or definition • Widely used in schools, homes, and businesses • 130,000–250,000 entries	• *Random House Dictionary* • *The American Heritage Dictionary* • *Webster's New World Dictionary*
School Dictionaries	• Definitions suitable for students' grade levels • Emphasizes common words • 100,000 or fewer entries	• *Macmillan School Dictionary* • Merriam-*Webster's School Dictionary*

Each page of a dictionary has guide words along the top of the page. Guide words indicate the first and last entries on the page. Using the guide words will help you locate an entry much more quickly than browsing will.

Every page or every two-page spread has a pronunciation key at the bottom. The pronunciation key shows you how to use the special pronunciation symbols found in the dictionary.

Guide words

First entry on the page

How does this illustration help convey the definition of *solar system?*

Last entry on the page

Pronunciation key

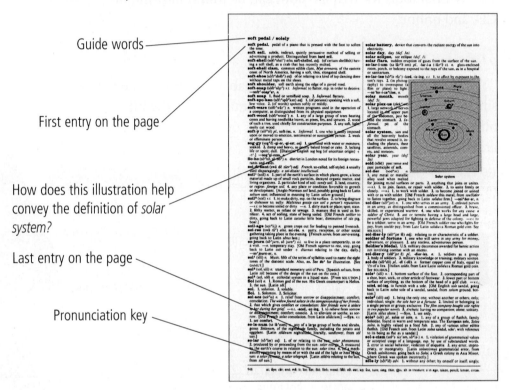

The Thesaurus

A thesaurus is a special type of dictionary that lists synonyms, or words with similar meanings. If you do word processing, your computer software may even include a thesaurus. You probably most often use a dictionary to find the meaning of a particular word. When you use a thesaurus, you already know the meaning you want to convey. However, you need to find the word that best expresses that meaning. For example, you want to write that you were tired. But how tired were you? A thesaurus would give you *drained, exhausted, fatigued, tired, wearied, worn-out,* and more such words.

In a thesaurus entry, each definition is followed by several synonyms. The entry may also include a cross-reference to one or more other major entries. If you look up a cross-reference entry, you will find more synonyms for the word listed. Following is an example of a thesaurus entry.

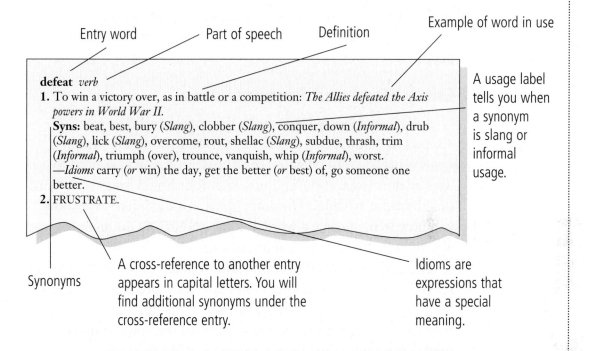

Entry word — Part of speech — Definition — Example of word in use

defeat *verb*
1. To win a victory over, as in battle or a competition: *The Allies defeated the Axis powers in World War II.*
Syns: beat, best, bury (*Slang*), clobber (*Slang*), conquer, down (*Informal*), drub (*Slang*), lick (*Slang*), overcome, rout, shellac (*Slang*), subdue, thrash, trim (*Informal*), triumph (over), trounce, vanquish, whip (*Informal*), worst.
—*Idioms* carry (*or* win) the day, get the better (*or* best) of, go someone one better.
2. FRUSTRATE.

A usage label tells you when a synonym is slang or informal usage.

Synonyms

A cross-reference to another entry appears in capital letters. You will find additional synonyms under the cross-reference entry.

Idioms are expressions that have a special meaning.

Exercise 7

Use a dictionary or a dictionary-style thesaurus to answer these questions.

1. What guide words are on the dictionary page that contains each of the following words?
   a. crackle   **c.** municipal
   b. groan   **d.** solarize
2. Other than at the bottoms of pages, where can you find a guide to pronunciation in a dictionary? Tell which dictionary you used to answer the question.
3. Does the word *deign* rhyme with *mine, mean,* or *main?*
4. What synonyms for *friendly* are listed in the thesaurus? Give at least three.
5. What are six synonyms for *sad?*

The dictionary offers much more than the definitions of words. In a dictionary, you can find out how to divide a word into syllables. You can get information about a word's spelling and pronunciation, its part of speech, and its history. Many dictionaries have entries for places (like cities, countries, and rivers) and famous people.

Entry Word and Pronunciation

A dictionary entry begins with the entry word. The word appears in bold type so that it stands out. In addition, the entry word is broken into syllables. In your writing, you may need to hyphenate a word at the end of a line. You should break up a word only between syllables. The entry word in a dictionary will show you how to hyphenate a word. Online and CD-ROM dictionaries also usually offer audio pronunciations.

The guide to a word's pronunciation follows the entry word. A special set of sound symbols shows how the word is pronounced. Simple words in the pronunciation key at the bottom of the page help you pronounce each symbol. Some of the vowel sounds might be shown in the pronunciation key like this:

fat, āpe, cär; ten, ēven; is, bīte, gō, hôrn, fŏŏl, ūse

You also can find a complete pronunciation key at the front of the dictionary. Try using the sound symbols to pronounce the following word:

in•noc•u•ous   (i nok′ ū əs)

> Note that the last syllable has the schwa (ə) sound, which sounds like the *a* in ago.

Part of Speech

Dictionaries also indicate a word's part of speech. In the entry on the following page, for example, *partition* is first defined as a noun (*n.*) and then as a transitive verb (*v.t.*). You'll find a complete list of abbreviations used for the parts of speech at the front of the dictionary. The example shows the word's meanings for both parts of speech.

> **par·ti·tion** (pär tish´ən) *n.* **1.** a dividing or being divided into shares or distinct parts; division or distribution of portions: *the partition of territory between rival states.* **2.** section or part into which a thing is divided. **3.** that which divides, as an interior wall separating parts of a room.—*v.t.* **1.** to divide into shares or distinct parts: *to partition land for sale, to partition office space into small cubicles.* **2.** to separate by a partition (with *off*): *to partition off a space for storage.* [Latin *partītiō* division.]

Note that *partition* as a noun means "a division." *Partition* as a verb means "to divide something into parts."

The dictionary provides examples illustrating many of the word's definitions.

Definition

Many words have more than one meaning. Some words, in fact, have more than a dozen different meanings. Each definition in an entry is numbered, as shown above. In most school dictionaries, definitions are arranged from the most common to the least common.

Word Origins

Most dictionaries indicate a word's origin and history at the beginning or end of an entry. This brief account tells how the word entered the English language. Sometimes the entry traces the word back through several stages. It shows how the word changed as it passed from language to language.

> **bom·bard** (bom bärd´) *v.t.* **1.** to attack with artillery or bombs. **2.** to subject to a vigorous or persistent attack: *He bombarded her with questions.* **3.** Physics. to subject (atomic nuclei) to a stream of high-speed subatomic particles. [French *bombarder,* from *bombarde* cannon, from Medieval Latin *bombarda* weapon for hurling stones, from Latin *bombus.* See BOMB.]

This word is traced back first to French, the language from which it was borrowed into English. Then the word is traced back to its Latin origin.

Dictionaries often use abbreviations, such as *L.* for *Latin* or *Fr.* for *French,* to show a word's language of origin. You can find a list of these abbreviations at the front of the dictionary. The chart on the next page shows the origins of some English words.

The Origins of Some English Words		
English Word	**Origin**	**Word of Origin**
cookie	Dutch	*koeje*, meaning "small cake"
gumbo	Bantu	*gumbo*, referring to okra, the vegetable
judo	Japanese	*ju*, meaning "gentle" + *do*, meaning "way"
thesaurus	Greek	*thesauros*, meaning "treasure" or "storehouse"

Synonyms

A thesaurus is one place to look for synonyms. A dictionary may also offer a list of synonyms for some words. Some dictionaries give definitions to help you understand the differences in meaning among synonyms. Following is an example.

> **Syn. Excessive, immoderate, inordinate, intemperate, exorbitant** mean going beyond what is normal or proper. **Excessive** suggests an amount or quantity too great for what is required: *The summer rains were excessive and flooded the fields.* **Immoderate** implies going beyond bounds, esp. in emotional matters: *His speech was received by the opposition with immoderate laughter.* **Inordinate** suggests lack of judgment or regulation: *They asked an inordinate price for the house.* **Intemperate** implies lack of control: *His talk turned out to be an intemperate attack on bankers.* **Exorbitant** suggests a rather sharp divergence from the normal: *The new job made exorbitant demands on his time.*

An example sentence helps you understand the meaning of each synonym.

Exercise 8

Use a dictionary to answer the following questions.

1. How is the word *peculiarity* divided into syllables?
2. From what language did the word *pecan* come?
3. What synonyms are given for *era*? List at least three.
4. What part of speech is the word *obstreperous*?

UNIT
23
Vocabulary and Spelling

LOG ON ▶ **Writing** Online   For research tools and additional skills practice, go to glencoe.com and enter QuickPass code WC77680p3.

653

23.1 Borrowed Words

How do languages grow and change? One way is through borrowing words from other languages. When people interact with each other, they're likely to borrow some of one another's words. This can happen even when they speak different languages. This kind of word borrowing into English began when the language was still young.

Early Word Borrowings

In the middle of the fifth century A.D., Germanic tribes from northwestern Europe settled in England. Today we refer to these people as Anglo-Saxons. Their language, now called Old English, was the earliest form of English.

In the late 500s, Christian missionaries came to England from Rome. They began to convert the Anglo-Saxons to Christianity. These missionaries brought to England not only their religion, but also their language—Latin. Many words still in use today were borrowed into Old English from Latin. Some examples are *candle, altar, temple,* and *school.*

A few hundred years later, in A.D. 1066, English came under another important influence.

Detail from Bayeux Tapestry, *William of Normandy's Ship Before Pevensey Shore,* c. 1066

In that year the French-speaking Normans invaded England and conquered the Anglo-Saxons. Over the next few hundred years, many French words came into the English language. The chart on the following page shows some words borrowed from early French.

English Borrowings from French	
Government and Law	city, authority, tax, prison, crime, suit, jury, bail
The Military	army, navy, soldier, sergeant, lieutenant, captain, assault
Dining and Food	dinner, table, fork, plate, roast, sausage, veal, pork
The Arts	music, art, beauty, color, design, theater, poem
Trades	barber, butcher, grocer, painter, tailor, carpenter
Religion	saint, grace, mercy, salvation, clergy, preach

Words from Many Lands

Not long after the Norman invasion, European traders began traveling regularly to the Middle East. Arab traders there sold them silk, spices, and other goods from Asia. Often, the Arabic words for these goods were passed on as well. Some English words that came from Arabic include *alcohol, cotton, mattress, orange, sugar,* and *syrup.*

In the late 1400s, European traders and explorers began traveling even farther. They found new sea routes, explored new lands, and brought back new products— and new words. Portuguese sailors set up trade routes to Africa and Asia. Other Europeans—explorers, sailors, soldiers, missionaries, and colonists—traveled to the Americas. They brought back foods new to Europeans, such as chocolate, potatoes, turkeys, and maize (corn). The words for these foods were added to the English language.

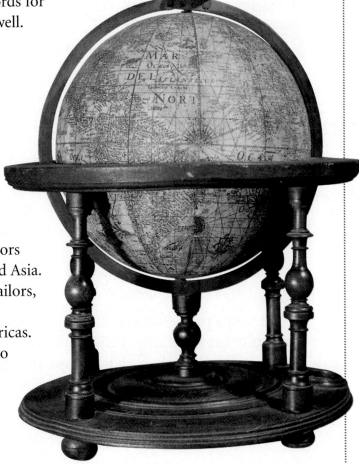

The chart below shows some words that were borrowed from cultures around the world. A few of these words came directly into English. Most were borrowed by other European languages first and then borrowed into English. For example, *banana* began as an African word. The word was picked up in West Africa by traders from Portugal. Later, it was borrowed from Portuguese into Spanish. Then, after bananas were brought into England, the English started using the word. It became part of the English language.

English Words Borrowed from Other Lands	
Africa	banana, chimpanzee, gorilla, okra, zebra
Australia & New Zealand	boomerang, kangaroo, kiwi, koala
India	bandanna, cot, ginger, jungle, loot, pepper, shampoo
Malaya & Polynesia	bamboo, ketchup, paddy, rattan, taboo, tattoo
Mexico & Caribbean	canoe, chocolate, cocoa, coyote, hammock, tomato
Persia (now Iran)	caravan, musk, pajamas, scarlet, shawl

Exercise 1

Look up each of the following words in a dictionary. Tell what language each word was borrowed from.

1. boss
2. zinc
3. yak
4. bungalow
5. spaghetti
6. hurricane

Exercise 2

Work with a partner or a small group. Do some research on European traders or explorers active between the 1100s and the 1800s. Find two new products they brought back to Europe. In a dictionary look up the words that name those products. Tell what language or languages each word came from.

WORDWORKS

FAMILY RESEMBLANCES

Perhaps you've been told that you have your grandmother's eyes, your father's voice, or your aunt's kind nature. Similarities in appearance and personality often show up in families.

Languages belong to families, too. English is part of the language family called Indo-European. Most European languages plus many languages spoken in India belong to this family.

Words from different languages in the same family sometimes have family resemblances. These words, which look similar and often have the same meaning, are called cognates. But don't confuse them with borrowed words. Cognates are words that have descended from the same older language. For example, the English word *mother* has cognates in German (*mutter*), Latin (*mater*), Swedish and Danish (*moder*), French (*mère*), and Italian (*madre*).

Because they often began in very early languages, cognates usually refer to something basic about human relations or culture. Many cognates refer to body parts, family relationships, and plants and animals. The numbers one to ten in most Indo-European languages are cognates. For example, English *ten* has cognates in Latin (*decem*), Greek (*deka*), Spanish (*diez*), Welsh (*deg*), and Dutch (*tien*).

FATHER
Latin–Pater
Greek–Patér
Spanish–Padre
German–Vater
French–Père
Dutch–Vader

Challenge

Can you figure out the English words for the cognates in this sentence?

The vind blew snø against the Haus.

ACTIVITY

Pick A Number

Following are the numbers one through five in different languages. Which word in each item is not a cognate?

1. en, uno, yksi, een
2. två, dos, due, dva
3. tres, kolme, tri, tre
4. fire, vier, ctyri, four
5. cinq, cinco, cinque, fem

Vocabulary and Spelling

23.2 Using Context Clues

Imagine this. You're reading a book and doing fine until you come across the word *exobiologist*. You have no idea what *exobiologist* means, and you don't have a dictionary handy. What do you do? One thing you could do is look for clues in the words and the sentences that surround the unfamiliar word. When you use those surrounding clues, you are using context.

Context Clues

Writers often give clues to the meaning of an unfamiliar word. Sometimes they even tell you what the word means. In the paragraph above, for example, you are told what the word *context* means. The chart below shows some types of context clues.

Interpreting Clue Words		
Type of Context Clue	**Clue Words**	**Examples**
Definition The meaning of the word is given in the sentence.	that is in other words or which means	Janet put the wet clay pot in the *kiln,* **or** oven, to harden.
Example The unfamiliar word is explained through familiar examples.	like such as for example for instance	The new program has been *beneficial* for the school; **for example,** test scores are up and absences are down.
Comparison The unfamiliar word is compared to a familiar word or phrase.	too also likewise similarly resembling	Maria thought the dress was *gaudy.* Lisa, **too,** thought it was excessively flashy.
Contrast The unfamiliar word is contrasted to a familiar word or phrase.	but on the other hand unlike however	Robins are *migratory* birds, **unlike** sparrows, which live in the same region all year round.

Using the General Context

Sometimes you'll have to look for less specific clues in the context. The surrounding sentences may give you subtle clues to the meaning of the unfamiliar word. Look at the passage below. Notice the clues in the general context that help you figure out the meaning of *exobiologist*.

> Maryann was determined to become an exobiologist. She knew that there was no proof that any forms of life existed on other planets. However, she knew it was possible that life *could* have developed beyond our planet. Maryann had been interested in space exploration ever since her childhood. She felt that the study of exobiology was an exciting new field, and she wanted to be part of it.

You can tell from the sentence structure that exobiologist is a noun that names a person.

These clues show that it has something to do with life on other planets.

These clues show that exobiology, a word related to exobiologist, is a field of study.

You know from the other clues that the word has to do with life on other planets. You can figure out that an exobiologist studies life on other planets.

Exercise 3

Use context clues to figure out the meaning of the italicized word in each passage. Write the meaning of the word. Then tell what context clue or clues you used.

1. Their pet dog, Topper, had been like a member of the family for more than ten years. It was no surprise, then, that Jeff's whole family *lamented* Topper's death.
2. Nikolai is *conscientious* about cleaning his room. Andrew, on the other hand, must be reminded again and again to clean up his room.
3. Julie, a straight-A student, is *exempt* from final exams. Carlos, another straight-A student, is also excused from taking the exams.
4. The film must be completely *immersed,* or covered with fluid.
5. The little boy was *naive*. For instance, he believed the stories older boys told him about space aliens.

Vocabulary and Spelling

WORDWORKS

DOES THIS MAKE ¢¢¢ 2 U?

Have you ever played the picture game in which you draw a picture to represent a word? Your teammates must guess the word by looking at your drawing. The game is fun because not all words are easy to draw or guess.

What if you always had to use pictures when writing? You'd have something in common with people living about 5,500 years ago, when writing systems were first developing. Pictographic writing was one of the earliest forms of writing—before any alphabet was developed. In pictographic writing, a picture of a tree would mean "tree" and a picture of the sun would mean "sun." There are limitations to pictographic writing, though. Try creating a simple picture to mean "hungry" or "thinking" or "dizzy." You'll soon find that a picture isn't always worth a thousand words.

> ### Challenge
> *Figure out the question in the rebus below.*

As pictographic writing developed further, people used pictures to represent the sounds of words. For example, if you used pictographs today, a picture of the sun could mean "sun" or "son."

A picture could also be used in place of just one syllable of a word. Using a picture of a key to stand for the second part of *lucky* would be one example.

A picture that represents a part of a word or phrase is called a *rebus.* The use of rebuses was a big step toward the development of modern writing systems. The rebus is now popular in games and puzzles.

ACTIVITY

Pictoplay

Using pictographs and rebuses, work with a partner to rewrite the note below. See how many syllables and words you can replace with pictures.

Would you like to go to the store with me? I need to get some potatoes, corn, and beans for dinner tonight.

Roots, Prefixes, and Suffixes

Like pieces of a puzzle, parts of words can be fitted together to make a whole word. Unlike a puzzle, however, the same word piece can be put together with many other pieces. Thus, a few word parts can make many different words.

The main part of a word is the root. Prefixes and suffixes are other pieces that can be attached to a root to change its meaning. The diagram below shows how prefixes, roots, and suffixes fit together to make new words.

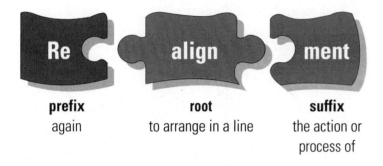

| **prefix** | **root** | **suffix** |
| again | to arrange in a line | the action or process of |

Roots

The **root** of a word carries the main meaning. Some roots, like the word *align,* above, can stand alone. Other roots must have other parts attached to make a complete word. For example, the root *ject* ("throw") is useless by itself. But combined with a prefix it can become *reject, project,* or *inject.* Add a suffix and you get *rejection, projection,* or *injection.*

Knowing the meanings of common roots can help you figure out the meanings of unfamiliar words. The following chart shows two more helpful roots. Can you think of some other words that contain these roots?

ROOTS	WORDS AND MEANINGS	
script means "writing"	*scripture*	sacred writing
	transcript	a written record
phon means "sound" or "voice"	*telephone*	instrument for sending voices
	phonics	the study or science of sounds

Prefixes

Prefixes are syllables attached before a root. Prefixes can change, or even reverse, the meaning of a word. Two or more prefixes may have the same, or nearly the same, meaning. A single prefix may have more than one meaning. The chart below shows the meanings of some common prefixes. For example, *un-* (as in *unknown*) and *il-* (as in *illegal*) both can mean "not" or "the opposite of."

Prefixes	Prefixes	Words	Meanings
Prefixes that reverse meaning	*un-* means "not" or "the opposite of"	unnatural unhappy	not natural not happy
	il- means "not" or "the opposite of"	illegal illogical	not legal not logical
Prefixes that show relations	*re-* means "again"	rebuild reconsider	to build again to consider again
	super- means "beyond, above, or more"	superfine superhuman	extra fine more than human
Prefixes that show judgment	*pro-* means "in favor of" or "on the side of"	progovernment	in favor of the government
	anti- means "against" or "opposite"	antiaircraft	against aircraft (as in "antiaircraft gun")
Prefixes that show number	*semi-* means "half" or "partial"	semiyearly semisweet	twice a year somewhat sweet
	uni- means "one"	unicycle unilateral	one-wheeled vehicle one-sided
	bi- means "two"	biweekly bicycle	every two weeks cycle with two wheels
	tri- means "three"	triangle tripod	having three angles three-legged stand
	deci- means "ten"	decade decimal system	period of ten years system based on tens

Suffixes

A **suffix** is a syllable added to the end of a root that changes the meaning of the root. Many suffixes also change the part of speech of a root word. Learning the meanings and uses of suffixes can help you build your vocabulary. As with prefixes, two or more suffixes can have the same or a similar meaning.

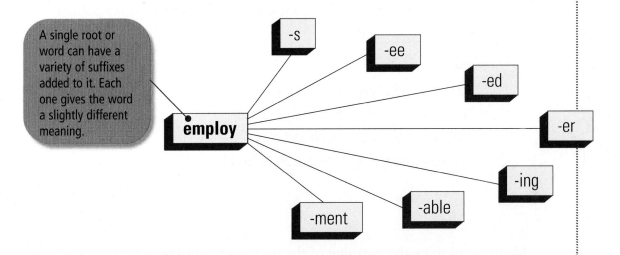

A single root or word can have a variety of suffixes added to it. Each one gives the word a slightly different meaning.

employ — -s, -ee, -ed, -er, -ing, -able, -ment

Suffixes			
	Suffixes	**Words**	**Meanings**
Suffixes that show state of being	*-ship* means "state or condition of"	leadership friendship	state of being a leader state of being a friend
	-hood means "state or condition of"	childhood nationhood	condition of being a child condition of being a nation
Suffixes that mean "one who"	*-ist* means "one who"	archaeologist physicist	one who studies archaeology one who studies physics
	-ian means "belonging to" or "characteristic of"	librarian Bostonian	worker in a library person who lives in Boston
Suffixes that mean "related to"	*-ish* means "relating to" or "like"	childish boyish	like a child like a boy
	-al means "relating to"	global tropical	relating to the globe relating to the tropics

Notice that sometimes the spelling of a word is changed when a suffix is added to it. For example, the ending of *library* is changed to make the word *librarian.* Look at pages 673, 674, and 677 to learn more about spelling words with suffixes.

Words seldom have more than a single prefix added to them. However, more than one suffix can be added to the same word. Each added suffix can change the word's part of speech as well as its meaning. The following examples show how suffixes can change a single root word.

peace (noun)
peace + -ful = peaceful (adjective)
peace + -ful + -ly = peacefully (adverb)
peace + -able = peaceable (adjective)
peace + -able + -ly = peaceably (adverb)

Exercise 4

Identify and write the meaning of the root in each of the following words. Then write the definition of each word. Use your dictionary for help if necessary.

1. prescription
2. objection
3. phonetic
4. manuscript
5. phonetician
6. microphone

Exercise 5 ◆

Add a prefix, a suffix, or both to each of the following words. Use prefixes and suffixes from the charts in this lesson. Then write the definition of the new word. Use a dictionary to check your definitions.

1. legible
2. nature
3. form
4. war
5. done
6. highway
7. weekly
8. fresh
9. cycle
10. violin

WORDWORKS

"MAN TURNS INTO SEA MONSTER"

The newspaper headline "Man eating lobster wrecks restaurant" probably wouldn't worry you. But "Man-eating lobster wrecks restaurant" might send you into a panic. The two headlines look similar, but their meanings are obviously very different. Why is that?

Like all other languages, English has the capacity to grow, or add new words. One way to add words is through compounding, or joining words to make new words. The compound *man-eating* comes from joining *man* and *eating*.

Often the meanings of the words that make up a compound give a clue to its meaning. For example, *doghouse* means "a house for a dog."

Sometimes, though, the meaning of the compound is more than the sum of its parts. The word *underdog,* for instance, doesn't refer to something under a dog but to a predicted loser in a competition.

Words that form compounds can be spelled closed (*troublemaker*), open (*high school*), or hyphenated (*man-eating*). Compounds can be made with most parts of speech—noun plus noun (*fire drill*), verb plus verb (*blow-dry*), adjective plus noun (*fast food*), and so on. The compounds themselves can be almost any part of speech.

Challenge

Pronounce hothouse *and* hot house. *Do you pronounce them differently? Try other similar compounds. How do we indicate compounds in speech?*

ACTIVITY

Get It Together

See how many compounds you can form by joining words from opposite columns.

bird	blue
over	house
light	dog
air	night
watch	flow

Vocabulary and Spelling

23.4 | Synonyms and Antonyms

As a writer, you want to present your ideas as clearly as possible. You also want your writing to be interesting and lively. A knowledge of synonyms and antonyms can improve your vocabulary and your writing.

The trouble began on a *sizzling* August day.

sizzling
blistering
scalding
sultry
torrid
scorching
red-hot
boiling

Synonyms

Synonyms are words that have the same, or nearly the same, meaning. Synonyms can make your writing more colorful. When you describe something, you want to make your readers "see" what you describe. One way to do that is to avoid dull, overused words. For example, suppose you're describing a tired old dog walking across the street. You could simply write "The tired old dog walked across the street." Or you could write "The worn-out, ancient mutt hobbled across the street." Choosing the right synonyms for overused words can make your writing livelier.

A dictionary gives synonyms for some words. However, the best place to find synonyms is in a dictionary of synonyms. Such a book is also called a thesaurus. (See pages 647–649 for more information about using a thesaurus.) Remember that synonyms rarely mean exactly the same thing. For example, *weary, worn-out, drained,* and *exhausted* are all synonyms for *tired.* However, each word has a slightly different meaning. Check the meanings of synonyms to make sure the one you choose is the right one.

Antonyms

Antonyms are words with opposite, or nearly opposite, meanings. *Up* and *down,* and *tall* and *short* are examples of antonyms. While many English words have synonyms, antonyms are less common.

Antonyms are often formed by adding a prefix meaning "not." *Un-, il-, dis-, in-,* and *non-* are all prefixes that can reverse meaning to form antonyms. For example, you can easily form antonyms for the words *happy, legal, comfort, complete,* and *fattening.* Just add the prefixes above in the order listed.

When adding a prefix to make an antonym, make sure you know the exact meaning of the new word. For example, you can add the prefix *dis-* to the word *ease.* However, the word formed, *disease,* is no longer an antonym for *ease,* as it was formerly.

Exercise 6

In each of the following sentences, replace the underlined word with a synonym. Use a thesaurus if you wish. Hint: When checking a verb in the thesaurus, look for the present-tense form.

1. The horse <u>ran</u> around the track.
2. The flower was a <u>pretty</u> color.
3. Carla stood at the <u>top</u> of the mountain.
4. Jake waxed and <u>polished</u> his new car.
5. Rochelle <u>looked</u> out the window.
6. It was a <u>hard</u> test.
7. The meal was <u>tasty</u>.
8. We picked some of the <u>good</u> peaches.
9. Leon listened to the two men <u>talking</u>.
10. <u>Grab</u> the other end of the rope.

Exercise 7

Think of an antonym for each of the following words. Then write a sentence, using the antonym. Underline the antonym in the sentence. Remember that many antonyms can be made by adding prefixes that reverse meaning.

1. cruel
2. friendly
3. dull
4. common
5. cheerful

Vocabulary and Spelling

WORDWORKS

THE CAT WANTS HIS PAJAMAS BACK

"Those red sleepers are the cat's pajamas." Suppose a father said this to his young daughter about what she wanted to wear to bed one night. Should she try to scrounge up something else to wear so that she won't upset the cat? Or should she accept the compliment? It might help to know that at one time, *the cat's pajamas* meant "something good or desirable."

Challenge

The passage below uses 1960s slang. What do the underlined slang words mean? What slang words would you use instead?

<u>Get</u> <u>with</u> <u>it</u>, and go to the dance. It'll be a <u>blast</u>! I really <u>dig</u> school dances. They're <u>boss</u>.

The *cat's pajamas* is an example of slang, the informal vocabulary of a group of people. Slang usually begins with a small group of people, who use it almost as a code for group identity. Over time more and more people may use it.

Slang goes in and out of style. Have you heard *rat fink*, meaning "someone who gives information behind another's back"? Does *swinging*, meaning "lively and up-to-date," ring a bell? These two phrases were popular in the 1950s and 1960s but aren't used now.

Some words begin as slang and later become accepted into the language. *Hot dog* and *fan* both began as slang. Other slang words simply remain so. One current exam-

ple of a slang expression is " I'm out of here," meaning "I'm leaving."

What's the Word

Put your ears on "slang alert" for a day. Listen for examples of slang that you, your friends, or even characters on TV use. Take notes as you listen. Create an American "Slanglish-English" dictionary. Write each word and its "translation," as in a foreign-language dictionary.

Homonyms

Did you ever play the *bass* or catch a *bass* in the lake? Did you ever shed a *tear* when you found a *tear* in your favorite shirt? Pairs (not *pears*) of words that sound alike or are spelled alike are called homonyms. Homonyms can be divided into two groups. One group contains words called homographs.

Homographs

The word *homograph* is made up of two roots: *homo* (same) and *graph* (writing). Homographs are words that are spelled alike. However, the words have different meanings and may have different pronunciations. *Bass* (pronounced to rhyme with *face*) is a musical instrument or type of voice. (He sang in the *bass* section of the chorus.) *Bass* (pronounced to rhyme with *lass*) is a kind of fish. (I caught an eight-pound striped *bass*.) The chart shows some more examples of homographs.

Homographs		
Word	**Meaning**	**Example**
object (ob' jekt)	a thing	What is that strange *object*?
object (əb jekt')	to oppose	"I *object!*" the lawyer shouted.
sow (sō)	to plant	Farmers *sow* their crops.
sow (sou)	a female pig	The *sow* has five piglets.
lead (lēd)	to go in advance	Will you *lead* the way?
lead (led)	a kind of metal	This pipe is made of *lead*.
dove (duv)	a type of bird	The *dove* is a symbol of peace.
dove (dōv)	past tense of *dive*	He *dove* into the lake.
bow (bō)	a knot with two loops	The child learned to tie a *bow*.
bow (bou)	to bend at the waist	She refused to *bow* to the king.
wind (wind)	air that moves	Listen to the *wind* in the trees.
wind (wīnd)	to wrap around	Help me *wind* up this ball of string.
wound (woond)	an injury	Cover the *wound* with gauze.
wound (wound)	past tense of *wind*	He *wound* the gauze around his hand.

Homophones

Homophones are a second type of homonym. Homophones are words that sound alike. *Bass* (the instrument) sounds the same as *base* (as in *first base*). *Pair, pare,* and *pear* are another group of homophones.

Homophones sound alike but have different spellings and different meanings. That's why they're often confused. Always check a dictionary if you're unsure about which homophone to use. The chart below shows some common homophones. Can you think of any additional examples?

See

HOMOPHONES
to, too, two
meat, meet
here, hear
there, their, they're
deer, dear
sail, sale
for, four

Sea

Exercise 8

In each sentence below, find as many words as you can that have homophones. Write each word you find. Then write its homophone or homophones.

1. Angela sat on the shore, waiting to see the sun come up over the horizon.
2. How much will the sail for the new boat cost?
3. I need to buy a necktie and a pair of shoes.
4. The boys will wait in here, and the girls will wait over there.
5. Would you like four more of those?

WORDWORKS

CAN YOU PICK A FLOUR?

"How is bread made?"

"I know that!" Alice cried eagerly. "You take some flour—"

"Where do you pick the flower?" the White Queen asked. "In a garden, or in the hedges?"

"Well, it isn't picked at all," Alice explained: "it's ground—"

"How many acres of ground?" said the White Queen.

In this passage from *Through the Looking Glass,* Lewis Carroll plays with homophones, words having the same sounds but different meanings.

Most of today's homophones didn't always sound alike. *Bear* and *bare* began as English words with the same meanings as today—a *bear* was an animal, and *bare* meant "uncovered." However, hundreds of years ago *bear* and *bare* didn't sound the same at all. The word *bear,* spelled *bera,* had two syllables. The word *bare,* spelled *bær,* had the vowel sound of the *a* in *bat.* Gradually, the pronunciations grew closer until the words became homophones.

Grate, which was borrowed from French originally had the same meaning as it does today, "a metal lattice to cover a window or fire." The English word *great,* which originally meant "thick" or "coarse," had two syllables. Later, the second syllable was lost, so that today we have another pair of homophones.

Challenge

"Cinderella opened a photo shop and waited for her prints to come." Think of another silly joke that depends upon homophones. Better yet, make one up.

Get It Together

Give the homophones for each pair of clues.

1. a story; what a dog wags
2. it stops your bike; a crack in a vase
3. bread before baking; female deer
4. a dark time; a medieval warrior
5. animal feet; a short rest

23.6 Spelling Rules I

What would you think of a letter or an essay full of misspelled words? You might think that the writer was careless. You might even have trouble understanding the writer's ideas. Good writing includes careful attention to details such as spelling.

Do you have trouble with spelling? One reason for the problem may be that the spelling of English words doesn't always make sense. For example, pronounce the words *through, dough, ought, bough, cough,* and *rough.* Did you notice that the letters ough are pronounced differently in each word? Worse yet, the same sound can be spelled several ways. For example, pronounce oh. Some other ways to spell the same sound are *oe (doe), ou (soul), ew (sew),* and *oa (road).*

The best way to avoid spelling errors is to check your spelling against a dictionary. However, you won't always have a dictionary handy. Learning a few spelling rules will help you master the spelling of thousands of words.

Spelling *ie* and *ei*

The letters *ie* and *ei* are contained in many English words. They often cause confusion. The following rhyme can help you remember how to spell words with these letter combinations. There are so few exceptions to this rule that you can easily memorize all the important ones.

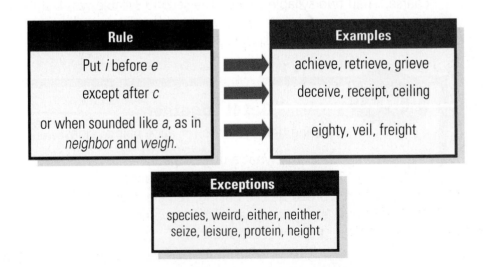

Rule	Examples
Put *i* before *e*	achieve, retrieve, grieve
except after *c*	deceive, receipt, ceiling
or when sounded like *a*, as in *neighbor* and *weigh.*	eighty, veil, freight

Exceptions
species, weird, either, neither, seize, leisure, protein, height

Spelling Unstressed Vowels

English is full of words with an unstressed vowel sound. In dictionaries this sound is represented by a special symbol called a schwa (ə). Say the word *about* aloud, listening to the sound of the vowel in the first syllable. This unstressed vowel always *sounds* the same (*uh*), but it can be spelled *a, e, i, o, u,* or more than a dozen other ways. Listen for the sounds of the underlined letters in the words *c<u>a</u>nal, ang<u>e</u>l, penc<u>i</u>l, pers<u>o</u>n, circ<u>u</u>s, mount<u>ai</u>n,* and *serg<u>ea</u>nt.* All these words have the same unstressed vowel sound.

As you can see, words with this vowel sound can cause spelling problems. You can't just "spell it the way it sounds." Sometimes, however, you can get around the difficulty. Think of a related word in which the vowel is stressed. When the vowel is stressed, it may not be as great a spelling problem. For example, you may not be sure whether *legal* or *legel* is the correct spelling. However, you may know the related word *legality* (notice the stress). You can see that the vowel letter you want is *a.* The chart below shows some additional examples of how you can use this strategy.

Spelling Unstressed Vowels		
Unknown Letter	**Related Word**	**Correct Spelling**
opp_site	opp<u>o</u>se	opposite
rid_cule	rid<u>i</u>culous	ridicule
phot_graph	phot<u>o</u>graphy	photograph
observ_nt	observ<u>a</u>tion	observant
inform_tive	inform<u>a</u>tion	informative

Suffixes and the Silent e

Many English words end with a silent letter *e.* When you add a suffix to words that end in a silent *e,* the *e* is often dropped. However, sometimes the silent *e* is kept. The following chart shows the rules for suffixes and the silent *e.*

Adding Suffixes to Words That End with Silent *e*

Rule	Example
When adding a suffix that begins with a consonant to a word that ends with a silent *e*, keep the *e*.	safe + -ly = safely hope + -ful = hopeful **Common exceptions** awe + -ful = awful judge + -ment = judgment
When adding *-ly* to a word that ends with an *l* plus a silent *e*, always drop the *e* and one *l*.	incredible + -ly = incredibly laughable + -ly = laughably
When adding a suffix that begins with a vowel or *y* to a word that ends with a silent *e*, usually drop the *e*. Sometimes the *e* is kept to avoid changing the sound or confusing the meaning of the original word.	shape + -ing = shaping rose + -y = rosy **Common exceptions** dye + -ing = dyeing mile + -age = mileage
When adding a suffix that begins with *a* or *o* to a word that ends with *ce* or *ge*, keep the *e* so that the word will keep the soft *c* or *g* sound.	trace + -able = traceable change + -able = changeable
When adding a suffix that begins with a vowel to a word that ends in *ee* or *oe*, keep the *e*.	agree + -able = agreeable canoe + -ing = canoeing

Suffixes and the Final *y*

Adding suffixes to words that end in *y* can often cause spelling problems. Follow these rules for adding suffixes to such words.

- When a word ends in a vowel + *y*, keep the *y*.

  play + -ful = playful   pray + -ing = praying
enjoy + -ment = enjoyment

- When a word ends in a consonant + *y*, change the *y* to *i*.

  fry + -ed = fried   try + -ed = tried
happy + -ness = happiness

- BUT if the suffix begins with an *i*, keep the *y* so that two *i*'s don't come together.

  fry + -ing = frying   carry + -ing = carrying

Adding Prefixes

The addition of a prefix doesn't change the spelling of a word. This is a rule you can remember easily.

- When you add a prefix to a word, do not change the spelling of the word or the prefix.

pre- + pay = prepay	re- + act = react
dis- + able = disable	im- + possible = impossible
un- + natural = unnatural	de- + odorize = deodorize
il- + legal = illegal	co- + operate = cooperate

Exercise 9

There is one misspelled word in each of the following sentences. Find the word, and write its correct spelling.

1. Luckily, our tickets were exchangable for a performance on another night.
2. Winning the trophy for the third straight year was a tremendous acheivement for our team.
3. The two friends were inseparible when they were children.
4. Attending the play was an agreable experience.
5. Jack tryed canoeing through white water, but he regretted it.

Exercise 10

Look at each set of words below. Find the one misspelled word in each set, and write it correctly.

1. shoeing, changable, freeing
2. judgeing, safely, wholly
3. ilogical, immediate, correspond
4. relieve, deceive, hieght
5. grading, rosey, dyeing.

WORDWORKS

LEFTOVER LETTERS

English spelling can seem strange. Why, for example, is there a _w_ in _two_ and _answer_? What is _gh_ doing in _thought_ and _though_? Where did we get all those silent _e_'s?

The answers lie in the history of English. Like all languages, English has changed over time, and one major change has occurred in its pronunciation. Until about five hundred years ago, most of today's leftover letters stood for sounds.

Consider an old friend, silent _e_. Originally the final _e_ in words like _bake_ and _time_ wasn't silent. It stood for an unstressed sound much like the final sound in _Rita._ The pronunciation changed, but not the spelling.

Silent _gh_ is harder to explain since the sound it once stood for no longer exists in English. The letters _gh_ spelled a rough, throat-clearing _k_ sound. That sound is gone, but not the spelling.

You may wonder why all these leftover letters didn't disappear once pronunciations changed. The printing press, invented in 1440, was one reason. By then pronunciation had begun to change, but spelling had not. Printers used the familiar spellings, which became standard as more and more people read books. Thus, printing helped to freeze many early spellings of English words.

Challenge

Some people have wanted to simplify the English spelling system, changing though _to_ tho, _for example. What pro and con arguments can you think of for this proposal?_

sign	signal
bomb	bombard
hymn	hymnal

ACTIVITY

Can You Speak Old English?

Imitate early pronunciations of English words. Try to make each consonant letter stand for a sound.

1. folk
2. gnat
3. answer

4. two (long _o_)
5. light (short _i_)
6. knight (short _i_)

Spelling Rules II

The rules in the last lesson and in this one will help you improve your spelling skills. You probably won't memorize all these rules right away. However, reviewing them from time to time should help you improve your spelling.

Doubling the Final Consonant

Adding suffixes to words that end in a consonant can be confusing. In some cases you double the final consonant when adding the suffix. In other cases you don't double it. The following rules can help you avoid many spelling errors.

Double the final consonant when a word ends in a single consonant following one vowel and

- the word is one syllable

  run + -ing = running   ship + -ing = shipping
  mad + -er = madder   top + -ed = topped

- the word has an accent on the last syllable and the accent stays there after the suffix is added

  regret + -ed = regretted   prefer + -ed = preferred
  forget + -able = forgettable   commit + -ing = committing

Do not double the final consonant when

- the accent is not on the last syllable

  number + -ed = numbered   differ + -ed = differed

- the accent moves when the suffix is added

  prefer + -ence = preference   fatal + -ity = fatality

- the word ends in two consonants

  hang + -er = hanger   haunt + -ed = haunted

- the suffix begins with a consonant

  light + -ness = lightness   real + -ly = really

Special case: When a word ends in *ll*, and the suffix *-ly* is added, drop one *l*.

  full + -ly = fully   dull + -ly = dully

Forming Plurals

The usual way to form plurals in English is to add *-s* or *-es.* However, there are other ways to form plurals. The following chart shows the general rules for plurals.

General Rules for Plurals		
If the Noun Ends in	**Then Generally**	**Examples**
s, *sh,* *ch,* *x,* or *z*	add *-es*	bus → buses rush → rushes match → matches tax → taxes buzz → buzzes
a consonant + *y*	change *y* to *i* and add *-es*	buddy → buddies candy → candies
a vowel + *y*	add *-s*	boy → boys way → ways
a vowel + *o*	add *-s*	stereo → stereos studio → studios
a consonant + *o*	generally add *-s* **Common exceptions** but sometimes add *-es*	solo → solos photo → photos cargo → cargoes hero → heroes tomato → tomatoes
f or *ff*	add *-s* **Common exceptions** change *f* to *v* and add *-es*	roof → roofs cuff → cuffs thief → thieves hoof → hooves wolf → wolves
lf	change *f* to *v* and add *-es*	shelf → shelves calf → calves
fe	change *f* to *v* and add *-s*	wife → wives knife → knives

Some nouns don't follow the general rules in the chart on page 678. They form plurals in a special way. Most of these special rules are easy to remember. Some of them resemble the general rules. The following chart includes examples of each rule.

Special Rules for Plurals	
Special Case	**Example**
To form the plurals of most proper names, add -*s*. But add -es if the name ends in *s, ch, sh, x,* or *z*.	Troy → Troys Smith → Smiths James → Jameses Thatch → Thatches Rush → Rushes Marx → Marxes Jiminez → Jiminezes
To form the plural of one-word compound nouns, follow the general rules for plurals.	pocketknife → pocketknives gooseberry → gooseberries schoolbag → schoolbags pickax → pickaxes
To form the plural of hyphenated compound nouns or compound nouns of more than one word, make the most important word plural.	sister-in-law → sisters-in-law head of state → heads of state court-martial → courts-martial
Some nouns have irregular plural forms and do not follow any rules. You simply have to remember these plural forms.	goose → geese mouse → mice child → children woman → women
Some nouns have the same singular and plural forms.	fish → fish moose → moose dozen → dozen Sioux → Sioux

Forming Compound Words

The rule for spelling compound words is simple. Keep the original spelling of both words, no matter how the words begin or end.

surf + board = surfboard
green + house = greenhouse
easy + going = easygoing
side + walk = sidewalk

night + time = nighttime
inn + keeper = innkeeper
house + boat = houseboat
home + made = homemade

horse + shoe = horseshoe

Exercise 11

Find the one misspelled word in each of the following sentences, and write its correct spelling.

1. Mrs. Hart's grandaughter will perform two solos.
2. The calfs were injured when the barn ceiling collapsed.
3. The autumn leafs dropped slowly as gentle breezes shook the branches.
4. Two of the chief of staffs met with the president.
5. The truckload of noisy cattle frightened the gooses, which ran about the barnyard in a panic.

Exercise 12

Look at each set of words below. Find the one misspelled word in each set, and write it correctly.

1. halves, puffs, elfs
2. fully, bookeeping, brothers-in-law
3. deer, mouses, children
4. permited, hopped, preferred
5. reelism, houseboat, observant

23.8 Spelling Problem Words

Do you often forget whether *tomorrow* has one *m* or two? Is the correct spelling *advertise* or *advertize*? Most people have trouble spelling certain words. But there are ways in which you can learn to spell even the most difficult words.

Improving Spelling Skills

Here is a spelling strategy that will help you master the spelling of new or difficult words. As you write, note words that you have trouble spelling. When reading, note unfamiliar words or words that look hard to spell. Then use the following steps to learn to spell them.

Say It	**Visualize It**	**Write It**	**Check It**
Look at the printed word, and say it out loud. Say it a second time, pronouncing each syllable clearly.	Without looking at the word, imagine seeing it printed or written. Try to picture the word spelled correctly.	Look at the printed word, and write it two or three times. Then write it without looking at the printed word.	Check what you have written against the printed word. Did you spell the word correctly? If not, try the process again.

Remember also that your dictionary can be an important tool for improving your spelling. You might say, "How can I look up a word if I can't spell it?" You probably can spell enough of a word's beginning to locate it in your dictionary. Look up one spelling, and if you don't find the word, consider alternative letter combinations that could make the sounds you hear, and try again. Once you've located the word, use the four-step spelling method to learn it.

Another way to learn difficult words is to use memory devices, or tricks for remembering. Rhymes, such as *i before e except after c,* are good memory devices. You also can think up clues about how to spell a certain word. For example, if you have trouble remembering that *mathematics* has an *e,* remind yourself that there is *them* in *mathematics.*

Try to think of other tricks, sentences, or rhymes that help you remember how to spell the hard parts of troublesome words.

Keeping a personal word list of difficult words is another way to improve your spelling. You should keep your list up-to-date, adding new words as you come across them. Delete words from the list once you have mastered them. Study the words a few at a time, using the four-step spelling method.

Easily Confused Words

Certain words sound alike or nearly alike but have different spellings and meanings. Look at the following example:

affect   "to bring a change in"
              How does acid rain affect *the forests?*

effect   "a result"
              This test will have a bad effect *on my final grade.*

If you don't know the difference between the two words, you're likely to use the wrong word and therefore the wrong spelling. Some of these easily confused words are listed below.

Words Often Confused	
accept, except	loose, lose
affect, effect	than, then
all ready, already	their, there, they're
all together, altogether	to, too, two
choose, chose	whose, who's
its, it's	your, you're

Frequently Misspelled Words

The following words are often misspelled. Look for your "problem" words on this list. What other words would you add to the list?

Words Often Misspelled

absence	convenient	jewelry	receipt
accidentally	definite	laboratory	recognize
accommodate	disease	leisure	recommend
adviser	dissatisfied	library	restaurant
all right	embarrass	license	rhythm
analyze	environment	misspell	schedule
answer	essential	molasses	separate
beautiful	February	muscle	sincerely
beginning	foreign	necessary	succeed
blaze	forty	neighborhood	technology
business	funeral	niece	theory
cafeteria	genius	noticeable	tomorrow
canceled	government	nuisance	traffic
canoe	grammar	occasion	truly
cemetery	guarantee	original	usually
choir	height	parallel	vacuum
commercial	humorous	permanent	variety
colonel	immediate	physician	Wednesday

Exercise 13

On a separate piece of paper, write the word in the parentheses that correctly completes each sentence.

1. The team was (all together, altogether) satisfied with the outcome of the game.
2. Is this (your, you're) glove?
3. Do you think that Janet will (except, accept) the gift?
4. The car needs to have (its, it's) brakes replaced.
5. If it's not Kim's, then (whose, who's) is it?
6. How will this loss (effect, affect) the playoffs?
7. We can't afford to (lose, loose) the next game.
8. I think dogs are smarter (then, than) cats.
9. We (choose, chose) to see the movie last night.
10. The farmers harvested (their, there, they're) crops.

UNIT 24 Study Skills

24.1 The Parts of a Book

When doing research, you may find more books on your topic than you can read. How do you decide which books will be the most useful? How do you find out if a book has the information you need? Certain pages in the front and the back of a book can help you. These pages can give you clues about whether the information in the book is up-to-date and reliable.

In the Front of the Book

The pages shown below are found in the front part of the book, before the main text. They can help you see whether the book contains what you need.

The **title page** gives the title of the book. It also names the book's author, authors, or editor.

The **contents** lists the names of the book's parts, chapters, sections, and so on. It tells you the page on which each one begins.

The date on the **copyright page** tells you when the book was published.

In the Back of the Book

The glossary and the index are found in the back of a book. Glossaries are found especially in books that use many specialized or technical terms. You often find glossaries in books on science or technology and in some textbooks.

The **index** contains an alphabetical list of topics in the book, including important people, places, events, and terms. Page numbers are given for each entry.

The **glossary** is an alphabetical list of special or unfamiliar terms in the book. Each term is defined.

Exercise 1

Use this textbook as needed to answer the questions. Tell where you found each answer.

1. On what page or pages are prefixes discussed in *Writer's Choice*?
2. What information besides the title can you find on the title page of *Writer's Choice*?
3. What unit in this book discusses capitalization?
4. Suppose you had a book called *An Introduction to Computers* and wanted to find a definition of *system disk*. Where would you look first to find it?
5. Where would you look to discover whether the book *An Introduction to Computers* was up-to-date?

24.2 Reading Strategies

Suppose you needed information about the structure of a plant cell or the events leading up to the Crusades. What would you do? Chances are you would read something. Reading is your most important tool for gaining information. However, there are different ways of reading. Using the best reading strategy for your purpose can save you time.

Skimming

When you skim a piece of writing, you glance over the text rapidly to get a general overview of the material presented. In skimming a textbook, for example, you might look at all the headings and illustrations and any words that are highlighted in bold type. You might also read the first sentence of each paragraph.

You can use skimming to preview material before beginning to read or to study for a test. You can also skim to find out if a book contains information you need.

Scanning

When you scan, your eyes move over the text rapidly, looking for particular information. For example, you may be looking for a name, a date, a figure, or a definition. You might scan to review key terms or main ideas for a test. You often scan to see if a book has any information on a specific topic. Keeping your topic in mind, you would look for words that relate to it. While scanning, you're interested only in finding out if a topic is covered. You'll learn what the book or article actually says about the topic during your careful reading.

Careful Reading

Careful reading means reading the text slowly and carefully to make sure you fully understand the information presented. You need to read carefully when learning material for the first time. Studying a new chapter in one of your textbooks would require careful reading.

Careful reading requires that you pay attention to whether you understand the material. You may need to read difficult passages more than once. For example, you need to read technical or scientific material very slowly and carefully to make sure you understand the ideas. If the material contains unfamiliar or technical terms, be sure to define and clarify those words or phrases. If the book has no glossary, keep a dictionary handy to look up unfamiliar terms.

Three Strategies for Reading		
Strategy	**Purpose**	**Examples of Purpose**
Skimming	Looking over a piece of writing fairly quickly to get an overall view of its content	Will I like this book of short stories? What is this article about? What are the main ideas of this chapter? How is this unit organized? What will I learn from this lesson?
Scanning	Looking rapidly over a piece of writing to find a particular piece or type of information	Does this book tell about the Trail of Tears? What are the characteristics of a sonnet? What key terms will I need to know to understand this chapter? Will I learn anything from this book about African Americans in the Civil War?
Careful Reading	Slowly and carefully reading a piece of writing in order to fully understand its content	What is the purpose of this article? What happens to the characters in this novel? What is this writer trying to say about changes in the English language? What can I learn about computers from this book?

Exercise 2

List some of the reading you have done, both for classes and for yourself, in the past several weeks. Next to each assignment write which of the three reading strategies listed above you would use, and tell why. Meet with a small group of your classmates to compare and discuss your lists.

24.3 | Writing Summaries

Have you ever told a friend about a movie you saw or a book you read? Have you ever explained to a classmate what was covered in a class he or she missed? Summarizing—telling the main ideas of something—saves time. Imagine trying to tell someone every single detail about a movie. It could take longer than the movie itself.

Summarizing in your own words also helps you to organize and remember ideas. After preparing a written summary of something, you'll find that you understand it better.

When to Summarize

Summarizing can help you almost anytime you need to understand and remember ideas or facts. The following chart shows some situations in which you might need to prepare a written summary of some sort.

Summarizing	
SITUATION	**KINDS OF SUMMARIES**
Preparing a written or oral research report	Brief restatements of the important facts and ideas from the various sources you used
Listening to lectures, speeches, or discussions	Notes on the main ideas from the lecture, speech, or discussion
Viewing a film or video documentary	Notes on the main ideas or techniques of the documentary
Reading textbook material	A restatement of the most important information in the textbook

How to Summarize

When you summarize a movie for a friend, you include all the important ideas or events. However, you leave out most of the details. In the same way, a good written summary includes only the main ideas. It leaves out examples and other supporting details.

When you write a summary, you should put the ideas in your own words. Using the author's words is quoting directly, not summarizing. Occasionally you may wish to quote a sentence or a phrase from the author. If you do so, be sure to use quotation marks around the author's words.

Compare the student summary below with the original text shown. Notice how the summary shortens the original but still includes the most important information.

Ferdinand Magellan (1480?–152... ...manded the first European voyage to sai... around the world, Magellan wa... his expedition was backed by t... monarch Charles I. What Ma... find for Spain was a westwar...

The Spice Islands (the M... lured Magellan on his histo... thought he could reach the... sailing west across the Atl...

The voyage began in 1... three years later in 1522,... crew members and one... the voyage and returned to Spain. Mag... himself was killed in the Philippines in April 1521. Nevertheless, he is remembered as a great navigator and the first to command an around-the-world voyage.

Portuguese navigator Ferdinand Magellan commanded a 1519–1522 Spanish voyage to the Spice Islands. Magellan did not live to complete the voyage. However, he is remembered for being the first to show that it was possible to sail around the world.

Exercise 3

Find a short, interesting article in an encyclopedia or some other written source. If you wish, you can select about three or four paragraphs from a longer article. Write a brief summary of the selection you choose. Remember to use your own words.

24.4 Making a Study Plan

Imagine having extra time each week to do what you want without losing study time. One way to gain additional free time is by learning efficient study habits. To get the most out of your study time, try making a study plan.

Setting Goals

Music, art, or physical education classes might not require much work outside the classroom. On the other hand, you could have daily homework in math or many pages to read weekly in social studies. Begin by making a chart of all your classes that require some study time. Next to each class, write any assignments you have received. Then set your goals for each class.

A goal is an objective you want to achieve. Learning to play the piano is a goal. Understanding the rules of grammar is another goal. Simply completing any school assignment, such as reading twenty pages of a textbook, can be a goal.

Get in the habit of always studying in the same place. That will help you concentrate when you sit down to study.

Keep your study supplies—pencils, notebooks, dictionary—at your study place so you don't waste time looking for them.

Always check a calendar that shows assignment due dates and the dates on which you will complete your goals.

Divide school assignments into short-term goals and long-term goals. Short-term goals are those that can be completed in one study session. Learning ten new spelling words or reading a few pages in a textbook are short-term goals. A long-term goal might be completing a research report, reading a novel, or preparing for a unit test.

Long-term goals can be broken down into smaller tasks. For example, studying for a unit test might require reviewing one chapter per study session. Completing a research report would include many short-term tasks. Looking for resources, gathering information, listing and outlining ideas, and writing a rough draft are some examples. Be realistic about what you can do in a study session of one or two hours. For instance, you probably can't read a novel or plan and write a report in one session.

Scheduling Study Time

Setting goals is important, but just as important is setting deadlines to reach your goals. The tool that will help you reach your goals is a study-plan calendar. After you have listed your goals, write each one on your calendar. For long-term goals, first write the final due date. For example, if you have a unit test on the nineteenth, write that on your calendar. Then work backward from the final due date and write each short-term goal on the date that you will work on it. You might want to set goals of reviewing, say, one chapter each day for a week.

You may have a test in science and an oral report in English both due on Monday. If so, you need to carefully balance your study time for both so that you are not overwhelmed. Also, remember to write your goals on your study calendar as soon as you receive your assignments. You don't want to remember some night as you go to bed that you have an English test the following morning!

Be sure to write other important activities, such as sports, music lessons, or school club meetings, on your calendar as well. You probably wouldn't want to schedule writing a draft of a report on the same day that you have a band recital. The calendar on the next page shows a student's study calendar. You can use it as a model for one of your own.

Monthly Planner

Visual Organizers Inc.

Sunday	Monday	Tuesday	Wednesday	Thursday	Friday	Saturday	Top Priority List
				1	**2**	**3**	
4	**5** Study for social studies quiz	**6** Social studies quiz. Read the story "To Build a Fire"	**7** Library research for science report	**8** Study new vocabulary words, English complete exercise 12, math	**9** Do outline of science report English quiz on vocabulary words Hand in exercise 12, math	**10**	
11	**12** Start rough draft of science report	**13** write rough draft of science report	**14** Read chapter 26, social studies	**15** Revise rough draft, science report	**16** Learn new vocabulary words, English Complete exercise 13, math	**17**	Important Phone Calls
18	**19** Type finished science report English quiz on vocabulary words Hand in exercise 13, math	**20** Proofread science report	**21** Hand in science report	**22**	**23**	**24**	
25	**26**	**27**	**28**	**29**	**30**	**31**	Messages – Reminders

Visual Organizers, Inc. © 1987

No. HT-1502 – Monthly P

Exercise 4

Work with a classmate to make a list of your classes and the assignments due in each class. Discuss what special activities, such as sports or music lessons, you should include. Discuss with each other ways of breaking down long-term goals into several short-term goals. Discuss what amount of time should be given to each goal. Then prepare an assignment calendar for one month, based on the list you develop.

24.5 | Using the SQ3R Method

Good study habits involve working efficiently and using an appropriate study strategy. The SQ3R study method will make your study time more productive. The SQ3R method is based on five steps: **S**urvey, **Q**uestion, **R**ead, **R**ecord, **R**eview.

You can use the SQ3R method with any subject. Once you have learned the method and use it regularly, it will become a habit. Using the method, you will remember more of what you read and will understand it better. You will also be better prepared to participate in class.

You **survey** by skimming the text quickly. (See pages 687–688 for hints on skimming.) Remember, look for the main ideas in the material. Pay attention to any sentences or terms that are highlighted. Also look at all photographs, graphs, maps, and other illustrations. Think about how the graphic material is related to the main ideas.

The next step is to **question.** Write out a list of questions that you want to have answered when you read the material. For example, suppose you are studying a section on Ferdinand Magellan in your social studies text. You might write such questions as, Who was Ferdinand Magellan? What was Magellan looking for on his voyage? Why was his voyage important? If you are studying a textbook that has its own review questions, add those to your list. Having a list of questions before you begin reading will help you focus on important ideas in the material.

Read through the material slowly and carefully. As you read, take notes about the main ideas and look for answers to your questions. Also, as you read, you may add questions to your list. Make sure you understand each paragraph or passage.

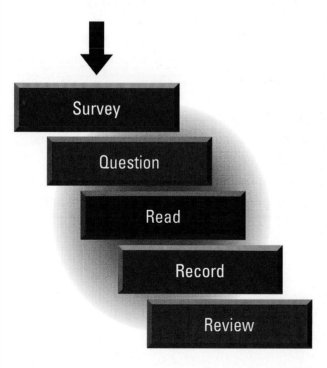

Survey

Question

Read

Record

Review

After you have carefully read the material, **record** the answers to your questions. Don't look in the book. Rely on your memory of what you have read to answer the questions. In this way, you will test whether you have really learned the material. If you have to struggle to answer the questions, you may need to reread the material.

After answering the questions, check your answers against the material you have read. If you have missed any answers, **review** that section again. Following your review, rephrase your questions, or write new ones that cover the same material. Continue rewriting questions and reviewing the material until you are able to answer all questions correctly. Keep your review questions and answers in your notebook. You can use this material later to study or to review for tests.

Exercise 5

Choose from history a famous person who interests you. Read an encyclopedia article about that person, using the SQ3R method. Be sure you take notes, and prepare and answer your review questions carefully. After you have studied the material using the SQ3R method, answer the following questions. Try to do so without referring to your notes.

1. What was the full name of the person you read about?
2. What accomplishment is this person most noted for?
3. What inspired this person to achieve?
4. When did this person live, and when did this person achieve something notable?
5. Where was this person born, or where did this person live most of his or her life?
6. Where did this person make his or her most important accomplishment?
7. Why is this person important in history?
8. How, if at all, is your life different because of this person?

Study Skills

24.6　Taking Notes and Outlining

Suppose someone asked you to go to the grocery store to pick up ten different items. What would you do to be sure you remembered all the items? Write them down, of course! Most people don't remember *everything* they read or hear, or even *most* of what they read or hear. That's why taking notes is important.

Taking Notes

As a student, you will need to remember many things. What was said in a classroom discussion? What main ideas were presented in a video documentary shown in class? What important ideas did you find when researching a topic for a report?

While Listening　Taking notes during classroom lectures or discussions or while viewing films will help you remember what you hear. You can't write down every word that is said. Instead, listen for ideas the speaker emphasizes. Write the key words of those main ideas. Then write the key words for each supporting detail or example the speaker gives to support a main idea.

Highlight or star major ideas or categories of information. Underline important ideas or examples.

Don't try to write notes in complete sentences. Use numbers, dashes, abbreviations, and symbols to save time.

☆ *Water pollution*
   1. *oil spills–tankers*
   2. *chemical wastes–industry*
☆ *Air pollution*
   1. *exhaust fumes–autos*
   2. *carbon dioxide–factories, forest fires*
☆ *Land pollution*
   1. *garbage–landfills*
   2. *industrial waste–dumping*

Study Skills

While Reading   Naturally, you don't want to copy down everything you read when doing research for a report. Have a specific topic or theme in mind when you begin your research. Take notes on just the information you think is important to your topic. Summarize that information in your own words, using as few words as possible.

Write your notes on 3 x 5 note cards. Use a new card for each source or each bit of information you read. At the top of the card write the name of your source, its author, and the page numbers where you found the information. You will need this information for your report. You may also need to go back to a source to look for further information.

Avoid copying long direct quotations. When using a quotation, make sure you copy the words exactly as they appear in the source. Enclose them in quotation marks, and include the name of the person being quoted.

Michael Wyeth, The Story of Romulus and
Remus, pp.127–140.
    According to legend they were twin boys
brought up by a fer
decided to build a n
Tiber River. Romul
argument. Then he

Janet Harper, The City of Rome, pp. 23--25.
Rome has been an important city for more
than 2,000 years. According to legend it was
founded by twin brothers Romulus and
Remus, 753 B.C. Rome began as a small
village built on seven hills along the Tiber
River in Italy.

Always record the source of your information, that is, the title, author, and page numbers of the book or article.

Summarize the information in your own words. Write only the main ideas and important supporting details.

Outlining

After you finish your research, organize the information on your note cards. Examine the information on each card, and group cards with similar ideas together. Each group can be a main topic. Within each group, separate cards into subgroups. These will become subtopics in your outline.

You might try several ways of organizing your cards to see which works best. The order you use will depend on your topic. A history of early Rome would probably require chronological order, or the order in which events happened. A science paper on pollution could be ordered by cause and effect, showing how one thing causes another.

Following is an example of the start of an outline.

Use Roman numerals to number your main topics. Main topics are the "big ideas."

Indent and use letters and numbers for subtopics and their divisions. If a main topic has subtopics, there must be at least two of them.

If you divide a subtopic, there must be at least two divisions.

> The Eternal City
> I. The Founding of Rome
>   A. The Myth of Romulus and Remus
>   1. Twins cared for by wolf
>   2. Romulus kills Remus and builds Rome
>   B. Began as small village built on seven hills
> II. Rome Becomes Powerful
>   A. Romans defeat Etruscans
>   B. Conquer neighbors in Italy

Exercise 6

Work with a small group of classmates. Brainstorm to make a list of topics for a report. As a group, choose one of the topics. Then have group members read and take notes about the topic from a variety of resources. Look over the group's notes and decide on a method of organization for the material. Then, as a group, prepare an outline for a report on the topic.

Study Skills

Understanding Graphic Information

Have you ever read so many facts at once that you had trouble grasping them? A paragraph containing many numbers, for example, could leave you wondering what the main point is. Tables, graphs, and other graphic aids often do a better job of organizing information for you than text.

Tables

Tables organize information by putting it into categories arranged into columns and rows. You can read a table from top to bottom in columns or from left to right across rows. Look at the table below. Suppose you need information about the regions from which most U.S. immigrants have migrated in recent years. Find the headings 2004, 2005, and 2006 at the top of the table and read down the columns. Read across the table to see how immigration numbers have changed for a particular region. For instance, to see how African immigration fluctuated from 2004 to 2006, read across the row labeled Africa.

The title tells you what kind of information the table contains.

Immigration to the United States by Region (Numbers in 1,000s)			
REGION	**2004**	**2005**	**2006**
Africa	66.4	85.1	117.4
Asia	334.5	400.1	422.3
The Americas	756.1	794.3	966.2
Europe	133.2	176.6	164.3
Oceania	6	6.5	7.4
Unknown	3.2	5.3	2.7

Source: U.S. Department of Homeland Security, Office of Immigration Statistics.

Headings along the top and labels at the left side help you locate the information you need.

Note that numbers are given in 1,000s. The number 117.4, therefore, means 117,400 immigrants.

Graphs

Graphs are used to show groups of numbers. The numbers in a table, in fact, can often be turned into a graph. Two types of graphs you will see often in your schoolwork are bar graphs and circle graphs. Examples of both types of graphs are shown on the following page.

Study Skills

Bar Graphs Each number in a bar graph is represented by a bar. The graph can have horizontal (left to right) or vertical (bottom to top) bars. The length or height of the bar indicates the size of the number. The bar graph below shows some of the same information that the table on page 699 shows. Notice how the heights of the bars allow you to compare the numbers easily.

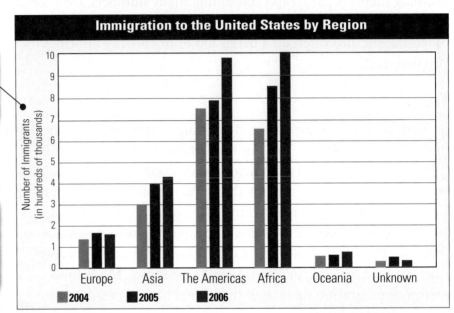

The scale at the left tells what the numbers mean. It also allows you to measure how much or how many of something each bar stands for.

You can quickly see that immigration fluctuates from year to year. From what region has the number of immigrants increased the most between 2004 and 2006?

Immigration to the United States by Region

Number of Immigrants (in hundreds of thousands)

Europe   Asia   The Americas   Africa   Oceania   Unknown

■ 2004   ■ 2005   ■ 2006

Circle Graphs In a circle graph, information is presented as slices of a "pie." (Circle graphs are sometimes called pie charts.) The graph begins with a circle that stands for the whole of something. For example, the whole circle could represent the world population. Each slice of the circle shows a part of the whole. If the whole circle is the world's immigrant population, each slice could show the immigrant population of one region.

U.S. Immigrants by Region, 2004–2006

The Americas **35.5%**

Africa **37.9%**

Unknown **1.5%**

Oceania **2.8%**

Europe **6.5%**

Asia **15.8%**

Notice how easy it is to compare the sizes of the slices. Which two regions come closest in numbers of immigrants?

Source: Department of Homeland Security, 2006

Study Skills

Since a circle graph shows parts of a whole, the slices are often marked as percentages. The whole circle is 100 percent—or *all*. The percentages of all the slices add up to 100 percent. The circle graph on the previous page shows information taken from the table on page 699.

Maps

Maps show a portion of the earth's surface. Maps can show a variety of information. Physical maps show natural features of the earth's surface, such as rivers and mountains. Political maps show the boundaries of countries, states, and other political divisions, as well as cities. Physical and political features are often combined on a single map. Historical maps may show areas held by particular groups during a certain period in history. They may show changes in boundaries over time or other historical information.

The title of the map tells what its subject is. The title of a historical map will tell what period of history the map shows.

Most maps have a legend, or key, to explain the features they show. This map key explains how colors are used to show each period of growth of the Roman Empire.

A map scale lets you measure distances on the map.

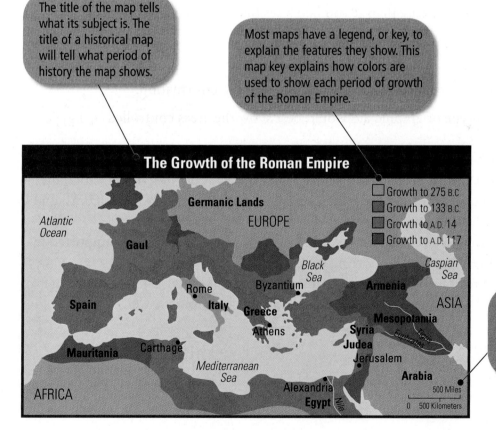

The Growth of the Roman Empire

Growth to 275 B.C.
Growth to 133 B.C.
Growth to A.D. 14
Growth to A.D. 117

Diagrams

Has someone ever tried to describe an unfamiliar object or process to you? Perhaps you had trouble understanding it until he or she drew

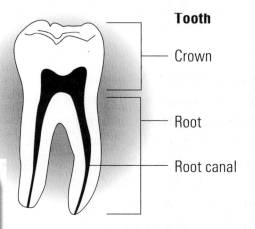

Tooth

Crown

Root

Root canal

a picture. Being able to picture the parts of an object or to picture how the object works can help you understand it. That's why we use diagrams.

Diagrams are pictures that show a process or show relationships among parts of an object. In some diagrams, each part of an object is labeled. A label may include

Many diagrams are cutaways that show the inside of something you would not normally see.

an explanation of what that part does or how it relates to the whole. Diagrams help you understand an object much more easily than if you had a written or spoken description.

Exercise 7

Answer the following questions about graphic information.

1. Which type of graphic aid would best show the areas controlled by Egypt in 1800 B.C.?
2. Which type of graphic aid would best show how the space shuttle works?
3. Which type of graphic aid would best show what portion of your total diet is made up of fruits and vegetables, protein foods, dairy products, grains, and other foods?
4. Which type of graphic aid would best show the amounts of oil imported by the five biggest oil-importing countries?
5. What region contributed the most immigrants to the United States in the period 1981–1990? Use a graphic aid in this lesson to answer.

24.8 Using Memory

Think of the trouble you'd have multiplying 1,634 x 391 if you didn't know the multiplication tables. (You may not always have a pocket calculator handy.) Memorizing certain information helps you in your schoolwork. It saves you the time of looking up the same facts over and over.

How to Memorize

The most often-used memory technique is repetition—just repeating something over and over. Putting a group of items in some order can make them easier to remember. Alphabetical order, smallest to largest, and nearest to farthest are some possible ways of ordering items.

Writing out what you want to memorize is a good technique. Writing out poems, sayings, or long lists and saying them aloud as you write will help you memorize them.

Tricks for Remembering

Another way of remembering material is by using tricks such as sayings or rhymes. The chart shows a few examples.

Tricks for Remembering	
Purpose	**Memory Aid**
To remember the year Columbus sailed to the Americas	In fourteen hundred and ninety-two, Columbus sailed the ocean blue.
To remember that the order of the planets from the Sun is <u>M</u>ercury, <u>V</u>enus, <u>E</u>arth, <u>M</u>ars, Jupiter, <u>S</u>aturn, <u>U</u>ranus, and <u>N</u>eptune	<u>M</u>y <u>v</u>ery <u>e</u>xcellent <u>m</u>other just <u>s</u>erved <u>us</u> <u>n</u>ectarines.
To remember that the order of colors in a rainbow is <u>r</u>ed, <u>o</u>range, <u>y</u>ellow, <u>g</u>reen, <u>b</u>lue, <u>i</u>ndigo, and <u>v</u>iolet	Roy G. Biv
To remember that the person who runs a school is a princi<u>pal</u>, not a princi<u>ple</u>	The princi<u>pal</u> is my pal.

The memory aids in the chart are just a few of the common ones. You can make up your own tricks to help you remember information. For example, you may need to memorize the scientific classifications of living things: kingdom, phylum, class, order, family, genus, and species. You could make up a sentence in which the first letter of each word is the same as the first letter of each category. Try to use the names of familiar people or places. Using familiar names will make it easier to remember your sentence.

Rhymes are especially effective memory tricks. Poetry can be easier to remember than prose. Another effective trick is to see if the first letters of the items in a list spell a word or a name. For example, atoms contain <u>p</u>rotons, <u>e</u>lectrons, and a <u>n</u>ucleus. Think of a <u>pen</u> to remember that fact. The name Roy G. Biv in the chart on page 703 is another example. It's even easier if the items do not have to be memorized in order.

Experiment with these techniques the next time you need to memorize information. Try tricks of your own as well. You may find just the right techniques for your own use.

Exercise 8

Work with one or two classmates. Develop a memory trick to remember the names of the five Great Lakes from east to west: Ontario, Erie, Huron, Michigan, and Superior. Experiment with several of the techniques you learned in this lesson.

Exercise 9

With one or two classmates brainstorm some item of information that should be memorized, such as members of the animal kingdom or the names of important navigators during the Age of Exploration. Decide on the best technique for memorizing the information. Then develop a memory trick to remember it.

Study Skills

UNIT 25

Taking Tests

LOG ON ▶ **Writing** Online | For research tools and additional skills practice, go to **glencoe.com** and enter QuickPass code WC77680p3.

705

25.1 | Test-Taking Strategies

Your teacher has just announced you will have an English test in two weeks. How will you get ready for it? Careful attention to daily classroom assignments and discussions is the best way to be prepared. However, you can also get ready by learning how to take a test. Effective test-taking involves budgeting your time wisely both before and during the test.

Preparing for a Test

You can prepare for a test as soon as it is announced. First, note when the test will be given, and find out what it will cover. Then make a study plan that allows you to organize your time effectively. For suggestions on making a study plan, see pages 691–693.

Once you've decided how to budget your study time, start reviewing the material. Look over your textbook, class notes, homework assignments, and quizzes. Write a list of study questions as you review. If possible, get together with other students and work in a study group. Quiz one another with the questions each of you has prepared.

Taking a Test

The day of the test has arrived. You've prepared wisely, and your hard work should pay off. Keep in mind, however, that tests usually last one class period or less. Since the time is limited, you will need to use your time efficiently during the test. The following page has some tips that will help you.

Taking Tests

Tips on Managing Your Time During a Test

1. Read the directions carefully before you begin. Understanding the directions will help you answer items correctly.

2. Answer all the items you are sure of first. Skipping hard items will give you time to answer all of the items you know.

3. After you have finished the easier items, go back and try the items you skipped. Give the best answers you can.

4. Allow time to check your answers before you turn in your test. This review will decrease your chances of making simple errors.

Exercise 1

Choose the response that best completes each of the following statements:

1. A good way to prepare for a test is to make a _____.
   - **a.** class schedule
   - **b.** study break
   - **c.** study plan
   - **d.** summary

2. It's a good idea to review your _____.
   - **a.** homework
   - **b.** textbook
   - **c.** quizzes
   - **d.** all of the above

3. When a test is announced, one of the first things to find out is _____.
   - **a.** whether you will need a pencil or a pen
   - **b.** what the test will cover
   - **c.** the teacher's name
   - **d.** how the test will be graded

4. When taking a test, it is a good idea to skip the _____ until you have completed the other items.
   - **a.** first few items
   - **b.** even-numbered items
   - **c.** easy items
   - **d.** difficult items

5. Allow time to _____ your answers before you turn in your test.
   - **a.** remove
   - **b.** check
   - **c.** rearrange
   - **d.** none of the above

25.2 Types of Test Items

Your teacher has just informed the class of an upcoming test. It will contain true-false, multiple-choice, matching, fill-in, and short-answer items. Don't panic. There are strategies you can learn that will help you answer each of these types of test items.

True-False Items

A true-false item asks you to decide whether a statement is true or false. A single true-false statement may contain some information that is true and some that is false. However, the item should be marked true only if the *entire* statement is true. If *any* part of the statement is false, you should mark it false. Look at the following example.

> The first part of this sentence is true, but the second part is not. Columbus landed in what is now the Bahamas. The statement is false.

Columbus sailed westward from Spain in 1492 and landed at the site of present-day New York City on October 12.

Multiple-Choice Items

Multiple-choice test items are the kind you will encounter most often. Each item includes an incomplete sentence or a question and several responses. You must choose the response that best completes the sentence or answers the question. Read all of the responses before writing your answer. Eliminate those you know are incorrect. This method will help you zero in on the correct response.

Be careful about choosing responses that contain absolute words, such as *always, never, all,* or *none.* Since most statements have exceptions, absolute statements are often incorrect.

The following multiple-choice item might appear on an English test. As you read it, decide how you would select the correct answer.

Taking Tests

Which statement concerning the book *Julie of the Wolves* is accurate?

a. It was written by Jean Craighead George.
b. It takes place in North America.
c. It is the story of a girl and wild animals.
d. all of the above

> You probably know that response *a* is correct. However, read all of the responses before answering.

> Select this response only if you are sure that at least two of the responses are correct. In this case, *d* is correct.

Matching Items

In a matching activity you are given two lists of items. You must match items in the first list with items from the second list. Before you begin, notice whether each list contains the same number of items. Often the second column will contain more items than the first column. When that is so, some items in column 2 will not be used.

If each item is to be used only once, make a note of each item as you use it. (If you are permitted to write on the test, cross it out.) Complete the easy matches first. Then there will be fewer items to choose from when you try the more difficult matches.

Match each city with the name of its state.

___ 1. Chicago   a. Alaska
___ 2. Dallas   b. Florida
___ 3. Miami   c. Georgia
___ 4. Atlanta   d. Illinois
___ 5. Fairbanks   e. Texas
                       f. Wisconsin

> On your test paper or answer sheet you must write the correct letter from column 2 for each item in column 1.

> Column 2 has one more item than column 1. One item in column 2 will not be used.

Fill-in Items

Fill-in items usually consist of a sentence with one or more blanks for you to fill in. The number of blanks usually shows how many words will be needed for the response. Your answer should make the statement both true and grammatically correct. Check your choice by rereading the sentence with your answer included. Try answering the following fill-in item.

Notice that four names are needed. The correct fill-in answers are *George Washington*, *Thomas Jefferson*, *Abraham Lincoln*, and *Theodore Roosevelt*.

The United States presidents carved on Mount Rushmore are _____, _____, _____, and _____.

Short-Answer Items

Short-answer questions ask you for specific information. Always read the question carefully to be sure you understand what is being asked. Unless you are told not to, answer each question with a complete sentence. Look at the following question, which might appear on a social studies test.

First, think out your answer. You can compose the sentence in your head before you begin writing.

Why did the early colonists risk the dangerous voyage across the Atlantic Ocean to settle in America?

Be sure you understand the question before you begin your answer. In this case, you will need to give the reasons early colonists came to America.

Rephrase the question to answer with a complete sentence. For example: *The early colonists settled in America to gain religious and political freedom and economic opportunity.*

Practice the test-taking skills you covered in this lesson. Read the passage below. Then answer the test items that follow the passage.

Although he never sailed himself, Prince Henry of Portugal (1394–1460) was an important influence on early exploration. Prince Henry's crews sailed the oceans more than five hundred years ago. They used their knowledge of water currents, winds, and the sun and stars to get them to their destinations.

These sailors also used instruments. Henry, often called the Navigator, set up a school of navigation in Portugal. He brought together experts who worked to improve the compass and the astrolabe. A compass shows directions. With an astrolabe, sailors can tell latitude, or distance from the equator. Led by Henry, the Portuguese developed a fast, maneuverable ship called a caravel. In addition, sailors kept careful records of all they saw. These records added to the information map makers needed and sailors used for later voyages.

1. True or False: Portuguese sailors depended on experience, not on instruments.
2. Why was Prince Henry called the Navigator?
   a. He sailed on many overseas voyages.
   b. He was the king of Portugal.
   c. He encouraged improvements in navigation.
   d. all of the above
3. Match each item with the correct description.
   1. astrolabe   a. indicates direction
   2. caravel   b. shows latitude
   3. compass   c. fast, maneuverable ship
4. Fill in the blanks: Map makers used information from _____ kept by Portuguese _____.
5. Write a short answer: How did Portugal contribute to future world exploration by Europeans?

Taking Tests

You have probably taken standardized tests, which are given to groups of students throughout the country. In order to do your best, you need to be familiar with the types of test items on these exams. Learning how to answer standardized test items will make you feel more relaxed and confident.

Reading Comprehension

Reading comprehension test items measure how well you understand what you read. These items usually include a passage about a specific topic followed by questions. The questions may ask you to identify main ideas or to recognize supporting details. The questions may also ask you to draw conclusions based on the passage. The following is an example of an item from a reading-comprehension test.

The titles in *a* and *b* describe only supporting details. Item *d* is not specific enough. Item *c* focuses on the passage's specific topic and is the correct choice.

Women artists have long been respected in Native American culture. Women in the Great Plains nations have created beautiful ceremonial robes and pottery. In traditional Navaho culture women artists wove magnificent rugs with bold designs and patterns. Cheyenne women developed the art of sewing porcupine and bird quills into elaborate symbols and designs. Some of these women even formed an organization called the Sacred Quillworker's Guild. Members of the organization teach the art to other Cheyenne women.

What would be the best title for this passage?
a. The Sacred Quillworker's Guild
b. Basketry, Weaving, and Design
c. Native American Women Artists
d. Native American Artists

Taking Tests

Vocabulary

Standardized tests often include vocabulary items. One type of vocabulary item asks you to complete a sentence with one of several multiple-choice items. To complete the sentence correctly, you need to know the meaning of a particular word.

Sometimes you can use your knowledge of word parts to identify a word's meaning. See if you can analyze the parts of *preface* to complete the item below.

1. A book's preface appears _____ .

   a. at the end of the book
   b. at the beginning of the book
   c. in the middle of the book
   d. just before the book's index

Notice that *preface* contains the prefix *pre-*, which means "before." You can use this knowledge to determine that the correct answer is *b*.

In another type of vocabulary item, you show that you understand a word's meaning by choosing a synonym for it. In the following example you must choose the word closest in meaning to the underlined word in the sentence.

By trying each choice in the sentence, you can eliminate *worry*, *attack*, and probably *ignore*. The best synonym for *expunge* is *remove*.

In delivering his speech, the senator decided to expunge the part that attacked the vice president.

a. ignore   b. remove   c. worry   d. attack

Taking Tests

Analogies

Analogy items test your understanding of relationships between things or ideas. For example, think about the relationship between *strong* and *weak*. The words are antonyms—words that have opposite meanings. A test item may begin with a pair, such as *strong* and *weak*. You must then choose another pair of words with a similar relationship. Since *strong* and *weak* are opposites, the second pair of words should also be opposites.

Big and *large* have the same meaning. *Red* is not the opposite of *pink* nor is *athletic* the opposite of *musical*. Only *young* and *old*, choice c, are antonyms.

Strong is to weak as

a. big is to large

b. red is to pink

c. young is to old

d. athletic is to musical

Sometimes colons are used to shorten analogies. A single colon separates the words in each pair, and a double colon separates the two pairs. For example, "strong is to weak as young is to old" is shown as "strong : weak :: young : old." What is the relationship in the item below?

Remember, you read the single colon as though it said "is to" and the double colon as "as." This item begins "Kitten is to cat as . . ."

kitten : cat ::

a. book : play

b. computer : calculator

c. horse : donkey

d. calf : cow

Taking Tests

If the relationship is unclear, try making up a sentence that describes the relationship between the first pair of words. For instance, in the example above you might say, "A kitten is a baby cat." Then try substituting each pair of words in that sentence. After trying each pair of words in the example above, you should find that *d* makes the most sense.

Grammar, Usage, and Mechanics

Standardized tests often include sections that test your knowledge of grammar, usage, and mechanics. These items often present a sentence divided into several underlined sections. Each section is marked with a letter. You must tell which of the underlined sections contains an error. You can also indicate that there is no error.

Another type of item gives a sentence with only one section underlined. The sentence is followed by several possible corrections. One of the choices may be the same as the underlined part. Examples of both types are shown on the following page.

1. <u>Each of the girls</u> <u>checked</u> <u>their own book</u>
         a   b   c

   <u>out of the library.</u> <u>no error</u>
       d   e

2. Aaron is <u>the biggest</u> of the two boys.

   a. the biggest   c. the more bigger
   b. the bigger   d. the most biggest

In this item you must decide if the sentence contains an error. If it does, you must indicate which underlined section contains the error. In this example, section *c* contains the error.

In this type of item, you choose the response that best replaces the underlined part. One of the choices may be the same as the underlined part. The correct choice here is *b*.

Exercise 3

Use the test-taking strategies described in this lesson to complete the following items.

1. A transparent piece of glass is one that _____.
   a. cannot be seen through   c. is easily broken
   b. is clear   d. is very thick

2. dentist : teeth :: _____
   a. mechanic : engines   c. dog : bone
   b. doctor : nurse   d. student : pencil

3. Choose the letter of the underlined section that needs to be corrected in the following sentence. Choose *e* if no correction is needed.

   The captain past the ball to another member of
       a   b   c

   the basketball team. no error
           d   e

4. Decide whether the underlined section in the following sentence needs correction. Then choose the best correction from the choices listed.

   Meg has taken the dog out for a run in the park.
   a. has taken   c. has took
   b. take   d. taking

Standardized Test Practice

Introduction

The following pages of exercises have been designed to familiarize you with the standardized writing tests that you may take during the school year. These exercises are very similar to the actual tests in how they look and what they ask you to do. Completing these exercises will not only provide you with practice, but also will make you aware of areas you might need to work on.

These writing exercises—just like the actual standardized writing tests—are divided into three sections.

Sentence Structure In this section, pages 718 to 725, you will be given a short passage in which some of the sentences are underlined. Each underlined sentence is numbered. After you finish reading the passage, you will be asked questions about the underlined sections. The underlined sections will be either incomplete sentences, run-on sentences, correctly written sentences that should be combined, or correctly written sentences that do not need to be rewritten. You will need to select which is best from the four choices provided.

Usage In this section, pages 726 to 733, you will also be asked to read a short passage. However, in these exercises, a word or words in the passage will be omitted and a numbered blank space will be in their place. After reading the passage, you will need to determine which of the four provided words or groups of words best belongs in each numbered space.

Mechanics Finally, in the third section, pages 734 to 741, the short passages will have parts that are underlined. You will need to determine if, in the underlined sections, there is a spelling error, capitalization error, punctuation error, or no error at all.

Writing well is a skill that you will use the rest of your life. You will be able to write more accurate letters to your friends and family, better papers in school, and more interesting stories. You will be able to express yourself and your ideas more clearly and in a way that is interesting and engaging. These exercises should help to improve your writing and to make you comfortable with the format and types of questions you will see on standardized writing tests.

Standardized Test Practice

Read each passage. Some sections are underlined. The underlined sections may be one of the following:

- Incomplete sentences
- Run-on sentences
- Correctly written sentences that should be combined
- Correctly written sentences that do not need to be rewritten

Choose the best way to write each underlined section and mark the letter for your answer. If the underlined section needs no change, mark the choice "Correct as is" on your paper.

"Genius is two per cent inspiration and ninety-eight per cent perspiration." Thomas Alva Edison, the most famous American inventor, said this in relation to his own work. <u>Edison invented the electric lightbulb. He did this in 1879.</u> He seemed to have limitless patience and energy. <u>He worked in his laboratory. For as long as nineteen hours a day without stopping.</u> His hard work paid off in many important inventions, (2) including the phonograph, the motion picture projector, and the alkaline battery. <u>By the time of his death in 1931, he had patented 1,093 inventions.</u>
(3)

(1)

---

1 A In 1879 Edison invented the electric light-bulb.

  B In 1879 Edison invented the electric light-bulb, and that's when he invented it.

  C Edison invented in 1879 the electric light-bulb.

  D Edison invented the electric lightbulb since 1879.

2 F He worked in his laboratory for as long as nineteen hours a day. Without stopping.

  G He worked in his laboratory, he worked for as long as nineteen hours a day without stopping.

  H He worked in his laboratory for as long as nineteen hours a day without stopping.

  J Correct as is

3 A By the time of his death, in 1931, patenting 1,093 inventions.

  B By the time of his death it was in 1931, he had patented 1,093 inventions.

  C By the time of his death in 1931. He had patented 1,093 inventions.

  D Correct as is

In 1849, <u>Harriet Tubman was an enslaved person on a plantation in the South. When she decided to escape to the North.</u> (1) To avoid capture, she traveled only by night. <u>She was assisted by the Underground Railroad. It was a secret system of people who helped enslaved people escape to the northern states and Canada.</u> (2) In 1850, Harriet made the first of nineteen courageous trips back to the South to help other enslaved people. <u>She led her parents, most of her brothers and sisters, and hundreds of other enslaved people to freedom.</u> (3) Harriet Tubman was never captured.

1 A In 1849, Harriet Tubman was an enslaved person on a plantation, then she decided to escape to the North.

B In 1849, Harriet Tubman being an enslaved person on a plantation when she decided to escape to the North.

C In 1849, Harriet Tubman was an enslaved person on a plantation when she decided to escape to the North.

D Correct as is

2 F She and the Underground Railroad were assisted by a secret system of people who helped enslaved people escape to the northern states and Canada.

G She was a secret system of people who helped enslaved people escape to the northern states and Canada, assisted by the Underground Railroad.

H She was assisted by the Underground Railroad, a secret system of people who helped enslaved people escape to the northern states and Canada.

J She was assisted by the Underground Railroad, it being a secret system of people who helped enslaved people escape to the northern states and Canada.

3 A She leading her parents, most of her brothers and sisters, and hundreds of other enslaved people to freedom.

B She led her parents, most of her brothers and sisters, and hundreds of other enslaved people. To freedom.

C She led her parents, and she also led most of her brothers and sisters, and hundreds of other enslaved people to freedom.

D Correct as is

STOP

Standardized Test Practice

Read each passage. Some sections are underlined. The underlined sections may be one of the following:

- Incomplete sentences
- Run-on sentences
- Correctly written sentences that should be combined
- Correctly written sentences that do not need to be rewritten

Choose the best way to write each underlined section and mark the letter for your answer.
If the underlined section needs no change, mark the choice "Correct as is" on your paper.

Can you imagine cowboys of the Old West quoting Shakespeare? It sounds strange, but it was not uncommon. <u>Throughout the nineteenth century, theater companies from the East headed West with Shakespeare's plays. To perform them for the people of the frontier.</u> (1) These plays were performed in a variety of settings and were quite popular. <u>Western audiences, however, were not used to watching plays, they didn't like to sit quietly.</u> (2) They would often yell suggestions to the actors in the middle of the show. <u>Some audience members threw money at good performers. Some audience members threw fruit and vegetables at bad performers.</u> (3)

---

1 A Throughout the nineteenth century, theater companies from the East headed West with Shakespeare's plays, they wanted to perform them for the people of the frontier.

B Throughout the nineteenth century, theater companies from the East headed West with Shakespeare's plays to perform them. For the people of the frontier.

C Throughout the nineteenth century, theater companies from the East headed West with Shakespeare's plays to perform them for the people of the frontier.

D Correct as is

2 F Western audiences, however, were not used to watching plays. And didn't like to sit quietly.

G Western audiences, however, were not used to watching plays and didn't like to sit quietly.

H Western audiences, however, not used to watching plays. They didn't like to sit quietly to watch the plays.

J Correct as is

3 A Some audience members threw money, or other audience members threw fruit and vegetables at bad performers.

B Some audience members threw money at good performers, while others threw fruit and vegetables at bad performers.

C Some audience members and others threw money or fruit and vegetables.

D Some audience members threw money at good performers, because others threw fruit and vegetables at bad performers.

Mrs. Rosenberg, the eighth-grade French teacher, took papers out of her bag and set them down they
were on her desk. She told her students to stop talking because she had something to discuss with them.
(1)

It was just after the midterm. The students were nervous and worried.
(2)
"I want to talk about your midterm exams," Mrs. Rosenberg said.

Finally, she broke into a huge smile and told the class what was on her mind. She explained that the test
scores had been especially good and she wanted to reward them. With French cookies that she had baked.
(3)
The students congratulated each other. They ate the whole plate of cookies, which were delicious.

---

1 A Mrs. Rosenberg, the eighth-grade French teacher, took papers out of her bag and set them down on her desk.

B Mrs. Rosenberg, the eighth-grade French teacher. She took papers out of her bag and set them down on her desk.

C Mrs. Rosenberg, the eighth-grade French teacher, took papers out of her bag and set them down. On her desk.

D Correct as is

2 F Just after the midterm the students were nervous and worried.

G It was just after the midterm, and they were nervous and worried, and it was the students.

H It was just after the midterm, and the students were nervous and worried.

J It was just after the midterm because the students were nervous and worried.

3 A She explained that the test scores especially good, and she wanted to reward them with French cookies that she had baked for them.

B She explained that the test scores had been especially good, and she wanted to reward them with French cookies that she had baked for them.

C She explained that the test scores wanted to reward them with French cookies that she had baked for them especially good.

D Correct as is

Standardized Test Practice

Read each passage. Some sections are underlined. The underlined sections may be one of the following:

- Incomplete sentences
- Run-on sentences
- Correctly written sentences that should be combined
- Correctly written sentences that do not need to be rewritten

Choose the best way to write each underlined section and mark the letter for your answer.
If the underlined section needs no change, mark the choice "Correct as is" on your paper.

<u>For thousands of years, people in desert regions have made adobe buildings, they made them out of mud.</u> (1) Adobe, or sun-dried clay, is formed into bricks to create dwellings. <u>First, sandy clay is mixed with water and then bits of straw or grass are added.</u> (2) The straw or grass helps the mud to stick together. <u>To create the bricks. The mixture is set into wooden forms and left to solidify.</u> (3) It may take several days for the bricks to cure, or harden. <u>The hardened bricks are then baked in the sun. They are baked in the sun for about two weeks.</u> (4) In the desert, there is little rain or freezing weather to melt or crack the hardened mud houses.

---

1 A For thousands of years, people in desert regions have made adobe buildings. They made them out of mud.
  B For thousands of years, people in desert regions have made adobe buildings. Out of mud.
  C For thousands of years, people in desert regions have made adobe buildings out of mud.
  D Correct as is

2 F First, sandy clay is mixed with water and then bits of straw or grass added.
  G First, sandy clay is mixed with water. And then bits of straw or grass are added.
  H First, sandy clay is mixed with water, added then are bits of straw or grass.
  J Correct as is

3 A To create the bricks the mixture is set. Into wooden forms and left to solidify.
  B To create the bricks, the mixture is set into wooden forms and left to solidify.
  C To create the bricks, the mixture is set it goes into wooden forms and is left to solidify.
  D Correct as is

4 F The hardened bricks are then baked in the sun for about two weeks.
  G The hardened bricks are then baked in the sun, and the sun bakes them for about two weeks.
  H The hardened bricks are then in the sun for about two weeks baked.
  J The hardened bricks are then baked in the sun that is for about two weeks.

What is the most popular team sport in the world? If you guessed soccer, you are almost right. <u>Officially, football is the most popular sport. Because what Americans call soccer is called football in the rest of the world.</u> ₍₁₎ Soccer is played almost everywhere. There are records of soccer-type sports played in China and other countries over 2,000 years ago. <u>By creating uniform rules for play in 1863. England became the</u> ₍₂₎ <u>birthplace of soccer as we know it today.</u> More than 140 nations are members of the international soccer community. <u>There are more soccer players throughout the world than people who play basketball, baseball,</u> ₍₃₎ <u>or golf.</u>

1 A Officially, football is the most popular sport, so what Americans call soccer is called football. In the rest of the world.

B Officially, football is the most popular sport because what Americans call soccer is called football in the rest of the world.

C Officially, football is the most popular sport, this is because what Americans call soccer is called football in the rest of the world.

D Correct as is

2 F By creating uniform rules for play in 1863, England became the birthplace of soccer as we know it today.

G By creating uniform rules for play in 1863, England it is becoming, the birthplace of soccer as we know it today.

H By creating uniform rules for play in 1863, England became. The birthplace of soccer as we know it today.

J Correct as is

3 A There are more soccer players throughout the world than people who basketball, baseball, or golf.

B There are more soccer players throughout the world. They play basketball, baseball, or golf.

C There are more soccer players throughout the world than people who play basketball, there are also more than play baseball, or golf.

D Correct as is

STOP

Standardized Test Practice

Read each passage. Some sections are underlined. The underlined sections may be one of the following:

- Incomplete sentences
- Run-on sentences
- Correctly written sentences that should be combined
- Correctly written sentences that do not need to be rewritten

Choose the best way to write each underlined section and mark the letter for your answer.
If the underlined section needs no change, mark the choice "Correct as is" on your paper.

<u>Tim and Lily were walking to school when a man sped by them in a wheelchair.</u>
(1)
"What was that?" asked Tim, in amazement.

Lily explained that the man was using a wheelchair especially designed for handicapped athletes. <u>Lily said that her uncle had a wheelchair like that, he used it to play tennis.</u> These new wheelchairs are lighter
(2)
than traditional ones, so they can move more quickly. <u>Lily said that people in wheelchairs can play basket-</u>
(3)
<u>ball today. She also said that people in wheelchairs can enter marathons.</u> Lily and Tim decided to watch the

marathon on television because there would be several wheelchair athletes competing.

---

1 A Tim and Lily were walking to school. When a man sped by them in a wheelchair.
  B Tim and Lily were walking to school, a man sped by them in a wheelchair.
  C Tim and Lily were walking to school when a man sped by them. In a wheelchair.
  D Correct as is

2 F Lily saying that her uncle had a wheelchair like that. He used to play tennis.
  G Lily said that her uncle had a wheelchair like that. Which he used to play tennis.
  H Lily said that her uncle had a wheelchair like that, in which he used to play tennis.
  J Correct as is

3 A Lily said that people in wheelchairs, who can play basketball, can also enter marathons today.
  B Lily said that people in wheelchairs can play basketball and enter marathons today.
  C Lily said that people in wheelchairs can play basketball today, and she also said that people in wheelchairs can enter marathons.
  D Lily said that people in wheelchairs can play basketball today and marathons.

Karen had planned what she would wear. She was going to wear her favorite blue shirt and a blue skirt that matched. It was the first eighth-grade dance of the year, and Karen had every detail thought out. At eight o'clock, Karen's father dropped her off at the school gym, her friends were standing outside waiting for her. As they went inside, they talked about how much fun the seventh-grade dances had been. The music had been great and lots of kids had danced. They hoped this dance would be the same as the seventh-grade dances. The only difference would be that now they were the older kids.

(Underlined with numbers: (1) under "She was going to wear her favorite blue shirt and a blue skirt that matched." (2) under "At eight o'clock, Karen's father dropped her off at the school gym, her friends were standing outside waiting for her." (3) under "They hoped this dance would be the same as the seventh-grade dances.")

1 A Karen had planned what she would wear that it was her favorite blue shirt and a blue skirt that matched

B Karen had planned what she would wear, and she was going to wear her favorite blue shirt and a blue skirt that matched.

C Karen had planned to wear her favorite blue shirt and a blue skirt that matched.

D Karen had planned to wear what matched and was going to wear her favorite blue shirt and a blue skirt that matched

2 F At eight o'clock, Karen's father dropped her off at the school gym. Where her friends were standing outside waiting for her.

G At eight o'clock, Karen's father dropped her off at the school gym. Her friends standing outside waiting for her.

H At eight o'clock, Karen's father dropped her off at the school gym where her friends were standing outside waiting for her.

J Correct as is

3 A They hoped this dance. Would be the same as the seventh-grade dances.

B They hoped this dance would be the same. As the seventh-grade dances.

C They hoped this dance the same as the seventh-grade dances.

D Correct as is

STOP

Standardized Test Practice

Read each passage and choose the word or group of words that belongs in each space. Mark the letter for your answer on your paper.

What is the ___(1)___ engineering and construction project ever tackled? The honor belongs to the Great Wall of China. The Wall reaches about 1,500 miles across China and is made of dirt, brick, and stone.

Segments of the Wall date from the fourth century B.C., but the majority of the work ___(2)___ in the Ch'in Dynasty, between 221 and 206 B.C. China was unified in 214 B.C. and the existing segments of wall ___(3)___ to form one long wall. The Wall was designed to act as fortification against attacking nomads, or roving tribes. The Great Wall no longer serves as protection, but it still exists and is ___(4)___ the largest tourist attraction in China.

1 A enormousest
   B more enormous
   C enormous
   D most enormous

2 F happened
   G happens
   H has happened
   J will happen

3 A has been connected
   B is connected
   C was connected
   D were connected

4 F certainly
   G more certainly
   H certain
   J most certain

Have you ever eaten a durian? Chances are that you would remember if you had. The durian is a fruit that has a terrible odor, but a delicious flavor. They have a custardy texture and many people prize ___(1)___ as exotic delicacies.

Durians ___(2)___ in Southeast Asia on trees. These trees can ___(3)___ 130 feet tall. They are expensive because they ripen quickly and are only ripe for a very short time before they are inedible. The only way to know whether or not they are ripe is to smell them. A horrible smell means that the durian is ___(4)___ ripe!

1 A its
   B our
   C them
   D they

2 F have been grown
   G is grown
   H are grown
   J were grown

3 A reach
   B reached
   C had reached
   D will reach

4 F perfectly
   G perfect
   H more perfect
   J most perfect

STOP

Standardized Test Practice

Read each passage and choose the word or group of words that belongs in each space. Mark the letter for your answer on your paper.

Nancy Lopez was more than just a good golfer, she ___(1)___ better than any other female golfer in the history of the sport. Before turning professional, she won the New Mexico Women's Amateur when she was just 12 years old. She also won the U.S. Junior Girls and Western Junior titles three years in a row. In addition, she ___(2)___ for second place in the U.S. Women's Open when she was still an amateur.

When Nancy turned professional in 1978, she had a ___(3)___ rookie year. She won rookie of the year, player of the year, and a trophy for the best scoring average. The world of women's golf ___(4)___ see a player as successful as Nancy Lopez for a long time.

1 A plays
 B played
 C is playing
 D was playing

2 F has tied
 G tied
 H is tying
 J was tying

3 A remarked
 B remarkability
 C remarkable
 D remarkably

4 F will scarcely never
 G will probably never
 H will hardly never
 J will not never

Three years ago, Julia Kramer noticed a vacant lot down the street from her apartment building. It was full of garbage. Julia was an avid gardener, but since she lived in the city, she didn't have many opportunities to garden. She __(1)__ that the empty lot might be a great spot for a garden.

Julia organized a meeting of __(2)__ neighbors to talk about creating a garden. The project became a cooperative community undertaking as local schools and organizations chipped in to help clean up the lot and plant the garden. A local plant shop even __(3)__ trees and plants. Due to the efforts __(4)__ put in, the people of Julia's neighborhood are now able to sit and play in a beautiful garden.

1 A thought
  B think
  C is thinking
  D has thought

2 F his
  G your
  H her
  J us

3 A donated
  B donate
  C had donated
  D are donating

4 F their
  G they
  H theirs
  J them

STOP

Standardized Test Practice

Read each passage and choose the word or group of words that belongs in each space. Mark the letter for your answer on your paper.

Emily Dickinson was born in 1830 in Amherst, Massachusetts. She was one of the most productive poets in all of American literature. She __(1)__ nearly 1,800 poems, many of which were only discovered after her death in 1886.

Dickinson __(2)__ traveled or even left her house. She didn't even like to leave her room to greet visitors. She used __(3)__ language and generally wrote poems that are composed of brief four-line stanzas. Her poems, although short, explored large issues like the search for knowledge, the concept of time, and the meaning of life. Through her poetry, Emily Dickinson __(4)__ in affecting the world outside of her little house in Amherst.

---

1 A writes
  B wrote
  C had written
  D was writing

2 F barely never
  G almost never
  H not never
  J hardly never

3 A simplify
  B simpleness
  C simple
  D simply

4 F succeeded
  G will succeed
  H succeed
  J are succeeding

Red lined cleaning shrimp are among the most peculiar and helpful creatures in the sea. The strange thing about them is how they gather __(1)__ food. They get food by cleaning __(2)__ organisms off fishes' bodies. The fish depend upon the shrimp to free them of parasites. The shrimp wave their antennae to call to any fish in need of a cleaning. When an interested fish comes along, the shrimp __(3)__ any stray parasites from the fish's skin. When the fish is clean, it will swim away. The shrimp sleep at night, and clean and eat all day. It is __(4)__ a strange but practical way to live.

1 A their
  B his
  C our
  D its

2 F tiny
  G tiniest
  H most tiny
  J more tiny

3 A was eating
  B ate
  C eat
  D had eaten

4 F definitely
  G most definiter
  H more definite
  J definite

STOP

Standardized Test Practice

Read each passage and choose the word or group of words that belongs in each space. Mark the letter for your answer on your paper.

Kevin and Marco sat in their classroom before school and talked about their __(1)__ with the pollution in the stream where they liked to fish. Kevin said, "That stream __(2)__ by the whole town. Why doesn't anyone do anything about it?"

"It's easy to put responsibility onto others," said Mr. Leery, their teacher. "But you'll get results __(3)__ if you take it upon yourselves to improve things."

Kevin and Marco explained the situation to the other students in the class. Everyone volunteered to help clean the stream. By the end of the day, the trash __(4)__ from the stream and it looked a lot better.

1 **A** irritate
   B irritation
   C irritating
   D irritated

2 **F** are owned
   G have been owned
   H is owned
   J were owned

3 **A** faster
   B more fast
   C fastly
   D most fast

4 **F** has been removed
   G is being removed
   H had been removed
   J will be removed

"You grew up in the city?" Ellen said with amazement as she looked at the boyhood pictures of her father in the photo album.

Her father replied, "Of course I did. I was a real city boy. I ___(1)___ a tree until I was eight years old."

"But, Dad," Ellen exclaimed, "There are parks in every city in the country. There must have been one where you lived."

"You're right, Ellen, I was just teasing you about the tree," answered Dad. "We used to go to the park every afternoon after school to play baseball. We liked to think of it as ___(2)___ private park." Dad continued nostalgically, "I loved playing baseball with my friends. We ___(3)___ quite a good team and would play other neighborhood teams. It was the ___(4)___ time of my life."

1 **A** had never seen
   B hadn't never seen
   C hadn't barely seen
   D hadn't never hardly seen

2 **F** his
   G our
   H your
   J their

3 **A** assembles
   B assembling
   C assembled
   D assembler

4 **F** most exciting
   G exciting
   H more exciting
   J excitingest

Standardized Test Practice

Read each passage and decide which type of error, if any, appears in each underlined section. Mark the letter for your answer on your paper.

Norman Rockwell is one of the most popular artists of the 20th century. <u>Rockwell began working at the Saturday Evening post in 1916.</u> He soon became <u>the newspapers top draftsman. Over</u> the next 47 years, he
(1)   (2)

illustrated 322 covers for the newspaper. <u>Rockwell also ilustrated advertisements for popular products</u> like
                                                                  (3)

Crest and Jell-O.

<u>Rockwell lived in Stockbridge Massachusetts with his wife.</u> He died in 1978. Stockbridge is the home of
                                 (4)

the Rockwell Museum.

<u>Rockwell's art depicts small town America.</u> His subjects are ordinary people in everyday situations. Some
                 (5)

examples of the scenes he illustrated are a woman taking her daughter for <u>a ride in a horse-drawn carriage a new television antenna being installed on the roof of a Victorian house, and a mom and dad</u> driving
                                               (6)

grandma and the kids to their summer vacation.

Rockwell brought great joy to many people over his long career as an artist.

---

1 A Spelling error
   B Capitalization error
   C Punctuation error
   D No error

2 F Spelling error
   G Capitalization error
   H Punctuation error
   J No error

3 A Spelling error
   B Capitalization error
   C Punctuation error
   D No error

4 F Spelling error
   G Capitalization error
   H Punctuation error
   J No error

5 A Spelling error
   B Capitalization error
   C Punctuation error
   D No error

6 F Spelling error
   G Capitalization error
   H Punctuation error
   J No error

The Olympic Games began in greece in the year 776 B.C. The first Olympics had only one event: a 200-
(1)
yard dash. Later, other events such as longer races, wrestling discus throwing, javelin throwing, boxing, and
(2)
chariot races were added.

Political problems between the Greeks and Romans caused the Olympics to be abolished in A.D. 394.
(3)
However, they were revived in the late nineteenth century, and the first modern summer Olympics opened
(4)
in Athens, Greece on Sunday March 24, 1896.

The Olympics are now held every four years and feature the best athletes from almost every country in
(5)
the world. The goals of the Olympic Games are to encourage physical fitness and to promote good will
(6)
among the Nations of the world.

1 A Spelling error
  B Capitalization error
  C Punctuation error
  D No error

2 F Spelling error
  G Capitalization error
  H Punctuation error
  J No error

3 A Spelling error
  B Capitalization error
  C Punctuation error
  D No error

4 F Spelling error
  G Capitalization error
  H Punctuation error
  J No error

5 A Spelling error
  B Capitalization error
  C Punctuation error
  D No error

6 F Spelling error
  G Capitalization error
  H Punctuation error
  J No error

STOP

Standardized Test Practice

Read each passage and decide which type of error, if any, appears in each underlined section. Mark the letter for your answer on your paper.

<u>Louis Braille was born in france in 1809.</u> At the age of three, he was accidentally blinded and his <u>parents</u>
(1)
<u>arranged for him to go to a special school for blind children.</u> When he was older, <u>Louis goal was to create an</u>
(2)   (3)
<u>alphabet</u> that would allow blind people to read and write more easily. He had <u>heard about Charles barbier, a</u>
(4)
<u>French army</u> captain, who had developed a way of <u>writing that involved useing raised dots to permit</u>
(5)
<u>soldiers to communicate at night without light.</u>

Louis worked with the method ceaselessly. <u>By the time he was fifteen years old he had developed</u> the six-
(6)
dot and standard spelling method that is used by millions of blind people today. The method is called
Braille, after Louis.

1 **A** Spelling error
   B Capitalization error
   C Punctuation error
   D No error

2 **F** Spelling error
   G Capitalization error
   H Punctuation error
   J No error

3 **A** Spelling error
   B Capitalization error
   C Punctuation error
   D No error

4 **F** Spelling error
   G Capitalization error
   H Punctuation error
   J No error

5 **A** Spelling error
   B Capitalization error
   C Punctuation error
   D No error

6 **F** Spelling error
   G Capitalization error
   H Punctuation error
   J No error

Michael was staring at the ceiling. "Shouldn't you be doing your homework?" his grandmother asked.

"I am doing my homework, Grandma." Michael replied.
                                    (1)
His grandmother put down her crossword puzzle "You are just staring at the ceiling. I have never heard
                                              (2)
of homework like that. Are you sure you're following your teacher's instructions?"

"I promise that I am doing exactly what my Teacher asked me to do, Grandma."
                                        (3)
"I beleive you, but that's the strangest way of studying I've ever seen!"
        (4)
Michael smiled as he reveeled his secret. "I am supposed to think about what I will do over Winter
                    (5)   (6)
vacation and then write about it. I'm doing the thinking part now!"

1 A Spelling error
   B Capitalization error
   C Punctuation error
   D No error

2 F Spelling error
   G Capitalization error
   H Punctuation error
   J No error

3 A Spelling error
   B Capitalization error
   C Punctuation error
   D No error

4 F Spelling error
   G Capitalization error
   H Punctuation error
   J No error

5 A Spelling error
   B Capitalization error
   C Punctuation error
   D No error

6 F Spelling error
   G Capitalization error
   H Punctuation error
   J No error

STOP

Standardized Test Practice

Read each passage and decide which type of error, if any, appears in each underlined section. Mark the letter for your answer on your paper.

One day Darryl began to think about what he might like to do with his future. First, of course, <u>he had to graduate from george Washington High School</u> and then he had to pick a college to attend. <u>He thought he might study medicine.</u>
(1)
(2)
<u>Darryl had often considered becomming a doctor.</u> It would mean many <u>more years of school, studying, and hard work but Darryl thought it would</u> be worth it. He would be able to help sick people get better, <u>and maybe even find a cure for a diseaze.</u> Darryl <u>could not think of a better Career.</u>
(3)
(4)
(5)
(6)

1 A Spelling error
   B Capitalization error
   C Punctuation error
   D No error

2 F Spelling error
   G Capitalization error
   H Punctuation error
   J No error

3 A Spelling error
   B Capitalization error
   C Punctuation error
   D No error

4 F Spelling error
   G Capitalization error
   H Punctuation error
   J No error

5 A Spelling error
   B Capitalization error
   C Punctuation error
   D No error

6 F Spelling error
   G Capitalization error
   H Punctuation error
   J No error

An almanac is an annual publication that includes information <u>such as weather forecasts tide tables, and</u> <u>astronomical information.</u> The most famous almanac is *The Old Farmer's Almanac.* It was first published in
(1)
1792. The almanac provided reliable <u>weather forcasts that were said to be eighty-percent acurate.</u>
(2)

The emphasis of the book was changed 1861. <u>The editor at that time, Charles l. Flint, encouraged more</u> <u>articles on farming.</u> By 1900, general features about modern life and nature replaced many of the
(3)
agriculture articles.

<u>During World war II, a German spy was captured by the FBI. He had</u> landed on the coast of Long
(4)
Island, New York. <u>What was suprising was that the spy had a copy of the almanac in his coat pocket! The</u>
(5)
government guessed that the Germans were using the book's weather predictions.

<u>The almanac is still published each year in Dublin, New hampshire.</u> *The Old Farmer's Almanac* has not
(6)
missed a publication for over two hundred years.

1 **A** Spelling error
B Capitalization error
C Punctuation error
D No error

2 **F** Spelling error
G Capitalization error
H Punctuation error
J No error

3 **A** Spelling error
B Capitalization error
C Punctuation error
D No error

4 **F** Spelling error
G Capitalization error
H Punctuation error
J No error

5 **A** Spelling error
B Capitalization error
C Punctuation error
D No error

6 **F** Spelling error
G Capitalization error
H Punctuation error
J No error

STOP

Standardized Test Practice

Read each passage and decide which type of error, if any, appears in each underlined section. Mark the letter for your answer on your paper.

<u>Claudias father told her that they were going to fly to Chicago</u> to visit his sister Carol. <u>Claudia was exited</u>

(1)

<u>because she had never been</u> on an airplane before. <u>She had been on several car trips but never a trip so far</u>

(2)   (3)

away that she had to take a plane. She could not wait for the day of the trip to arrive.

    <u>On the day of the trip, Claudia and her Father took a taxi to the airport.</u> When they got to the gate, she

(4)

looked out the window and became mesmerized by the aircraft. <u>The captain smiled at her as she boarded</u>

(5)

<u>the plane.</u> At that moment, Claudia decided that she wanted to be a captain and she spent the rest of the

flight dreaming about flying. <u>The plane landed at o'hare International Airport. Aunt Carol</u> was waiting at

(6)

the gate for them.

---

1 A Spelling error
  B Capitalization error
  C Punctuation error
  D No error

2 F Spelling error
  G Capitalization error
  H Punctuation error
  J No error

3 A Spelling error
  B Capitalization error
  C Punctuation error
  D No error

4 F Spelling error
  G Capitalization error
  H Punctuation error
  J No error

5 A Spelling error
  B Capitalization error
  C Punctuation error
  D No error

6 F Spelling error
  G Capitalization error
  H Punctuation error
  J No error

In the spring, <u>twenty eighth-graders took a trip to see the Statue of Liberty in New York City New York.</u>
(1)
It was their first time in New York and they were excited to see the statue. Their teacher, <u>Mrs. costas, led</u>

<u>them up the 142 steps of the spiral staircase</u> and told them about the history of the statue.
(2)

She explained that <u>the statue had been given to the United States by france</u> to commemorate the hun-
(3)
dredth anniversary of the signing of <u>the Declaration of Independance. She also told them</u> that the statue is
(4)
over 151 feet and weighs 204 tons. <u>"We will climb to the crown, she said. "There</u> is an observation deck."
(5)
<u>From the deck, they would have a breathtaking view of New York.</u>
(6)

1 **A** Spelling error
  B Capitalization error
  C Punctuation error
  D No error

2 **F** Spelling error
  G Capitalization error
  H Punctuation error
  J No error

3 **A** Spelling error
  B Capitalization error
  C Punctuation error
  D No error

4 **F** Spelling error
  G Capitalization error
  H Punctuation error
  J No error

5 **A** Spelling error
  B Capitalization error
  C Punctuation error
  D No error

6 **F** Spelling error
  G Capitalization error
  H Punctuation error
  J No error

STOP

UNIT 26

Listening and Speaking

LOG ON ▶ **Writing** Online   For research tools and additional skills practice, go to **glencoe.com** and enter QuickPass code WC77680p3.

26.1 How to Listen

As you turn on the radio to listen to your favorite station, you run into a problem. You're ready to listen to music, but all you hear is static. When there's interference, it's difficult to enjoy or understand what you're listening to.

You may face forms of mental "interference" every day. Ignoring the static, though, will help you listen.

Listening in Class

Does your mind ever wander during school? Maybe you can't stop thinking about your bad morning. Maybe the sun is shining, and you'd like to be outside. You have to get your thoughts back on track. You know you need to listen if you're going to learn. These tips will help you get started.

Tips for Effective Listening

1. Sort out any interference, such as classroom noise or wandering thoughts. Focus your attention completely on the speaker.

2. Determine your purpose for listening. Are you trying to obtain information? Are you trying to solve a problem? Are you listening for enjoyment?

3. Identify main ideas as you listen. Then write them down in your own words. These are the most important points to remember.

4. Put a star or check mark next to any ideas that your teacher tells you are especially important or that might appear on a test.

5. Review your notes after class. Do you have any questions? Clear them up right away to avoid confusion later.

Interpreting Special Clues Gestures and tone of voice often indicate which information is important. Sometimes your teacher may speak certain words or phrases more loudly than others. Write those down. Hand and body movements also tell you to pay special attention to what's being said.

Listening to Persuasive Speech

Television commercials, political speeches, and editorials on the evening news all have one thing in common. Each speaker wants to convince you that what you're hearing is the truth. Don't listen without thinking, though. You must decide if the speaker is saying something you can believe.

Fact Versus Opinion   Identifying the speaker's attitude is very important. Do you know when you're hearing facts and when you're hearing opinions? A fact is something that can be proven. An opinion is what someone *believes* to be true. In the following examples try to separate the facts from the opinions.

Evaluating News Statements	
Heard on the Evening News	**Questions to Ask Yourself**
Today when both candidates met, Smith grudgingly shook hands with his opponent.	What one word tells me how the news reporter thinks the candidate feels? Is this necessarily true?
Twenty-seven boy scouts camped in the mountains last weekend.	Does this story introduction try to convince me of anything?
Last night a ferocious dog attacked a gas station attendant.	Would I feel differently if the dog were described as frightened rather than ferocious?
Local high school girls are taking a stand against their new band uniforms.	Does this statement try to persuade me of something, or does it just give me information?

Persuasive Speeches   Speakers often try to sway you to their point of view. They use emotional words and actions to make you feel strongly about what they're saying. The emotional words they use are often adjectives and adverbs. Would you feel good about something described in such terms as *dreary, rotten, foul-smelling, eerie, dingy?* Probably not. Now think about these: *golden, shiny, energetic, wonderful, pure.* These words would probably make you feel good.

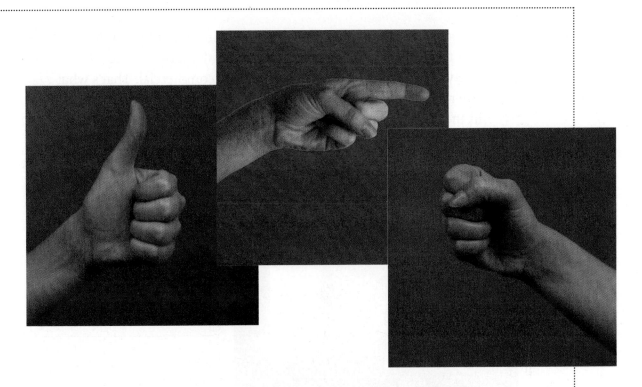

Speakers often use actions to accompany their emotional words. In these cases, you need to "listen" with your eyes. They might make eye contact with you and smile. They could nod their heads or move their arms or hands.

Emotional words and actions are good to use, but you need to think through what's being said. Speakers might be sincere, or they might be trying to force their messages on you. It's up to you to decide what their intentions are.

Listening to Commercials   Commercials bombard us every day. Though they sometimes give information, their main function is to boost sales. They do this by delivering two messages—one is obvious, and the other is hidden. The obvious message is *what* you hear or see. The hidden message comes through in *how* the information is presented.

Have you ever heard a commercial declare that its product is new and improved? To know exactly what this means, you need to know what it was like before the improvement. If the product was poor to begin with, it may still be poor. Beware of words like *more, better, whiter, brighter, longer-lasting,* and so on.

Commercials also may give information that only *sounds* true. Your dog may eat the dog food advertised. But that doesn't mean that your dog will look as healthy as the dog in the commercial. That's what you're supposed to believe, though. Can you catch the faulty reasoning in the sample commercials in the chart below?

Advertising: Believe it or Not	
Advertisement	**Think It Through**
A girl wearing the advertiser's product sits among a group of friends, laughing and talking.	What is the hidden message here? If you wear this product, you will be as popular as the girl in the commercial. Is this true?
You are told that the bike advertised is the best in its class.	What class is the advertiser talking about? Maybe you do not need that kind of bike. Maybe it is not worth the money.
A famous actor tells you that the car in the television commercial is simply the best.	An actor may know about performing, but does that make him an expert on a car's performance? Should you believe him?
A group of athletes are shown celebrating a win while drinking a particular soft drink.	What idea are you being asked to accept? You are supposed to believe that if you drink the same soft drink, you will be a winner.

Evaluating What You Hear   Faulty reasoning can exist in any form of persuasion. You may hear it in editorials on the news. You may hear it from your friends. At times you may even hear it from your own mouth. Look at the examples in the following chart. Do you recognize the faulty reasoning in each example? Where might you hear each form?

Recognizing Forms of Faulty Thinking	
Testimonial	Fred Jackson, a famous water polo player, says, "After I get out of the pool, I dry my hair with an All Hot Air hair dryer."
Bandwagon	"Hot Fish Lips is the hottest band to come to town," the D.J. says. "The concert will be a sellout. Get your tickets now."
Name Calling	"The other candidate is a total loser. If he gets elected, it won't be long until he messes up our country."
Faulty Cause and Effect	"Mom didn't buy me new basketball shoes. I didn't make the team. I'd be a starter, though, if she'd bought me the shoes."
Generalization	"Six out of ten people chose Brighty Bright toothpaste over Brand X. Brighty Bright is the best toothpaste you can buy."

Exercise 1

Listen carefully to any radio or television advertising, television editorials, and conversations you hear this week. Try to determine what is really being said. Can you sort out the facts and opinions? Which ones use faulty reasoning to persuade the listener? Find at least two examples of the forms of faulty reasoning listed in the chart above. Compare your responses with those of your classmates, and discuss why you believe or do not believe the messages.

Interviewing a person is a good way to get information. Information from an interview can add life to a paper or speech. It also makes research more fun. By talking with someone, you may find useful information that you wouldn't find in a book. If you improve your interviewing skills, you may never have trouble finding information again.

When to Interview

Not every topic lends itself to interviewing. For example, let's say your oral report is on Christopher Columbus. Finding someone who sailed on the *Santa María* might be difficult. The library or museum is the place to go for that kind of report. Often, though, there are experts in the field you're researching, and they're right under your nose. You just have to look for them.

Let's say you're researching basketball rules. You might find information by asking the physical education teacher or the basketball coach. Or maybe you know someone who is a referee. When thinking about resources, don't overlook the people in your family, your school, or your community. Look at the chart below for examples of topics and possible sources of information about them.

Subjects for Interviews	
Topic	**Resources**
The history of your town	Mayor's office; local historian; oldest resident
How ice cream is made	Ice cream shop owner; parents; restaurant manager
Fly-cast fishing	Family and friends; local bait-and-tackle store owner; fly-cast fisher
Laws about children	Lawyer or judge at juvenile court; law department professor at local university; social worker
Dog breeding	Local kennel; dog breeder; veterinarian

When you interview someone, you become a reporter. Keep in mind the six favorite words of every good reporter: *who, what, where, when, why,* and *how.* These words are like the signs along a road. You need them if you want to get where you want to go. Otherwise you might get lost in your interview.

Preparing to Interview

When you find someone to interview, write or call that person to request a meeting. Introduce yourself and your topic, and ask if there's a time you can meet. When you decide on a time, write it down and get ready.

Before you interview someone, find out all you can about your topic. Use encyclopedias, books, newspapers, and magazines to find basic background information. If you know something about your topic before the interview, you can focus the purpose of your interview and ask more relevant questions.

Write out those questions. Then review them before you meet with your subject. You want to make sure you haven't left out anything important.

Some materials you may need for the interview include the following:

- a tape recorder (ask if it's OK to use it)
- a notebook (tape recorders don't always work)
- a couple of pens or pencils

The more prepared and professional you are in your interview, the better it will go.

For a helpful interview, you need to ask good questions. For example, if you interviewed a firefighter in your town, here are some questions you might ask.

List of Sample Questions to Ask a Firefighter

1. What were you like as a child? Was it your childhood dream to be a firefighter?

2. When did you decide to be a firefighter?

3. Where did you attend school to learn to fight fires? What was the training like?

4. What is the scariest thing about fighting fires? Have you ever been close to losing your life?

5. What was the worst fire you ever fought? How long did it take to put it out?

6. What tasks do you have to perform when you're not fighting fires?

Conducting an Interview

Check the questions from your notes, and take them to the interview. Then listen closely, take good notes, and ask follow-up questions. Also, be sure to relax. If you're at ease, chances are the person you're interviewing will be relaxed, too.

Ask Open-ended Questions   Open-ended questions can't be answered with a simple yes or no. The point of an interview is to get your subject to talk freely. Ask, "What's it like to ride a bronco?" rather than, "Is it frightening to ride a bronco?" The first question will encourage your subject to describe how bronco riding feels. You will get more information with questions like that. You'll also find more questions to ask as you go along.

Avoid Saying Too Much   Don't start a conversation with the person you're interviewing. You're there to listen. Don't get sidetracked into giving your own opinions about the topic. Just ask your questions, and then listen. Look at the following list of interviewing tips. Keep these in mind as you plan and conduct your interview.

Interviewing Tips

1. Have a general idea of the information you want to gain from the interview. Review your questions. Make sure they flow in a logical order.

2. Eliminate distractions that might impede your ability to listen and your subject's ability to speak.

3. Start with the most important questions. Be friendly, but stick to business. Keep the interview going in the right direction. Remain in charge, and stay focused.

4. If you do not understand something, ask for clarification. If you want additional information about something that was said, ask a follow-up question.

5. Pay attention as you take notes. Jot down important points, but do not get overly involved in note-taking. Eye contact is a must. You can fill in the blanks later.

6. Thank the person when the interview is over. Ask whether you may phone if you think of additional questions. You may also want to send a thank-you note.

Exercise 2

Choose several careers that interest you, and list local people in those fields. Find out the *who, what, where, when,* and *why* of each person on your list.

Begin by writing down the names of people who might provide information. Call them to see whether you could interview them. Then find as much background information as you can. Use the library or any family files for your research. Next, write out questions you can ask each person.

Conduct your interviews, using the guidelines in this lesson. Write a short biography of each person you interviewed, and add a summary telling which careers you might pursue and why. Present your results to the class.

You engage in informal speaking many times every day. You talk with your friends in the lunchroom or at your locker. You speak to your parents or your neighbors. These are all examples of informal speech. The tone is casual, and everyone involved usually joins in. Here are some tips on speaking informally.

Tips on Speaking Informally		
Type	**Description**	**Hint**
Conversation	This is the most informal type of speech. Each person is free to listen and speak spontaneously.	Courtesy is very important. Do not interrupt another speaker. Listen until he or she has finished.
Discussion	A discussion generally concerns one topic. One person may be chosen to act as discussion leader. The leader's job is to keep the group focused on the topic.	Letting each person speak in turn will help the group fully develop its ideas about the topic.
Announcement	Announcements are descriptions of upcoming events or activities. They should be brief but should provide all the important information.	After your announcement ask if there are questions. You want to be sure that everyone understands what you have announced.
Demonstration	The speaker explains how a process works or how something is made.	Demonstrate the steps of a process in the correct order. Number the steps so that your audience can follow the process.
Storytelling	Stories are usually meant to entertain, to teach a moral, or to make a point. You could tell a story about almost anything.	Let your enthusiasm for your story show in how you tell it. Act out the parts. Re-create the story. Draw your audience in.

Listening and Speaking

Participating in a Discussion

You probably take part in discussions of some kind every day. You may have them in classes, on sports teams, in choir, and so on. You probably also have discussions with your family or among friends.

Often in discussions groups try to make decisions. Discussion leaders are needed then, because people don't always agree. Leaders aren't the only people who help discussions run smoothly, though. It's the job of everyone involved. Here are some tips for taking part in an informal discussion.

Tips for Participating in a Discussion

1. Let everyone take turns speaking. Do not interrupt when someone else is talking.

2. Pay attention to the discussion leader. If it is time to move on or quiet down, be cooperative.

3. Listen to what everyone says. Jot down notes on points you want to remember.

4. When it is your turn to talk, look at everyone around you. If you state an opinion, clarify and support it with evidence or examples.

5. If something is unclear to you, ask a question.

6. Help the group stick to the topic under discussion. Make sure your comments relate directly to it.

Explaining a Process

Building a model airplane and making blueberry muffins may not seem to have anything in common, but they do. Both are processes that require step-by-step directions.

When giving directions, explain the process in a simple and clear way, and in the correct order. If you don't give good directions, your blueberry muffins may end up tasting like the model airplane. On the next page you'll find step-by-step directions for explaining things.

> **How to Give Step-By-Step Directions**
>
> 1. Determine your audience and the information they will need to understand the process.
>
> 2. Write out the process on a piece of paper. Make a diagram to use as a visual aid if you think that will help make the process clear.
>
> 3. Go back and fill in any steps you have forgotten.
>
> 4. Review the steps, and rearrange any that are out of order.
>
> 5. Reword each step so that it is simply and clearly stated.

Making Announcements

If you had to make an announcement to your class about an upcoming event, would you know what to do? Making a good announcement requires you to consider three things. First of all, you must understand your audience. What do they need to hear? Second, consider the announcement itself. What are the facts? How can you make sure you state all the facts clearly and briefly? Finally, you need to decide how you can strengthen the persuasiveness of your announcement. How can you make people *want* to hear what you say?

> **Tips for Making Announcements**
>
> 1. Write down the most important points. The name of the event and the date, time, and place are necessary, so include them.
>
> 2. If you can, add a little life to what you have written. Think of your audience— what would make them want to attend the event?
>
> 3. Make sure everyone is quiet before you begin speaking. Look over your audience to get everyone's attention.
>
> 4. While speaking, look at your audience to convey your message.
>
> 5. Speak slowly and in a normal voice. Be sure that everyone has heard the entire message.
>
> 6. When you have finished, ask if there are any questions.

Exercise 3

Imagine that the following announcement came over your school's public address system. Meet with a small group to discuss the announcement. Have one group member read it aloud to judge its effectiveness. What is good about the announcement? What is not so good about it? Has anything been left out? Working as a group, rewrite the announcement so that it is as effective as you can make it.

> *A dance will be held in the gym this Friday after the basketball game. If you attend the game, you get into the dance free. Our basketball team's record so far this season is 4–0. It's our school's best start in ten years. We're playing our biggest rival. Tip-off is at seven o'clock. The dance will follow immediately and go until midnight. The bleachers will be pushed back, and music will be played through the gym's sound system. If you want to come, you must have a permission slip filled out by a parent or guardian.*

Exercise 4

Break into small groups to make a list of events that would require announcements. The events can be real or imaginary. Allow each member to choose one event and work independently. Make a list, including as much information about your event as you can. Don't actually write the announcement. Just list the information.

When your list is complete, fold your paper and put it into a container. Each group member should pick a list from the container and write a short announcement for it. Read the announcements aloud in your group, and discuss their effectiveness.

Speaking Formally

Writing a formal speech is similar to writing a research paper, but it can be more satisfying. When you write a paper for a class, your teacher is probably the only one who reads it. But if you give a speech on the same topic, your whole class gets to hear it. Speeches are great opportunities to share with others what you've learned and what you believe in. You'll find that speeches are easy to give if you use the three steps of preparation, practice, and delivery. These steps all lead to a well-researched, well-organized, and successful presentation.

Preparing a Speech

Preparation is the most important part of writing a speech. It's the foundation on which everything is built. A weak foundation almost always makes for a weak house. The same is true of speeches. Put a lot of time and effort into the preparation of your speech. Make it as strong as you can. If you do, you'll be able to write and deliver a strong speech.

Prewriting   You first need to consider the purpose of your speech. What are you attempting to do? Inform? Persuade? Then think of your audience. What do they already know about your topic? What don't they know? Use this information to help you adapt your language to your audience and purpose.

Next, narrow the topic. A subject such as "Dogs of the World" is too broad. Maybe selecting one breed would be wise. You might further narrow the topic to either the characteristics or the history of the dog.

Drafting   Once you feel comfortable with your topic, audience, and purpose, it's time to move on. Write out your main point in one sentence. This is your thesis statement. It summarizes the entire speech. Your thesis statement might read, "Cocker spaniels are good pets for children." Everything in your speech should then support this statement.

With your thesis statement written, start drafting. Like a research paper, a formal speech usually contains three main parts. The introduction is first; it sets up the speech. Next comes the body, containing your main ideas and supporting details. Last, the conclusion wraps up everything. There are two ways to compose your speech. You can write it out exactly as you'll say it, or you can use note cards. Outlining your main points and supporting details on note cards usually works better.

You can refer to what you need to say without having to read your speech word for word.

Revising At this point you want to take an X-ray of your speech. Look at its skeleton—the structure you've built out of words. Do your words support the ideas you want to get across? Does your speech flow logically from one idea to the next? Do all your ideas lead toward a conclusion? If you find areas where the structure breaks down, rework them. Don't be surprised if you go back and forth between drafting and revising. It takes time to fine-tune a speech.

Also, use strong transitions. You don't want to lose your audience when you move to the next thought. For example, you could begin another main point with, "*Another* way in which the cocker spaniel is a good pet . . ."

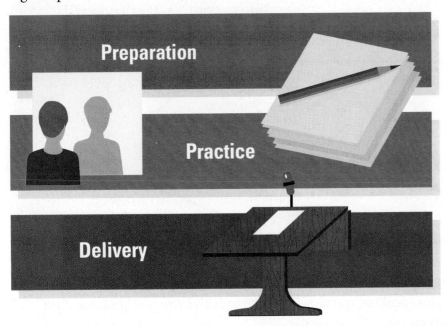

As you prepare your oral report, use the diagram on the next page to help you structure it. Notice the writing stages shown in the box between Prewriting and Presenting. You'll spend most of your time in the Drafting, Revising, and Practicing stages. Move back and forth among these until you're ready to present your report.

Practicing a Speech

Once you write your speech, practice it as much as you can. If your speech is supposed to be a certain length, time yourself. This will help you speed it up or slow it down. Also, practice delivering your speech

Prewriting
- Determine your purpose and audience.
- Decide on a topic and narrow it.

Drafting
- Make an outline of the important points.
- Fill in the supporting details.
- Write out what you want to say.

Revising
- Review your report. Does it flow logically from one point to the next?
- Reword unclear statements.
- Write an outline on note cards to make practicing easier.

Practicing
- Practice your report out loud and alone, then again in front of a friend or family member.
- Ask for advice and accept it to improve your report.
- Time the report if it needs to be a certain length.

Presenting
- Relax as you stand before your audience.
- Make eye contact with the audience at all times.
- Speak up and speak clearly.

in front of a mirror. Look for unnatural gestures or exaggerated movements. If you can, practice giving your speech into a tape recorder. Listen to your voice. Are you emphasizing important words and ideas? Are you speaking too slowly or too quickly? Are you pronouncing words clearly and distinctly?

Rehearse your speech in front of a few friends or relatives. Ask for comments on what is strong and what needs work. Don't be afraid of criticism. Consider the changes they suggest, and make the changes if you feel comfortable doing so.

If you can, practice your speech at the site where you'll later give it. That way, the surroundings will be familiar, and you'll feel comfortable when you deliver the speech.

Use your notes to remind yourself of the main points. Your note cards shouldn't serve as script, though. If you just read your speech, your audience may lose interest.

Delivering a Speech

You've prepared and practiced your speech. Now it's important that you remember to relax. Be yourself in front of the audience. It's the best way to capture and hold people's attention. If you enjoy giving your speech, your audience will enjoy listening.

If you're a bit nervous, don't worry. Use that uneasiness to your advantage. Athletes, stage actors, and singers all know how to use "butterflies" to make their performance more energetic and full of life. You can do the same thing.

Before the Speech   At the last minute, just before you deliver your speech, you may be tempted to make changes. That could be a bad idea, though. You've drafted, revised, and rehearsed your speech. Changes might upset the careful preparation you've just completed. Change only what positively needs improvement in your speech.

Tips for Relating to Your Audience		
Audience Signals	**Interpretation**	**Speaker Response**
People in your audience are moving around in their chairs or staring off into space.	You may have lost their attention.	You may recapture their interest by raising and lowering your voice or adding gestures. Perhaps you need to speed up your delivery.
Your audience seems puzzled. Some are talking with a neighbor.	They may not have understood something you said.	You may need to back up and explain a portion of your speech again. Briefly review your main ideas before continuing.
You notice some people trying to get closer to you. A few are leaning forward in their chairs.	They may be unable to hear you.	Speak up. Maybe some other noises are preventing people from hearing. Ask the audience if you need to repeat anything.
Your audience is listening attentively and nodding.	You have their full attention.	You are doing well. Do not change a thing. Keep up the good work.

Just before you speak, take a moment to look at your audience. You created your speech just for them. Keeping that in mind will help you deliver your speech confidently.

During the Speech   As you begin speaking, remember to make eye contact with your audience. Try talking to each person in turn. As you focus on each member of the audience, tell yourself that you're speaking directly to that person. Think about what you're saying and to whom you're saying it. When you take your mind off yourself, you become more relaxed.

Keep an eye out, too, for audience signals. No matter how well you plan, something unexpected can always occur. Think about what went wrong and how you can make it right. Above all, don't panic if something goes wrong. Below are some tips that will help you identify possible problems.

Deliver your speech with all the gestures and voice variations you've practiced. You can also respond to your audience. If they smile, smile back. Whatever happens, though, don't allow yourself to be distracted. Use your note cards, and keep up the rhythm and flow of your speech. Stay focused on what you're saying, and you'll deliver a successful speech. Following are a few more tips for speaking effectively.

Tips for Speaking Effectively

1. After you make an important point, pause a moment. A pause allows your audience to think about what you have said. It also creates a dramatic break that will capture people's attention.

2. Look around the room as you speak, making eye contact with each person in the audience. Think of your own experience. You probably dislike it when a speaker talks at you rather than to you.

3. Use your arms and hands while speaking. If you just stand there stiffly, your voice may also turn flat. Avoid going overboard. You do not want your gestures to be unnatural, but you do want them to strengthen your words.

4. To make sure you are speaking loudly enough, start out by speaking directly to someone in the last row of your audience.

Choose a partner to work with throughout this exercise. Together choose a topic for a formal speech. Pick one from the list below, or use another of your choice.

- the history of the trombone (or of another instrument)
- the extinct mammoth
- sign language: the language of the deaf
- the northern lights
- what you should know about cars
- the joy of computers

After you have narrowed and researched the topic together, you should each write and practice your own speech. Your speech can either inform or persuade. When you are finished, deliver them to each other. Express your ideas fluently, using Standard American English. Discuss how your speeches are alike and different. What are the strong points and weak points? Make suggestions to each other for improving your speeches.

Listening and Speaking

26.5 Presenting a Dramatic Interpretation

The impulse to tell a story, whether in the form of a poem, a song, a myth, or an epic, has always been a part of human culture. Such stories, often passed from one generation to the next, tell the hopes, the sorrows, and the history of a culture. In ancient Greece and Rome, bards, or traveling poets, presented their works at public festivals. At festivals today, poets and storytellers continue to entertain and delight their audiences.

The art of reciting or reading poetry aloud is not limited to poets; anyone can prepare and deliver an oral interpretation of a favorite poem. Choose a poem and follow these steps as you prepare to present a poem to your class.

Preparing a Poetry Reading

1. Think about who the speaker might be. Whose "voice" do you hear? What is the speaker's tone, or attitude, toward the subject? How might you use your voice to convey that tone?
2. Read through the poem again, this time focusing on your own reaction to it. What emotions do you feel? What ideas and questions come to mind? Jot down your responses to the poem, and look up any unfamiliar words. Make notes about how the poet's choice of language and imagery helps convey the intended meaning. Which words, phrases, or sentences will you emphasize in your oral interpretation?
3. Notice sound devices such as rhyme, rhythm, and repetition. Consider how you will emphasize sound devices as you recite or read the poem aloud.
4. Decide where you will pause to take a breath. Pause at the end of a line only if there is a punctuation mark or a natural pause. Otherwise, read through the ends of lines—even rhyming lines—until you reach a good place to pause.
5. Experiment with volume and speed to convey feeling.

Giving a Poetry Reading

Think of your presentation as an opportunity to give yourself, as well as your classmates, a better understanding and greater appreciation of the poem.

1. Eliminate any distractions that might disrupt the flow of your reading or your classmates' ability to concentrate.
2. The way you present your poem will depend on how you have interpreted it. However, you should always speak clearly and loudly enough so that all of your classmates can hear you.
3. Make eye contact with your audience to help them feel involved in your performance.
4. After you share your oral interpretation with your class, ask for questions or comments. Compare your understanding of the poem with your audience's interpretation.
5. Remember that poetry is open to many interpretations. Insights from your classmates may even help to expand your understanding of the poem further.

Exercise 6

In groups of three, generate criteria for evaluating poetry readings. Think about tone, rate of speaking, rhythm, volume, and pitch. How might these factors affect the presentation of the poem's meaning? Then, as a group, choose a poem to use for a poetry reading. Individually, prepare your own reading of the poem and tape record it. Regroup and listen to each reading of the same poem. How are they the same? Different? Discuss the similarities and differences and the reasons for them. Use your list of criteria to judge the effectiveness of each reading.

Exercise 7

Think about reasons why poetry has often been used to carry on oral traditions in many cultures. What purpose do you think poetry might have served in these cultures? Then think about the role of poetry in your culture. What purposes might it serve? Share your ideas with a group.

Viewing and Representing

LOG ON ▶ **Writing** Online   For research tools and additional skills practice, go to glencoe.com and enter QuickPass code WC77680p3.

Studies show that young people spend an average of one thousand hours a year watching television. That's almost three hours every day. Added to that are the many hours they spend watching movies, playing video games, reading magazines, listening to CDs and the radio, and surfing the Web. For better or worse, young people, far more than their parents and grandparents, have become very attached to **mass media.**

The term *mass media* means "a form of communication that is widely available to many people." Examples include newspapers, magazines, television, radio, movies, videos, and the Internet. Most of such forms of mass media also contain advertisements, messages that have only one purpose: to persuade readers or viewers to buy a certain product.

The various forms of mass media will have a great influence on your life. The influences can bring both positive and negative messages and results. Some forms of the media will enable you to learn new skills and explore new ideas and opportunities. Others will bring you inspiring or exciting entertainment. However, some forms of the media, if you are not careful, can mislead you, confuse you, and even endanger you.

The media often present difficult challenges. How can readers and viewers decide which media messages are valuable and truthful, and which messages are harmful, unfair, or just plain junk? Knowledge is power! Learning how to interpret, analyze, and evaluate the many messages that are sent to you—by the press, the radio and television, the movie and video game industry, the advertisers, and the Web— will give you the power and the skills to enjoy the media's benefits and discard the media junk. This unit will help.

Viewing and Representing

27.1 Interpreting Visual Messages

Radio is the only example of mass media that does not contain pictures. Just like written text, pictures carry messages. Every photograph, painting, cartoon, drawing, advertisement, and computer graphic is created carefully to send a distinct visual message. If you understand how artists and photographers craft pictures to send messages, you will be able to "read" each message and evaluate its value and truthfulness.

Understanding Visual Design

The colors, shapes, and various types of lines make up the **visual design** of a picture. The arrangement of features in a picture is called **composition.** The following chart lists some basic elements in the visual design and composition of a picture. It also describes how the artist or photographer can manipulate, or work with, these elements to send different visual messages that convey distinct thoughts, feelings, and moods.

Elements of Visual Design and Composition	
Element	**Possible Effect**
Lines	
Heavy, thick lines	Suggest boldness or power
Thin or broken lines	Suggest weakness or lightness
Straight lines	Point in a direction, or lead the eye, to something else
Curved lines	Suggest motion, warmth
Vertical lines	Suggest power, status
Horizontal lines	Suggest peace, stillness
Diagonal lines	Suggest tension, action, energy
Shapes	
Round	Suggest wholeness, happiness
Square	Suggest firmness, stability
Colors	
Cool colors (blue, green, gray)	Convey a sense of calm and coldness
Warm colors (orange, yellow, red)	Convey a sense of energy and vibrancy
Bright colors	Create a sense of warmth and joyfulness
Subdued or pastel colors	Suggest innocence or softness
Repetition of color	Can suggest a pattern or assign a value to what is portrayed

Elements of Visual Design and Composition *continued*	
Element	**Possible Effect**
Position of subjects	
Center of picture	Suggests strength, dominance; draws attention to the subject
Top of picture	Suggests power, importance
Bottom of picture	Suggests weakness, lack of power
Space	
Large space around subject	Draws attention to subject; can suggest loneliness, vastness
Small amount of space around subject	Makes subject seem very powerful

Study this photograph. The bright, warm colors suggest energy and joyfulness. The girl is positioned in the center top of the picture. Your eye is drawn immediately to her face, and her facial expression matches the message sent by the design and composition: She is having fun! Note also that the round snow tube and its shadow take up almost all the space in the photograph. This makes the subject seem very powerful. So does the head-on shot. You relate to the girl's feelings because she is looking right into your eyes. How might the visual message, or mood of this picture be different if the photographer had taken it from the sidelines as the girl raced by?

Exercise 1

Use the Elements of Visual Design and Composition chart to help you interpret the visual message contained in the photograph to the left. Explain how shapes and position, as well as colors and facial expression, work together to send that message.

Many artists and photographers choose to work in black and white rather than in color. The absence of color lets them emphasize dark and light. Study the chart on the next page to understand how light and shadow often send visual messages.

Visual Messages of Light and Shadow	
Use of Light	**Possible Effect**
Brightly lit areas	Draw the eye to them; create a cheerful mood
Dimly lit areas or shadows	Give a sense of mystery, sadness, or doom

Study this photograph. It was taken in 1909. At that time, many children worked in factories and mills. Laws to protect them had not yet been passed. Lewis Hine took this photograph of a young mill worker. He used it to illustrate

a report he wrote that urged lawmakers to pass protective child-labor laws. Note that the objects shown in the top of the photograph are brightly lit, while the objects in the lower half of the photograph are dark and heavy. The photographer purposely used this contrast of light and dark. He wanted to draw the viewer's attention to the child's face. He also used the sunlight on her face to represent youth and innocence. Then he plunged most of the child's body, and the heavy machinery surrounding her, into darkness.

Exercise 2

Think about the photographer's use of light and darkness in this photograph. Summarize in your own words the visual message that he wanted to send. Then refer to the Elements of Visual Design and Composition chart. Explain how the photographer used lines, position, and space to stress or extend his visual message.

Finally, compare and contrast the visual design of this photograph with one of the others used in this section. How did both photographers manipulate the elements of visual design and composition to send entirely different messages?

Understanding Film Techniques

Like a short story or novel, a movie or television show tells a story. Also like written literature, films use dialogue to tell much of the story. However, films also use a variety of techniques that go beyond what can be done on the written page. Think back to stories that you have both read and seen performed in a film or television version. How did the two versions compare? What, if anything, did the film techniques add to your understanding or enjoyment of the story?

The following chart lists some of the special visual techniques that directors of movies and television shows use to extend or emphasize the mood or message of the film.

Film Techniques for Sending Visual Messages

Technique	Possible Effect
Camera angles	
High (looking down on subjects)	Often makes subject seem smaller, less important, or more at risk
Low (looking up at subject)	Emphasizes subject's importance or power
Straight-on (eye level)	Puts viewer on equal level with subject; can make viewer identify with subject
Camera shots	
Close-up (picture of subject's face)	Emphasizes character's facial expressions; leads viewer to identify with him or her
Long shot (wide view, showing character within larger setting)	Shows relationship between character and setting
Lighting	
High, bright lighting	Creates cheerful, optimistic tone
Low, shadowy lighting	Creates gloomy, mysterious tone
Lit from above	Makes subject seem to glow with power or strength
Lit from below	Often creates tone of tension or fear
Editing	
Quick transitions between frames	Speed up pace; increase suspense or excitement
Slow dissolve or fade out	Often shows that a change in time has taken place
Special effects	
Slow motion	Emphasizes movement and builds drama
Blurred motion	Suggests speed or confusion
Background music	Arouses audience's emotional response

Throughout his long film career, actor John Wayne continually played the strong, no-nonsense hero—characteristically in Westerns and in war movies. Study the movie still at left from the 1959 classic John Wayne Western, *Rio Bravo*. Note that the director, Howard Hawks, used a low camera angle, shooting up at Wayne. This gives the character added height, and emphasizes his power and strength. Note also that Wayne is lit from above; the bright sun emphasizes the whiteness of his hat, leading viewers to perceive him as the "good guy." Then note elements in the Elements of Visual Design and Composition chart that Hawks used. He has probably instructed Wayne to stand as straight as possible, using the vertical line of that stance to emphasize the character's power and status.

What message do you think the director sends through Wayne's facial expression? At what pace do you think Wayne is walking? If you were on the creative staff of this movie, what type of background music would you choose for this scene?

Exercise 3

Study this movie still from *The Lion King*. Use the Film Techniques for Sending Visual Messages chart, as well as the Elements of Visual Design and Composition chart on pages 766–767, to describe the visual messages that the animator and director aim to send to viewers. In your answer, include such features as lines, shapes, color, lighting, camera angle, and camera shot. Then describe the type of background music you imagine in this scene. Explain your choice.

27.2 Analyzing Media Messages

Photographs, movies, and television programs often seem "true to life." In other words, they show scenes and actions that seem realistic. However, all media messages are constructed carefully to emphasize a particular point of view. Even a factual film documentary or a public service message on such topics as the environment or personal health uses carefully chosen colors, lines, and camera angles to present information from a certain perspective.

The artist, photographer, or director makes many decisions about what pictures and information to include, what camera angles will prove most effective, and what information should not be included because it might support another point of view. Every time you view an example of mass communications, analyze it carefully. Begin by using these steps.

Key Questions to Ask Yourself About Media Messages

To analyze a media message, ask yourself these Key Questions:

- What message is this visual (photo, drawing, cartoon, television program, video) trying to send to viewers?
- What techniques were used to present the information from a particular viewpoint?
- What do I already know about this subject?
- How can I use what I already know to judge whether this message is
    —fair or unfair?
    —based on reality or fantasy?
    —based on facts or opinions?
- What additional sources might I use to find other viewpoints that I can trust on this subject?
    —parent, teacher, or other trustworthy adult
    —reliable books or other reference sources

Then, on the basis of your answers to the questions and of other trusted viewpoints that you find, make a decision about the visual message. Make sure that you can support that decision with well-thought-out reasons.
    —I agree with the visual message because . . . .
    —I disagree with the visual message because . . . .

If our population growth continues, we'll have drastic shortages of water, land, roads, and housing.

Practice using the **Key Questions** by examining this photograph and its caption.

- **WHAT THE MESSAGE IS:** The writer of the article in which this photograph appears wants the viewer to accept the point of view that the United States faces serious shortages brought about by population growth.

- **WHAT TECHNIQUES WERE USED:** The photograph is almost totally filled with trash at a landfill. The low camera angle emphasizes the amount of trash. The use of black-and-white rather than color photography emphasizes the drabness and ugliness of trash. In addition, the use of a landfill as the focus of the message plays right into the public's knowledge about the problems of trash disposal. In other words, the writer is selling a point of view by tying it to a point of view the public has already accepted.

- **WHAT YOU KNOW:** You know that trash is a problem, but you also know that the problem isn't related only to population growth.

- **HOW YOU CAN USE WHAT YOU KNOW:** You can question the fairness of this picture and this line of reasoning. You can decide to learn more before accepting the writer's point of view.

- **OTHER SOURCES YOU MIGHT USE TO FIND OTHER VIEWPOINTS THAT YOU CAN TRUST:** Ask a parent or other trusted adult to give his or her point of view. Use reference materials to find facts that support—or *don't* support—the visual message. In addition, use reference sources to help you learn about the writer. Find out whether you can trust the writer to deliver fair and truthful messages.

Decision time! Now you can make a well-thought-out decision, based on your analysis, to agree or disagree with the writer's visual message. Your decision will be valuable because *it is backed up by careful analysis.*

Exercise 4

Working with a partner, find a public-service announcement or paid political message in a current newspaper or newsmagazine. With your partner, use the Key Questions to help you analyze the fairness of the message. Present your findings to the class.

Analyzing Movies, Music, and Television Shows

You can use the Key Questions to help you analyze and evaluate a variety of different types of mass-media messages. In this section, use the Key Questions to help you analyze the messages that the producers of movies, music videos, and television shows send viewers.

Actors in movies and television shows play fictional characters. Some characters in music videos exist only in fantasy settings. What visual messages do such characters and settings send viewers, and are these messages valuable and fair? Use the Key Questions to help you decide.

Exercise 5

Watch carefully as your teacher plays a scene or two from a popular movie or television show. Then work together as a class to use the Key Questions to help you analyze and evaluate the visual messages you received.

Key Questions to Ask Yourself About Media Evaluation

To analyze a variety of media, ask yourself these Key Questions:

- How does this particular medium present messages to viewers?
- What techniques were used to persuade viewers to agree with that message?
- What do I already know about this subject?
- How can I use what I already know to judge whether this message is
  —fair or unfair?
  —based on reality or fantasy?
  —based on facts or opinions?
- What additional sources might I use to find other viewpoints that I can trust on this subject?
  —parent, teacher, or other trustworthy adult
  —reliable books or other reference sources

Then, on the basis of your answers to the questions and of trusted viewpoints that you find, make a decision about the visual message. Make sure that you can support that decision with strong facts and reasons.
  —I agree with the visual message because . . . .
  —I disagree with the visual message because . . . .

Choose a favorite movie, television show, music video, or video game. Use the Key Questions to analyze and evaluate its visual messages. Write a brief report on your findings and conclusions.

Analyzing Advertisements and Commercials

You can also use the Key Questions to help you analyze and evaluate the media messages appearing in advertisements, in newspapers and magazines, on computer Web sites, and in television commercials.

More than any other form of media, advertisements and commercials have one and *only* one goal: *to persuade the viewer to buy the product being advertised.* To accomplish that goal, advertisers often use techniques included in the Elements of Visual Design and Composition listed on pages 766–767 and the Film Techniques for Sending Visual Messages listed on page 769. In addition, they often use one or more of the following advertising techniques.

Common Advertising Techniques		
Technique	**Description**	**Example**
Bandwagon: "Jump on the bandwagon and join in the fun!"	showing through visual images or carefully chosen words that everybody, especially "every popular, attractive, well-liked person," uses this product	an advertisement for a certain soft drink, showing attractive, smiling people enjoying each other's company as they drink it
Testimonial: "Be like your favorite celebrity!"	showing a popular star of movies or television, a famous athlete, or a leading musical performer using the product	an advertisement for a car, showing a popular television or movie star driving it
Partial truth: "Use this for incredible results!"	using oils, dyes, and other substances to make the results of using the product seem "too good to be true"	an advertisement for a certain facial cosmetic, showing an attractive teenager with perfect skin who claims to have used the product
Card stacking: "Leading experts are convinced that you should use this product."	using actors to pretend that they are doctors, dentists, and other experts to present only what supports the advertiser's opinion	an advertisement for a certain medicine, in which an actor portrays a doctor who recommends using it

Viewing and Representing

Common Advertising Techniques		
Technique	**Description**	**Example**
Name calling or appeal to guilt: "Do you still use those paper towels that are harming the beauty of our countryside?"	manipulating scientific terms, statistics, or other data to convince viewers that using another product would be foolish or wasteful	an advertisement for paper products that claims that using any other brand of paper product will be harmful to the environment

Although commercials and advertisements often include a few convincing facts, those facts are surrounded by persuasive words and often unrealistic claims. Remember: Knowledge is power! Viewers can use a version of the Key Questions to help them "cut through" the glossy language and promises of advertisements and commercials. Then viewers can make informed, wise decisions about which products to buy. As an example, examine the following model of an advertisement.

Exercise 7

Use the Key Questions that follow to help you analyze and evaluate this advertisement. Discuss your findings with classmates.

Key Questions to Ask Yourself About Commercial Messages

To analyze a commercial message, ask yourself these Key Questions:

- What message is this commercial trying to send to readers or viewers?
- What visual techniques were used to extend the written message and persuade readers or viewers to agree?
- What do I already know about this subject?
- How can I use what I already know to judge whether this message is
  —fair or unfair?
  —based on reality or fantasy?
  —based on facts or opinions?
- What additional sources might I use to find other viewpoints that I can trust on this subject?
  —parent, teacher, or other trustworthy adult, such as an expert in the field
  —reference sources, including magazines such as *Consumer Reports* and *Consumer's Digest*

Then, on the basis of your answers to the questions and of trusted viewpoints that you find, make a decision about the visual message. Make sure that you can support that decision with strong facts and reasons.
  —I agree with the visual message because . . . .
  —I disagree with the visual message because . . . .

Exercise 8

Watch carefully as your teacher plays a video clip of one or more television commercials. Then work as a class to use the Key Questions to identify, analyze, and evaluate the messages that the commercials convey.

Producing Media Messages

Another way to increase your understanding of media messages is to apply the techniques that artists, filmmakers, and advertisers use. Produce your own media messages! This section will help you to create two of them: a printed public service announcement and a television commercial.

Creating a Public Service Announcement

What changes would you like to see in your community or among your peers? Newspapers and magazines often contain public service announcements, or PSAs. There are two kinds of PSAs:

- **free advertisements** created by government agencies, charities, or community groups to convey useful information to the community and urge viewers to take action

Example: The United States Department of Education might place a full-page announcement in a family-oriented magazine, using written text and one or more photographs to convey why it is important for young children to learn to read. The purpose would be to urge parents to set aside time every day to read to their young children.

- **Paid advertisements** sponsored by a business, political party, or political action committee to convey useful information to the community and urge viewers to take action. Such ads also subtly mention the name of the sponsor to encourage viewers to form a good opinion of it.

Example: A fast-food restaurant chain might place a full-page announcement in a young people's magazine, with text that provides information about the tragic state of the nation's homeless. It would then urge readers to sign up for a road race to benefit the homeless. A photograph might include a group of healthy, attractive teenagers running in a model race, wearing T-shirts with the restaurant's familiar logo.

Follow these tips to plan and create a PSA of your own.

Tips for Creating a PSA for a Newspaper or Magazine

1. **BEGIN BY BRAINSTORMING.** Think about causes that you support or concerns that you have about such issues as the environment, education, or health. Jot down several ideas and then pick one to develop into a public service announcement.

2. **IDENTIFY YOUR PURPOSE AND MESSAGE.** What underlying message do you want your PSA to send to your readers? What action would you like your readers to take, once they understand and agree with your point of view? On notebook paper, write a sentence that states your purpose. Then write another sentence that states your message. Keep both in mind as you decide what facts you will include in your message.

3. **LIST YOUR FACTS.** List the facts that you plan to include in your PSA. Be sure to check reference sources to make sure your facts are accurate and up-to-date. Note the sources of your facts. Your PSA may carry greater weight if you quote experts or provide supportive statistics from reliable sources. Once your list is complete, examine each fact carefully. Decide which facts strongly support your point of view and which ones do not. Cross out any that seem weak.

4. **DECIDE ON THE VISUAL IMAGES.** Art is very important because it will catch the reader's attention and will extend and emphasize the message you want to send. On scrap paper, draw sketches of the art you might include or look through magazines for photographs you might use. Refer to the Elements of Visual Design and Composition chart on page 766 for ideas about use of lines, colors, and positions of your subjects. Experiment with different elements and techniques, always keeping your purpose and message in mind.

5. **DRAFT AND REVISE YOUR TEXT.** Turn your list of facts into full sentences, catchy slogans, and persuasive language that sends your message clearly. Reread your text several times to make sure your language is strong. You might ask a friend to read it and offer suggestions too.

6. **DECIDE ON A LAYOUT.** Sketch various page designs—experimenting with the position of the art and text. Select a page design that will draw the readers in and will encourage them to read and understand your message.

7. **MAKE YOUR FINAL COPY.** When you are satisfied with your art choice, your text, and your page layout, make a final copy of your public service announcement.

8. **PUBLISH YOUR PUBLIC SERVICE ANNOUNCEMENT.** Share your PSA with viewers—friends, members of the school community, neighbors, and family members. You might publish it in the school newspaper, hang it as a poster in the school, or post it on a community bulletin board. Ask for comments and suggestions. Find out whether your viewers understood and agreed with your message.

Exercise 9

Use the tips to create your own public service announcement.

Creating a Television Commercial

What product would you like to convince viewers to buy? How can you most effectively combine visual images, persuasive language, background music, and such film techniques as camera angles, camera shots, and lighting to make viewers understand and agree with your media message? Follow these tips to create an effective television commercial.

Tips for Creating a Television Commercial

1. **BUILD A PRODUCTION TEAM.** The creation of a filmed message requires the skills and cooperative effort of a group of people. Each member of the production team is responsible for one or more of the following jobs, based on his or her skills and interests.
   - **Director**—leads the group, overseeing the work of all team members and supervising the filming.
   - **Scriptwriter**—writes and revises the facts, opinions, and persuasive language included in the spoken message.
   - **Organizer and layout expert**—creates a series of simple sketches, showing each scene in the commercial and outlines the format of the commercial, from beginning to end. He or she creates a plan for the director, actors, camera operator, and music arranger to follow during the filming.

- **On- and off-camera actor(s)**—appear in the commercial. The on-camera actor or actors might speak the script, or they may act out a scene while an off-camera actor does a "voice-over," narrating the scene and delivering the spoken commercial message.
- **Lighting expert**—follows the director's plan for creating the proper lighting during the filming
- **Video operator**—videotapes the commercial
- **Music arranger**—works with the director to choose any background music that may be used and follows the director's cue to start the music at the appropriate time during the filming

2. **BEGIN BY THINKING ABOUT, OR VIEWING, OTHER COMMERCIALS.** Work with your group to view and discuss existing television commercials. Evaluate the techniques, agreeing on those that seem particularly interesting and effective in persuading viewers to buy the advertised product.

3. **BRAINSTORM.** Jot down everyone's ideas about products that you would enjoy promoting. The group's enthusiasm for the product will help you to write and produce a convincing commercial. Select one product.

4. **WORK COOPERATIVELY TO PLAN THE COMMERCIAL.** Work together to decide upon persuasive language, visual images, the roles that actors might play, and other issues. For guidance in your planning, refer to the charts on pages 766, 769, and 774. Then work independently to plan and prepare your assigned part. Come together to review and revise ideas until everyone is satisfied.

5. **REHEARSE.** Do several run-throughs of the commercial before actually taping it. At this point, the director should be in charge, planning the camera shots and angles, the lighting, the movements and positions of the actors, and the voice and music cues.

6. **SHOOT!** Create your commercial, following the plan that you perfected during rehearsals.

7. **PRESENT YOUR COMMERCIAL.** Play the commercial for classmates and friends. Invite members of the audience to comment and make suggestions on your message and your techniques.

Exercise 10

Use the tips to create an effective television commercial.

UNIT 28 Electronic Resources

LOG ON ▶ **Writing** Online For research tools and additional skills practice, go to **glencoe.com** and enter QuickPass code WC77680p3.

781

28.1 The Internet

The **Internet** is an electronic connection to a world of information and services that you can tap into with a computer. It uses telephone lines, cable lines, and satellites to link your computer to computers all over the world. Today, the Internet is for many people a common resource for research, up-to-the-minute news, shopping, socializing and entertainment.

The Internet, often referred to simply as the Net, is a collaborative enterprise. No one organization or company owns it. A few organizations work together to set standards and keep the Internet running smoothly.

The first Internet was established with Department of Defense funding in 1969 for research, educational, and government purposes. It linked computers at four university sites, three of them in California. Most of the users were computer experts, scientists, and engineers. Commands had to be given in difficult computer language.

From this limited beginning, the Internet expanded in response to the need for information. In less than two decades, most universities and government offices were using the Internet for communication and research. By that time, inexpensive desktop computers had been developed and were finding their way into average American homes. By the early 1990s, after the introduction of user-friendly browsers, the Internet became a widely used avenue of knowledge for the average person. By 2010 about 1.8 billion people worldwide will be using the Internet.

When most people speak of the Internet, they mean that part of the Internet called the World Wide Web. The **World Wide Web** makes it easy to connect to millions of different Web sites that may include video, graphics, animation, and sound as well as text.

The Internet has revolutionized not only research but also business and social communication, shopping, and even recreation. Here are a few of the ways in which people use the Internet.

- **NEWS REPORTS:** A user can have access to the latest news within minutes of its being reported. All major newspapers and television news departments have Web sites.

- **SHOPPING:** Just about everything you might need can be ordered online, including books, games, computer equipment, clothing, and groceries.

- **WORK:** Businesses can communicate with other businesses, clients, or customers via e-mail or through instant messaging.
- **CLASS WORK:** College students can access lectures and lecture notes and even take open-book tests without leaving their homes or dormitories. Numerous middle schools and high schools have established their own student-operated Web sites.
- **SOCIAL LIFE:** People can make new friends, keep in touch with old ones, and share thoughts and ideas with others through e-mail, instant messaging, discussion forums, and chat rooms.
- **ENTERTAINMENT:** Besides listening to music and reading news and reviews of movies, plays, concerts, and other performances, Internet users can play games with opponents who are miles, or even continents, away.

Exercise 1

Work with a small group to make an Internet time line that shows the history of the Internet. Use Internet, classroom, and library resources to help create the time line. Combine your group's time line with those of other groups to create a classroom "Internet Time Line." You might use e-mail to share information about the project with other students your age. Display the time line in your classroom or in one of the common areas of the school.

28.2 Using the Internet

How can you access the Internet? Besides the computer itself, you need a modem, an Internet service provider, and a browser.

- A **modem** (derived from MOdulation plus DEModulation) is a device that allows a computer to communicate and share information with another computer over telephone or cable lines. Most computers now come with a built-in modem.
- An **Internet service provider**, or ISP, provides a service (for a fee) that allows your computer to connect to the Internet by way

of existing telephone lines. Newer service methods, already in place in some locations, use TV cable lines or wireless transmission for the signals. Instead of an ISP, online services, such as America Online or Microsoft Network, will let you access the Internet as well as their own private services. For example, America Online users can use private chat rooms and message boards where members can exchange messages.

- To display the contents of a Web site, your computer must have a browser. A **browser** is a software program that displays Web pages that can include text, graphics, pictures, and video. The best-known browsers are Microsoft Internet Explorer, Mozilla Firefox, Safari, Opera, and Netscape Navigator. A browser enables you to get around the Web. With a browser, you can also use plug-ins. These software programs extend the abilities of your browser—for example, to play sounds or display movies from an Internet site.

Even if you don't have your own computer, you can probably access the Internet at your school or in a public library. Most libraries now have Internet terminals that their patrons can use.

Searching the Internet

When writing a report, doing research, or just using the Internet for amusement, you may want to find specific information. The fastest way to find the Web sites you are looking for is to use a search engine. A **search engine** lets you look for information on the Web by searching for keywords. A **keyword** is a word or phrase that describes your topic.

If you haven't narrowed your search to a specific topic, you can start with a subject directory. A **subject directory** lists general topics, such as arts and humanities, science, education, entertainment, sports, and health. After you select a broad topic, the directory will offer a list of possible subtopics from which to choose. Several search engines and subject directories, such as Google, Yahoo!, and Excite, are available on the Internet. A **metasearch engine,** such as Dogpile or Metacrawler, will let you search several search engines at the same time.

You can do a more precise search by using the **Boolean search** method. The following chart will help you to use this technique.

TIPS FOR DOING A BOOLEAN SEARCH

A Boolean search uses the operators AND, OR, and NOT between keywords to further limit the terms of a search.

AND Link two keywords with AND to find only Web sites that contain both words (galaxy AND Jupiter). You will get fewer matches, but most of them will relate to your topic. Some programs use a plus sign instead of AND (galaxy + Jupiter).

OR The command OR tells the search engine to look for Web pages that use one term *or* the other (Mars OR Jupiter). You will get hits for every site that uses either word.

NOT If there is information that you do not want, use NOT between the two keywords (planets NOT Jupiter). You will get information about other planets but not about the planet Jupiter. Some programs use a minus sign instead of NOT (planets – Jupiter).

Addresses

If you use a search engine or a subject directory, your list of hits will include hyperlinks to each site. All you need to do to reach a site is to click on its hyperlink. Otherwise, to get to a particular Web site you need to know its address. Every Web site on the Internet has a unique address or URL. **URL** stands for Uniform Resource Locator. No two Web sites can have the same URL.

As an Internet user, you may want to keep track of some Web sites that you visit. You can keep a record of them by making a bookmark of them or by naming sites as "favorites." This option lets you keep a file of your favorite sites. Instead of typing the address each time you want to view a Web site, you simply go to the bookmark or favorites menu on your browser and click on the site's name.

Electronic Resources

URL Components

Following is a typical URL. Notice that it is typed with no spaces between its parts and usually (but not always) is in all lowercase letters.

http://www.domainname.com/path/filename

http://—stands for hypertext transfer protocol, the rules for moving text over the Web. This protocol allows your computer to get information from any other computer hooked to the Web.

domain name—identifies the Web site. The part before the dot names the site owner. After the dot comes a suffix identifying the type of domain (see list of domain types below).

path—identifies the path within the site that leads to a specific document

file name—names the specific file that you are looking for

Domain Types

The following suffixes found in domain names identify the type of domain.

.com	for-profit company	.tv	television
.edu	educational institution	.biz	business
.gov	government body	.au	Australia
.mil	military site	.de	Germany
.net	network or internet service provider	.es	Spain
.org	nonprofit organization	.us	United States

Hyperlinks

You may notice as you begin to investigate various Web sites that some words or phrases are underlined or are in a different color from the rest of the text (or both). These words or phrases are hyperlinks. **Hyperlinks** are text or graphics (often buttons) that, when clicked on, take you to a specific page of a Web site or to a related Web site. Sometimes it may be difficult to find a hyperlink on a Web page. If you are not sure whether a part of the text or graphics contains a hyperlink, drag the arrow cursor over it. If your arrow changes to a pointing finger, you've found a hyperlink.

Exercise 2

On a sheet of paper, create a four-column chart. In each column, write one of the headings *Animals, History, Sports,* and *Art.* If you used any of these general words as keywords you would get far too many hits to be useful. Under each heading, write more-specific keywords you could use to search for information within that topic. Write at least five terms in each column. Then compare lists with your group or the class.

Exercise 3

Use a search engine to find Web sites that provide information about the nine known planets in the solar system. Write down the URLs of each Web site that you visit and record information that you learn about the planets on note cards. After you have information about all nine planets, present your findings to the class.

28.3 Using E-mail

One of the most popular and useful features of the Internet is the ability to send and receive **e-mail**, or electronic mail. With the click of a button, you can send a message to anyone in the world. You can also attach other computer files to your e-mail message. You can send pictures of yourself to your family, send a sound clip of your favorite song to a friend, or send a story you have written to one of your teachers.

For many people, e-mail has replaced regular mail or telephone as the preferred medium of communication for personal and business use. It reaches its destination, no matter how far, in a matter of seconds. When used to transmit complex data, it is less likely to be misunderstood than a voice-mail message and can be printed out for reference.

To send e-mail, you need a unique e-mail address. Your Internet service provider will provide you with one. You can also use another service, such as Yahoo!, to provide you with an e-mail account.

A typical e-mail address has four parts. The first part is the user name. This is the name that you choose or that is assigned to you by your

This is the name that you choose or that is assigned to you by your Internet service provider. The second part is the @ symbol, which stands for "at." This symbol separates the user name from the rest of the e-mail address. The third part is the domain name, which is the name of your ISP's computer or the service that hosts your e-mail account. The last part of an e-mail address is the suffix, usually *.net* if you use an ISP. The suffix indicates the type of organization that provides your e-mail service.

With most e-mail programs, you can store frequently used e-mail addresses in an address book. When you want to send a message to a person whose address is in your address book, you simply begin typing the person's name and the e-mail application "autofills" the name and address for you. You can also store additional information, such as the person's street address, birthday, and phone number in your address book.

Just as you can send an e-mail message to any address in the world, anyone in the world can send an e-mail message to you. Sometimes you will receive junk e-mail, or **spam**. Advertisements are the main form of spam. E-mail can also contain software viruses disguised as attachments that, when downloaded and opened, can harm your computer. Anti-virus utilities can help protect from such viruses. If you receive an e-mail from someone whose e-mail address you don't recognize, show it to an adult, and do reply back unless the adult gives you permission. Some people send links to Web sites through e-mail. If you receive a message with a link to a Web site, show it to an adult before clicking on the link.

E-mail Pen Pals

You've probably worked with partners or small groups many times in school. E-mail allows you to collaborate with people who are not in the same room, the same school, or even the same country. Imagine comparing descriptions of your school day with a student from Australia. How about having your class collaborate on a project with a class from South Africa? With e-mail, the whole world can be at your fingertips. Talk to your teacher about finding a class in a "sister school" you can work with or about seeking e-mail pen pals.

E-mail Etiquette

When sending e-mail, follow these rules of e-mail etiquette.

- Use the subject line wisely. Be as brief as you can, but let the recipient know what your message is about.

- When responding to a long message, don't include the entire message in your response. Quote just enough of it to let your correspondent know what you are responding to.
- Keep messages short and to the point.
- Use appropriate capitalization. Using all capital letters is considered SHOUTING.
- Avoid sending unfriendly e-mail. Sending an unfriendly e-mail message is called "flaming."
- It is important to use correct spelling.
- Consider including your name and contact information at the end of your message. This is typically referred to as a signature.
- Be careful when using humor or sarcasm. It is difficult to convey some emotions in print. Use "smileys" if you want to show emotion (see next page).
- Remember that good behavior on the Internet is no different from good behavior in face-to-face situations. Treat others as you would like them to treat you.

Mailing Lists

If there is a particular subject that you need to research, you might want to consider subscribing to a mailing list. A **mailing list** is like a bulletin board on which you exchange information through e-mail. Type "mailing list" into a search engine along with your topic of interest, such as "baseball" or "astronomy." Choose a search result that interests you. You may want to be specific when choosing a topic. For example, instead of typing "baseball," you could type "St. Louis Cardinals." Once you have found a mailing list that interests you, follow the directions to subscribe to the list.

Once you subscribe to a mailing list, you will receive e-mail messages from people discussing your subject of interest. Before you post your own messages on the mailing list, read the postings already there until you are familiar with the type of discussion the group is having. Post a message only when you have something new to say, and remember to keep your posts brief and to the point. Be sure to follow the rules of e-mail etiquette. You can cancel your subscription to a mailing list at any time.

EMOTICONS AND ACRONYMS

Emoticons, (icons that show emotion), can be used to give expression to online messages that you send. They are created with the characters on your keyboard.

:-)	smile
;-)	wink
:-(	frown/unhappy
:-D	laughing
:-o	wow!
:*)	clowning around
:-P	tongue out
:-/	confused
0:-)	angel (with halo)

Acronyms are words formed from the first letters of other words. Many people use special acronyms to save typing time and space in their e-mail. These are a few of the most commonly used ones.

BTW	By the way
FAQ	Frequently asked questions
FYI	For your information
GMTA	Great minds think alike
IMHO	In my humble opinion
LOL	Laugh out loud
ROFL	Rolling on the floor laughing
TYVM	Thank you very much

Exercise 4

Using a search engine, find and subscribe to a mailing list that discusses a topic of interest to you. Create a mailing-list log to keep track of the correspondence that the mailing list generates. Keep the log for a week and then share what you've learned with the class.

Exercise 5

Working with the class, create a United States map or a world map to show all the places from which you and your classmates have received e-mail. Use colored thumbtacks to show where the e-mail originated. Keep track of incoming e-mail for the next month and update the maps as necessary.

Electronic Resources

Selecting and Evaluating Internet Sources

Before you even begin searching the Internet, you need to decide what kinds of information you are looking for. Is it personal information, such as learning more about a hobby, or is it related to your school work? These types of information can overlap, of course, but having a particular goal in mind will help you in the search process.

Personal Information

Whatever your interest, there is probably a Web site—more likely several of them—devoted to it. Do you have a favorite computer game? You can probably find a few sites and discussion groups devoted to it. On these sites, you can chat with other players, learn new strategies, find out about upgrades or when a new version of the game will be released, and perhaps even find people to play the game with on the Web.

Think of a hobby, one you currently have or one you're just considering. Try a keyword search and see how many sites you can find devoted to that hobby. You may be surprised, possibly even bowled over, by the results.

Are you interested in music, movies, books, sports? The number of sites for any of these topics is overwhelming. Your only challenge will be finding the site or sites that best suit your needs.

Would you like information about teen-related topics, such as getting along in school, dating, or *your* music, clothing, and values? Hundred of teen sites are available for your special interests. Check with your teacher, librarian, or computer lab head for suggestions.

School Work

Suppose you need to find information for a research project. You may use print resources, such as books, magazines, and newspapers, or you may decide to access the wealth of information available to you on the Web. Two general categories of sites can give you the help you need. One group consists of the millions of sites devoted to particular topics. To find these, you'll need to use a search engine or subject directory. The second group includes the many sites devoted to general reference sources, such as dictionaries, encyclopedias, and electronic "handbooks."

For a start, look for a Web site that contains links to a variety of other reference sources. One example of such a site is B. J. Pinchbeck's Homework Helper (www.bjpinchbeck.com). It contains links to dozens of good reference sources, including several dictionary and encyclopedia sites, sites for converting currencies or units of measure, directories of various kinds, and sources of statistics. Many of these links contain still more useful links. Another useful site is the Internet Public Library (www.ipl.org). Try the School and Homework Help of its teen division. When you find a site that you know will be useful for your school work, bookmark it.

Exercise 6

Think of three questions that have short answers but would require some research to answer. (For example: How many acres are there in a mile? What's the meaning of *xenophobic*? Who was Akira Kurosawa?) Write your questions on a piece of paper. Then exchange questions with a partner. Use one of the Internet sites mentioned above for help in finding the answers to your partner's questions.

Evaluation

Whether you use print or electronic sources, you are responsible for verifying the accuracy of the information you gather. One way to check the reliability of a Web site is to find out who owns it or who created it. For instance, if you are looking for the average snowfall in Boston during December, you can probably rely on the National Weather Service Web site to be accurate. However, if you find the information on a site created by a student in California, you might need to verify it in another source.

Criteria for Evaluation In evaluating any information source, ask the following questions.

1. What person, organization, or company created the information? Is that source well known? Is it considered reliable? Generally (but not always), you can expect a government or university site to be more accurate than an individual's site. If the source is not given, you have reason to question the authenticity of the material.

2. How current is the information you have found? If it is important for the information to be current, look for the date of publication. If you are researching a topic in medicine, science, or technology, it is important that you use up-to-date information. In areas such

as literature and history, older material may be as good as current data.

3. What is the purpose of the information? If it is obvious that the purpose of the information is to entertain or persuade or if it was provided by a group with a particular bias, you may want to be cautious in how you use the information.

4. Has the material been reviewed? It is often relatively easy to find a review of printed material, but it is more difficult to determine whether there is any review process for material on a Web site. It is probably safe to assume that material from a government or university site has undergone some form of review.

5. Is the material suitable for your purpose? Be sure that the information you use is written in a way that you (or your intended audience) can understand. If it contains difficult-to-understand ideas or vocabulary, consider looking for another source.

Exercise 7

Choose a famous current or historical event and find a Web site that provides information about the event. Record the URL and five to ten facts that you learned about the event on the Web site. Check the accuracy of the facts in another source, such as an encyclopedia. Then report to the class on the accuracy of the Web site.

28.5 CDs and Other Electronic Resources

Besides the resources available to you on the Internet, a computer can help you access a wide variety of information from compact discs (CDs), digital video discs (DVDs), CD-Rs, and CD-RWs. CD-R stands for "compact disc recordable," and CD-RW stands for "compact disc rewritable." These items can be viewed at and sometimes borrowed from a library. The number and variety of topics covered in them is constantly growing. If your family is considering the purchase of a new computer, be sure that the computer can accommodate these informational items.

CDs (CD-R and CD-RW)

Writeable **CDs** (CD-R and CD-RW), look like audio compact discs, but store more than just audio information. Once data has been written onto a CD, it cannot be removed and can only be read. CD-R

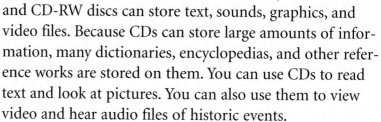

and CD-RW discs can store text, sounds, graphics, and video files. Because CDs can store large amounts of information, many dictionaries, encyclopedias, and other reference works are stored on them. You can use CDs to read text and look at pictures. You can also use them to view video and hear audio files of historic events.

To use a CD, your computer must have a CD drive. CD drives are standard on most new computers.

DVDs

A **DVD** can store up to six times the data of a CD on the same surface area. Similar in size and shape to a CD, a DVD can hold enough information for a full-length movie. A DVD player can be used to watch movies, and like a CD, a DVD requires a special drive on a computer. Although a DVD drive can play CDs, a CD drive cannot play DVDs.

Removable Storage

Your computer uses a built-in hard drive that stores information. All computers also include a drive for removable discs that can increase your storage capacity. You can insert a removable disc into another computer and transfer files to it. These removable discs can also be used to send information to someone else or to store files as a backup in case your hard drive crashes and you lose the information there.

The average computer user uses CDs and flash drives to store information, although most software is now being distributed on a CD. Flash drives are removable, rewritable devices. Small and lightweight, most are about the size of a pack of gum. They are also convenient and portable and can be carried in your pocket, on a key fob, or on a lanyard around your neck. These devices are popular with those who use more than one PC and need to move personal data or work files from one place to another.

External writable CD and DVD drives, also called burners, make it possible to record music or data from a computer or other CD or DVD. These drives are standard equipment with new PCs. Because of the widespread practice of burning CDs and DVDs, laws against illegal copying of music and movies are being enforced.

Exercise 8

Find a book and a CD on the same subject at your neighborhood or school library. If you were writing a report on this subject, which source would be the most helpful? Create a chart listing the advantages and disadvantages of each.

Troubleshooting Guide

As you work on the Web, you may need help in dealing with possible problems. Here are some error messages that you might see as you spend time on the Web. They are followed by their possible causes and some suggestions for eliminating the errors.

Message: Unable to connect to server. The server may be down. Try connecting again later.

Possible Causes: The server is having technical problems. The site is being updated or is not communicating properly with your browser.

Suggestion: It usually helps if you try again in a few minutes; however, it could be a few days before the server is working properly.

Message: Unable to locate the server: www.server.com. The server does not have a DNS (Domain Name System) entry. Check the server name in the URL and try again.

Possible Causes: You have typed in the URL incorrectly, or the site no longer exists.

Suggestion: Be sure you have entered the URL correctly—check for proper capitalization and punctuation. If you have entered it correctly, try using a search engine to find the site.

Keep in mind, though, the possibility that the site may have been abandoned.

Message: File Not Found: The requested URL was not found on this server.

Possible Causes: You have reached the server, but that particular file no longer exists or you have entered the path or file name incorrectly.

Suggestion: Check the URL again. If you have entered it correctly, try searching for the page from the server's home page.

Message: Network connection refused by the server. There was no response.

Possible Causes: You have reached the server, but it is too busy (too many other people are trying to access it) or temporarily shut down.

Suggestion: Try to access the site later.

Message: Connection timed out.

Possible Causes: Your browser attempted to contact the host, but the host took too long to reply.

Suggestion: Try to access the site later.

Message: Access denied. You do not have permission to open this item.

Possible Causes: The URL has moved, the Webmaster no longer allows public access to the site, or you have been denied access to the site.

Suggestion: Contact the Webmaster to verify the URL or try the site again in a few days. Sometimes there is nothing you can do if access has been denied.

Message: You do not have the proper plug-in installed to view this content.

Possible causes: You have attempted to access content that your Web browser is not equipped to view.

Suggestion: The Web site that requires the plug-in will usually provide instructions for downloading and installing the plug-in. Before you download and install the plug-in, evaluate the reliability of these instructions. Some of the popular plug-ins are Flash player, Quicktime, RealPlayer, and Windows Media Player.

WRITING AND LANGUAGE GLOSSARY

This glossary will help you quickly find definitions used in writing and grammar.

A

Adjective. A word that modifies, or describes, a noun or a pronoun. An adjective may tell *what kind, which one, how many,* or *how much.*

The **comparative degree** of an adjective compares two people, places, things, or ideas. (*worse, sadder)*

The **superlative degree** of an adjective compares more than two people, places, things, or ideas. (*worst, saddest)*

A **possessive adjective** is a possessive pronoun used before a noun.

A **predicate adjective** always follows a linking verb. It modifies the subject of the sentence.

A **proper adjective** is formed from a proper noun. It always begins with a capital letter.

A **demonstrative adjective** is the word *this, that, these,* or *those* used before a noun.

Adjective clause. A dependent clause that modifies a noun or pronoun.

Adverb. A word that modifies a verb, an adjective, or another adverb. Adverbs may tell *how, when, where, in what manner,* and *how often.* Some adverbs have different forms to indicate **comparative** and **superlative degrees.** (*loud, louder, loudest; sweetly, more sweetly, most sweetly)*

Adverb clause. A dependent clause that modifies a verb, an adjective, or an adverb.

Allusion. A reference in a piece of writing to a well-known character, place, or situation from a work of literature, music, or art or from history.

Analysis. The act of breaking down a subject into separate parts to determine its meaning.

Anecdote. A short story or incident usually presented as part of a longer narrative.

Antecedent. *See* Pronoun.

Appositive. A noun placed next to another noun to identify it or add information about it. (My basketball coach, *Ms. Lopes,* called for a time out.)

Argument. A statement, reason, or fact for or against a point; a piece of writing intended to persuade.

Article. The adjectives *a, an,* and *the. A* and *an* are **indefinite articles.** They refer to any one item of a group. *The* is a **definite article.** It indicates that the noun it precedes is a specific person, place or thing.

Audience. The person(s) who reads or listens to what the writer or speaker says.

B

Base form. *See* Verb tense.

Bias. A tendency to think a certain way. Bias may affect the way a writer or speaker presents his or her ideas.

Bibliography. A list of the books, articles, and other sources used as reference sources in a research paper.

Body. The central part of a composition that communicates and explains the main idea identified in the introduction.

Bookmarks/favorites. The feature on many Web browsers that allows the user to save addresses of Internet sites so that the sites can be accessed quickly.

Brainstorming. A group activity in which people generate as many ideas as possible without stopping to judge them.

C

Case. The form of a noun or pronoun that is determined by its use in a sentence. A noun or pronoun is in the **nominative** case when it is used as a subject, in the **objective** case when it is used as an object, and in the **possessive** case when it is used to show possession.

Cause-and-effect chain. A series of events in which one cause leads to an effect that in turn leads to another effect, and so on.

Characterization. The methods a writer uses to develop the personality of the character. A writer may make direct statements about a character's personality or reveal it through the character's words and actions or through what other characters think and say about the character.

Chronological order. The arrangement of details according to when events or actions take place.

Clarity. The quality of a piece of writing that makes it easy to understand.

Clause. A group of words that has a subject and a predicate and that is used as part of a sentence.

> An **independent clause,** also called a **main clause,** has a subject and a predicate and can stand alone as a sentence.

> A **dependent clause,** also called a **subordinate clause,** has a subject and a predicate, but it makes sense only when attached to a main clause.

Cliché. An overused expression. (*white as snow*)

Clustering. The grouping together of related items as a way of organizing information.

Coherence. A quality of logical connection between the parts of a paragraph or composition.

Cohesive writing. A type of writing in which sentences and paragraphs are logically connected to one another.

Collaboration. The process of working with others on writing or other projects.

Colloquialism. A casual, colorful expression used in everyday conversation.

Comparative degree. *See* Adjective; Adverb.

Comparison-and-contrast organization. A way of organizing ideas by illustrating their similarities and differences.

Complement. A word or phrase that completes the meaning of a verb. Three kinds of complements are **direct objects**, **indirect objects,** and **subject complements.**

Conceptual map. A graphic device that develops a central concept by surrounding it with examples or related ideas in a weblike arrangement.

Conclusion. A restatement or summing up of the ideas in a composition that brings it to a definite close.

Conflict. The struggle between two opposing forces that lies at the center of the plot in a story or drama.

Conjunction. A word that joins single words or groups of words.

> A **coordinating conjunction** (*and, but, or, nor, for, yet*) joins words or groups of words

that are equal in grammatical importance. **Correlative conjunctions** (*both . . . and, just as . . . so, not only . . . but also, either . . . or, neither . . . nor*) are pairs of words used to connect words or phrases in a sentence.

Connotation. The thoughts and feelings associated with a word, rather than its dictionary definition.

Constructive criticism. Comments on another person's writing made with the intention of helping the writer improve a particular draft.

Context. The words and sentences that come before and after a specific word and help to explain its meaning.

Conventions. Correct spelling, grammar, usage, and mechanics.

Coordinating conjunction. *See* Conjunction.

Correlative conjunction. *See* Conjunction.

Credibility. The quality of a speaker or writer that makes that person's words believable.

Declarative sentence. A sentence that makes a statement.

Deductive reasoning. A way of thinking or explaining that begins with a general statement or principle and applies that principle to specific instances.

Definite article. *See* Article.

Demonstrative adjective. *See* Adjective.

Denotation. The dictionary definition of a word.

Dependent clause. *See* Clause.

Descriptive writing. Writing that uses sensory detail to convey a dominant impression of, for example, a setting, a person, an animal, and so on.

Desktop publishing. The use of computer programs to format and produce a document that may include written text, graphics, and/or images.

Dialect. A variation of a language spoken by a particular group of people. A dialect may be regional (based on location) or ethnic (based on cultural heritage).

Dialogue. The conversation between characters in a written work.

Diction. A writer's choice of words and the arrangement of those words in phrases, sentences, or lines of a poem.

Direct object. *See* Complement.

Documentation. Identification of the sources used in writing research or other informative papers; usually in the form of endnotes or footnotes, or using parenthetical documentation.

Drafting. One of the steps in the writing process; the transforming of thoughts, words, and phrases into sentences and paragraphs.

E–F

Editing. One of the steps in the writing process in which a revised draft is checked for standard usage, varied sentence structure, and appropriate word choice.

Editorial. An article in a newspaper or other form of media that expresses an opinion about a topic of general interest.

Elaboration. The support or development of a main idea with facts, statistics, sensory details, incidents, anecdotes, examples, or quotations.

Ellipsis. A mark of punctuation, consisting of three spaced periods, that shows the omission of a word or words.

E-mail. Short for electronic mail. Messages, usually text, sent from one person to another by way of computer.

Evaluating. Making a judgment about the strengths and weaknesses of a draft in content, organization, and style.

Evidence. Facts or examples from reliable sources that can be used to support statements made in speaking or writing.

Exclamatory sentence. A sentence that expresses strong or sudden emotion.

Explanatory writing. *See* Expository writing.

Expository writing. A kind of writing that aims at informing and explaining. Examples of expository writing are news articles, how-to instructions, and research papers.

Expressive writing. Writing that emphasizes and conveys the writer's feelings.

Fact. A piece of information that can be verified.

Feedback. The response a listener or reader gives to a speaker or writer about his or her work.

Figurative language. Words used for descriptive effect that express some truth beyond the literal level. Figures of speech such as similes, metaphors, or personification are examples of figurative language.

Formal language. Language that uses correct grammar and omits slang expressions and contractions. It is especially common in non-fiction writing that is not personal.

Fragment. An incomplete sentence punctuated as if it were complete.

Freewriting. A way of finding ideas by writing freely, without stopping or limiting the flow of ideas, often for a specific length of time.

Future tense. *See* Verb tense.

Generalization. A statement that presents a conclusion about a subject without going into details or specifics.

Genre. A division of literature. The main literary genres are prose, poetry, and drama. Each of these is further divided into subgenres.

Gerund. A verb form ending in *–ing* that is used as a noun.

Graphic organizer. A visual way of organizing information; types of graphic organizers are charts, graphs, clusters, and idea trees.

Home page. The location on a Web site by which a user normally enters the site. A typical home page may explain the site, summarize the content, and provide links to other sites.

Hyperlink. Highlighted or underlined phrases or words on a Web page that, when clicked, move the user to another part of the page or to another Web page.

Hypertext. Links in some electronic text that take the user to another document or to a different section in the same document.

Ideas. In writing, the message or theme and the details that elaborate upon that message or theme.

Idiom. A word or phrase that has a special meaning different from its standard or dictionary meaning. (*Burning the midnight oil* is an idiom that means "staying up late.")

Imagery. Language that emphasizes sensory impressions that can help the reader of a literary work to see, hear, feel, smell, and taste the scenes described in the work.

Imperative sentence. A sentence that makes a request or gives a command.

Indefinite article. *See* Article.

Indefinite pronoun. *See* Pronoun.

Independent clause. *See* Clause.

Inductive reasoning. A way of thinking or explaining that begins with a series of examples and uses them to arrive at a general statement.

Infinitive. A verbal made up of the word *to* and the base form of a word. An infinitive often functions as a noun in a sentence.

Informative writing. A kind of writing that explains something, such as a process or an idea. *See also* Expository writing.

Intensifier. An adverb that emphasizes an adjective or another adverb. (*very* important; *quite* easily)

Interjection. A word or phrase that expresses strong feeling. An interjection has no grammatical connection to other words in the sentence.

Internet. A worldwide computer network that allows users to link to any computer on the network electronically for social, commercial, research, and other purposes.

Interpretation. An explanation of the meaning of a piece of writing, a visual representation, or any other type of communication.

Interview. A question-and-answer dialogue that has the specific purpose of gathering up-to-date or expert information.

Intransitive verb. *See* Verb.

Introduction. The beginning part of a piece of writing, in which a writer identifies the subject and gives a general idea of what the body of the composition will contain.

Inverted order. The placement of a predicate before the subject in a sentence. In most sentences in English, the subject comes before the predicate.

Irregular verb. *See* Verb tense.

J

Jargon. Special words and phrases used by a particular trade, profession, or other group of people.

Journal. A personal notebook in which a person can freewrite, collect ideas, and record thoughts and experiences.

L–M

Learning log. A journal used for clarifying ideas about concepts covered in various classes.

Lexicon. A wordbook or dictionary.

Listing. A technique for finding ideas for writing.

Literary analysis. The act of examining the different elements of a piece of literature in order to evaluate it.

Logical fallacy. An error in reasoning often found in advertising or persuasive writing. Either-or reasoning and glittering generalities are types of logical fallacies.

Main clause. *See* Clause.

Main idea. *See* Thesis statement.

Main verb. The most important word in a verb phrase.

Media. The forms of communication used to reach an audience; forms such as newspapers, radio, TV, and the Internet reach large audiences and so are known as mass media.

Memoir. A type of narrative nonfiction that presents an account of an event or period in history, emphasizing the narrator's personal experience.

Metaphor. A figure of speech that compares seemingly unlike things without using words such as *like* or *as*. (*He is a rock.*)

Mood. The feeling or atmosphere of a piece of writing.

Multimedia presentation. The use of a variety of media, such as video, sound, written text, and visual art to present ideas or information.

N

Narrative writing. A type of writing that tells about events or actions as they change over a period of time and often includes story elements such as character, setting, and plot.

Nonfiction. Prose writing about real people, places, and events.

Noun. A word that names a person, a place, a thing, an idea, a quality, or a characteristic.

Noun clause. A dependent clause used as a noun.

Number. The form of a noun, pronoun, or verb that indicates whether it refers to one (**singular**) or more than one (**plural**).

O

Object. *See* Complement.

Onomatopoeia. The use of a word or phrase that imitates or suggests the sound of what it describes. (*rattle, boom*)

Opinion. A belief or attitude that cannot be proven true or false.

Oral tradition. Literature that passes by word of mouth from one generation to the next. The oral tradition of a culture may reflect the cultural values of the people.

Order of importance. A way of arranging details in a paragraph or other piece of writing according to their importance.

Organization. The arrangement of main points and supporting details in a piece of writing.

Outline. A systematic arrangement of main and supporting ideas, using Roman numerals, letters, and numbers, for a written or an oral presentation.

P

Paragraph. A unit of writing that consists of related sentences.

Parallel construction. The use of a series of words, phrases, or sentences that have similar grammatical form.

Paraphrase. A restatement of someone's ideas in words that are different from the original passage but retain its ideas, tone, and general length.

Parenthetical documentation. A specific reference to the source of a piece of information, placed in parenthesis directly after the information appears in a piece of writing.

Participle. A verb form that can function as an adjective. Present participles always end in *-ing*. Although past participles often end in *-ed*, they can take other forms as well.

Peer response. The suggestions and comments provided by peers, or classmates, about a piece of writing or another type of presentation.

Personal pronoun. *See* Pronoun.

Personal writing. Writing that expresses the writer's own thoughts and feelings.

Personification. A figure of speech that gives human qualities to an animal, object, or idea.

Perspective. *See* Point of view.

Persuasion. A type of writing that aims at convincing people to think or act in a certain way.

Phrase. A group of words that acts in a sentence as a single part of speech.

A **prepositional phrase** begins with a preposition and ends with a noun or a pronoun.

A **verb phrase** consists of one or more auxiliary verbs followed by a main verb.

Plagiarism. The dishonest presentation of another's words or ideas as one's own.

Plot. The series of events that follow one another in a story, novel, or play.

Plural. *See* Number.

Poetry. A form of literary expression that emphasizes the line as the unit of composition. Traditional poetry contains emotional, imaginative language and a regular rhythm.

Point of view. The angle, or perspective, from which a story is told, such as first- or third-person.

Portfolio. A collection of various pieces of writing, which may include finished pieces and works in progress.

Predicate. The verb or verb phrase and any of its modifiers that make an essential statement about the subject of a sentence.

Predicate adjective. *See* Adjective.

Preposition. A word that shows the relationship of a noun or pronoun to some other word in the sentence.

Prepositional phrase. *See* Phrase.

Presentation. The way words and design elements look on the page.

Presenting/Publishing. The last step in the writing process; involves sharing the final writing product with others in some way.

Present tense. *See* Verb tense.

Prewriting. The first stage in the writing process; includes deciding what to write about, collecting ideas and details, and making an outline or a plan. Prewriting strategies include brainstorming and using graphic organizers, notes, and logs.

Prior knowledge. The facts, ideas, and experiences that a writer, reader, or viewer brings to a new activity.

Progressive form. *See* Verb tense.

Pronoun. A word that takes the place of a noun, a group of words acting as a noun, or another pronoun. The word or group of words that a pronoun refers to is called its **antecedent**.

A **personal pronoun** refers to a specific person or thing.

Pronoun case. *See* Case.

Proofreading. The final part of the editing process that involves checking work to discover typographical and other errors.

Propaganda. Information aimed at influencing thoughts and actions; it is usually of a political nature and may contain distortions of truth.

Proper adjective. *See* Adjective.

Prose. Writing that is similar to everyday speech and written language, as opposed to poetry and drama.

Publishing. The preparation of a finished piece of writing often involving available technology, so that it can be presented to a larger audience.

Purpose. The aim of writing, which may be to express, discover, record, develop, reflect on ideas, problem solve, entertain, influence, inform, or describe.

R

Regular verb. *See* Verb tense.

Representation. A way in which information or ideas are presented to an audience.

Research. The search for information on a topic.

Review. The analysis and interpretation of a subject, often presented through the mass media.

Revising. The stage of the writing process in which a writer goes over a draft, making changes in its content, organization, and style in order to improve it. Revision techniques include adding, elaborating, deleting, combining, and rearranging text.

Root. The part of a word that carries the main meaning.

Run-on sentence. Two or more sentences or clauses run together without appropriate punctuation.

S

Sensory details. Language that appeals to the senses; sensory details are important elements of descriptive writing, especially of poetry.

Sentence. A group of words expressing a complete thought. Every sentence has a **subject** and a **predicate.** *See also* Subject; Predicate; Clause.

A **simple sentence** has only one main clause and no subordinate clauses.

A **compound sentence** has two or more main clauses. Each main clause of a compound sentence has its own subject and predicate, and these main clauses are usually joined by a comma and a coordinating conjunction. A semicolon can also be used to join the main clauses in a compound sentence.

A **complex sentence** has one main clause and one or more subordinate clauses.

Sentence fluency. The smooth rhythm and flow of sentences that vary in length and style.

Sentence variety. The use of different types of sentences to add interest to writing.

Setting. The time and place in which the events of a story, novel, or play takes place.

Simile. A figure of speech that compares two basically unlike things, using words such as *like* or *as.*

Simple sentence. *See* Sentence.

Spatial order. A way of presenting the details of a setting according to their location—for example, from left to right or from top to bottom.

Standard English. The most widely used and accepted form of the English language

Style. The writer's choice and arrangement of words and sentences.

Subject. The noun or pronoun that tells who or what the sentence is about.

Subordinate clause. *See* Clause.

Summary. A brief statement of the main idea of a composition.

Supporting evidence. *See* Evidence.

Suspense. A literary device that creates growing interest and excitement leading up to the climax and resolution of a story. A writer creates suspense by providing clues to the resolution without revealing too much information.

Symbol. An object, a person, a place, or an experience that represents something else, usually something abstract.

T

Tense. *See* Verb tense.

Theme. The main idea or message of a piece of writing.

Thesis statement. A one- or two-sentence statement of the main idea or purpose of a piece of writing.

Time order. The arrangement of details in a piece of writing based on when they occurred.

Tone. A reflection of a writer's or speaker's attitude toward a subject.

Topic sentence. A sentence that expresses the main idea of a paragraph.

Transition. A connecting word or phrase that clarifies relationships between details, sentences, or paragraphs.

U–V

Unity. A quality of oneness in a paragraph or composition that exists when all the sentences or paragraphs work together to express or support one main idea.

URL. The standard form of an Internet address; stands for Uniform Resource Locator.

Venn diagram. A graphic organizer consisting of two overlapping circles; used to compare two items that have both similar and different traits.

Verb. A word that expresses an action or a state of being and is necessary to make a statement.

Verbal. A verb form that functions in a sentence as a noun, an adjective, or an adverb. The three kinds of verbals are participles, gerunds, and infinitives. *See also* Gerund; Infinitive; Participle.

Verb phrase. *See* Phrase.

Verb tense. The form a verb takes to show when an action takes place. The **present tense** names an action that happens regularly. The **past tense** names an action that has happened, and the **future tense** names an action that will take place in the future. All the verb tenses are formed from the four principal parts of a verb: a **base form** (*freeze*), a **present participle** (*freezing*), a **simple past** form (*froze*) and a **past participle** (*frozen*). A **regular verb** forms its simple past and past participle by adding -*ed* to the base form. Verbs that form their past and past participle in some other way are called **irregular verbs**.

In addition to present, past, and future tense, there are three perfect tenses—present perfect, past perfect, and future perfect. Each of the six tenses has a **progressive** form that expresses a continuing action.

Voice. A writer's unique way of using tone and style to communicate with the audience.

W

Web site. A location on the World Wide Web that can be reached through links or by accessing a Web address, or URL. *See* URL.

Word choice. The vocabulary a writer chooses to convey meaning.

Word Processing. The use of a computer for the writing and editing of written text.

World Wide Web. A global system that uses the Internet and allows users to create, link, and access fields of information. *See* Internet.

Writing process. The series of stages or steps that a writer goes through to develop ideas and to communicate them.

GLOSARIO
DE ESCRITURA Y LENGUAJE

Este glosario permite encontrar fácilmente definiciones de gramática inglesa y términos que usan los escritores.

Adjective/Adjetivo. Palabra que modifica, o describe, un nombre (*noun*) o pronombre (*pronoun*). Un adjetivo *indica qué tipo, cuál, cuántos o cuánto.*

   Comparative degree/Grado comparativo. Adjetivo que compara a dos personas, lugares, cosas o ideas (*worse, sadder;* en español: *peor, más triste*).

   Superlative degree/Grado superlativo. Adjetivo que compara más de dos personas, lugares, cosas o ideas (*worst, saddest;* en español: *el peor, la más triste*).

   Possessive adjective/Adjetivo posesivo. Pronombre posesivo que va antes del nombre.

   Predicative adjective/Adjetivo predicativo. Siempre va después de un verbo copulativo y modifica al sujeto de la oración.

   Proper adjective/Adjetivo propio*. Adjetivo que se deriva de un nombre propio; en inglés siempre se escribe con mayúscula.

   Demonstrative adjective/Adjetivo demostrativo. Se usa antes del nombre: *this, that, these, those (este, ese, aquel, estos, esos, aquellos).*

Adjective clause/Proposición adjetiva. Proposición dependiente que modifica un nombre o un pronombre.

Adverb/Adverbio. Palabra que modifica a un verbo, adjetivo u otro adverbio. Los adverbios indican *cómo, cuándo, dónde, de qué manera* y *qué tan seguido* sucede algo. Algunos adverbios tienen diferentes formas para indicar los grados **comparativo** (*comparative*) y **superlativo** (*superlative*) (*loud, louder, loudest; sweetly, more sweetly, most sweetly;* en español: *fuerte, más fuerte, lo más fuerte; dulcemente, más dulcemente, lo más dulcemente*).

Adverb clause/Proposición adverbial. Proposición dependiente que modifica un verbo, un adjetivo o un adverbio.

Allusion/Alusión. Referencia en un texto escrito a un personaje, lugar o situación muy conocidos de una obra literaria, musical, artística o histórica.

Analysis/Análisis. Acción de descomponer un tema o escrito en distintas partes para encontrar su significado.

Anecdote/Anécdota. Narración breve o incidente que se presenta como parte de una narrativa más larga.

Antecedent/Antecedente. *Ver Pronoun.*

Appositive/Apositivo. Nombre colocado junto a otro para identificarlo o agregar información sobre él. (Mi entrenadora de baloncesto, *Ms. Lopes*, pidió tiempo fuera.)

Argument/Argumento. Afirmación, razón o hecho en favor o en contra de algún comentario; texto escrito que trata de persuadir.

Article/Artículo. Nombre dado a las palabras *a, an* y *the* (en español: *un, uno/a, el, la*). *A* y *an* son artículos **indefinidos** (*indefinite articles*), que se refieren a cualquier cosa de un grupo. *The* es un artículo **definido** (*definite article*); indica que el nombre al que precede es una persona, lugar o cosa específicos.

Audience/Público. Persona (o personas) que lee o escucha lo que dicen un escritor o un hablante.

B

Base form/Base derivativa. *Ver Verb tense.*

Bias/Tendencia. Inclinación a pensar de cierta manera. La tendencia influye en la manera en que un escritor o hablante presenta sus ideas.

Bibliography/Bibliografía. Lista de los libros, artículos y otras fuentes que se utilizan como referencia en una investigación.

Body/Cuerpo. Parte central de una composición que comunica la idea principal identificada en la introducción.

Bookmarks/favorites/Marcadores/favoritos. Característica de muchos buscadores de red que permiten guardar direcciones de Internet para entrar a ellas rápidamente.

Brainstorming/Lluvia de ideas. Actividad de grupo en que se generan tantas ideas como sea posible sin detenerse a analizarlas.

C

Case/Caso. Forma de un nombre o pronombre que está determinado por su uso en la oración. El nombre o pronombre está en caso **nominativo** (*nominative case*) cuando se utiliza como sujeto; en caso **acusativo** y **dativo** (*objective case*) cuando recibe la acción del verbo, y en caso **posesivo*** (*possessive case*)

cuando se utiliza para indicar posesión o propiedad.

Cause-and-effect chain/Cadena de causa y efecto. Serie de acontecimientos en que una causa lleva a un efecto que, a su vez, lleva a otro efecto, y así sucesivamente.

Characterization/Caracterización. Métodos que utiliza un escritor para crear sus personajes. Puede ser describiendo directamente su personalidad, o revelándola con sus palabras y acciones, o bien a partir de lo que otros personajes piensan y dicen de él.

Chronological order/Orden cronológico. Organización de detalles de acuerdo con el tiempo en que sucedieron los acontecimientos o acciones.

Clarity/Claridad. Cualidad de un escrito que lo hace fácil de entender.

Clause/Proposición. Grupo de palabras que consta de sujeto y predicado, y que se usa como parte de una oración compuesta.

> **Independent clause/Proposición independiente.** También llamada proposición principal (*main clause*); tiene sujeto y predicado y hace sentido por sí misma.
> **Dependent clause/Proposición dependiente.** También llamada proposición subordinada (*subordinate clause*); tiene sujeto y predicado pero depende de la proposición principal.

Cliché/Cliché. Expresión usada con demasiada frecuencia (*blanco como la nieve*).

Clustering/Agrupamiento. Reunión de temas relacionados para organizar la información.

Coherence/Coherencia. Relación lógica entre las partes de un párrafo o composición.

Cohesive writing/Escritura coherente. Tipo de escritura en que las oraciones y párrafos están lógicamente relacionados entre sí.

Collaboration/Colaboración. Proceso de trabajar en equipo para escribir un texto o realizar un proyecto.

Colloquialism/Expresión coloquial. Expresión informal y pintoresca que se utiliza en la conversación diaria.

Comparative degree/Grado comparativo. *Ver Adjective; Adverb.*

Comparison-and-contrast/Comparación y contraste. Manera de organizar ideas, señalando sus similitudes y diferencias.

Complement/Complemento (u objeto). Palabra o frase que complementa el significado de un verbo. Tres complementos son: **directo** (*direct object*), **indirecto** (*indirect object*) y **predicativo (atributo)** (*subject complement*).

Conceptual map/Mapa conceptual. Recurso gráfico que desarrolla un concepto central rodeándolo con ejemplos o ideas relacionadas a manera de red.

Conclusion/Conclusión. Afirmación que resume las ideas de una composición, antes de ponerle punto final.

Conflict/Conflicto. Lucha entre dos fuerzas opuestas que constituye el elemento central de la trama en un cuento u obra de teatro.

Conjunction/Conjunción. Palabra que une palabras o grupos de palabras.

> **Coordinating conjunction/Conjunción coordinante.** Las palabras *and, but, or, nor, for, yet* (*y, pero, o, no, para, aun*) unen palabras o grupos de palabras que tienen igual importancia gramatical.
>
> **Correlative conjunction/Conjunción correlativa*.** Las palabras *both . . . and, just as . . . so, not only . . . but also, either . . . or, neither . . . nor* (*tanto . . . como, así como, no sólo . . . sino, o . . . o*) son palabras en pares que vinculan palabras o frases en una oración.

Connotation/Connotación. Pensamientos y sentimientos relacionados con una palabra, más que con su definición de diccionario.

Constructive criticism/Crítica constructiva. Comentario sobre lo que escribe otra persona, con la intención de ayudar a que mejore el borrador.

Context/Contexto. Palabras y oraciones que vienen antes y después de una palabra y ayudan a explicar su significado.

Conventions/Reglas de escritura. Normas que regulan la ortografía, la gramática, el uso y la puntuación de un escrito.

Coordinating conjunction/Conjunción coordinante. *Ver Conjunction.*

Correlative conjunction/Conjunción correlativa*. *Ver Conjunction.*

Credibility/Credibilidad. Cualidad de un hablante o escritor que hace creer sus palabras.

Declarative sentence/Oración afirmativa. Oración que declara algo.

Deductive reasoning/Razonamiento deductivo. Pensamiento o explicación que parte de una afirmación o principio generales y los aplica a casos específicos.

Definite article/Artículo definido. *Ver Article.*

Demonstrative adjective/Adjetivo demostrativo. *Ver Adjective.*

Denotation/Denotación. Definición de una palabra que da el diccionario.

Dependent clause/Proposición dependiente. *Ver Clause.*

Descriptive writing/Escritura descriptiva. Tipo de escritura que ofrece detalles sensoriales para comunicar la impresión de un escenario, persona, animal, etcétera.

Desktop publishing/Edición por computadora. Uso de programas de computadora para formar un documento con texto escrito, gráficas y/o imágenes.

Dialect/Dialecto. Variedad de lenguaje hablado que usa un grupo particular. Un dialecto puede ser regional (de un lugar) o étnico (de un grupo cultural).

Dialogue/Diálogo. Conversación entre personajes en un escrito.

Diction/Dicción. Palabras que escoge un escritor y cómo las utiliza en frases, oraciones o versos.

Direct object/Complemento directo. *Ver Complement.*

Documentation/Documentación. Identificación de las fuentes que se emplean para escribir un artículo u otros textos informativos; generalmente se ponen como notas al pie, al final del texto o entre paréntesis.

Drafting/Borrador. Paso del proceso de escritura; transformación de ideas, palabras y frases a oraciones y párrafos.

E

Editing/Edición. Paso del proceso de escritura en que se revisa que el borrador corregido tenga un lenguaje estándar, una estructura sintáctica variada y la elección adecuada de palabras.

Editorial/Editorial. Artículo en un periódico u otro medio que expresa una opinión sobre un tema de interés general.

Elaboration/Elaboración. Sustento o desarrollo de una idea principal con hechos, estadísticas, detalles sensoriales, incidentes, anécdotas, ejemplos o citas.

Ellipsis/Puntos suspensivos. Signo de puntuación que consiste en dejar tres puntos para indicar que se están suprimiendo una o varias palabras.

E-mail/Correo electrónico. Mensajes, generalmente textos, que se envían por computadora.

Evaluating/Evaluación. Juicio sobre las fallas y aciertos de un borrador en cuanto a contenido, organización y estilo.

Evidence/Evidencia. Datos o ejemplos de fuentes confiables que sirven para sustentar afirmaciones escritas o habladas.

Exclamatory sentence/Oración exclamativa. Oración que expresa una emoción fuerte o repentina.

Explanatory writing/Texto explicativo. *Ver Descriptive text.*

Expository writing/Texto descriptivo. Tipo de escritura que informa o explica, como artículos periodísticos, instrucciones y artículos de investigación.

Expressive writing/Texto expresivo. Texto que realza y transmite los sentimientos del escritor.

F

Fact/Hecho. Información que puede comprobarse.

Feedback/Retroalimentación. Respuesta del escucha o lector al mensaje de un hablante o escritor.

Figurative language/Lenguaje figurado. Palabras usadas con un efecto descriptivo que expresa una verdad más allá del nivel literal. Los tropos, como el símil, la metáfora y la personificación, son ejemplos de lenguaje figurado.

Formal language/Lenguaje formal. Lenguaje que utiliza una gramática correcta y omite contracciones y expresiones coloquiales. Es común en textos de no ficción, que no son de carácter personal.

Fragment/Fragmento. Oración incompleta con puntuación de oración completa.

Freewriting/Escritura libre. Búsqueda de ideas escribiendo durante un tiempo determinado, sin detenerse ni limitar el flujo de ideas.

Future tense/Tiempo futuro. *Ver Verb tense.*

G-H

Generalization/Generalización. Afirmación que presenta una conclusión sobre un tema sin dar detalles específicos.

Genre/Género. Clasificación literaria o de otro medio. Los principales géneros literarios son la prosa, la poesía y el drama. Cada uno se divide en subgéneros.

Gerund/Gerundio. Verboide que termina en –*ing* y se usa como nombre (en inglés).

Graphic organizer/Organizador gráfico. Manera visual de organizar la información, como las tablas, las gráficas, las redes y los árboles de ideas.

Home page/Página principal. Página por medio de la cual un usuario entra normalmente a un sitio de Web. Por lo general, explica el sitio, resume el contenido y proporciona vínculos con otros sitios.

Hyperlink/Hipervínculo. Oraciones o palabras sombreadas o subrayadas en una página en red que al activarse con un clic conectan con otra parte de la página o con otra página de la red.

Hypertext/Hipertexto. Vínculos en textos electrónicos que llevan a otro documento o a una sección distinta del mismo documento.

I-J

Ideas/Ideas. En composición, el mensaje o tema y los detalles que lo elaboran.

Idiom/Modismo. Palabra o frase cuyo significado es diferente del significado estándar o de diccionario. (*Se le pegaron las sábanas* es un modismo que significa "se levantó muy tarde").

Imagery/Imaginería. Lenguaje que describe impresiones sensoriales para que el lector de un texto literario pueda ver, oír, sentir, oler y gustar las escenas descritas.

Imperative sentence/Oración imperativa. Oración que exige u ordena algo.

Indefinite article/Artículo indefinido. *Ver Article.*

Indefinite pronoun/Pronombre indefinido. *Ver Pronoun.*

Independent clause/Proposición independiente. *Ver Clause.*

Inductive reasoning/Razonamiento inductivo. Pensamiento o explicación que parte de varios ejemplos para llegar a una afirmación general.

Infinitive/Infinitivo. Verboide que consta de la palabra *to* y la base del verbo (en español terminan en -*ar, -er* o -*ir*). Se usa como sustantivo en la oración.

Informative writing/Texto informativo. Texto que explica un proceso o una idea. *Ver también Descriptive text.*

Intensifier/Intensificador. Adverbio que refuerza un adjetivo u otro adverbio (*very* important, *quite* easily; *muy* importante, *bastante* fácil).

Interjection/Interjección. Palabra o frase que expresa un sentimiento muy fuerte. La interjección no tiene relación gramatical con las demás palabras de la oración.

Internet/Internet. Red mundial computarizada que permite comunicarse electrónicamente con cualquier computadora de la red para buscar información social, comercial, de investigación y de otro tipo.

Interpretation/Interpretación. Explicación del significado de un texto, de una representación visual o de cualquier otro tipo de comunicación.

Interview/Entrevista. Diálogo a base de preguntas y respuestas cuyo propósito es obtener información actualizada o de expertos.

Intransitive Verb/Verbo intransitivo. *Ver Verb.*

Introduction/Introducción. Sección inicial de un texto en la que el escritor identifica el tema y da la idea general de lo que contendrá el cuerpo del mismo.

Inverted order/Orden invertido. Colocación del predicado antes del sujeto. En la mayoría de las oraciones en inglés, el sujeto va antes del predicado.

Irregular verb/Verbo irregular. *Ver Verb tense.*

Jargon/Jerga. Palabras y frases que usa un determinado grupo.

Journal/Diario. Libreta personal en la que con toda libertad se anotan ideas, pensamientos y experiencias.

L

Learning log/Registro de aprendizaje. Diario para aclarar ideas sobre conceptos tratados en varias clases.

Lexicon/Léxico. Diccionario.

Listing/Lista. Técnica para generar ideas a partir de las cuales se escribe un texto.

Literary analysis/Análisis literario. Examen de las diferentes partes de una obra literaria a fin de evaluarla.

Logical fallacy/Falacia lógica. Error de razonamiento que se encuentra con frecuencia en publicidad o en escritos persuasivos, como razonamientos con dos alternativas opuestas o generalidades muy llamativas.

M

Main clause/Proposición principal. *Ver Clause.*

Main idea/Idea principal. *Ver Thesis statement.*

Main verb/Verbo principal. La palabra más importante de una frase verbal.

Media/Medios. Formas de comunicación usadas para llegar a un público. Los periódicos, la radio, la televisión y la Internet llegan a públicos muy grandes, por lo que se conocen como medios de comunicación masiva.

Memoir/Memoria. Tipo de narrativa de no ficción que presenta el relato de un hecho o período de la historia, resaltando la experiencia personal del narrador.

Metaphor/Metáfora. Tropo que compara dos cosas aparentemente distintas sin usar las palabra *like* o *as (como)*. (*Él es una roca.*)

Mood/Atmósfera. Sentimiento o ambiente de un texto escrito.

Multimedia presentation/Presentación multimedia. Uso de una variedad de medios como video, sonido, texto escrito y artes visuales para presentar ideas e información.

N

Narrative writing/Narrativa. Tipo de escritura que narra sucesos o acciones que cambian con el paso del tiempo; por lo general tiene personajes, escenario y trama.

Nonfiction/No ficción. Texto en prosa acerca de personas, lugares y sucesos reales.

Noun/Nombre (o sustantivo). Palabra que nombra a una persona, lugar, cosa, o a una idea, cualidad o característica.

Noun clause/Proposición nominal. Proposición dependiente que se usa como nombre.

Number/Número. Forma del nombre, pronombre o verbo que indica si se refiere a uno (**singular**) o a más de uno (**plural**).

Object/Objeto. *Ver Complement.*

Onomatopoeia/Onomatopeya. Palabra o frase que imita o sugiere el sonido que describe (*rattle, boom;* en español: *pum, zas*).

Opinion/Opinión. Creencia o actitud; no puede comprobarse si es falsa o verdadera.

Oral tradition/Tradición oral. Literatura que se transmite de boca en boca de una generación a otra. Puede representar los valores culturales de un pueblo.

Order of importance/Orden de importancia. Forma de acomodar los detalles en un párrafo o en otro texto escrito según su importancia.

Organization/Organización. La disposición y el orden de los puntos principales y los detalles de apoyo en un escrito.

Outline/Esquema. Organización sistemática de ideas principales y secundarias con números romanos, letras y números arábigos para una presentación oral o escrita.

Paragraph/Párrafo. Una unidad de un texto que consta de oraciones relacionadas.

Parallel construction/Construcción paralela. Serie de palabras, frases y oraciones que tienen una forma gramatical similar.

Paraphrase/Parafrasear. Repetir las ideas de otro con palabras diferentes del original pero conservando las ideas, el tono y la longitud general.

Parenthetical documentation/Documentación parentética. Referencia específica a la fuente de la información que se pone entre paréntesis directamente después de ésta.

Participle/Participio. Verboide que se usa como adjetivo. El participio presente siempre termina en *–ing* y el participio pasado por lo general termina en *–ed*.

Peer response/Respuesta de compañeros. Sugerencias y comentarios que dan los compañeros de clase sobre un texto escrito u otro tipo de presentación.

Personal pronoun/Pronombre personal. *Ver Pronoun.*

Personal writing/Escritura personal. Texto que expresa los pensamientos y sentimientos del autor.

Personification/Personificación. Tropo que da cualidades humanas a un animal, objeto o idea.

Perspective/Perspectiva. *Ver Point of view.*

Persuasion/Persuasión. Tipo de escritura encaminado a convencer a pensar o actuar de cierta manera.

Phrase/Frase. Grupo de palabras que forma una unidad en una oración.

    Prepositional phrase/Frase preposicional. Comienza con una preposición y termina con un nombre o un pronombre.

    Verb phrase/Frase verbal. Consta de uno o más **verbos auxiliares** (*auxiliary verbs*) seguidos del verbo principal.

Plagiarism/Plagio. Presentación deshonesta de palabras o ideas ajenas como si fueran propias.

Plot/Trama. Serie de sucesos en secuencia en un cuento, novela u obra de teatro.

Plural/Plural. *Ver Number.*

Poetry/Poesía. Forma de expresión literaria compuesta por versos. La poesía tradicional contiene un lenguaje emotivo e imaginativo y un ritmo regular.

Point of view/Punto de vista. Ángulo o perspectiva desde el cual se cuenta una historia; por ejemplo, primera o tercera persona.

Portfolio/Portafolio. Colección de varias obras escritas de un estudiante, que puede tener obras terminadas y otras en proceso.

Predicate/Predicado. Verbo o frase verbal y sus modificadores que hacen una afirmación esencial sobre el sujeto de la oración.

Predicate adjective/Adjetivo predicativo. *Ver Adjective.*

Preposition/Preposición. Palabra que muestra la relación de un nombre o pronombre con otra palabra en la oración.

Prepositional phrase/Frase preposicional. *Ver Phrase.*

Presentación. La forma en que se ven en una página las palabras y los elementos de diseño.

Presenting/Publishing/Presentación/ Publicacíon. Último paso del proceso de escritura que implica compartir con otros lo que se ha escrito.

Present tense/Tiempo presente. *Ver Verb tense.*

Prewriting/Preescritura. Primer paso del proceso de escritura: decidir sobre qué se va a escribir, reunir ideas y detalles, y elaborar un plan para presentar las ideas; usa estrategias como lluvia de ideas, organizadores gráficos, notas y registros.

Prior knowledge/Conocimiento previo. Hechos, ideas y experiencias que un escritor, lector u observador lleva a una nueva actividad.

Progressive form/Durativo. *Ver Verb tense.*

Pronoun/Pronombre. Palabra que va en lugar del nombre; grupo de palabras que funcionan como un nombre u otro pronombre. La palabra o grupo de palabras a que se refiere un pronombre se llama **antecedente** (*antecedent*).

   Personal pronoun/Pronombre personal. Se refiere a una persona o cosa específica.

Pronoun case/Caso del pronombre. *Ver Case.*

Proofreading/Corrección de pruebas. Último paso del proceso editorial en que se revisa el texto en busca de errores tipográficos y de otra naturaleza.

Propaganda/Propaganda. Información encaminada a influir en los pensamientos o acciones; en general es de naturaleza política y puede distorsionar la verdad.

Proper adjective/Adjetivo propio*. *Ver Adjective.*

Prose/Prosa. Escritura similar al lenguaje cotidiano tanto oral como escrito, a diferencia de la poesía y el teatro.

Publishing/Publicación. Presentación de una obra escrita terminada mediante el uso de la tecnología, para darla a conocer a un público amplio.

Purpose/Finalidad. Objetivo de la escritura: expresar, descubrir, registrar, desarrollar o reflexionar sobre ideas, resolver problemas, entretener, influir, informar o describir.

Regular verb/Verbo regular. *Ver Verb tense.*

Representation/Representación. Forma en que se presenta información o ideas al público.

Research/Investigación. Proceso de localizar información sobre un tema.

Review/Reseña. Análisis e interpretación de un tema presentado por lo general a través de los medios de comunicación masiva.

Revising/Revisión. Paso del proceso de escritura en que el autor repasa el borrador, cambia el contenido, la organización y el estilo para mejorar el texto. Las técnicas de revisión son agregar, elaborar, eliminar, combinar y reacomodar el texto.

Root/Raíz. Parte de una palabra que contiene el significado principal.

Run-on sentence/Oración mal puntuada. Dos o más oraciones o proposiciones seguidas, cuyo significado es confuso debido a su inadecuada puntuación.

S

Sensory details/Detalles sensoriales. Lenguaje que apela a los sentidos; los detalles sensoriales son elementos importantes de la escritura descriptiva, sobre todo en la poesía.

Sentence/Oración. Grupo de palabras que expresa un pensamiento completo. Cada oración tiene **sujeto** (*subject*) y **predicado** (*predicate*). *Ver también Subject; Predicate; Clause.*

> **Simple sentence/Oración simple.** Consta de una proposición principal y no tiene proposiciones subordinadas.
> **Compound sentence/Oración compuesta.** Tiene dos o más proposiciones principales, cada una con su propio sujeto y predicado; por lo general van unidas por una coma y una conjunción coordinante, o por un punto y coma.
> **Complex sentence/Oración compleja.** Tiene una proposición principal y una o más proposiciones subordinadas.

Sentence Fluency/Fluidez oracional. El vitmo suave y suelto de las oraciones que varían en longitud y estilo.

Sentence variety/Variedad de oraciones. Uso de diferentes tipos de oraciones para agregar interés al texto.

Setting/Escenario. Tiempo y lugar en que ocurren los sucesos de un cuento, novela u obra de teatro.

Simile/Símil. Tropo que compara dos cosas esencialmente distintas, usando las palabras *like* o *as* (*como*). (*Su pelo era como hilo de seda.*)

Simple predicate/Predicado simple. *Ver Predicate; Sentence; Subject.*

Simple sentence/Oración simple. *Ver Sentence.*

Spatial order/Orden espacial. Forma de presentar los detalles de un escenario según su ubicación: de izquierda a derecha o de arriba hacia abajo.

Standard English/Inglés estándar. La forma más ampliamente usada y aceptada del idioma inglés.

Style/Estilo. Forma en que un escritor elige y organiza las palabras y oraciones.

Subject/Sujeto. Nombre o pronombre principal que informa sobre quién o sobre qué trata la oración.

Subordinate clause/Proposición subordinada. *Ver Clause.*

Summary/Resumen. Breve explicación de la idea principal de una composición.

Supporting evidence/Sustento. *Ver Evidence.*

Suspense/Suspenso. Recurso literario que genera interés y emoción para llegar al clímax o desenlace de una historia. Un escritor crea suspenso al proporcionar pistas sobre el desenlace pero sin revelar demasiada información.

Symbol/Símbolo. Objeto, persona, lugar o experiencia que representa algo más, por lo general, abstracto.

Tense/Tiempo. *Ver Verb tense.*

Theme/Tema. Idea o mensaje principal de una obra escrita.

Thesis statement/Exposición de tesis. Exposición de la **idea principal** o finalidad de una obra en una o dos oraciones.

Time order/Orden temporal. Organización de detalles en un texto escrito según el momento en que ocurrieron.

Tone/Tono. Reflejo de la actitud del escritor o hablante hacia un sujeto.

Topic sentence/Oración temática. Oración que expresa la idea principal de un párrafo.

Transition/Transición. Palabra o frase de enlace que aclara las relaciones entre los detalles, oraciones o párrafos.

U-V

Unity/Unidad. Integridad de un párrafo o composición; coherencia entre todas las oraciones o párrafos para expresar o sustentar una idea principal.

URL/URL. Forma estándar de una dirección de Internet. (Son iniciales de *Uniform Resource Locator.*)

Venn diagram/Diagrama de Venn. Organizador gráfico que consta de dos círculos que se traslapan, usado para comparar dos cosas con características comunes y diferentes.

Verb/Verbo. Palabra que expresa acción o estado y que es necesaria para hacer una afirmación.

Verbal/Verboide. Forma del verbo que funciona como nombre, adjetivo o adverbio en la oración. Los verboides son: participio *(participles)*, gerundio *(gerunds)* e infinitivo *(infinitives)*.

Verb phrase/Frase verbal. *Ver Phrase.*

Verb tense/Tiempo verbal. El tiempo de un verbo indica cuándo ocurre la acción.

> **Present tense/Presente.** Indica una acción que sucede regularmente.
> **Past tense/Pasado.** Indica una acción que ya sucedió.
> **Future tense/Futuro.** Indica una acción que va a suceder.
> En inglés todos los tiempos verbales están formados por las cuatro partes principales del verbo: **base derivativa** *(base form)* *(freeze, congelar)*, **participio presente** *(present participle) (freezing, congelando)*, **pretérito simple** *(simple past form) (froze, congeló)* y **participio pasado** *(past participle) (frozen, congelado)*.
> Un **verbo regular** *(regular verb)* forma su pretérito simple y su participio pasado agregando la terminación *ed* al infinitivo. Los verbos que forman su pretérito y participio pasado de otra forma se llaman **verbos irregulares** *(irregular verbs)*.
> Además de los tiempos presente, pasado y futuro hay tres tiempos perfectos: **presente perfecto** *(present perfect)*, **pretérito perfecto** *(past perfect)* y **futuro perfecto** *(future perfect)*.
> Cada uno de los seis tiempos tiene una forma **durativa** *(progressive form)* que expresa acción continua.

Voice/Voz. La forma única que tiene un escritor o escritora de usar el tono y el estilo para comunicarse con los lectores.

Web site/Sitio Web. Sitio de World Wide Web que puede ser alcanzado mediante vínculos o una dirección Web o URL. *Ver también URL; World Wide Web.*

Word Choice/Léxico. El vocabulario que selecciona una escritora o escritor para presentar un significado.

Word processing/Procesador de palabras. Programa de computadora para escribir y editar un texto.

World Wide Web/World Wide Web. Sistema global que usa Internet y permite a los usuarios crear, vincularse y entrar a campos de información. *Ver también Internet.*

Writing process/Proceso de escritura. Serie de pasos o etapas por los que atraviesa un escritor para desarrollar sus ideas y comunicarlas.

*Este término o explicación solamente se aplica a la gramática inglesa.

*W*hat are the basic tools for building strong sentences, paragraphs, compositions, and research papers? You'll find them in this handbook—an easy-to-use "tool kit" for writers like you. Check out the helpful explanations, examples, and tips as you complete your writing assignments.

Writing Good Sentences

A sentence is a group of words that expresses a complete thought. Every sentence has a subject and a predicate.

Using Various Types of Sentences

How you craft a sentence—as a statement, question, command, or exclamation—depends on the job you want the sentence to do.

Type	Job It Does	Ways to Use It
Declarative	Makes a statement	Report information *October is National Pizza Month.*
Interrogative	Asks a question	Make your readers curious *Why is pizza so popular?*
Imperative	Gives a command or makes a request	Tell how to do something *Spread the toppings on the pizza dough.*
Exclamatory	Expresses strong feeling	Emphasize a startling fact *Every second, Americans eat about 350 slices of pizza!*

Varying Sentence Structure and Length

Many sentences in a row that look and sound alike can be boring. Vary your sentence openers to make your writing interesting.

- **Start a sentence with an adjective or an adverb.**
  Suddenly the sky turned dark.

- **Start a sentence with a phrase.**
  Like a fireworks show, lightning streaked across the sky.

- **Start a sentence with a clause.**
  As the thunderstorm began, people ran for cover.

Many short sentences in a row make writing sound choppy and dull. To make your writing sound pleasing, vary the sentence length.

Check It Out

For more about how to vary sentence length and structure, review Unit 21, Sentence Combining, pages 618–627.

- **Combine short sentences into longer ones.**

    Tornadoes are also called twisters. They are spinning clouds. The clouds are funnel shaped.

    Tornadoes, also called twisters, are spinning funnel-shaped clouds.

- **Alternate shorter sentences with longer sentences.**

    Tornado winds are powerful. They can hurl cows into the air, tear trees from their roots, and turn cars upside down.

Using Parallelism

Parallelism is the use of a pair or a series of words, phrases, or sentences that have the same grammatical structure. Use parallelism to call attention to the items in the series and to create unity in writing.

Not Parallel Gymnasts are strong, flexible, and move gracefully.
Parallel Gymnasts are strong, flexible, and graceful.

Not Parallel Do warm-up exercises to prevent sports injuries and for stretching your muscles.
Parallel Do warm-up exercises to prevent sports injuries and to stretch your muscles.

Not Parallel Stand on one leg, bend the other leg, and you should pull your heel.
Parallel Stand on one leg, bend the other leg, and pull your heel.

Revising Wordy Sentences

Revise wordy sentences to make every word count.

- **Cut needless words.**

    Wordy We need to have bike lanes in streets due to the fact that people like to ride their bikes to work and school, and it's not safe otherwise.
    Concise We need bike lanes in streets so that people can safely ride to work and school.

- **Rewrite sentences opening with the word *there*.**

    Wordy There are many kids riding their bikes in the street.
    Concise Many kids ride their bikes in the street.

- **Change verbs in passive voice to active voice.**

    Wordy Bikes are also ridden by grown-ups who want to keep fit.
    Concise Grown-ups who want to keep fit also ride bikes.

Writing Good Paragraphs

A paragraph is a group of sentences that relate to one main idea. A good paragraph develops a single idea and brings that idea into sharp focus. All the sentences flow smoothly from the beginning to the end of the paragraph.

Writing Unified Paragraphs

A paragraph has **unity** when the sentences belong together and center on a single main idea. One way to build a unified paragraph is to state the main idea in a topic sentence and then add related details.

Writing Topic Sentences A **topic sentence** gives your readers the "big picture"—a clear view of the most important idea you want them to know. Many effective expository paragraphs (paragraphs that convey information) start with a topic sentence that tells the key point right away.

Elaborating Topic Sentences Elaboration gives your readers a specific, more detailed picture of the main idea stated in your topic sentence. Elaboration is a technique you can use to include details that develop, support, or explain the main idea. The following chart shows various kinds of elaboration you might try.

> **Revising Tip**
>
> To make a paragraph unified, leave out details that do not relate to the topic sentence.

Topic Sentence: The state of Florida is known for its alligators.	
Descriptions	Alligators look like dinosaurs from millions of years ago.
Facts and statistics	Alligators can weigh as much as six hundred pounds.
Examples	Alligators eat a wide variety of foods, such as fish, insects, turtles, frogs, and small mammals.
Anecdotes (brief stories)	Silvia almost fainted when she came home to find an alligator paddling around in her swimming pool.
Reasons	Face-to-face encounters with alligators are now common because people have built golf courses over the animals' habitat.

Writing Coherent Paragraphs

A paragraph has **coherence** when all the sentences flow smoothly and logically from one to the next. All the sentences in a paragraph *cohere*, or "stick together," in a way that makes sense. To be sure your writing is coherent, choose a pattern of organization that fits your topic and use transition words and phrases to link ideas.

Organizing Paragraphs A few basic patterns of organization are listed below. Choose the pattern that helps you meet your specific writing goal.

- Use **chronological order,** or time order, to tell a story or to explain the steps in a process.
- Use **spatial order** to order your description of places, people, and things. You might describe the details in the order you see them—for example, from top to bottom or from near to far.
- Use **order of importance** to show how you rank opinions, facts, or details from the most to least important or the reverse.

Using Transitions Linking words and phrases, called **transitions,** act like bridges between sentences or between paragraphs. Transitions, such as the ones shown below, can make the organization of your paragraphs stronger by showing how ideas are logically related.

To show time order or sequence
after, at the beginning, finally, first, last year, later, meanwhile, next, now, second, sometimes, soon, yesterday

To show spatial relationships
above, ahead, around, at the top, below, beyond, down, here, inside, near, on top of, opposite, outside, over, there, under, within

To show importance or degree
above all, first, furthermore, in addition, mainly, most important, second

Check It Out

For more about transitions, see page 72.

TRY IT OUT

Copy the following paragraph on your paper. Underline the topic sentence. Cross out the sentence that is unrelated to the topic sentence. Add a transition to make a clear connection between two of the sentences.

A local artist creates weird and funny sculptures from fruits and vegetables. First he uses a sharp knife to carve faces that look like animals, such as bears and pigs. He glues on tiny beans to make eyes. Finally he uses beet juice to paint the mouth. Although the process sounds easy, it requires great imagination. The octopus sculpted from a banana is the silliest work of art I've ever seen.

Writing Good Compositions

A composition is a short paper made up of several paragraphs, with a clear introduction, body, and conclusion. A good composition presents a clear, complete message about a specific topic. Ideas flow logically from one sentence to the next and from one paragraph to the next.

Making a Plan

The suggestions in the chart below can help you shape the information in each part of your composition to suit your writing purpose.

Introductory Paragraph

Your introduction should interest readers in your topic and capture their attention. You may

- give background
- use a quotation
- ask a question
- tell an anecdote, or brief story

Include a **thesis statement,** a sentence or two stating the main idea you will develop in the composition.

Body Paragraphs

Elaborate on your thesis statement in the body paragraphs. You may

- offer proof
- give examples
- explain ideas

Stay focused and keep your body paragraphs on track. Remember to

- develop a single idea in each body paragraph
- arrange the paragraphs in a logical order
- use transitions to link one paragraph to the next

Concluding Paragraph

Your conclusion should bring your composition to a satisfying close. You may

- sum up main points
- tie the ending to the beginning by restating the main idea or thesis in different words
- make a call to action if your goal is to persuade readers

Drafting Tip

You may need two paragraphs to introduce your topic. The first can tell an anecdote; the second can include your thesis statement. See page 831 for an example.

Drafting Tip

A good conclusion follows logically from the rest of the piece of writing and leaves the reader with something to think about. Make sure that you do not introduce new or unrelated material in a conclusion.

Using the 6+1 Trait® Model

What are some basic terms you can use to discuss your writing with your teacher or classmates? What should you focus on as you revise and edit your compositions? Check out the following seven terms, or traits, that describe the qualities of strong writing. Learn the meaning of each trait and find out how using the traits can improve your writing.

Ideas The message or the theme and the details that develop it

Writing is clear when readers can grasp the meaning of your ideas right away. Check to see whether you're getting your message across.

- ✔ Does the title suggest the theme of the composition?
- ✔ Does the composition focus on a single narrow topic?
- ✔ Is the thesis, or main idea, clearly stated?
- ✔ Do well-chosen details elaborate the main idea?

Organization The arrangement of main points and supporting details

A good plan of organization steers your readers in the right direction and guides them easily through your composition—from start to finish. Find a structure, or order, that best suits your topic and writing purpose. Check to see whether you've ordered your key ideas and details in a way that keeps your readers on track.

- ✔ Are the beginning, middle, and end clearly linked?
- ✔ Is the order of ideas easy to follow?
- ✔ Does the introduction capture your readers' attention?
- ✔ Do sentences and paragraphs flow from one to the next in a way that makes sense?
- ✔ Does the conclusion wrap up the composition?

Voice A writer's unique way of using tone and style

Your writing voice comes through when your readers sense that a real person is communicating with them. Readers will respond to the **tone,** or the attitude, that you express toward a topic and to the **style,** the way that you use language and write sentences. Read your work aloud to see whether your writing voice comes through.

- ✔ Does your writing sound interesting when you read it aloud?
- ✔ Does your writing show what you think about your topic?
- ✔ Does your writing sound like you—or does it sound like you're imitating someone else?

Revising Tip

Use the cut-and-paste features of your word processing program to experiment with the structure—the arrangement of sentences or paragraphs. Choose the clearest, most logical order for your final draft.

6+1 Trait® is a registered trademark of Northwest Regional Educational Laboratory, which does not endorse this product.

Word Choice The vocabulary a writer uses to convey meaning

Words work hard. They carry the weight of your meaning, so make sure you choose them carefully. Check to see whether the words you choose are doing their jobs well.

- ✔ Do you use lively verbs to show action?
- ✔ Do you use vivid words to create word pictures in your readers' minds?
- ✔ Do you use precise words to explain your ideas simply and clearly?

Sentence Fluency The smooth rhythm and flow of sentences that vary in length and style

The best writing is made up of sentences that flow smoothly from one sentence to the next. Writing that is graceful also sounds musical—rhythmical rather than choppy. Check for sentence fluency by reading your writing aloud.

- ✔ Do your sentences vary in length and structure?
- ✔ Do transition words and phrases show connections between ideas and sentences?
- ✔ Does parallelism help balance and unify related ideas?

Conventions Correct spelling, grammar, usage, and mechanics

A composition free of errors makes a good impression on your readers. Mistakes can be distracting, and they can blur your message. Try working with a partner to spot errors and correct them. Use this checklist to help you.

- ✔ Are all words spelled correctly?
- ✔ Are all proper nouns—as well as the first word of every sentence—capitalized?
- ✔ Is your composition free of sentence fragments?
- ✔ Is your composition free of run-on sentences?
- ✔ Are punctuation marks—such as apostrophes, commas, and end marks—inserted in the right places?

Presentation The way words and design elements look on a page

Appearance matters, so make your compositions inviting to read. Handwritten papers should be neat and legible. If you're using a word processor, double-space the lines of text and choose a readable font. Other design elements—such as boldfaced headings, bulleted lists, pictures, and charts—can help you present information effectively as well as make your papers look good.

Revising Tip

Listen carefully to the way your sentences sound when someone else reads them aloud. If you don't like what you hear, revise for sentence fluency. You might try adding variety to your sentence openers or combining sentences to make them sound less choppy.

Check It Out

See the Troubleshooter, pages 304–327, for help in correcting common errors in your writing.

Evaluating a Composition Read this sample composition, which has been evaluated using the 6+1 Trait® model.

Ideas The focus is clear from the start. The thesis statement suggests the organizational structure of the composition.

Sentence Fluency A variety of sentence types helps the writing flow smoothly.

Conventions The composition is free of errors in spelling, grammar, usage, and mechanics.

Word Choice Notice the use of strong, vivid verbs, such as *persevered, diagnosed,* and *defied.*

Organization Paragraphs follow the order suggested in the introduction. The repetition of key words links ideas from one paragraph to the next.

Voice The writer's values and attitude toward the topic are clearly expressed.

True Courage

Are you courageous? According to *Webster's Dictionary,* if you have the "mental or moral strength to venture, persevere, and withstand danger, fear, or difficulty," you are. Three people who have shown mental or moral strength are Stacy Allison, Lou Gehrig, and Rosa Parks. Although the challenges they faced were different, their responses were similar. Their actions define what courage truly is.

For Stacy Allison, courage came one step at a time. In 1987 she tried to climb Mount Everest, the tallest mountain in the world. She and three other experienced climbers had spent two years carefully planning the climb. However, they couldn't have planned on a heavy snowstorm, which forced them down the mountain. After such a disappointing defeat, most people would have given up their dream, but Allison was not like most people. The following year, she returned to Everest, and despite the dangers and difficulties, she persevered. Her courage paid off, and she became the first woman from the United States to reach the summit of Mount Everest.

Baseball great Lou Gehrig had another kind of mountain to climb. Gehrig began playing first base for the New York Yankees in 1925. In the years that followed, he set many records, some of which stood until the 1990s. He left baseball in 1939 when he was diagnosed with a deadly disease called ALS. But he didn't leave life then. He bravely battled his disease and even gave a speech at Yankee Stadium, though he was too weak to stand without support. Less than two years later he was gone, but his courage is still remembered.

Rosa Parks's courage is also unforgettable. To me, she is the most courageous person of all. On December 1, 1955, Parks defied Alabama law and refused to give up her seat on a bus to a white person. She was arrested, but she took her case all the way to the Supreme Court. The Court later ruled that segregated buses were unconstitutional. Unlike Allison, Parks did not plan to make history. Unlike Gehrig, she was not already famous and admired. She was just an ordinary working woman who found the moral strength to challenge an unfair law. She stands as an everlasting example of what courage can do.

Stacy Allison, Lou Gehrig, and Rosa Parks had the mental and moral strength to persevere. Instead of giving in to difficulty or fear, they managed to overcome their challenges with dignity. Do you have what it takes to be courageous? If you follow their examples, you might find that you do.

Writing Good Research Papers

A research paper reports facts and ideas gathered from various sources about a specific topic. A good research paper blends information from reliable sources with the writer's original thoughts and ideas. The final draft follows a standard format for presenting information and citing sources.

Exploring a Variety of Sources

Once you've narrowed the topic of your research paper, you'll need to hunt for the best information. You might start by reading an encyclopedia article on your topic to learn some basic information. Then widen your search to include both primary and secondary sources.

- **Primary sources** are records of events by the people who witnessed them. Examples include diaries, letters, speeches, photos, posters, interviews, and radio and TV news broadcasts that include eyewitness interviews.
- **Secondary sources** contain information that is often based on primary sources. The creators of secondary sources conduct original research and then report their findings. Examples include encyclopedias, textbooks, biographies, magazine articles, Web site articles, and educational films.

When you find a secondary source that you can use for your report, check to see whether the author has given credit to his or her sources of information in **footnotes, endnotes,** or a **bibliography.** Tracking down such sources can lead you to more information you can use.

If you're exploring your topic on the Internet, look for Web sites that are sponsored by government institutions, famous museums, and reliable organizations. If you find a helpful site, check to see whether it contains links to other Web sites you can use.

> **Research Tip**
>
> Look for footnotes at the bottom of a page. Look for endnotes at the end of a chapter or a book. Look for a bibliography at the end of a book.

Evaluating Sources

As you conduct your research, do a little detective work and investigate the sources you find. Begin by asking some key questions so you can decide whether you've tracked down reliable resources that are suitable for your purpose. Some important questions to ask about your sources are listed in the box on the next page.

Ask Questions About Your Sources

✔ **Is the information useful?**
Find sources that are closely related to your research topic.

✔ **Is the information easy to understand?**
Look for sources that are geared toward readers your age.

✔ **Is the information new enough?**
Look for sources that were recently published if you need the most current facts and figures.

✔ **Is the information trustworthy and true?**
Check to see whether the author documents the source of facts and supports opinions with reasons and evidence. Also check out the background of the authors. They should be well-known experts on the topic that you're researching.

✔ **Is the information balanced and fair?**
Read with a critical eye. Does the source try to persuade readers with a one-sided presentation of information? Or is the source balanced, approaching a topic from various perspectives? Be on the lookout for **propaganda** and for sources that reflect an author's **bias,** or prejudice. Make sure that you learn about a topic from more than one angle by reviewing several sources of information.

Giving Credit Where Credit Is Due

When you write a research paper, you support your own ideas with information that you've gleaned from your primary and secondary sources. But presenting someone else's ideas as if they were your own is **plagiarism,** a form of cheating. You can avoid plagiarism by citing, or identifying, the sources of your information within the text of your paper. The chart below tells what kinds of information you do and don't need to cite in your paper.

DO credit the source of . . .	DON'T credit the source of . . .
• direct quotations	• information that can be found in many places—dates, facts, ideas, and concepts that are considered common knowledge
• summaries and paraphrases, or restatements, of someone else's viewpoints, original ideas, and conclusions	
• photos, art, charts, and other visuals	• your own unique ideas
• little-known facts or statistics	

Citing Sources Within Your Paper The most common method of crediting sources is with parenthetical documentation within the text. Generally a reference to the source and page number is included in parentheses at the end of each quotation, paraphrase, or summary of information borrowed from a source. An in-text citation points readers to a corresponding entry in your **works-cited list**—a list of all your sources, complete with publication information, that will appear as the final page of your paper. The Modern Language Association (MLA) recommends the following guidelines for crediting sources in text.

✓ **Check It Out**

Study the sample research paper on pages 831–832 to see the relationship between parenthetical documentation and a works-cited list.

- **Put in parentheses the author's last name and the page number where you found the information.**
  All too often the injury becomes infected, and then the manatee dies (Clark 35).

- **If the author's name is mentioned in the sentence, put only the page number in parentheses.**
  Margaret G. Clark says that it's common for manatees to die from infected injuries (35).

- **If no author is listed, put the title or a shortened version of the title in parentheses. Include a page number if you have one.**
  Accidents involving floodgates and canal locks are the second leading cause of manatee deaths ("Manatee Mortality").

Preparing the Final Draft

Ask your teacher how to format the final draft. Most English teachers will ask you to follow the MLA guidelines listed below.

- Put a heading in the upper left-hand corner of the first page with your name, your teacher's name, and the date on separate lines.
- Center the title on the line below the heading.
- Number the pages one-half inch from the top in the right-hand corner. After page one, put your last name before the page number.
- Set one-inch margins on all sides of every page; double-space the lines of text.
- Include an alphabetized, double-spaced works-cited list as the last page of your final draft. All sources noted in parenthetical citations in the paper must be listed.

On the next three pages, you'll find sample style sheets that can help you prepare the list of sources—the final page of the research paper. Use the one your teacher prefers.

MLA Style

MLA style is most often used in English and social studies classes. Center the title *Works Cited* at the top of your list.

Source	Style
Book with one author	Price-Groff, Claire. *The Manatee.* Farmington Hills: Lucent, 1999.
Book with two or three authors	Tennant, Alan, Gerard T. Salmon, and Richard B. King. *Snakes of North America.* Lanham: Lone Star Books, 2003. [If a book has more than three authors, name only the first author and then write "et al." (Latin abbreviation for "and others").]
Book with an editor	Follett, C. B., ed. *Grrrrr: A Collection of Poems About Bears.* Sausalito: Arctos, 2000.
Book with organization or group as author or editor	National Air and Space Museum. *The Official Guide to the Smithsonian Air and Space Museum.* Washington: Smithsonian Institution Press, 2002.
Work from an anthology	Soto, Gary. "To Be a Man." *Hispanic American Literature: An Anthology.* Ed. Rodolfo Cortina. Lincolnwood: NTC, 1998. 340–341.
Introduction in a published book	Weintraub, Stanley. Introduction. *Great Expectations.* By Charles Dickens. New York: Signet, 1998. v–xii.
Encyclopedia article	"Whales." *World Book Encyclopedia.* 2003.
Weekly magazine article	Trillin, Calvin. "Newshound." *New Yorker* 29 Sept. 2003: 70–81.
Monthly magazine article	Knott, Cheryl. "Code Red." *National Geographic* Oct. 2003: 76–81.
Online magazine article	Rauch, Jonathan. "Will Frankenfood Save the Planet?" *Atlantic Online* 292.3 (Oct. 2003). 15 Dec. 2003 <http://www.theatlantic.com/issues/2003/10/rauch.htm>.
Newspaper article	Bertram, Jeffrey. "African Bees: Fact or Myth?" *Orlando Sentinel* 18 Aug. 1999: D2.
Unsigned article	"Party-Line Snoops." *Washington Post* 24 Sept. 2003: A28.
Internet	"Manatees." *SeaWorld/Busch Gardens Animal Information Database.* 2002. Busch Entertainment Corp. 3 Oct. 2003 <http://www.seaworld.org/infobooks/Manatee/home.html>.
Radio or TV program	"Orcas." *Champions of the Wild.* Animal Planet. Discovery Channel. 21 Oct. 2003.
Videotape or DVD	*Living with Tigers.* DVD. Discovery, 2003. [For a videotape (VHS) version, replace "DVD" with "Videocassette."]
Interview	Salinas, Antonia. E-mail interview. 23–24 Oct. 2003. [If an interview takes place in person, replace "E-mail" with "Personal"; if it takes place on the telephone, use "Telephone."]

CMS Style

CMS style was created by the University of Chicago Press to meet its publishing needs. This style, which is detailed in *The Chicago Manual of Style* (CMS), is used in a number of subject areas. Center the title *Bibliography* at the top of your list.

Source	Style
Book with one author	Price-Groff, Claire. *The Manatee.* Farmington Hills, MI: Lucent, 1999.
Book with multiple authors	Tennant, Alan, Gerard T. Salmon, and Richard B. King. *Snakes of North America.* Lanham, TX: Lone Star Books, 2003. [For a book with more than ten authors, name only the first seven authors and then write "et al." (Latin abbreviation for "and others").]
Book with an editor	Follett, C. B., ed. *Grrrrr: A Collection of Poems About Bears.* Sausalito, CA: Arctos, 2000.
Book with organization or group as author or editor	National Air and Space Museum. *The Official Guide to the Smithsonian Air and Space Museum.* Washington, DC: Smithsonian Institution Press, 2002.
Work from an anthology	Soto, Gary. "To Be a Man." *Hispanic American Literature: An Anthology,* edited by Rodolfo Cortina, 340–341. Lincolnwood, IL: NTC, 1998.
Introduction in a published book	Dickens, Charles. *Great Expectations.* New introduction by Stanley Weintraub. New York: Signet, 1998.
Encyclopedia article	[Credit for encyclopedia articles goes in your text, not in your bibliography.]
Weekly magazine article	Trillin, Calvin. "Newshound." *New Yorker,* September 29, 2003, 70–81.
Monthly magazine article	Knott, Cheryl. "Code Red." *National Geographic,* October 2003, 76–81.
Online magazine article	Rauch, Jonathan. "Will Frankenfood Save the Planet?" *Atlantic Online* 292, no. 3 (October 2003). http://www.theatlantic.com/issues/2003/10/rauch.htm.
Newspaper article	[Credit for newspaper articles goes in your text, not in your bibliography.]
Unsigned article	[Credit for unsigned newspaper articles goes in your text, not in your bibliography.]
Internet	Busch Entertainment Corp. "Manatees." *SeaWorld/Busch Gardens Animal Information Database.* http://www.seaworld.org/infobooks/Manatee/home.html.
Radio or TV program	[Credit for radio and TV programs goes in your text, not in your bibliography.]
Videotape or DVD	*Living with Tigers.* Discovery, 2003. DVD. [For a videotape (VHS) version, replace "DVD" with "Videocassette."]
Interview	[Credit for interviews goes in your text, not in your bibliography.]

APA Style

The American Psychological Association (APA) style is commonly used in the sciences. Center the title *References* at the top of your list.

Source	Style
Book with one author	Price-Groff, Claire. (1999). *The manatee.* Farmington Hills, MI: Lucent.
Book with multiple authors	Tennant, A., Salmon, G. T., & King, R. B. (2003). *Snakes of North America.* Lanham, TX: Lone Star Books. [For a book with more than six authors, name only the first six authors and then write "et al." (Latin abbreviation for "and others").]
Book with an editor	Follett, C. B. (Ed.). (2000). *Grrrrr: A collection of poems about bears.* Sausalito, CA: Arctos.
Book with organization or group as author or editor	National Air and Space Museum. (2002). *The official guide to the Smithsonian Air and Space Museum.* Washington, DC: Smithsonian Institution Press.
Work from an anthology	Soto, G. (1998). To be a man. In R. Cortina (Ed.), *Hispanic American literature: An anthology* (pp. 340–341). Lincolnwood, IL: NTC.
Introduction in a published book	[Credit for introductions goes in your text, not in your references.]
Encyclopedia article	Whales. (2003). In *World Book encyclopedia.* Chicago: World Book.
Weekly magazine article	Trillin, C. (2003, September 29). Newshound. *The New Yorker,* 70–81.
Monthly magazine article	Knott, C. (2003, October). Code red. *National Geographic, 204,* 76–81.
Online magazine article	Rauch, J. (2003, October). Will Frankenfood save the planet? *Atlantic Online, 292.* Retrieved from http://www.theatlantic.com/issues/2003/10/rauch.htm
Newspaper article	Bertram, J. (1999, August 18). African bees: Fact or myth? *The Orlando Sentinel,* p. D2.
Unsigned article	Party-line snoops. (2003, September 24). *The Washington Post,* p. A28.
Internet	Busch Entertainment Corp. (2003). Manatees. In *SeaWorld/Busch Gardens animal information database.* Retrieved October 3, 2003, from http://www.seaworld.org/infobooks/Manatee/home.html
Radio or TV program	Orcas. (2003, October 21). *Champions of the wild* [Television series episode]. Animal Planet. Silver Spring, MD: Discovery Channel.
Videotape or DVD	*Living with tigers.* (2003). [DVD]. Discovery. [For a videotape (VHS) version, replace "DVD" with "Videocassette."]
Interview	[Credit for interviews goes in your text, not in your references.]

Evaluating a Research Paper Read this sample research paper, which has been evaluated using the 6+1 Trait® model.

The Endangered Manatee

When Christopher Columbus sailed to the New World, he thought he saw mermaids, but they didn't look like the ones he'd seen in paintings. In his journal, he wrote that these mermaids were "not so beautiful as they are painted, since in some ways they have a face like a man" (Ellis 88). Columbus was most likely describing West Indian manatees. These gentle gray-brown sea mammals have hairy snouts, and they weigh about a thousand pounds.

Manatees still live in Florida's warm waters, but possibly not for much longer. The number of manatees in the region has been declining. As of July 2000, only about twenty-four hundred manatees remained (Sawicki 6). The manatees are still dying off, even though environmental laws have been passed to help them survive. What is responsible for the decline of this gentle giant? Sadly, the answer is people. The development of Florida's coastal areas spelled trouble for manatees. Boats, canal locks, and pollution are the top three causes of manatee injuries and deaths.

Boating is fun for people, but it can be harmful to manatees. In fact, the chief cause of manatee deaths in recent years has been collisions with boats ("Manatee Mortality"). Manatees eat plants that grow deep in the water, but like seals and other water mammals, they must rise to the surface to breathe. As they rise to the surface, they sometimes swim into the path of an oncoming motorboat or another water craft. Because manatees are slow swimmers, they cannot get out of the way. And even if they could, they might not know which direction they should swim. Scientists believe that manatees cannot hear low-frequency sounds, such as the hum of a motorboat. As a result, manatees are often hit and killed by boats. Not every accident is deadly: The Mote Marine Laboratory in Sarasota, Florida, estimates that 80 percent of Florida's manatees have been hit at least once by marine craft (Koeppel 68).

Accidents involving floodgates and canal locks are the second leading cause of manatee deaths ("Manatee Mortality"). To understand why these accidents occur, picture what floodgates and canal locks look like and what they do. Try to imagine large underwater walls that can be raised and lowered or opened and closed to control water levels. When those walls are opened, the rushing water creates a strong current. That current is strong enough to pull in just about anything around it, including slow-moving manatees. Some manatees drown when they are pulled in by the current and cannot get to the surface of the water to breathe. Others caught between the gates are crushed or trapped and drowned (Clark 37). *(continued)*

Organization The opening paragraph captures readers' attention with an interesting anecdote.

Ideas The thesis statement clearly states the main point or central idea.

Organization The body paragraphs follow the order suggested in the thesis statement.

Ideas Carefully chosen details support the paragraph's main idea. The writer uses parenthetical citations (MLA style) to document the sources of information.

Conventions The composition is free of errors in grammar, usage, spelling, and mechanics.

Sentence Fluency Sentence openings vary, and the writing flows smoothly from one idea to the next.

Objects that people put in the water also cause problems that can result in injury or death of manatees. For example, fishermen set small floating objects called buoys at the water's surface to warn boaters of the crab traps below. The fishermen attach the traps to the buoys with wires or strong plastic lines that can tangle around a manatee's flippers. When the manatee struggles to free itself, it can be injured. All too often the injury becomes infected, and then the manatee dies (Clark 35). Manatees have also been known to choke to death on fishhooks and on garbage that people have thrown into the water.

Sentence Fluency The use of parallelism effectively ties together related ideas.

Environmental laws are supposed to protect the manatee from all these dangers. But according to Judith Valle of Save the Manatee Club, a group that works to protect manatees, enforcement of those laws is currently "pathetic" (Sawicki 6). What can we do to save the manatee? We can begin by putting an end to water pollution that kills manatees and other organisms, large and small. We can avoid boating in areas where manatees commonly swim. And we can invest in new technologies that will help keep manatees safe. For example, scientists are working on warning devices that could be attached to boats and canal locks that would keep manatees away. These devices send out high-frequency sounds that manatees can hear (Eliot). If people are responsible for the decline of manatees, then we must also be responsible for their ultimate survival.

Voice The writer's attitude toward the topic shines through.

Presentation A properly formatted works-cited list is part of every good research report. This one follows MLA style (see page 828). Remember to double-space your entire report and to put your works-cited list on a separate sheet of paper.

Works Cited

Clark, Margaret Goff. *The Vanishing Manatee.* New York: Cobblehill, 1990.

Eliot, John L. "Deaf to Danger: Manatees Can't Hear Boats." *National Geographic* Feb. 2000: Earth Almanac section.

Ellis, Richard. *Monsters of the Sea.* New York: Knopf, 1994.

Koeppel, Dan. "Kiss of the Manatee." *Travel Holiday* Feb. 1999: 66–69.

"Manatee Mortality." *Save the Manatee Club.* Save the Manatee Club, Inc. 31 Oct. 2003 <http://www.savethemanatee.org/mort.htm>.

Sawicki, Stephen. "Manatee Protectors Turn to the Courts." *Animals* July 2000: 6.

INDEX

E

F

411, 805
Prompts. *See* Writing prompts
Pronoun-antecedent agreement, 132, 431
Pronouns, 803
  antecedents for, 132, 431
  as compound direct object, 433
  as compound subject, 433
  definition of, 429
  indefinite, 437, 541
  intensive, 439
  interrogative, 441
  object, 429, 481
  as objects of prepositions, 429, 481
  personal, 162, 429
  possessive, 435
  as predicate nominative, 405
  reflexive, 439
  relative, 505, 623
  subject, 429
  Troubleshooter for, 316–317
  using, 433
Pronunciation, 650
Proofreading, 80, 803
  practice, 375–376, 395, 425, 447–448, 475, 497, 517–518, 531, 549, 559–560, 585–586, 615
  symbols for, 80, 847
  TIME Facing the Blank Page, 99, 106
  See also Editing; Revising; Troubleshooter
Propaganda, 747, 803
Proper adjectives, 453, 797
  capitalization of, 453
Proper nouns, 379, 575
  capitalization of, 379, 575, 577, 579
Proposal, 345-348
Prose, 803
Publishing, 803. *See* Presenting
Punctuation
  apostrophes, 601
  colons, 597
  commas, 591, 593, 595
  dashes, 603
  end marks, 357, 589
  exclamation points, 367, 589
  hyphens, 603
  italics, 599
  parentheses, 603
  periods, 357, 589
  question marks, 357, 589
  quotation marks, 599

semicolons, 597
See also specific marks
Purpose, determining, for writing, 54–57, 803

Question marks, 357, 589
Questions
  diagraming, 564
  for interview, 230
  open-ended, 750
  research, to guide, 225, 227
  See also Interrogative sentences
Quotation
  capitalization of first words of, 573
  commas with, 595, 599
  direct, 573, 595, 599
  indirect, 573
  punctuating, 599
  in reports, 226
Quotation marks
  for dialogue, 169, 170
  with direct quotations, 599
  with divided quotations, 599
  with other marks of punctuation, 599
  with title of short works, 599

R

Raise, rise, 555
Readers' Guide to Periodical Literature, 645
Reading
  methods of, 687–688
  note taking while, 697
Reading comprehension on standardized tests, 712
Reason, as type of evidence, 271
Rebus, 660
Recalling details, 697
Reference works, 225
  almanac, 641–642
  atlas, 640–641
  dictionary, 647–651
  encyclopedia, 225, 639–640
  thesaurus, 648–649, 652
Reflexive pronouns, 439
Regular verbs, 407, 409, 411, 413
Relative pronouns, 505, 623
Research reports
  APA style, 830
  citing sources, 827
  CMS style, 829
  collecting information for,

224–227
  conducting interviews for, 228–231
  drafting, 221, 232–235
  editing, 237
  evaluating sources, 825
  MLA style, 828
  note cards, 226
  outline for, 233
  parts of, 234
  presenting, 227, 236–239, 247
  prewriting, 224–231
  primary sources, 225, 825
  proofreading, 237, 246
  questions to guide research, 224
  research for, 224–227
  revising, 236–238
  secondary sources, 225, 825
  student model, 238, 831–832
  thesis statement, 232–233, 821
Responding to literature. *See* Literature, responding to
Revising, 73, 239, 804
  checklist for, 30, 67, 68, 88, 140, 186, 246, 296
  considering audience in, 229
  creating variety in sentences in, 74–77
  descriptive writing, 112, 115, 140
  evaluating draft in, 66–69
  expository writing, 198, 236–238, 246
  feature writing, 42
  feedback from teacher, implementing, 30, 88, 140, 186, 296
  making paragraphs more effective in, 70–73
  narrative writing, 166, 177, 178, 186
  oral reports, 756–760
  personal writing, 6, 30
  persuasive writing, 268, 275, 296
  research reports, 225, 236–238
  speeches, 758
  TIME Facing the Blank Page, 99, 104–105
  in writing process, 43–44, 48, 66–77, 88
  See also Editing; Proofreading
Rhythm, *134*
Rise, raise, 555
Roots, 661, 804
Rubrics. *See* Writing rubrics
Run-on sentence, 804
  Troubleshooter for, 308–309

ACKNOWLEDGMENTS

Text

UNIT ONE From *The Diary of Latoya Hunter.* Copyright © 1992 by Latoya Hunter. Reprinted by permission of Crown Publishers, a division of Random House, Inc.

UNIT TWO From "Smart, Cool and on the Air" by Maisha Maurant, reprinted by permission of the Detroit Free Press and Copyright Clearance Center.

From *The Clay Marble* by Minfong Ho. Copyright © 1991 by Minfong Ho. Reprinted by permission of Farrar Straus Giroux.

From "Ode to la Tortilla" by Gary Soto, from *Neighborhood Odes: Poems by Gary Soto.* Copyright © 1992 by Gary Soto. Reprinted by permission of Harcourt, Inc.

UNIT THREE From *Song of the Gargoyle,* by Zilpha Keatley Snyder. Copyright © 1991 by Zilpha Keatley Snyder. Used by permission of Dell Publishing, a division of Random House, Inc.

From *The Gathering* by Virginia Hamilton. Copyright © 1981 by Virginia Hamilton. By permission of Greenwillow Books, a division of HarperCollins Publishers, Inc.

UNIT FOUR "User Friendly" by T. Ernesto Bethancourt, copyright © 1989 by T. Ernesto Bethancourt, from *Connections: Short Stories* by Donald R. Gallo, Editor. Used by permission of Delacorte Press, a division of Random House, Inc.

"A Huge Black Umbrella" by Marjorie Agosin. Reprinted by permission.

UNIT FIVE From *Living Treasure* by Laurence Pringle. Copyright © 1991 by Laurence Pringle. By permission of Morrow Junior Books, a division of HarperCollins Publishers, Inc.

UNIT SIX Taken from *Gifted Hands* by Ben Carson. Copyright © 1990 by Review & Herald Publishing Association. Used by permission of Zondervan Publishing House.

"The Liberry" by Bel Kaufman. Reprinted by permission of the author.

Photo

1. Herscovici/Art Resource,NY; **2-3** © Don Hammond/Design Pics/CORBIS; **4** Allan Landau; **5** Art Wise; **8 (1st 2 images)** Jose Luis Pelaez, Inc. /Getty Images, (guitar)Photodisc/Getty Images, (shopper) Thomas Northcut/Getty Images, (wheelchair) Rayman/Getty Images; **9 through 12** Ralph J. Brunke; **13** Bruce Laurance/Getty Images; **16** (t)David Woo/Stock Boston, (b)Ralph J. Brunke; **17 18** Ralph J. Brunke; **20** Tom Walker/Stock Boston; **21** Ralph J. Brunke; **23** Gilson Ribeiro; **24** Selection reprinted by permission of HarperCollins Publishers. Photo by Ralph J. Brunke; **26** Ralph J. Brunke; **28** Bob Daemmrich/The Image Works; **31** Richard Hutchings/PhotoEdit; **35** Giraudon/Art Resource, NY; **36** file photo; **40-41** Travelpix Ltd./Getty Images; **42** William Jordan; **46 50** Allan Landau; **53** Picnic in Washington Park, Pat Thomas, Milwaukee, WI, Acrylic over oil on masonite. Dated 1975. 20 1/2" x 27 1/2". Collection of The Museum of American Folk Art, New York City; Gift of Rose Winters; **56 58 59** Allen Landau; **61** © 1992 Sucession H. Matisse/ARS, New York; **62 63 64** Allan Landau; **65** National Museum of American Art, Washington DC/Art Resource, NY; **66 70 74 75** Allan Landau; **77** Hirshhorn Museum and Sculpture Garden, Smithsonian Institution, Gift of the Joseph H. Hirshhorn Foundation, 1974. Photograph by Lee Stalsworth; **78 82 83** Allan Landau; **86** Bob Daemmrich/The Image Works; **92** The Phillips Collection, Washington DC; **94** Courtesy Bernice Steinbaum gallery; **108-109** © Gallo Images-Roger De La Harpe/Getty Images; **112 113** Ralph J. Brunke; **114** Charles Seaborn/Odyssey Productions, Chicago; **116** Ralph J. Brunke; **118** *Fruit of the Spirit,* Martin Charlot, © 1983; **122** John Elk III/Stock Boston; **124** (l)Robert Brenner/PhotoEdit, (r) Debby Davis/PhotoEdit; **126** Pete Saloutos/Photographic Resources; **128** Gayna Hoffman/Stock Boston; **130** Laura Derichs; **131** (t)Laura Derichs, (b)Ralph J. Brunke; **132** (t) Laura Derichs, (b)Ralph J. Brunke; **134 135** Ralph J. Brunke; **138** Amy Etra/PhotoEdit; **143** Scala/Art Resource, NY; **144** Peter Blume. "Light of the World," 1935. Oil on composition board. 18 x 20 1/4 inches. (45.7 cm x 51.4 cm). Collection of the Whitney Museum of American Art. Purchase 33.5; **150-151** Alan Marsh/Design Pics/CORBIS; **152** (l)Tom Tondee, (r) Laura Derichs; **153 154** Laura Derichs; **156** Photofest; **160** Florence H.G. Ward; **168** From Alice's Adventures in Wonderland by Lewis Carroll, illustration, S. Michelle Wiggins © 1983 by Armand Eisen. Reprinted by permission of Alfred A. Knopf, Inc; **172** Calvin and Hobbes © 1986 Watterson. Reprinted with permission of Universal Press Syndicate. All rights reserved; **176** NASA; **179** Boston Athenaeum; **181** Nathaniel Bruns; **191** Bridgeman/Art Resource, NY; **194-195** Purestock/Superstock; **196** (t) Courtesy Monterey Bay Aquarium, (b) Charles Seaborn/Odyssey Productions, Chicago; **198 199** Ralph J. Brunke; **208** (l)Carl Roesser/Animals Animals, (r) Richard Kolar/Animals Animals; **212** Courtesy the estate of Rube Goldberg; **216** Maresa Pryor/Earth Scenes; **220 222 226** Allan Landau; **228** © Jim Craigmyle/CORBIS; **230 232** Allan Landau; **236** Ralph J. Brunke; **241** (l)BET, (r) Focus on Sports; **247** Lawrence Migdale/Stock Boston; **249** Courtesy of Patricia Gonzales; **251** Courtesy of Kathryn Stewart; **256-257** © Stuart Westmorland/CORBIS; **258** Christine Armstrong. @ Review and Herald; **259** (t) Ralph J. Brunke, (b) William De Kay © Detroit Free Press; **260** Ralph J. Brunke; **261** Art Wise; **262** James D. Watt/Animals Animals; **270** Allan Landau; **273** John Weber Gallery; **274 278 290** Allan Landau; **294** Bob Daemmrich/The Image Works; **300** National Museum of American Art, Washington D.C./Art Resource, NY; **304-305** © Chung Sun-Jun/Staff/Getty Images; **354-355** CNAC/MNAM/Dist. Reunion des Musees Nationaux/Art Resource, NY; **357** (t)Mark Burnett/Stock Boston, (bl)Greenlar/The Image Works,(bc) John Cancalosi/Natural Selection,(br)Neal Mishler/Natural Selection; **375** American Museum of Natural History #4587, (2)Photo by Lynton Gardiner; **387** Bob Daemmrich; **395** Courtesy of Robert McCall; **399** Ralph J. Brunke; **426** Courtesy R.H. Love Gallery; **447** Michael Holford; **463** Malcolm S. Kirk/Peter Arnold, Inc.; **475** © 1992 Charles Simonds, ARS, New York; **487** Robert Frerck/ Getty Images; **489** SEF/Art Resource; **497** © 1986, Helen Oji; **507** Focus on Sports; **517** Courtesy Phyllis Kind Gallery, New York/Chicago; **532** Courtesy Brooke Alexander Gallery; **539** (t)Bob Daemmrich, (b)Tony Freeman/PhotoEdit; **549** Giraudon/Art Resource, NY; **559** Scala/Art Resource, NY; **574** Tony Freeman/PhotoEdit; **585** Courtesy Elaine Horwitch Galleries, Scottsdale, Arizona; **589** Tony Freeman/PhotoEdit; **616** Phyllis Kind gallery, New York/Chicago; **628-629** Art Resource, NY; **631** Bill Bachman/Photographic Resources; **636** DIL/Jupiterimages; **640** From The World Book

Proofreading Symbols

Symbol	Example	Meaning
⊙	Lieut Brown	Insert a period.
∧	No one came to the party.	Insert a letter or a word.
⌃;	The bell rang the students left for home.	Insert a semicolon.
≡	I enjoyed paris.	Capitalize a letter.
/	The Class ran a bake sale.	Make a capital letter lowercase.
⌒	The campers are home sick.	Close up a space.
⟨sp⟩	They visited N.Y. sp	Spell out.
⋀	Sue please help.	Insert a comma.
∩	He enjoyed faild day.	Transpose the position of letters or words.
#	alltogether	Insert a space.
୬	We went to to Boston.	Delete letters or words.
⌄ ⌄	She asked, Who's coming?	Insert quotation marks.
/=/	mid January	Insert a hyphen.
¶	"Where?" asked Karl. "Over there," said Ray.	Begin a new paragraph.
⌄	She liked Sarah's glasses.	Insert an apostrophe.